Women's Christian Temperance Union is established; heroin is discovered.

Amphetamine is synthesized for the first time.

Drug regulation gets its start in the Pure Food and Drug Act.

Workmen's compensation laws contribute to the support of Prohibition by big business.

1861–1865 **1874** **1884** **1887** **1893** **1906** **1909** **1911–1920**

During the Civil War, morphine is widely used to treat the wounded.

Sigmund Freud begins using cocaine.

Anti-Saloon League is organized and launches a political action campaign.

First International Opium Conference is held in Shanghai.

Media campaigns against marijuana use; use of amphetamines spreads.

Marijuana Tax Act virtually prohibits marijuana use.

World War II ends, and there is fear of a drug epidemic as soldiers return home.

Great Depression begins.

1925 **1929** **1930** **1930s** **1933** **1937** **1941** **1945**

Linder v. United States rules that physicians can prescribe small doses of heroin for the relief of addiction.

Uniform Drug Act provides a model for state laws.

Prohibition is repealed.

United States enters World War II.

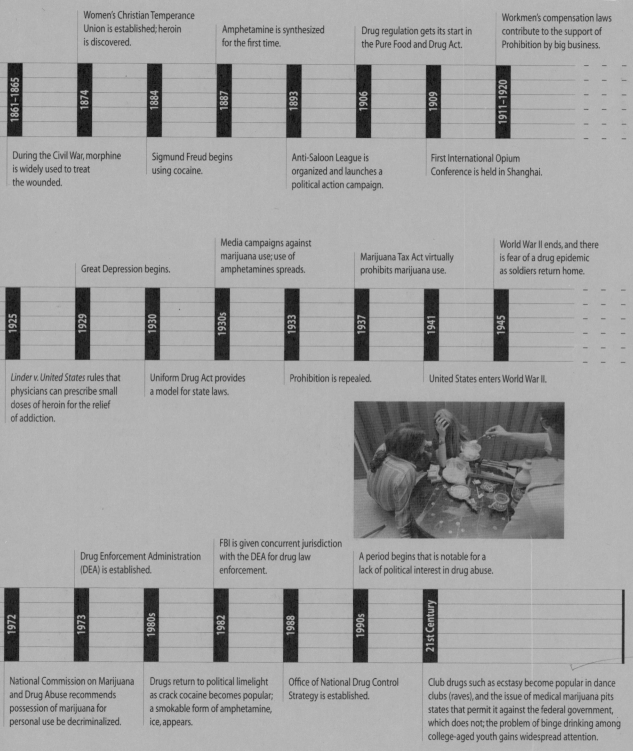

Drug Enforcement Administration (DEA) is established.

FBI is given concurrent jurisdiction with the DEA for drug law enforcement.

A period begins that is notable for a lack of political interest in drug abuse.

1972 **1973** **1980s** **1982** **1988** **1990s** **21st Century**

National Commission on Marijuana and Drug Abuse recommends possession of marijuana for personal use be decriminalized.

Drugs return to political limelight as crack cocaine becomes popular; a smokable form of amphetamine, ice, appears.

Office of National Drug Control Strategy is established.

Club drugs such as ecstasy become popular in dance clubs (raves), and the issue of medical marijuana pits states that permit it against the federal government, which does not; the problem of binge drinking among college-aged youth gains widespread attention.

DRUGS

AN INTRODUCTION

FIFTH EDITION

Howard Abadinsky

St. John's University

THOMSON
™
WADSWORTH

Australia • Canada • Mexico • Singapore • Spain • United Kingdon • United States

THOMSON

™

WADSWORTH

Senior Acquisitions Editor, Criminal Justice: Jay Whitney
Editorial Assistant: Paul Massicotte
Technology Project Manager: Susan DeVanna
Marketing Manager: Dory Shaeffer
Marketing Assistant: Neena Chandra
Advertising Project Manager: Stacey Purviance
Project Manager, Editorial Production: Jennie Redwitz
Print/Media Buyer: Karen Hunt
Permissions Editor: Bob Kauser
Production Service: Linda Jupiter, Jupiter Productions
Text Designer: Lisa Mirski Devenish

Endsheet Timeline Designer: Adriane Bosworth
Photo Permissions: Roberta Spieckerman
Copy Editor: Judith Brown
Illustrator: John and Judy Waller
Proofreader: Henrietta Bensussen
Cover Designer: Yvo Riezebos
Cover Image: © Fred Tomaselli, Courtesy of
James Cohan Gallery, New York
Compositor: Carlisle Communications, Ltd.
Text and Cover Printer: Phoenix Color Corp

Printed in the United States of America
3 4 5 6 7 07 06 05 04

For more information about our products, contact us at:
Thomson Learning Academic Resource Center
1-800-423-0563
For permission to use material from this text, contact us by:
Phone: 1-800-730-2214
Fax: 1-800-730-2215
Web: http://www.thomsonrights.com

Library of Congress Control Number: 2003106629
ISBN 0-534-61515-5

Wadsworth/Thomson Learning
10 Davis Drive
Belmont, CA 94002-3098
USA

Asia
Thomson Learning
5 Shenton Way #01-01
UIC Building
Singapore 068808

Australia/New Zealand
Thomson Learning
102 Dodds Street
Southbank, Victoria 3006
Australia

Canada
Nelson
1120 Birchmount Road
Toronto, Ontario M1K 5G4
Canada

Europe/Middle East/Africa
Thomson Learning
High Holborn House
50/51 Bedford Row
London WC1R 4LR
United Kingdom

Brief Contents

Contents

CHAPTER 4

CHAPTER 5

Stimulants 112

CHAPTER 8   **The Psychology of Drug Abuse 186**

CHAPTER 9   **Drug Abuse Treatment 203**

CHAPTER 10

Drug Abuse Prevention 246

CHAPTER 13

Preface

While there are numerous texts on drug abuse, they focus on a particular aspect or aspects of the issue: pharmacology, psychology, sociology, treatment, the business of drugs, prevention, laws and law enforcement, policy. None are comprehensive. This book strives to provide the reader with a thorough understanding of drug abuse policy. In order to accomplish that goal, it is necessary to examine drug history; biological, psychological, and sociological explanations; the various types of treatment and prevention programs; the business of drugs; and drug laws and law enforcement. Without an understanding of these topics, an informed discussion of policy is not possible. Without an understanding of the dynamics of drug abuse, a discussion of the problem becomes an exercise equivalent to the proverbial blind men attempting to describe an elephant—each can accurately portray only that part he can touch—hence, the logic for the comprehensive nature of this book.

Because the subject transcends so many disciplines—history, law, neuropharmacology, political science, social work, counseling, psychology, and sociology—the literature is massive and diverse. Putting together all aspects of drug abuse in a single book is a daunting task. This fifth edition continues the comprehensive approach, updating and adding information on pharmacology, inhalants, herbal stimulants, "club drugs," the changing nature of the drug business, and recent developments in policy. The book is organized into fourteen chapters using a syllabus format for ease of classroom presentation. There is an instructor's manual with extensive test questions.

New to the Fifth Edition

Drug History Time Line

Open to the front of the book to see the new "Drug History Time Line," which helps students understand drugs in context, from the U.S. Surgeon General's hue and cry over high-proof alcohol abuse in 1885 to the remarkable lack of political interest in drug abuse during the 1990s.

Club Drugs

Chapter 6, "Hallucinogens, Club Drugs, and Marijuana," now includes extensive coverage of MDMA, or ecstasy, and other current club drugs.

Extended Glossary

Key terms and concepts appear in an extended glossary at the end of the text for easy study access and reference for students.

Web Sites

A list of Web sites appears in "Internet Connections" at each chapter's end, affording opportunities for further learning of the chapter topics.

New Research

Chapter 3, "Drugs and the Nervous System," includes new research on neurotransmitters, with a focus on the role of dopamine.

International Coverage

Chapter 14, "Drug Maintenance, Decriminalization, and Harm Reduction," features coverage on the latest international developments in drug policy, including the popularity of the harm reduction approach in Europe.

Organization of the Text

Chapter 1 explores the drug use continuum from abstinence to dependence and the slippery term *drug abuse*. Categories of drugs and methods for estimating their prevalence are explained, as well as the relationship between drugs, crime, and violence.

Chapter 2 presents a history of the drugs of abuse, beginning with the temperance movement and Prohibition, the patent medicine problem, and the intertwining of foreign affairs, the Opium Wars, and the Harrison Act. The chapter reviews the opiates, the erratic popularity of cocaine in its various forms, the marijuana saga, and the history of artificial depressants and stimulants, natural and artificial hallucinogens. There is an examination of U.S. policy as it moved from indifference to the "war on drugs."

Chapter 3 explores the complex world of neurology—but explanatory diagrams and easily understood prose reveal that it is "science for poets." This prepares the student for examining, in Chapters 4, 5, and 6, how each of the drugs of abuse manipulates the organism to produce its effects. Chapter 3 examines the disease model, arousal theory, genetic predisposition, as well as the role of setting and expectations in producing a drug's effects.

Chapter 4 focuses on depressants ranging from opiates and alcohol to sedatives and inhalants, identifying the role of neurotransmitters, which, while they can produce profound positive effects—euphoria, reduction of stress and pain—can also result in dependence, addiction, and death.

Chapter 5 focuses on stimulants ranging from caffeine and nicotine to cocaine and amphetamines, again, identifying the role of neurotransmitters, which, while they can produce profound positive effects—euphoria, increased energy levels, enhanced mood—can also lead to dependence, damage to critical organs, and death.

Chapter 6 examines hallucinogens and marijuana, which have depressing, stimulating, and hallucinogenic characteristics. So-called *psychedelics* overwhelm the nervous system's ability to modulate sensory input, producing altered perceptions of reality, sensory illusions, and hallucinations. These substances range from those used in religious ceremonies by Native Americans, to LSD, PCP, and so-called club drugs—MDA and MDMA/ecstasy.

Chapter 7 examines sociological studies and theories that consider psychoactive drugs in their social context, characterizes their stages, and suggests explanations for their abuse. Combined with the biological views of Chapters 3 to 6, this chapter and the psychological views expressed in Chapter 8 provide the full range of knowledge critical to an informed view of the causes of drug abuse.

Chapter 8 moves the study of drug abuse to the field of psychology, examining the two major branches of that discipline, one based on psychoanalytic theory, the other on behavior/learning theory, and their explanations for drug abuse.

Chapter 9 reviews the various treatment approaches to drug abuse, reflecting explanations explored in Chapters 3 to 8. Programs—ranging from methadone to mandatory, private and public in- and outpatient, 12-step, and the therapeutic community—are described, and their theoretical underpinnings discussed. There is an analysis of the difficulties in evaluating drug-program effectiveness and the lack of research support for much of what is offered in the form of substance abuse treatment.

Chapter 10 explores the relatively new and often illusory field of drug abuse prevention through a critique of basic premises and a description of the leading programs. Research on prevention is analyzed, and the technical problems and criticisms of prevention programs are discussed.

Chapter 11 provides a tour of the drug economy, which is characterized by freebooting capitalism that responds only to market conditions of supply and demand, as influenced by competitive violence and law enforcement efforts. There is an examination of the business of drugs, a world filled with private armies and violence, from its highest "international" levels down through mid-level wholesalers and finally, the retail—street—level. The chapter ends with a discussion of money laundering and its various methods.

Chapter 12 looks at the law enforcement response to the business of drugs as constrained by the U.S. Constitution and jurisdictional limitations. There is an examination of the various statutes used to investigate and prosecute drug offenders, such as conspiracy, RICO, tax, and money-laundering laws, as well as the investigative agencies and the techniques of drug-law enforcement. The chapter concludes with an analysis of these techniques.

Chapter 13 ties together all of the previous chapters with an examination and critical analysis of U.S. policy with respect to drug abuse.

Chapter 14 extends the drug policy issue beyond U.S. borders by examining the approach taken in Great Britain and the European alternative referred to as harm reduction. The chapter concludes with a comparative critique of drug decriminalization/legalization.

Since the language of drugs and drug abuse can be confusing, an extensive *Glossary* is presented after Chapter 14.

The author welcomes correspondence about his work, and can be reached at abadinsky@att.net.

Acknowledgments

I would like to thank

> Robin J. Adler, Northeastern University
> Tammy Anderson, University of Delaware
> Joseph R. Caton, University of Wisconsin–Milwaukee
> Tory Caeti, University of North Texas
> Peter B. Kraska, Eastern Kentucky University
> Bernadette Muscat, York College of Pennsylvania
> David E. Olson, Loyola University–Chicago

for their careful reviews and suggestions for this edition. I would like to thank previous reviewers: Wayman C. Mullins, James Yenan, Bruce D. Johnson, Bryan J. Vila, Laura E. Nagy, and Rick Aniskewiscz. I would like to thank Sabra Horne, senior executive editor at Wadsworth, for her confidence in me, and Jennie Redwitz, production editor, for her interest and careful attention to detail. Thanks also to Linda Jupiter, production service, for her careful attention to detail, and to Judith Brown, copy editor and Henrietta Bensussen, proofreader, for their outstanding work.

About the Author

Howard Abadinsky is professor of criminal justice at St. John's University. He was an inspector for the Cook County, IL, Sheriff's Office for eight years and a New York State parole officer and senior parole officer for 15 years. The author holds a B.A. from Queens College of the City University of New York, an M.S.W. from Fordham University, and a Ph.D. from New York University. He is the author of several books, including *Probation and Parole,* 8th edition, *Organized Crime,* 7th edition, and *Law and Justice,* 5th edition.

Dr. Abadinsky can be reached at abadinsky@att.net and encourages comments about his work.

Dedication

To Carolyn and Morgan

CHAPTER 1 — An Introduction to Drug Abuse

Our society makes artificial distinctions among addictive drugs. We foster the false impression that because nicotine and alcohol are legal, they must be less dangerous and less addictive than the illicit drugs. —*Avram Goldstein (2001: 4)*

Study behavior you regard as pathological and you will find pathological motivations. We should not be asking, "Why do people use drugs? Rather, we should ask, "How do some people maintain healthy relationships with drugs, and how do some develop unhealthy relationships?" —*Kevin W. Whiteacre and Hal Pepinsky (2002: 26)*

This book is concerned with psychoactive drugs that have the potential to harm their users, who may in turn harm others, e.g., the intoxicated driver. While statutes distinguish between lawful drugs such as nicotine and alcohol and illegal drugs such as heroin and cocaine, biology recognizes no such distinction. Nicotine is a drug that meets the rigorous criteria for abuse liability and dependence potential, and "cigarettes are one of the major drugs of addiction in the United States and in the world and are responsible for more premature deaths than all of the other drugs of abuse combined" (Schuster 1993: 40).

Nicotine Dependence/Addiction

Nicotine dependence is the most common substance use disorder in the United States. Approximately 60% to 80% of current smokers fulfill classic criteria for drug dependence; e.g., they have difficulty stopping, have withdrawal when they stop, are tolerant, and continue despite knowledge of personal harm. Nicotine appears to have a dependence potential at least equal to that of other drugs. For example, among persons who experiment with alcohol, 10% to 15% will meet criteria for alcohol dependence at some point in their life. Among persons who experiment with cigarettes, 20% to 30% will meet criteria for nicotine dependence in their lifetime (American Psychiatric Association 1995). If addiction is defined as compulsive drug-seeking behavior, even in the face of negative health consequences, then tobacco use is certainly addiction ("Nicotine Addiction" 2001).

Not a Happy New Year

The 17-year-old high school student in Lake County, Illinois, joined a group of friends celebrating New Year's Eve. Over a 3-hour period he consumed almost a quart of vodka. He subsequently passed out and died before paramedics arrived (Santana 1996).

But They're Not Using Pot

Each weekend, three to ten students at the University of Virginia drink so much they need medical treatment (Winerip 1998).

An Illegal Drug (for Adolescents)

The Missouri Division of Alcohol and Drug Abuse (1999) reports that in their state 86% of adolescents have used alcohol by the time they have reached the twelfth grade.

Danger to Others

Alcohol disturbs behavior in a way that "threatens the safety of others even when used occasionally and not compulsively" (A. Goldstein 2001: 5).

Suspected of being intoxicated, a teenager attempts to walk a straight line for law enforcement. Statistics prove that youth who experiment with alcohol are most likely to use marijuana and other drugs later on.

© Richard Hutchings/PhotoEdit

According to scientific and pharmacological data used to classify dangerous substances for the protection of society, alcohol should be a Schedule II narcotic, a Drug Enforcement Administration category referring to a substance that is highly addictive and available only with a government narcotic registry number. The cost of alcohol abuse is twice the social cost of all illegal drug abuse. Alcohol is reputed to be the direct cause of 80,000 to 100,000 deaths annually, and alcohol-related auto accidents are the leading cause of death for teenagers (Wicker 1987; Li, Smith, and Baker 1994). But alcohol for recreational use is permitted to be legally manufactured, imported, sold, and possessed. Because of this reality, while it has been associated with a myriad of social problems, since the repeal of Prohibition in 1933 trafficking in alcohol has not been associated with rampant violence and corruption. Indeed, the repeal of Prohibition resulted in a dramatic decrease in the murder rate in the United States, which began to increase in the 1960s along with the prevalence of illicit drug use (L. Myers 1995).

Distinctions between alcohol and other psychoactive drugs reflect neither reality nor science (N. Miller 1995). Indeed, heroin users have typically used marijuana and alcohol while adolescents, and heavy-alcohol-use-to-injecting-heroin is a typical sequence for most addicts (Inciardi, McBride, and Surratt 1998).

The Gateway to Illegal Drug Abuse

"Both tobacco and alcohol share a role as 'gateway drugs' that presage use of other psychoactive drugs; in other words, alcohol and/or tobacco use precedes most subsequent use of marijuana and cocaine" (Shiffman and Balabanis 1995: 18). Thus, "there is a fairly consistent progression of adolescent substance use beginning with the licit drugs alcohol and/or cigarettes, moving on to illicit substances initiating with marijuana and progressing to cocaine and 'harder,' more problematic drugs" (P. Johnson, Boles, and Kleber 2000: 79).

"Each day, more than 3,000 young persons smoke their first cigarette, and the likelihood of becoming addicted to nicotine is higher for these young smokers than for those who begin later in life" (Zickler 2002: 7). Nearly one in four high school seniors smokes every day, and more than one in eight smokes a half-pack or more each day ("Update . . ." 2000). "Young people age twelve to seventeen who smoke are about twelve times more likely to use illegal drugs and sixteen times more likely to drink heavily than youths who did not smoke. Young people use alcohol more than illegal drugs and the younger a person is when alcohol use begins, the greater the risk of developing alcohol abuse or dependence later in life. . . . Alcohol use among the young strongly correlates with adult drug use. For example, adults who started drinking at early ages are nearly eight times more likely to use cocaine than adults who did not drink as children" (Office of National Drug Control Policy 2000: 10).

Alcohol?

"Drug abuse and related crime permeate every corner of our society, afflicting inner cities, affluent suburbs, and rural communities. Drugs affect the rich and poor, educated and uneducated, professionals and blue-collar workers, young and old" (Office of National Drug Control Policy 2001:3).

Hypocrisy?

In England, the government notes that "drug prevention policies which ignore licit drugs [alcohol and tobacco] lack credibility" (Advisory Council on the Misuse of Drugs 1998:*xi*). In 1999, the U.S. Congress defeated an administration plan to include antidrinking messages in federal efforts to keep youngsters from using illicit drugs. There are an estimated 14 million people in the United States addicted to alcohol; that is, they suffer from Jellinek's Disease (Ynclan 2002).

With these incongruities serving as a backdrop, this opening chapter will begin by describing the problems inherent in defining terms such as drugs and drug abuse, the drug use continuum from abstinence to dependency, measuring the extent of drug use, and the connection between drugs and crime.

Drugs—Reaching a Definition

The term *drug* is derived from the fourteenth-century French word *drogue,* meaning a dry substance—most pharmaceuticals at that time were prepared from dried herbs (Palfai and Jankiewicz 1991). There is no completely satisfying way of delineating what is and what is not a drug—for example, the differences between water, vitamin supplements, and penicillin (Goode 1989). Thus, some feel it appropriate to refer to *chemical* or *substance* abuse. Imprecision in the use of the term *drug* has had serious social consequences.

Because alcohol is excluded from most people's definition of *drug,* the public is conditioned to regard a martini as something fundamentally different from a marijuana cigarette, a barbiturate capsule, or a bag of heroin. Similarly, because the meaning of the word *drug* differs so widely in therapeutic and social contexts, the public is conditioned to believe that "street" drugs act according to entirely different principles than "medical" drugs, alcohol, and nicotine, with the result that the risks of the former are exaggerated and the risks of the latter are overlooked (Uelmen and Haddox 1983).

"In contemporary society the word *drug* has two connotations—one positive, explaining its crucial role in medicine, and one negative, reflecting, not the natural and synthetic makeup of these chemicals, but the self-destruction and socially deleterious patterns of misuse" (Jones, Shainberg, and Byer 1979: 1). In this book the term **drug** will refer to substances having mood-altering, psychotropic (or **psychoactive**) effects. This definition includes caffeine, nicotine, and alcohol, as well as illegal chemicals such as marijuana and heroin.

Drug Abuse and Addiction

Drug abuse implies the misuse of certain substances—it is a moral, not a scientific, term: "An unstandardized, value-laden, and highly relative term used with a great deal of imprecision and confusion, generally implying drug use that is excessive, dangerous, or undesirable to the individual or community and that ought to be modified" (Nelson et al. 1982: 33). Drug abuse "implies willful, improper use due to an underlying disorder or a quest for hedonistic or immoral pleasure" (N. Miller 1995: 10). Numerous definitions of drug abuse reflect social values, not scientific insight: "One reason for the prevalence of definitions of drug abuse that are neither logical nor scientific is the strength of Puritan moralism in American culture which frowns on the pleasure and recreation provided by intoxicants" (Zinberg 1984: 33). Such definitions typically refer to:

1. the nonmedical use of a substance,
2. to alter the mental state,

3. in a manner that is detrimental to the individual or the community, and/or
4. that is illegal.

For example, the American Social Health Association (1972: 1) defines drug abuse as the "use of mood modifying chemicals outside of medical supervision, and in a manner which is harmful to the person and the community." Other definitions, such as those offered by the World Health Organization and the American Medical Association, include references to physical and/or psychological dependency (Zinberg 1984).

In fact drug abuse may be defined from a number of perspectives: "The legal definition equates drug use with the mere act of using a proscribed drug or using a drug under proscribed conditions. The moral definition is similar, but greater emphasis is placed on the motivation or purpose for which the drug is used. The medical model opposes unsupervised usage but emphasizes the physical and mental consequences for the user, and the social definition stresses social responsibility and adverse effects on others" (Balter 1974: 5).

The Drug Use Continuum

Substance Abuse

The American Psychiatric Association (1994: 182) refers to **substance abuse** as a "maladaptive pattern of substance use manifested by recurrent and significant adverse consequences related to the repeated use of substances," including "repeated failure to fulfill major role obligations, repeated use in situations in which it is physically hazardous, multiple legal problems, and recurrent social and interpersonal problems."

The use of psychoactive chemicals, licit or illicit, can objectively be labeled **drug abuse** only when the user becomes dysfunctional as a consequence; for example, is unable to maintain employment; has impaired social relationships; exhibits dangerous—reckless or aggressive—behavior; and/or significantly endangers his or her health. Thus, drug *use*, as opposed to drug *abuse* can be viewed as a continuum—see Figure 1.1. At one end is the nonuser who has never used prohibited or abused lawful psychoactive drugs. Along the continuum are experimental use and culturally endorsed use, which includes the use of drugs—wine or peyote, for example—in religious ceremonies. "Regardless of the duration of use, such people tend not to escalate their use to uncontrollable amounts.[1] For example, long-term cocaine users have found that recreational patterns can be maintained for a decade or more without loss of control. Such use tends to occur in weekly or biweekly episodes and users perceive that the effects facilitate social functioning" (R. Siegel 1989: 222–23). At the far end of the drug use continuum is the drug-dependent, compulsive user whose life often revolves around obtaining, maintaining, and using a supply of drugs. For the compulsive user, failure to ingest an adequate supply of the desired drug results in psychological stress and discomfort, and there may also be physical withdrawal symptoms.

Understanding the use of psychoactive substances as a continuum allows the issue of drugs to be placed in its proper perspective: There is nothing inherently evil or virtuous about the use of psychoactive substances. For some—actually many—persons, they make life more enjoyable; hence the widespread use of tobacco and alcohol without serious unpleasant effects. For others, drugs become a burden as dependence brings dysfunction. In between these two extremes are a variety of drug *users* such as the underage

---

[1]For the story of a recreational heroin user who was not dysfunctional, see Marlowe 1999.

FIGURE 1.1
Drug Use Continuum

adolescent using tobacco or alcohol on occasion, which is common in our society. Adults may experiment with illegal drugs, marijuana and cocaine, for example, without moving up to more frequent, that is, recreational use. The recreational user enjoys a beer or cocktails on a regular basis, or ingests cocaine or heroin just before or at social events, during which the drug eases social interaction for this actor. Outside of this specific social setting, the recreational user abstains and, thereby, is in control of his or her use of drugs. For some, recreational use crosses into compulsive use marked by a preoccupation with securing and using drugs in the face of negative consequences, such as losing a job, severe disruption of social relationships, and/or involvement with the criminal justice system.

What we know about those who use psychoactive drugs is skewed toward compulsive users, particularly with respect to illegal drugs: Noncompulsive users have received very little research attention because they are hard to find. "Much data on users are gathered from treatment, law enforcement, and correctional institutions, and from other institutions allied with them. Naturally these data sources provide a highly selected sample of users: those who have encountered significant personal, medical, social, or legal problems in conjunction with their drug use, and thus represent the pathological end of the using spectrum" (Zinberg et al. 1978: 13). Such data "cannot be used to support a causal interpretation because of the absence of information on individuals who may have ingested a drug but had minimal or no negative consequences" (Newcomb and Bentler 1988: 13). This includes the recreational user.

Addiction

Norman Miller (1995) avoids using the term *drug abuse* and opts, instead, for **addiction**[2] characterized by:

1. *Preoccupation.* The addict assigns a high priority to acquiring drugs. Social relationships and employment are jeopardized in the quest for drugs and the consequences of use.
2. *Compulsion.* The addict continues to use drugs despite serious adverse consequences. He or she will often deny the connection between the adverse consequences and the use of drugs.
3. *Relapse.* In the face of adverse consequences, addicts discontinue drugs but subsequently return to abnormal use.

Dennis Donovan (1988: 6) conceives of addiction as a "complex, progressive behavior pattern having biological, psychological, sociological, and behavioral components. What sets this behavior apart from others is the individual's overwhelmingly pathological involvement in or attachment to it, subjective compulsion to continue it, and reduced ability to exert personal control over it. . . . The behavior pattern continues despite its negative impact on the physical, psychological, and social function of the individual."

---

[2]*Addiction* is from the Latin verb *addicere:* to bind a person to one thing or another.

Definition Determines Response

A variety of lawful substances are addicting and have been abused by any number of "respectable persons," including major government officials. Social expectations and definitions determine what kind of drug-taking is appropriate and the social situations that are approved and disapproved for drug use. The use of drugs is neither inherently bad nor inherently good—these are socially determined values (Goode 1989). Thus, Mormons and Christian Scientists consider use of tea and coffee "abusive," while Moslems and some Protestant denominations have the same view of alcohol, although they permit tobacco smoking. The National Commission on Marijuana and Drug Abuse (1973: 13) argues that *drug abuse* "must be deleted from official pronouncements and public policy dialogue" because the "term has no functional utility and has become no more than an arbitrary codeword for that drug use which is presently considered wrong." As the history in Chapter 2 informs us, moderate use of a drug will be defined as "abuse"—and illegal—or it will be socially acceptable—and lawful—if society so determines, regardless of the relative danger inherent in the substance. In other words: How society defines drug abuse determines how society responds to drug use.

Drugs of Abuse

In this book we will examine psychoactive drugs in each of three categories according to their primary effect on the central nervous system: depressants, stimulants, and hallucinogens. (Some chemicals, such as cannabis and MDMA/ecstasy, have a combination of these characteristics.) A drug can have at least three different names: chemical, generic, and trade, and those that have a legitimate medical use may be marketed under a variety of trade names. Trade names begin with a capital letter, while chemical or generic titles are in lowercase.

Depressants

Depressants depress the central nervous system (CNS) and can reduce pain. The most frequently used drug in this category is alcohol; the most frequently used illegal drug is the opiate derivative heroin. Other depressants, all of which have some medical use, include morphine, codeine, methadone, barbiturates, methaqualone, and tranquilizers. These substances can cause physical and psychological dependence—a craving—and withdrawal results in physical and psychological stress. Opiate derivatives (heroin, morphine, codeine) and opiumlike drugs such as methadone are often referred to as **narcotics.** The depressant category also includes **inhalants,** a variety of readily available products routinely kept in the home, such as glue, paint thinner, hair spray, and nail polish remover. They produce vapors that when inhaled can cause an intoxication similar to that of alcohol.

Stimulants

Stimulants elevate mood—produce feelings of well-being—by stimulating the central nervous system. The most frequently used drugs in this category are caffeine and nicotine; the most frequently used illegal stimulant is cocaine, which, along with amphetamines, has some limited medical use.

Hallucinogens

These drugs alter perceptual functions: the term **hallucinogen,** rather than, for example, psychoactive or psychedelic, is a value-laden one. The most frequently used hallucinogens are LSD (lysergic acid diethylamide) and PCP (phencyclidine). Both are produced chemically, and neither has any legitimate medical use. There are also organic hallucinogens such as mescaline, which is found in the peyote cactus. The lawful use of peyote is limited to the religious ceremonies of the Native American church, which some, but not all, states exempt from their controlled substances statutes. Cannabis, frequently used in the form of marijuana, exhibits some of the characteristics of hallucinogens, depressants, and even stimulants. Its lawful use (in the liquid form of THC, its psychoactive ingredient) is limited to the treatment of glaucoma and to reduce some of the side effects of cancer chemotherapy.

Estimating the Extent of the Drug Problem

Information on the drug problem in the United States is derived from six indicators, each providing a different perspective on the problem, and they complement one another. Although the indicators have recognized limitations and deficiencies that affect the quality of information, the agencies that prepare them believe the data can reliably portray general trends. Richard Rosenfeld and Scott Decker (1999) found a high correlation between drug use measurements that rely on the criminal justice system (Arrestee Drug Abuse Monitoring) and those based on reports from hospitals and medical examiners (Drug Abuse Warning Network). The fact that these two different indicators tell basically the same story raises confidence in their validity. Those indicators using self-reports (National Household and Monitoring the Future) raise questions since they have been found to be least valid for the more stigmatized drugs such as heroin and cocaine (General Accounting Office 1998; hereafter GAO).

Efforts to determine the prevalence of heroin use have a long history with precise estimates remaining difficult to determine. Standard methods of measuring prevalence such as household surveys are not adequate—heroin use is rare in the general population so that only a small number of users would be included in a household survey. Survey-based estimates substantially underestimate prevalence because of difficulties in locating heroin abusers (e.g., many of them are not living in stable households). In addition, because heroin use is an illegal activity, heroin users may not accurately report their use.

National Household Survey on Drug Abuse

The National Household Survey on Drug Abuse (**NHSDA**) is funded by the National Institute of Drug Abuse (**NIDA**). Between 1972 and 1990, NHSDA was conducted every two or three years, and annually since 1990. The survey provides data on incidence, prevalence, and trends of drug use for persons aged 12 and older living in households. Results are based on about 9,000 interviews with persons randomly selected from the household population, who record their responses on self-administered answer sheets. In 1991, the NHSDA sample was increased to more than 30,000 and in 1999, to 70,000 interviews.

Household Survey data are used in conjunction with Monitoring the Future survey data (discussed below) to describe levels of drug use in specific segments of the population. Household Survey data may also be used in conjunction with DAWN data (discussed below) to describe long-term trends in drug abuse. In the past, self-report surveys on drug use have been found to be reasonably trustworthy (Oetting and Beauvais 1990), but more recently questions have been raised about their accuracy (GAO 1998).

Survey limitations include the fact that the homeless and persons living in military installations, dormitories, and institutions such as jails, prisons, and hospitals are not covered, although the survey attempts to approximate these populations by using a controversial "imputation" procedure (GAO 1993). Also, some people refuse to participate. Because the survey is voluntary and the questionnaires are self-administered, the results may be biased (and probably understate the scope of the drug problem). Concern has also been expressed over privacy and comprehension issues. During the interviews of 25–30 percent of respondents aged 12 to 17 at the time the survey was administered, there was a third person present. And any number of persons have difficulty with English or with understanding the drug-use jargon employed by the survey (GAO 1993).

Monitoring the Future

The Monitoring the Future study is conducted by the Institute for Social Research at the University of Michigan for the National Institute of Drug Abuse. Annual surveys of high school seniors began in 1975, and eighth- and tenth-grade students were added in 1991. Students are drawn to be representative of all students in U.S. public and private schools. About 40,000 students located in about 400 schools complete questionnaires in their classrooms every spring.

Primary uses of the data include: (1) assessing the prevalence and trends of drug use among high school seniors; and (2) gaining a better understanding of the lifestyles and value orientations associated with patterns of drug use and monitoring how these orientations are shifting over time. Follow-up surveys of representative subsamples of the original graduates, which have been conducted for over a decade, provide data on young adults and college students. According to the survey, adolescent drug use began increasing dramatically in the late 1960s, peaking in 1979. It then fell throughout the 1980s, hitting a low in 1991 and 1992 before beginning to climb again (Ho 1999). By the end of the decade, it remained steady, with only minor fluctuations. In 2001, MTF marked the fifth year in a row that drug and alcohol use among eighth, ninth, and twelfth graders remained stable or, in some cases, such as cigarette smoking, decreased. In 2002, for the first time, smoking, drinking, and the use of illegal drugs among adolescents fell simultaneously. The survey also found that the use of MDMA (ecstasy) showed statistically significant declines for the first time after rising rapidly in recent years. The only significant increases in drug use were crack use by tenth graders in the past year and use of sedatives by twelfth graders in the past year. Fifty-three percent of high school seniors reported using an illicit drug at least once in their lives, 41 percent within the past year, and 25 percent within the last month (Drug Use Summary 2003).

The survey has several limitations. High school dropouts (about 30 percent of students), who are associated with higher rates of drug use, are not part of the sampled universe. Chronic absentees, who may also have higher rates of abuse, are less likely to be surveyed (Liu 1994). In Texas, for example, youths entering that state's detention facilities are nearly twelve times as likely to have used cocaine as youngsters in school (Fredlund et al. 1990). Conscious or unconscious distortions in self-reporting information can also bias results. In addition, new trends in drug abuse, such as the use of crack, may not be initially detected because the survey is designed to measure only drugs abused at significant levels. Questions about crack were asked for the first time in the 1986 survey, and questions about ecstasy (MDMA) were first asked in 1996. There is also concern over the lack of anonymity: The name, address, and telephone number of the respondent appears on the questionnaire's cover sheet in order to facilitate follow-up surveys.

Drug Abuse Warning Network (DAWN)

DAWN, which was initiated in 1972 and funded by NIDA, is a large-scale drug abuse data collection system designed as an early-warning indicator of the nation's drug abuse problem. An episode report is submitted for each drug abuse patient who visits the emergency room of a hospital participating in DAWN and for each drug abuse death encountered by a participating medical examiner or coroner. In a single emergency room "episode," a patient may "mention" having ingested more than one drug. DAWN records each drug a patient reports having used within four days before the hospital visit and relays the information to the Drug Enforcement Administration (DEA). Data are collected from a nonrandom sample in about twenty selected metropolitan areas throughout the country representing approximately one-third of the U.S. population.

While standard definitions and data collection procedures exist, variations among individual reporters may occur. Incomplete reporting, turnover of reporting facilities and personnel, and reporting delays of up to one year (primarily for medical examiner data) are some of the system's limitations. For hospital emergencies, the National Narcotics Intelligence Consumers Committee (NNICC), in its last two publications, has used data from the DAWN Consistent Panel rather than from the Total Panel. The Consistent Panel includes only those hospitals reporting on a consistent basis (specifically, 90 percent or more of each year). Data representing the total DAWN system were not used for trend analysis by NNICC because of reporting fluctuations. While medical examiner/coroner data are not subject to the same inconsistencies, reports are so small compared with the total DAWN system that they are not considered a valid trend indicator. (For a discussion of the uses and abuses of DAWN data, see Caulkins, Ebener, and McCaffrey 1995.)

Arrestee Drug Abuse Monitoring (ADAM)

Drug Use Forecasting, now called Arrestee Drug Abuse Monitoring (**ADAM**), began in New York City in 1987, and by 1990, twenty-five of the largest cities in the United States were involved. By 2000, there were more than thirty-nine sites, most of them in large urban areas. ADAM measures the extent of drug use in the high-risk population who have been arrested. Demographic, drug use and purchase, housing, method of support, and health insurance data are collected in central police booking facilities in each city. For approximately fourteen consecutive evenings each quarter, staff obtain voluntary and anonymous urine specimens and interviews from a new sample of arrestees. In each site approximately 225 males are sampled. All female arrestees, regardless of charge, are included in the sample because of the small number of female arrestees available. Responses are consistently high: Over 90 percent agree to be interviewed, and more than 80 percent of those interviewed provide urine specimens.

To obtain samples with a sufficient distribution of arrest charges, the number of male arrestees in each sample who are charged with drug-related offenses (sale or possession) is limited—one out of five; such persons are most likely to be using drugs at the time of their arrest and thus are undersampled. ADAM statistics are minimum estimates of drug use by male arrestees.

Urine samples are analyzed for ten drugs: cocaine, opiates, marijuana, PCP, methadone, benzodiazepine (Valium), methaqualone, propoxyphene (Darvon), barbiturates, and amphetamines. Except for marijuana and PCP, which can be detected several weeks after use, urine tests detect use in the previous two to three days. The ADAM data reveal that cocaine continues to be the substance of choice of a majority of those arrested, with heroin remaining important but far less popular. Amphetamines were detected in less than 10 percent of the arrestees, and were most likely to be found in western states.

A number of validation issues arise with respect to ADAM. Central booking facilities, where the samples are selected, serve different areas of a city or county. This makes generalizing to the wider population of arrestees unreliable. The busy, if not frantic, pace of most central booking facilities makes respondent-selection procedures difficult, leading to questions about sampling techniques. And a study by the General Accounting Office (1993) revealed that ADAM standards in selecting arrestees have not been applied uniformly across sites. Further, the nature of lockups in booking facilities makes confidentiality difficult to achieve.

Peter Reuter (1999: 18) concludes that each of the four drug use indicators provides useful information: "Monitoring the Future provided early indications of the cocaine epidemic, while ADAM did a good job in tracking its later stages. DAWN has shown that drug problems can increase even as the rate of drug use in the population stabilizes and has provided compelling evidence that drug problems are disproportionately borne by poor and urban minority populations. The National Household Survey on Drug Abuse has provided an essential measure of the decline in drug use in the general population through the 1980s."

National Narcotics Intelligence Estimates

The National Narcotics Intelligence Consumers Committee (**NNICC**) is a federal interagency mechanism for coordinating drug intelligence collection requirements and producing joint intelligence estimates. NNICC issues periodic reports on the worldwide illicit drug situation. The report contains estimates of illegal drug production and availability and discusses four major drug categories: marijuana, cocaine, opiates, and synthetic drugs. The report also contains information on drug-trafficking routes and methods and on the flow of drug-related money.

Estimates of illegal drug quantities are very difficult to make because little reliable data exist. NNICC obtains drug production data for individual countries from host country records, local contacts, informants, and sophisticated intelligence-gathering techniques. It derives drug availability and consumption estimates from sample surveys, drug seizures, drug price and purity data, drug-related hospital emergencies, and other data.

Retail Price/Purity

The price and purity levels of illegal drugs at the retail (consumer) level are key values in the NNICC estimating process. The DEA gathers these data, which are used as an indicator of drug availability. Drug prices are derived from a computerized database containing reports on purchases of, and negotiations to purchase, illegal drugs by undercover federal, state, and local law enforcement officers. Purity levels for heroin and cocaine are determined through laboratory analysis. (Purity levels are not applicable to marijuana and most synthetic drugs.) The limited number of reports and lack of randomness are problems that have plagued these indicators in the past (Comptroller General 1988a). In addition, the price paid by undercover officers is affected by quantity discounts, thus underestimating the actual per dose retail price; or the officers may pay a premium price because they are not known to their dealers, and new customers are typically charged more (Caulkins 1994).

Drug Use: How Many, How Much?

What do these indicators reveal? More than 14 million Americans use illicit drugs—for about 60 percent it is marijuana—this is about half of the 1979 peak year. In 1979, nearly 30 million people used marijuana at least once; that number stabilized by 2000 to about 19 million (Haynes 2002). An estimated 10 percent of youths aged 12–17 report using an illicit drug at least once in the past 30 days; for about 80 percent it was marijuana. Teen inhalant use is about 1 percent. There are more than 1 million estimated hallucinogen users.

NHSDA
Monitoring the Future
DAWN
ADAM
NNICC
Retail Price

There are an estimated 230,000 "casual" and 500,000 "heavy" users of heroin. About 3 million persons have used heroin at least once in their lifetime. An estimated 1.8 million Americans aged 12 and older are users of cocaine—cocaine use reached a peak of 5.7 million in 1985. The National Household Survey reveals that about 9 million persons have tried methamphetamine at least once, and about 8 percent of high school seniors report taking it at least once. About 12 percent of high school seniors report trying ecstasy, which has stimulating and hallucinogenic properties. The rate for college students is 13 percent (*MDMA* 2002). Except for an increase in the use of ecstasy—probably explained by its increasing availability—overall use of illicit drugs among teenagers generally remained unchanged for the last few years.

Smoking (nicotine) rates in the United States have remained virtually unchanged in more than a decade, although the rate among young adults aged 18–25 has increased to more than 40 percent.

An estimated 60 million Americans aged 12 and older smoke cigarettes; about 4 million are under 18. About 5 percent of youths aged 12–17 smoke cigars. Adults who live below the poverty line are more likely to smoke than those living above the poverty line, and high school dropouts are three times more likely to smoke than college graduates. About 44.5 million adults describe themselves as smokers who had quit.

According to the National Household Survey on Drug Abuse, in 2002 more than half of the United States population aged 12 and older used alcohol. Thirty percent engage in binge drinking (drinking five or more drinks on the same occasion on at least 1 day in the past 30 days), and more than 10 percent are heavy drinkers. Among youth aged 12–17, the rate of alcohol use was about 50 percent in 1979 but has fallen to less than 20 percent. The rate of binge drinking among young adults aged 18–25 is more than 30 percent, and heavy alcohol use is about 14 percent. After decreasing to about 38 percent in 1998, the proportion of tenth graders who reported having "been drunk" sometime during the past year increased to almost 41 percent in 1999. An estimated 46 million persons aged 12 or older are binge drinkers. Almost one in five underage persons aged 12–20 is a binge drinker. The rate of binge drinking among underage persons is almost as high as among adults aged 21 or older.

The national survey of drug use among high school students has been tracking the use of inhalants by eighth and tenth graders since 1991. Inhalant use for all grades appears to have peaked in 1995. Inhalant use continues to be more prevalent among eighth graders than students in the tenth or twelfth grade. Lifetime use of inhalants among eighth graders decreased from 19.7 percent in 1999 to 17.9 percent in 2000. During the 10 years that data have been collected for eighth graders, inhalant use was highest in 1995, with percentages of 21.6 for lifetime use, 12.8 for past year use, and 6.1 for past month use. In 2002, 7.7 percent of eighth graders, 5.8 percent of tenth graders, and 4.5 percent of twelfth graders used inhalants in the past year (*Inhalants* 2003). A survey by the National Parents' Resource Institute for Drug Education of 100,000 students in grades six to twelve in rural and suburban school districts revealed that while the overall percentage of students using illegal drugs like cocaine, heroin, and marijuana fell to an 8-year low, the percentage using cocaine and heroin monthly remained the same for sixth, eighth, and twelfth graders ("Teenage Drug Use . . ." 2002).

Estimates

There are roughly 175,000 emergency room incidents related to cocaine each year, while heroin and marijuana are each implicated in roughly 97,000 incidents. Estimates based on the Household Survey indicate 2.8 million Americans are "dependent" on illegal drugs, while an additional 1.5 million fall in the less severe "abuser" category (*National Drug Control Strategy* 2002).

Most Commonly Abused Prescription Drugs

Although many prescription drugs can be abused or misused, three classes of prescription drugs are most commonly abused:

1. **Opioids,** which are most often prescribed to treat pain;
2. CNS depressants, which are used to treat anxiety and sleep disorders;
3. Stimulants, which are prescribed to treat the sleep disorder narcolepsy, attention-deficit hyperactivity disorder (ADHD), and obesity.

Source: National Institute on Drug Abuse

These estimates may not account for the abuse of prescription drugs, painkillers, and sedatives, typically by white persons of at least middle-class status. For these persons such drugs are easier to acquire than their illegal street counterparts. And they are cheaper than street drugs such as heroin and cocaine. The cost of an evening's worth of cocaine or heroin can run into hundreds of dollars, whereas in Miami, for example, dealers sell Vicodin, Valium, Xanax, and oxycodone, a painkiller often given to cancer patients, for as little as three to four dollars a pill.

In addition, these drugs are popular because, even without a doctor's prescription, access is increasing. Restocking trips are often taken to Mexico, where the black market continues to grow. It is estimated that Tijuana alone has about 1,700 pharmacies, many of which sell controlled substances illegally over the counter. And in some instances, doctors in Mexico sell prescriptions (Kirsebbaum 2002).

What Is the Connection Between Drugs and Crime?

The traditional way of considering the question of drugs and crime is the tripartite model offered by Paul Goldstein (1985):

1. *Offenses that are psychopharmacology induced.* The result of a response to the intoxicating effects of a drug, including biological features (discussed in Chapter 3)
2. *Economic-compulsive.* Crime driven by a need to buy drugs
3. *Systemic.* Drug use as part of a pattern of criminal behaviors but not driven by or the result of drug use (violence associated with the business of drugs, for example)

The outlawing of certain drugs created criminal opportunities for those daring enough to enter this market (discussed in Chapter 11). Participants become actors in a business that has no mechanisms for resolving disputes except violence. The outlawing of certain drugs also makes criminals of those who use (actually the crime is "possession")

Healthy Drug Use?
"Acknowledging potentially healthy relationships with drugs allows us to better identify unhealthy ones. This may sound heretical to the professionals who readily categorize all illicit drug use as abuse. But the refusal to recognize healthy relationships with stigmatized drugs hinders our understanding of drug-related problems and healthy relationships with them. This refusal can even increase negative drug use by failing to consider broader circumstances such as poverty, exclusion, and marginalization itself, which may influence one's relationship with drugs" (Whiteacre and Pepinsky 2002: 27).

these chemicals while substantially inflating the cost of the substances to the consumer. To secure their preferred substance, abusers of illegal drugs typically target salable property but will also commit robbery and/or sell drugs. There is a criminal population whose nondrug law violations are based only on their desire to secure drugs. However, it is also clear that an unknown percentage, perhaps a majority, of drug abusers, particularly those addicted to heroin, were criminals whose drug abuse is simply part of a pattern of hedonistic and antisocial behavior. George Vaillant (1970: 488) reports that no matter what their class origins, most persons who use narcotics "have a greater tendency than their socioeconomic peers to be delinquent," and even drug-abusing physicians "are relatively irresponsible before drug addiction."[3] In a study of drug addicts in a treatment program, drug use played an earlier role than in offender-based studies. But among the general population, "other forms of deviance or criminality precede the onset of illicit drug use (Farabee, Joshi, and Anglin 2001).

Research on Adolescents

Research has determined that "youngsters who have conduct problems are more likely than others to be exposed to illicit drugs" (Swan n.d.: 1). Adolescents with emotional and behavioral problems are more likely to abuse alcohol, tobacco, and illicit drugs, according to a study by the Substance Abuse and Mental Health Services Administration (1999). The study found that adolescents inclined toward substance abuse admitted to delinquent behaviors such as stealing, cutting classes or skipping school, and hanging around with others who get into trouble. They also reported poor peer and parental relations and such problems as difficulty concentrating in school or focusing attention on tasks at home, at part-time work, or even when involved in sports.

When compared to adolescents having fewer, or less serious, behavioral problems, adolescents who repeatedly stole, showed physical aggression, or ran away from home were seven times more likely to be dependent on alcohol or illicit drugs. They were more than four times as likely to have used marijuana in the past month, and seven times more likely to have used other illicit drugs. They were nearly three times as likely to have used alcohol in the past month; three times as likely to have smoked cigarettes in the past month; and nearly nine times as likely to need treatment for drug abuse. According to the 2001 National Household Survey on Drug Abuse (discussed earlier), youths who engaged in violent behaviors during the past year were more likely to report past month alcohol and illicit drug use than youths who did not engage in violent behaviors during the past year.

---

[3]Concern over the abuse of morphine by medical doctors dates back to at least the latter part of the nineteenth century (Mattison 1883), and in 1964 Charles Winick wrote of the physician addict, a loner who does not knowingly associate with other addicts. In fact, drug abuse is a significant problem for the medical profession, with the addiction rate for physicians estimated at anywhere from 30 to 100 times that for the population at large (Grosswirth 1982). In more recent years the drug of choice for use by physicians tends to be the powerful synthetic opiate fentanyl (Kennedy 1995).

A study of male adolescent ninth and tenth graders in Washington, D.C., found that for about half of those who used drugs (mostly marijuana), criminal behavior preceded use; for the other half, criminal behavior followed drug use. However, "those both using and selling drugs were more than twice as likely to have started using drugs before committing crimes as were those using but not selling drugs" (Brounstein et al. 1990: 3–4). In fact, we cannot be sure whether drug abuse leads to crime, or criminals tend to abuse drugs. Or perhaps neither—there are variables that lead to drug abuse and the same variables lead to crime—see Figure 1.2 (McBride and McCoy 1981; also Speckart and Anglin 1985, 1987). Indeed, areas with high levels of delinquency and crime also have high levels of drug usage, while the reverse is also true. In their study, Cheryl Carpenter and her colleagues (1988) found that the most seriously delinquent adolescents also abused drugs, but crime and drug use appeared to be independent of one another—both apparently related to other causal variables. In fact, extensive research informs us that a relatively small segment of youths commit a disproportionate amount of juvenile crime, and "the majority of serious crimes committed by youths are concentrated among serious delinquents who are also heavy users of alcohol and other drugs" (B. D. Johnson et al. 1991: 206). For these persons, both drug use and crime appear to be part of a troubled lifestyle.

Research on Adults

There is undoubtedly a high correlation between drug use and nondrug crime (e.g., Gandossy et al. 1980; B. D. Johnson et al. 1985; Nurco et al. 1985; Inciardi 1986; Wish and Johnson 1986). One study found that more than half of the men arrested in twelve major cities tested positive for recent use of illicit drugs (Kerr 1988). "A strong consensus has emerged in the research literature that the most frequent, serious offenders are also the heaviest drug users" (Visher 1990: 330). However, is it drug use that leads to criminal behavior?

FIGURE 1.2
Relationship Between Drugs and Crime: Three Possibilities

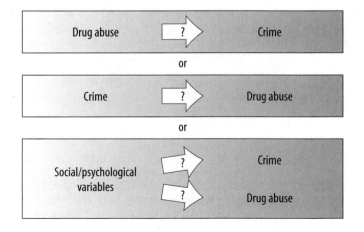

The question of whether crime is a pre- or postdrug use phenomenon is actually an oversimplification, and James Inciardi (1981: 59) argues that "the pursuit of some simple cause-and-effect relationship may be futile." His data found, for example:

> Among the males, there seems to be a clear progression from alcohol to crime, to drug abuse, to arrest, and then to heroin use. But upon closer inspection, the pattern is not altogether clear. At one level, for example, criminal activity can be viewed as predating one's drug-using career, because the median point of the first crime is slightly below that of first drug abuse, and is considerably before the onset of heroin use. But, at the same time, if alcohol intoxication at a median age of 13.3 years were to be considered substance abuse, then crime is clearly a phenomenon that succeeds substance abuse. Among the females, the description is even more complex. In the population of female heroin users, criminal activity occurred after both alcohol and other drug abuse and marijuana use, but before involvement with the more debilitating barbiturates and heroin.

A study of heroin addicts in Wilmington, Delaware, revealed criminal and drug careers rather independent of one another, the two merging as the use of heroin became overarching (Faupel and Klockars 1987).

This issue has serious policy implications. If drug abusers simply continue in crime after they have given up drug abuse, efforts to reduce crime by reducing drug abuse are doomed to fail. As James Q. Wilson (1975: 137) points out, perhaps "some addicts who steal to support their habit come to regard crime as more profitable than normal employment. They would probably continue to steal to provide themselves with an income even after they no longer needed to use part of that income to buy heroin" or any other illegal substance. M. Douglas Anglin and George Speckart (1988: 223) found, however, "that levels of criminality after the addiction career [is over] are near zero, a finding that is compatible with data presented by other authors and is illustrative of the 'maturing out' phase of the addiction career 'life cycle.' "

In fact, the sequence of drug use and crime has produced contradictory findings (Huizinga, Menard, and Elliott 1989). For example, James Vorenberg and Irving Lukoff (1973) found that the criminal careers of a substantial segment of the heroin addicts they studied antedated the onset of heroin use. Furthermore, they found that those whose criminality preceded heroin use tended to be more involved in violent criminal behavior. Anglin and Speckart (1988) report that between 60 and 75 percent of the addicts in their samples had arrest histories that preceded addiction. Paul Cushman (1974: 43) found, however, that the heroin addicts he studied were predominantly noncriminal before addiction, and experienced "progressively increased rates of annual arrests after addiction started." (Of course, this finding could be the result of addicts being less adept at crime.) Whatever the relationship—drug abuse leading to crime or criminals becoming drug abusers—some researchers (Ball et al. 1979; Johnson, Lipton, and Wish 1986) have found that the amount of criminality tends to be sharply reduced when persons who have been narcotic addicts are no longer addicted. Furthermore, Bruce Johnson and his colleagues (1985; 1989) and Anglin and Speckart (1988) found that the more frequent the drug use, the more serious the types of crime committed; for example, burglary and robbery instead of shoplifting and other larcenies. (For a summary of research findings on this issue, see Chaiken and Chaiken 1990.)

The crime–drug abuse question has typically been related to the abuse of heroin, not cocaine. During the time that this writer was a parole officer in New York (1964–1978), offenders who had used cocaine were rare, while studies by the New York State Division of Parole indicated that those who had used heroin were a substantial majority of parole clientele in the New York City area. Three decades ago, Troy Duster (1970: 42) was able to state that "cocaine usage is rare in the United States." However, during the 1980s the abuse of cocaine dramatically increased in the same populations that have traditionally been the major consumers of heroin. During these years cocaine use crossed social class lines and the age of onset dropped considerably. Furthermore:

> Until recently it has been assumed that cocaine was not a criminogenic force toward income-generating crime because cocaine does not have the physiological addictive power of heroin and because cocaine users were viewed as unlikely to come from population groups with high crime rates. Cocaine was thought to be a drug of the middle and upper class. These assumptions appear to be unjustified. Weekly and daily cocaine use are associated with high levels of illegal income. (J. Collins, Hubbard, and Rachel 1985: 759)

During the 1980s, cocaine, however—in the smokable form of crack—not heroin, became the "in" drug among young adults aged 18–25 in low-income areas of New York City. This was a dramatic change from the drug scene of the late 1960s and early 1970s, when heroin was the major problem. Furthermore, heroin abusers typically use cocaine, many as frequently as they do heroin, in a combination known as a "speedball." The use of these substances, David Smith (1986) notes, is part of a lifestyle that also includes abuse of alcohol, marijuana, barbiturates, and amphetamines—and crime. In one study of 105 drug abusers, cocaine was the primary drug of choice, and 50 percent also abused alcohol (B. D. Johnson, Anderson, and Wish 1989). And one study found that the business of crack is crime-intensive in that it "leads serious delinquents to become even more seriously involved in crime" (Inciardi and Pottieger 1991: 268). It appears that crack intensifies the criminal behaviors in which users were actively involved before initiation into crack use, except for women; they moved from property crimes to prostitution (Chin and Fagan 1990). Indeed, the significant drop in homicides in some major cities, New York in particular, is, at least in part, attributed to the decline in crack use by young persons.

The National Institute of Justice concludes: "Assessing the nature and extent of the influence of drugs on crime requires that reliable information about the offense and the offender be available, and that definitions be consistent. In face of problematic evidence, it is impossible to say quantitatively how much drugs influence the occurrence of crime" (*Fact Sheet: Drug Related Crime* 1995: 3). While "there is a generally consistent overall pattern of positive and sometimes quite strong associations between illegal drug use and criminal behavior of other types," research has not been able to validate a causal link between drug use and criminal behavior (Anthony and Forman 2000: 27). While many different data sources establish a raw correlation between drug use and criminal offenses, correlation does not equal causation. Thus, drug use might cause (promote, encourage) crime; or criminality might cause (promote, encourage) drug use; and/or both may be caused (promoted, encouraged) by other variables—environmental, situational, and/or biological (MacCoun, Kilmer, and Reuter 2002).

Drugs and Violence

More than three decades ago, Edwin Schur (1965) argued that narcotic addiction in the United States seems to reduce the inclination to engage in violent crime. However, a more recent research effort found that heroin users (not necessarily addicts) are at least as violent as, and perhaps more violent than, their nondrug- or nonheroin-using criminal counterparts (B. D. Johnson, Lipton, Wish 1986), which is consistent with this writer's experience as a parole officer. In fact, the researchers report, "About half of the most violent criminals are heroin abusers" (1986b: 3). It is difficult to determine whether this is simply a problem of changing definitions or a changing drug population. While there is no evidence that crime results from the direct effects of heroin itself—indeed, the substance appears to have a pacifying effect—the irritability resulting from withdrawal symptoms has been known to lead to violence (P. Goldstein 1985).

This writer dealt with heroin addicts for 14 years and found many, if not most, to be quite capable of committing violent acts including homicide—they were frequently convicted of violent crimes. In addition, as we shall discuss in Chapter 11, the heroin distribution subculture at every level—from wholesaling to street sale—is permeated with extreme levels of violence. And, as noted earlier, many drug abusers use more than one psychoactive chemical (polydrug abuse), thus expanding the possible behavioral effects of the different combinations. If the additional substance is alcohol, which is relatively inexpensive, the drug-crime nexus is mitigated, at least for income-generating crimes; a great deal of violent noneconomic crime is known to be linked to alcohol intoxication. Crimes against persons and violence by drug users are often related to their use of alcohol (Dembo et al. 1991; P. Goldstein et al. 1991). And a Canadian study found that alcohol-dependent prison inmates were twice as likely to have committed violent crimes as their most serious crime, compared with those dependent on drugs ("Canadian Study Quantifies Link . . ." 2002).

Alcohol is an important element in a great deal of crime: Drunk driving is the cause of about 16,000 deaths annually; more than 60 percent of homicides involve alcohol use by both offender and victim; and about 65 percent of aggressive sexual acts against women involve alcohol use by the offender. Research has revealed that the pharmacological effects of alcohol can cause aggression in some persons, and alcohol is a factor in nearly half of America's murders, suicides, and accidental deaths. It is a factor in nearly 40 percent of violent crimes ("Coming to Grips with Alcoholism" 1987; Chermack and Taylor 1995; Associated Press 1998; Greenfeld 1998; Associated Press 1999a).

More than 20 percent of prison inmates incarcerated for violent crimes were under the influence of alcohol when they committed their crime (*Behind Bars* . . . 1998). But is there a causal link: Would the crimes have been committed in the absence of alcohol? Was alcohol used to provide "courage" for an act that was being planned? We know that alcohol consumption can lead to disinhibition, but what distinguishes "the life of the party" from the felonious assailant? Alcohol can also impair the processing of information and judgment, thus causing a misinterpretation of events or the behavior of others, resulting, for example, in assault and/or aggressive sexual behavior (e.g., date rape).

Other drugs (PCP and cocaine, for example) may involve otherwise normal persons in violent behavior. The Detroit medical examiner's office reported that 37 percent of that city's homicide victims had cocaine in their blood samples (Franklin 1987), indicating that cocaine users either engage in dangerous behavior or expose themselves to places or situations where violence is likely to occur. And persons intent on committing violent crimes, such as robbery, may ingest alcohol or stimulants for courage—alcohol in small doses acts as a stimulant (W. Hunt 1983). "The relationship between drugs and violence has been consistently documented in both the popular press and in social scientific research" (P. Goldstein 1985: 494).

Research has found that crack users are more likely to commit crimes against persons than against property. Crack sellers also appear to be more violent than other drug sellers, and their violence is not limited to drug transactions (Belenko and Chin 1989; Fagan and Chin 1991). There was a surge in children beaten and killed by their crack-abusing parents (Kerr 1988). However, a study in Kansas City, Missouri, of almost 1,500 arrestees, about half of whom abused cocaine, found "no reason to believe that drug using offenders, especially those characterized by heavy or addictive use, are more likely to be arrested for serious or violent offenses than nondrug using offenders. At the very least, it appears that nondrug using offenders commit a relatively higher rate of violent and predatory crimes" (Whitlock, Collings, and Burnett 1990: 21).

Now that we have been introduced to the topic, in Chapter 2 we will examine the history of drugs and drug abuse.

SUMMARY

The drug use continuum helps in defining the slippery term *drug abuse,* but the important point is that how society defines drug abuse determines how it responds to drug use. Drugs—substances with mood-altering, psychoactive effects—can be categorized by their primary effect on the central nervous system: depressants, stimulants, and hallucinogens. Drug use measurements in the United States come from six sources: two using self-reports, hospital reporting, central police booking reporting, NNICC estimates, and retail price/purity information. Drug abuse and crime are connected, but the relationship is not clear: Does drug abuse cause crime, does crime cause drug abuse, or are there other variables that cause both?

 **INTERNET CONNECTIONS**   Arrestee Drug Abuse Monitoring Program (ADAM): www.adam-nij.net
Drug Abuse Warning Network (DAWN): www.sangas.gov/oas/dawn.htm

Monitoring the Future: www.monitoringthefuture.org
National Institute on Drug Abuse: www.nida.gov
Texas Commission on Alcohol and Drug Abuse: www.tcada.state.tx.us/research

REVIEW QUESTIONS

1. Why is *drug abuse* not a scientific term?
2. What are the four variables that typically enter into a definition of drug abuse?
3. What are the three categories of drugs of abuse?
4. Why have noncompulsive drug users received little research attention?
5. What factors determine whether the moderate use of a psychoactive substance will be defined as drug abuse?
6. What is the difference between drug abuse and drug addiction?
7. What are the methods used to estimate the amount of drug use in the United States?
8. What are the shortcomings of these efforts?
9. How does polydrug use make the issue of drug abuse more complicated?
10. What are the three possible relationships between drugs and criminal behavior?
11. What has research determined with respect to adolescent drug use?
12. What is the relationship between drugs and violence?
13. What policy implications flow from the relationship between drugs and criminal behavior?

CHAPTER 2   Drug Use and Legislation: A History

The United States of America during the nineteenth century could quite properly be described as a dope fiend's paradise. —*Edward M. Brecher (1972: 3)*

American concern with narcotics is more than a medical or legal problem—it is in the fullest sense a political problem. The energy that has given impetus to drug control and prohibition came from profound tensions among socioeconomic groups, ethnic minorities, and generations—as well as the psychological attraction of certain drugs. The form of this control has been shaped by the gradual evolution of federal police powers. The bad results of drug use and the number of drug users have often been exaggerated for partisan advantage. Public demand for action against drug abuse has led to regulative decisions that lack a true regard for the reality of drug use. —*David Musto (1973: 244)*

The history of drug use and attempts at control provide insight into the complexity of more contemporary control, enforcement, and social issues on this subject.[1] As with many attempts at historical analyses, we are handicapped by the lack of adequate data on a number of items, particularly the extent of drug abuse at earlier periods in our history and of alcohol during Prohibition. Providing an empirically based analysis of changing policies with respect to drugs is difficult without the ability to measure the effect of these changes, and in fact, we cannot provide such measurements. Even today the number of persons abusing various substances, from alcohol to heroin, is the subject of debate.

Policy decisions, as we shall see in this chapter, have frequently been based on perceptions, beliefs, and attitudes with little empirical foundation. They have often reflected popular prejudices against a variety of racial and ethnic groups: "What we think about addiction very much depends on who is addicted" (Courtwright 1982: 3). And sometimes policy has reflected concern over issues of international, rather than domestic, politics. Since the earliest drug prohibitions in the United States reflected a concern with alcohol, we will begin our examination with a history of that substance.

---

[1]For an excellent history of global drug use, see Davenport-Hines (2002).

Alcohol and the Temperance Movement

Bad—and Thus to Be Banned—for All

"The temperance ideology differed from the modern alcoholism movement in that it maintained that alcohol is inevitably danger-ous for everyone. That is, some people might believe they can drink moderately, but it is only a matter of time before they en-counter increasing problems and completely lose control of their drinking. As strange as it seems to us today, the temperance message thus was that alcohol is inevitably addicting, in the same way that we now think of narcotics" (Peele 1995:37).

Drinking alcoholic beverages for recreational purposes has an ancient history, with records of such use dating back more than 5,000 years. The Bible records that Noah planted a vineyard and drank of the wine "and was drunken" (*Genesis* 9: 21). Later we are told that the daughters of Lot made their father drunk with wine in order to trick him into propagating the family line (*Genesis* 19: 32–36). This unseemly use of alcohol could certainly serve as an object lesson against its use, but the practice of drinking alcoholic beverages appears to be nearly universal.

The people of the United States have traditionally consumed large quantities of alco-hol. "Early Americans drank alcohol at home and at work, and alcohol was ever-present in colonial social life" (W. White 1998: 1). In 1785 Dr. Benjamin Rush, the Surgeon Gen-eral of the Continental Army and a signer of the Declaration of Independence, authored a pamphlet decrying the use of high-proof alcohol, which he claimed caused, among other maladies, moral degeneration, poverty, and crime. This helped fuel the move toward pro-hibition and inspired the establishment in 1808 of the Union Temperance Society, the first of many such organizations (Musto 1998). The Society was superseded by the American Temperance Union in 1836, and the work of the Union was supported by Protestant churches throughout the country. But the movement was divided over appropriate goals and strategies: Should moderation be preached, or should abstinence be forced through prohibition? "Between 1825 and 1850, the tide turned toward abstinence as a goal and legal alcohol prohibition as the means" (W. White 1998: 5).

U.S. opposition to alcohol was often intertwined with **nativism,** and efforts against alcohol and other psychoactive drugs were often a thinly veiled reaction to minority groups. (The early temperance movement, however, was strongly abolitionist.) Prohibi-tionists were typically rural white Protestants antagonistic to urban Roman Catholics, particularly the Irish, who used the social world of the saloon to gain political power in large cities such as New York and Chicago (Abadinsky 2003a).

Political and Business Support for Prohibition

The temperance movement made great progress everywhere in the country, and it often rode, or coincided, with the anti-immigrant sentiment that swept over the United States during the 1840s and early 1850s. In 1843 this led to the formation of the American Republican Party in New York, which spread nationally as the Native American party or the "Know-Nothings." (Many clubs were secret, and when outsiders inquired about the group, they were met with the response: "I know nothing.") Allied with a faction of the Whig Party, the Know-Nothings almost captured New York in 1854, and they did suc-ceed in carrying Delaware and Massachusetts. They also won important victories in Pennsylvania, Rhode Island, New Hampshire, Connecticut, Maryland, Kentucky, and California. In 1855 voters in Chicago elected a Know-Nothing mayor, and prohibition legislation was enacted in the Illinois legislature (but was defeated in a public referen-dum that same year [Asbury 1950]). By 1855, about a third of the United States had prohibition laws, and other states were considering their enactment (Musto 1998). Slavery and abolition and the ensuing Civil War subsequently took the place of temperance as the day's most pressing issues (Buchanan 1992).

In 1869 the Prohibition Party attempted, with limited success, to make alcohol a national issue. In 1874 the Women's Christian Temperance Union was established. Issues of temperance and nativism arose again strongly during the 1880s, leading to the formation of the American Protective Association, a rural-based organization that was strongly anti-Catholic and anti-Semitic. (For an excellent history of nativism in the United States, see D. Bennett 1988.) In 1893 the Anti-Saloon League was organized.

Around the turn of the twentieth century, these groups moved from efforts to change individual behavior to a campaign for national prohibition. After a period of dormancy, the prohibition movement was revived in the years 1907–1919 (Humphries and Greenberg 1981). By 1910 the Anti-Saloon League had become one of the most effective political action groups in U.S. history. It had mobilized Protestant churches behind a single purpose: to enact national prohibition (Tindall 1988). In 1915, nativism and prohibitionism fueled the rise of the Ku Klux Klan, and this time the KKK spread into northern states and exerted a great deal of political influence. During World War I an additional element, anti-German xenophobia, was added, because brewing and distilling were associated with German immigrants (Cashman 1981).

Big business was also interested in prohibition; alcohol contributed to industrial inefficiency, labor strife, and the saloon, which served the interests of machine politics:

> Around 1908, just as the Anti-Saloon League was preparing for a broad state-by-state drive toward national prohibition, a number of businessmen contributed the funds essential for an effective campaign. The series of quick successes that followed coincided with an equally impressive number of wealthy converts, so that as the movement entered its final stage after 1913, it employed not only ample financing but a sudden urban respectability as well. Substantial citizens now spoke about a new discipline with the disappearance of the saloon and the rampaging drunk. Significantly, prominent Southerners with one eye to the Negro and another to the poorer whites were using exactly the same arguments. (Wiebe 1967: 290–91)

Workmen's compensation laws also helped stimulate business support for temperance. Between 1911 and 1920, forty-one states had enacted workmen's compensation laws, and Sean Cashman (1981: 6) points out: "By making employers compensate workers for industrial accidents the law obligated them to campaign for safety through sobriety. In 1914 the National Safety Council adopted a resolution condemning alcohol as a cause of industrial accidents."

National Prohibition

The acrimony between rural and urban America, between Protestants and Catholics, between Republicans and (non-southern) Democrats, between "native" Americans and more recent immigrants, and between business and labor reached a pinnacle with the ratification in 1919 of the Eighteenth Amendment. According to William Chambliss (1973: 10), **Prohibition** was accomplished by the political efforts of an economically declining segment of the American middle class: "By effort and some good luck this class was able to impose its will on the majority of the population through rather dramatic changes in the law." Andrew Sinclair (1962: 163) points out that "in fact, national prohibition was a measure passed by village America against urban America." We could add, by much of Protestant America against Catholic (and, to a lesser extent, Jewish) America: "Thousands of Protestant churches held thanksgiving prayer meetings. To many of the people who attended, prohibition represented the triumph of America's towns and rural districts over the sinful cities" (Coffey 1975: 7; Gusfield 1963; A. Sinclair 1962).

The Eighteenth Amendment to the Constitution was ratified by the thirty-sixth state, Nebraska, on January 16, 1919. According to its own terms, the amendment became effective on January 16, 1920. Ten months after ratification, over a veto by President Woodrow Wilson, Congress passed the National Prohibition Act, usually referred to as the **Volstead Act** after its sponsor, Congressman Andrew Volstead of Minnesota. The Volstead Act strengthened the language of the amendment and defined as intoxicating all beverages containing more than 0.5 percent alcohol; it also provided for federal enforcement. Thus, the Prohibition Bureau, an arm of the Treasury Department, was created, soon becoming notorious for employing agents on the basis of political patronage.

In addition to being inept and corrupt, bureau agents were a public menace. By 1930, 86 federal agents and 200 civilians had been killed, many of them innocent women and children. Prohibition agents set up illegal roadblocks and searched cars; drivers who protested were in danger of being shot. Agents who killed innocent civilians were rarely brought to justice—when they were indicted by local grand juries, the cases were simply transferred and the agents escaped punishment (Woodiwiss 1988). The bureau was viewed as a training school for bootleggers because agents frequently left the service to join their wealthy adversaries.

The response of a large segment of the American population also proved to be a problem. People do not necessarily acquiesce to new criminal prohibitions, and general resistance can be fatal to the new norm (Packer 1968). Moreover, primary resistance or opposition to a new law such as Prohibition can result, secondarily, in disregard for laws in general: *negative contagion*. During Prohibition, notes Sinclair (1962: 292), a "general tolerance of the bootlegger and a disrespect for federal law were translated into a widespread contempt for the process and duties of democracy." This was exemplified by the general lawlessness that reigned in Chicago:

Banks all over Chicago were robbed in broad daylight by bandits who scorned to wear masks. Desk sergeants at police stations grew weary of recording holdups—from one hundred to two hundred were reported every night. Burglars marked out sections of the city as their own and embarked upon a course of systematic plundering, going from house to house night after night without hindrance. . . . Payroll robberies were a weekly occurrence and necessitated the introduction of armored cars and armed guards for the delivery of money from banks to business houses. Automobiles were stolen by the thousands. Motorists were forced to the curbs on busy streets and boldly robbed. Women who displayed jewelry in night clubs or at the theater were followed and held up. Wealthy women seldom left their homes unless accompanied by armed escorts. (Asbury 1950: 339)

The murder rate in the United States went from 6.8 per 100,000 persons in 1920, to 9.7 in 1933, the year Prohibition was repealed (Chapman 1991), after which it began to decline.

And while the United States had local organized crime before Prohibition, there were no large crime syndicates (King 1969). Pre-Prohibition crime, insofar as it was organized, centered around corrupt political machines, vice-entrepreneurs, and, at the bottom, gangs. The "Great Experiment," of Prohibition provided an opportunity for organized crime, especially violent forms, to blossom into an important force. Prohibition acted as a catalyst for the mobilization of criminal elements in an unprecedented manner, unleashing an unparalleled level of competitive violence and reversing the order between the criminal gangs and the politicians. It also led to an unparalleled level of criminal organization (Abadinsky 2003a). When the repeal of Prohibition left a critical void in their business portfolios, these criminal organizations would look to the drug trade.

Opium: A Long History

The earliest "war against drugs" (other than alcohol) in the United States was a response to opium—a depressant and pain reliever. **Opium** is the gum from the partially ripe seedpod of the opium poppy. There is no agreement on where the plant originated, and a great deal of debate surrounds its earliest use as a drug, which may date back to the Old Stone Age. The young leaves of the plant have been used as a potherb and salad vegetable, and its small, oily seeds, which are high in nutritional value, can be eaten, pressed to make an edible oil, baked into poppy seed cakes, ground into poppy flour, or used as lamp oil. As a vegetal fat source "the seed oil could have been a major factor attracting early human groups to the opium poppy" (Merlin 1984: 89). Archaeologists have discovered ancient art relics that may depict opium use in Egyptian religious rituals as early as 3500 B.C.E. (Inverarity, Lauderdale, and Field 1983).

By 1500 B.C.E the Egyptians had definitely discovered the medical uses of opium, because they list it as a pain reliever in the Ebers Papyrus. From Egypt its use spread to Greece (O'Brien and Cohen 1984). Opium is discussed by Homer in the *Odyssey* (circa 700 B.C.E.), and the term *opium* is derived from the Greek word *opion,* meaning the juice of the poppy (Bresler 1980). Opium was used by doctors in classical Greece and ancient Rome. Later, Arab physicians used it, and the Crusaders picked it up from them and brought it back to Europe, where it became a standard medicine. It is mentioned by Shakespeare in Othello, by Chaucer, Sir Thomas Browne, and Robert Burton. In the early sixteenth century the physician Paracelsus made a tincture of opium—powdered opium dissolved in alcohol—that he called *laudanum,* and until the end of the nineteenth century it proved to be a popular medication (O'Brien and Cohen 1984). De Quincey (1952) noted that opium was often cheaper than alcohol.

Two centuries ago, opium was generally available as a cure for everything. It was like aspirin; every household had some, usually in the form of laudanum. Naturally, the general availability of opium and the medical profession's enthusiasm for it helped create addicts, some of them very famous: Samuel Taylor Coleridge (1772–1834) and Thomas De Quincy (1785–1859) are the best known. At the time, medicine was primitive, doctors had no concept of addiction, and opium became the essential ingredient of innumerable remedies dispensed in Europe and America for the treatment of diarrhea, dysentery, asthma, rheumatism, diabetes, malaria, cholera, fevers, bronchitis, insomnia, and pain of any kind (Fay 1975). There was nothing to alert patients to the dangers of the patent medicines doctors prescribed or to prepare them for the side effects. As a result, there was no more stigma attached to the opium habit than to alcoholism; it was an unfortunate weakness, not a vice. Wherever it was known, opium use was both medicinal and recreational (Alvarez 2001).

In explaining the popularity of opium, Charles Terry and Mildred Pellens (1928: 58) state: "When we realize that the chief end of medicine up to the beginning of the [nineteenth] century was to relieve pain, that therapeutic agents were directed at symptoms rather than cause, it is not difficult to understand the wide popularity of a drug which either singly or combined so eminently was suited to the needs of so many medical situations."

Opium is a labor-intensive product. To produce an appreciable quantity requires repeated incisions of a great number of poppy capsules: about 18,000 capsules—one acre—to yield 20 pounds of opium (Fay 1975). Accordingly, supplies of opium were rather limited in Europe until the eighteenth century when improvements in plantation farming increased opium production. Attempts to produce domestic opium in the United States were not successful. While the poppy could be grown in many sections of the United States, particularly the South, Southwest, and California, labor costs and an opium gum that proved low in potency led to a reliance on imported opium (H. W. Morgan 1981).

As the primary ingredient in many *patent medicines*—actually secret formulas that carried no patent at all—opiates were readily available in the United States until 1914, and quacks prescribed and promoted them for general symptoms as well as for specific diseases. People who were not really ill were frightened into the patent medicine habit (J. Young 1961). Patients who were actually sick received the false impression that they were on the road to recovery. Of course, because scientific medical treatment was most often absent for even the mildest of diseases, a feeling of well-being was at least psychologically, and perhaps by extension physiologically, beneficial. However, babies born to opiate-using mothers were often small, and they experienced the distress of withdrawal. Harried mothers often responded by relieving them with infant remedies that contained opium.

The smoking of opium was popularized by Chinese immigrants, who brought the habit with them to the United States. During the latter part of the nineteenth and early twentieth centuries they also operated commercial *opium dens,* which attracted the attention of the police, "not because of the use of narcotics but because they became gathering places for thieves, footpads [highwaymen] and gangsters." In fact, "opium dens were regarded as in a class with saloons and, for many years, were no more illegal" (Katcher 1959: 287).

The Opium Derivatives: Morphine and Heroin

At the end of the eighteenth century (Latimer and Goldberg 1981) or early in the nineteenth (Merlin 1984; Nelson et al. 1982; Musto 1987b; Bresler 1980), a German pharmacist poured liquid ammonia over opium and obtained an alkaloid—a white powder that he found to be many times more powerful than opium. Frederich W. Serturner named the substance *morphium* after Morpheus, the Greek god of sleep and dreams. Ten parts of opium can be refined into one part of **morphine** (Bresler 1980). It was not until 1817, however, that articles published in scientific journals popularized the new drug, resulting in widespread use by doctors. Quite incorrectly, as it turned out, the medical profession viewed morphine as an opiate without negative side effects.

By the 1850s morphine tablets and a variety of morphine products were readily available without prescription. In 1856 the hypodermic method of injecting morphine directly into the bloodstream was introduced to U.S. medicine. The popularity of morphine rose during the Civil War when the intravenous use of the drug to treat battlefield casualties was rather indiscriminate (Terry and Pellens 1928). Following the war, morphine use among ex-soldiers was so common as to give rise to the term *army disease.* "Medical journals were replete with glowing descriptions of the effectiveness of the drug during wartime and its obvious advantages for peacetime medical practice" (Cloyd 1982: 21). Hypodermic kits became widely available, and the use of unsterile needles by many doctors and laypersons led to abscesses or disease (H. W. Morgan 1981).

In the 1870s morphine was exceedingly cheap—cheaper than alcohol—with pharmacies and general stores carrying preparations that appealed to a wide segment of the population, whatever the individual emotional quirk or physical ailment. Anyone who visited nearly any physician for any complaint, from a toothache to consumption, would be prescribed morphine (Latimer and Goldberg 1981), and the substance was widely abused by physicians themselves. Morphine abuse in the latter part of the nineteenth century was apparently widespread in rural America (Terry and Pellens 1928).

Starting in the 1870s, doctors injected women with morphine to numb the pain of "female troubles" or to turn the "willful hysteric" into a manageable invalid. By the 1890s, when the first drug epidemic peaked, female medical addicts made up almost half of all addicts in the United States. In the twentieth century, the drug scene shifted to underworld elements of urban America, the disreputable "sporting class": prostitutes, pimps, thieves, gamblers, gangsters, entertainers, active homosexuals, and youths who admired the sporting men and women (Stearns 1998).

In 1874, a British chemist experimenting with morphine synthesized diacetylmorphine, and the most powerful of opiates came into being: "Commercial promotion of the new drug had to wait until 1898 when the highly respected German pharmaceutical combine Bayer, in perfectly good faith but perhaps without sufficient prior care, launched upon an unsuspecting world public this new substance, for which they coined the trade name 'heroin' and which they marketed as—of all things—a 'sedative for coughs' " (Bresler 1980: 11). Jack Nelson and his colleagues (1982) state that **heroin** was actually isolated in 1898 in Germany by Heinrich Dreser, who was searching for a nonhabit-forming pain reliever to take the place of morphine. Dreser named it after the German word *heroisch,* meaning large and powerful.

Opiates, including morphine and heroin, were readily available in the United States until 1914. In 1900, 628,177 pounds of opiates were imported into the United States (Bonnie and Whitebread 1970). The President's Commission on Organized Crime (1986; hereafter **PCOC**) notes that between the Civil War and 1914 there was a substantial increase in persons using opiates, the consequence of a number of factors including:

- The spread of opium smoking from Chinese immigrants into the wider community.
- An increase in morphine addiction as a result of its indiscriminate use to treat battlefield casualties during the Civil War.
- The widespread administration of morphine by hypodermic syringe.
- The widespread use of opium derivatives by the American patent medicine industry.
- Beginning in 1898, the marketing of heroin as a safe, powerful, and nonaddictive substitute for the opium derivatives morphine and codeine.

China and the Opium Wars

Until the sixteenth century, China was a military power whose naval fleet surpassed any that the world had ever known. A fifteenth-century power struggle ultimately led to a regime dominated by Confucian scholars; in 1525, they ordered the destruction of all oceangoing ships and set China on a course that would lead to poverty, defeat, and decline (Kristoff 1999).

In 1626, a British warship appeared off China, and its captain imposed his will on Canton (now Guangzhou) with a bombardment. In response to the danger posed by British ships, the emperor opened the city of Canton to trade, and Britain granted the British East India Company a monopoly over the China trade. Particularly important to this trade was the shipping of tea to England. By the 1820s, the trade situation between England and China paralleled trade between the United States and Japan today—while British consumers had an insatiable appetite for Chinese tea, the Chinese desired few English goods. The British attempted to introduce alcohol, but a large percentage of Asians have enzyme systems that make drinking alcohol extremely unpleasant. Opium was the exception (Beeching 1975). Poppy cultivation was an important source of revenue for the Moghul emperors (Muslim rulers of India between 1526 and 1857). When the Moghul empire fell apart, the British East India Company salvaged and improved upon the system of state control of opium. In addition to the domestic market, the British supplied Indian opium to China.

Opium was first prohibited by Peking (Beijing) in 1729, when only small amounts of the substance were reaching China. Ninety years earlier, tobacco had been similarly banned as a pernicious foreign article. Opium use was strongly condemned in China as a violation of Confucian principles, and for many years the imperial decree against opium was generally supported by the population (Beeching 1975). In 1782 an attempt by a British merchant ship to sell 1,601 chests of opium resulted in a total loss, as no purchasers could be found. By 1799, however, a growing traffic in opium led to an imperial decree condemning the trade. Dean Latimer and Jeff Goldberg (1981) doubt that opium addiction was extensive or particularly harmful to China as a whole. The poorer classes, the authors note, could afford only adulterated opium, which was unlikely to produce addiction. "Just why the Chinese chose to obtain their supplies from India," states Peter Fay (1975: 11–12), "is no clearer than why, having obtained it, they smoked it instead of ate it." In the end, he notes, the Chinese came to prefer the Indian product to their own. However, because the preference was to smoke opium, it had to be specially prepared by being boiled in water, filtered, and boiled again until it reached the consistency of molasses, thereby becoming "smoking opium."

Like the ban on tobacco, the one on opium was not successful (official corruption was endemic in China). As consumption of imported opium increased and the method of ingestion shifted from eating to smoking, official declarations against opium increased, and so did smuggling. "When opium left Calcutta, stored in the holds of country ships and consigned to agents in Canton, it was an entirely legitimate article. It remained an entirely legitimate article all the way up to the China sea. But the instant it reached the coast of China it became something different. It became contraband" (Fay 1975: 45). In fact, the actual shipping of opium to China was accomplished by independent British or Parsee merchants. Thus, notes Beeching, "the Honourable East India Company was able to wash its hands of all formal responsibility for the illegal drug trade" (1975: 26).

Opium furnished the British with the silver needed to buy tea. Because opium was illegal in China, however, its importation—smuggling—brought China no tariff revenue. Before 1830 opium was transported to the coast of China, where it was offloaded and smuggled by the Chinese themselves. The outlawing of opium by the Chinese government led to the development of an organized underworld; gangs became secret societies—*triads*—that still move heroin out of the Far East to destinations all over the world (Latimer and Goldberg 1981; this will be discussed in Chapter 11). The armed opium ships were safe from Chinese government intervention, and the British were able to remain aloof from the smuggling itself.

In the 1830s the shippers grew bolder and entered Chinese territorial waters with their opium cargo. The British East India Company, now in competition with other opium merchants, sought to flood China with cheap opium and drive out the competition (Beeching 1975). In 1837 the emperor ordered his officials to move against opium smugglers, but the campaign was a failure and the smugglers grew even bolder. The following year the emperor changed his strategy and moved against Chinese traffickers and drug abusers, as only a total despot could do, helping to dry up the market for opium. As a result, the price fell significantly (Fay 1975).

The First Opium War. In 1839, in dramatic fashion, Chinese authorities laid siege to the port city of Canton, confiscating and destroying all opium awaiting offloading from foreign ships. The merchantmen agreed to stop importing opium into China, and the siege was lifted. The British merchants petitioned the Crown for compensation and retribution. The reigning Parliamentary Whig majority, however, was very weak, and compensating the opium merchants was not politically or financially feasible. Instead, the cabinet, without Parliamentary approval, decided on a war that would result in the seizure of Chinese property (Fay 1975).

In 1840, a British expedition attacked the poorly armed and poorly organized Chinese forces. In the rout that followed, the Emperor was forced to pay $6 million for the opium his officials had seized and $12 million as compensation for the war. Hong Kong became a Crown colony, and the ports of Canton, Amoy (Xiamen), Foochow (Fuzhou), Ningpo, and Shanghai were opened to British trade. Opium was not mentioned in the peace (surrender) treaty, but the trade resumed with new vigor. In a remarkable reversal of the balance of trade, by the mid-1840s China had an opium debt of about 2 million pounds sterling (Latimer and Goldberg 1981). In the wake of the First Opium War, China was laid open to extensive missionary efforts by Protestant evangelicals who, although they opposed the opium trade, viewed saving souls as their primary goal. Christianity, they believed, would save China from opium (Fay 1975). Unfortunately, morphine was actively promoted by Catholic and Protestant missionaries as an agent for detoxifying opium addicts (Latimer and Goldberg 1981).

The Second Opium War. The Second Opium War began in 1856, when the balance of payments once again favored China. In that year a minor incident between the British and Chinese governments was used as an excuse to force China into making further treaty concessions. And this time the foreign powers seeking to exploit a militarily weak China included Russia, the United States, and particularly France, which was jealous of the British success. Canton was sacked, and a combined fleet of British and French warships sailed right up the Grand Canal to Peking and proceeded to sack and burn the imperial summer palace. The emperor was forced to indemnify the British 20,000 pounds sterling, more than enough to offset the balance of trade, which was the real cause of the war. A commission was appointed to legalize and regulate the opium trade (Latimer and Goldberg 1981), which increased from less than 59,000 chests a year in 1860 to more than 105,000 by 1880 (Beeching 1975). Until 1946 the British permitted the use of opiates in its Crown colony of Hong Kong, first under an official monopoly and after 1913 directly by the government (Lamour and Lamberti 1974). During Japan's occupation of China, which began a few years before its attack on Pearl Harbor, large amounts of heroin were trafficked by the Imperial army's "special services branch," which helped finance the cost of the occupation (Karch 1998).

The "Chinese Problem" and the American Response

Chinese were originally brought into the United States after 1848 to work in the gold fields, particularly in those aspects of mining that were most dangerous because few white men were willing to engage in blasting shafts, placing beams, and laying track lines in the gold mines. Chinese immigrants also helped build the western railroad lines at pay that few whites would accept—"coolie wages." After their work was completed, the Chinese were often banned from the rural counties and, by the 1860s, were clustering in cities on the Pacific coast where they established Chinatowns—and smoked opium.

The British opium monopoly in China was challenged in the 1870s by opium imported from Persia and cultivated in China itself. In response, British colonial authorities, heavily dependent on a profitable opium trade, increased the output of Indian opium, causing a decline in prices that was aimed at driving the competition out of business. The resulting oversupply increased the amount of opium entering the United States for the Chinese population.

Beginning in 1875 there was an economic depression in California. As a result, the first significant piece of prohibitionary drug legislation in the United States was enacted by the city of San Francisco. "The primary event that precipitated the campaign against the Chinese and against opium was the sudden onset of economic depression, high unemployment levels, and the disintegration of working-class standards of living" (Helmer 1975: 32). The San Francisco ordinance prohibited the operation of opium dens, commercial establishments for the smoking of opium, "not because of health concerns as such, but because it was believed that the drug stimulated coolies into working harder than non-smoking whites" (Latimer and Goldberg 1981: 208).

Depressed economic conditions and xenophobia led one western state after another to follow San Francisco's lead and enact anti-Chinese legislation that often included prohibiting the smoking of opium. The anti-Chinese nature of the legislation was noted in some early court decisions. In 1886 an Oregon district court, responding to a petition for habeas corpus filed by Yung Jon, who had been convicted of opium violations, stated: "Smoking opium is not our vice, and therefore it may be that this legislation proceeds more from a desire to vex and annoy the 'Heathen Chinese' in this respect, than to protect the people from the evil habit. But the motives of legislators cannot be the subject of judicial investigation for the purpose of affecting the validity of their acts" (Bonnie and Whitebread 1970: 997).

"After 1870 a new type of addict began to emerge, the white opium smoker drawn primarily from the underworld of pimps and prostitutes, gamblers, and thieves" (Courtwright 1982: 64). In Chicago during the 1890s, Chinatown was located in the notorious First Ward, whose politicians grew powerful and wealthy by protecting almost every vice known to man. But First Ward alderman John "Bathhouse" Coughlin "couldn't stomach" opium smokers and threatened to raid the dens himself if necessary. There was constant police harassment, and in 1894 the city enacted an anti-opium ordinance. By 1895 the last of the dens had been raided out of business (Sawyers 1988).

Anti-Chinese efforts were supported and advanced by Samuel Gompers (1850–1924) as part of his effort to establish the American Federation of Labor. The Chinese served as scapegoats for organized labor, which depicted the "yellow devils" as undercutting wages and breaking strikes. Anti-opium legislation was also fostered by stories of white women being seduced by Chinese white-slavers through the use of opium.[2] In 1882, the Chinese

---

[2]Similar anti-Chinese hysteria, especially the diatribe that they used opium to seduce white women, led to anti-opium legislation in Australia at the end of the nineteenth century (Manderson 1999).

Exclusion Act banned the entry of Chinese laborers into the United States. (It was not until 1943, when the United States was allied with China in a war against Japan, that citizenship rights were extended to Chinese immigrants and China was permitted an annual immigration of 105 persons.)

In 1883, Congress raised the tariff on the importation of smoking opium. In 1887, apparently in response to obligations imposed on the United States by a Chinese-American commercial treaty negotiated in 1880 and becoming effective in 1887, Congress banned the importation of smoking opium by Chinese subjects. Americans, however, were still permitted to import the substance, and many did so, selling it to both Chinese and American citizens (PCOC 1986). The Tariff Act of 1890 increased the rate on smoking opium to $12 per pound, resulting in a substantial increase in opium smuggling and the diversion of medicinal opium for manufacture into smoking opium. In response, in 1897 the tariff was reduced to $6 per pound (PCOC 1986).

During the nineteenth century opiates were not associated with crime in the public mind. While opium use may have been frowned upon by some as immoral,

> employees were not fired for addiction. Wives did not divorce their addicted husbands, or husbands their addicted wives. Children were not taken from their homes and lodged in foster homes or institutions because one or both parents were addicted. Addicts continued to participate fully in the life of the community. Addicted children and young people continued to go to school, Sunday School, and college. Thus, the nineteenth century avoided one of the most disastrous effects of current narcotic laws and attitudes—the rise of a deviant addict subculture, cut off from respectable society and without a "road back" to respectability. (Brecher 1972: 6–7)

Twentieth-Century Efforts and Legislation

The Pure Food and Drug Act

National efforts against opiates (and cocaine) were part of a larger campaign to regulate drugs and the contents of food substances; in 1879 a bill was introduced in Congress to accomplish national food and drug regulation. These efforts were opposed by the Proprietary Association of America, which represented the patent medicine industry. The medical profession was more interested in dealing with quacks within the profession than with quack medicines, and the American Pharmaceutical Association was of a mixed mind: Its members, in addition to being scientists, were merchants who found the sale of proprietary remedies bulking large in their gross income (J. Young 1961). Toward the end of the nineteenth century, the campaign for drug regulation was assisted by agricultural chemists, who decried the use of chemicals to defraud consumers into buying spoiled canned and packaged food. In 1884 state-employed chemists formed the Association of Official Agricultural Chemists to combat this widespread practice. They began to expand their efforts into nonfoodstuffs, including patent medicines.

The nation's newspapers and magazines made a considerable amount of money from advertising patent medicines. Toward the turn of the century, however, a few periodicals, in particular *Ladies Home Journal* and *Collier's,* began vigorous investigations and denunciations of patent medicines. Eventually, the American Medical Association (AMA, founded in 1847), which was a rather weak organization at the close of the nineteenth century because the vast majority of doctors were not members (Musto 1973), began to campaign in earnest for drug regulation.

U.S. Senate hearings on the pure food issue gained a great deal of newspaper coverage and aroused the public (J. Young 1961). The dramatic event that quickly led to the adoption of the Pure Food and Drug Act, however, was the 1906 publication of Upton Sinclair's *The Jungle.* Sinclair, in a novelistic description of the meat industry in Chicago, exposed the filthy, unsanitary, and unsafe conditions under which food reached the consumer. The sale of meat fell by almost 50 percent, and President Theodore Roosevelt dispatched two investigators to Chicago to check on Sinclair's charges. Their "report not only confirmed Sinclair's allegations, but added additional ones. Congress was forced by public opinion to consider a strong bill" (Ihde 1982: 42). The result was the Pure Food and Drug Act passed later that same year, which required medicines to list certain drugs and their amounts, including alcohol and opiates.

China and the International Opium Conference

The international U.S. response to drugs in the early twentieth century was directly related to its trade with China. To increase its influence in China and thus improve its trade position, the United States supported the International Reform Bureau (**IRB**), a temperance organization representing over thirty missionary societies in the Far East, which was seeking a ban on opiates. As a result, in 1901 Congress enacted the Native Races Act, which prohibited the sale of alcohol and opium to "aboriginal tribes and uncivilized races." The provisions of the act were later expanded to include "uncivilized elements" in the United States proper: Indians, Eskimos, and Chinese (Latimer and Goldberg 1981).

As a result of the Spanish-American War in 1898, the Philippines were ceded to the United States. At the time of Spanish colonialism, opium smoking was widespread among Chinese workers on the islands. Canadian-born Reverend Charles Henry Brent (1862–1929), a supporter of the IRB, arrived in the Philippines as the Episcopal bishop during a cholera epidemic that began in 1902 and that reportedly had led to an increase in the use of opium. As a result of his efforts, in 1905 Congress enacted a ban against sales of opium to Filipino natives except for medicinal purposes; 3 years later the ban was extended to all residents of the Philippines. It appears that the legislation was ineffective, and smoking opium remained widely available (Musto 1973). "Reformers attributed to drugs much of the appalling poverty, ignorance, and debilitation they encountered in the Orient. Opium was strongly identified with the problems afflicting an apparently moribund China. Eradication of drug abuse was part of America's white man's burden and a way to demonstrate the New World's superiority" (H. W. Morgan 1974: 32).

Bishop Brent proposed the formation of an international opium commission, to meet in Shanghai in 1909. This plan was supported by President Theodore Roosevelt who saw it as a way of assuaging Chinese anger at the passage of the Chinese Exclusionary Act (Latimer and Goldberg 1981). The International Opium Commission, chaired by Brent and consisting of representatives from thirteen nations, convened in Shanghai on February 1. Brent was successful in rallying the conferees around the U.S. position that opium was evil and had no nonmedical use. The commission unanimously adopted a number of vague resolutions, the most important being (Terry and Pellens 1928):

1. That each government take action to suppress the smoking of opium at home and in overseas possessions and settlements;
2. That opium has no use outside of medicine, and accordingly, that each country should move toward increasingly stringent regulations concerning opiates;
3. That measures should be taken to prevent the exporting of opium and its derivatives to countries that prohibit its importation.

Revisionist History or Historical Ignorance?

"Addictive drugs were criminalized because they were harmful; they are not harmful because they were criminalized" (Office of National Drug Control Policy 2001:56).

Only the United States and China, however, were eager for future conferences, and legislative efforts against opium following the conference were generally unsuccessful. Southerners were distrustful of federal enforcement, and the drug industry was opposed. Efforts to gain southern support for antidrug legislation focused on the alleged abuse of cocaine by African Americans—the substance was reputed to make them uncontrollable. While there already existed tariff legislation with respect to opium, Terry and Pellens note that its purpose was to generate income. The first federal legislation to control the domestic use of opium was passed in 1909 as a result of the Shanghai conference. "An Act to prohibit the importation and use of opium for other than medicinal purposes" failed to regulate domestic opium production and manufacture; nor did it control the interstate shipment of opium products, which continued to be widely available through retail and mail order outlets (PCOC 1986).

A second conference was held in The Hague in 1912, with the United States, Turkey, Great Britain, France, Portugal, Japan, Russia, Italy, Germany, Persia, the Netherlands, and China in attendance. A number of problems stood in the way of an international agreement: Germany wished to protect her burgeoning pharmaceutical industry and insisted on a unanimous vote before any action could be agreed upon; Portugal insisted on retaining the Macao opium trade; the Dutch demanded to maintain their opium trade in the West Indies; and Persia and Russia wanted to keep on growing opium poppies. Righteous U.S. appeals to the delegates were rebuffed with allusions to domestic usage and the lack of laws in the United States (Latimer and Goldberg 1981). Nevertheless, the conference managed to put together a patchwork of agreements known as the International Opium Convention, which was ratified by Congress on October 18, 1913. The signatories committed themselves to enacting laws aimed at suppressing the abuse of opium, morphine, and cocaine as well as drugs prepared or derived from these substances (PCOC 1986). On December 17, 1914, the Harrison Act, which represented this country's attempt to carry out the provisions of the Hague Convention, was approved by President Woodrow Wilson.

The Harrison Act

The Harrison Act provided that any person in the business of dealing in drugs covered by the act, including the opium derivatives morphine and heroin, as well as cocaine, was required to register annually and to pay a special annual tax of $1. The statute made it illegal to sell or give away opium or opium derivatives and coca or its derivatives without a written order on a form issued by the commissioner of revenue. Persons who were not registered were prohibited from engaging in interstate traffic in the drugs, and no one could possess any of the drugs who had not registered and paid the special tax, under a penalty of up to 5 years imprisonment and a fine of no more than $2,000. Rules promulgated by the Treasury Department permitted only medical professionals to register, and they had to maintain records of the drugs they dispensed. Within the first year more than 200,000 medical professionals registered, and the small staff of treasury agents could not scrutinize the number of prescription records that were generated (Musto 1973).

It was concern with federalism—constitutional limitation on the police powers of the central government—that led Congress to use the taxing authority of the federal government to control drugs. While few people today would question the Drug Enforcement Administration's right to register physicians and pharmacists and control what drugs they can prescribe and dispense, at the beginning of the twentieth century, federal authority to regulate narcotics and the prescription practices of physicians was generally thought to be unconstitutional (Musto 1998). In 1919 the use of taxing authority to regulate drugs was upheld by the Supreme Court (*United States v. Doremus* 249 U.S. 86):

> If the legislation enacted has some reasonable relation to the exercise of the taxing authority conferred by the Constitution, it cannot be invalidated because of the supposed motives which induced it. . . . The Act may not be declared unconstitutional because its effect may be to accomplish another purpose as well as the raising of revenue. If the legislation is within the taxing authority of Congress—that is sufficient to sustain it.

The Harrison Act was enacted with the support of the AMA and the American Pharmaceutical Association, both of which had grown more powerful and influential in the first two decades of the twentieth century, since the medical profession had been granted a monopoly on dispensing opiates and cocaine. The Harrison Act also had the effect of imposing a stamp of illegitimacy on the use of most narcotics, fostering an image of the immoral and degenerate "dope fiend" (Bonnie and Whitebread 1970). At this time, according to Courtwright's (1982) estimates, there were about 300,000 opiate addicts in the United States. But, he notes, the addict population was already changing. The medical profession had, by and large, abandoned its liberal use of opiates—imports of medicinal opiates declined dramatically during the first decade of the twentieth century—and the public mind came to associate heroin with urban vice and crime. Opiate users of the twentieth century were increasingly male habitues of pool halls and bowling alleys, denizens of the underworld, and they typically used heroin (Kinlock, Hanlon, and Nurco 1998). As in the case of minority groups, this marginal population was an easy target of drug laws and drug law enforcement.

The commissioner of the Internal Revenue Service was placed in charge of upholding the Harrison Act, and in 1915, 162 collectors and agents of the Miscellaneous Division of the Internal Revenue Service were given the responsibility for enforcing drug laws. In 1919 the Narcotics Division was created within the Bureau of Prohibition with a staff of 170 agents and an appropriation of $270,000. The Narcotics Division, however, was tainted by its association with the notoriously inept and corrupt Prohibition Bureau and suffered from a corruption scandal of its own: "The public dissatisfaction intensified because of a scandal involving falsification of arrest records and charges relating to payoffs by, and [in] collusion with, drug dealers" (PCOC 1986: 204). In response, in 1930 Congress removed drug enforcement from the Bureau of Prohibition and established the Federal Bureau of Narcotics (**FBN**) as a separate agency within the Department of the Treasury. "Although the FBN was primarily responsible for the enforcement of the Harrison Act and related drug laws, the task of preventing and interdicting the illegal importation and smuggling of drugs remained with the Bureau of Customs" (PCOC 1986: 205).

Case Law Results. In 1916 the Court ruled in favor of a physician (Dr. Moy) who had provided maintenance doses of morphine to an addict (*United States v. Jin Fuey Moy* 241 U.S. 394). In 1919, however, the Court ruled (*Webb v. United States* 249 U.S. 96) that a prescription for morphine issued to an habitual user who was not under a physician's care, that was not intended to cure but to maintain the habit is not a prescription and thus violates the Harrison Act. However, private physicians found it impossible to handle the large drug clientele that was suddenly created: They could do nothing "more than sign prescriptions" (Duster 1970: 16).

In *United States v. Behrman* (258 U.S. 280, 289, 1922) the Court ruled that a physician was not entitled to prescribe large doses of proscribed drugs for self-administration, *even* if the addict was under the physician's care. The Court stated that "prescriptions in the regular course of practice did not include the indiscriminate doling out of narcotics in such quantity as charged in the indictments." In 1925 the Court limited the application of *Behrman* when it found that a physician who had prescribed small doses of drugs for the relief of an addict did not violate the Harrison Act (*Linder v. United States* 268 U.S. 5). In reversing the physician's conviction the Court distinguished between *Linder* and excesses shown in the case of *Behrman:*

> The enormous quantities of drugs ordered, considered in connection with the recipient's character, without explanation, seemed enough to show prohibited sales and to exclude the idea of *bona fide* professional activity. The opinion [in *Behrman*] cannot be accepted as authority for holding that a physician, who acts *fide bona* and according to fair medical standards, may never give an addict moderate amounts of drugs for self-administration in order to relieve conditions incident to addiction. Enforcement of the tax demands no such drastic rule, and if the Act had such scope it would certainly encounter grave constitutional guarantees.

In fact, the powers of the Narcotics Division were clear and limited to the enforcement of registration and record-keeping regulations. "The large number of addicts who secured their drugs from physicians were excluded from the Division's jurisdiction. Furthermore, "the public's attitude toward drug use," notes Donald Dickson (1977: 39), "had not much changed with the passage of the Act—there was some opposition to drug use, some support of it, and a great many who did not care one way or the other. The Harrison Act was actually passed with very little publicity or news coverage."

Richard Bonnie and Charles Whitebread (1970: 976) note the similarities between the temperance and antinarcotics movements. "Both were first directed against the evils of large scale use and only later against all use. Most of the rhetoric was the same: These euphoriants produced crime, pauperism and insanity." However, "the temperance movement was a matter of vigorous public debate; the anti-narcotics movement was not. Temperance legislation was the product of a highly organized nationwide lobby; narcotics legislation was largely ad hoc. Temperance legislation was designed to eradicate known evils resulting from alcohol abuse; narcotics legislation was largely anticipatory." In fact, notes H. Wayne Morgan (1981), comparisons between alcohol and opiates—until the nature of addiction became clear—were often favorable to opium. It was not public sentiment that led to antidrug legislation, but nevertheless, the result of such legislation was an increasing public perception of the danger of certain drugs (Bonnie and Whitehead 1970). As we will see, this perception was fanned by officials of the federal drug enforcement agency.

Narcotic Clinics and Enforcement. Writing in 1916, Pearce Bailey noted that the passage of the Act "spread dismay among the heroin takers":

> They saw in advance the increased difficulty and expense of obtaining heroin as a result of this law; then the drug stores shut down, and the purveyors who sell heroin on the street corners and in doorways became terrified, and for a time illicit trade in the drug almost ceased. . . . Once the law was established the traffic was resumed, but under very different circumstances. The price of heroin soared [900 percent, and was sold in adulterated form]. This put it beyond the easy reach of the majority of adherents, most of whom do not earn more than twelve or fourteen dollars a week. Being no longer able to procure it with any money that they could lay their hands on honestly, many were forced to apply for treatment for illness brought about by result of arrest for violation of the law. (1974: 173–74)

Beginning in 1918 narcotic clinics opened in almost every major city. Information about them is sketchy (Duster 1970), and there is a great deal of controversy over their operations. While they were never very popular with the general public, most clinics were well run under medical supervision (H. W. Morgan 1981). While some clinics were guilty of a variety of abuses, the good ones enabled addicts to continue their normal lives without being drawn into the black market in drugs (Duster 1970). The troubled clinics, however, such as in New York where the number of patients overwhelmed the medical staff, generated a great deal of newspaper coverage, resulting in an outraged public.

Following World War I and the Bolshevik Revolution, xenophobia and prohibitionism began to sweep the nation. The United States severely restricted immigration, and alcohol and drug use were increasingly associated with an alien population. In 1922 federal narcotic agents closed the drug clinics and began to arrest physicians and pharmacists who provided drugs for maintenance. At issue was section 8 of the Harrison Act, which permitted the possession of controlled substances if prescribed "in good faith" by a registered physician, dentist, or veterinarian in accord with "professional practice." The law did not define "good faith" or "professional practice." Under a policy developed by the federal narcotic agency, thousands of persons, including many physicians—more than 25,000 between 1914 and 1938 (White 1998)[3]—were charged with violations: "Whether conviction followed or not mattered little as the effects of press publicity dealing with what were supposedly willful violations of a beneficent law were most disastrous to those concerned" (Terry and Pellens 1928: 90). "Once a strict antidrug policy had been established, both the public's and policymakers' curiosity about the details of a drug's biological effects faded. Federal scientists also feared their research findings might conflict with official policies, so they avoided some areas of investigation" (Musto 1998: 62).

The medical profession withdrew from dispensing drugs to addicts, forcing them to look to illicit sources and giving rise to an enormous illegal business in drugs. Persons addicted to opium smoking eventually found their favorite drug unavailable—the bulky smoking opium was difficult to smuggle—and they turned to the more readily available heroin which was prepared for intravenous use and would produce a more intense effect (Courtwright 1982). The criminal syndicates that resulted from Prohibition added heroin trafficking to their business portfolios. When Prohibition was repealed in 1933, profits from bootlegging disappeared accordingly, but drug trafficking remained as an important source of revenue for organized criminal groups. (The business of drugs is discussed in Chapter 11.) Law enforcement efforts against drugs have proven as ineffectual as efforts against alcohol during Prohibition, with similar problems of corruption.

The federal government shaped vague and conflicting court decisions into definitive pronouncements reflecting the drug enforcement agency's own version of its proper role: "American administrative regulations took on the force of ruling law" (Trebach 1982: 132). The drug agency also embarked on a vigorous campaign to convince the public and Congress of the dangers of drugs and, thereby, to justify its approach to the problem of drug abuse. According to Bonnie and Whitebread (1970: 990), the existence of a separate federal narcotics bureau "anxious to fulfill its role as crusader against the evils of narcotics" has been *the* single major factor in the legislative history of drug control in the United States since 1930.

The actions of the federal government toward drug use must be understood within the context of the times. The years immediately following World War I were characterized by pervasive attitudes of nationalism and nativism and by a fear of anarchy and communism. The Bolshevik Revolution in Russia, a police strike in Boston (see Russell 1975), and widespread labor unrest and violence were the backdrop for the infamous Palmer

---

[3]There continues to be a stigma within the medical profession attached to physicians who treat drug abusers (S. Gilbert 1996).

Raids of 1919, in which Attorney General A. Mitchel Palmer, disregarding a host of constitutional protections, ordered the arrest of thousands of "radicals." That same year the Prohibition Amendment was ratified, and soon legislation ended large-scale (legal) immigration. Drug addiction—morphinism/heroinism—was added to the un-American "isms" of alcoholism, anarchism, and communism (Musto 1973). In 1918 there were only 888 federal arrests for narcotic law violations; in 1920 there were 3,477. In 1925, the year the clinics were closed, there were 10,297 (Cloyd 1982).

According to William White (1998: 113), Treasury Department opposition to prescribing drugs for addicts was based on a belief in the prevailing propaganda of the day with respect to alcohol treatment. "The Treasury Department opposed ambulatory treatment because, for many patients, it turned into sustained maintenance, and also because the remaining inebriate hospitals and asylums of the day were still boasting 95% success rates. After all, leaders of the Treasury Department argued, why should someone be maintained on morphine when all he or she had to do was to take the cure? It was through such misrepresentation of success rates that the inebriate asylums and private treatment sanitariums contributed inadvertently to the criminalization of narcotic addiction in the U.S."

In 1923, legislation was introduced to curtail the importation of opium for the manufacture of heroin, resulting in a virtual ban on heroin in the United States. (In 1956 Congress declared all heroin to be contraband.) Among the few witnesses who testified before Congress, all supported the legislation. The AMA had already condemned the use of heroin by physicians, and the substance was described as the most dangerous of all habit-forming drugs, some witnesses arguing that the psychological effects of heroin use serve as a stimulus to crime. Much of the medical testimony, in light of what is now known about heroin, was erroneous, but the law won easy passage in 1924 (Musto 1973). A pamphlet published the same year by the prestigious Foreign Policy Association summarized contemporary thinking about heroin (cited in Trebach 1982: 48). Heroin

- is unnecessary in the practice of medicine
- destroys all sense of moral responsibility
- is the drug of the criminal
- recruits its army among youths

The use of opiates, except for narrow medical purposes, was now thoroughly criminalized, both in law and in practice. The law defined drug users as criminals, and the public viewed heroin use as the behavior of a deviant criminal class.

The Uniform Drug Act

Until 1930 efforts against drugs were primarily federal. Only a few states had drug-control statutes, and these were generally ineffective (Musto 1973). At the urging of federal authorities, many states enacted their own antidrug legislation. By 1931 every state restricted the sale of cocaine, and all but two restricted the sale of opiates. State statutes, however, were far from uniform. As early as 1927, this lack of uniformity, combined with the growing hysteria about dope fiends and criminality, resulted in several requests for a uniform state narcotic law. The diversity of state drug statutes was not an anachronism. The need for greater uniformity in state statutes was recognized in the first half of the nineteenth century, when a prominent New York attorney, David Dudley Field (1805–1894), campaigned for a uniform code of procedure for both civil and criminal matters. During the 1890s the American Bar Association set up the National Conference of Commissioners on Uniform State Laws, whose efforts resulted in a variety of uniform codes that were adopted by virtually all jurisdictions (Abadinsky 2003b).

A uniform drug act for the states was the goal of both the Committee on the Uniform Narcotic Act and representatives of the American Medical Association because doctors wanted uniformity of legal obligations. Their first two drafts copied a 1927 New York statute that listed coca, opium, and cannabis products as habit-forming drugs to be regulated or prohibited. Because of opposition to its inclusion on the habit-forming list, cannabis was dropped from later drafts with a note indicating each state was free to include cannabis or not in its own legislation without affecting the rest of the act. The final draft also used the 1927 New York statute as a model and included suggestions from the newly appointed commissioner of the Federal Bureau of Narcotics (FBN), Harry Anslinger. It was adopted overwhelmingly by the National Conference of Commissioners on Uniform State Laws, to which each governor had appointed two representatives. By 1937, thirty-five states had enacted the Uniform Drug Act, and every state had enacted statutes relating to marijuana. Despite propagandizing efforts by the FBN, "The laws went unnoticed by legal commentators, the press and the public at large" (Bonnie and Whitebread 1970: 1034).

The lack of public concern is related to the demographics of drug abuse, which was concentrated in minority, lower-class areas and the criminal subculture. Before the Harrison Act there was considerable use in rural areas, and in the South, where drugs often substituted for alcohol in dry areas, more opiates were used than in other parts of the country. After the Harrison Act, addicts in rural areas were attended to quietly by sympathetic doctors. Heroin was heavily concentrated in urban areas of poverty. For example, during the early decades of the twentieth century, heroin use in New York was heaviest in the Jewish and Italian areas of the Lower East Side. As these two groups climbed up the economic ladder and moved out, they were replaced by African Americans looking for affordable housing; this group then became the addict population (Helmer 1975). Demographics intensified the problem—African Americans had a higher birthrate than Jews and Italians, and an extraordinary number of youngsters were at the age of highest risk for addiction, 16.

Pointing to the similarities between the prohibition against alcohol and that against other drugs, David Courtwright (1982: 144) asks why, since both reform efforts had ended in failure, did the public withdraw its support for one and increase its support of the other? "One factor (in addition to economic and political considerations) must have been that alcohol use was relatively widespread and cut across class lines. It seemed unreasonable for the government to deny a broad spectrum of otherwise normal persons access to drink. By 1930 opiate addiction, by contrast, was perceived to be concentrated in a small criminal subculture; it did not seem unreasonable for that same government to deny the morbid cravings of a deviant group."

World War II had a dramatic impact on the supply of heroin in the United States. The Japanese invasion of China interrupted supplies from that country, while the disruption of shipping routes by German submarines and attack battleships reduced the amount of heroin moving from Turkey to Marseilles to the United States. When the United States entered the war, security measures "designed to prevent infiltration of foreign spies and sabotage to naval installations made smuggling into the United States virtually impossible." As a result, "at the end of World War II, there was an excellent chance that heroin addiction could be eliminated in the United States" (A. W. McCoy 1972: 15). Obviously, this did not happen; the reasons will be discussed later in this chapter and in Chapter 11.

Cocaine: From Coca Leaf to Crack

Cocaine is a stimulant, an alkaloid found in significant quantities only in the leaves of two species of coca shrub that are indigenous to certain sections of South America, although it has been grown elsewhere.[4] "For over 4,000 years among the native Andean population, the coca leaf has been used in ancient rituals and for everyday gift giving. Holding spiritual, economic and cultural significance, coca is seen as an important medium for social integration and human solidarity in the face of adverse conditions" (Wheat and Green 1999: 42). To the Incas, the plant was of divine origin reserved for those who believed themselves descendants of the gods. In Bolivia, it is drunk as *mate* (coca tea) and chewed for hours by farmers and miners along with an alkaloid that helps release the active ingredients. "The result is similar to a prolonged caffeine or tobacco buzz. But it is more than that. It improves stamina, is a sacred symbol central to community life and provides essential nutrients" (Wheat and Green 1999: 43).

European experience with chewing coca coincided with Spanish exploration of the New World. While the early Spanish explorers, obsessed with gold, referred to coca-leaf chewing with scorn, later reports about the effects of coca on Indians were more enthusiastic. Nevertheless, the chewing of coca leaves was not adopted by Europeans until the nineteenth century (Grinspoon 1979). A "mixture of ignorance and moral hauteur played an important role in the long delay between the time Europeans first became acquainted with cocaine—in the form of coca—and the time they began to use it" (Ashley 1975: 3). The coca leaves tasted bitter and were favored by pagans—Peruvian Indians—"an obviously inferior lot who had allowed their great Inca Empire to be conquered by Pizarro and fewer than two hundred Spaniards." Early records indicate that the effects of coca—stamina and energy—were ascribed not to the drug but to a pact the Indians had made with the devil, or simply to delusion—the Indian is sustained by the *belief* that chewing coca gives him extra strength.

---

[4]During the 1920s, Indonesia exported more coca leaf than did Latin America (Karch 1996).

Nineteenth-Century Use of Cocaine

Alkaloidal cocaine was isolated from the coca leaf by German scientists in the decade before the American Civil War, and the German chemical manufacturer Merck began to
produce small amounts (Karch 1998). Scientists experimenting with the substance noted
that it showed promise as a local anesthetic and had an effect opposite to that caused by
morphine. Indeed, at first cocaine was used to treat morphine addiction, but the result
was often a morphine addict who was also dependent on cocaine (Van Dyke and Byck
1982). Enthusiasm for cocaine spread across the United States, and by the late 1880s a
feel-good pharmacology based on the coca plant and its derivative cocaine emerged, as
the substance was hawked for everything from headaches to hysteria. "Catarrh powders
for sinus trouble and headaches—a few were nearly pure cocaine—introduced the concept of snorting" (Gomez 1984: 58). Patent medicines frequently contained significant
amounts of cocaine.

One popular product was the coca wine *Vin Mariani,* which contained two ounces of
fresh coca leaves in a pint of Bordeaux wine; another, *Peruvian Wine of Coca,* was available for $1 a bottle through the 1902 Sears, Roebuck catalog. The most famous beverage
containing coca, however, was first bottled in 1894, and an advertisement for Coca-Cola
in *Scientific American* in 1906 publicized the use of coca as an important tonic in this
"healthful drink" (May 1988b: 29). A 1908 government report listed more than forty
brands of soft drinks containing cocaine (Helmer 1975). As opposed to the patent medicines, however, these beverages, including wine and Coca-Cola, contained only small, typically trivial, amounts of cocaine (Karch 1998).

In 1884 Sigmund Freud began taking cocaine and soon afterward began to treat his
friend Ernst von Fleischl-Marxow, who had become a morphine addict, with cocaine.
The following year, von Fleischl-Marxow suffered from toxic psychosis as a result of taking increasing amounts of cocaine by subcutaneous injection, and Freud wrote that the
misuse of the substance had hastened his friend's death. While Freud continued the
recreational use of cocaine as late as 1895, his enthusiasm for its therapeutic value
waned (Byck 1974).

After the flush of enthusiasm for cocaine in the 1880s, its direct use declined. Cocaine
continued to be used in a variety of potions and tonics, but unlike morphine and heroin,
did not develop a separate appeal (H. W. Morgan 1981). Indeed, it gained a reputation for
inducing bizarre and unpredictable behavior.

Cocaine in the Twentieth Century

After the turn of the twentieth century, cocaine, like heroin, became identified with the
urban underworld and, in the South, with African Americans. "As with Chinese opium,
southern blacks became a target for class conflict, and drug use became one point of
tension in this larger sociopolitical struggle" (Cloyd 1982: 35). The campaign against
cocaine took on bizarre aspects aimed at winning support for antidrug legislation
among Southern politicians who traditionally resisted federal efforts that interfered with
their concept of states' rights. Without any research support, a spate of articles alleged

widespread abuse of cocaine by African Americans, often associating such abuse with violence and the rape of white women (Helmer 1975). Ultimately, notes Jerald Cloyd (1982: 54), "Southerners were more afraid of African-Americans than of increased federal power to regulate these drugs." At the time of the Harrison Act there was considerable discussion—but no evidence—of substantial cocaine use by blacks in northern cities (H. W. Morgan 1981).

As with opiates, the legal use of cocaine was affected by the Pure Food and Drug Act of 1906 and finally by the Harrison Act in 1914. Before this federal legislation, many states passed laws restricting the sale of cocaine, beginning with Oregon in 1887. By 1914, forty-six states had such laws, while only twenty-nine had similar laws with respect to opiates (Grinspoon 1979). With its dangers well known, by the end of World War I the medical community had largely lost interest in cocaine (Karch 1998), and in 1922 Congress officially defined cocaine as a narcotic and prohibited the importation of most cocaine and coca leaves. This caused an increase in law enforcement efforts, and the price of cocaine increased accordingly. In 1932, amphetamines became available, and this cheap legal stimulant helped to further decrease user interest in cocaine (Cintron 1986).

In the United States, from 1930 until the 1960s, there was limited demand for cocaine and, accordingly, only limited supply.[5] Cocaine use was associated with deviants at the fringes of society—jazz musicians and the denizens of the underworld—and sources were typically diverted from medical supplies. During the late 1960s and early 1970s, attitudes toward recreational drug use became more liberal because of the wide acceptance of marijuana. Cocaine was no longer associated with deviants, and the media played a significant role in shaping public attitudes:

> By publicizing and glamorizing the lifestyle of affluent, upper-class drug dealers and the use of cocaine by celebrities and athletes, all forms of mass media created an effective advertising campaign for cocaine, and many people were taught to perceive cocaine as chic, exclusive, daring, and nonaddicting. In television specials about cocaine abuse, scientists talked about the intense euphoria produced by cocaine and the compulsive craving that people (and animals) develop for it. Thus, an image of cocaine as being extraordinarily powerful, and a (therefore desirable) euphoriant was promoted. (Wesson and Smith 1985: 193)

Cocaine soon became associated with a privileged elite, and the new demand was sufficient to generate new sources. Refining and marketing networks outside of medical channels (Grinspoon 1979) led to the development of the criminal organizations discussed in Chapter 11.

During the 1980s a new form of cocaine—called **crack**—became popular in a number of cities, particularly New York. Its popularity dramatically altered the drug market at the consumer level: both users and sellers were much younger than was typical in

---

[5] This was not the case in Europe and the Far East, where major drug firms provided cocaine—often surreptitiously—for sale in the drug black market (Karch 1998).

Drug Hysteria

According to Steven Belenko (1993: 24), all drug scares have four common elements:

1. The scope of the problem is never as great as originally portrayed in the media.
2. Despite the media portrayals, compulsive use and addiction are not inevitable consequences of using the drug.
3. The violent behavior associated with the use of the drug is not as common as initially believed, nor is it necessarily caused by the drug.
4. The popularity of the particular drug waxes and wanes over time, and prevalence rates do not continue to increase.

---

the heroin business. Younger retailers and a competitive market increased the level of violence associated with the drug business. The appearance of this new form of cocaine, which is smoked, set off a frenzy of media interest. Elected officials responded by increasing penalties for this form of the substance as opposed to the powdered form, which is typically sniffed.

By 1987 the rapid expansion of crack use stopped, and by 1989 its popularity began to diminish. The hysteria with which the media and public officials had greeted this "new scourge" was subjected to research and reflection: "Crack itself was never instantly addictive or totally devastating as asserted by the media, political speeches, and statements of public policy. In particular, it did not draw the naive and young in droves into this new and dangerous lifestyle." Indeed, crack use was centered in those populations in which drug abuse has always been endemic—the urban underclass (B. D. Johnson, Golub, and Fagan 1995: 291).

Cocaine has very limited medical use as a local anesthetic for ear, nose, and throat surgery. Its early use, however, led to the development of procaine (Novocain), which in 1905 was introduced into medicine and continues to be used today, particularly in dentistry (Snyder 1986). Novocain and other synthetic drugs have, for the most part, replaced cocaine as a local anesthetic. Coca leaves are legally imported into the United States by a single chemical company, which extracts the cocaine for pharmaceutical purposes. The remaining leaf material, which contains no psychoactive agents, is prepared as a flavoring for Coca-Cola.

Marijuana: From Immigrants to the Counterculture

Cannabis sativa L., the hemp plant from which **marijuana** and hashish are derived, grows wild throughout most tropical and temperate regions of the world; it has

For the Birds

In 1998, Canada declared hemp a legal crop, joining several European nations that also have commercial hemp industries. When a Canadian producer of birdseed shipped nearly twenty tons of his product to the United States, it was seized by U.S. Customs agents—the shipment consisted of sterilized seeds produced from industrial hemp (Wren 1999f).

been cultivated for at least 5,000 years for a variety of purposes including the manufacture of rope and paint. There is a great deal of interest in the cultivation of hemp for its fiber, particularly in the American apparel and paper industries (Mintz 1997).

Marijuana's use as an intoxicant was brought to Africa by Arab traders, and the plant was introduced into Brazil through the slave trade in the 1600s. The word *marijuana* is derived from the Spanish term for any substance that produces intoxication: *maraguano*. Until the early 1900s recreational use of marijuana was popular chiefly among Mexican laborers in the Southwest and certain fringe groups such as jazz musicians (Weisheit 1990).

When the dried leaves of the marijuana plant are smoked like tobacco, perceptual changes occur that vary widely according to the strength of the substance, the person smoking the marijuana, and the environmental conditions. In the past most of the cannabis growing wild in the United States derived from plants originally cultivated for their fiber rather than their drug content, so their psychoactive potency was quite weak (R. C. Peterson 1980). In more recent years entrepreneurial horticulturists in the United States began producing more powerful strains of the plant.

Early Marijuana Legislation and Literature

As already discussed in this chapter, race, religion, and ethnicity have been closely identified with the reaction to drugs in the United States: the Irish and alcohol; the Chinese and opium; African Americans and cocaine; and, finally, Mexicans and marijuana. Bonnie and Whitebread (1970) state that the most prominent influence in marijuana legislation was racism: State laws against marijuana, they argue, were often part of a reaction to Mexican immigration. Before 1930 sixteen states with relatively large Mexican populations had enacted antimarijuana legislation. "Chicanos in the Southwest were believed to be incited to violence by smoking it" (Musto 1973: 65). Jerome Himmelstein (1983: 29) argues, however, that the "crucial link between Mexicans and federal marihuana policy was not locally based political pressure from the Southwest, but a specific image of marihuana that emerged from the context of marihuana use by Mexicans and was used to justify anti-marihuana legislation. Because Mexican laborers and other lower-class groups were identified as typical marihuana users, the drug was believed to cause the kinds of antisocial behavior associated with those groups, especially violent crime." Because of marijuana's association with suspect marginal groups—Mexicans, artists, intellectuals, jazz musicians, bohemians, and petty criminals—it became an easy target for regulation (Morgan 1981). In the eastern United States marijuana was erroneously believed to be addictive and would serve as a substitute for narcotics that were outlawed by the Harrison Act.

In light of more contemporary research into marijuana (which will be reviewed in Chapter 6), the hysterical antimarijuana literature produced during the 1930s can often seem amusing. Earle and Robert Rowell (1939: 49) wrote, for example, that marijuana "seems to superimpose upon the user's character and personality a devilish form. He is one individual when normal, and an entirely different one after using marijuana." Marijuana "has led to some of the most revolting cases of sadistic rape and murder of modern times." In 1936 the Federal Bureau of Narcotics presented a summary of cases that illustrate "the homicidal tendencies and the generally debasing effects which arise from the use of marijuana" (Uelmen and Haddox 1983: 1–11). The 1936 motion picture *Reefer Madness* presented a frightening portrait of the marijuana user.

"It is clear," note Bonnie and Whitebread (1970: 1021–22), "that no state undertook any empirical or scientific study of the effects of the drug. Instead they relied on lurid and often unfounded accounts of marijuana's dangers as presented in what little newspaper coverage the drug received." By 1931, twenty-two states had marijuana legislation that was often part of a general-purpose statute against narcotics (Bonnie and Whitebread 1970). Despite its being outlawed, marijuana was never an important issue in the United States until the 1960s: "It hardly ever made headlines or became the subject of highly publicized hearings and reports. Few persons knew or cared about it, and marihuana laws were passed with minimal attention" (Himmelstein 1983: 38).

The Federal Bureau of Narcotics, operating on a Depression-era budget, was reluctant to take on the additional responsibilities that would result from outlawing marijuana at the federal level. Harry J. Anslinger, FBN commissioner from 1930 until his retirement in 1962, hoped that the states would act against marijuana, leaving the bureau free to concentrate on heroin and cocaine. In order to get the states to act, the bureau dramatized the dangers of marijuana. But in such trying economic times, the states were reluctant to take on additional work, and the FBN's own propaganda forced it to act (Himmelstein 1983).

At the urging of Anslinger, Congress passed the Marijuana Tax Act of 1937. Because of uncertainty over the federal government's ability to outlaw marijuana, the act placed a prohibitive tax on cannabis—$100 an ounce—rather than prohibit the substance outright. This tax act was a result of three days of congressional hearings that Bonnie and Whitebread (1970: 1054) characterize as "a case study in legislative carelessness." Commissioner Anslinger was able to orchestrate an undocumented and hysterical presentation before the House Ways and Means Committee on the dangers of marijuana, and the floor debate on the bill, they argue, represented a near-comic example of dereliction of legislative responsibility. Anslinger (with Tompkins 1953: 20–21) maintained that marijuana was "a scourge which undermines its victims and degrades them mentally, morally, and physically." The AMA's opposition to the bill was ridiculed by members of the Ways and Means Committee. Marijuana was being treated like just another narcotic (Bonnie and Whitebread 1970). The states followed the federal lead and increased their penalties for drug violations, including marijuana. In 1951 penalties for possession and trafficking in marijuana were substantially increased—along with those for other controlled substances—with the passage of the Boggs Act (discussed below).

Counterculture Use and Changing Laws

During the 1960s public attitudes toward marijuana underwent considerable change. A nonconformist counterculture, whose members were often from the white middle class, emerged. The rebellious nature of the hippies encouraged greater experimentation with sex and drugs, marijuana in particular. In fact, note Charles Lidz and Andrew Walker (1980), marijuana use helped tie diverse interests—civil rights, antiwar, antiestablishment—together: Its primary import was as a membership ritual for an otherwise very diffuse and disorganized group. No longer confined to minority or subcultural groups—Chicanos, African Americans, Beatniks, musicians—marijuana soon found widespread acceptance among persons of the middle and upper classes. This led to significant scientific inquiry into the effects of marijuana, and toward the latter part of the 1960s it became clear that whatever its dangers might be, the substance was simply not in the same class as heroin or cocaine on any important pharmacological dimension. Young, white, middle-class users, however, like their ghetto counterparts, were being subjected to the significant penalties that obtained for heroin and cocaine.

The rise of middle-class marijuana users offered the public a new view of the phenomenon in *Life* magazine's October 31, 1969 issue. Marijuana was the lead story, and the magazine presented photographs of white, middle-class persons enjoying marijuana in a variety of congenial social settings. Also included was an in-depth story of a young man from Nashville, Tennessee, a long-distance runner and prep school graduate attending the University of Virginia on an athletic scholarship. He was arrested for possession of 3 pounds of marijuana and in a Virginia state court received a sentence of 20 years. The same issue of *Life* contains an article by the former director of the United States Food and Drug Administration, James L. Goddard, who stated: "Our laws governing marijuana are a mixture of bad science and poor understanding of the role of law as a deterrent force. They are unenforceable, excessively severe, scientifically incorrect and revealing our ignorance of human behavior" (p. 34). The following year Robert Kennedy, Jr. and R. Sargent Shriver III, juveniles at the time, were arrested for possession of marijuana. Public pressure soon caused legislators to reconsider state and federal penalties for marijuana.

"As of 1965, marihuana laws still bore the mark of the harsh legislation of the 1950s. Simple possession carried penalties of two years for the first offense, five for the second, and ten for the third" (Himmelstein 1983: 103). By the end of the 1960s penalties on the state level had been significantly reduced. However, the Comprehensive Drug Abuse Prevention and Control Act of 1970 established five schedules for controlled substances, and marijuana, along with heroin, was placed in the highest category, Schedule I:

- The drug or other substance has a high potential for abuse.
- The drug or other substance has no currently accepted medical use in treatment in the United States.
- There is a lack of accepted safety for the use of the drug or other substance under medical supervision.

While the penalties remained as high as imprisonment for 5 years for nonnarcotic drugs, i.e., marijuana, such sentences are reserved for possession of large amounts with intent to sell—for wholesale traffickers, the only type of offender traditionally of interest to federal drug law enforcement. Simple possession was made a misdemeanor, a crime punishable by imprisonment for not more than 1 year. The major elements of the federal law were copied by most states.

In 1972 the (presidentially appointed) National Commission on Marijuana and Drug Abuse recommended that possession of marijuana for personal use or noncommercial distribution be decriminalized. The following year Oregon became the first state to abolish criminal penalties for the possession of one ounce or less of marijuana, replacing incarceration with relatively small fines. In 1975 California made possession of one ounce or less of marijuana a citable misdemeanor with a maximum penalty of $100, and there were no increased penalties for recidivists. By 1978 eleven states had decriminalized marijuana, a position supported by President Jimmy Carter (Himmelstein 1983) but opposed by the President's Commission on Organized Crime (1986), which was appointed by President Ronald Reagan. Alaska, after 15 years, has made it illegal again, the result of a ballot initiative in 1990.

In more recent years there has been some medical use of the active ingredient in marijuana—but not marijuana itself—to control the side effects of chemotherapy and to treat glaucoma. Despite vigorous opposition at the federal level, in 1997 voters in California and Arizona passed referendums authorizing physicians to prescribe marijuana; Maine voters did the same in 1999.

Amphetamines: Speed and Ice

First synthesized in 1887, **amphetamine** was introduced into clinical use in the 1930s and eventually offered as a "cure-all" for just about every ailment. Between 1932 and 1946 there were thirty-nine generally accepted medical uses for amphetamines, including the treatment of schizophrenia, morphine addiction, low blood pressure, and caffeine and tobacco dependence (D. Smith 1979). Manufactured under the trade name Benzedrine, in 1932 amphetamine was marketed as an inhalant for use as a nasal decongestant. "Amphetamines were unique: never before had a powerful psychoactive drug been introduced in such quantities in so short a period of time, and never before had a drug with such a high addictive potential and capability of causing long-term or irreversible physical and psychological damage been so enthusiastically embraced by the medical profession as a panacea or so extravagantly promoted by the drug industry" (Grinspoon and Hedblom 1975: 13).

By the end of the decade, as their stimulating properties became widely known, amphetamines were used primarily as *analeptics*—stimulating drugs. Many amphetamine-based inhalants appeared on the market and were widely available without prescription. These quickly became the subject of widespread abuse. During World War II, British, German, and Japanese governments issued amphetamines to soldiers to elevate mood and to counteract fatigue and pain, and American military personnel were exposed to their use through contact with the British military. During the Korean conflict the United States authorized the distribution of amphetamines to military personnel. The first major wave of abuse appeared when American servicemen in Korea and Japan mixed the substance with heroin to create "speedballs," which were taken intravenously (Grinspoon and Hedblom 1975).

Dextroamphetamine, a more potent version of Benzedrine, was marketed as Dexedrine; and methamphetamine, manufactured under the trade name Methadrine, is an even more potent analeptic. Currently the drug of choice for street abusers, who refer to it by the brand name Methadrine, or "meth," "crank," "speed," or "ice," methamphetamine is injected, snorted, or smoked. Reports of its abuse by businessmen and athletes appeared as early as 1940, and a black market in the substance—"pep pills"—began to develop. It was (is?) particularly popular among long-distance truck drivers and college students trying to stay awake. Amphetamines were widely prescribed in the 1950s and 1960s as an aid in dieting, leading to abuse by housewives taking "diet pills."

In the 1960s a widespread anti-amphetamine campaign with the slogan "Speed Kills" was launched by the Food and Drug Administration (O'Brien and Cohen 1984), and in 1971 federal laws restricted the conditions under which amphetamines could be prescribed. During the late 1980s the smokable crystal methamphetamine called *ice* appeared on the drug scene. Media and political concern over the possible spread of this new form of drug led to a new drug scare. Widespread abuse continues, and a significant increase in illegal methamphetamine use is being experienced in California and the Southwest, where the drug is cheaper than cocaine.

Barbiturates

Barbiturates are sedating drugs synthesized from barbituric acid. Barbituric acid was first synthesized in Germany in 1863 by Nobel Prize-winning chemist Adolf von Baeyer. The first barbiturate was synthesized in 1882 but not marketed until 1903 (McKim 1991). Accounts vary as to how barbituric acid acquired its name. In 1903 it was released under the trade name Veronal, a name derived from the Italian city of Verona. It is known generically in the United States as barbital (Wesson and Smith 1977).

Barbiturates were used to induce sleep, replacing other aids such as alcohol and opiates. Since the appearance of phenobarbital in 1912, thousands of barbituric acid derivatives have been synthesized, although only about a dozen are commonly used; these are marketed under a variety of brand names. Barbiturates were widely prescribed in the United States during the 1930s when their toxic effects were not fully understood. By 1942 there were campaigns against the nonmedical use of barbiturates, and by the 1950s it was one of the major drugs of abuse among adults in the United States. In the 1960s its abuse quickly spread to the youth population (O'Brien and Cohen 1984). Nonmedical abuse is usually the result of diverting licit supplies through theft or burglary, forged prescriptions, or illegal manufacture in other countries, particularly Mexico. Supplies diverted from licit sources may be repackaged in nondescript capsules, thus disguising their source (Wesson and Smith 1977).

Tranquilizers and Sedatives

In the 1960s many doctors routinely prescribed a variety of substances, along with amphetamines and barbiturates, to reduce anxiety. Tranquilizers or sedatives such as Miltown and Valium enabled millions of housewives to "get by with a little help from their friends." These substances were the subject of heavy advertising, much of it depicting women in need of relief from tension and anxiety, by drug companies who offered their products as aids in coping with the normal problems of life. Consumers often became so dependent on these substances that they could not function without them, having lost the ability to deal with normal levels of stress. As a result of unfavorable attention by health and consumer organizations and a congressional hearing in 1979, the manufacturers of Valium and other tranquilizers shifted their focus to promote these substances' ability to ease the stress of modern living. In 1980 the Food and Drug Administration required tranquilizers to be labeled as generally not appropriate for anxiety or tension associated with the stress of everyday life. Nevertheless, they continue to be widely prescribed for patients experiencing "troubling times."

Hallucinogens

Hallucinogens such as LSD became popular during the 1960s, particularly among rebellious college students and people who identified themselves as antiestablishment. Lester Grinspoon (1979: 57) states that "it is impossible to write an adequate history of such an amorphous phenomenon [LSD] without discussing the whole cultural rebellion of the 1960s." LSD was first synthesized in Switzerland in 1938, but its hallucinogenic qualities did not become apparent until its discoverer took his first "trip" in 1943. During the 1950s the army and the Central Intelligence Agency conducted LSD experiments on soldiers and civilians, without their knowledge or consent, to test its suitability for chemical warfare and its utility as a "truth serum" (Henderson 1994a).

Although LSD arrived in America from Europe in 1949 for experimental use in treating psychiatric disorders (Stevens 1987), before 1962 it was virtually unknown except by a small number of psychiatrists and psychologists (Brecher 1972). Two psychologists at Harvard, Timothy Leary and Richard Alpert, were experimenting with the hallucinogenic mushroom psilocybin. Although the "Psilo-cybin Project" began as a scientific endeavor, it ended as casual use of the drug by many friends and acquaintances, including a small clique of psychedelic enthusiasts. Among them were authors Aldous Huxley (*Brave New World*) and Ken Kesey (*One Flew Over the Cuckoo's Nest*), and the poet Allen Ginsberg. (See Wolfe 1968 for a look at Kesey and his Merry Pranksters' psychedelic world.) Experiments that Leary and Alpert conducted on inmates at Concord State Prison suggested that aggressive and hardened inmates became introspective and caring under the influence of psilocybin. Leary began encouraging his psychology students to use psilocybin. Word of their activities spread beyond the Harvard community when it was picked up by newspapers as a result of a story in the *Harvard Crimson*. Federal agencies began making inquiries. School officials were anxious to rid themselves of Leary and Alpert, so their research, and control over psilocybin, was placed under a faculty committee while the school awaited the expiration of Leary's and Alpert's teaching contracts. No matter, they had been introduced to LSD.

"In a major city like Los Angeles," notes Jay Stevens (1987: 171), "it was as easy to go on an LSD trip as it was to visit Disneyland. Interested parties could either contact the growing number of therapists who were using LSD in practice, or they could offer themselves as guinea pigs to any of the dozens of research projects that were under way at places like UCLA." Therapists were using LSD "to heighten the traditional psychotherapeutic values of recall, abreaction, and emotional release," in most cases with apparent success and without negative side effects (1987: 180). However, the reaction of mainstream, establishment medicine and psychiatry toward LSD was generally negative, particularly when it was utilized by nonphysicians such as psychologists. Stevens refers to the resulting conflict as a turf war between medically trained practitioners and all other therapists. LSD was also widely used without the guise of any therapeutic milieu, such as at the "LSD colony" in Hollywood, where, according to Leary (R. Rosenbaum 1988: 135), "Cary Grant was the high cardinal."

In 1962 Congress enacted legislation that gave the Food and Drug Administration control over all new investigational drugs. Although aimed at amphetamines, the legislation also applied to LSD (Stevens 1987). That same year Leary, Alpert, and thirty-five disciples moved to Zihuatanejo, Mexico, where they used LSD freely. The two psychologists established the International Foundation for Internal Freedom and "Freedom Center" at a small hotel in Zihuatanejo. A second headquarters was opened in Newton, Massachusetts, just outside of Boston: Their goal was to "turn on America." Leary popularized the use of LSD, and as a result of his Harvard connection, LSD gained the attention of the mass media (Grinspoon 1979). As a self-appointed High Priest of LSD (the title of Leary's book), he traveled widely and lectured on the virtues of using acid to "turn on, tune in, and drop out." Acid rock songs, such as "White Rabbit" by the Jefferson Airplane, "Sunshine Superman" by Donovan, and the Beatles' "Magical Mystery Tour" and "Lucy in the Sky with Diamonds," became top hits. The books of Nobel Prize-winner Hermann Hesse (1877–1962) were popular among the youth of the sixties, and his work helped to popularize the "psychedelic" experience (Engel 1974). Psychedelic jargon and colors became fashionable, and the media reported on the activities of hippies in New York's Greenwich Village and San Francisco's Haight-Ashbury district. LSD use became part of the counterculture and antiwar movement.

In 1963 an editorial attacking LSD appeared in the *Journal of the American Medical Association,* and in 1965 LSD was outlawed. In 1963 Leary and Alpert were discharged from Harvard; that same year the Mexican authorities closed down Freedom Center, and Leary was deported. In 1965 Leary was returning to the United States from a trip to Mexico with three other persons, one of whom had secreted marijuana in her undergarments. When the drug was discovered during a strip search, Leary blurted out, "I'll take responsibility for the marijuana." At the time possession of marijuana was a serious crime in Texas. Despite his defense that the use of drugs was part of his religious liberty,

Leary was convicted and sentenced to 30 years in prison. Leary appealed; in the meantime his harassment by law enforcement agencies resulted in numerous arrests. In 1969 the U.S. Supreme Court ordered his marijuana case to be retried. In 1970 Leary was convicted again and sentenced to 10 years. Leary appealed, but several weeks later he was convicted of another drug-related charge in California, where he received a 1- to 10-year sentence. He was immediately remanded to a minimum-security prison.

Facing further trials in other states, later that year the 49-year-old Leary escaped from prison and subsequently reappeared in Algeria, where he found refuge with the Black Panthers. After being placed under house arrest for purposes of "revolutionary discipline," Leary fled again, this time to Switzerland. Eventually he made his way to Afghanistan, where he was captured by U.S. drug enforcement agents. Leary wound up in the maximum-security prison at Folsom, California. After reportedly agreeing to provide information to the government, Leary was released in 1976 (R. Rosenbaum 1988). For a number of years he was popular on the collegiate lecture circuit, often appearing with G. Gordon Liddy, of Watergate fame, who was responsible for much of the harassment to which Leary had been subjected (Stevens 1987). In 1996, at 75, Leary died of prostate cancer (Mansnerus 1996).

Government Action After World War II

In the years immediately before World War II, the Federal Bureau of Narcotics seemed to have the drug problem well under control. Commissioner Anslinger released statistics indicating a significant drop in the addict population. Then came the war. Opiate smuggling dwindled, and those Americans of an age most susceptible to drug use were in Europe and Asia. Drug use was viewed as unpatriotic as well as illegal. Alcohol, barbiturates, and amphetamines were the substances most widely abused during the war years, when the price of opiates increased dramatically. The addict population appeared to reach an all-time low.

At the end of the war there was fear of an epidemic of drug use as U.S. soldiers began to return from Far Eastern locations where opiate use was endemic. The epidemic failed to materialize. The FBN became a victim of its own propaganda and apparent success, and Congress would not increase the drug-fighting budget (H. W. Morgan 1981). Then in 1950 and 1951 a spate of news stories on drug abuse reported that the use of heroin was spilling out of the ghetto and into middle-class environs, where it was poisoning the minds and bodies of America's (white) youth. Musto (1973) points out a parallel between the periods following World War I and World War II: Both were characterized by an atmosphere of hostility to radicals and Communists, and both led to punitive sanctions against drug addicts. Any expression of tolerance for radical political ideas or drug addicts was un-American. In a timely stroke of political genius, the Federal Bureau of Narcotics linked heroin trafficking to Red China.

Anslinger accused the People's Republic of selling opium and heroin to the free nations of the world in order to finance overseas ambitions (Cloyd 1982). As we shall see in

Chapter 11, Far Eastern heroin was, and continues to be, the business of Chinese Nationalists, triads, Thais, and Burmese insurgents—*not* the People's Republic, which routinely executes drug traffickers. Indeed, "at the time of the Communist takeover in 1949, China was the world's largest producer and consumer of narcotic drugs" (Lee 1995: 194).

On the basis of statistics showing that between 1946 and 1950 there had been a 100 percent increase in the number of narcotic laws-related arrests, and that over a 5-year period the average age of persons committed to a Public Health Service hospital had declined from 37.5 to 26.7 years, Congress concluded that drug addiction was increasing and that penalties for drug trafficking were inadequate. In 1951 Congress passed the Boggs Act, which increased penalties for violations of drug laws. Once again, using rather dubious statistical data, Congress concluded that the increased penalties of the Boggs Act had been quite successful in reducing drug trafficking. As a result, in 1956 Congress passed the Narcotic Control Act, which further increased the penalties for drug violations—for example, the sale of heroin to individuals under 18 years of age was made a capital offense—and increased the authority of the Federal Bureau of Narcotics and agents of the Customs Bureau (PCOC 1986). State legislatures, responding to the federal initiative, significantly increased penalties for drug violations.

"Public concern over the problem of drug abuse, which had been relatively dormant during the 1940s and 1950s, flared again during the 1960s. The intensification of national concern resulted in increasing pressure for federal initiatives in the area. In response to this development, a White House Conference on Narcotics and Drug Abuse was convened in 1962, which resulted in the establishment of the President's Advisory Commission on Narcotics and Drug Abuse (Prettyman Commission) on January 15, 1963" (PCOC 1986: 215). The commission recommended discarding the antiquated legal notion that drug control was simply a taxing measure, and they suggested that the responsibilities of the Federal Bureau of Narcotics be transferred to the Department of Justice. On the other hand, the commission recommended that the regulation of marijuana and lawful narcotic drugs be transferred from the FBN to the Department of Health, Education, and Welfare (**HEW**). It also recommended increasing the number of federal drug agents and enacting legislation for the strict control of nonnarcotic drugs capable of producing psychotoxic effects when abused.

In the 1960s concern increased over the diversion of dangerous drugs from licit sources. As a result, Congress passed the Drug Abuse Control Amendments of 1965, which, among other things, mandated record-keeping and inspection requirements for depressant and stimulant drugs throughout the chain of distribution, from the basic manufacturer to (but not including) the consumer. Enforcement of the 1965 legislation was left to a newly created agency within HEW's Food and Drug Administration, the Bureau of Drug Abuse Control. The Treasury Department's monopoly over drug enforcement had ended (PCOC 1986).

A Turn Toward Treatment

During the 1960s the medical profession began to reassert itself on the issue of drug abuse in both treatment and research. Treating disciplines—psychology and social work—and researchers in sociology and public health began to focus on the drug issue as a social—not simply a law enforcement—problem. The social activism of the 1960s also influenced the perspective on drug abuse (H. W. Morgan 1981), and a new strategic approach was implemented: reducing demand by rehabilitating large numbers of drug addicts. Arnold Trebach (1982: 226) argues that this approach was facilitated by the resignation of Harry Anslinger as commissioner of the FBN ("which had been accomplished with the active encouragement of the Kennedy brothers"). Anslinger was replaced by Harry Giordano, a pharmacist, and the pendulum of drug policy began to shift away from a law enforcement model toward a treatment model. The 1963 Prettyman Commission recommended the relaxation of mandatory prison sentences for drug convictions, greater research, and the dismantling of the Federal Bureau of Narcotics, whose functions were to be divided between the Department of Health, Education, and Welfare (prevention and treatment) and the Department of Justice (law enforcement).

In 1961 California established a civil commitment program in which drug addicts were taken into custody and committed—like mentally ill in need of hospitalization—to a nonpunitive period of confinement and drug treatment. Confinement was followed by a period of aftercare/parole supervision. In 1966 New York established the Narcotic Addiction Control Commission, a large-scale effort whose goal was to confine as many drug addicts as possible under civil commitment statutes. As in California, whose lead New York was following, confinement was followed by a period of parole supervision. (This writer was employed briefly as a senior narcotic parole officer for the Narcotic Addiction Control Commission. This agency, which expended billions of dollars, was dismantled during the 1970s as a very costly failure.) In 1966, Congress passed the Narcotic Addict Rehabilitation Act, which in lieu of prosecution authorized federal district courts to order the voluntary and involuntary civil commitment of certain defendants found to be drug addicts, and mandated the Surgeon General to establish rehabilitation and posthospitalization care programs for drug addicts. The legislation also authorized the financing of state efforts to treat addicts.

Between 1969 and 1974 the number of federally funded drug rehabilitation programs dramatically increased from 16 at the beginning of 1969 to 926 in 1974. Federal expenditures on drug treatment rose from about $80 million to about $800 million during that period. About half of the 80,000 clients in these programs were being maintained on methadone (Moss 1977), a synthetic opiate. During the 1960s a pilot program of methadone maintenance was initiated at Rockefeller University in New York. The drug, which was taken orally, prevented withdrawal symptoms in heroin addicts who were maintained with daily doses. Trebach (1982: 227) refers to this approach to heroin addiction as the "greatest theoretical and practical departure in American rehabilitation strategies and clinical attitudes since the early 1920s." While the program was successful in aiding the rehabilitation of certain kinds of drug users, methadone when ingested intravenously produces a heroinlike euphoria, and by the early 1970s large quantities had been diverted to the illegal street market. In response, Congress passed the Narcotic Treatment Act in 1974, which required annual registration by practitioners dispensing narcotic drugs and imposed new standards for the legal dispensing of dangerous drugs (PCOC 1986).

The 1960s and 1970s also experienced a rise in the popularity of the therapeutic-community approach to treating addiction, the best known being Synanon in California and Daytop Village in New York. Operated by recovered addicts, these drug-free centers use a variety of talking and confrontational therapies mixed with aspects of behavior modification. (Methadone, therapeutic communities, and other approaches to the treatment of drug abusers will be discussed in Chapter 9.)

Comprehensive Drug Abuse Prevention and Control Act of 1970

As the turn of the decade approached, alarming statistics (of dubious validity) about drug abuse were publicized. The drug problem was quickly becoming a major political issue. In 1968 President Lyndon Johnson decried the fragmented approach to drug-law enforcement. With congressional approval, the president abolished the Federal Bureau of Narcotics and the Bureau of Drug Abuse Control and transferred their responsibilities to a newly created agency, the Bureau of Narcotics and Dangerous Drugs (**BNDD**), in the Department of Justice. Revenue and importation aspects of drug trafficking remained within the Treasury Department's Internal Revenue Service and Bureau of Customs. In 1970 President Richard Nixon clarified the responsibilities of the federal agencies involved in drug control, announcing that BNDD "controls all investigations involving violations of the laws of the United States relating to narcotics, marijuana and dangerous drugs, both within the United States and beyond its borders." Several months later guidelines were promulgated that provided increased authority for Customs officials at ports and borders.

The two-pronged approach to dealing with drug abuse—*reducing availability* by investigating and prosecuting traffickers, and *reducing demand* by preventing addiction and treating addicts—was now firm policy. The Comprehensive Drug Abuse Prevention and Control Act of 1970 authorized HEW to increase its efforts at prevention and rehabilitation through a program of grants to special projects and made the HEW National Institute on Drug Abuse (NIDA) the agency with primary responsibility for drug education and prevention activities. The legislation also established five schedules into which all controlled substances could be placed according to their potential for abuse (discussed in Chapter 12); imposed additional reporting requirements for manufacturers, distributors, and dispensers; promulgated new regulations for the importation of controlled substances; and established the Commission on Marijuana and Drug Abuse. BNDD was authorized to increase its strength by 300 agents.

The 1970 legislation represented a new legal approach to federal drug policy. It was predicated, not on the constitutional power to tax, but on federal authority over interstate commerce. The PCOC (1986: 228) notes that this shift had enormous implications for the way the federal government would approach drug enforcement in the future. The act "set the stage for an innovation in Federal drug law enforcement techniques. That innovation was the assigning of large numbers of Federal narcotic agents to work in local communities. No longer was it necessary to demonstrate interstate traffic to justify Federal participation in combating illegal drug use." The new approach was upheld by decisions of the Supreme Court, and the National Conference of Commissioners on Uniform State Laws drafted a model act based on the 1970 statutes, which has been adopted by most states.

A 1973 reorganization plan led to the creation of the Drug Enforcement Administration (**DEA**) within the Department of Justice. All drug-control investigative and enforcement responsibilities, except those related to ports of entry and borders, were given over to the new agency. In 1982 the Federal Bureau of Investigation (FBI) was given concurrent jurisdiction with DEA for drug investigation and law enforcement. In addition, the DEA director was required to report to the director of the FBI, who was given responsibility for supervising drug-law enforcement efforts and policies. That same year the Department of Defense Authorization Act contained a provision outlining military cooperation with civilian authorities. This provision was aimed at improving the level of cooperation by delineating precisely what assistance military commanders could provide. It also permits military personnel to operate military equipment that had been lent to civilian drug enforcement agencies (PCOC 1986). (In 1988 the military's role in drug-law enforcement was substantially increased; this is discussed in Chapter 12.)

The Drug Scare of the 1980s

As 1980 approached, the lack of public interest in and even tolerance of drug use showed signs of shifting as grassroots parent groups began to influence the political landscape. A mother "who later presided over the National Federation of Parents for Drug-Free Youth, attended a rock concert in 1978 with her two young children and discovered rampant drug use all around them. Her anger, shared by others she contacted, apparently was a major factor in the defeat of her Congressman, . . . who had sponsored a bill favoring the decriminalization of an ounce of marijuana. That a broad base of parents were antagonistic to drugs and that they were now organizing their political power had been demonstrated" (Musto 1987b: 271). With encouragement from Dr. Robert L. DuPont, then director of the National Institute on Drug Abuse, an "antipot" handbook for parents was published. The antidrug theme was soon picked up by the Reagan Administration.

The issue of drug abuse is politically safe and useful because no one is in favor of it. During the presidency of Ronald Reagan, drugs again became a major political issue. On 19 June 1986 Len Bias, a basketball star from the University of Maryland, died of a cocaine overdose; on 27 June, Don Rogers, a defensive back for the Cleveland Browns, also died of a cocaine overdose. These widely reported incidents, occurring within a short time of each other and less than five months before congressional elections, led to an intensification of antidrug efforts, a widespread public relations effort utilizing sports and entertainment personalities whose message to television viewers was "Just Say No!" (to drugs). Not to be outdone, Congress responded with huge allocations to combat this scourge, and politicians scrambled for partisan advantage. "Len Bias' death brought together the political and human aspects of drug abuse. His death accentuated that attention placed on drugs after the announcement of the 'war on drugs.' Although consensus about the need to 'do something' was generally accepted, politicians continued to argue over the best approach"

(Merriam 1989: 25). With the elections over and Congress in the hands of the Democrats, the president significantly scaled back the allocations.

The fight against drugs and drug abuse was an important issue in the presidential campaign of 1988. The heat of the national campaign led to the enactment of an omnibus drug bill (Anti-Drug Abuse Act of 1988) in the final days of the 100th Congress. The legislation states: "It is the declared policy of the United States Government to create a Drug-Free America by 1995." The bipartisan measure, which was approved overwhelmingly, increased antidrug spending earmarking 50 percent for treatment, a figure that was to increase to 60 percent over the next few years. On both federal and state levels, penalty distinctions between marijuana and drugs such as heroin and cocaine have been erased—"zero tolerance" (Pollan 1995).

The statute mandated greater controls over precursor chemicals and devices used to manufacture drugs, such as encapsulating machinery. It also created a complex and extensive body of civil penalties aimed at casual users, including fines and ineligibility for federal benefits such as educational loans and mortgage guarantees, and/or the loss of a maritime, pilot, or stockbroker license for a number of years. Penalties for selling drugs to minors were enhanced, and a judge can impose the death penalty for murders committed as part of a continuing criminal enterprise or for the murder of a law enforcement officer during an arrest for a drug-related felony.

The legislation also established the Office of National Drug Control Policy (**ONDCP**) headed by a director ("drug czar") appointed by the president. The director is charged with coordinating federal drug supply reduction efforts, including international control, intelligence, interdiction, domestic drug-law enforcement, treatment, education, and research, and also serves as a liaison between the federal government and state and local drug control efforts. The first director was William J. Bennett, who served as drug czar for twenty-two months, using the position primarily as a rhetorical platform to focus attention on the issue of drug abuse as seen by the administration. His approach attracted extensive media attention, but the powers of the director are so circumscribed that he accomplished little else.

Drug Abuse in the 1990s and Early 2000s

The 1990s were remarkable for the lack of political interest in drug abuse. Indeed, as officials began to recognize the extent of prison overcrowding resulting from our drug policies, statutory and administrative remedies were formulated that placed more drug offenders in diversion/drug treatment programs, probation, and on parole. Laws providing significantly greater prison sentences for the sellers of crack cocaine than for sellers of powdered cocaine came under fire—the former is more likely to be used by minorities, the latter by middle-class whites. There is a mandatory 5-year minimum for selling 5 grams of crack or 500 grams of powdered cocaine; 10 years for selling 50 grams of crack or 5,000 grams of powdered cocaine.

The cocaine market was impacted by crack, because many crack users were purchasing the powdered form (cocaine hydrochloride) in large doses and converting it to crack themselves, reducing the demand for street-level crack, which many users believed inferior to what they could produce themselves. The use of methamphetamine increased, with new supplies coming from Mexico. In some areas, methamphetamine was almost as popular as cocaine. Marijuana remained readily available, and both its use and sale transcend ethnic, racial, and gender boundaries. Users of marijuana tend to be under 20 years old (ONDCP 1995b).

While cocaine remained the dominant (illegal) drug of abuse, heroin, prepared for smoking and snorting, began to make a comeback, particularly outside its typical core clientele, the urban poor. This revival, fueled by the availability of high-grade heroin, particularly from Colombia, is following a pattern set by cocaine in the 1970s. The abundance of heroin is reflected in the purity levels found at the retail level.

In sum, this country moved from a century of permissiveness to draconian sanctions as the result of foreign affairs, the policy of a single federal agency, and a volatile mix of racism and politics. This has led to two drug problems in the United States:

1. The drug problem of the affluent: "It is by no means insignificant, and it has caused more than its share of personal tragedies. But it is a *manageable* problem, and it has been steadily decreasing for several years, for reasons unrelated to the war on drugs."
2. The drug problem of America's have-nots: "That problem has grown malignantly in the face of the drug war—and it is much further from solution than it was when that war began" (Currie 1993: 3).

Now that we have completed our review of the evolution of the problem of drug abuse in the United States, in the next chapter we will examine the neurology of psychoactive substances.

SUMMARY

The temperance movement in the United States in the nineteenth century culminated in passage of the Eighteenth Amendment—Prohibition—in 1919. Opium was used for centuries in Europe and Asia, but it became part of international commerce when Britain forced open trade with China and smuggled opium into that country after its ruler banned its use. China lost the Opium Wars in 1840 and 1856 and was forced to allow legalization and regulation of the opium trade.

The first anti-opium legislation in the United States was the Pure Food and Drug Act of 1906, which required that medicines be labeled if they contained alcohol, opiates, or cocaine. To increase its influence in China and thus improve its trade position, the United States supported international efforts to ban opium shipments to China. These efforts led to an International Opium Convention in The Hague in 1912, which committed participants to enact laws aimed at suppressing the abuse of opium, morphine, and cocaine. The Harrison Act of 1914 represented this country's attempt to carry out the provisions of the Hague Convention. The act required anyone who sold the drugs covered by the law to register annually and pay an annual tax. This roundabout drug legislation occurred because at the time Congress had taxing authority but not the authority to directly regulate narcotics or the prescription practices of physicians.

In the years after World War II concern about drug use prompted Congress to pass the Boggs Act in 1951 and the Narcotic Control Act in 1956, which increased penalties for drug-law violations. With the shift in the 1960s toward treatment, Congress passed the Comprehensive Drug Abuse Prevention and Control Act of 1970, a two-pronged approach that tried to reduce availability through prosecution and to reduce demand through prevention and treatment. In the 1980s concerns of middle-class parents and the drug-overdose deaths of sports stars pushed Congress to pass further antidrug legislation. The 1990s can be characterized as relatively inactive, although a revival of cocaine use has magnified differences between rich and poor in the enforcement of drug policy in the United States, while the popularity of ecstasy in the twenty-first century reveals that the next new drug fad is always "just around the corner."

INTERNET CONNECTIONS

Drug Enforcement Administration: www.usdoj.gov/dea
Lycaeum (drug information site): www.leda.lycaeum.org
Web of Addictions (information resource for drugs): www.well.com/user/woa

---

REVIEW QUESTIONS

1. What was the relationship between nativism and Prohibition?
2. How can Prohibition be explained in terms of rural versus urban America?
3. Why did the end of Prohibition lead to an increase in drug trafficking?
4. Why can the United States during the nineteenth century be described as a "dope fiend's paradise"?
5. How was recreational use of opium popularized in Europe during the late eighteenth and early nineteenth centuries?
6. How did the primitive state of medicine explain the popularity of opium into the nineteenth century?
7. Why was the production of opium unsuccessful in the United States?
8. What was the patent medicine problem?
9. What was the relationship between the Civil War and the popularity of morphine?
10. What was the primary cause of the Opium Wars?
11. What was the relationship between the Chinese immigrants and legislation controlling opiates at state and local levels in the United States?
12. What international events led to the enactment of the Harrison Act?
13. What were the important events that led to the passage of the Pure Food and Drug Act?
14. How can the efforts of the temperance movement and the U.S. response to drugs be explained, at least in part, in terms of racial prejudice?
15. What were the major provisions of the Harrison Act?
16. What was the relationship between the development of the Harrison Act and a concern for federalism?

17. After the Harrison Act was passed, what was the Supreme Court's attitude toward physicians who dispensed opiates?
18. What was the role of federal drug enforcement officials in determining the U.S. policy toward drugs?
19. What was the relationship between prevailing political attitudes after World War I and our reaction to drug users?
20. What led to the development of the Uniform Drug Act?
21. What accounted for the general lack of public concern about drug abuse before World War II?
22. How did World War II affect drug use in the United States?
23. Why did Spanish explorers have a negative view of coca chewing?
24. What was the relationship between the campaign against cocaine and African Americans in the South?
25. What led to the sudden popularity of cocaine beginning in the 1960s?
26. Why has the domestic cannabis crop in the United States until recently been unattractive to potential smokers?
27. What has made domestic cannabis more appealing to potential smokers?
28. What was the relationship between racial and ethnic prejudice and efforts to outlaw marijuana?
29. What was the relationship between the military and the promotion of amphetamines?
30. Why are the properties of amphetamines popular among some students and truck drivers?
31. What was the connection between Timothy Leary and the popularizing of LSD?
32. What was the relationship between public attitudes in the post-World War II era and the U.S. response to drugs?
33. What led to the turn toward treatment of drug abuse during the 1960s?
34. What is the purpose of the Office of National Drug Control Policy (the "drug czar") ?
35. Why has the issue of drugs proven so popular with politicians?
36. What distinguishes the 1980s from the 1990s with respect to the problem of drug abuse?

CHAPTER 3

Drugs and the Nervous System

The legal distinction between licit and illicit drugs is sometimes treated as if it had pharmacological significance. Vendors of licit drugs and proponents of a "drug-free society" share an interest in convincing tobacco smokers and alcohol drinkers that smoking and drinking are radically different than "drug abuse." But a nicotine addict can be just as hooked as a heroin addict, and the victim of an alcohol overdose is just as dead as the victim of a cocaine overdose. —*Mark A. R. Kleiman (1992: 7)*

Advances in science are rapidly dispelling both popular and clinical myths about drug abuse and addiction and what to do about them [although] scientific understanding has not yet totally displaced the moralizing that continues to shadow any discussion on this topic. —*Alan I. Leshner (1999a: 1)*

Distinctions between the neurology and pharmacology (discussed in Chapters 3, 4, 5, and 6), the sociology (Chapter 7), and the psychology (Chapter 8) of drug use are quite artificial (Peele 1985). While the explanatory value of each by itself is limited, the interaction of these three dimensions can explain drug use. Their separation into different chapters, therefore, is for pedagogical rather than scientific purposes. (The neurology of drug abuse also has important treatment and policy implications—topics of subsequent chapters.) In this chapter we will examine how psychoactive drugs impact the central nervous system. In subsequent chapters we will apply this information to specific drugs—depressants, stimulants, hallucinogens, and marijuana.

Neurological Theories of Drug Abuse

A theory helps us explain events. It organizes events so that they can be placed in perspective, explains the causes of past events, and predicts when, where, and how future events will occur. "A theory consists of a set of assumptions; concepts regarding events, situations, individuals, and groups; and propositions that describe the interrelationships among the various assumptions and concepts" (Binder and Geis 1983: 3). Theory is the basic building block for the advancement of human knowledge. In the physical sciences, such as chemistry and physics, theory can usually be subjected to rigorous testing and replication. However, testing neurological theories of drug abuse is limited to work with laboratory animals and to observing and examining current users. We could not give

---

Drug Effects

The effects of *any* drug depend on:

- the amount taken
- the user's past drug experience
- the manner in which the drug is taken
- the circumstances under which the drug is taken (the place, the user's psychological and emotional stability, the presence of other people, the simultaneous use of alcohol or other drugs)

Source: Alcoholism and Drug Addiction Research Foundation, Toronto

---

nondrug-using human beings varying doses of drugs in order to find out how their central nervous system responds (which may also require an autopsy).

The Disease Model

Drug abuse is often discussed in terms such as "overpowering desire," "compulsion," or even "enslavement," as if the substance had a power all its own to "hook" persons foolish enough to ingest it. Such theories emphasize the involuntary nature of drug use—use based on a *craving*—that has found some support in laboratory experiments with animals. Indeed, with the exception of marijuana and hallucinogens, animals will abuse the same chemicals that humans do (Friedman 1993). According to this approach, sometimes referred to as the **disease model,** the drug-dependent person is a victim of forces beyond his or her control. This theoretical approach has treatment implications. For example, it would support two very different approaches to substance abuse: the use of methadone detoxification and maintenance and the Alcoholics Anonymous (AA) chemical-free approach that emphasizes a need for total abstinence. (Methadone and AA will be discussed in Chapter 9.)

Scientists have discovered reward pathways located in the mesolimbic area of the brain that are activated by a variety of psychoactive substances. Drugs such as heroin, nicotine, cocaine, and amphetamines appear to affect these pathways through the release of the neurotransmitter dopamine (discussed later), a common element in continued use. "Dopamine effects in the reward pathway are enhanced not only by cocaine, amphetamines, and opiates, but also by nicotine and alcohol." The "stimulation of a dopaminergic reward pathway is what makes a drug addictive" (A. Goldstein 2001: 66).

Some psychoactive chemicals alter the central nervous system, creating what appears to be a compulsion to use the drug to restore a sense of well-being. Prolonged opiate use, for example, causes pervasive changes in brain function that persist long after the individual stops taking the drug. Heroin addicts themselves state they take the drug to "feel normal." Thus, to the heroin addict, notes John Irwin (1970: 19), "it is the fix that cures the sickness, and it is the fix that is central to the whole dope life." After a period of abstinence an addict returning to heroin use is likely to state: " 'It makes me feel normal again'—that is, it relieves the ex-addict's chronic triad of anxiety, depression, and craving" (Brecher 1972: 14). While drug use might begin through experimentation, dependence would be the inevitable result of these physiological changes.

Arousal Theory

Some neurological theories describe the drug abuser as a person whose body is malfunctioning with respect to the production of crucial neurotransmitters, making drug use **self-medicating.** According to this view, the user's choice of drug is the result of an interaction between its pharmacological properties and the primary feeling state experienced. Thus, according to *arousal theory,* those whose central nervous system quickly habituates to incoming stimuli due to a neurotransmitter malfunction are most apt to be reinforced for engaging in antisocial behavior and less likely to learn alternative behavior patterns. Subjectively, such persons regard many ordinary environments as boring and unpleasant and would thus be more motivated than most people to seek novel and/or intense sensory stimulation. The behavior of such persons would include impulsivity, risk taking, and an inclination to use psychoactive substances (Ellis 1990). While social factors may determine whether a person is exposed to drugs, genetics may help explain why only a segment of those exposed become drug dependent.

Genetic Predisposition

More than a century ago genetic explanations were proposed to explain addiction: The addict inherits a nervous system that has more energy or perhaps more actual nerve fiber; drugs provide such nervous systems with a substance necessary but deficient; when the user finds that a drug satisfies this deficiency, repeated drug use naturally follows. A complementary theory views drug users as having an inherited predisposition to "nervous weakness" for which the use of drugs compensates. Other observers conceived of a lack of hereditary endowments that leaves some persons ill-equipped to deal with the fast pace of societal change, with drug use providing chemical compensation.

In more contemporary times, the National Institute on Drug Abuse has been funding studies on this issue, and evidence uncovered reveals that an individual's genetic makeup is a major factor in vulnerability to drug abuse (NIDA 1998c). NIDA-funded researchers found that while family and social environmental factors determine whether an individual will begin using drugs, progression from use to dependence was largely due to genetic factors, particularly for males, and the genetic influence for heroin addiction surpassed that of any other drug (Zickler 1999). While drug abuse is the result of a complex interplay of environmental, social, psychological, and biochemical factors, genetic factors play an important role in the vulnerability to drug abuse—the more severe the abuse, the greater the role of genetic factors (Comings 1996).

Limitations in the Neurological Study of Drug Abuse

The Complexities of Drug Effects

"Drug effects are strongly influenced by the amount taken, how much has been taken before, what the user wants and expects to happen, the surroundings in which it is taken, and the reactions of other people. All of these influences are themselves tied up with social and cultural attitudes and beliefs about drugs as well as more general social conditions. Even the same person will react differently at different times" (Institute for the Study of Drug Dependence (1987: 1).

Our discussion of the neurology of psychoactive drugs will necessarily have limitations—there is a great deal that is not known about the details of how these drugs actually affect the nervous system. There is evidence, for example, that the same substance can have a different impact on different people. The social context (the setting in which the drug is ingested) and the user's expectations can influence a drug's effects (Becker 1967, 1977; Schnoll 1979). Whether a person will interpret the effect of a drug like marijuana, LSD, or an opiate, especially the first few times he or she takes it, as euphoria or pleasure depends very much on the setting and other complex psychological and social conditions (Grinspoon and Hedblom 1975). In other words, use of the substances discussed in this book is not *automatically* pleasurable. Many, if not most, people who have been exposed to morphine or heroin, for example, find the initial experience distinctly unpleasant: "not everyone responds to the analgesic experience the same way. Some people find a narcosis tremendously alluring, while others report that the sensations of helplessness are disturbing and distinctly unappealing" (Peele 1980: 143). Thus, "one person's dysphoria may be another person's euphoria" (Schnoll 1979: 256). Some people get "high" from dangerous pursuits, others from chemicals, and still others seek to avoid both.

Laboratory studies, which form the basis for much of our knowledge of psychoactive drugs, fail to reproduce social context, and their results are accordingly limited. The dependence potential of various drugs is typically based on laboratory studies with monkeys and rats, although research has discovered that there are interspecies differences in the effects of cocaine on the brains of rodents and primates. The discrepancy in findings between rodents and primate studies illustrates the limitations of animal models of drug abuse (Bolla, Cadet, and London 1998). Furthermore, in experimental environments these animals can also become addicted to stinging electric shocks delivered to the tail or the paws (W. Bennett 1988). Indeed, researchers have discovered that with animals "almost any environmental stimulus can serve as a reinforcer or punisher under the right environmental conditions" (Dworkin and Pitts 1994: 106).

Experimentation on human subjects is obviously limited by ethical considerations. Thus, with respect to a lawful drug, alcohol, "because of ethical considerations, prospective studies of ethanol reactivity in children and young adolescents (before they have initiated regular drinking) have not been conducted" (Sher 1991: 86). And laboratory studies also cannot actually replicate street use in which any of the substances under discussion may be abused with alcohol or in some other combination. This leads to our next topic.

Polydrug Use

Understanding the neurology of psychoactive drugs is also complicated by the phenomenon of **polydrug use**—abusers consuming more than one type of psychoactive chemical. Research shows overwhelmingly that compulsive users use more than one drug, so this is a major difficulty in studying drug abuse. Heroin addicts are very often polydrug users abusing alcohol and other drugs (McFarland 1989; Vaillant 1970; Johnson, Lipton, and Wish 1986). Bruce Johnson and his colleagues found that 90 percent of the heroin addicts they studied also abused alcohol and cocaine (Johnson, Lipton, and Wish 1986). Joan Epstein and Joseph Gfroerer (1997) report that a large proportion of heroin users also use heroin in combination with other drugs, especially cocaine and alcohol. In a study of heroin addicts in San Antonio, it was discovered that 100 percent used alcohol, almost half on a daily basis (Maddux and Desmond 1981). Almost 19 percent of the persons admitted for heroin abuse treatment in Colorado also reported the use of cocaine (Colorado Alcohol and Drug Abuse Division 1987). Mark Gold and his colleagues (1986: 55) found that "most cocaine abusers are concurrently abusing alcohol or other sedative-hypnotics to alleviate the unpleasant side effects of cocaine." Crack users frequently "administer heroin because it enhances the euphoric effect while ameliorating the intense stimulant effects of cocaine" (*Trends in Heroin* 1994: 1). In the District of Columbia, alcohol is frequently used to moderate the effects of cocaine. In Colorado more than 35 percent of cocaine users admitted for treatment report the use of alcohol (Mendelson and Harrison 1989).

The New York State Division of Substance Abuse Services (1986: 14–15) reported that the "use of more than one substance continues to be the predominant pattern of abuse. Both heroin and cocaine are commonly used with one drug ameliorating the undesired effects of the other; PCP is used by some heroin abusers to heighten the effect of heroin. Alcohol use is almost always involved." In San Antonio, approximately two-thirds of substance-related deaths have involved both cocaine and heroin (Spence 1989). In Minnesota, polydrug use, which includes alcohol, is widespread among that state's chemical-abusing population (Minnesota Department of Human Services 1987).

Ethnographers have reported that "criss-crossing" (lines of cocaine and heroin are alternately inhaled) is becoming more common and is gaining in popularity among drug enthusiasts in New York. They have also reported that some users are snorting heroin and smoking crack in combination. In this combination, it is believed that the primary drug is crack and heroin is used to ease agitation associated with crack. Finally, drug users unable to secure their preferred substance because of insufficient funds or connections when the supply is scarce often seek available substitutes.

According to Schnoll (1979), mixing drugs can have the following neurological effects:

1. *Additive.* Two drugs having similar actions are ingested, so the effect is cumulative. $(1 + 1 = 2)$
2. *Synergistic.* Two drugs having similar actions are ingested, but the effect of their joint action is more than cumulative. $(1 + 1 = 3)$
3. *Potentiating.* Two drugs have different actions, but when taken together, one enhances the effects of the other. $(1 + 1 = 4)$
4. *Antagonistic.* Two or more drugs are taken together, and one counteracts the effects of the other(s). $(1 + 1 = 0)$

Drugs prepared for street sale are typically impure or a mixture of psychoactive chemicals. "The users of illegally purchased drugs are often totally unaware of the actual chemical substance, the dose being purchased, and the contaminants that may be present in the sample." Many of these contaminants can produce toxic reactions in their own right (Schnoll 1979: 257).

Psychoactive Substances and the Central Nervous System

All of the substances we are interested in affect the central nervous system (CNS): depressants, stimulants, hallucinogens, and cannabis, which produces all three effects. The body consists of cells organized into tissues, and specialized cells along the surface of the body receive information about the environment that is translated into electrochemical signals we experience as sight, sound, smell, and touch. Information from the internal and external environment—stimuli—is received by the **central nervous system** (CNS), consisting of the brain and the spinal cord whose cells—neurons—send information to a specific processing center of the brain.

The Brain

The brain, a dense mass weighing about 3 pounds and consisting of 10–50 billion anatomically independent but functionally interrelated neurons, is connected to the spinal cord by fibers and cells (the **peripheral nervous system**) that carry sensory information and muscle commands to the rest of the body (Figure 3.1). "This single organ controls all body activities, ranging from heart rate and sexual function to emotion, learning and memory" (Society for Neuroscience 2002: 5). After receiving and processing information, the brain sends commands to muscles and glands through three processes:

1. *Behavior processes.* These include voluntary movements such as walking and talking, and the autonomic bodily functions (such as those of the heart, lungs, and digestive system). These involuntary functions are regulated by the **autonomic nervous system,** which in turn has two divisions having opposite effects:

   a. The **sympathetic nervous system** acts (actually reacts) to mobilize the organism for action—for example, for "fight" or "flight." The release of the neurotransmitter norepinephrine (NE) into the blood system or of drugs that mimic NE (stimulants such as cocaine) activates the sympathetic nervous system.

   b. The **parasympathetic nervous system** is concerned with the digestive system and acts to conserve bodily resources. The effects of various psychoactive drugs on the digestive system are related to this nervous system.

2. *Affective processes.* These govern mood, feelings, and emotions.

3. *Thought processes.* These involve the ability to reason, categorize, organize, abstract, and pay attention.

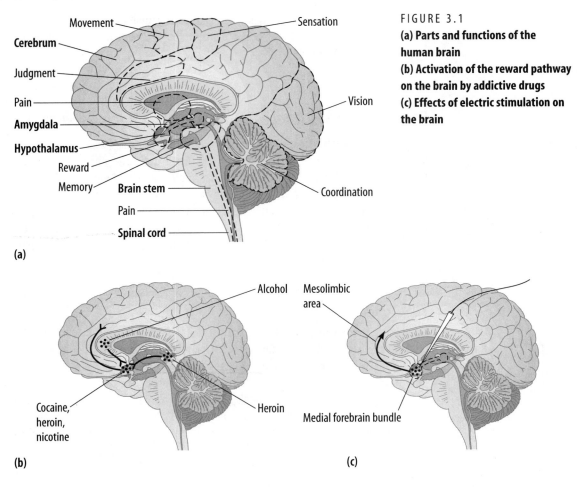

FIGURE 3.1
(a) Parts and functions of the human brain
(b) Activation of the reward pathway on the brain by addictive drugs
(c) Effects of electric stimulation on the brain

The brain contains areas that produce pleasurable sensations—*reward pathways.* The pharmacological activation of brain reward systems is largely responsible for producing a psychoactive chemical's potent addictive properties. Direct electrical stimulation of the **medial forebrain bundle** (MFB) produces intensely rewarding effects, while stimulants and depressants can activate this reward system by their pharmacological actions.

Neurons

A neuron is the basic working unit of the central nervous system, a specialized cell designed to transmit information from the brain to other nerve cells, muscle, or gland cells. **Neurons** come in many sizes and shapes and form chains of specialized and excitable cells. They differ from other body cells in that they can conduct information in the form

Drugs and the Brain's Reward System

"Almost all abused drugs produce pleasure by activating a specific network of neurons called the brain reward system. The circuit is normally involved in an important type of learning that helps us to stay alive. It is activated when we fulfill survival functions, such as eating when we are hungry or drinking when we are thirsty. In turn, our brain rewards us with pleasurable feelings that teach us to repeat the task. Because the drugs inappropriately turn on this reward circuit, people want to repeat drug use" (Society for Neuroscience 2002: 33).

of electrical impulses over long distances. There are over 100 billion neurons in the body and across them, from neuron to neuron, move signals or impulses—information in the form of electrical activity.

A neuron consists of a **cell body** (*soma*) containing the nucleus and an electricity-conducting fiber; the **axon,** which also gives rise to many smaller axon branches before ending at nerve terminals; **synapses,** contact points where one neuron communicates with another; and **dendrites,** which appear as branches of a tree and extend from the neuron cell body and receive messages from other neurons (Figure 3.2). "The dendrites and cell body are covered with synapses formed by the ends of axons of other neurons" (Society for Neuroscience 2002: 7). Each neuron has multiple dendrites that form structural networks for receiving information from another neuron or from the environment in the form of light, sound, smell, etc., and converting it (through transduction) into electrical activity that is transmitted to the axon.

Axons may be long or short. Neurons in the brain stem have axons that extend down into the spinal cord, where they divide into thousands of branches, making contact with different receiving neurons. The axon conducts ("fires") electrical impulses to terminals, which react by releasing neurotransmitters that are stored in synaptic buttons, or vesicles, at the end of the axon. These neurotransmitters move across the synaptic gap to receptor sites on the dendrites on the other side, triggering activity—the release of secondary messengers—in the next neuron. Through this mechanism, an impulse is directed to the spinal cord and into the proper circuit for transmission to the brain.

FIGURE 3.2
Neuron, showing synapse, neurotransmitters, and receptor sites

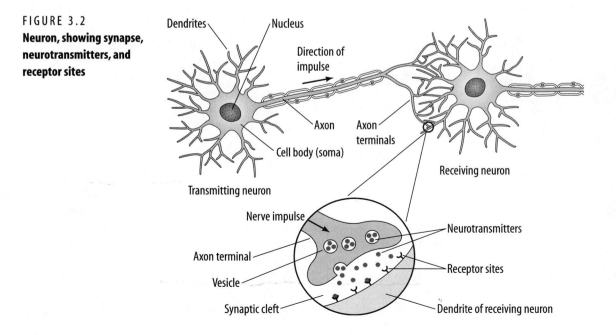

Nerve Cell Communication

"Nerve signals often travel over long distances in the body. For example, if you step barefooted on a sharp object, the sensory information is relayed from your foot all the way to the brain; from there, nerve signals travel back to the leg muscles and cause them to contract, drawing back the foot. Dozens of neurons can be involved in such a circuit, necessitating a sophisticated communication system to rapidly convey signals between cells. Also, because individual neurons can be up to three feet long, a rapid-relay mechanism within the neurons themselves is required to transmit each signal from the site where it is received to the site where it is passed on to a neighboring cell. Two mechanisms have evolved to transmit nerve signals. First, within cells, electrical signals are conveyed along the cell membrane. Second, for communication between cells, the electrical signals generally are converted into chemical signals conveyed by small messenger molecules called neurotransmitters" ("Principles of Nerve Cell Communication" 1997: 107).

Neurons do not interlock but instead are separated by synapses, which are fluid-filled microscopic gaps (.0002 mm) that provide a chemical bridge for signals in the form of charged particles or ions from one neuron to another. A neuron may have over 10,000 synapses. There are two functional types of synapses: (1) *excitatory* synapses, which enhance electrical impulses, and (2) *inhibitory* synapses, which retard electrical impulses. Depressants reduce synaptic transmission by inhibiting nerve impulse conduction at synapses; this causes a reduction in sensory pain signals received by the brain (Tortora 1983). Stimulants facilitate synaptic transmission. A large concentration of positively charged particles entering a receiving neuron tells it to pass on the message. On the other hand, a large concentration of negatively charged particles entering the neuron will inhibit it from passing on the message (Society for Neuroscience information).

Neurotransmitters

Central nervous system information is carried by **neurotransmitters,** chemicals (drugs) released from sacs (vesicles) clustered in the synaptic terminals at the end of axons of neurons. On reaching the ends of an axon, these voltage changes trigger the release of neurotransmitters (chemical messengers). Neurotransmitters are released at nerve ending terminals and bind to receptors on the surface of the target neuron (Society for Neuroscience 2002).

Neurotransmitters inhibit or enhance the release of ions—electrical charges similar to those of a battery—and communication occurs when a sufficient number of synapses are activated by these electrical impulses. About one hundred neurotransmitters are found in the central nervous system. Some (**catecholamines:** dopamine, **epinephrine, norepinephrine**) excite (speed "firing") and others (such as endorphins) inhibit (slow "firing"). The body uses these chemicals to trigger such effects as anger or to regulate the operation of different organs. Each neurotransmitter has a receptor site—proteins located on the surfaces of nerve cells, or neurons—designed to receive it, and the ensuing reaction may cause the stimulation or inhibition of a specific function. "Of greatest interest for addiction would be the presence of a neurotransmitter in the midbrain reward pathway, where dopamine neurons are thought to play a key role in mediating pleasurable (hedonic) effects" (A. Goldstein 2001: 33).

Dopamine (DA), one of a number of neurotransmitters found in the central nervous system, has received special attention from psychopharmacologists because of its apparent role in the regulation of mood and affect, and because of its role in motivation and reward processes. Studies have revealed that the reinforcing effects of psychoactive drugs in humans is associated with increases in brain dopamine (Volkow et al. 1999b). "Although drugs affect a variety of neurotransmitters, virtually all of them increase the levels of dopamine in the brain's mesolimbic region, which is involved in pleasure, reward and motivation" (Carroll 2000: D6). Although there are several dopamine systems in the brain, the mesolimbic dopamine system appears to be the most important for motivational processes. Some addictive drugs produce their potent effects on behavior by enhancing mesolimbic dopamine activity.

Dopamine is necessary to sustain life. A DA deficiency is believed to cause **Parkinson's disease;**[1] an excess is believed to cause Tourette syndrome.[2] The brains of schizophrenics are high in dopamine, and antischizophrenic (neuroleptic) drugs work because of their ability to block dopamine (Snyder 1986). Cocaine and the DA **agonist** (a drug having a similar effect) amphetamine can cause schizophrenic symptoms because these substances interfere with the **reuptake** of dopamine (Palfai and Jankiewicz 1991; Bloom 1993). The failure of the reuptake system (the process by which released neurotransmitters are absorbed for subsequent reuse) increases the concentration of dopamine in the brain, particularly within pleasure centers. *Ecopipam,* a potent **antagonist** of dopamine D_1 and D_5 receptors, is able to block stimulant and reinforcing properties of cocaine and may play a potential role in treatment of cocaine dependence (Romach et al. 1999).

Cells in the mesolimbic dopamine system are spontaneously active, releasing small amounts of dopamine into the synaptic cleft. The levels of dopamine produced when the cells are active at this low rate may be responsible for maintaining normal affective tone and mood. Neurotransmitter level is controlled by chemicals in the presynaptic terminal known as **monoamine oxidases** (MAO). Scientists speculate that some forms of clinical depression may result from unusually low dopamine levels. See Figure 3.3.

---

[1]Clinical studies of cocaine users in their 30s show an increase in symptoms of Parkinson's—tremors or stiffness—apparently the result of a decrease of dopamine receptors (Hartel 1993). Flupentixol, a drug that blocks dopamine, reduces the effects of cocaine, but cannot be used for drug treatment because it also produces symptoms of Parkinson's (Bloom 1993).

[2]Tourette syndrome is an incurable genetic affliction, the symptoms of which can range from mild tics to *coprolalia*—periodic outbursts of foul language (Brody 1995).

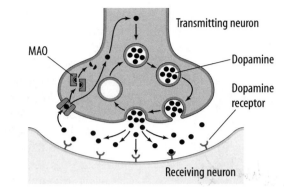

FIGURE 3.3
Dopamine's normal action. After being released into the synapse, dopamine attaches to receptor sites on the receiving neuron. Then the dopamine is either quickly recycled by a transporter or broken down by MAO.

It has also been revealed that pathological obesity and drug addiction often share a common element, a brain deficient in nerve cell (D_2) receptors, which dopamine activates to stimulate pleasurable feelings. This deficiency may contribute to overeating as compensation for reduced stimulation of brain reward circuits.

Repeated use of psychomotor stimulants like cocaine and depressants like heroin produces changes in the mesolimbic dopamine system. Specifically, repeated use of cocaine or heroin can deplete dopamine from this system. These dopamine depletions may cause normal rewards to lose their motivational significance. At the same time, the mesolimbic dopamine system becomes even more sensitive to pharmacological activation by psychoactive substances (Addiction Research Unit/SUNY at Buffalo 1998).

Abstinence from drugs such as cocaine or from morphine after repeated administration may decrease dopamine levels in this brain system, and this diminished dopamine function may be related to the intense craving associated with withdrawal in drug-dependent humans. The subjective experience of craving is related to relapse into drug-taking behavior following abstinence and therefore is an important factor in drug addiction.

Serotonin is found in many tissues, including the lining of the digestive tract and the brain. Serotonin is involved in sleep, mood, depression, and anxiety and serves to moderate primitive drives, aggression, sex, and eating, while improving the ability to interact socially. The medically prescribed antidepressant Prozac (fluoxetine) inhibits the reuptake of serotonin.

Norepinephrine governs arousal reactions and appears to play a role in elevating mood; NE agonists such as cocaine and amphetamine produce a "high."

Receptor Sites

Receptor sites consist of large molecules on the surface of cells where neurotransmitters attach, creating a lock-and-key effect and causing chemical substances to interact and produce pharmacological actions. Receptors are sensory specific and distinguish between substances. Upon receiving the correct substance (creating a chemical fit), they transmit signals that bring about pharmacological action in the target tissue. Many psychoactive drugs (agonists—substances that stimulate receptor sites) mimic the action of neurotransmitters and "fool" the receptor into accepting it. Competing drugs (antagonists—substances that inhibit the action of a receptor site) can counteract the effect of an agonist by their ability to occupy receptor sites without triggering activity, providing a basis for using chemicals to deal with drug abuse. Low levels of the dopamine D_2 receptors have been found to predispose[3] persons to enjoy the effects of stimulating drugs, which may compensate for this receptor deficiency by increasing the activation of reward circuits (Volkow et al. 1999a).

Drugs exert their principal effects upon individual cells in the brain where receptor sites controlling particular organs have an affinity for certain psychoactive substances. Opiates, for example, will lock into brain receptor sites controlling such autonomic functions as breathing and blood pressure.

Once they have performed their assigned task—conveying messages to nearby neurons—neurotransmitters are recycled by the sending neuron in the reuptake process. This process conserves the neurotransmitters by bringing them back into the presynaptic terminal for storage so they can be used again. Proteins called **transporters,** located on the surface of the sending neurons, latch onto the neurotransmitters and transport them back inside for use at a later time. Psychoactive substances not only cause the release of neurotransmitters, but they may inhibit the transporters from performing their reuptake task so that the neurotransmitters continue to stimulate the receiving neuron.

Terms Describing Drug Abuse

The entire volume of human blood—11.6 pints for an average-sized male; 9.5 for an average-sized female—makes a complete circulation about every 60 seconds. Psychoactive drugs are absorbed into the bloodstream and quickly carried to the central nervous system. Eventually they pass the **blood-brain barrier,** causing the release of neurotransmitters in the brain. The barrier acts as a gatekeeper, preventing certain substances from entering brain tissue, for example, penicillin (because it would cause convulsions) but readily admits psychoactive substances (and general anesthetics). Since the blood-brain barrier in infants has not matured, they are particularly vulnerable to the effects of psychoactive chemicals.[4]

---

[3]It should be noted that this predisposition alone is not sufficient to explain drug use: The experimental subjects who found stimulants rewarding were not drug users.

[4]A fetus is also vulnerable because the placental barrier is more permeable than the blood-brain barrier. Infants also lack a fully functioning liver and, therefore, cannot readily deactivate and eliminate psychoactive chemicals.

Drug Ingestion

Drugs enter the bloodstream in one of three ways, and the route of administration affects how fast the substance will enter the brain and thus assert a psychoactive response:

1. *Oral ingestion.* The substance is swallowed and enters the bloodstream through the gastrointestinal tract, the slowest route of administration.
2. *Inhalation.* The substance is sniffed and rapidly reaches the bloodstream through mucous membranes of the nose or sinus cavities, or it is smoked and quickly absorbed through the linings of the lungs, which are surrounded by capillaries.
3. *Injection.* The substance is injected into a vein (intravenous), and all of the drug enters the bloodstream. Some is carried directly to the brain, producing an effect within seconds. Injecting a drug under the skin (subcutaneous) increases the time required for the substance to enter the bloodstream and thus produces a delayed and reduced effect.

Some drugs can be ingested in a number of ways—different forms of heroin and cocaine can be sniffed, smoked, or injected—while other drugs can be taken in only one way—marijuana must be smoked.

A drug taken intravenously is carried to the right chamber of the heart, where it mixes with blood returning from the rest of the body and is then pumped through the lungs, returns to the heart, and is delivered to the brain. This takes about 16 seconds, and when the drug arrives at the brain it is greatly diluted. A substance that is smoked results in some passing directly into the bloodstream through membranes of the mouth. With deep inhalations, however, most of the drug will spread through the fine membranes of the lungs—all of the blood in the body moves through the lungs—and pass directly into the blood carrying drug molecules to the left side of the heart, where it is pumped directly to the brain without dilution. This takes about 3 seconds. And each breath produces an immediate drug spike in the brain, an immediate euphoric effect more powerful than the intravenous route. Inhalation also avoids the danger of overdose. Oral ingestion results in slow absorption from stomach and intestine and is the method least favored by drug users (A. Goldstein 2001).

Half-Life

The amount of time it takes for the substance to be eliminated from the body is measured in terms of **half-life,** the time it takes for one-half of the drug to be eliminated through the liver[5] and primarily into the kidneys for urination. The half-life of some drugs may be as short as a few minutes, while traces of other drugs may remain in the system for several weeks. Drugs that are lipid-soluble will be absorbed by body fat and subsequently released into the bloodstream in small doses over a relatively longer period of time—greater half-life. This explains why the percentage of body fat is a factor in the effect of

---

[5]Advanced alcoholism may impair the liver's ability to deactivate and eliminate alcohol.

drugs. The greater the half-life, the less severe are withdrawal symptoms after the use of the drug has been discontinued. The greater the time a drug remains in the bloodstream, the less likely tolerance will occur.

Tolerance

The continued use of certain drugs, particularly depressants, produces **tolerance,** "a progressive increase in the ability of the body to adapt to the effects of a drug that is used at regular and frequent intervals. It is manifested in two ways: (1) progressively larger doses must be administered to produce the same effects; and (2) eventually as much as ten or more times the original lethal dose can be safely taken" as the metabolism adapts to the substance (Ausubel 1978: 14).

> Tolerance develops as the body becomes progressively immune to the chemical effects of the drug at the cellular level. Should usage continue, a physiological dependence on the narcotic will occur as the affected tissues and cells accommodate the chemically induced processes that result from the introduction of the drug. The *homeostatic* processes of the body adjust to the narcotic and bring about a new physiological equilibrium. If the equilibrium and normal functioning are to be maintained at the physiological level, regular and stable amounts of the drug [or a similar drug— **cross-tolerance**[6]] must be taken. (Biernacki 1986: 9; italics added)

Homeostasis refers to a state of equilibrium achieved through the self-adjusting characteristics of the body. Through homeostasis, complex organisms adapt themselves to changes in the environment by means of, for example, changes in body temperature, blood sugar level, and heart rate. The physiology and biochemistry of the body change according to information received and processed by the nervous system, particularly the central nervous system, and the endocrine system (glands such as the thyroid and adrenal). With respect to both neurotransmitters and receptors, the brain behaves as if trying to maintain all its operating systems on an even keel. Psychoactive substances upset this normal balance (A. Goldstein 2001).

The toxicity of a drug is affected by tolerance. Thus, an alcoholic—someone addicted to alcohol—can ingest quantities of alcohol that would be potentially fatal for an occasional user. Some psychoactive drugs do not produce tolerance (marijuana), while others may produce various degrees of tolerance, from hardly perceptible to severe. There is also **selective tolerance:** For example, tolerance to the "nod" experienced by heroin users develops rapidly, while the "rush" will always be experienced by heroin users no matter how high their level of tolerance. There is also some evidence of **reverse tolerance,** referred to as *kindling,* to certain drugs: becoming *more* sensitive to the same or lesser dosage over time. When tolerance develops, the failure to ingest enough of a drug on a timely basis will disrupt homeostasis and cause the onset of **withdrawal** symptoms.

---

[6]Cross-tolerance refers to the ability of one drug (an agonist) to substitute for another.

These symptoms can manifest themselves in a number of ways, all of them unpleasant to the person being subjected to them, usually taking the form of being directly opposite of the effects produced by the drug. While in withdrawal, the addict may experience extreme anxiety, hyperactivity, shaking, cold sweat, and severe depression.

Drug Cues and Sexual Dysfunction

Brain imaging and other modern technologies show that the addicted brain is distinctly different from the nonaddictive brain, manifested by changes in brain metabolic activity, receptor availability, gene expression, and responsiveness to environmental cues. It appears that the intensity of the drug euphoria burns emotional memories into brain circuits, making that person vulnerable to the appearance of drug *cues.* These memories are encoded into a part of the brain—**amygdala**—that operates outside of conscious control to cause intense cravings for re-creating the euphoric experience. Research has discovered a connection between cues and reversion to drug use (Childress et al. 1999). Even tolerance and withdrawal symptoms in laboratory animals are affected by environmental cues (Hinson 1985; Bloom 1993). Indeed, a person who has been removed from his or her drug-seeking environment in order to treat addiction but then is returned to the former environment gets secondary associations that may in fact induce the person to go back to using drugs (Bloom 1993).

In approximately two-thirds of cocaine-dependent subjects in a lab setting, drug cues increased craving for cocaine (Avants et al. 1995). In another research effort, cocaine users who viewed items related to their drug use, such as glass crack pipe, mirror, razor blade, straw, rolled $20 bill, lactose powder, and simulated crack rocks, elicited a higher degree of craving, as measured by brain scans, than had been previously reported, and while it involved the amygdala, extended to other parts of the brain (Bonson et al. 2002).

Drug abuse is characterized by a pattern of sexual dysfunction. Drugs can substitute for sexual activity through corresponding stimulation of pleasure regions of the brain. "Cocaine abusers may experience a powerful urge to take the drug when they encounter environmental cues such as people, places, or paraphernalia that they associate with drug use. This cue-induced behavior may be accompanied by physical sensations—light-headedness, increased heart rate, or mild druglike 'high'—like those produced by cocaine" (Zickler 2001b: 1). These same brain regions that are activated by the cocaine cues are also activated by sexual stimuli and sexual activity through corresponding stimulation of pleasure regions of the brain. There is also a disruption of hormonal balance in the hypothalamus and pituitary glands.

The **hypothalamus,** a small gland located near the base of the brain, integrates information from many sources and is the control center for the autonomic nervous system. It is also the primary point of contact between the nervous system and the endocrine system, sending messages in the form of impulses to appropriate control centers to restore normal levels of blood chemicals in line with the *homeostatic* needs of the body.

Many drugs enter the brain in high concentrations at the blood-rich hypothalamus, creating initial autonomic effects on consciousness and mood. The hypothalamus controls

such basic drives as sexual activity. It regulates the release of hormones from the pituitary gland located directly below. These hormones act directly on adrenal, glands, testes, and ovaries. Disruptions in the normal flow of hormones from the pituitary can adversely affect sexual function, and chronic drug use upsets hormonal balance by decreasing dopamine secretion from the hypothalamus ("Sexual Dysfunction and Addiction Treatment" 2000).

If addiction is, at its core, a consequence of fundamental changes in brain function, a goal of treatment must be either to reverse or compensate for those brain changes (J. Cooper 1998). While drug addicts may not be able to control their cravings, through behavior therapy (discussed in chapter 9), they may be able to control the way they respond to them (Grady 1998).

Now that we have examined the neurology of drug abuse, in the next chapter we will apply this dimension to depressants.

SUMMARY

Neurological theories that attempt to explain drug abuse include the disease model, arousal theory, and genetic predisposition. The study of the impact of drug abuse on the central nervous system is limited by the differential reactions of people to the same drug, the inability of scientists to replicate street use, ethical considerations, and polydrug use. Nevertheless, the addicted brain is distinctly different from the nonaddictive brain. Drugs have their main effects within the neurons of the central nervous system by stimulating or inhibiting release of neurotransmitters, such as dopamine, serotonin, and norepinephrine, or by blocking the receptor sites for those neurotransmitters. Deficiencies in neurotransmission systems help to explain why some people use drugs. How drugs enter the bloodstream—oral ingestion, inhalation, or injection—is a significant factor in their effects. The body has its own ways of adjusting to the ingestion of drugs, and different people have different levels of tolerance.

INTERNET CONNECTIONS

About Alcoholism: www.alcoholism.about.com
Addiction Research Unit (university research group): www.wings.buffalo.edu/aru/arulinks.htm
Addiction Technology Transfer Center — Virginia: www.views.vcu.edu/vattc
Brown Center for Alcohol and Addiction Studies: www.caas.brown.edu
Lycaeum: www.leda.lycaeum.org/Contacts
MedLinePlus (drug abuse topics): www.nlm.nih.gov/medlineplus/substanceabuse.html
Society for Neuroscience: www.web.snf.org
Whole Brain Atlas: www.med.Harvard.edu/AANLIB/home.html

REVIEW QUESTIONS

1. Besides dosage, what variables determine a drug's impact on an individual?
2. Why is laboratory testing of drugs on humans of limited value in determining the impact of these substances on actual substance abusers?

3. Why can't the findings of laboratory studies on animals be generalized to humans?
4. What are neurotransmitters?
5. What are receptor sites in the brain?
6. What is the relationship between drug abuse and pleasure centers of the brain?
7. What are transporters?
8. What is the blood-brain barrier?
9. What is the relationship between homeostasis and tolerance?
10. What is reverse tolerance?
11. How does body fat affect half-life?

CHAPTER 4

Depressants

> In determination of a drug's status, more than abuse potential should be considered. What are the toxicities of the drug? What are the chances of becoming dependent on the drug? Is dependency on a drug necessarily bad? Sometimes these questions are difficult to answer. Certainly, two of the most toxic drugs we know are alcohol and tobacco (nicotine). These drugs are sold legally.... Dependency to both of these drugs develops, as it does to caffeine.... Why are we so concerned about dependency on opiates and not caffeine? Heroin, if given in pure form for long periods of time, has few toxic effects.
>
> —*Sidney H. Schnoll (1979: 255)*

This category of drugs—the depressants—includes alcohol, barbiturates, sedatives/tranquilizers, and the narcotics. The latter may be natural (opium derivatives such as morphine and codeine), semisynthetic (such as heroin), or synthetic (such as methadone and Demoral).[1] Depressants are typically addicting, and studies have indicated the possibility of a relationship between certain chemical deficiencies and the propensity for addiction to depressants.

Endorphins

During the 1970s a number of scientists, working independently, discovered material and analgesics in brain and body tissues generally referred to as **endorphins,** a contraction of "endogenous morphine." Three families of endorphins (enkephalins, dynorphins, beta-endorphins) have many of the characteristics of morphine, and the body contains receptor sites programmed to receive these neurotransmitters. When they reach the receptor sites in the central nervous system (CNS), endorphins relieve pain. Pain is the result of a trauma experienced by the body, information about which is detected by sensors that send impulses along the nervous system, through neurons and across synapses as they move toward the brain. The subsequent release of endorphins in the brain inhibits pain impulses. Eventually, endorphins are destroyed by enzymes.

---

[1]As opposed to depressants, which act centrally on the brain, analgesics such as acetaminophen (for example, Tylenol, Panadol, and Anacin-3), ibuprofen (for example, Nuprin, Mediprin, and Advil), and aspirin relieve pain via localized action. They are not addictive (Brody 1988).

When people stub a toe or injure a finger, they usually grit their teeth and clench their fists, activities that apparently cause the release of these naturally occurring opiates that reduce sensations of pain. The athlete's ability to overcome pain during competition and the soldier's ability to perform heroic feats while severely wounded can be explained by the endorphin-receptor phenomenon, as can success in treating pain with acupuncture (Snyder 1977; 1989; Davis 1984; J. Goldberg 1988).[2] While these receptor sites are programmed to receive endorphins, they are also receptive to external chemicals such as opiates.

These opioid receptors are found in the brain's reward pathways and distributed widely throughout the nervous system and in the nerves that supply the extremities, the skin, the blood vessels, and most internal organs. These receptors are found along pain pathways and when activated interrupt the pain pathway to the brain, diminishing the perception of pain (A. Goldstein 2001).

Endorphins also enable the organism (including many animals) to deal with psychological stress by curbing an autonomic overreaction and producing calm: They slow breathing, reduce blood pressure, and lower the level of motor activity (Davis 1984). A "deficiency in an endorphin system that ordinarily would support feelings of pleasure and reinforcement might lead to feelings of inadequacy and sadness" (Levinthal 1988: 149), a phenomenon that would render the use of depressants essentially a form of self-medication.[3] As noted in Chapter 3, the use of psychoactive substances does not automatically produce a pleasurable response. However, persons at risk for addiction may suffer from an endorphin deficiency. For such persons, addiction would be the result of a genetically acquired deficiency or of a temporary or permanent impairment of the body's ability to produce endorphins. "This point of view would help account for the puzzling variability from individual to individual in the addictive power of opiate drugs. If an endorphin deficiency exists, however, the question would still remain as to what precipitating circumstances would lead to such a deficiency and whether these circumstances were environmental, inherited genetically, or a product of both" (Levinthal 1988: 154).

The ingestion of large amounts of heroin or some other opiate may also cause this deficiency (Snyder 1977). Thus, an abstaining addict would be unusually sensitive to feelings of pain or stress and would be inclined to use narcotic drugs again. In other words, receptors become increasingly dependent on external depressants, which in turn further reduce the production of endorphins, leaving the receptors increasingly dependent on substances from the outside. "If the opiate drug is later withdrawn, the receptors are now left without a supply from any source at all, and the symptoms of withdrawal are a consequence of this physiological dilemma" (Levinthal 1988: 156).

---

[2]In one study, treating drug abusers with acupuncture was not found to be beneficial (Latessa and Moon 1992). Another study found it effective in detoxification treatment (Brewington, Smith, and Lipton 1994).

[3]Mark Gold (1994) disputes the self-medication thesis.

Stress and Addiction

Depressants such as heroin inhibit stress hormones (such as cortisol and adrenalin) and stress-related neurotransmitters. A person having difficulties dealing with stress who is exposed to opiates is likely to find them rewarding and, thus, become addicted. In the absence of stress, many persons taking heroin over long periods of time do so without becoming addicted, and hospital patients self-administering morphine for pain do not increase their intake over time, nor do they suffer from a morphine craving when the pain subsides and they no longer have access to the drug (Peele 1985; E. Rosenthal 1993). One study found that only 4 out of more than 12,000 patients who were given opioids for acute pain actually became addicted to the drugs. Even long-term morphine use has limited potential for addiction. In a study of thirty-eight chronic pain patients, most of whom received opioids for 4 to 7 years, only two patients actually became addicted, and both had a prior history of drug abuse (NIDA data).

Drug addicts trying to remain off drugs can often resist the cravings brought on by seeing reminders (cues) of their former drug life. For months they can walk past the street corner where they used to buy drugs and not succumb. But then there is a sudden relapse, which addicts explain by stating: "Well, things weren't going well at my job," or "I broke up with my girlfriend." Sometimes the problem is as simple as a delayed welfare check. That they often relapse, apparently in response to what most people would consider mild stressors, suggests that addicts may be more sensitive than nonaddicts to stress. This hypersensitivity "may exist before drug abusers start taking drugs and may contribute to their initial drug use, or it could result from the effects of chronic drug use on the brain, or its existence could be due to a combination of both" (Jeanne Kreek quoted in Stocker 1999: 12). Chronic use of heroin, however, may increase hypersensitivity to stress and trigger a cycle of continued drug use when the effects of heroin wear off.

Research has shown that during withdrawal, the level of stress hormones rises in the blood and stress-related neurotransmitters are released in the brain. These chemicals trigger emotions perceived as highly unpleasant, driving the addict to take more drugs. Because the effects of heroin last only 4 to 6 hours, addicts often experience withdrawal three or four times a day. This constant switching on and off of the stress systems of the body heightens whatever hypersensitivity these systems may have had before the person started taking drugs. The result is that these stress chemicals are on a sort of hair-trigger release, surging at the slightest provocation (Kreek in Stocker 1999).

The body reacts to stress by secreting two types of chemical messengers: hormones in the blood and neurotransmitters in the brain. Some of the hormones travel throughout the body, altering the metabolism of food so that the brain and muscles have sufficient stores of metabolic fuel for activities, such as fighting or fleeing, that help the person cope with the source of the stress. In the brain, the neurotransmitters trigger emotions, such as aggression or anxiety, that prompt the person to take action.

Normally, stress hormones are released in small amounts throughout the day, but when the body is under stress the level of these hormones increases dramatically. Endorphins inhibit these stress hormones, thereby inhibiting stressful emotions. Heroin and

Morphine
Uses and Effects

Classification:	Narcotic
CSA Schedule*:	Schedule II
Trade or Other Names:	Duramorph, MS-Contin, Roxanol, Oramorph SR
Medical Uses:	Analgesic
Physical Dependence:	High for nonmedical use, low for medical patients in pain
Psychological Dependence:	High
Tolerance:	Yes
Duration (hours):	3–6
Usual Method:	Oral; smoked; injected
Possible Effects:	Euphoria, drowsiness, respiratory depression, constricted pupils, nausea
Effects of Overdose:	Slow and shallow breathing, clammy skin, convulsions, coma, possible death
Withdrawal Syndrome:	Watery eyes, runny nose, yawning, loss of appetite, irritability, tremors, panic, cramps, nausea, chills, and sweating

Source: U.S. Drug Enforcement Administration

*Controlled Substances Act, the common name for the Comprehensive Drug Abuse Prevention and Control Act of 1970 (see Chapter 12).

morphine inhibit the stress hormone cycle and presumably the release of stress-related neurotransmitters just as endorphins do. Thus, when people take heroin or morphine, the drugs add to the inhibition already being provided by the endorphins.

Heroin

The opium poppy,[4] *papaver somniferum,* requires a hot, dry climate and very careful cultivation (Wishart 1974). Poppy seeds are scattered across the surface of freshly culti-

---

[4]Sales of poppy seeds for cultivation, not culinary use—they often appear on bagels—has been illegal in the United States since 1970. The Drug Enforcement Administration has been conducting an ineffectual campaign against the cultivation of the pretty red flower, which looks elegant when dried (Vest 1997).

Poppy seeds mature in three months, producing brightly colored flowers. When the flower petals fall off, field workers cut a slit in each seedpod so that raw opium can ooze, harden, and be scraped off.

© Ric Ergenbright/CORBIS

vated fields. Three months later when the poppy is mature, the green stem is topped by a brightly colored flower. Gradually the flower petals fall off leaving a seedpod about the size of a small egg. Incisions are made in the seedpod just after the petals have fallen but before it is fully ripe. A milky-white fluid oozes out and hardens on the surface into a dark brown gum—raw opium. The raw opium is collected by scraping the pod with a flat, dull knife—a labor-intensive process. "Because the yield per acre is small and because laborious care is required in collecting the juice, it can only be grown profitably where both land and labor are cheap" (Ausubel 1978: 9).

Raw or cooked opium contains more than thirty-five different alkaloids, including morphine and codeine. In mainland Southeast Asia, the morphine alkaloid alone accounts for approximately 10 percent of the total weight of opium. Heroin manufacturers must first extract the morphine from the opium, before converting the morphine to heroin. The extraction is a simple process, requiring only a few chemicals and a supply of water. Morphine sometimes is extracted from opium in small clandestine laboratories, which are typically set up near the opium poppy fields. Since the morphine base is about one-tenth the weight and volume of raw opium, it is desirable to reduce the opium to morphine before transporting the product from the field to a heroin laboratory.

The process of extracting morphine from opium involves dissolving opium in boiling water, adding lime (calcium oxide), or slaked lime (calcium hydroxide), or limestone (calcium carbonate) to precipitate nonmorphine alkaloids, and then pouring off the morphine in solution. Ammonium chloride is then added to the solution to precipitate morphine from the solution. The chemicals used to process opium to morphine have a number of legitimate purposes and are widely available on the open market. An empty oil drum, some cooking pots, and filter cloths or filter paper are needed.

The conversion of morphine to heroin base is a relatively simple and inexpensive procedure. The necessary chemicals for conversion to heroin are commonly available as industrial chemicals. The equipment is very basic and quite portable. Heroin conversion laboratories are generally located in isolated, rural areas due to the telltale odors of the laboratory's chemicals. Acetic anhydride, in particular, is a key chemical with a very pungent odor resembling vinegar. Thai-speakers in the Golden Triangle area commonly refer to acetic anhydride as *nam-som* (vinegar).

Heroin synthesis from morphine (either morphine base or morphine hydrochloride) is a two-step process that requires between 4 and 6 hours to complete. Heroin base is the intermediate product. Typically, morphine hydrochloride bricks are pulverized, and the dried powder is then placed in an enamel pot. Acetic anhydride is added, which then reacts with the morphine to form heroin acetate. (This acetylation process will work either with morphine hydrochloride or morphine base.) The pot lid is tied or clamped on, using a damp towel for a gasket. The pot is carefully heated for about 2 hours, below boiling, at a constant temperature of 185° Fahrenheit. It is never allowed to boil or to become so hot as to vent fumes into the room. The mixture is agitated by tilting and rotation until all of the morphine has dissolved. When cooking is completed, the pot is cooled and opened. During this step, morphine and the anhydride become chemically bonded, creating an impure form of diacetylmorphine (heroin).

Water is added to the thick, soupy mixture, and the mixture is stirred as the heroin dissolves in the solution. Sodium carbonate (a crystalline powder) is dissolved in hot water and then added slowly to the heroin solution until effervescence stops. This precipitates heroin base, which is then filtered and dried by heating in a steam bath. For each kilogram of morphine, 685 grams to 937 grams of crude heroin base is formed, depending on the quantity of morphine.

The tan-colored heroin base (about 70 percent pure heroin) may be dried, packed, and transported to a heroin-refining laboratory, or it may be purified further before conversion to heroin hydrochloride (a water-soluble salt form of heroin) at the same site.

Mainland Southeast Asian heroin base is an intermediate product that can be further converted to either "smoking heroin" (heroin no. 3) or "injectable heroin" (heroin no. 4) (Drug Enforcement Administration information), a powder between 80 and 99 percent pure.

Lawfully produced morphine is usually harvested by the more modern industrial poppy straw process of extracting alkaloid from the mature dried plant. The extract may be either liquid, solid, or powder (*Drugs of Abuse* 1989). In equivalent doses, heroin is about two-and-a-half times as potent as morphine because it more easily penetrates the blood-brain barrier. Once heroin reaches the brain, however, it is converted back into morphine (Royal College of Psychiatrists 1987). The Drug Enforcement Administration (DEA) reports that more than 400 tons of opium or its equivalent in poppy straw concentrate are legally imported each year into the United States. Part of this quantity is used to extract codeine (an opiate alkaloid about 20 percent as potent as morphine), an ingredient used in many cough medicines.

1919 ✳
harrison act.

chippers - get high
occ.

intensity
potency
effectiveness

Codeine
Uses and Effects

Classification:	Narcotic
CSA Schedule:	Schedule II, III, V
Trade or Other Names:	Tylenol w/Codeine, Empirin w/Codeine, Robitussin A-C, Fiorinal w/Codeine, APAP w/Codeine
Medical Uses:	Analgesic, antitussive (cough suppressant)
Physical Dependence:	Moderate
Psychological Dependence:	Moderate
Tolerance:	Yes
Duration (hours):	3–6
Usual Method:	Oral, injected
Possible Effects:	Euphoria, drowsiness, respiratory depression, constricted pupils, nausea
Effects of Overdose:	Slow and shallow breathing, clammy skin, convulsions, coma, possible death
Withdrawal Syndrome:	Watery eyes, runny nose, yawning, loss of appetite, irritability, tremors, panic, cramps, nausea, chills, and sweating

Source: U.S. Drug Enforcement Administration

Pure heroin is a white powder with a bitter taste and little odor, but street heroin comes in many different forms, depending on how it was made and what has been added to it. Street heroin can be white, tan, brown, gray, or black. It can be a fine, fluffy powder, course like sand, chunky, or a solid mass that is either gummy or rock hard (black tar heroin). It can smell like vinegar, vitamins, or medicine—or have no smell. No matter what color or form, all heroin is either heroin salt or heroin base. Heroin salt dissolves easily in water, so it is easy to inject or sniff. Heroin base (like cocaine base) is easy to smoke but needs to be mixed with an acid like vitamin C in order to dissolve. White powder and black tar heroin are usually heroin salt, and brown heroin is usually heroin base. "White powder" refers to heroin "salt," mostly snorted or injected (China white, number 4). "Brown base" refers to heroin "base" (Persian, brown sugar, Pakistani) that can be smoked but needs to be heated in a solution of water and mild acid to inject, and "tar" is the black, sticky, gumlike substance (chiva, Mexican tar, or black tar heroin), mostly smoked or injected (Harm Reduction Coalition information). For street sale heroin is typically diluted ("stepped on" or "cut") with any powdery substance that dissolves when heated, such as lactose, quinine, flour, or cornstarch. Until the 1990s, consumer-available heroin prepared for intravenous use usually had a purity of less than 5 percent.[5] In recent years, purity levels of retail heroin sold in New York City has averaged above 60 percent, revealing that heroin is being subjected to little cutting before it reaches the consumer level. Increased purity makes smoking and sniffing feasible; the substance prepared for sniffing or smoking is generally 40 percent heroin. The increased purity and the concern about AIDS may be causing the shift from injecting to smoking and sniffing among heroin users (Epstein and Gfroerer 1997; Adrade, Sifaneck, and Neaigus 1999). Numerous reports have suggested a rise in heroin use in recent years, attributed to young people who are smoking or sniffing rather than injecting.

Effects of Heroin

Heroin has analgesic and euphoric properties. While brief, sharp, localized (phasic) pain is poorly relieved by opiates, duller, more chronic and less localized (tonic) pain is effectively relieved (Snyder 1977; Melzack 1990). As with all opiates, heroin "acts chiefly on the central and autonomic nervous systems and, to some extent, directly on smooth muscles. Effects on the central nervous system are primarily depressant, although larger doses may bring out stimulant properties, especially at the spinal level of reaction. . . . The depressant actions include analgesia (relief of pain, sedation, freedom from anxiety, muscular relaxation, decreased motor activity), hypnosis (drowsiness and lethargy), and euphoria (a sense of well-being and contentment). Unlike anesthetics, opiates are able to produce marked analgesia without excessive drowsiness, muscular weakness, confusion, or loss of consciousness" (Ausubel 1978: 11).[6]

Heroin is typically ingested intravenously, although some users inject it just under the skin—"skinpopping." Powdered heroin is placed in a "cooker"—a spoon or bottle cap. A small amount of water is added, and the mixture is heated with a match or lighter until the heroin is dissolved. The mixture is drawn up into a hypodermic needle and inserted into a vein that has been distended by being tied with a tourniquet. The user may bring blood back into the hypodermic, where it can mix with the heroin, a process known as "booting." Heroin can also be sniffed like cocaine and even smoked. When

---

[5]A low purity level does not necessarily indicate diluting/cutting, but may simply be the result of processing. Thus, a sample with a purity level of 50 percent heroin may be devoid of any adulterants but contain many by-products of heroin manufacture (Coomber 1999).

[6]The effects of opiates vary with species; for instance, in cats and horses morphine produces intense stimulation and is sometimes used (illegally) to "dope" race horses for a better performance (Harris 1993).

Heroin users pour the powdered drug onto a spoon, add a small amount of water, then heat the concoction with a match or lighter. The liquid heroin is then drawn into a syringe and injected into an available vein.

© Grant LeDuc/Stock, Boston

smoked—"chasing the dragon"—heroin is heated and the fumes inhaled, usually through a small tube.

Michael Agar (1973) points out that the "junkie" can experience four different effects from ingesting heroin:

1. *The Rush.* Heroin produces euphoria, referred to as the "rush": "About 10 seconds after the beginning of an injection of heroin the subjects had a typical narcotic 'rush,' including a wave of euphoric feelings, visceral sensations, a facial flush and a deepening of the voice" (Dole 1980: 146). Heroin (and cocaine) activate brain systems responsible for the reinforcing properties of such natural rewards as food and sex—male and female users describe the euphoric rush produced by heroin and cocaine as similar to, but several times stronger than, sexual orgasm (*Problems of Drug Dependence 1997*). Agar (1973) notes that while heroin is believed to have no effect on an addict after his or her tolerance builds up, the heroin user actually experiences the rush no matter how addicted he or she is. Addicts frequently describe the rush in sexual terms: "I felt like I died and went to heaven. My whole body was like one giant fucking incredible orgasm" (Inciardi 1986: 61). Indeed, heroin use substitutes for sex, in which the addict usually has little or no interest. Typically, the onset of heroin-using behavior coincides with adolescence, and remission usually occurs, with or without treatment, as the sex drive is reduced—there are few heroin addicts in the 40-years-to-senior-citizen population.

**The Adolescent Brain
and Drugs**
Different regions of the brain develop on different timetables. One
of the last parts to mature deals
with the ability to make sound
judgments and calm unruly emotions. Along with surges in testos-
terone at puberty, this may
account for the rise in aggressiveness and irritability seen in adolescents. On the other hand, the
developing adolescent brain
drives an interest in novelty that
vastly exceeds that of children or
adults. The choice of "novelty"
often depends on the youngster's
environment: Middle-class youth
are more likely to have access to
activities such as skiing and scuba
diving, while for many others,
crime, sex, and drugs are the most
viable outlets (Brownlee 1999).

2. *The High.* Described by addicts as a feeling of general well-being, the **high** decreases with increased tolerance; thus, increasing dosages are required to achieve the high. While the rush is experienced over a period of seconds, the high can last for several hours.

3. *The Nod.* This is described by addicts as being "out of it," in a state of unawareness, oblivious to one's surroundings—an escape from reality. The nod ranges from a slight dropping of the eyelids and jaw to complete unconsciousness: "they become calm, contented, and detached. They appeared to be quite uninterested in external events" (Dole 1980: 146). One addict provides this description: "It just knocks you completely into another dimension. The nod is like—you know, it's not describable. There's not words to express the feeling. The feeling is *that* good. So good that once hooked you never really live the feeling down" (Rettig, Torres, and Garrett 1977: 35). Tolerance affects the nod dramatically, and doses greater than that required for the high are needed to sustain the nod.

4. *Being Straight.* This is how addicts describe their condition when they are not sick; that is, not suffering the onset of withdrawal symptoms—homeostatic. Unless an addict has been tricked into buying a "blank," he or she will get a rush and get straight, although not necessarily experience a high or the nod (Agar 1973).

Heroin impairs homeostatic functions. There is a slight decrease in body temperature, although a dilation of blood vessels gives the user a feeling of warmth. The body retains fluids; there is also a decrease in the secretion of digestive fluids, and a depression of bowel activity, and the user suffers from constipation. Heroin also causes a dilation of the pupils, which explains why addicts frequently wear sunglasses. At relatively high doses the sedating effects cause a semistuporous, lethargic, and dreamy state—"nodding"—in which there is a feeling of extreme contentment. Unlike alcohol, heroin depresses aggression and also stimulates the brain area controlling nausea and vomiting. Instead of euphoria, some initial users experience nausea and vomiting: "I got such a bad pain in my head that I thought I was fucking brain damaged. I puked my guts out" (Inciardi 1986: 61). However, the vomiting caused by opiates "is not accompanied by the usual adverse feelings that nausea and vomiting produce in most people" (Harris 1993: 87).

A very dangerous side effect of heroin is that it depresses the respiratory centers in the brain. Thus an overdose can result in respiratory arrest and death from lack of oxygen to the brain. (Physicians use the antagonist Naloxone to undo the heroin-induced depressed respiration rate.) It is believed that there are millions of occasional users of heroin—**chippers** or *weekenders,* whose use parallels that of persons who drink heavily only on weekends or at parties; they appear to avoid addiction.

Tolerance for Heroin

Tolerance to some aspects of heroin use, in particular the "high," requires an increase in the dosage in order to gain the same level of response. In other words, a maintenance dose of morphine or some other narcotic will prevent physical withdrawal symptoms.

Those seeking the "high," however, must keep increasing the dosage until it is no longer feasible (that is, economically possible) to do so. They may then seek some way to reduce the level of tolerance, possibly by entering a drug rehabilitation program. With a lowered level of tolerance, the addict can resume low-dose usage and gain the sought-after response. There is also cross-tolerance; that is, tolerance to heroin carries over to other narcotic drugs, such as morphine and methadone (which will be discussed in Chapter 9), but not to other depressants such as alcohol or barbiturates. (Alcohol withdrawal symptoms—the delirium tremens, or DTs, convulsions, and hallucinations—can be relieved, however, by barbiturates or sedatives because of cross-tolerance.) However, as mentioned earlier, rapid physical tolerance does not develop in medical patients who take morphine for physical pain (Melzack 1990).

Heroin Withdrawal

The neuro-adaptation we refer to as tolerance often results in *rebounding* when the substance is withdrawn. The withdrawal symptoms tend to be the opposite of effects produced by the drug. "Thus, withdrawal from a depressant drug will give rise to brain excitation as adrenergic neurons that have been unnaturally inhibited by a drug such as heroin in its absence become hyperactive and cause anxiety, shaking, and cold sweat" (Royal College of Psychiatrists 1987: 34) and sometimes spontaneous orgasm. Heroin depletes the neurotransmitter dopamine, and in withdrawal the dramatic increase in dopamine activity intensifies other unpleasant symptoms (Fishbein and Pease 1990). Clonidine, a nonaddicting drug (discussed in Chapter 9), is often used by physicians to slow down these neurons and thereby relieve withdrawal symptoms (Davis 1984). Withdrawal symptoms, David Ausubel notes, while undoubtedly uncomfortable, "are seldom more severe than a bad case of gastrointestinal influenza" (1978: 16). Symptoms subside in about a week, although the psychological symptoms may persist indefinitely.

Children born to addicted mothers, in addition to having a host of other physical problems—small size, anemia, heart disease, hepatitis, pneumonia—also suffer from withdrawal symptoms (O'Brien and Cohen 1984), although this view is challenged by Stanton Peele (1985). Peele argues that the symptoms exhibited by the newborn of heroin addicts—undue crying and ineffective feeding, followed cyclically by restless periods of sleep—are not the result of heroin withdrawal but manifest themselves from the cumulative effects of the mother's unhealthy lifestyle. The National Institute on Drug Abuse (NIDA) reports that infants born to heroin-abusing mothers frequently suffer from Neonatal Abstinence Syndrome—withdrawal symptoms that may require medication.

Medical Use of Heroin

Since 1924 heroin has been virtually banned in the United States, even for medical use as an analgesic. The prohibition against the use of heroin under any circumstances, even to alleviate the intractable pain experienced by some cancer patients, is controversial. Arnold

---

Signs and Symptoms of Opioid Withdrawal

In temporal order of appearance (Ginzburg 1986):

1. Several hours after last use: anxiety, restlessness, irritability, drug craving
2. After 8–15 hours since last use: yawning, perspiration
3. After 16–24 hours since last use: sneezing, sniffles, anorexia (severe appetite loss), vomiting, abdominal cramps, bone pains, tremors, weakness, insomnia, goose flesh, convulsions (very rarely), cardiovascular collapse

---

Trebach (1982: 79) argues that heroin should be made available under such circumstances. "For some patients, heroin is superior to other medicines for the control of pain, anxiety, and related conditions." John Kaplan (1983b) states that while most patients cannot tell the difference between heroin and morphine in equivalent doses, patients (in England where such use is legal) who take the drug intravenously tend to prefer heroin. The greater euphoric effect of intravenous heroin appears to provide some relief for terminal patients whose painful existence is often measured in weeks, days, or hours. Heroin, however, is not the most powerful of the narcotics. The synthetic chemical etorphine is 5,000 to 10,000 times more potent than morphine. Because of its potency, etorphine is usually used only by veterinarians to immobilize large wild animals (Snyder 1977; *Drugs of Abuse* 1989).

Oxycodone. A synthetic version of morphine, **oxycodone,** was first introduced in December 1995 and marketed under the trade name OxyContin (produced by Purdue Pharma of Connecticut). Sold in tablets that contain 40 to 160 milligrams in a time-released formulation, the 160 milligram tablet is intended to work for up to 12 hours (Clines and Meier 2001). This powerful depressant is prescribed and very effective for severe and chronic pain, but has been linked to numerous overdose fatalities, resulting in its diversion to the substance abuse market. Although OxyContin is a time-released medication, abusers crush the pills and swallow, inhale, or inject it to produce an immediate and intense reaction (Meier 2001; Meier and Peterson 2001).

Dangers of Heroin Use

Ingesting heroin significantly more pure than the user's level of tolerance leads to overdose reactions that can include respiratory arrest and death. And because heroin is illegal, there is no way for the user to determine the level of purity. Indeed, the "hot shot" is used as a relatively easy way of eliminating addicts who have become police informers. Another danger is that heroin cut for street sale may contain adulterants, or the user may mix the substance with other drugs, such as the stimulants cocaine and amphetamine, to enhance the euphoric reaction (potentiating effect). This combination can be fatal to some abusers.

Heroin
Uses and Effects

Classification:	Narcotic
CSA Schedule:	Schedule I
Trade or Other Names:	Diacetylmorphine, horse, smack
Medical Uses:	None in United States, analgesic, antitussive
Physical Dependence:	High
Psychological Dependence:	High
Tolerance:	Yes
Duration (hours):	3–6
Usual Method:	Injected, sniffed, smoked
Possible Effects:	Euphoria, drowsiness, respiratory depression, constricted pupils, nausea
Effects of Overdose:	Slow and shallow breathing, clammy skin, convulsions, coma, possible death
Withdrawal Syndrome:	Watery eyes, runny nose, yawning, loss of appetite, irritability, tremors, panic, cramps, nausea, chills, and sweating

Source: U.S. Drug Enforcement Administration

Users also face the dangers associated with diseases that are transmitted by shared hypodermic needles, particularly hepatitis and AIDS. In New York City, where there are believed to be about 200,000 heroin addicts, as many as 60 percent may be infected with the AIDS virus, and addicts are the leading cause of the spread of AIDS. In addition to the threat of shared needles, infected addicts spread the disease through sexual relations with nonaddicts.

Barbiturates

There are about 2,500 derivatives of barbituric acid and dozens of brand names. Lawfully produced barbiturates are found in tablet or capsule form; illegal barbiturates may be found in liquid form for intravenous use because barbiturates are poorly soluble in water. Classified as sedative/hypnotics, they include amobarbital (e.g., Amytal), pentobarbital (e.g., Nembutal), phenobarbital (e.g., Luminal), secobarbital (e.g., Seconal), and the combination amobarbital-secobarbital (e.g., Tuinal).

Effects of Barbiturates

"Barbiturates depress the sensory cortex, decrease motor activity, alter cerebellar function, and produce drowsiness, sedation, and hypnosis" (*Physicians' Desk Reference* 2003: 480; hereafter PDR). They inhibit seizure activity and can induce unconsciousness in the form of sleep or surgical anesthesia. Unlike opiates, barbiturates do not decrease, and may actually increase, reaction to pain. They can produce a variety of alterations in the central nervous system, ranging from mild sedation to hypnosis and deep coma. In high enough dosage they can induce anesthesia, and an overdose can be fatal. Although they are CNS depressants, in some persons, they produce excitation (PDR 2003). The user's *expectations* have a marked influence on the drug's effect: "For instance, the person who takes 200 mg of secobarbital and expects to fall asleep will usually sleep, if provided with a suitable environment. Another individual, who takes the same amount of secobarbital and expects to have a good time in a stimulating environment, may experience a state of paradoxical stimulation or disinhibition euphoria" (Wesson and Smith 1977: 28).

Barbiturates are often used for their intoxicating effects. Some people take them in addition to alcohol, or as a substitute. Heavy users of other drugs sometimes turn to them if their usual drugs are not available, or to counteract the effects of large doses of stimulants such as amphetamines or cocaine. Barbiturates are known generally on the street as "downers" or "barbs." Many are named for the colors of their brand name versions: blues or blue heavens (Amytal), yellow jackets (Nembutal), red birds or red devils (Seconal), and rainbows or reds and blues (Tuinal).

A small dose (e.g., 50 mg or less) may relieve anxiety and tension. A somewhat larger dose (e.g., 100 to 200 mg) will, in a tranquil setting, usually induce sleep. An equivalent dose in a social setting, however, may produce effects similar to those of drunkenness—a "high" feeling, slurred speech, staggering, slowed reactions, loss of inhibition, and intense emotions often expressed in an extreme and unpredictable manner. High doses characteristically produce slow, shallow, and irregular breathing, and can result in death from respiratory arrest. Barbiturate use during pregnancy has been associated with birth defects.

Barbiturates are classified according to the speed with which they are metabolized (broken down chemically) in the liver and eliminated by the kidneys: slow, intermediate, fast, and ultrafast. In low dosage, barbiturates may actually increase the reaction to painful stimuli. The fast-acting barbiturates, particularly Nembutal (sodium pentobarbital), Amytal (amobarbital sodium), Seconal (secobarbital sodium), and Tuinal (secobarbital sodium and amobarbital sodium combined) are most likely to be abused (O'Brien and Cohen 1984). Exactly how barbiturates cause their neurophysiological effects is not fully understood, but the substance impairs the postsynaptic action of excitatory neurotransmitters (McKim 1991). Barbiturates serve as a positive reinforcer for laboratory animals.

Barbiturate Tolerance and Withdrawal

As with opiates, tolerance develops to barbiturates; but in contrast to opiates, there is a fatal dosage level, and the margin between an intoxicating dosage and a fatal dosage

Barbiturates
Uses and Effects

Classification:	Depressant
CSA Schedule:	Schedule II, III, IV
Trade or Other Names:	Amytal, Florinal, Nembutal, Seconal, Tuinal, Phenobarbital, Pentobarbital
Medical Uses:	Anesthetic, anticonvulsant, sedative, hypnotic, veterinary euthanasia agent
Physical Dependence:	High–Moderate
Psychological Dependence:	High–Moderate
Tolerance:	Yes
Duration (hours):	5–8
Usual Method:	Oral, injected
Possible Effects:	Slurred speech, disorientation, drunken behavior without odor of alcohol
Effects of Overdose:	Shallow respiration, clammy skin, dilated pupils, weak and rapid pulse, coma, possible death
Withdrawal Syndrome:	Anxiety, insomnia, tremors, delirium, convulsions, possible death

Source: U.S. Drug Enforcement Administration

becomes smaller with continued use. "Tolerance to a fatal dosage, however, does not increase more than twofold. As this occurs, the margin between an intoxicating dosage and a fatal dosage becomes smaller" (PDR 2003: 482). Drinking alcohol can further reduce that margin because alcohol "may result in additional CNS depressant effects" (481). When under the influence of small amounts of barbiturates or a combination of alcohol and barbiturates, a "person may 'forget' that he has already taken barbiturates and continue to ingest them until he reaches a lethal dose." Such overdoses often appear, incorrectly, to be suicidal (Wesson and Smith 1977: 24).

Withdrawal symptoms range from mild—muscle twitching, tremors, weakness, dizziness, visual distortion, nausea, vomiting, insomnia—to major—delirium, convulsions, and possibly death (PDR 2003).

Medical Use of Barbiturates

Barbiturates are used primarily as sedatives for the treatment of insomnia and as anticonvulsants to help prevent or mitigate epileptic seizures. The ultrafast barbiturates—the best known being sodium pentothal—are used to induce unconsciousness in a few minutes. At relatively high dosage, they are used as anesthetics for minor surgery and to induce anesthesia before the administration of slow-acting barbiturates.

Because of the risks associated with barbiturate abuse, and because new and safer drugs such as the tranquilizers/benzodiazepines are now available, barbiturates are less frequently prescribed than in the past. Nonetheless, they are still available both by prescription and illegally.

Dangers of Barbiturate Use

The disinhibition euphoria that can follow barbiturate intake is what makes them appealing as intoxicants (Wesson and Smith 1977). Intoxication results in slurred speech, unsteady gait, confusion, poor judgment, and a marked impairment of motor skills. Unlike opiates, barbiturates make it dangerous to operate a motor vehicle. With continuous intoxication at high doses, the user typically neglects his or her appearance, bathing infrequently and becoming unkempt and dirty, as well as irritable and aggressive (McKim 1991). Like opiates, barbiturates are addicting, with both psychological and physiological dependence. High doses characteristically produce slow, shallow, and irregular breathing, and can result in death from respiratory arrest. "Following a large overdose of secobarbital or phenobarbital (short-acting barbiturates), an individual may be in coma for several days" (Wesson and Smith 1977: 20).

Taking barbiturates with other CNS depressants (e.g., alcohol, tranquilizers), such opioids as heroin, morphine, meperidine (Demerol), codeine, or methadone, or with antihistamines (found in cold, cough, and allergy remedies) can be extremely dangerous, even lethal. Long-term high dosage produces chronic inebriation; the impairment of memory and judgment; hostility, depression, or mood swings; chronic fatigue; and stimulation of preexisting emotional disorders, which may result in paranoia or thoughts of suicide. The prescribing of barbiturates has declined notably since the safer benzodiazepine tranquilizers (discussed below) were introduced (Alcoholism and Drug Addiction Research Foundation, Toronto).

Benzodiazepines (ben-zo-di-az-a-pins)

Benzodiazepines, minor tranquilizers or **sedatives**—referred to pharmacologically as *sedative-hypnotics*—are among the most widely prescribed of all drugs. The best-known are Valium (diazepam), Librium (chlordiazepoxide), and Equanil and Miltown (meprobamate). The full extent of the nonmedical use of sedatives is not known, although it appears that their abuse is often in combination with other controlled substances. They produce effects subjectively similar to alcohol and barbiturates, but unlike these other depressants, benzodiazepines have few effects outside the CNS (McKim 1991). Major or antipsychotic tranquilizers such as Thorazine (chlorpromazine) do not produce euphoria and thus are rarely used nonmedically (Nelson et al. 1982).

Effects of Tranquilizers

Minor tranquilizers are absorbed into the bloodstream and affect the central nervous system, slowing down physical, mental, and emotional responses. The CNS contains benzodiazepine receptors that (through a complex process involving certain [GABA] receptors) inhibit the brain's limbic system, which regulates emotions (Smith and Wesson 1994). Although it has yet to be discovered, scientists believe that the body produces its own benzodiazepine-like substance that controls anxiety.

Medical Use of Benzodiazepines

Minor tranquilizers are usually prescribed for anxiety or sleep problems. They can be used to treat panic disorders and muscle spasms. Sometimes referred to as "sleeping pills," these CNS depressants have largely replaced barbiturates, which reportedly have a significantly greater potential for abuse and risk for fatal overdose. In laboratory animals, benzodiazepines have proven to be less effective reinforcers than barbiturates (NIDA 1991). Benzodiazepines have an upper limit of effectiveness—after a certain point, increasing the dosage will not increase the effect, and overdoses are rarely fatal (McKim 1991): "Even when a benzodiazepine is taken in an overdose of 50–100 times the usual therapeutic dose, fatalities from respiratory depression are rare" (Smith and Wesson 1994: 180).

Valium is often prescribed to relieve stress, because it produces a sense of calm and well-being. It is also addictive. Benzodiazepines are not effective for treating anxiety beyond four months, and the drug can generate intense and severe secondary anxiety. Thus, if the underlying cause of the anxiety is not treated, benzodiazepines may worsen the condition and increase the risk of suicide (Miller and Gold 1990). The drug has a very long half-life (24–48 hours), which means that even after it is discontinued, Valium stays in the system metabolizing slowly (Bluhm 1987). A benzodiazepine known as *Versed* is 10 times more potent than Valium and used to induce "twilight sleep" for surgery patients who need to be relaxed but conscious.

Benzodiazepine Tolerance and Withdrawal

When used as sleeping pills, tolerance develops rapidly, and effectiveness may wear off after three nights. Because of tolerance, even if the dosage is increased, benzodiazepines are not effective for treating anxiety beyond 4 months.

Repeated use leads to dependence, and discontinuing tranquilizers *can*—although it is unclear in what proportion of users—produce withdrawal symptoms that include anxiety, insomnia, agitation, anorexia, tremor, muscle twitching, nausea/vomiting, hypersensitivity to sensory stimuli and other perceptual disturbances, and depersonalization.

Benzodiazepines
Uses and Effects

Classification:	Depressant
CSA Schedule:	Schedule IV
Trade or Other Names:	Ativan, Dalmane, Diazepam, Librium, Xanax, Serax, Valium, Tranxene, Verstran, Versed, Halcion, Paxpam, Restoril
Medical Uses:	Anti-anxiety, sedative, anticonvulsant, hypnotic
Physical Dependence:	Low
Psychological Dependence:	Low
Tolerance:	Yes
Duration (hours):	4–8
Usual Method:	Oral, injected
Possible Effects:	Slurred speech, disorientation, drunken behavior without odor of alcohol
Effects of Overdose:	Shallow respiration, clammy skin, dilated pupils, weak and rapid pulse, coma, possible death
Withdrawal Syndrome:	Anxiety, insomnia, tremors, delirium, convulsions, possible death

Source: U.S. Drug Enforcement Administration

Discontinuing use after prolonged exposure to high doses can produce hallucinations, delirium, grand mal convulsions, and, on rare occasions, death (NIDA 1987; Smith and Wesson 1994). Valium withdrawal symptoms may first appear after 7 to 10 days, and may be quite serious and even life threatening (Bluhm 1987). Someone using minor tranquilizers under medical supervision for more than 2 or 3 weeks is usually withdrawn gradually over a period of months.

Dangers of Tranquilizer Use

Common short-term effects include drowsiness, dizziness, confusion, and mood swings. Common long-term effects include lethargy, irritability, nausea, loss of sexual interest, increased appetite, and weight gain. Regular use of minor tranquilizers can produce both psychological and physical dependence. Combining minor tranquilizers with alcohol, painkillers, or drugs containing antihistamines such as cough, cold, and allergy medications can result in unconsciousness and failure to breathe. A life-endangering CNS depression can result when benzodiazepines are used in conjunction with alcohol. In some persons, benzodiazepines can induce hostility and even aggression (McKim 1991). Valium overdose is the second-leading cause of drug-related emergency room admissions in the United States. Some tranquilizers block receptors for the neurotransmitter dopamine (which can lead to symptoms of Parkinson's disease).

Methaqualone

Such drugs as glutethimide (Doriden), methyprylon (Noludar), ethchlorvynol (Placidyl), and methaqualone (found in Mandrax) were introduced as barbiturate substitutes, in the belief they would be safer. It was soon found, however, that they shared problems similar to those of barbiturates, including abuse leading to overdose and interaction with other CNS depressants. The same caution necessary in using barbiturates thus applies to these other sedative/hypnotics as well.

Methaqualone was first synthesized in 1951 in India, where it was introduced as an antimalarial drug but proved to be ineffective. At the same time, its sedating effects caused it to be introduced in Great Britain as a safe, nonbarbiturate "sleeping pill." The substance subsequently found its way into street abuse, and similar patterns occurred in Germany and Japan. In 1965 methaqualone was introduced into the United States as the prescription drugs Sopors and Quaalude without any restrictions—it was not listed as a scheduled (controlled) drug. By the early 1970s "ludes" and "sopors" were part of the drug culture. Physicians were overprescribing the drug for anxiety and insomnia, believing that it was safer than barbiturates. Street sales were primarily diversions from legitimate sources.

Eight years after it was first introduced into the United States, the drug's serious dangers became evident, and in 1973 it was placed on the DEA's Schedule II list. Although chemically unrelated to barbiturates, methaqualone intoxication is similar to barbiturate intoxication. Addiction develops rapidly, and an overdose can be fatal. However, while similar to barbiturates in its effect, methaqualone produces an even greater loss of motor coordination, which is why it is sometimes referred to as a "wallbanger." Methaqualone is now illegally manufactured in Colombia and smuggled into the United States.

Alcohol

Two out of every three adult Americans consume alcohol.[7] It is a potentially dangerous drug used by mainstream religions such as Judaism and Catholicism (although prohibited

---

[7]Unless otherwise noted, information in this section is from the Office of Substance Abuse Studies, University of Maryland; Missouri Division of Alcohol and Drug Abuse; Alcoholism and Drug Addiction Research Foundation, Toronto, Canada; Canadian Centre on Substance Abuse, Ottawa, Canada; and the Centre for Education and Information on Drugs and Alcohol in New South Wales.

by Islam and several Protestant denominations), whose recreational use in moderation is an accepted part of American culture.

Alcohols are compounds used in perfumes, paints, and many other products. Ethyl alcohol (ethanol) is used as a beverage. A natural substance, ethyl alcohol is formed by the **fermentation** that occurs when sugar reacts with yeast. It can be made by distillation or by fermenting fruits, vegetables, or grains. In pure form the substance is colorless and has a bitter taste. While some people apparently enjoy the taste of beverages containing alcohol, many others ingest the drug *despite* its taste. The substance can produce feelings of well-being, sedation, intoxication, or unconsciousness, depending on the amount and the manner in which it is consumed.

Extensive research indicates that alcohol taken in moderate amounts—more than 5 grams but not more than 30 grams of pure alcohol[8] (Burros 1996)—can help protect against heart disease by raising the level of high-density lipoproteins (so-called good cholesterol), which help cleanse the arteries of fatty deposits (Angier 1991).[9] More recent research has revealed that as little as a single glass of wine or beer per week can significantly reduce the risk of ischemic stroke, which is the most common type and is caused by clots that reduce blood flow to the brain—600,000 people in the United States suffer a stroke each year (Greenberg 1999).

Alcohol is a *regulated* rather than *controlled* substance—it can be purchased and possessed with only a few restrictions. There are three major classes of alcoholic beverage:

1. *Beer.* Beer is produced by the fermentation of barley malt or other grains (brewing). It is usually flavored with hops or other aromatic bitters. In the United States beer generally contains no more than 5 percent alcohol (10 percent proof), although some "ice" beers contain closer to 6 or (mostly foreign brews) 7 percent.[10] A variant of beer known as "malt liquor" can contain 8 percent alcohol (16 proof). There are also "light" beers (about 3 percent alcohol) and nonalcoholic (or "near") beers (about .05 percent alcohol).

2. *Wine.* Wine is obtained from the fermentation of the juice of grapes (and sometimes other fruits). It usually contains 6 to 14 percent alcohol (12 to 28 proof). Wine coolers—mixtures of wine and fruit juice—range from 5 to 8 percent alcohol. There are also fortified wines that have added alcohol. Port and sherry wines are examples of high-quality fortified wines. Low-priced fortified wines are produced by adding grain alcohol to low-grade wine often sold in screw-top bottles—a favorite of low-income alcoholics and of youth, since they produce more intoxication at less cost than other types of alcoholic beverages.

---

[8]A 6-ounce glass of wine has about 11 grams of alcohol; a 12-ounce can of beer about 13 grams; and a 1-ounce shot of liquor about 15 grams.

[9]For a review of this issue, see the Spring 1994 edition of *Contemporary Drug Problems* 21.

[10]In 1935, fearing that beer manufacturers would attempt to lure customers by raising the amount of alcohol in their brews, Congress enacted legislation that prohibited the listing of alcohol content on beer labels. In 1995 the Supreme Court ruled that law unconstitutional.

The Basics of Bourbon

In 1776, Virginia named its western frontier Kentucky County, which, after the Revolution, became Bourbon County in honor of France's help in the war. Bourbon, which by law must be derived from at least 51 percent corn—as distinct from rye whiskey—receives its color and almost all of its taste from the charred barrels in which it is stored for at least 2 years. The Tennessee version, Jack Daniel's and George Dickel, is the result of slow filtering over the course of several days through maple charcoal (Allen 1998). In order for the substance to be labeled *bourbon,* according to U.S. law, the barrels can only be used once.

In the United States Scotch is aged for 3 years in used barrels, mostly bourbon barrels from Kentucky (Allen 1998; Kummer 1999).

3. *Liquor.* When alcohol produced by fermentation (of corn, malt, grains, molasses, potatoes) reaches about 15 percent, it kills the alcohol-producing yeast cells. To obtain higher concentrations of alcohol, **distillation** is necessary: The mix is heated—alcohol has a lower boiling point than the other liquids—and its cooling vapors are collected. After several distillations, nearly pure alcohol can be obtained. The colorless liquid is usually mixed with water, coloring, and flavoring agents. It contains at least 25 percent alcohol (50 percent proof) but may be as high as 50 percent alcohol (100 proof). This category includes whiskey (the Kentucky version known as bourbon; the American or Scottish version known as Scotch), brandy, rum, gin, and vodka.

Alcohol is absorbed primarily through the small intestine. The rate of absorption depends on the type and amount of foods in the stomach—foods, especially solid and fatty foods, slow the absorption process. Body weight and gender also influence the effects of alcohol: Heavier persons have more bodily fluids and thus dilute more of the substance; women have less gastric acid and will absorb about 30 percent more alcohol than men. Once absorbed into the bloodstream, alcohol moves to wherever there is water in the body, including inside cells of the CNS.

Alcohol and Tobacco

"Alcohol and tobacco seem to go together. Consumers of one drug are likely to consume the other. Moreover, alcohol and tobacco often are used at the same time" (Shiffman and Balabanis 1995: 17).

Effects of Alcohol

Alcohol is a psychoactive/mind-altering chemical that, like heroin and tranquilizers, depresses the central nervous system. It is an efficient tranquilizer with the ability to reduce short-term anxiety (Willoughby 1988). However, alcohol first affects the part of the brain that controls inhibitions: drinkers talk more, exude self-confidence, and may get foolish or even rowdy—there is a general loss of self-restraint (Valenzuela 1997).

The mechanism by which alcohol does this involves two receptors: **GABA** receptors restrain neuron activity so that chaotic communication is avoided; **NMDA** receptors promote communication necessary to encode memories, generate thoughts, and make decisions. Alcohol reinforces GABA activity while reducing NMDA activity, thereby slowing communication between neurons (Kotulak 2002b). As the dose increases, so do the effects, the brain experiencing greater difficulty communicating with nerves and muscles. This results in slurred speech, staggering, and a loss of emotional control. Further ingestion can lead to stupor from which arousal is difficult, and severe respiratory depression, coma, and death can result.

Alcohol is a complex substance affecting a number of neurotransmitter and receptor systems in the brain: endorphin, dopamine, serotonin, and glutamine. When alcoholics imbibe, their brains release elevated levels of endorphins, triggering rewarding sensations enticing the person to drink more. However, at low doses alcohol acts as a stimulant, and initially the user of alcohol often experiences it as an energizer with euphoric effects (Bukstein, Brent, and Kaminer 1989). As with most other psychoactive substances, this is the result of alcohol stimulating the dopaminergic reward pathway in the brain (Dettling et al. 1995).

As with other drugs, the influence of alcohol is mediated through setting and expectations. Imbibers at a funeral will act differently than they would at a wedding or other happy occasion. The two effects—stimulation-sedation—appear to be influenced by the degree of excitability of the central nervous system at the time of ingestion, which depends on the setting in which alcohol is used, as well as the personality of the user. In a quiet environment, the excitatory influence may be impaired, and alcohol produces sedation and drowsiness. If the environment is loud and lively, the drinker demonstrates excitement.

Similar reactions have been found with respect to alcohol and sexual arousal. Increasing doses of alcohol suppress physiological arousal for both men and women. But subjective sexual arousal is affected not only by blood alcohol concentration but also by a person's beliefs about the effects of alcohol. Thus, in men, but not women, the culturally transmitted connection between sex and alcohol enhances arousal. Culturally transmitted beliefs and expectations exert a powerful influence over sexuality in drinking situations. That is, expectancies about the relationship between alcohol and sex generated by the culture influence how a person believes he or she will respond to sexual stimuli (George and Norris n.d.).

Regular use of moderate daily amounts of alcohol can produce psychological dependence, the lack of alcohol resulting in anxiety and mild panic attacks. Prolonged or chronic drinking produces both psychological and physical dependence. The stronger depressant effect lasts about 2 hours, while a weaker stimulation of the central nervous system lasts about six times as long. As the time since the last drink increases, the longer-lasting stimulating effect becomes dominant and the drinker becomes agitated—the "morning-after hangover." This is the start of the drinker's withdrawal syndrome. Because of alcohol's primary depressant effect, calm can be temporarily restored by more drinking. For the alcoholic, the morning drink has a calming effect that is part of a vicious cycle of continued alcohol use.

Blood Alcohol Level. Almost all alcohol is burned as fuel. Unlike other drugs of abuse, alcohol provides calories and is technically a food, with some eliminated through

Alcohol and Aging

At age 65 the body's ability to respond to alcohol is quite different from that at 45. Thus, older adults get into trouble with alcohol with an amount that would not be considered immoderate at an earlier age. As people age, they lose muscle and bone, lean body mass, and acquire a greater percentage of body fat. As a result, there is a decrease in body water in which alcohol is soluble, replaced by fat in which alcohol is not soluble. Aging also results in a decline in a stomach enzyme that breaks down alcohol before it reaches the bloodstream. As a result, there is greater burden on the liver where most alcohol metabolism takes place. And advancing age also causes a decline in the blood flow through the liver so alcohol is eliminated more slowly from the blood. Thus, blood alcohol levels in older people are 30 to 40 percent higher than in younger people (M. Wald 2002).

the lungs and in urine. Breathalyzer tests measure the **blood alcohol level** (BAL)—the amount of alcohol in the blood—because alcohol in the air exhaled closely parallels concentrations in the blood. In most states, a BAL of .10 is the legal standard for intoxication, although a number of states have lowered the level to .08. Alcohol produces tolerance, and persons with high levels of alcohol tolerance can perform tasks with a BAL that would render a nontolerant person "a falling-down drunk." Alcohol has a cross-tolerance with barbiturates and benzodiazepines. It appears to act on the CNS in the same manner as benzodiazepines—that is, it acts on benzodiazepine receptors, which are inhibitory.

The alcohol impairment charts in Table 4.1a and 4.1b show a person's approximate BAL based on weight and the number of drinks he or she has consumed. Separate charts are shown for men and women because a woman drinking an equal amount of alcohol in the same period of time as a man of the same weight may have a higher BAL than that man. In the charts, you can see that impairment begins with the first drink, and by the second drink, most people have impaired balance, motor coordination, vision, and self-control.

Genetic Influence on Alcohol Use. A wide variety of studies clearly indicate that genetic factors influence the development of alcoholism, but the studies differ in their estimate of the degree of genetic influence. While *genes* (segments of chromosomes that code for the production of specific proteins) are important in the control of behavior, they do not directly cause a person to become alcoholic or drug dependent, although they are believed to produce a tendency or predisposition to respond to drugs (including alcohol) in a certain manner. "If you are the son of a male alcoholic who began his alcoholism in early adolescence or early adulthood, the chance of your becoming an alcoholic is 7 to 10 times greater than that of the average population. If you are the twin of a male alcoholic, the chance of your becoming an alcoholic is about 70 percent. This means there is some

TABLE 4.1a **Alcohol Impairment Chart, Men**

Body Weight[2]	Approximate Blood Alcohol Percentage[1]								
	100	120	140	160	180	200	220	240	
Drinks[3] 0	.00	.00	.00	.00	.00	.00	.00	.00	**Only safe driving limit**
1	.04	.03	.03	.02	.02	.02	.02	.02	Impairment begins
2	.08	.06	.05	.05	.04	.04	.03	.03	**Driving skills significantly affected**
3	.11	.09	.08	.07	.06	.06	.05	.05	
4	.15	.12	.11	.09	.08	.08	.07	.06	
5	.19	.16	.13	.12	.11	.09	.09	.08	**Possible criminal penalties**
6	.23	.19	.16	.14	.13	.11	.10	.09	
7	.26	.22	.19	.16	.15	.13	.12	.11	**Legally intoxicated**
8	.30	.25	.21	.19	.17	.15	.14	.13	
9	.34	.28	.24	.21	.19	.17	.15	.14	**Criminal penalties**
10	.38	.31	.27	.23	.21	.19	.17	.16	

TABLE 4.1b **Alcohol Impairment Chart, Women**

Body Weight[2]	Approximate Blood Alcohol Percentage[1]									
	90	100	120	140	160	180	200	220	240	
Drinks[3] 0	.00	.00	.00	.00	.00	.00	.00	.00	00	**Only safe driving limit**
1	.05	.05	.04	.03	.03	.03	.02	.02	.02	Impairment begins
2	.10	.09	.08	.07	.06	.05	.05	.04	.04	**Driving skills significantly affected**
3	.15	.14	.11	.10	.09	.08	.07	.06	.06	
4	.20	.18	.15	.13	.11	.10	.09	.08	.08	**Possible criminal penalties**
5	.25	.23	.19	.16	.14	.13	.11	.10	.09	
6	.30	.27	.23	.19	.17	.15	.14	.12	.11	**Legally intoxicated**
7	.38	.32	.27	.23	.20	.18	.16	.14	.13	
8	.40	.36	.30	.26	.23	.20	.18	.17	.15	**Criminal penalties**
9	.45	.41	.34	.29	.26	.23	.20	.19	17	
10	.51	.45	.38	.32	.28	.25	.23	.21	19	

[1]Subtract .01% for each 40 minutes of drinking.

[2]In pounds.

[3]One drink is 1.25 ounces of 80 proof liquor, 12 ounces of beer, or 5 ounces of table wine.

Source: Data supplied by the Pennsylvania Liquor Control Board.

Under the Influence

After one drink, a person weighing 120 pounds has a blood alcohol level of about .04; a person weighing 140 pounds, .03; a person weighing 240 pounds, .02. The effects at different levels are as follows:

.02–.03: Slight euphoria and loss of inhibition

.04–.06: Feeling of well-being, relaxed, sensation of warmth; minor impairment of reasoning and lowering of caution

.07–.09: Slight impairment of balance, motor coordination, vision, and self-control; slurred speech

.10–.12: Significant impairment of motor coordination, balance, vision, and reaction time; loss of good judgment

.30–.40: Loss of consciousness and possible death from respiratory arrest

factor, or factors, passed to the male offspring that make them more vulnerable to the actions of alcoholism" (Bloom 1993: 24). Research that compared fraternal and identical male twins supports the role of genetic factors in alcoholism. The researchers also found that environmental factors had little influence on the development of alcoholism (Prescott and Kendler 1999).

Studies have revealed that some persons with particular inherited characteristics are at greater risk for addiction than persons without these characteristics. "Researchers have identified as important influences such inherited characteristics as how an individual metabolizes alcohol, hormonal and behavioral effects of alcohol and tolerance of high levels of alcohol in the blood" (Brody 1987: 14; also see Tarter, Alterman, and Edwards (1985) and Tarter (1988) for a review of research on behavioral traits and predisposition to substance abuse). Studies have shown that first-degree relatives of alcoholics are more likely to be alcoholics than close blood relatives of nonalcoholics. Adopted children with alcoholic natural parents are more likely to become alcoholics than adopted children with nonalcoholic natural parents (Schuckit 1985).

Research (Blum et al. 1990) reveals that the genetic component of alcoholism appears to be related to an abnormality of a dopamine receptor gene. Persons having this defect are at potentially greater risk for the disease than the general population. While another study (Gelernter, Goldman, and Risch 1993) disputes the Blum et al. findings,[11] subsequent research identified a specific genetic (dopamine-related) abnormality associated with a susceptibility for alcoholism (Dettling et al. 1995; Guardia et al. 2000). It has been shown that

---

[11]"Individuals who become alcoholic or severely alcoholic probably do so for a variety of different reasons, and for the majority of alcoholics the causation may not even be primarily genetic" (Gelernter, Goldman, and Risch 1993: 1677).

another stimulating neurotransmitter, serotonin, also influences drinking behavior (Gulley et al. 1995), and a deficiency in serotonin or serotonin receptors has been linked to a predisposition to alcoholism (Goleman 1990). The ability of alcohol to produce both depressant and stimulant effects may be related to the fact that, as opposed to other psychoactive substances, alcohol is able to affect many different parts of the CNS (Kotulak 1997).

Alcohol Tolerance and Withdrawal

While tolerance to alcohol's rewarding effects does not develop, people who drink on a regular basis become tolerant to many of the unpleasant effects of alcohol, and are thus able to drink more before suffering these effects (NIAAA 1997). Even with increased consumption, many such drinkers don't appear intoxicated.

In the liver, alcohol is converted to **acetaldehyde,** which in high levels causes permanent liver damage. In the alcoholic—though not in persons not addicted to alcohol—acetaldehyde builds up and is transported through the blood-brain barrier, where it combines with neurotransmitters to produce TIQs (tetrahydroisoquinolines). TIQs attach to CNS receptors to produce a feeling of well-being similar to that produced by morphine. This activity causes brain cell membranes to become abnormally thickened and to require a constant supply of alcohol. Thus, the brain cells have become addicted to alcohol. In its absence, membranes function poorly, and the alcoholic experiences withdrawal symptoms (Catanzarite 1992; Kotulak 2002b).

A physically dependent alcoholic who abruptly stops drinking will experience a withdrawal syndrome that can range from very mild to life threatening. If large amounts of alcohol are consumed for a long time, withdrawal symptoms will often be severe and far more dangerous than withdrawal from heroin. By contrast, the morning-after hangover may result from a single bout of alcohol abuse—nausea, shakiness, headache.

In the typical course of withdrawal, symptoms begin within the first 24 hours after the last drink, reach their peak intensity within 2 or 3 days, and disappear within 1 or 2 weeks. As the alcohol blood level begins to drop, the person may experience headaches, anxiety, involuntary twitching of muscles, tremor of hands, weakness, insomnia, nausea, anxiety, rapid heart rate, and increased blood pressure. At this point, the alcoholic usually craves alcohol. The second stage of alcohol withdrawal includes hallucinations, usually visual, but they may include auditory or olfactory (smell) as well. If hallucinations develop, they may persist for hours, days, or even weeks.

The third stage occurs during the next 48 hours as symptoms become progressively more intense. There may be a fall in blood pressure, fever, delirium characterized by disorientation, delusions and visual hallucinations, and convulsions similar to those exhibited in grand mal epileptic seizures. The fever, delirium, and convulsions are the most serious symptoms and can be fatal.

If the person remains untreated, the syndrome may progress to **delirium tremens** (DTs): profound confusion, disorientation, hallucinations, hyperactivity, and extreme cardiovascular disturbances. Without close medical management, the person may harm him- or herself or others, or die from the medical complications. Prevention of the DTs involves the use of sedatives such as Valium, since once the DTs begin, no known medical treatment is able to stop them. If left untreated, DTs can be fatal.

Dangers of Alcohol Use

Alcohol has a pervasive effect on the body's gastrointestinal tract, liver, bloodstream, brain and nervous system, heart, muscles, and endocrine system. Some harmful consequences are primary—they result directly from prolonged exposure to alcohol's toxic effects (such as heart and liver disease or inflammation of the stomach). Others are secondary—indirectly related to chronic alcohol abuse, they include loss of appetite, vitamin deficiencies, infections, and sexual impotence or menstrual irregularities. Because alcohol can be utilized as a source of energy, this supply of calories often suppresses appetite, leading to dietary deficiencies that may be responsible in part for the pathologic conditions seen in chronic alcoholism. The risk of serious disease increases with the amount of alcohol consumed:

- loss of control of eye muscles
- hypoglycemia (low level of glucose in the blood)
- gastritis (chronic inflammation of the stomach)
- increased susceptibility to infections
- cardiac arrhythmia (irregularity)
- anemia (red blood cell deficiency)
- neuritis (nerve inflammation)
- pancreatitis (inflammation of the pancreas)
- increased blood pressure

Chronic alcohol drinking produces even more severe conditions, some of which may be irreversible:

- **Korsakoff syndrome** (vitamin B deficiency)
- brain damage
- cardiomyopathy (heart muscle disorder)
- cancer of the tongue, mouth, pharynx, hypopharynx, esophagus, and liver
- decreased white blood cells
- weakened immune system
- liver damage; in more extreme cases, **cirrhosis**
- depletion of vitamins and minerals
- lowered hormone levels, leading to sexual dysfunction
- fetal alcohol syndrome

As already noted, withdrawal from chronic alcohol use results in serious complications that can be fatal.

Fetal Alcohol Syndrome. Researchers have discovered that even moderate drinking by pregnant women can impair a child's intellectual ability in school (Goleman 1989), and alcohol has been linked to a tenfold increased risk of developing leukemia during infancy ("New Hazard of Drinking in Pregnancy Is Found" 1996). Pregnant women who drink risk having babies with **fetal alcohol syndrome** (FAS). The most serious of these effects include mental retardation, growth deficiency, head and facial deformities, joint and limb abnormalities, and heart defects. While it is known that the risk of bearing an FAS-afflicted child increases with the amount of alcohol consumed, a safe level of consumption has not been determined. When an FAS baby is born it may withdraw from alcohol, exhibiting tremors, irritability, fits, and a bloated stomach. The fetus is at greatest risk of harm during the first 3 months of pregnancy, as the major organs and limbs are starting to form during that time. Research indicates that ethanol induces the destruction of large numbers of neurons from several regions of the developing brain (Ikonomidou et al. 2000).

Whether an individual child will have FAS appears to depend on a number of factors in addition to alcohol, including parental health, other drug use, lifestyle, and other socioeconomic factors. Some of the factors contributing to FAS may be male-mediated. This influence may occur biologically through damage to the sperm, or physically and psychologically through violence or other abuse to the mother.

Inhalants

The term *inhalants* refers to more than a thousand household and commercial products such as commercial adhesives, lighter fluids, cleaning solvents, and paint. They can be abused by inhaling them through the mouth or nose for an intoxicating effect. Inhalant users can ingest substances in various ways that include inhaling directly from containers for products such as rubber cement or correction fluid, sniffing fumes from plastic bags held over the mouth and nose, or sniffing a cloth that is saturated with the substance. The substance may be inhaled directly from an aerosol can or out of an alternative container such as a balloon filled with nitrous oxide. Some volatile substances release intoxicating vapors when heated (*Inhalants* 2003).

Commonly abused inhalants are usually volatile hydrocarbon solvents produced from petroleum and natural gas; the two main exceptions are amyl nitrite and nitrous oxide. (*Volatile* means the hydrocarbons evaporate when exposed to air, and *solvents* refers to their capacity, in liquid form, to dissolve many other substances.) Inhalants include a variety of readily available products often kept in the home. They can be divided into four classes:

1. Volatile solvents, such as glue, paint thinner, cleaning fluid, nail polish remover, and gasoline
2. Aerosols, such as hair spray, spray paint, frying pan lubricants, and deodorants
3. Anesthetics, such as nitrous oxide ("laughing gas" used as a whipped cream propellant) and ether
4. Volatile nitrates, such as amyl nitrate, a prescription drug used to treat angina, and butyl nitrate, used in room deodorizers

Toluene (methyl benzene), a common ingredient of most solvents, has the greatest abuse potential, and some industries have added mustard oil to their toluene-rich products so that the nasal irritation it causes will deter abusers.

Effects of Inhalants and Solvents

With some exceptions, these products are usually not produced for their psychoactive qualities, but when used for mind-altering purposes they are *drugs*. In general, these chemicals are abused by young (preadolescent and adolescent) males; although some, such as the volatile nitrites, are popular among anal sex aficionados because they relax the sphincter muscles; they are also reputed to increase the intensity of orgasm. Inhaled vapors from solvents and propellants enter the bloodstream directly from the lungs and are then rapidly distributed to the brain and liver, organs with the largest blood supply. Most volatile hydrocarbons are fat soluble and are thus absorbed quickly into the central nervous system.

Upon inhalation, the body becomes starved of oxygen, forcing the heart to beat more rapidly in an attempt to increase blood flow to the brain. The user initially experiences stimulation, a loss of inhibition, and a distorted perception of reality and spatial relations. After a few minutes the senses become depressed, and a sense of lethargy arises as the body attempts to stabilize blood flow to the brain, usually referred to as a "head rush." Users can become intoxicated several times over a few hours because of a chemical's short-acting, rapid-onset effect. Many users also experience headaches, nausea, vomiting, slurred speech, loss of coordination, and wheezing (*Inhalants* 2003).

While some volatile hydrocarbons are metabolized and then excreted through the kidneys, many are eliminated from the body unchanged, primarily through the lungs. The odor of solvents may therefore remain on the breath for several hours following inhalation. The complete elimination of volatile hydrocarbons may take some time, since they are released slowly from fatty tissues back into the blood.

Inhalant Tolerance and Withdrawal

Regular users can become dependent on volatile substances, as the substances become important in their daily lives. But even with extended use, the possibility of developing tolerance is very small. It is also rare for withdrawal symptoms to occur when a person stops using (Hormes, Filley, and Rosenberg 1986). Very heavy users, however, may experience headaches, muscular cramps, and abdominal pain.

Heavy or sustained use of inhalants can cause tolerance and physical withdrawal symptoms within several hours to a few days after use. Withdrawal symptoms may include sweating, rapid pulse, hand tremors, insomnia, nausea, vomiting, physical agitation, anxiety, hallucinations, and grand mal seizures.

Dangers of Inhalant Use

Research evidence suggests that short-term use of volatile substances rarely causes permanent damage, and effects are reversible if the person stops using inhalants. While the dangers of inhalants have often been exaggerated, long-term use of aerosols and cleaning fluids can damage the kidneys, liver, and the brain, but this is rare. Perception and coordination become impaired, and heavy use can cause unconsciousness. The "high" may be accompanied by sedation, hallucinations, and delusions. High dosage can result in vomiting, paralysis, and coma. A common method of use, a plastic bag covering the head, can lead to unconsciousness and death by suffocation.

The long term use of leaded petrol can cause leukemia and various types of cancers, because the lead accumulates in the body. Other physical effects of petrol sniffing can also include: anorexia, seizure, and sudden sniffing syndrome. *Sudden sniffing syndrome* is caused by heart failure that may happen if a person does strenuous exercise or has a sudden fright immediately after sniffing. However, this is rare and is usually associated with aerosols, butane gas, and cleaning fluid. The harms most associated with volatile substances are in how and where they are sniffed. Deaths or accidents can occur as a result of sniffing in unsafe places—on a roof or by a railway line (information from the Centre for Education and Information on Drugs and Alcohol in New South Wales).

Research sponsored by the National Institute on Drug Abuse (Mathias 2002) revealed that chronic inhalant abuse is associated with brain abnormalities and cognitive impairment considerably more severe than that experienced by cocaine abusers.

Analogs and Designer Drugs

Many chemical variations, or **analogs,** of the drugs discussed in this chapter have been found or developed. These include semisynthetic opiates such as hydromorphine, oxycondone, etorphine, and diprenorphine, and synthetic opiates such as pethidine, methadone, and propoxyphene (Darvon). The synthetic drug **fentanyl** citrate, which is often used intravenously in major surgery, works exactly like the opiates: It kills pain and produces euphoria and, if abused, leads to addiction. The substance is easily produced by persons skilled in chemistry.

Fentanyl compounds are often sold as **China white** (the street name for the finest Southeast Asian heroin) to addicts who cannot tell the difference. Those who know the difference may actually prefer fentanyl because it is usually cheaper than heroin and more readily available, and some users believe it contains fewer adulterants than heroin (Roberton 1986). However, fentanyl compounds are quite potent and difficult for street dealers to cut properly, a situation that can lead to overdose and death. One derivative, 3-methyl fentanyl, is extremely potent (approximately 3,000 times as potent as morphine) and is thought to be responsible for a number of overdose deaths. In 1988, 3-methyl

Fentanyl
Uses and Effects

Classification:	Narcotic
CSA Schedule:	Schedule I, II
Trade or Other Names:	Innovar, Sublimaze, Alfenta, Sufenta, Duragesic
Medical Uses:	Analgesic, adjunct to anesthesia, anesthetic
Physical Dependence:	High
Psychological Dependence:	High
Tolerance:	Yes
Duration (hours):	10–72
Usual Method:	Injected, transdermal patch
Possible Effects:	Euphoria, drowsiness, respiratory depression, dilated pupils, nausea
Effects of Overdose:	Slow and shallow breathing, clammy skin, convulsions, coma, possible death
Withdrawal Syndrome:	Watery eyes, runny nose, yawning, loss of appetite, irritability, tremors, panic, cramps, nausea, chills, and sweating

Source: U.S. Drug Enforcement Administration

fentanyl led to the death of eighteen people in the Pittsburgh area. A local chemist without a criminal record was found to be the source—he apparently got the idea from a television news report. In 1991 the drug killed ten persons in one weekend in four Northeastern cities (Nieves 1991). Fentanyl has been used (illegally) to "dope" race horses because the substance is very difficult to detect in urine or blood.

Analogs designed by underground chemists (**designer drugs**) to mimic controlled substances are an emerging problem: "These chemists change the molecular structure of a drug and thus make the drug legally unrestricted. Since the passage of the Anti-Drug Abuse Act of 1986 all analogs of controlled substances have themselves become controlled substances. The changes in chemical structure may also change its potency, length of action, euphoric effects, and toxicity" (NIDA 1987: 27).

SUMMARY

Endorphins are natural pain relievers in the human body, and more study is needed to uncover their possible connection to opiate addiction. Depressants inhibit the release of stress hormones and stress-related neurotransmitters, a stress-reduction method that becomes addicting in some people. Heroin's effects include the rush, the high, the nod, and being straight, but tolerance reduces or eliminates the high and the nod. The dangers of heroin include overdose as well as the risk of hepatitis and AIDS through the use of shared needles. Barbiturate effects vary significantly by user (and user expectation), but drug abusers often take them in addition to alcohol or other drugs or to counteract the effects of stimulant drugs. Barbiturate use with other CNS depressants is extremely dangerous and even lethal. Benzodiazepines are prescribed for sleep or anxiety problems, and their abuse is often in combination with other controlled substances. Alcohol is a more complex substance than other depressants, affecting several neurotransmitters and receptor sites in the brain and acting as a stimulant in low doses before the onset of its depressant effect. Chronic use of alcohol negatively affects all the body's organs and systems: brain and nervous system, heart and circulatory system, liver and digestive system, and endocrine system. Inhalants are generally household products, and their abuse produces mild euphoria, lightheadedness, and exhilaration. Chemical variations of drugs have been developed over the years—sometimes to get around restrictions on controlled drugs. They can be as potent or more so than other drugs.

INTERNET CONNECTIONS

Center for Substance Abuse Research: www.cesar.umd.edu
College on Problems of Drug Dependence: www.views.vcu.edu/cpdd
National Institute on Alcohol Abuse and Alcoholism: www.niaaa.nih.gov
Rutgers University Center of Alcohol Studies: www.rci.Rutgers.edu
Society for the Study of Addiction: www.addiction-ssa.org
UCLA Drug Abuse Research Center: www.medsch.ucla.edu/som/npi/DARC

REVIEW QUESTIONS

1. What is the relationship between pain and endorphins?
2. How can a deficiency in endorphins explain heroin use?
3. How does heroin affect the user?
4. How does the concept of tolerance help explain addiction?
5. Why would heroin addicts who do not intend to abandon the use of heroin enter a drug treatment program without being coerced?
6. For heroin users, what are the differences between the "rush," the "high," and the "nod"?
7. How does heroin impair homeostatic functions?
8. Why is a heroin overdose life threatening?
9. What is the effect of barbiturates on the user?
10. How are the different barbiturates classified?
11. How does methaqualone affect the user?
12. What are the medical uses of sedatives?
13. Why is alcohol considered a food?

14. What are the three classes of alcohol?
15. Why is alcohol referred to as a regulated drug?
16. How is alcohol similar to heroin?
17. How does alcohol differ from heroin?
18. What are the dangers of alcohol abuse?
19. What are the effects of inhalants and solvents?
20. What are the dangers involved in using inhalants and solvents?
21. What are designer drugs?

CHAPTER 5

Stimulants

Stimulants produce profound subjective well-being with alertness. Normal pleasures are magnified and anxiety is decreased. Self-confidence and self-perceptions of mastery increase. Social inhibitions are reduced and interpersonal communication is facilitated. All aspects of the personal environment take on intensified qualities but without hallucinatory perceptual distortions. Emotionality and sexual feelings are enhanced.

—Frank Gawin, M. Elena Khalsa, and Everett Elinwood, Jr. (1994: 113)

As the term *stimulants* indicates, substances in this category stimulate the central nervous system. In moderation they enhance mood, increase alertness, and relieve fatigue. Two commonly used stimulants are nicotine, found in tobacco products, and caffeine, an active ingredient in coffee, tea, and some soft drinks. Used in moderation, these substances tend to relieve malaise and increase alertness.

More powerful stimulants such as cocaine and amphetamines are taken orally, sniffed, smoked, and injected. Smoking, snorting, or injecting stimulants produces a sudden sensation known as a "rush" or a "flash." Abuse is often associated with a pattern of binge use, that is, consuming large doses of stimulants sporadically. Heavy users may inject themselves every few hours, continuing until they have depleted their drug supply or reached a point of delirium, psychosis, and physical exhaustion. During this period of heavy use, all other interests become secondary to re-creating the initial euphoric rush. Tolerance can develop rapidly, and both physical and psychological dependence occur. Abrupt cessation, even after a weekend binge, is commonly followed by depression, anxiety, drug craving, and extreme fatigue ("crash").

It has been hypothesized that stimulants such as cocaine and amphetamine may compensate for a deficiency in three neurotransmitters—dopamine (DA), norepinephrine (NE), which acts with epinephrine (**adrenaline**), and serotonin (SE)—that can otherwise result in apathy and depression (Khantzian 1985; Nunes and Rosecan 1987), bolstering the theory of drug use as being self-medication.

As discussed in Chapter 3, in the presynaptic terminals of normal persons, monoamine oxidases, or MAO, control the level of neurotransmitters. In some individuals an excess of MAO lowers the amount of dopamine, norepinephrine, and serotonin, which results in depression (Sunderwirth 1985). Indeed, MAO-inhibiting drugs such as Nardil (phenelzine) are medically prescribed to treat depression. The use of powerful stimulants by some persons and not others, given that both groups have equal access to these drugs, may be explained by physiological deficiencies, much as the use of insulin by diabetics can be explained—nondiabetics will not find the ingestion of insulin a positive experience. The users of stimulants, according to this view, are attempting to reduce inner tension and increase energy and activity levels (see, for example, Fishbein, Lozovsky, and Jaffe 1989).

At the other extreme, in persons who are highly extroverted, perhaps even manic, stimulants make more dopamine available to the brain and are thus highly rewarding even in small doses, making such persons susceptible to addiction (Goleman 1990). In 1995, a variant of the dopamine receptor D_4 was found to be associated with "novelty seeking": persons with this genetic factor tend to be extroverted, quick-tempered, impulsive, and easily bored (Angier 1995). Several teams of researchers working independently have reported that such persons possess a gene that makes them especially responsive to dopamine, and this is believed related to participation in extreme sports such as skydiving and ice climbing, as well as drug use (Koerber 1997).

Scientists have also discovered a mechanism that appears to account for the different levels of euphoria people experience when taking a stimulant. People who have lower levels of dopamine D_2 receptors in their brains were found to be more inclined to like the effects of a mild stimulant than those who have higher levels of these receptors, who were found to dislike the drug's effects (NIDA 1999d). Dopamine deficiencies in the brain cannot be remedied by introducing corrective substances because the blood-brain barrier prevents most substances from reaching it.

Cocaine

Coca is a flowering bush or shrub (*Erythroxylon coca*) that in cultivation stands 3 to 6 feet high, and yields at most 4 ounces of waxy, elliptical leaves that are about 1 percent cocaine by weight. Conversion into cocaine hydrochloride—powdered cocaine—requires several steps. Immediately after harvesting, the leaves are pulverized, soaked, and shaken in a mixture of alcohol and benzene (a coal tar derivative) for about three days. After the liquid is drained, sulfuric or hydrochloric acid—depending on the alkaloid content of the leaves—is added, and the solution is again shaken. Sodium carbonate is added, forming a precipitate, which is washed with kerosene and chilled, leaving behind crystals of crude cocaine known as coca paste, which is allowed to dry.

Between 200 and 500 kilograms of coca leaves are required to make 1 kilo of paste; 2.5 kilos of coca paste are converted into 1 kilo of cocaine base—a malodorous, rough, greenish yellow powder of more than 66 percent purity—and finally into cocaine hydrochloride by being treated with ether, acetone, and hydrochloric acid. One kilo of cocaine base is synthesized into 1 kilo of cocaine hydrochloride, a white crystalline powder that is about 95 percent pure. Those who process the substance are exposed to noxious fumes and the real danger of an explosion.

In the United States cocaine hydrochloride is "cut" (diluted) for street sale by adding sugars (such as lactose, inositol, and mannitol) or talcum powder, borax, or other neutral substances, as well as local anesthetics such as procaine hydrochloride (Novocain) or lidocaine hydrochloride. (Novocain is sometimes mixed with mannitol or lactose and

---

Ingredients for Producing Cocaine Hydrochloride

- Coca leaves
- Acetone (paint and varnish solvent)
- Benzene (common solvent)
- Sulfuric or hydrochloric acid (used in batteries, for cleaning metal, and preparing food products)
- Sodium carbonate (used in glass, soap, and cleaners)
- Kerosene (available as a cleaning agent and as fuel for lamps and stoves)
- Ammonia (commonly used to make cleaning agents, fertilizers, and synthetic fibers)
- Lime (used to make bricks and mortar)
- Potassium permanganate (used for purifying water and tanning leather)
- Ethyl ether (a widely used solvent)

The Drug Enforcement Administration monitors the sales of some of these precursor chemicals. Manufacturers are required to report their domestic sales of more than 50 gallons a month and foreign sales of more than 500 gallons a month.

---

sold as cocaine.) After cutting, cocaine typically has a consumer sale purity of less than 20 percent, although huge increases in the availability of cocaine can result in a level as high as 50 percent and a concomitant increase in the number of emergency room admissions for cocaine overdoses.

Effects of Cocaine

The substance typically enters the bloodstream by being snorted into the nostrils through a straw or rolled paper or from a "coke spoon." "Because cocaine is a vasoconstrictor, it inhibits its own absorption, and the time it takes to reach peak concentration gets longer as the dose gets larger" (Karch 1996: 19). Some abusers will take it intravenously, which is the only way to ingest 100 percent of the drug. Because this is a more efficient method, users with limited funds may buy and inject cocaine as a group. In Brazil, the result of this practice has been a dramatic increase in the number of AIDS cases (Brooke 1991a). Cocaine may also be absorbed through genital or rectal application, during which its anesthetic properties prolong vaginal intercourse or suppress the discomfort of anal intercourse. This extremely dangerous practice can lead to seizure, coma, and death (Karch 1998). Inhaled, the drug's effects peak in 15 to 20 minutes, and disappear in 60 to 90 minutes. Intravenous use results in an intense feeling of euphoria that crests in 3 to 5 minutes, and wanes in 30 to 40 minutes. (Smoking crack cocaine is discussed later.)

Cocaine
Uses and Effects

Classification:	Stimulant
CSA Schedule:	Schedule II
Trade or Other Names:	Coke, flake, snow, crack
Medical Uses:	Local anesthetic
Physical Dependence:	Possible
Psychological Dependence:	High
Tolerance:	Yes
Duration (hours):	1–2
Usual Method:	Sniffed, smoked, injected
Possible Effects:	Increased alertness, excitation, euphoria, increased pulse rate and blood pressure, insomnia, loss of appetite
Effects of Overdose:	Agitation, increased body temperature, hallucinations, convulsions, possible death
Withdrawal Syndrome:	Apathy, long periods of sleep, irritability, depression, disorientation

Source: U.S. Drug Enforcement Administration

Neurological Effects. Cocaine binds to specific receptor sites on brain membranes (Hanbauer 1988), and it is theorized that this triggers the release of dopamine, serotonin, and norepinephrine (Weiss and Mirin 1987). These neurotransmitters enhance mood and at high enough doses produce feelings of euphoria by activating the sympathetic nervous system, giving rise to increased heart rate, blood pressure, breathing rate, body temperature, and blood sugar (Washton 1989). The substance also acts on the hypothalamus to decrease appetite and reduces the need for sleep by inducing the release of stimulant neurotransmitters. In addition to stimulating their release, cocaine also blocks or inhibits the reabsorption of dopamine, norepinephrine, and serotonin by the discharging neurons, by preventing a reuptake transporter from performing its usual function (Figure 5.1).[1] As a result, neurotransmitters continue to bombard their receptor sites. The neurons remain in

---

[1] A strain of mice bred for the absence of the dopamine transporter are impervious to cocaine; they are also highly active, fail to eat, and often die from exhaustion (Grady 1996).

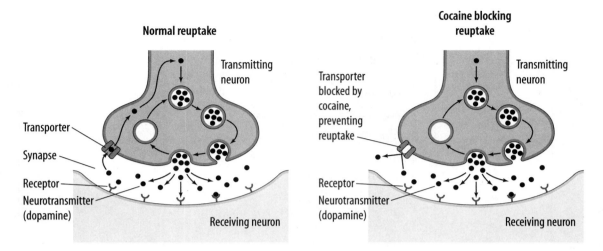

FIGURE 5.1

Cocaine blocking reuptake of neurotransmitters such as dopamine, norepinephrine, and serotonin. This results in their accumulation in the synapse, stimulating the receiving neuron.

a state of excitement, the brain is stimulated accordingly, and euphoria increases (Holloway 1991; Sunderwirth 1985).

Roy Wise reports that DA is the key to cocaine's euphoric qualities: "Cocaine also blocks noradrenaline and serotonin reuptake, but these actions and cocaine's well-known anesthetic effects appear to contribute little, if anything, to the rewarding effects of cocaine" (1994: 191). As the supply of dopamine depletes, however, depression sets in. And research has discovered that cocaine-dependent persons have fewer DA receptors than normal controls, which also helps explain why they feel depressed when not on cocaine (Holloway 1991).

In 1998, however, new studies pointed to the importance of serotonin: A deficiency in this neurotransmitter was found to be linked to a desire for cocaine (Blakeslee 1998; Rocha et al. 1998; Parsons, Weiss, and Koob 1998). It was also revealed that genetically altered mice continued to find cocaine rewarding even when it failed to increase their (already high) levels of dopamine (NIDA 1999c). Depletion of both DA and SE in specific brain regions that control drive and affect may contribute to craving and depression evident in the aftermath of cocaine abuse; "but when cocaine is readministered, frontal brain regions may be reactivated, again contributing to the compulsion to use cocaine" (Bolla, Cadet, and London 1998: 281). While the case for dopamine's centrality remains airtight, another neurotransmitter, glutamate (or mGluR5) appears to play an independent role in the rewarding qualities of cocaine. Indeed, research in Geneva, Switzerland, reveals that glutamate's role in cocaine dependence is even more central than dopamine's (Hollon 2002).

Certain regions within the brain, when stimulated, produce feelings of pleasure. One neural system that appears to be most affected by cocaine originates in this region (ventral tegmental area—VTA) located deep within the brain. Cocaine short-circuits the reward pathways of the brain (Dunwiddie 1988), and in laboratory animals cocaine has usurped other rewards such as food and sex. In laboratory tests monkeys pressed a bar as

When inhaled, the effects of cocaine peak in about 20 minutes but disappear within 90 minutes. Users have an initial sense of euphoria, with illusions of increased mental alertness. When the drug wears off, depression usually follows.

© J. Pickerell/The Image Works

many as 12,800 times for an infusion of 0.5 milligrams of cocaine. "No other drug, including opiates and amphetamine, has been reported to be more potent than cocaine in such tests" (Geary 1987: 31). The ultimate consequence of unlimited access to cocaine is death. Without unlimited access, however, monkeys are able to self-regulate their cocaine use (Siegel 1989).

Would monkeys in the wild succumb to the allure of unlimited amounts of cocaine? Laboratory conditions do not replicate the animals' natural environment, nor are the results of such experiments readily generalizable to humans who have such species-exclusive traits as a sense of values and a desire for self-control (Peele 1985). Some dopamine agonists are self-administered by and rewarding to animals while they do not produce euphoria in humans (Rothman 1994). Furthermore, we know that the use of cocaine is related to behavioral stress (*Problems of Drug Dependence* 1997), and monkeys in the laboratory setting are under considerable stress.

Physiological Effects. In small doses, cocaine will bring about extreme euphoria and indifference to pain, along with illusions of increased mental and sensory alertness, and physical strength: "A few hundredths of a gram of cocaine hydrochloride, chopped finely and arranged on a smooth surface into several lines, or rows of powder, can be snorted into the nose through a rolled piece of paper in a few seconds. The inhalation shortly gives rise to feelings of elation and a sense of clarity or power of thought, feelings that pass away for most people in about half an hour" (Van Dyke and Byck 1982: 128). At higher doses, however, the drug has the potential "to produce megalomania and feelings of omnipotence in most individuals" (M. Gold et al. 1986: 44). Cocaine causes the body to feel as if there were an impending threat, a response to stimuli that causes the release of stimulating neurotransmitters (dopamine and norepinephrine): "In essence the co-caine stimulated reactions in the body are mimicking a natural physiological stress re-sponse; the generalized adrenergic discharge stimulates the energy producing mechanisms to prepare the CNS and skeletal muscles for 'fight' or 'flight.' The body feels the chemistry of fright, tension and anxiety, but the brain gives the message that everything is better than fine" (M. Gold et al. 1986: 38).

Studies suggest that cocaine actually heightens the body's sensitivity to stress, al-though the user fails to recognize that this is occurring. Cocaine activates stress systems, much like when an opiate addict goes into withdrawal, but the person perceives this as part of the cocaine rush because cocaine is also stimulating the parts of the brain that are involved in feeling pleasure. When cocaine's effects wear off and the addict goes into with-drawal, the stress systems are again activated. This time, the cocaine addict perceives the activation as unpleasant because cocaine is no longer stimulating the pleasure circuits in the brain. Because cocaine switches on the stress systems both when it is active and dur-ing withdrawal, these systems rapidly become hypersensitive (Kreek 1997).

Chemically similar substances such as lidocaine (Xylocaine) and procaine (Novo-cain)—as dental patients recognize—eliminate all feeling when applied topically or subcutaneously. Single small doses of procaine, when taken intranasally or smoked, pro-duce the same euphoric response as does cocaine in experienced cocaine users. Users can-not distinguish between the two substances, and tests indicate that laboratory animals will work as hard for procaine as they will for cocaine (Van Dyke and Byck 1982). In lab-oratory tests with animals, however, while procaine served as a reinforcer similar to co-caine, lidocaine did not (Balster 1988).

Coca Paste and Cocaine Combinations

Versions of the drug other than cocaine hydrochloride have become popular among cer-tain abusers. Coca paste, which is typically smoked with either tobacco or marijuana products, is used extensively in cocaine-processing countries. Because it requires less pro-cessing than cocaine, coca paste—called *bazuco*—is popular among low-income groups in these countries and has become a major abuse problem in Colombia. In the late 1980s the substance made its way into the United States, where it became known as "bubble gum" to young abusers because of the phonetic association of *bazuco* with Bazooka bubble gum. The substance usually results from an error in the water/sulfuric acid ratio. The paste has at least traces of a host of dangerous chemicals used in its pro-duction, including kerosene, sulfuric acid, leaded gasoline, and potassium perman-ganate, which can cause irreversible damage to liver, lungs, and brain.

Some intravenous abusers combine cocaine with heroin—a practice known as "speedballing." This was the combination that led to the death of comedian John Belushi in 1982. It appears that heroin enhances the subjective effects of cocaine, al-though the neurobiology of the interaction is unclear. Because heroin and cocaine work on different parts of the mesolimbic dopamine neurons, they can be combined to pro-duce even more intense dopamine activation. The heroin increases cell firing and dopamine release, while the cocaine keeps the released dopamine in the synaptic cleft longer, thereby intensifying and prolonging its effects; users show very rapid psychological and physiological deterioration. Although speedball use produces extremely intense activation of brain reward systems, it is often short-lived because this drug combination is associated with a very high fatality rate—the combination of cocaine and heroin is perhaps the most dangerous form of illicit substance use (information from the Addiction Research Unit/SUNY at Buffalo). Some cocaine users also ingest heroin to soften and prolong the impact of cocaine.

Crack

Crack, the drug abuser's answer to fast food, became popular among young men and women during the 1980s.[2] The drug is relatively cheap, $5 to $10 a "rock," although those hooked on crack report spending between $100 and $200 a day on the substance.[3] Crack is generally sold on the street in small glass vials or tiny plastic bags.[4] Versions of crack may contain any combination of freebase residue, concentrated caffeine, or different amphetamines.

While cocaine hydrochloride cannot easily be smoked—the melting and vaporization point is very high (195° Centigrade)—freeing the alkaloid from the hydrochloride attachment (**freebase**) will produce purified crystals of cocaine base that readily vaporize at 98° Centigrade. Cocaine cooked in a mixture of sodium bicarbonate (baking soda) and water becomes hard when heat-dried—this is what is called crack. The soaplike substance is then cut into bars or chips (sometimes called "quarter rocks") and smoked. This freebase cocaine can be crushed and smoked in a special glass pipe or sprinkled on a tobacco or marijuana product. The term *crack* refers to the crackling sound heard when the mixture is smoked (heated), presumably from the sodium bicarbonate.

Dennis Watlington, a former crack user, states that crack is typically smoked in a glass pipe about 5 inches long and a quarter inch in diameter with a metal screen at the top to hold a small clump of the substance. When lit, the substance melts and clings to the screen with some of it oozing down inside the stem where it dries and forms a hard residue that can later be scraped off and smoked. "The most satisfying way to smoke crack," he notes, "is to insert this stem into a glass bowl the size of an espresso cup. Through a second pipe inserted into the side of the bowl, the smoker pulls the smoke after it collects in quantity in the bowl" (1987: 150).

Because crack is inhaled directly into the lungs, bypassing much of the circulatory system en route to the brain, it takes about 5 seconds to impact—even faster than intra-

---

[2]For a thorough examination of the different facets of crack, see Chitwood, Rivera, and Inciardi (1996).

[3]For a discussion of the comparative costs of crack and cocaine hydrochloride, see Caulkins (1997).

[4]Crack is frequently smoked in "crack houses." For a look at the social organization of crack houses, see Elifson and Elifson (1993).

When cocaine is cooked with sodium bicarbonate and water, it becomes crack. Popular in the 1980s and considered the "fast food" of drugs, the crack high is achieved in about five seconds and is often described as a sexual euphoria.

© Schwartz/Black Star

venous ingestion. When "crack is heated, the drug crosses the blood-brain barrier in only a few seconds, providing a virtually instantaneous 'high' and intense gratification, often described as a 'sexual euphoria,' or orgasm" (McCoy, Miles, and Inciardi 1995: 172). "Crack can excite sexual desires while inhibiting the ability to achieve orgasm, creating sexual encounters that are prolonged and more conducive to the spread of AIDS" (Drug Enforcement Administration 1994: 3).

The vapors first produce a potent *rush*: "This 'rush' lasts a few seconds, and is replaced by a euphoric excitation that lasts for several minutes. A five to twenty minute period of less pleasurable hyperexcitability follows. Then the 'ultimate high' degenerates into the ultimate low" (NIDA 1986: 4). "After smoking crack repeatedly, the user develops an intense craving for more. Although it can take months or even years for a nasal cocaine user to progress from recreational to compulsive use, this can happen within days to weeks with crack" (Rosecan, Spitz, and Gross 1987: 299).

Interviews with crack users in drug treatment programs revealed the apparent power of this substance:

Despite the many years of using other drugs, the experience with Crack was quite different. Most respondents had been in control of their drug use, even those who had been using very heavily. The majority (63 percent) had never needed treatment for their drug use before using Crack. The experience with Crack, however, was very much a jolt, for which these users were not prepared in spite of their past experience. For many it was a very frightening experience. Respondents remembered feelings and behaviors under the influence of Crack that they had never experienced before—the irritability, rage, and aggression. Most of the clients had held jobs and valued the money they earned. Now, in retrospect, the loss of so much spent on Crack was incomprehensible to them. (Frank et al. 1987: 12)

That crack is smoked rather than injected has increased its appeal. Indeed, it constitutes the first psychoactive drug experience of many young abusers, who try it even before alcohol and marijuana (Rosecan, Spitz, and Gross 1987). Unfortunately, "because of the large, concentrated doses that reach the brain, seizures are more likely to occur from smoking cocaine than from snorting it, and smoking can lead more easily to respiratory failure and/or cardiac arrest" (Washton 1989: 16). It was crack that led to the death of college basketball star Len Bias, 22 years old, and professional football player Don Rogers, 23.

Reports—some would say hysteria—about the power of crack to produce dependence have subsided, and today it is rarely mentioned in the media. While crack is admittedly a strongly dependence-producing substance, recent research indicates that it is not the all-powerful drug the media had portrayed. Crack appears to be less addictive than nicotine, although more addictive than alcohol (Kolata 1989c; Egan 1999b). A study of seventy-nine crack users in Toronto revealed a "lack of strong evidence to support the view that use of the drug is necessarily compulsive. Over half of the respondents had never or rarely experienced a craving to take crack" (Cheung, Erickson, and Landau 1991: 133). There has been a dramatic change in the crack-using population, as adolescents began to reject the substance and "crackheads," no longer considered "cool," became outcasts. Crack users today are more likely to be older—late twenties, early thirties—males.

Cocaine Tolerance

Many researchers have reported that tolerance to the euphoric effects of cocaine occurs with repeated use, although the biological basis underlying sensitization or tolerance to cocaine is not yet fully understood (Izenwasser and Unterwald 1994; Zahniser et al. 1988; Grinspoon and Bakalar 1985; O'Brien and Cohen 1984). This tolerance causes the abuser to increase the dosage. "Chronic users often find themselves caught in a futile, obsessive chase to recapture the original cocaine 'high,' but as dosages and frequency increase, so does the user's tolerance to the euphoric effects" (Washton, Stone, and Henrickson 1988: 367). And "in face of dose escalation, one might eventually achieve blood levels of cocaine high enough to induce toxic local anesthetic effects" that include panic attacks and the risk of seizures (Post and Weiss 1988: 232). However, Steven Karch (1996), a medical examiner, reports that because of tolerance, chronic cocaine users may consume massive amounts without apparent ill effects. There is evidence of cocaine tolerance in binge-type ingestion (Kreek 1997).

Roger Weiss and Steven Mirin report a form of reverse tolerance: "long-term users may experience more excitatory effects from the same, or even smaller, doses of the drug," a phenomenon referred to as **kindling** (1987: 48).

Cocaine Withdrawal

After frequent and high doses of cocaine, the failure to continue ingestion produces a withdrawal syndrome characterized by psychological depression, irritability, extreme fatigue, and prolonged periods of restless sleep. James Inciardi states that this syndrome is not necessarily physiological—it may simply be the result of an emotional letdown when heavy abusers try to discontinue the drug—"they *think* they have a physical need for cocaine" (1986: 79).

Strong cravings for the substance and the malaise that follows cessation are possibly brain-mediated behavioral changes indicating physical dependence, and the elevation in reward thresholds as a result of cocaine use could trigger a withdrawal effect after use is discontinued (Koob et al. 1994). "When the cocaine- or amphetamine-dependent person is not taking one of these drugs, dopamine release will be diminished to levels lower than normal, which could contribute to the **anhedonia** [inability to enjoy routine pleasures], dysphoria [chronic discontent], and other symptoms of withdrawal that motivate repeated drug taking" (Hyman and Nestler 1996: 158). Chronic overstimulation of postsynaptic DA receptors could lead to a new adaptive state so that continued use of the drug would be required to maintain homeostasis (Bolla, Cadet, and London 1998). Despite the lack of signs of physical dependence, animals given free access to cocaine will continue to self-administer the drug until death, something they will not do for opiates (Geary 1987). The *Merck Manual* refers to cocaine as "probably the best example of a drug to which neither tolerance nor physical dependence develops, but to which psychic dependence develops that can lead to addiction" (Berkow 1982: 1427). While the cocaine withdrawal syndrome does not generally require medical treatment or pharmacotherapy, the risk of relapse is highest during withdrawal (McCance 1997).

"Withdrawal in [cocaine-] dependent subjects is not characterized by the obvious physical signs like those observed with opiates or sedative-hypnotics" (Koob et al. 1994: 7). Indeed, "there is no withdrawal syndrome after abruptly stopping cocaine. That is, the body has never developed a need for cocaine to maintain homeostasis" (Washton and Washton 1993: 17). "The absence of a clear-cut withdrawal syndrome and serious medical risk following abrupt cessation of the drug use obviates the need either for switching the cocaine-dependent patient to a substitute drug or for having to detoxify the patient by means of a gradual withdrawal procedure, as is routinely done in the treatment of heroin addicts and severe alcoholics" (Washton, Stone, and Henrickson 1988: 376). However, one study found evidence of cardiac and mood-related symptoms during short-term abstinence from chronic crack use that may indicate specific withdrawal phenomena (Kajdasz et al. 1999).

While tolerance can mask sensitization to cocaine-induced euphoria, craving persists. During early abstinence, persisting tolerance masks sensitization, but as tolerance wears off, sensitization becomes manifest as craving based on environmental cues increase (Bonson et al. 2002). Thus, abstinent cocaine users no longer experiencing withdrawal symptoms develop craving on returning to environments linked to the use of cocaine (discussed in Chapter 3).

Medical Use of Cocaine

In addition to its anesthetizing qualities, cocaine constricts blood vessels when applied topically. It is the only local anesthetic that has this effect, and cocaine was the anesthetic of choice for eye surgery because of this ability to limit the flow of blood. However, when it was discovered that the reduced flow could damage the surface of the eye, cocaine was no longer recommended for use in ophthalmology. It continues to be used in surgery of the mucous membranes of the ear, nose, and throat and for procedures that require passing a tube through the nose or throat (Van Dyke and Byck 1982), for which there are about 200,000 operations a year (P. White 1989). Plastic surgeons use it for nose alterations.

Dangers of Cocaine Use

In "very small and occasional doses," argues Inciardi, "cocaine is no more harmful than equally moderate doses of alcohol or marijuana" (1986: 79). One research effort found that "experimental use of cocaine during adolescence has benign consequences over a one-year period," although the researchers could not deny the possibility of long-term negative consequences (Newcomb and Bentler 1986: 273). Large doses of cocaine, how- ever, intensify each of the drug's reactions and can sometimes cause irrational behavior. In heavy abusers the euphoria is often accompanied by intensified heartbeat, sweating, dilation of pupils, and a rise in body temperature. After the initial euphoria, depression, irritability, insomnia, and in more serious instances, paranoia may result. Extreme reac- tions, such as delirium, hallucinations, muscle spasms, and chest pain, may appear. In a small of number of persons—the risk appears to be genetically determined—high levels of cocaine ingestion lead to a psychosis syndrome characterized by bizarre, paranoid ag- itation that frequently ends in death (Karch 1998).

Chronic users can also suffer from "cocaine bugs" (**formication,** known as Magnon's syndrome), a sensation similar to that of bugs crawling under the skin. In ex- treme cases, the sensation may become so great that the user will cut open his or her skin to get at "them." Less extreme reactions cause the user to scratch and pick at the "bugs," causing sores.

When people mix cocaine and alcohol consumption, they are compounding the danger each drug poses and unknowingly forming a complex chemical experiment within their bodies. Researchers have found that the human liver combines cocaine and alcohol and manufactures a third substance, cocaethylene, that intensifies co- caine's euphoric effects, while possibly increasing the risk of sudden death (*Crack and Cocaine* 2001).

Cardiac and Circulatory Dangers. Cocaine causes blood vessels to constrict and increases heart rate and blood pressure. As a result, the heart requires more oxygen-rich blood to nourish its muscle cells (Karch 1996). In persons whose coronary arteries are narrowed by atherosclerosis, reactions can range from mild angina to a fatal heart attack. Even in persons with normal coronary arteries, the ingesting of cocaine has resulted in angina and heart attacks believed to be a consequence of spasms that reduce or shut off the flow of the oxygenated blood that nourishes the heart.

There is also evidence that cocaine can painlessly and permanently damage heart muscles: "Cocaine causes vascular disease. Vessels throughout the body can be involved, but the brunt of the injury is borne by the heart" (Karch 1996: 83). Several thousand persons a year die as the result of sudden cardiac death induced by cocaine—the exact number is unknown because diagnosing the cause of death in such cases is quite difficult, and the mechanism(s) causing this fatal outcome is unknown (Karch 1996). Using advanced brain scanning techniques, researchers have found that the temporary narrowing of blood vessels caused by cocaine results in a cumulative effect—more cocaine use, more narrowing of the arteries. This suggests that heavy cocaine users are susceptible to strokes, bleeding inside the brain, thinking and memory deficits, and other brain disorders (NIDA 1998d; Bolla, Cadet, and London 1998). The American Heart Association (1999) reports that cocaine can lead to the development of aneurysms—ballooning-out of the wall of an artery—in heart arteries. An aneurysm in a heart artery may lead to a heart attack, while an aneurysm in an artery of the brain could burst and trigger a stroke. Some aneurysms do not cause symptoms, while others may cause chest pain and other coronary artery disease symptoms. The lack of judgment, unreliability, poor foresight, difficulty making decisions, disinhibition, apathy, euphoria, and irritability exhibited by chronic cocaine abusers appear to be related to damage caused by the drug in the part of the brain (prefrontal lobe) that controls or modifies these behaviors (Bolla, Cadet, and London 1998).

Since cocaine causes blood vessels to constrict, snorting can cause the cartilage in the middle of the nose to be deprived of oxygen. When the drug wears off, the tissue swells, which is why cocaine users frequently have stuffy, runny noses. Eventually, gradual deterioration of the nasal cartilage can cause the nose to collapse. The constriction of blood vessels in the nose also means a delay in the absorption of cocaine. Thus, intravenous injection of the drug is more efficient and quickly produces a powerful rush; it may also cause abscesses on the skin. This form of ingestion "produces the more debilitating effects of psychoses and paranoid delusions" (Inciardi 1986: 81), and is also more likely than other forms of ingestion to have fatal results.

Crack Babies.   Cocaine use by pregnant women has been linked to various abnormalities in their infants because the substance reduces the supply of blood and oxygen to the fetus (see, for example, Mayes 1992 and Woods 1993). Children born to crack-abusing mothers exhibit serious emotional difficulties that may hinder psychological and social development (Blakeslee 1989).

But these difficulties are more likely caused by poor prenatal nutrition and health than by the pharmacology of cocaine. Researchers have had difficulty isolating maternal drug use from the typically negative environment in which the children are raised: "If you grow up in such a lousy environment, things are so bad already that cocaine exposure doesn't seem to make much difference" (Barry Lester quoted in Begley 1999: 62). More recent research has revealed that "snow babies" are neither the emotional and cognitive cripples that many predicted, nor the perfectly normal kids that others have claimed. "Worries that 'crack babies' would never be able to function in society have turned out to be unfounded for the great majority" (Leshner 1999b: 3).

Crack/cocaine exposure in utero has not been demonstrated to affect physical growth and does not appear to independently affect developmental scores in the first 6 years (although there are insufficient data to assess this for infants born preterm). Findings are mixed regarding early motor development, but any effect appears to be transient and may, in fact, reflect tobacco exposure (Chavkin 2001). Preschool children of crack cocaine-using mothers do not appear to suffer any language or cognitive development problems. However, in one controlled study they exhibited higher rates of emotional and behavioral problems than children from similar backgrounds whose mothers did not use cocaine. It was not determined whether this is a function of the drug or the postnatal environment (Hawley et al. 1995).

"The 'crack baby' became a convenient symbol for an aggressive war on drug users because of the implication that anyone who is selfish enough to irreparably damage an innocent child for the sake of a quick high deserves retribution. This image, promoted by the mass media, makes it easier to advocate a simplistic punitive response than to address the complex causes of drug use" (Chavkin 2001).

Cocaine and Sex. Although cocaine has the reputation of being an aphrodisiac, heavy use may cause male abusers to become impotent or incapable of ejaculation, and females can experience difficulty in reaching an orgasm. Freebasing and intravenous use increase sexual desire but not performance. In fact, cocaine may produce spontaneous ejaculation without sexual activity and can replace the sex partner of either gender (M. Gold et al. 1986).[5] Arnold and Nanette Washton (1993) report that cocaine produced hypersexuality and sexual compulsivity in their patients, and "sexual feelings and fantasies often trigger powerful urges and cravings for cocaine." Crack cocaine has been associated with the spread of sexually transmitted diseases, especially AIDS, the result of young women having unsafe sex with multiple partners in exchange for crack (Chitwood, Rivera, Inciardi 1996).

Cognition. The detrimental effects of heavy cocaine use—two or more grams a week—on an individual's manual dexterity, problem solving, and other critical skills can last for up to a month after the drug was last taken. In one study, heavy cocaine users were outperformed by moderate users and nonusers on most tests measuring verbal memory, manual dexterity, and other cognitive skills. While the intensity (grams per week) of cocaine use was more closely associated with decreased performance than the duration of use, all cocaine users studied experienced reduced cognitive function. Dose-related effects were seen primarily on tasks involving the prefrontal cortex, which is the area of the brain most responsible for attention/concentration, planning, and reasoning. The heaviest cocaine users showed slower median reaction times and poorer attention and concentration (NIDA 1999e).

---

[5]Cocaine has anesthetic properties, however, and is sometimes applied directly to the head of the penis or to the clitoris to anesthetize the tissues, prolonging intercourse by retarding orgasm.

Cocaine for Recreational Use

"The justification for outlawing cocaine was mainly the supposed psychological and physiological consequences of prolonged use. But the law does not distinguish, as we must, between moderate and excessive doses. The more spectacular consequences of cocaine abuse are not typical of the drug's effects as it is normally used any more than the phenomena associated with alcoholism are typical of the ordinary consumption of that drug" (Grinspoon and Bakalar 1976: 119).

"Our findings do not indicate that occasional cocaine use inevitably leads to severe drug dependency and major dysfunction. However, it also cannot be concluded that occasional or so-called 'recreational' cocaine use is safe or harmless" (M. Gold et al. 1986: 49).

Amphetamines

"Among the commonly used psychoactive drugs," note Lester Grinspoon and Peter Hedblom, "the amphetamines have one of the most formidable potentials for psychological, physical, and social harm" (1975: 258). Unlike cocaine, amphetamines are products of the laboratory—synthetic drugs. Although their chemical structures are distinctly different (Snyder 1986) and amphetamine has no anesthetic properties, the effects of cocaine and amphetamines are similar. In fact, experienced intravenous cocaine users frequently identified amphetamine incorrectly as cocaine. In animal studies, cocaine and amphetamines often substitute for one another and have similar reinforcing patterns of self-administration (Balster 1988).

Legally produced amphetamine is taken in the form of tablets or capsules, while some abusers will crush the substance, dissolve it in water, and ingest it intravenously. There are three basic types of amphetamine, with the methyl-amphetamines having the greatest potential for abuse because they are fast acting and produce a rush. There are three types of methyl-amphetamine: dextro-methamphetamine (d-methamphetamine), dextro-levo methamphetamine (dl-methamphetamine), and levo-methamphetamine (l-methamphetamine). D-methamphetamine is the most potent and widely abused form of methamphetamine in the United States today. It is a white, odorless, and bitter-tasting crystalline powder that dissolves easily in water or alcohol ("Methamphetamine Abuse and Addiction" 2002).

According to the World Health Organization, **methamphetamine** is second only to marijuana as the most abused drug in the world. Methamphetamine is known by many street names such as speed, **crank,** go, crystal, crystal meth, and the "poor man's cocaine." It can be used by all of the common routes of illicit drug administration (inhalation, intranasal snorting, intravenous injection, or orally), but must be purified before it can be smoked. *Ice* is a purified form that is frequently sold as large crystals—*rocks*—

which are smoked. Like rock salt in size and appearance, ice produces a high reputed to last from 7 to 24 hours. Because of its purity, ice exaggerates all of the effects of methamphetamine, and overdoses are more common with ice because it is difficult for smokers to control the amount being inhaled. The substance could easily substitute for crack.

Ice rocks are made by melting methamphetamine crystals using a variety of techniques, but "the turkey bag method" is the most popular: Dry methamphetamine crystals are placed in an aluminum turkey roasting bag, which is then closed and dipped into boiling water until the methamphetamine melts. The melted material is then placed in cool water or in the refrigerator until it solidifies as a large crystal. The crystal is then cut into rocks that fit the various glass pipes used for smoking ice. Methamphetamine is usually smoked by inhaling it from a sheet of aluminum foil or through a glass pipe. When foil is used, the drug is heated in a crease of the foil until it vaporizes and is then inhaled via a straw. Pipes for smoking methamphetamine differ from those used for smoking crack—methamphetamine vaporizes at a much lower temperature than crack, so smoking it in a crack pipe at high heat would destroy it. Methamphetamine pipes have a large glass ball at the end for holding the methamphetamine, and a lighter is held under the ball to vaporize the drug. Air flow is regulated by a finger placed over a hole on top of the pipe. Some users reportedly prefer glass pipes for smoking methamphetamine because they fear developing Alzheimer's disease from using aluminum foil (Lukas 1996).

With $500 worth of chemicals, laboratory glassware, and a rudimentary knowledge of chemistry, an outlaw chemist can easily produce a pound of methamphetamine worth $20–30,000. As a result, hundreds of clandestine laboratories have sprouted up in remote regions throughout the United States. Recipes for manufacturing methamphetamine are widely available through pamphlets and the Internet. The clandestine manufacturing process has undergone substantial changes over the years. Phenyl-2-propanone (P2P), which was originally used in illegal manufacturing, is now controlled by the Drug Enforcement Administration as a bulk "immediate precursor" of methamphetamine. Accordingly, lab operators shifted to ephedrine, an ingredient common in over-the-counter cold and allergy remedies. Subsequent regulatory efforts led manufacturers to switch to the use of pseudoephedrine tablets. The yield from both methods is typically 70 percent of the precursor. Thus 1 kilogram of ephedrine yields 700 grams of methamphetamine.

During the 1980s, clandestine manufacturers using the precursor chemical pseudoephedrine created d-methamphetamine. For the user, d-methamphetamine is not only significantly more potent than other forms, but has fewer adverse side effects. D-methamphetamine eventually became the predominant form of methamphetamine illegally manufactured on the west coast of the United States during the late 1980s and is now widely associated with Mexican polydrug trafficking organizations (discussed in Chapter 11).

D-methamphetamine is clandestinely manufactured using the ephedrine or pseudoephedrine reduction method, producing quantities of up to 200 pounds at a time. Manufacturing is fairly simple—but quite dangerous—and almost all the ingredients needed are easily attainable either through commercial sources or by producing the chemicals clandestinely. Ephedrine, hydriodic acid, and red phosphorus are mixed and heated at various stages for about 12 hours to form d-methamphetamine in an acidic mixture. The mixture is strained through a bedsheet or pillowcase to remove the red phosphorus (which is not water soluble and could prove fatal if present in large doses). Sodium hydroxide is added to convert the acidic mixture to a basic one. Ice is then added to cool the resulting exothermic reaction to prevent evaporation or loss of product.

After this step, the mixture is transferred, most often to a 55-gallon drum with a spigot at its base. Freon (Coleman fuel or other solvents) is added to aid in the extraction of the d-methamphetamine from the sodium hydroxide solution. The Freon "drags" the d-methamphetamine to the bottom, and the clandestine lab cook drains it off. When treated with hydrogen chloride gas, the d-methamphetamine oil will convert into a white crystalline powder. Presses or mop buckets are used to remove excess Freon. Because Freon in its liquid state is heavier than water, the Freon along with the methamphetamine base goes to the bottom of the separatory vessel. However, if another solvent such as Coleman fuel is used, the methamphetamine base floats to the top because this solvent is lighter than water.

Some chemists die as a result of the toxic fumes produced or from explosions that can easily be ignited by a tiny spark or even the flip of a light switch. Illegal methamphetamine production also poses a serious environmental problem, because outlaws dump the chemical wastes into local streams or lakes or bury it in ditches. Methamphetamine labs are so contaminated that they pose a risk to law enforcement officers who seize them (Weingarten 1989).

Effects of Amphetamines

Methamphetamine increases the body's metabolism and produces euphoria, increases alertness, and gives the abuser a sense of increased energy. It can enable a shy person to become more outgoing and a tired person to become energized. Its ability to produce intensified feelings of sexual desire can, at least in part, explain its popularity. Although methamphetamine may impair the ability to operate a motor vehicle, it is often abused by truck drivers to stay awake during long hauls. The driver risks the danger of suddenly being rendered unconscious during the "crash" stage of methamphetamine use (discussed later).

Experiments have shown that animals, when given a choice, will readily operate pumps that inject them with amphetamine and will work hard to get more of the drug. Rhesus monkeys provided unlimited access to amphetamine will continually ingest the substance day and night, going almost completely without water, food, or sleep for 6 to 8 days, until they collapse into exhausted sleep for 2 days. Upon waking they show an immediate interest in food and water, and resume another week-long binge of amphetamine. When access to the drug is discontinued for a few weeks and the monkeys are returned to their cages, they will push the (now nonoperative) buttons for amphetamine an average of 4,000 times, indicating that a significant level of craving exists even in the absence of physiological dependence. When the substance is heroin, the monkeys will press the nonoperative buttons an average of 2,000 times, indicating that the craving for amphetamine is higher than for heroin (Grinspoon and Hedblom 1975).

Amphetamine/Methamphetamine
Uses and Effects

Classification:	Stimulant
CSA Schedule:	Schedule II
Trade or Other Names:	Biphetamine, Desoxyn, Dexedrine, Obetrol, ice, crank, speed
Medical Uses:	Attention deficit disorder, narcolepsy, weight control
Physical Dependence:	Possible
Psychological Dependence:	High
Tolerance:	Yes
Duration (hours):	2–4
Usual Method:	Oral, injected, smoked
Possible Effects:	Increased alertness, excitation, euphoria, increased pulse rate and blood pressure, insomnia, loss of appetite
Effects of Overdose:	Agitation, increased body temperature, hallucinations, convulsions, possible death
Withdrawal Syndrome:	Apathy, long periods of sleep, irritability, depression, disorientation

Source: Drug Enforcement Administration

Methamphetamine stimulates by triggering the release of dopamine, serotonin, and norepinephrine while inhibiting their reuptake (Selden et al. 1993—see Figure 5.2). Thus, like cocaine, methamphetamine mimics naturally occurring substances and causes a biochemical arousal—a "turn on"—without the presence of sensory input requiring such arousal. The body becomes physiologically activated, but it is a "false alarm." Because reuptake is blocked, the depletion of the body's stimulating neurotransmitters is believed responsible for the "crash" that results after the ingestion of high doses of amphetamine. The abuser becomes almost lifeless for one or more days, and the body uses the crash to replenish its depleted supply.

As with cocaine, in small doses methamphetamine will result in illusions of increased mental and sensory alertness and physical strength, an indifference to pain, and a "rush" or "flash" lasting a few minutes and described as extremely pleasurable. The rush is the

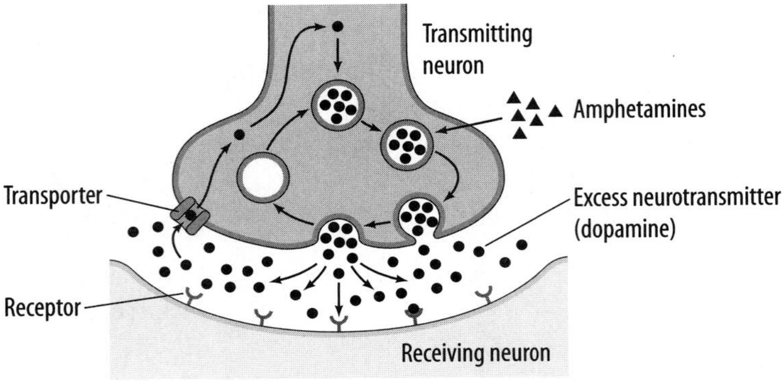

FIGURE 5.2
Methamphetamine stimulates the release of dopamine, serotonin, and norepinephrine but blocks their reuptake.

initial response the user feels when smoking or injecting methamphetamine and is the aspect of the drug that low-intensity users do not experience when snorting or swallowing the drug. During the rush, the user's heartbeat races, metabolism, blood pressure, and pulse soar, and users can experience feelings described in terms of multiple orgasms. Unlike the rush associated with crack cocaine, which lasts approximately 2–5 minutes, the methamphetamine rush can continue for 5–30 minutes. The rush is a result of methamphetamine triggering the adrenal gland to release epinephrine (adrenaline), a hormone that puts the body in a "fight or flight" mode. As with cocaine, the body feels the chemistry of fright, tension, and anxiety, but the brain gives the message that everything is better than fine because methamphetamine causes the explosive release of dopamine in the pleasure center of the brain. After the rush, a high ensues, during which the user feels both euphoric, energized, and aggressively smarter—he or she may become argumentative, often interrupting other people and finishing their sentences. The high can last 4–16 hours. Snorting or oral ingestion produces a high, but not an intense rush. Snorting produces effects within 3 to 5 minutes, and oral ingestion produces effects within 15 to 20 minutes.

Taken episodically and in low doses amphetamine can enhance sexual drive and performance; used habitually at high dosage it may impair sexual functioning and in some abusers provides a substitute for sex (D. Smith 1979). Grinspoon and Hedblom (1975: 103) state that while some people experience improved sexual performance, which may be an important reason for its popularity, "amphetamines are particularly dangerous in the hands of persons whose sexuality is abnormal or overtly perverse" because they appear to obliterate conventional restraints.

Methamphetamine Tolerance and Withdrawal

Tolerance does not develop to all effects of methamphetamine at the same rate; indeed, there may be increased sensitivity to some of them. With the high-intensity user, each successive rush becomes less euphoric, and it takes more methamphetamine to achieve it. Likewise, each high is not quite as strong as the one before, and the user needs more methamphetamine more often to get a high that is not as good as the last one he or she remembers. "Because tolerance for methamphetamine occurs within minutes—meaning that the pleasurable effects disappear even before the drug concentration in the blood falls significantly—users try to maintain the high by binging on the drug" (*Methamphetamine Abuse and Addiction* 1999: 3–4).

The most common symptoms of withdrawal among heavy amphetamine users are fatigue, long but troubled sleep, irritability, intense hunger, and moderate to severe depression, which may lead to suicidal behavior. Fits of violence may also occur. These disturbances can be temporarily reversed if the drug is taken again. With less systematic users, no acute, immediate symptoms of physical distress are evident with methamphetamine withdrawal, a stage that the abuser may slowly enter. Often 30 to 90 days must pass after the last drug use before the abuser realizes that he or she is in withdrawal. First, without really noticing, the individual becomes depressed, loses the ability to experience pleasure, becomes lethargic, and has no energy. Then the craving for more methamphetamine hits.

Medical Use of Amphetamines

Because amphetamines appear to act on the hypothalamus to suppress the appetite—although other CNS or metabolic effects may be involved—at one time they were widely prescribed to treat obesity. As opposed to more natural forms of dieting, however, the appetite returns with greater intensity after withdrawal from the drug, and it is only as a last resort that methamphetamine hydrochloride (Desoxyn) is used to treat obesity as one component of a weight-reduction regimen, and even then the treatment is limited to a few weeks.

As it became known that most of the benefits from treating many ailments with amphetamine were due to the drug's ability to elevate mood, medically accepted uses declined. Besides obesity, there are only two such uses in the United States: for treating narcolepsy, a sleeping disorder affecting about 250,000 Americans, usually treated with Dexedrine, and certain types of hyperactivity—hyperkinetic syndrome. The latter is for children with minimal brain damage or adolescent Attention Deficit Hyperkinetic Disorder (ADHD), when other remedies have proven insufficient. About 3 to 5 percent of the general population has the disorder, which is characterized by agitated behavior and an inability to focus on tasks. Paradoxically, in children with hyperkinetic (or hyperactive) syndrome, these drugs produce a calming effect and tolerance does not develop—they pose no exceptional risk for drug abuse problems in later life.

Ritalin (methylphenidate), which has effects similar to amphetamines but is less potent, is often the preferred drug for ADHD. Researchers speculate that methylphenidate amplifies the release of dopamine, thereby improving attention and focus in individuals who have dopamine signals that are weak, such as individuals with ADHD. When taken as prescribed, methylphenidate is a valuable medicine. Research shows that people with ADHD do not become addicted to stimulant medications when taken in the form prescribed and at treatment dosages. Another study found that ADHD boys treated with stimulants such as methylphenidate are significantly less likely to abuse drugs and alcohol when they are older than are nontreated ADHD boys.

Because of its stimulant properties, however, in recent years there have been reports of abuse of methylphenidate by people for whom it is not a medication. Some individuals abuse it for its stimulant effects: appetite suppression, wakefulness, increased focus/attentiveness, and euphoria. When abused, the tablets are either taken orally or crushed and snorted. Some abusers dissolve the tablets in water and inject the mixture. Complications can arise from this because insoluble fillers in the tablets can block small blood vessels ("Ritalin" 2001). There are reports of Ritalin being used illegally by college students, often as an aid in staying awake for late night studying during exam week (Zielbauer 2000).

Amphetamine continues to have military uses: the U.S. Air Force provided it to air crews during the Persian Gulf War. "More than sixty percent of the pilots who used the drug said it was 'essential' to accomplishing their mission" (Groopman 2001: 53; Rosenkranz 2003).

Dangers of Methamphetamine Use

A small amount can increase breathing and heart rate, cause heart palpitations, and anxiety or nervousness. Higher doses can make these effects more intense. Headaches, dizziness, and a rapid or irregular heartbeat may occur. Some people may become hostile and aggressive. Methamphetamine often causes hypothermia with renal failure that can be fatal. Although less common than with cocaine, methamphetamine use can lead to heart failure (Karch 1996). Using amphetamines over a long period of time can cause some health problems. With

---

Methamphetamine v. Cocaine

Methamphetamine is structurally similar to the neurotransmitter dopamine, but it is quite different from cocaine. Although these stimulants have similar behavioral and physiological effects, there are some major differences in the basic mechanisms of how they work at the level of the nerve cell. However, the bottom line is that methamphetamine, like cocaine, results in an accumulation of the neurotransmitter dopamine, and this excessive dopamine concentration appears to produce the stimulation and feelings of euphoria experienced by the user. In contrast to cocaine, which is quickly removed and almost completely metabolized in the body, methamphetamine has a much longer duration of action, and a larger percentage of the drug remains unchanged in the body. This results in methamphetamine being present in the brain longer, which ultimately leads to prolonged stimulant effects ("Methamphetamine: Abuse and Addiction" 2002).

Ritalin
Uses and Effects

Classification:	Stimulant
CSA Schedule:	Schedule II
Trade or Other Names:	Methylphenidate
Medical Uses:	Attention deficit disorder, narcolepsy
Physical Dependence:	Possible
Psychological Dependence:	High
Tolerance:	Yes
Duration (hours):	2–4
Usual Method:	Oral, injected
Possible Effects:	Increased alertness, excitation, euphoria, increased pulse rate and blood pressure, insomnia, loss of appetite
Effects of Overdose:	Agitation, increased body temperature, hallucinations, convulsions, possible death
Withdrawal Syndrome:	Apathy, long periods of sleep, irritability, depression, disorientation

Source: U.S. Drug Enforcement Administration

increased doses, users may become talkative, restless, and excited, and may feel a sense of power and superiority. With prolonged use, the short-term effects are exaggerated.

Because methamphetamine suppresses appetite, chronic heavy users generally fail to eat properly and thus develop various illnesses related to vitamin deficiencies and malnutrition. They may also be more prone to illness because they are generally run down, lack sleep, and live in an unhealthy environment. Chronic heavy users may also develop a drug-induced psychosis—a mental disturbance very similar to paranoid schizophrenia. The condition is an exaggeration of the short-term effects of high doses. Symptoms include hearing voices and paranoia—delusions that other people are threatening or persecuting them. Abusers may be prone to sudden, violent, and irrational acts. Herbert Meltzer notes that "normal volunteers screened to exclude any subjects with schizophrenic symptoms will become psychotic within 1 day if given repeated doses of amphetamine totaling several hundred milligrams" (1979: 156). Symptoms of psychosis at an abated level can persist for some time after the drug is discontinued (Institute for the Study of Drug Dependence 1987).

The heightened feelings of energy, combined with a significant lowering of social restraints on unconventional or aggressive behavior can, in some persons and/or in some situations, lead to extremely violent behavior: "Under the influence of speed even the most normally lethargic person *must* do something, even if it is as boring and repetitious as stringing beads for hours. When such a deep and insistent need to do *something* is thought to be disapproved or blocked, the speed abuser may attack the perceived thwarter with murderous rage" (Grinspoon and Hedblom 1975: 204). The symptoms usually disappear within a few days or weeks after drug use is stopped. Methamphetamine increases the libido and is associated with rougher sex, which may lead to bleeding and abrasions, increasing the danger of HIV/AIDS transmission ("Methamphetamine Abuse and Addiction" 2002).

Methamphetamine poisoning or overdose can cause brain hemorrhage, heart attack, high fever, coma, and occasionally, death. Most deaths, however, are due to accidents while under the influence of the drug. Methamphetamine may contain substances that do not easily dissolve in water. When users inject the drug, these particles can pass into the body and block small blood vessels or weaken the blood vessel walls. Kidney damage, lung problems, strokes, or other tissue injury may result. There is also the danger of acute lead poisoning because a common method of production uses lead acetate as a reagent ("Methamphetamine Abuse and Addiction" 2002).

Brain imaging research indicates that methamphetamine causes damage to nerve endings of dopamine-containing cells and persists for at least 3 years after drug use has stopped. The damage is similar to but less extensive than that caused by Parkinson's disease. In laboratory experiments, a single exposure to methamphetamine at high doses, or prolonged use at low doses, destroyed up to 50 percent of the brain cells that use dopamine. Although this damage may not be immediately apparent, scientists believe that with aging or exposure to other toxic agents, Parkinson symptoms may eventually emerge. These symptoms begin with lack of coordination and tremors and may eventually result in a form of paralysis. Methamphetamine users risk long-term brain damage since methamphetamine amplifies a process known as *apoptosis,* by which the brain culls defective cells, to the point where healthy cells are also eliminated (Zickler 2000; Mathias 2000a). These results provide evidence that methamphetamine at dose levels taken by human abusers of the drug leads to dopamine transporter reduction that is associated with motor and cognitive impairment (Volkow et al. 2001).

Little research has been done in humans into the effects of amphetamine use on pregnancy and fetal growth, although experiments with animals suggest that use during pregnancy may produce adverse behavioral effects.

Nicotine

Nicotine is one of more than 4,000 chemicals found in the smoke from tobacco; smokeless tobacco also contains a high level of nicotine (NIDA 1998a). About one percent of the weight of tobacco leaf is nicotine, and if all the nicotine in one cigarette were absorbed quickly into the body, the effect would be toxic and even fatal (A. Goldstein 2001). Most

American cigarettes contain at least 10 milligrams (mg) of nicotine, and the average smoker, through inhalation, takes in 1 to 2 mg per cigarette. Nicotine is absorbed through the skin and mucosal lining of the mouth and nose by inhalation in the lungs ("Nicotine Addiction" 2001).

Effects of Nicotine

After each inhalation of a cigarette, within 10 seconds the brain is swamped by a new drug spike (A. Goldstein 2001). The manner in which nicotine produces behavioral and cognitive effects is quite complex (see, for example, McGehee et al. 1995). Like other stimulants, particular CNS receptors have an affinity for nicotine (Figure 5.3). As is the case with other psychoactive drugs, nicotine attaches to these (nicotinic cholinergic) receptors located on the surface of neurons, triggering the release of stimulating neurotransmitters such as acetylcholine and glutamate. In addition, nicotine indirectly causes a release of dopamine in the brain regions that control pleasure and motivation. This reaction is similar to that seen with other drugs of abuse such as cocaine and heroin, and is thought to underlie the pleasurable sensations experienced by many smokers. Because of its ability to stimulate the release of dopamine, researchers are investigating the use of nicotine in the treatment of Parkinson's disease (Leary 1997; "Nicotine Addiction" 2001).

Immediately after exposure to nicotine, there is a "kick" caused in part by the drug's stimulation of the adrenal glands and resulting discharge of epinephrine (adrenaline). The rush of adrenaline stimulates the body and causes a sudden release of glucose as well as an increase in blood pressure, respiration, and heart rate. Nicotine also suppresses insulin output from the pancreas, which means that smokers are always slightly hyperglycemic. "In addition, nicotine indirectly causes a release of dopamine in the brain regions that control pleasure and motivation" (Society for Neuroscience 2002: 33). But, in addition, nicotine acts on a group of regulatory cells whose job is to control the dopamine response. When these mechanisms are disabled, the reward system continues to operate long after it should have normally shut down, causing a high that can last an hour (Kotulak 2002a).

FIGURE 5.3
Neurological effects of nicotine and cigarette smoke

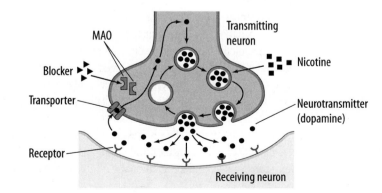

Cigarette smoking has also been found to decrease levels of the MAO enzyme, which exists in two forms, A and B. Cigarette smokers have a 40 percent MAO-B deficiency, causing the dopamine triggered by nicotine to remain active and thus enhancing its impact. This characteristic of smoking cigarettes indicates that it may be a **gateway drug** leading to addiction to other drugs of abuse (Glassman and Koob 1996); cigarette use typically precedes the use of illegal substances (Clymer 1994). Research has revealed that children who never smoked are certain not to use heroin or cocaine, while a significant proportion of children who smoke heavily have used these drugs and many of them have become drug dependent (Center on Addiction and Substance Abuse 1994).

As with other psychoactive substances, research has revealed that the use of nicotine may be a form of self-medication, smokers using nicotine to ward off depression—antidepressants can often help hard-core depressed smokers quit (Brody 1997). And, as is the case with alcohol (discussed in Chapter 4), genetics seem to play a role in the predisposition to nicotine dependence: "People with a gene variant in a particular enzyme metabolize or break down nicotine in the body more slowly and are significantly less likely to become addicted to nicotine than people without the variant" (Mathias 1999: 5). Research has discovered that prenatal exposure to tobacco is a significant risk factor for early substance abuse among preadolescents (*Problems of Drug Dependence* 1997).

In contrast to cocaine and amphetamine, nicotine can also exert a sedative effect, depending on the level of the smoker's nervous system arousal and the dose of nicotine taken. At high doses, there is evidence that nicotine may actually block cholinergic transmission, preventing the release of the neurotransmitter acetylcholine and producing sedation. Many users report a calming effect, and this may be related to nicotine's ability to activate cells in the spinal cord that reduce muscle tone and thus serve as a muscle relaxant. It also reduces appetite, although this may be at least partially offset by a decrease in metabolic rate.

Cigarette smoking "produces a rapid distribution of nicotine to the brain, with drug levels peaking with 10 seconds of inhalation. The acute effects of nicotine dissipate in a few minutes, causing the smoker to continue dosing frequently throughout the day to maintain the drug's pleasurable effects and prevent withdrawal." A typical smoker "will take 10 puffs on a cigarette over a period of 5 minutes that the cigarette is lit. Thus, a person who smokes about 1.5 packs (30 cigarettes) daily, gets 300 'hits' of nicotine to the brain each day" ("Nicotine Addiction" 2001: 2).

The addictive nature of nicotine is highlighted by the difficulty smokers exhibit in attempting abstinence: Less than 7 percent of those who try to quit on their own achieve more than 1 year of abstinence, and most relapse within a few days of attempting to quit: "Chronic use of nicotine products such as cigarettes produces physiological and/or psychological dependence." These smokers experience heightened stress between cigarettes, and smoking briefly restores their stress levels to normal—the apparent mood benefits reflect relief of withdrawal symptoms (Parrott 1999). An estimated 62 million Americans smoke, and an additional 6.8 million use smokeless tobacco ("Nicotine Addiction" 2001).

Bidis

In 1999, it was revealed that a version of cigarettes called *bidi* (pronounced "beedee" and also known as "beedis" or "beedies") was attracting a significant teenage audience. These small brown cigarettes consist of tobacco in tendu or temburni leaf, secured with a string at one end. They are handrolled in India, sweet flavored, and quite potent—three times the nicotine of conventional cigarettes—and at about two dollars a pack, cheaper than regular cigarettes. Their appearance—although legal they resemble marijuana joints—may account for at least some of the product's popularity among rebellious adolescents (C. Goldberg 1999; Center for Disease Control 1999). At the end of 1999, R. J. Reynold Tobacco Co. introduced vanilla, citrus, and spice Camel cigarettes (LaVelle 2000).

"Bidis must be puffed more frequently than regular cigarettes, and inhaling a bidi requires great pulmonary effort due to its shape and poor combustibility. Consequently, bidi smokers breathe in greater quantities of tar and other toxins than smokers of regular cigarettes" (Office of National Drug Control Policy 2000b: 11).

Smokeless Tobacco

Long associated with professional baseball (the original baseball cards advertised tobacco), chewing tobacco causes oral cancer and gum recession (Fields 2001).

Tobacco and Teenagers.   Major studies reveal a significant rise in smoking cigarettes among adolescents (Hilts 1995; Verhovek 1995). In 1996, it was revealed that the number of high school students smoking had increased sharply, with the highest increase among African American males (Feder 1996b). On August 10, 1995, then President Bill Clinton announced a major initiative to curb cigarette smoking by adolescents: "Cigarettes and smokeless tobacco are harmful, highly addictive and aggressively marketed to our young people." The $50 billion a year tobacco industry responded with a federal lawsuit.

Addiction to nicotine is influenced by gender. For men, the "compulsion to smoke is driven more strongly by nicotine's pharmacological effects on the brain, while women's addiction owes more to the visual, tactile, taste, and olfactory sensations" (Hanson 2002a: 4).

Nicotine Tolerance and Withdrawal

Repeated exposure to nicotine results in the development of tolerance, and higher doses of the drug are required to produce the same initial stimulation. Nicotine is metabolized fairly rapidly, disappearing from the body in a few hours. While some tolerance is lost overnight, smokers often report that the first cigarette of the day is the strongest and/or the "best" since it relieves the discomfort of withdrawal. As the day progresses, acute tolerance develops, and later cigarettes have less effect. Tolerance produces withdrawal symptoms when the consumption of nicotine ceases: slowing of brain activity, restless sleep, decreased heart rate and thyroid functioning, anxiety, and anger, cognitive and attentional deficits, and increased appetite (J. Hughes 1990).

Cigarettes

In his deposition, the plaintiff admitted that despite his illness, he still craved cigarettes. "At one point in his examination, lawyers asked him to demonstrate how he had smoked his cigarettes, and after putting one to his lips he declared: 'God, it feels good' "—a 56-year-old cancer patient who is suing a major cigarette company (Margolick 1991: B6).

The "lanky trial lawyer from Spring Valley, Wisc., who has been smoking for 47 years, since he was 13, who watched his cigarette-addicted father develop lung cancer when he was 50 and die of a heart attack at the age of 51, his cigarette-addicted brother die of emphysema and his father-in-law die of lung cancer," has had two heart attacks. Yet he still smokes (Kolata 1997: B9).

Withdrawal may begin within a few hours after the last cigarette, and symptoms peak within the first few days and may subside within a few weeks. For some people, however, symptoms may persist for months or longer (*Problems of Drug Dependence* 1997). "Dramatic changes in the brain's pleasure circuits during withdrawal from chronic nicotine use rival the magnitude and duration of similar changes observed during withdrawal from other abused drugs such as cocaine, opiates, amphetamines, and alcohol" (NIDA 1998b: 1). Failure to continue the ingestion of nicotine causes severe craving that may last for 6 months or longer—a major reason for relapse (NIDA 1998b).

The craving for nicotine is an important but poorly understood component of the withdrawal syndrome that has been described as a major obstacle to successful abstinence. While the withdrawal syndrome is related to the pharmacological effects of nicotine, many behavioral factors also can affect the severity of withdrawal symptoms. For some people, the feel, smell, and sight of a cigarette and the ritual of obtaining, handling, lighting, and smoking the cigarette are all associated with the pleasurable effects of smoking and can make withdrawal or craving worse. While nicotine gum and patches may alleviate the pharmacological aspects of withdrawal, cravings often persist (NIDA information).

Dangers of Nicotine Use

The medical consequences of nicotine exposure result from effects of both the nicotine itself and how it is taken. The most deleterious effects of nicotine addiction are the result of smoking cigarettes, which accounts for one-third of all cancers, particularly lung cancer. Cigarette smoking has been linked to about 90 percent of all lung cancer cases, and lung cancer is the nation's single leading cause of death and disability (Brody 2001). Smoking also causes lung diseases such as chronic bronchitis and emphysema,

Cost of Cigarettes

"The obituaries all said that [the Beatles] George Harrison died of cancer. But, in fact, what killed Mr. Harrison was smoking" (Brody 2001:D7).

and it has been found to exacerbate asthma symptoms in adults and children. Smoking is associated with cancers of the mouth, pharynx, larynx, esophagus, stomach, pancreas, cervix, kidney, ureter, and bladder. And smoking is a cancer hazard to those who are exposed to second-hand smoke. About 440,000 persons die annually from the deadly effects of tobacco smoke.

In 1999, it was revealed that cigar smokers are twice as likely as nonsmokers to get cancer of the mouth, throat, and lungs (Associated Press 1999d). The overall rates of death from cancer are twice as high among smokers as among nonsmokers, with heavy smokers having rates that are four times greater than those of nonsmokers (NIDA information).

Preliminary research has linked cigarette smoking by fathers with an increased risk of brain cancer and leukemia in their offspring, and children whose parents smoke are three to four times more likely to develop serious infectious diseases. An estimated 5,600 infant deaths are caused by smoking among pregnant women (Associated Press 1995). Nicotine affects the blood vessels in the placenta, interfering with oxygen supply to the fetus (A. Goldstein 2001). According to a study by Laurence Namur, newborns whose mothers smoke during pregnancy have the same nicotine level as adult smokers and spend the first few days of life going through withdrawal (Associated Press 1997a). In addition, research in 2001 found that prenatal exposure to smoke may predispose children to early smoking experimentation. The researchers speculate that maternal smoking during pregnancy causes disturbances in the neurophysiological functioning of the fetus (Thomas 2001). There is also considerable research indicating that children whose mothers smoke during pregnancy are at much greater risk than other children for drug abuse and conduct disorder (Varisco 2000).

In addition to its ability to cause cancer, cigarette smoking's relationship to coronary heart disease was first reported in the 1940s. Since that time, it has been well documented that smoking substantially increases the risk of heart disease, including stroke, heart attack, vascular disease, and aneurysm. It is estimated that nearly one-fifth of deaths from heart disease are attributable to smoking (NIDA information). There is also the problem of passive or secondary smoke, which is a major source of indoor air contaminants.

Nicotine causes blood vessels in the skin to constrict, reducing blood and oxygen supplies to the extremities—an obvious detriment in high-energy sports—and may be the reason why the skin of cigarette smokers tends to be more wrinkled than nonsmokers of the same age. As with heroin, nicotine stimulates centers of the brain cell that control vomiting, and new smokers may experience nausea.

According to researchers at the Centers for Disease Control and Prevention, because cigarette smoke makes it harder for the lungs to expel foreign material and easier for bacteria to stick, smokers are four times more likely than nonsmokers to get life-threatening blood infections or meningitis from bacteria that usually causes pneumonia. And the more cigarettes a person smokes, the higher the risk of an infection. The researchers noted that former smokers have an increased risk of the infection for at least 10 years after they quit (McConnaughey 2000).

What Happens to Your Body When You Quit Smoking?

- *20 minutes:* Blood pressure drops to normal, pulse rate returns to normal, and your body temperature increases to normal.
- *8 hours:* Carbon monoxide level in blood drops to normal, energy level in blood increases to normal.
- *24 hours:* Chance of heart attack decreases.
- *48 hours:* Nerve endings start regrowing, ability to smell and taste is enhanced to normal levels.
- *2 weeks:* Circulation improves, lung function increases up to 30%.
- *1–9 months:* Cilia regrow in lungs, which helps breathing and reduces infections; sinus congestion and coughing decreases; body's overall energy increases.
- *1 year:* Risk of coronary heart disease is half that of a smoker.
- *5 years:* Lung cancer death rate decreases by half, stroke risk is reduced to that of a nonsmoker, risk of mouth, throat and esophagus cancer is reduced by 50%.
- *15 years:* Risk of coronary heart disease is that of a nonsmoker.

Source: National Clearinghouse for Alcohol and Drug Information

Herbal Stimulants

So-called herbal stimulants, particularly *ephedra* (also known by its Chinese name *ma huang*) are used by young people as a "safe" alternative to illegal drugs. Ephedra, under a variety of brand names, is sold in the form of pills in many health food stores. Ephedra contains ephedrine, which is an amphetamine precursor and is produced as a stimulant in nonprescription asthma medicine and some cold and allergy medicines. Sometimes other ephedra derivatives and caffeine are added to increase its stimulating properties. Within 20 minutes of taking the substance, there is a jump in the heart rate and blood pressure. One popular brand is called Herbal Ecstasy, although it is not related to MDMA/ecstasy (discussed in Chapter 6).

Ephedra products are promoted as health and exercise supplements and have been linked to athlete deaths (Hobson 2002). Since it is classified as a dietary supplement—not a drug—ephedra is not subject to FDA regulation, although a number of states have passed restrictions because of reports of deaths believed related to herbal products containing ephedrine. The 1994 Dietary Supplement Health and Education Act was passed as the result of an effective lobbying campaign by the food supplement industry. The statute deregulated the industry and now permits the marketing of any supplement until the FDA is able to prove it is unsafe. The law also enables companies to make unrestrained and unjustified health claims.

Drug Free America?

In 1995, Dennis Hastert, now speaker of the United States House of Representatives, coauthored legislation to "help create a drug free America by the year 2002." That same year, Representative Hastert sponsored another bill allowing herbal products to bypass FDA regulations (Shenk 1999).

Adverse reactions of these herbal stimulants include liver failure, elevated blood pressure, heart palpitations, and strokes (Crowley 1996; Lambert 1996; Burros and Jay 1996; Kolata 1996). In 2003, following the death of a 23-year-old pitcher for the Baltimore Orioles in which ephedra is suspected of playing a role, the federal government ordered companies to stop advertising the drug as an athletic performance enhancer (Pear and Grady 2003).

Caffeine

Found in tea, coffee, many cola drinks, and cocoa products, caffeine is the most widely used psychoactive drug—about 90 percent of the adult North American population ingests caffeine regularly. After ingestion of caffeine, the chemical's compounds dissolve in the bloodstream and travel to the brain. Caffeine molecules are almost identical to the neurotransmitter adenosine, which controls the release of other chemicals that excite the central nervous system. Caffeine occupies adenosine receptor sites in the brain, neutralizing this control mechanism.

The result is an elevation of mood and a decrease in fatigue, and, in high doses, insomnia and a racing heart. Abrupt withdrawal of caffeine can result in headaches, lethargy, and depressionlike symptoms (Blakeslee 1991, 1994; Griffiths 1990; Griffiths et al. 1990; "Quitting Caffeine" 1991).

SUMMARY

Stimulants release dopamine and other stimulating neurotransmitters, and several block reuptake of these neurotransmitters, thus keeping the levels high; this pharmacology generates euphoria. Cocaine produces major euphoria and indifference to pain, along with illusions of increased alertness; crack is inhaled and thus works faster than powdered cocaine, producing a rush, which subsides to a high. Cocaine constricts the blood vessels and thus may damage the heart and cause vascular disease, and it affects sexual function and cognitive function. Methamphetamine is produced in illegal laboratories, using everyday chemicals, although the DEA controls bulk purchases of some of the precursor chemicals. Methamphetamine use results in euphoria and feelings of heightened energy, which sometimes leads to violent behavior. Nicotine has complex effects, including the stimulation of the adrenal glands resulting in an adrenaline surge and a sedative effect, unlike cocaine and amphetamine. Long-term nicotine use puts users at substantial risk for many cancers (particularly lung cancer), chronic bronchitis, emphysema, and heart disease. Herbal stimulants, especially ephedra, are a controversial group of drugs that have escaped regulation. Caffeine—by far the most widely used psychoactive drug—elevates mood and decreases fatigue but can also cause insomnia and racing heart.

INTERNET CONNECTIONS

Addiction Science (university-based research): www.ucsf.edu/cnba
Center for Disease Control Tobacco Information and Prevention Source: www.cdc.gov/tobacco
Institute of Behavioral Research (university-based drug research): www.ibr.tcu.edu
Virtual Clearinghouse (international group providing policy information): www.atod.org

REVIEW QUESTIONS

1. What impact do stimulants have on a user?
2. How can dependence on cocaine be explained by a neurotransmitter deficiency?
3. What naturally occurring phenomenon does cocaine imitate?
4. What is the typical reaction to small doses of cocaine?
5. What are the possible negative reactions to heavy use of cocaine?
6. Why do some cocaine users prefer crack?
7. What are the possible effects of cocaine on sexual activity?
8. What are the differences between the effect of cocaine hydrochloride and crack?
9. In what ways are the effects of methamphetamine and cocaine similar?
10. Why is the use of methamphetamine by certain persons dangerous?
11. How does nicotine differ from other CNS stimulants?
12. What are herbal stimulants?
13. How is caffeine similar to other CNS stimulants?

CHAPTER 6

Hallucinogens, Club Drugs, and Marijuana

Hallucination: Perception of visual, auditory, tactile, olfactory, or gustatory experiences without an external stimulus and with a compelling sense of their reality.

—American Heritage Dictionary *(2000: 782).*

"**A** hallucinogen is a drug that changes a person's state of awareness by modifying sensory inputs, loosening cognitive and creative restraints, and providing access to material normally hidden in memory or material of an unconscious nature" (Jacob and Shulgin 1994: 74). Hallucinogens can change a person's perception, making the person see or hear things that don't exist. They can also produce changes in thought, sense of time, and mood. According to Erich Goode (1972), the term *hallucinogen* implies something undesirable and suggests being "crazy." Supporters of the use of such chemicals prefer the term **psychedelic.** "Under the influence of hallucinogens, people see images, hear sounds, and feel sensations that seem real but do not exist" ("Hallucinogens and Dissociative Drugs" 2000: 1).

Hallucinogenic substances occur both naturally and synthetically. They excite the central nervous system—actually overwhelming its ability to modulate sensory input. Autonomic hyperactivity results in distortions of the perception of objective reality. These distortions include:

- *Depersonalization.* Having "out-of-body" experiences or misperceptions of reality
- *Sensisthesia.* "Seeing" sound and "hearing" visual input
- *Hallucinations.* Perceiving sounds, odors, tactile sensations, or visual images that arise from within the person

The sensory illusions produced by hallucinogens are often accompanied by mood alterations that are usually euphoric but sometimes severely depressive (*Drugs of Abuse* 1989) and that mimic severe mental illness (*Drug Abuse* 1987). Marked impairment of judgment can lead to poor decision making and serious accidents (Berkow 1982). A number of hallucinogens produce cross-tolerance. Unlike depressants and stimulants, hallucinogens do not function as reinforcers in animals (Winter 1994). Hallucinogens apparently have their own receptors ($5-HT_2$) in the central nervous system (Lin and Glennon 1994).

Club drugs is a general term for a number of illicit drugs, primarily synthetic, that are most commonly encountered at nightclubs and raves. The drugs include MDMA, ketamine, Rohypnol, GHB, and GBL.

Lysergic Acid Diethylamide (LSD)

LSD was synthesized in 1938. The first LSD "trip" was recorded by its discoverer, Albert Hofmann, a research chemist in Basel, Switzerland. In 1943, Hofmann accidentally ingested a minute quantity of the drug through the skin of his fingers (Grinspoon 1979). About this experience Hofmann relates:

> I had to leave my work in the laboratory and go home because I felt strangely restless and dizzy. Once there, I lay down and sank into a not unpleasant delirium which was marked by an extreme degree of fantasy. In sort of a trance with closed eyes . . . fantastic visions of extraordinary vividness accompanied by a kaleidoscopic play of intense coloration continuously swirled around me. After two hours this condition subsided. (quoted in Goode 1972: 98–99)

Three days later Hofmann experimented by swallowing 250 micrograms of LSD, not realizing that this was an extremely high dose; he soon became terrified, fearing that he would lose his mind or perhaps die (Grinspoon 1979).

LSD is produced from lysergic acid, a substance derived from the ergot fungus, which grows on wild rye or other grasses, or from lysergic acid amide, a chemical found in morning glory seeds. "Bread made from rye infected with the fungus causes a disease known as ergotism with hallucinatory as well as physiological symptoms" (Grinspoon 1979: 11). Although theoretically possible, manufacture from morning glory seeds is not economically feasible. In 1949, LSD was introduced into the United States as an experimental drug for treating psychiatric illnesses, but until 1954 it remained relatively rare and expensive because the ergot fungus was difficult to cultivate. That year the Eli Lily Company announced that it had succeeded in creating a totally synthetic version of LSD (Stevens 1987)—so had outlaw chemists.

While only a small amount of ergotamine tartrate is required to produce LSD in large batches, the substance is not readily available in the United States, and its purchase by other than established pharmaceutical firms is suspect. "Therefore, ergotamine tartrate used in clandestine LSD laboratories is believed to be acquired from sources abroad," and the difficulty in acquiring the chemical limits the number of independent manufacturers (Drug Enforcement Administration 1995: 4).

Cooking LSD is time consuming; it takes from 2 to 3 days to produce 1 to 4 ounces of crystal. Consequently, it is believed that LSD usually is not produced in large quantities, but rather in a series of small batches. Production of LSD in small batches also minimizes the loss of precursor chemicals should they become contaminated during the synthesis process. LSD crystal produced clandestinely can be as much as 95 to 100 percent pure. However, LSD degrades quickly when exposed to heat, light, and air and is most susceptible to degradation during the application process and once it is in paper form. As a result, under less than optimal real-life conditions, actual yields are significantly below the theoretically possible yield: 1 gram of LSD crystal generally yields 10,000 dosage units of LSD, or approximately 10 million dosage units per kilogram.

Pure, high-potency LSD is a clear or white, odorless crystalline material that is soluble in water. It is mixed with binding agents, such as spray-dried skim milk, for producing tablets or is dissolved and diluted in a solvent for application onto paper or other materials. Variations in the manufacturing process or the presence of precursors or by-products can cause LSD to range in color from clear or white, in its purest form, to tan or even black, indicating poor quality or degradation. To mask product deficiencies, distributors often apply LSD to off-white, tan, or yellow paper to disguise discoloration.

An odorless and almost tasteless white powder, LSD has a slightly bitter taste and is usually taken by mouth. Commonly referred to as "acid," LSD is sold on the street in tablets, capsules, and, occasionally, liquid form. LSD is often added to absorbent paper—"blotter acid"—and divided into small decorated squares, with each square representing one dose. It may be mixed with any number of substances, sugar, or gelatin sheets—"window panes." It only takes .01 milligram for LSD to have an effect.

Just how LSD works is not completely understood. "The molecular structure of LSD is similar to that of the neurotransmitter serotonin. LSD therefore has a high affinity for serotonin receptors and interferes with the normal functioning of these receptors" (Henderson 1994a: 42). Stimulation of serotonin receptors by agonists such as LSD and the hallucinogen psilocybin inhibits the activity of a mechanism (a neural system called the *raphe*) that modulates sensory input into the brain stem. This mechanism would normally integrate sensory inflow and the emotional and ideational state of the organism and suppress irrelevant information. Serotonin agonists occupy serotonin receptor sites in the brain and thereby cause a backup of serotonin that exceeds the ability of MAO to control serotonin. Serotonin overloads the sensory input systems of the CNS so that normal stimuli take on distorted images—the size of the signal delivered to the cerebral cortex is greatly enlarged. This combination—inhibition of control mechanisms and increasing signal size—overload the brain (Ray 1978). The result is actually a serotonin, rather than an LSD, trip and consists of intoxication for several hours (Palfai and Jankiewicz 1991).

Effects of LSD

LSD is absorbed easily from the gastrointestinal tract, and rapidly reaches a high concentration in the blood. It is circulated throughout the body and, subsequently, to the brain. LSD is metabolized in the liver and is excreted in the urine in about 24 hours. The effects of LSD range from blurred vision to a visual field filled with strange objects. Three-dimensional space appears to contract and enlarge, and light appears to fluctuate in intensity. Auditory effects also occur but to a lesser degree. All of these changes are episodic. Temperature sensitivity is altered, with the environment being perceived as abnormally cold or hot. Body images are altered (out-of-body experiences), and body parts appear to float. Time is sometimes perceived as running fast forward or backward. "Perceptually," notes Grinspoon, "LSD produces an especially brilliant and intense impact of sensory stimuli on consciousness. Normally unnoticed aspects of the environment capture the attention: ordinary objects are seen as if for the first time and with a sense of fascination or entrancement, as though they had unimagined depths of significance" (1979: 12). There is apparently selective recall of some aspects of the LSD experience: "During the period of drug activity the subject may report that he feels less friendly, more aggressive or agitated, or depressed. Much later, he will recall the experience as illuminating and pleasurable. He will rarely recall psychotic symptoms" (Meltzer 1979: 162).

A trip begins between 30 and 60 minutes after ingestion, peaks after 2 to 6 hours, and fades out after about 129 hours. There are "good acid trips" and "bad acid trips." They appear to be controlled by the attitude, mood, and expectations of the user and often depend on suggestions of those around him or her at the time of the trip. Favorable expectations produce good trips, while excessive apprehension is likely to produce the opposite. Because the substance appears to intensify feelings, the user may feel a magnified sense of love, lust, and joy, or anger, terror, and despair: "The extraordinary sensations and feelings may bring on fear of losing control, paranoia, and panic, or they may cause euphoria and even bliss" (Grinspoon 1979: 13). According to James MacDonald and Michael Agar (1994: 12), a "good trip," when everything is touched by magic but the user remains aware that reality will return when the drug wears off, turns into a "bad trip" when he or she "loses sight of this fact [that reality will return] for too long." The bad trip is the result of a failure to comprehend that reality has not changed, merely its perception while under the influence of LSD. Sensations and feelings change much more dramatically than the physical signs, which are as varied as the psychological and include dilation of the pupils (almost always); increased heart rate, blood pressure, and body temperature; mild dizziness or nausea; chills; trembling; slow deep breathing; loss of appetite; and insomnia (Grinspoon 1979).

The user may feel several different emotions at once or swing rapidly from one emotion to another. If taken in a large enough dose, the drug produces delusions and visual hallucinations. The user's sense of time and self changes. Sensations may seem to "cross over," giving the user the feeling of hearing colors and seeing sounds. These changes can be frightening and can cause panic. Although LSD has been used experimentally to treat a variety of psychological illnesses, it currently has no accepted medical use.

LSD Tolerance and Withdrawal

Tolerance develops rapidly, with repeated doses becoming completely ineffective after a few days of continuous use, and there is cross-tolerance to other hallucinogens. LSD is not addicting—there are no physical withdrawal symptoms (ISDD 1987).

Dangers of LSD Use

LSD use can produce *mydriasis* (prolonged dilation of the pupil of the eye), raised body temperature, rapid heartbeat, elevated blood pressure, increased blood sugar, salivation, tingling in fingers and toes, weakness, tremors, palpitations, facial flushing, chills, gooseflesh, profuse perspiration, nausea, dizziness, inappropriate speech, blurred vision, and intense anxiety. Death caused by the direct effect of LSD on the body is virtually impos-

LSD
Uses and Effects

Classification:	Hallucinogen
CSA Schedule:	Schedule I
Trade or Other Names:	Acid, microdot
Medical Uses:	None
Physical Dependence:	None
Psychological Dependence:	Unknown
Tolerance:	Yes
Duration (hours):	8–12
Usual Method:	Oral
Possible Effects:	Illusions and hallucinations, altered perception of time and distance
Effects of Overdose:	Longer, more intense "trip" episodes, psychosis, possible death
Withdrawal Syndrome:	Unknown

Source: U.S. Drug Enforcement Administration

sible. However, death related to LSD abuse has occurred as a result of the panic reactions, hallucinations, delusions, and paranoia experienced by users (Drug Enforcement Administration n.d.b).

There are no known physical dangers to long-term use, although psychosis has been reported in a few instances. Some users report experiencing severe, terrifying thoughts and feelings, fear of losing control, fear of insanity and death, and despair while using LSD. For those who knowingly ingest LSD at low doses there is usually mild euphoria and a loosening of inhibitions (Grinspoon 1979). Ingesting LSD unknowingly, however, can result in a highly traumatic experience, as the victim may feel that he or she has suddenly "gone crazy" (Brecher 1972). Fatal accidents have occurred during states of LSD intoxication.

Some LSD users—less than 25 percent (Abrahart 1998)—report recurring low-intensity trips—"flashbacks"—without ingesting the substance. This may be caused by LSD stored in and eventually released from fatty tissue. A flashback occurs suddenly, often without warning, and may occur within a few days or more than a year after the last use of LSD. Flashbacks usually occur in people who have used hallucinogens chronically or have an underlying personality problem; however, otherwise healthy people who use LSD occasionally may also have flashbacks. In normal (nonpsychotic) populations, more than half of those experiencing flashbacks report them as pleasant (Abrahart 1998). However, it remains to be established whether there are any causal links between flashbacks and LSD use—the link could be explained by the lack of control over what an LSD user is actually ingesting. LSD, like other illegally produced drugs, may contain any variety of additives, including methamphetamine, which appears to increase the likelihood of a bad trip (Ray 1978). Medically supervised LSD research would use pharmaceutically pure LSD, but since LSD use was prohibited in 1966, most research on adverse effects involved individuals who had obtained LSD on the black market, whose real composition, purity, and strength would be unknown (Abrahart 1998).

Most users of LSD voluntarily decrease or stop its use over time. LSD is not considered an addictive drug since it does not produce compulsive drug-seeking behavior. But, because tolerance develops rapidly, some users take progressively higher doses to achieve the state of intoxication that they had previously achieved, a dangerous practice, given the unpredictability of the substance.

Phencyclidine (PCP)

Phencyclidine was initially developed as a general anesthetic for surgery. While it produces distortions of sight and sound, and feelings of dissociation from the environment and self, these mind-altering effects are technically not hallucinations and are more properly known as "dissociative anesthetics" ("Hallucinogens and Dissociative Drugs" 2000). The drug is reported to have received the name PCP—"peace pill"—on the streets of San Francisco, where it was reputed to give illusions of everlasting peace. PCP is a white crystalline powder that has a distinctive bitter chemical taste. It is readily soluble in water or alcohol, and more than 100 variations (analogs) are produced easily and cheaply in clandestine laboratories (Lerner 1980). PCP can be mixed easily with dyes and turns up on the illicit drug market in liquid form and in a variety of tablets,

---

A Bad Trip

A bad trip is an acute anxiety or panic reaction following the ingestion of LSD. On a bad trip, painful or frightening feelings are intensified, just as pleasurable sensations are on a good trip. Distortion of the sense of time may cause this experience to seem almost unbearably long. The person may feel that he or she has lost control of the drug and that the trip will never end; he or she may exhibit paranoia or attempt to flee. A bad trip is an acute reaction to LSD, and it dissipates as the effects of the drug wear off (Henderson 1994b: 58).

capsules, and colored powders. Like any drug sold on the street, PCP is often mixed with other psychoactive substances, and it is sometimes sold as LSD. While it can be snorted or eaten, most commonly, PCP is applied to a leafy material such as mint, parsley, oregano, or marijuana—"killer joints" or "crystal supergrass"—and smoked.

PCP is typically made by mixing ingredients in three buckets for several hours. This is often accomplished in the back of a moving van to disperse the fumes produced. The ingredients must be poured from one bucket to the other, leading to the term "bucket chemists." PCP is sold on the street by such names as **"angel dust,"** "ozone," "whack," and "rocket fuel." The variety of street names for PCP reflects its bizarre and volatile effects.

Effects of PCP

PCP was first synthesized in 1956 and found to be an effective surgical anesthetic when tested on monkeys. As a *dissociative anesthetic,* it induces a lack of responsive awareness, not only of pain but to the general environment, without a corresponding depression of the autonomic nervous system (Dotson, Ackerman, and West 1995). Experiments on humans were carried out in 1957, and while PCP proved to work as an anesthetic, it had serious side effects. Some patients manifested agitation, excitement, and disorientation during the recovery period. Some male surgical patients became violent, while some females appeared to experience simple intoxication (Linder, Lerner, and Burns 1981). "When PCP was subsequently given to normal volunteers in smaller doses, it induced a psychotic-like state resembling schizophrenia. Volunteers experienced body image changes, depersonalization, and feelings of loneliness, isolation, and dependency. Their thinking was observed to become progressively disorganized" (Lerner 1980: 14).

There is evidence of PCP receptors in the brain, suggesting that an "important relationship exists between the chemical structure of the 'phencyclidines' and receptors in the CNS related to neurotransmitters" (Burns and Done 1980: 100). Exactly how PCP acts upon the body, however, is not completely known, although it appears that the release of dopamine is a critical piece of the puzzle (E. French, Levenson, and Ceci 1990). As opposed to other anesthetics, PCP increases respiration, heart rate, and blood pressure, qualities that make it useful for patients endangered by a depressed heart rate or low blood pressure. In the 1960s PCP became commercially available for use in veterinary medicine as an analgesic and anesthetic, but diversion to street use led the manufacturer to discontinue production in 1978.

Within 30 to 60 minutes of ingesting a moderate amount of PCP, the user experiences a sense of detachment, distance, and estrangement from his or her surroundings. There is also numbness, slurred speech, and a loss of coordination. These symptoms, which last up to 5 hours, are often accompanied by feelings of invulnerability. "A blank stare, rapid and involuntary eye movements, and an exaggerated gait are among the more common observable effects" (*Drugs of Abuse* 1989: 50). Under laboratory conditions, a subject may experience a feeling of "flying with angels" and "peace and tranquility" (R. Siegel 1989: 220). At low to moderate doses, physiological effects of PCP include a slight increase in breathing rate and a more pronounced rise in blood pressure and pulse rate. Respiration

---

Phencyclidine
Uses and Effects

Classification:	Hallucinogen
CSA Schedule:	Schedule I, II
Trade or Other Names:	PCE, PCPy, TCP, PCP, hog, loveboat, angel dust
Medical Uses:	None
Physical Dependence:	Unknown
Psychological Dependence:	High
Tolerance:	Yes
Duration (hours):	Days
Usual Method:	Oral, smoked
Possible Effects:	Illusions and hallucinations, altered perception of time and distance
Effects of Overdose:	Longer, more intense "trip" episodes, psychosis, possible death
Withdrawal Syndrome:	Unknown

Source: U.S. Drug Enforcement Administration

---

becomes shallow, and flushing and profuse sweating occur. Generalized numbness of the extremities and muscular incoordination also may occur. Psychological effects include distinct changes in body awareness, similar to those associated with alcohol intoxication.

PCP Tolerance and Withdrawal

PCP use does not seem to result in any significant tolerance or withdrawal symptoms ("Drug Abuse" 1991). "Generally 24–48 hours are required until the person again feels completely normal" (Lerner 1980: 16).

Dangers of PCP Use

PCP can result in mood disorders, acute anxiety, paranoia, and violent behavior. PCP-intoxicated persons can present severe management problems to treatment staff and law enforcement personnel because it activates stress hormones that allow users to demonstrate remarkable strength. Some reactions are similar to LSD intoxication: auditory hallucinations, image distortion—fun-house mirror images. "PCP is unique among popular drugs of abuse in its power to produce psychoses indistinguishable from schizophrenia" (*Drugs of Abuse* 1989: 50). As a result, "the phencyclidine intoxicated patient is often improperly diagnosed and treated by well-meaning uninformed personnel" (Lerner 1980: 13).

Use of PCP among adolescents may interfere with hormones related to normal growth and development as well as with the learning process. At high doses of PCP, there is a drop in blood pressure, pulse rate, and respiration. This may be accompanied by nausea, vomiting, blurred vision, flicking up and down of the eyes, drooling, loss of balance, and dizziness. High doses of PCP can also cause seizures, coma, and death (though death more often results from accidental injury or suicide during PCP intoxication). Speech is often sparse and garbled. People who use PCP for long periods report memory loss, difficulties with speech and thinking, depression, and weight loss. These symptoms can persist up to a year after cessation of PCP use. Mood disorders also have been reported. PCP has sedative effects, and interactions with other central nervous system depressants, such as alcohol and benzodiazepines, can lead to coma or accidental overdose (NIDA information).

Mushrooms and Cactus

In addition to the synthetic hallucinogens, some natural substances produce similar effects. **Mescaline** is the primary hallucinogenic ingredient of the fleshy part or buttons the size of a quarter to several inches across, of the small spineless peyote cactus. It has been used by Indians in Northern Mexico as part of their religious rites since prehistoric times. The Native American Church, with about 250,000 members, continues to use the cactus as part of religious ceremonies for which the church has been exempted from certain provisions of the federal Controlled Substances Act. Twenty-three states also exempt the sacramental use of peyote from criminal penalties.[1] Six persons are licensed by the state and federal governments to harvest peyote, which grows wild (cultivation is illegal) in South Texas 30 miles east of Laredo (Milloy 2002).

Peyote is usually ground into a powder and taken orally, although mescaline can also be produced synthetically. A typical dose of 350 to 500 milligrams produces illusions and hallucinations lasting anywhere from 5 to 12 hours (*Drugs of Abuse* 1989). In healthy volunteers half a gram of mescaline produced symptoms of psychosis indistinguishable from schizophrenia (Karch 1996). There have been no reports of fatal overdoses.

---

[1]In 1990 the Supreme Court, in an Oregon case, ruled 6–3 that states can prohibit the use of peyote by members of the American Indian Church, the First Amendment notwithstanding (Greenhouse 1990). In the wake of the Court decision, Congress enacted a statute providing a defense for people who use the substance "with good faith practice of a religious belief."

Mescaline and Peyote
Uses and Effects

Classification:	Hallucinogen
CSA Schedule:	Schedule I
Trade or Other Names:	Mescal, buttons, cactus
Medical Uses:	None
Physical Dependence:	None
Psychological Dependence:	Unknown
Tolerance:	Yes
Duration (hours):	8–12
Usual Method:	Oral
Possible Effects:	Illusions and hallucinations, altered perception of time and distance
Effects of Overdose:	Longer, more intense "trip" episodes, psychosis, possible death
Withdrawal Syndrome:	Unknown

Source: U.S. Drug Enforcement Administration

Psilocybe mushrooms have also been used for centuries in Native American religious ceremonies. The sacred or magic mushroom is typically eaten. Its active ingredients—**psilocybin** and psilocin—are chemically similar to LSD and can be produced synthetically. Like mescaline and LSD, they affect perceptions and mood (*Drugs of Abuse* 1989), and users cannot distinguish between psilocybin and LSD. There has been little research into this substance, and virtually none on human subjects (Karch 1996).

Dimethyltryptamine (DMT) is an hallucinogenic substance that occurs naturally in many plants and is used by Caribbean and Latin American Indians, and in Ololiuqui (the seeds of the morning glory plant), used by Indian priests in Latin America to produce delirium. Another hallucinogen is the magic mushroom of *Alice in Wonderland,* the **Amanita muscaria** of Russia and Scandinavia, where it was reputedly used by Vikings to increase their ferocity in battle (Ray 1978; although R. Blum 1969 disputes this). A brownish solid material that smells like mothballs, it must be smoked or injected—it is not activated when taken orally. It is typically placed at the end of a tobacco or marijuana cigarette. A single inhalation will produce a 5- to 10-minute trip. There has been little research into the substance, and toxic effects are unknown (Karch 1996).

Also known as MDMA, ecstasy became the drug of the 1990s as many young people gathered at rave parties where the hallucinogen was easily available and openly ingested. As the name implies, ecstasy brings on feelings of well-being.

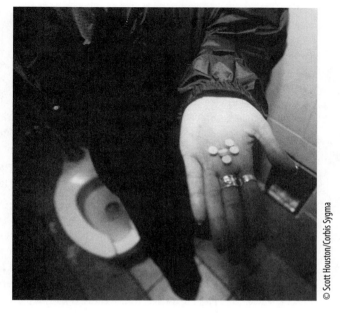

© Scott Houston/Corbis Sygma

Ecstasy

The common name for **MDMA** (3, 4-**M**ethylene**D**ioxy**M**eth**A**mphetamine) is **ecstasy.** It is a synthetic drug possessing stimulant and hallucinogenic properties. While MDMA does not cause overt hallucinations, many people report distorted time and exaggerated sensory perception while under the influence of the drug (Hanson 2001). Developed in Germany in 1914 as an appetite suppressant and for some psychiatric research (Nichols and Oberlender 1989; McNeil 2002), MDMA is but one of about 200 amphetamine analogs of the methylenedioxyamphetamine, or MDA. type. Accordingly, *ecstasy* is frequently used as a generic term for this family of substances.[2] It was used by some therapists in the 1970s to help patients explore their feelings for each other. In a controlled setting it was reputed to promote trust between patients and physicians (Karch 1996).

Ecstasy (or "X-TC") proved popular among white professionals—earning its nickname as a "yuppie drug"—and persons who consider themselves part of the New Age spiritual movement (Beck and Rosenbaum 1994). MDMA is usually ingested orally in tablet or capsule form. It is also available as a powder and is sometimes snorted and occasionally smoked but rarely injected. MDMA is reported to be popular on college campuses in the United States and at dance parties, or raves.

---

[2]GHB (gamma-hydroxybutyrate), discussed later, and its precursor GBL (gamma-butyrolactone) are sometimes sold as "liquid ecstasy."

Raves

Raves emerged in the late 1980s, starting amidst the party atmosphere of a Mediterranean island frequented by British youth on vacation. Rave music originated in the United States, mainly in Detroit, Chicago, and New York. The rave scene soon spread to other European countries, to Australia, to New Zealand, and elsewhere around the world. Raves vary in size: some draw a few hundred people, while others draw tens of thousands. They are commonly advertised in flyers distributed in clubs and music stores, and on Internet web sites.

Raves usually start late at night and continue into the morning. A well-known disk jockey is often the rave's main attraction. Ravers often wear or carry glow sticks or other brightly lit accessories, and eat lollipops and candy necklaces. Some wear painters' masks with mentholated vapor rub applied to the inside to enhance ecstasy's effects. Rave culture has become increasingly commercialized since its early days, and today accounts for a large part of the youth entertainment industry. So-called energy drinks (nonalcoholic beverages laced with amino acids) are often marketed at rave clubs. Bottled water is also prevalent at raves since participants drink a lot of water to keep their bodies hydrated and their body temperatures down.

In the early years, most raves were unlicensed, unregulated events held in clandestine locations—usually in remote sites like open fields, caves, or tunnels, and sometimes indoors in empty warehouses, airplane hangars, or barns. Rave locations were kept secret until the day of the event: Ticket holders called special telephone numbers to learn where to go. Largely due to police crackdowns on these unlicensed and unregulated clandestine raves, the rave scene moved to large clubs in urban and suburban areas. Raves attract a young crowd—as young as 13 at unlicensed raves, but more typically in the 17-to-early-20s range in licensed clubs. Younger ravers, sometimes called "candy ravers," are more likely to wear costumes. Different clubs promote different types of rave music and attract different races and sexual orientations (Scott 2002: 20–21).

Effects of Ecstasy

MDMA has a chemical structure similar to the stimulant methamphetamine and the hallucinogen mescaline. MDMA increases the activity levels of at least three neurotransmitters: serotonin, dopamine, and norepinephrine. Compared to the very potent stimulant, methamphetamine, MDMA causes greater serotonin release and somewhat lesser dopamine release (Hanson 2001).

During the 1950s, along with other hallucinogens, it was used—unsuccessfully—by the military as a "truth serum." It was not until its "rediscovery" in the late 1970s that ecstasy received a great deal of attention because of its purported ability to produce profound pleasurable effects: acute euphoria and long-lasting positive changes in attitude and self-confidence, with some symptoms resembling those caused by LSD but without the severe side effects typically associated with methamphetamine.

"The effects of MDMA usually become apparent twenty to sixty minutes following oral ingestion of an average dose (100–125 milligrams) on an empty stomach. The sudden and intense onset of the high experienced by many users is commonly referred to as the 'rush' (also the 'wave' or 'weird period'). This phase was often (particularly during initial use) experienced with a certain degree of trepidation, tension, stomach tightness, and/or mild nausea. This discomfort was generally transitory and melted away into a more relaxed state of being. Although novice users occasionally experienced some apprehension during this initial onset, anxiety levels typically decreased with subsequent use, allowing for increased enjoyment" (Beck and Rosenbaum 1994: 63). The total effects last from 3 to 6 hours.

The drug's rewarding effects vary with the individual taking it, the dose and purity, and the environment in which it is taken. MDMA can produce stimulant effects such as an enhanced sense of pleasure and self-confidence and increased energy—as with amphetamines, it increases heart rate and blood pressure. Its psychedelic effects include feelings of peacefulness, acceptance, and empathy. Users claim they experience feelings of closeness with others and a desire to touch them. Because MDMA engenders feelings of closeness and trust and has a short duration of action, some clinicians claim that the drug is potentially valuable as a psychotherapeutic agent. The mechanism by which the drug exerts its unique effects in humans is not well understood (Tancer and Schuster 1997). It is known that, as is the case with amphetamine, MDMA increases serotonin in the synapses, but it inhibits reuptake several times as much as amphetamine. To a lesser degree, MDMA inhibits dopamine reuptake. Research indicates that ecstasy destroys serotonin-producing neurons, which play a direct role in regulating aggression, mood, sexual activity, sleep, and sensitivity to pain. It is probably this action on the serotonin system that gives it purported properties of heightened sexual experience, tranquility, and conviviality.

Ecstasy Tolerance and Withdrawal

While tolerance to ecstasy develops, withdrawal symptoms, if any, are not known.

Dangers of MDMA

Ecstasy causes large increases in blood pressure, heart rate, and myocardial oxygen consumption, which can increase the risk for a cardiovascular catastrophe in people with preexisting heart disease (Mathias and Zickler 2001). Additional adverse effects include muscle tension, involuntary teeth clenching, nausea, blurred vision, feeling faint, tremors, rapid eye movement, and sweating or chills (*MDMA* 2002).

Animal laboratory evidence shows that MDMA use damages nerve cells, especially serotonergic axons, bringing on Parkinson's disease-like symptoms. In 1985, MDMA was

MDMA
Uses and Effects

Classification:	Hallucinogen
CSA Schedule:	Schedule I
Trade or Other Names:	2,5-DMA, STP, MDA, MDMA, ecstasy, DOM, DOB
Medical Uses:	None
Physical Dependence:	Unknown
Psychological Dependence:	Unknown
Tolerance:	Yes
Duration (hours):	Variable
Usual Method:	Oral, injected
Possible Effects:	Illusions and hallucinations, altered perception of time and distance
Effects of Overdose:	Longer, more intense "trip" episodes, psychosis, possible death
Withdrawal Syndrome:	Unknown

Source: U.S. Drug Enforcement Administration

placed on the DEA's Schedule I, although some medical supporters argue for its experimental use in psychotherapy. Indeed, the DEA has been criticized for placing MDMA in Schedule I, thereby precluding its use clinically, without methodical study of the substance (Shenk 1999). In 1985, scheduling hearings on MDMA were conducted, and the administrative law judge expressed his view that there was sufficient evidence for safe utilization under medical supervision and recommended Schedule III status. He was overruled by the director of the Drug Enforcement Administration, which in 1988 placed MDMA in Schedule I—high potential for abuse, no medically accepted use. Nevertheless, there is continued interest in testing the drug for such disorders as post-traumatic stress disorder (McNeil 2002).

In small doses, MDMA can greatly reduce the body's ability to metabolize the drug, which remains active in the body for longer periods. When users take multiple doses over a brief period, the increased toxic effects can lead to dehydration, hypothermia, and seizures (Mathias and Zickler 2001). In high doses, ecstasy may cause the body's temperature to increase markedly (malignant hyperthermia) leading to muscle breakdown and kidney and cardiovascular system failure, which in some cases has proven fatal. While

Two Dangers

There are two big problems with ecstasy. First, it is not always MDMA, which requires a stable laboratory condition, and impure samples can be lethal. The second problem is hypothermia. "MDMA gives you tons of energy to dance for five straight hours, raises your body temperature and causes dehydration. Though you are not hallucinating, you're so swept up in that terrific sense of well-being that you don't feel as though you're overheating, even when you are. And if you drink too much water to quench that terrific thirst, you can die from thinned-out blood." In effect, you drown yourself (Klam 2001: 43).

drinking water does not reduce the effects of ecstasy, it prevents dehydration. Drinking too much water, however, may lead to serious health complications in some people. Ecstasy may also produce a hangover effect: loss of appetite, insomnia, depression, and muscle aches. It can also make concentration difficult, particularly on the day after ecstasy is taken. Higher doses of ecstasy can produce hallucinations, irrational behavior, vomiting, and convulsions. Some evidence suggests that long-term use of ecstasy may cause damage to the brain, heart, and liver. "Ecstasy users at clubs and raves dance energetically in stuffy quarters, increasing the risk of exhaustion, which can result in dangerous dehydration leading to convulsions and, on occasion, death" (Stryker 2001: D5).

One research effort concluded that MDMA abuse could lead to chronic depression and other harmful effects. According to George Ricaurte (Blakeslee 1995), the drug destroys serotonin-carrying axons, which subsequently regenerate, making new connections to the brain. However, according to Ricaurte, in tests on monkeys and rats, these new connections are markedly abnormal. In a letter to the *New York Times,* two other researchers (Goldsmith and Doblin 1995) challenged Ricaurte's findings, along with other critics, who argue that the drugs used in his experiments on monkeys and rats were 45 times the usual recreational dosage for humans (McNeil 2002). A subsequent study by Ricaurte concluded that *heavy* use of MDMA caused significant decreases in neurons responsible for reabsorbing serotonin (Goode 1998). Human ecstasy users showed extensive damage to neurons that use serotonin to communicate with other neurons, and they scored lower on memory tests (NIDA 1999b). Learning and memory functions appear to be impaired by MDMA. There continues to be debate over the harmful effects of ecstasy to recreational users. Ricaurte insists that the amount taken in a single night may cause permanent brain damage and lead to symptoms like those of Parkinson's disease.

PMA (paramethoxyamphetamine), an illegal synthetic hallucinogen that has stimulant effects similar to MDMA, is sometimes sold as ecstasy. When users take PMA thinking they are ingesting MDMA, they often conclude they have taken weak ecstasy because PMA's effects take longer to appear. "They then ingest more of the substance to attain a better high, which can result in overdose and death" (*MDMA* 2002: 2).

Ketamine

Ketamine is a disassociative anesthetic similar to PCP, but produces less confusion, irrationality, and violence. Developed in the 1960s, ketamine is used as a surgical anesthetic for children, who are typically able to avoid unpleasant reactions, for battlefield injuries in which rapid onset is critical, and for repeated procedures such as chemotherapy and treatment of burns. It is also used in veterinary medicine, primarily to immobilize cats or monkeys. Its use in human surgery has declined with introduction of safer, more effective products.

The synthesis of ketamine is complicated, and to date, diversion of the legitimate product—particularly the burglary of veterinary facilities—is the only known source on the street. Street users often refer to the drug as "K" or "special K," and it is sold in powder, capsule, tablet, solutions, and some injectable forms. Ketamine powder can be snorted like cocaine, mixed into drinks, or smoked. The liquid is either injected, applied to smokable materials, or consumed in drinks. Its illegal use is associated with "acid house" music that also makes references to other hallucinogens such as LSD and MDMA. However, less is known about the extent of its abuse and dangers, although habituation can result in significant mental and emotional problems (Dotson, Ackerman, and West 1995).

A pharmaceutical vial of liquid contains the equivalent of about 1 gram of powder. A smaller quantity, called a "bump," is about 0.2 gram and costs about $20. Ketamine can produce a very wide range of effects, and users adjust the dosage depending on the effect desired. The drug's effect can be influenced by body size, tolerance, the presence of alcohol or other drugs, the method of administration, and the setting in which the drug is consumed. In the past several years, law enforcement has encountered ketamine powder packaged in small plastic bags, folded paper, aluminum foil, and capsules. These packets commonly contain 0.2 gram and, more recently, .07 gram. Some users inhale about .02 gram in each nostril, repeated in 5- to 10-minute intervals until the desired state is reached. A dose of .07 gram may produce intoxication. A larger dose of 0.2 gram may result in "Kland," a "mellow, colorful wonderworld." A dose of 0.5 gram can produce a "K-hole," or "out-of-body, near-death experience." With repeated daily exposure, users can develop tolerance and psychological dependence (Drug Enforcement Administration information). In 1999, ketamine was placed into Schedule III of the Controlled Substances Act.

Rohypnol

The benzodiazepine **Rohypnol** (flunitrazepam), although not approved for use in the United States, where it is classified as a Schedule III drug, is prescribed in about seventy countries for the short-term (4 weeks or less) treatment of insomnia. It is the most widely prescribed sedative in Europe (ONDCP 1998). It is ten times as potent as Valium. The effects begin within 20 minutes of administration and, depending on the amount ingested, may persist for more than 12 hours. The drug may be detected in urine for up to 72 hours (ONDCP 2002b).

Rohypnol is known on the street as rophies, roofies, rope, ruffies, R2, roofenol, roche, and roachies. The illegal flunitrazepam sold in the United States is typically diverted from legal sources in Mexico and South America. Usually sold here in the original bubble packs of 1- or 2-mg tablets, the drug is taken with alcohol or marijuana to enhance intoxication, and is popular in some adolescent/young adult crowds. Heroin abusers use flunitrazepam to enhance the effects of low-quality heroin, and cocaine abusers have reported using Rohypnol to ease down from a cocaine or crack binge. "Like other benzodiazepines, when taken alone, it is unlikely to cause problems. But, if combined even with a small amount of alcohol, the intoxication effects may be extreme, leading to severely impaired judgment and motor skills" (Fields 2001: 57). It may require 8 to 24 hours for recovery, and the person may have no memory of any events that transpired while under the influence.

Lethal overdose is unlikely, however, Rohypnol may be lethal when mixed with alcohol and/or other depressants. Like other benzodiazepines, prolonged use will result in physical dependence. Withdrawal symptoms include headache, muscle pain, and confusion. Severe withdrawal involving hallucinations and convulsions can occur. Seizures have been reported a week or more after last use. The substance, which can be ingested orally, snorted, or injected, induces muscle relaxation, short-term amnesia, and sleep. Rohypnol takes about 15 to 20 minutes to affect the CNS, lasts more than 8 hours, and induces tolerance (Navarro 1995). Adverse effects include drowsiness, hangover, dizziness, gastrointestinal upsets, confusion, and headaches.

Because it is colorless, odorless, and tasteless, Rohypnol has been implicated in cases of *date rape*—people may unknowingly be given the drug, which when mixed with alcohol, can incapacitate a victim and prevent her or him from resisting sexual assault. It can also cause a blackout and little if any memory of the assault. In response, in 1996, Congress passed the Drug-Induced Rape Prevention and Punishment Act, which provides for severe punishment for distribution of a controlled substance to an individual without that person's knowledge or consent and with the intent to commit a crime of violence, including rape (Navarro 1995; Seligmann and King 1996).

GHB and GBL

Similar to Rohypnol, **GHB** (gamma-hydroxybutyrate) and its precursor **GBL** (gamma-butyrolactone) are colorless, odorless, virtually tasteless, and in very low doses act as CNS depressants; in higher doses, they can produce unconsciousness and even respiratory failure. GBL was widely available as a dietary supplement in "health food" stores until an FDA recall in 1999. GBL is used as an industrial solvent, and tens of thousands of metric tons are produced each year and sold by its chemical name, 2(3H)-furanone dihydro (Brown 1999). Ingredients in GBL and GHB are found in a number of dietary supplements sold in health food stores, where they are promoted to induce sleep, build muscles, and enhance sexual performance. More than two dozen states have outlawed GHB, and at the beginning of 2000, it was placed in Schedule I of the Controlled Substances Act. It is typically manufactured from caustic chemicals such as paint or furniture polish remover, and when poorly prepared can cause severe chemical burns of the user's throat. An error in dosage of a tiny fraction of a gram can result in coma and death. GHB has been used by sexual predators since, in addition to rendering victims unconscious, it often causes them to forget what happened.

GHB Withdrawal

GHB has a withdrawal syndrome that has aspects of alcohol withdrawal (delirium tremens) and benzodiazepine withdrawal (long duration of symptoms). The syndrome appears to manifest itself in those patients who have self-administered GHB in an around-the-clock dosing schedule—that is, users who take GHB every 2–3 hours are at increased risk for the emergence of severe symptoms. GHB withdrawal can occur after several months of around-the-clock use. Due to the drug's short duration of action and rapid elimination, the signs and symptoms of GHB abstinence syndrome appear rapidly, generally within 1 to 6 hours after the last dose.

Withdrawal symptoms begin with anxiety, insomnia, tremor, and episodes of tachycardia (rapid heartbeat). Symptoms may rapidly progress to a state of uncontrolled delirium and agitation. According to Miotto and Roth (2001), the following symptoms can also occur:

- Anorexia, abdominal cramps
- Nightmares
- Impaired concentration, memory, and judgment
- Increased sensitivity to sounds and tactile sensations
- Delusions
- Elevated temperature
- Dehydration

Despite its apparent dangers, GHB has been useful in treating cataplexy, an illness experienced by about 50,000 persons who also suffer from narcolepsy, a serious sleeping disorder that afflicts more than 200,000 persons in the United States. *Cataplexy* results in muscle weakness that can cause victims to collapse without warning. GHB, under the brand name Xyrem, has been approved by the Food and Drug Administration for treatment of cataplexy and sold under severe restrictions (Reese 2000; "FDA: Date-Rape Drug Has Medical Use" 2002).

Cannabis

Marijuana does not fit easily into any of the categories we have already discussed, so accordingly we will consider it separately. Its scientific name *Cannabis sativa,* Latin for

Marijuana grows wild in most tropical and temperate regions, yet farmers cultivate it as an illegal crop. Growers kill male plants because only females produce the commercially valuable flowering buds of sticky resin. (The bigger the buds, the higher the profit.)

© Dennis Cody/Getty Images

"cultivated hemp," was given by the Swedish scientist Linnaeus, which accounts for the *L.* sometimes added to the term. The plant grows wild throughout most of the tropical and temperate regions of the world, including parts of the United States. It has been cultivated for the tough fiber of its stem, and its seed is used in feed mixtures and its oil in paint. The psychoactive part of the plant is an isomer of tetrahydrocannabinol (Delta9THC—hereafter THC), which is most highly concentrated in the leaves and resinous flowering tops.

The THC level of marijuana cigarettes varies considerably: Domestic marijuana has typically had less than 0.5 percent, although more recent plants have considerably higher levels. Indeed, the domestic cultivation of marijuana has spawned a significant market in horticultural equipment. These suppliers advertise in *High Times,* a magazine devoted to marijuana use. Much of the cultivation in the United States is accomplished indoors. "Care for these plants involves little more than watering during dry periods, light fertilizing, and weeding. The plants may grow to between sixteen and twenty feet tall. At harvest time these plants are cut at the base and hung upside down to dry so that they will not mold when packaged. The grower will sell both the leaves and any flowering tops, yielding as much as three pounds of marijuana per harvested plant" (Weisheit 1989: 7). The plant grows best under the same conditions that favor corn. THC in Jamaican, Colombian, and Mexican marijuana ranges from 0.5 to 4 percent; and the most select product, sinsemilla (from the Spanish, *sin semilla,* "without seed"), has been found to have as much as 8 percent. Male plants are killed so that the female plant, in seeking to trap pollen, produces more and more of the sticky resin that covers the buds. These buds grow

---

Marijuana
Uses and Effects

Classification:	Cannabis
CSA Schedule:	Schedule I
Trade or Other Names:	Pot, Acapulco Gold, grass, reefer, sinsemilla, Thai sticks
Medical Uses:	None
Physical Dependence:	Unknown
Psychological Dependence:	Moderate
Tolerance:	Yes
Duration (hours):	2–4
Usual Method:	Smoked, oral
Possible Effects:	Euphoria, relaxed inhibitions, increased appetite, disorientation
Effects of Overdose:	Fatigue, paranoia, possible psychosis
Withdrawal Syndrome:	Occasional reports of insomnia, hyperactivity, decreased appetite

Source: U.S. Drug Enforcement Administration

---

as large as a man's arm from the fingertips to the elbow. Growers concentrate on sinsemilla, selling these flowering tops; indeed, nowadays the leaves of the cannabis plant—"shake"—are typically discarded. Indoor cultivation has been aided by miniaturization—"marijuana bonsai"—of plants with an abundance of THC-rich buds (Pollan 1995).

Hashish, usually from the Middle East, contains the drug-rich resinous secretions of the cannabis plant, which are collected, dried, and then compressed into a variety of forms—balls, cakes, or cookielike sheets. It has a potency as high as 10 percent. Hashish is usually mixed with tobacco and smoked in a pipe. Hashish oil—a misnomer—is simply the result of repeated extractions of cannabis plant materials to yield a dark viscous liquid with a THC level as high as 20 percent. A drop or two on a cigarette has the effect of a single marijuana cigarette. Marijuana prepared for street sale may be diluted with oregano, catnip, or other ingredients and may also contain psychoactive substances such as LSD; marijuana from Vietnam often contained opium.

Effects of Cannabis

Cannabis preparations can be eaten or drunk in mixtures of resin and water or milk, a form known in India as *bhang*. In the United States marijuana is usually rolled in paper or inserted into a hollowed-out cigar—"blunting"—and smoked, the user typically inhaling the smoke deeply and holding it in the lungs for as long as possible. This tends to maximize the absorption of THC, about one-half of which is lost during smoking. THC appears to act as a dopamine agonist while also having an opiate-like effect on the brain's receptor system (M. Gold 1994). The psychoactive reaction occurs in 1 to 10 minutes and peaks in about 10 to 30 minutes, with a total duration of about 3 to 4 hours.

Exactly how marijuana affects the central nervous system is not entirely known. In 1990, researchers discovered cannabinoid receptors discretely located throughout the brain. These brain receptors are stimulated by the drug, indicating that there may be a naturally occurring THC neurotransmitter (Hilts 1990; Martin et al. 1994). It was subsequently discovered that, in fact, humans produce cannabinoids—*anandamide* (Harris 1999). Brain receptors react to anandamide as well as compounds in cannabis, triggering similar effects. In 1997, researchers found that marijuana triggers the release of dopamine, which stimulates pleasure centers of the brain and a craving for more marijuana (Blakeslee 1997; Carroll 2002).

The most important variables with respect to the drug's impact are the individual's experiences and expectations and the strength of the marijuana. Thus, the first-time user may not experience any significant reaction. In general, low doses tend to induce restlessness, an increasing sense of well-being, and gregariousness, followed by a dreamy state of relaxation and frequently hunger, especially for sweets. Higher doses may induce changes in sensory perception resulting in a more vivid sense of smell, sight, hearing, and taste, which may be accompanied by subtle alterations in thought formation and expression.

Although the substance has some use in medicine—for example, to relieve the pressure on the eyes of glaucoma patients, to control the nausea and vomiting that accompany cancer chemotherapy, and to control the muscle spasms of multiple sclerosis patients—its use remains illegal. Since 1982, however, there has been a legally available pharmaceutical for physicians in ophthalmology and cancer treatment, **Marinol** (dronabinol), which is 98.8 percent pure THC. There is some dispute as to whether or not oral THC is as effective as smoking marijuana (see, for example, Grinspoon 1987, and a response from Jourbert 1987; also in opposition to smoking marijuana, see Nahas and Pace 1993). In 1989 an administrative law judge for the Drug Enforcement Administration recommended that marijuana be placed on a less restricted schedule, one that would make it available by medical prescription. The judge called marijuana "one of the safest therapeutically active substances known to man." The DEA rejected the judge's recommendation ("U.S. Resists Easing Curb on Marijuana" 1989). In 1997, voters in Arizona and California approved referendums permitting the use of marijuana for medical purposes. The federal government responded by threatening to arrest any doctors who violate federal antimarijuana statutes.

Hashish
Uses and Effects

Classification:	Cannabis
CSA Schedule:	Schedule I
Trade or Other Names:	Hash, hash oil
Medical Uses:	None
Physical Dependence:	Unknown
Psychological Dependence:	Moderate
Tolerance:	Yes
Duration (hours):	2–4
Usual Method:	Smoked, oral
Possible Effects:	Euphoria, relaxed inhibitions, increased appetite, disorientation
Effects of Overdose:	Fatigue, paranoia, possible psychosis
Withdrawal Syndrome:	Occasional reports of insomnia, hyperactivity, decreased appetite

Source: U.S. Drug Enforcement Administration

In 2003, five jurors in a federal trial in California that convicted a medicinal marijuana advocate issued a public apology to him and demanded the judge grant him a new trial. The jurors said they had been unaware that the defendant, Ed Rosenthal, was growing marijuana for medical purposes when they convicted him on three federal counts of cultivation and conspiracy. The reason for Rosenthal's marijuana cultivation was ruled inadmissible at trial (Murphy 2003).

In 1999, a federally commissioned report by the Institute of Medicine stated that the active ingredient in marijuana is useful for treating pain, nausea, and the severe weight loss experienced by victims of AIDS. Because the smoke emitted by marijuana is even more toxic than tobacco, the report recommended use of the drug only on a short-time basis, under close supervision, for patients who failed to respond to other therapies (Stolberg 1999a). That same year, the Clinton administration announced that it would sell government-grown marijuana to researchers conducting high-quality research (Stolberg 1999b).

Marijuana Tolerance and Withdrawal

Animal and human studies conducted since the 1970s have revealed a marijuana withdrawal syndrome, which although less severe than that for alcohol, heroin, or cocaine, is characterized by insomnia, restlessness, loss of appetite, irritability, anger, and aggression (Carroll 2002). In 1999, a study found that people who have smoked marijuana daily for many years display more aggressive behavior when they stop smoking the drug (NIDA 1999a). However, THC has a very long half-life, working its way out of the body slowly over many days and, thereby, obviating severe withdrawal symptoms (Markel 2002). In fact, marijuana withdrawal is similar to that experienced by cigarette smokers when they quit (Carroll 2002; Zickler 2002).

Dangers of Marijuana Use

The negative short-term effects of marijuana seem quite limited: loss of inhibition, with some users also experiencing a loss of self-confidence, aggressiveness, and even auditory hallucinations. High doses impair learning, short-term memory, and reaction time (Misner and Sullivan 1999). And the more potent marijuana ingested by users today, as opposed to the heady days of Woodstock and the sixties, is more likely to bring on paranoia in some users (Markel 2002).

Marijuana causes a significant increase in heart rate that is, however, no more dangerous than the increase caused by using caffeine and nicotine. Casual use results in the same impairments that can be expected from equal amounts of alcohol (Abel 1978). The long-range effects are more controversial, some claiming no significant physical or psychological damage and others finding the opposite. While most marijuana users are able to quit, there appears to be a small portion of that population, 10–14 percent, who become strongly dependent (Carroll 2002).

SUMMARY

Hallucinogens overwhelm the nervous system's ability to modulate sensory input, resulting in altered perceptions of reality, sensory illusions, and hallucinations. LSD produces strong visual effects, with space appearing to contract and enlarge; it changes the user's sense of time and self, and appears to intensify feelings, thus making a "trip" highly susceptible to the expectations of the user. About 25 percent of former LSD users report flashbacks within a few days to several months after their last use. PCP users experience a sense of detachment from their surroundings and, often, a feeling of invulnerability. They are often difficult to handle because of PCP's bizarre effects, and users demonstrate remarkable strength and may exhibit anxiety, paranoia, and violent behavior. Mescaline and psilocybin are natural hallucinogens used for centuries in Native American religious rituals.

Ecstasy (MDMA)—the most popular of the club drugs—produces both stimulant and hallucinogenic effects, the stimulant effect being a rush and increased energy and the psychedelic effect being feelings of peacefulness and empathy with others. Ketamine is similar to PCP, but users experience less confusion and irrationality and are less prone to violence. Rohypnol is the most widely prescribed sedative in Europe but is illegal in the United States, partly because of its connection with date rape. GHB and its precursor GBL are similar to Rohypnol. Although GHB has dangerous effects and withdrawal symptoms, it is also a legal drug when used to treat cataplexy. Marijuana's effect depends on the user's expectations and the potency of the dose, but typically it induces a dreamy state of relaxation. Long-range effects have not been determined.

INTERNET CONNECTIONS

See "Internet Connections" in Chapters 1, 3, 4, and 5 for information on hallucinogens and marijuana.

REVIEW QUESTIONS

1. How do hallucinogens affect the central nervous system?
2. What determines whether an LSD trip will be a good one or a bad one?
3. How does PCP affect the user?
4. What are the dangers of PCP use?
5. How is mescaline produced?
6. What are the effects of peyote?
7. What is ketamine, and what are its effects?
8. What is MDMA? What are its dangers?
9. What is Rohypnol? What are its dangers?
10. What are GHB and GBL, and what are their dangers?
11. What are the effects of smoking cannabis?

CHAPTER 7

The Sociology of Drug Abuse

In order to be motivated to continue to experiment with the use of any drug, the individual must learn to use the drug appropriately and to experience its effects as pleasurable. This may depend partly on genetic predisposition, which influences whether drug use is pleasurable and to a large degree on contact with a peer/user network already socialized into these practices and understandings.

—*Advisory Council on the Misuse of Drugs (1998: 31)*

Since the discovery of drugs as a social problem (discussed in Chapter 2), attempts have been made to explain why some persons become dependent on chemicals while others, even those who use the same substances, do not. These explanations go beyond simply labeling abusers as "bad" or "weak" persons oriented toward a harmful vice: "Some believe it is a medical disease,[1] while others believe it is a behavioral problem. Some consider it to have genetic origins; others consider it to be primarily environmentally determined. Some examine it within a cultural context, others consider it to be an individual adjustment reaction. Some view it as a personality disorder, while others view it as a psychosocial problem" (Pickens and Thompson 1984: 53). In the biopsychosocial model, drug dependence is seen as being determined by the interaction of psychological, environmental, and physiological factors (Donovan 1988).

Theories of drug use typically depend on the discipline of the observer: neurology and pharmacology (discussed in Chapters 3, 4, 5, and 6), psychology (discussed in Chapter 8), and sociology, discussed in this chapter. While many theories of drug use presented by these disciplines may seem competitive or even conflicting, our examination will emphasize their complementary nature: Each provides a partial explanation for drug use and has important treatment and policy implications.

Sociological Theory

Since the social or behavioral sciences are concerned with behavior that is peculiarly human, (ethically based) testing is limited accordingly. We can subject rats to extreme

---

[1]"Moving etiological and rehabilitative issues from the context of morals to that of medicine offered many advantages. The legitimacy bestowed on substance abuse by treating it as a disease opened the way for more humane and effective treatment of patients. In addition, this view provided the impetus for scientific research into the condition" (Siegal et al. 1995: 67).

While many college students are focused on academics, others are learning to abuse alcohol and other drugs. The overindulgence of alcohol has become a social norm at college fraternities across America.

© Michael Jang/Getty Images

levels of physical stress and then study their reaction to morphine, but we cannot subject human beings to similar levels of stress, expose them to morphine, and then see if they become drug addicts. The social or behavioral sciences have to study the etiology of drug addiction in a more circuitous manner.

Sociological theory is concerned with social structures and social behavior, so it examines drug use in its social context. A sociological perspective often views drug use as the product of social conditions and relationships that cause despair, frustration, hopelessness, and general feelings of alienation in the most disadvantaged segments of the population (Biernacki 1986). The National Institute on Drug Abuse (*Drug Abuse* 1987) outlines factors that are associated positively with adolescent substance abuse, factors found more frequently in deprived socioeconomic environments:

1. Families whose members have a history of alcohol abuse and/or histories of antisocial behavior or criminality
2. Inconsistent parental supervision, with reactions that swing from permissiveness to severity
3. Parental approval or use of dangerous substances
4. Friends who abuse drugs
5. Children who fail in school during late elementary years and who show a lack of interest in school during early adolescence
6. Children who are alienated and rebellious
7. Antisocial behavior during early adolescence, particularly aggressive behavior

Many sociological studies have found that drug use among adolescents is motivated by intermittent feelings of boredom and depression, and like other aspects of adolescence,

Summary of Risk Factors for Drug Use

Culture and Society

- laws favorable to drug use
- social norms favorable to drug use
- availability of drugs
- extreme economic deprivations
- neighborhood disorganization

Interpersonal

- parent and family drug use
- positive family attitudes toward drug use
- poor/inconsistent family management practices
- family conflict and disruption
- peer rejection
- association with drug-using peers

Psychobehavioral

- early/persistent problem behavior
- academic failure
- low commitment to school
- alienation
- rebelliousness
- favorable attitudes toward drug use
- early onset of drug use

Biogenetic

- inherited susceptibility to drug abuse
- psychophysiological vulnerability to drug effects

Source: Newcomb (1995: 17)

it is typically abandoned upon reaching adulthood. Furthermore, contrary to conventional wisdom, research has found that drug use is typically a group activity of socially *well-integrated youngsters* (Glassner and Loughlin 1989). That is, contrary to some psychological views, the adolescent drug user is socially competent (or ego sufficient). Sociological studies often challenge the conflicting views of the adolescent drug user as either a deviant isolate or a peer-driven conformist. Sociology also cautions us to separate drug use that is situational and transitional from drug dependence or addiction, which is compulsive and dysfunctional. In England, the much smaller number of those adolescents who use illicit drugs regularly, as opposed to those who have tried illicit drugs, "reminds us that because a young person has tried an illicit drug does not mean that they will necessarily develop a pattern of long term misuse" (Advisory Council on the Misuse of Drugs 1998: xii). This has important policy implications.

> Treatment approaches based on sociological (and any variety of social-psychological) theories usually stress resocialization, the adopting of prosocial values, and/or submission to a peer culture that is strongly opposed to drug use. For example, according to a social stress model, adolescents initiate substance use as a means of coping with a variety of stressors and influences that may arise from within the family, the school, the peer group, or the community. [And] adolescents will be more resilient and, as such, less likely to engage in problematic early usage as a means of coping with these stressors if they are members of prosocial, supportive social networks. (Rhodes and Jason 1990: 396)

Studying the Stages of Drug Addiction

Sociologists have studied and labeled the stages that alcohol, heroin, and cocaine users go through on the path to addiction.

Alcohol

The alcoholic typically passes through several stages on the way to becoming addicted to alcohol (Catanzarite 1992):

- *Social drinking*. In this initial pattern, alcohol is used to enhance pleasant social situations. The drug is taken for relaxation and entertainment. For some individuals, drinking alcohol has a ritualistic dimension—a glass of wine or beer or a drink with a meal or as part of a religious ritual. Others may have an alcoholic beverage after work with colleagues—"a beer with the boys." The social drinker imbibes small amounts and does not experience harmful effects such as loss of control or impaired judgment. While social drinkers view alcohol as generating positive feelings, they do not need the substance for enjoyment. The social drinker observes societal conventions about when, where, and how much to drink.
- *Heavy drinking*. The heavy drinker uses alcohol to escape. For one type of drinker this critical step involves a circular problem—he or she experiences constantly high levels of stress and seeks relief by drinking alcohol, which creates additional stress that must be relieved by more alcohol. Another type resorts to heavy alcohol use when particular stressful problems are encountered and reduces drinking in their absence. By becoming intoxicated, both types of drinkers violate social conventions about the

use of alcohol and suffer negative side effects with respect to family, friends, and employment. They become defensive about their drinking and deny the influence of alcohol on their lives.

- *Dependent drinking*. The person is now addicted to alcohol and suffers from many consequences—an inability to function normally either socially, intellectually, or physically. He or she is not able to control drinking behavior and becomes obsessed and preoccupied with alcohol. Indeed, the person needs alcohol to "feel normal."

Heroin and Cocaine

Heroin and cocaine addiction have been studied extensively, with two general conclusions (Gerstein and Harwood 1990):

1. Initial use is experimental in nature and begins during adolescence.
2. Very few persons *begin* using drugs after reaching age 25 (unless drugs were not previously available).

The pattern has a familiar sequence: from tobacco and alcohol to marijuana and then to other illegal psychoactive substances such as heroin and cocaine. While most new users do not progress very far, the earlier the onset of use the more likely is dependence. "Individuals who do not initiate the use of alcohol or tobacco tend not to initiate the use of marijuana. Similarly, those who do not initiate the use of marijuana tend not to progress to hard drug use" (Golub and Johnson 1994: 404).

Heroin. The life of a heroin addict can be seen as a "career" with a number of stages:

- *Experimentation*. The individual, usually an adolescent, experiments with a variety of substances, including alcohol, cigarettes, marijuana, and perhaps barbiturates and amphetamines, and may snort or use heroin subcutaneously.
- *Initiation*. The drug abuser is initiated into intravenous use of heroin. Although the first use is often accompanied by unpleasant side effects such as vomiting, he or she learns to enjoy subsequent injections. Heroin use begins to be a center of existence.
- *Commitment*. The user is now an addict and takes on the social identity associated with the drug subculture, orienting his or her life toward the maintenance of a heroin habit.
- *Disjunction*. The addict's life is now characterized by crime, arrest, and imprisonment, interspersed with participation in drug treatment programs in response to court direction (to avoid imprisonment), or to reduce an expensive habit to manageable size, or to deal with severe physical ailments.
- *Maturation*. At some point, usually when the addict is closer to 40 years old than to 20, he or she typically begins to use only sporadically, gives up drugs completely as a result of treatment, or simply experiences spontaneous remission—or dies. While there are relatively few elderly (over the age of 50) addicts in the heroin-using population, one California study found that among hard-core addicts, by age 50 to 60

years, half of the 242 subjects tested positive for heroin (Hser et al. 2001). The "aging out" phenomenon is also found in other types of deviant behavior, such as crime in general.

"The addict lifestyle," notes Marsha Rosenbaum, "rotates around taking heroin for the purposes of alleviating withdrawal symptoms and/or getting high" (1981: 14). Heroin is quite costly and too expensive for most addicts to secure with only legitimate sources of income. Nevertheless, a habit requires intravenous use three, four, or five times daily, and the addict also requires funds for minimal life-support items such as food, clothing, and housing. If the addict is also a dealer, or is sufficiently organized, he or she is able to start the day with a fix. Few addicts, however, are able to plan even for the immediate future, so they rarely keep enough heroin in reserve to begin the day with a "wake-up fix." Without funds or drugs, the addict must begin the day "hustling" for money to get the first fix.

After a "connection" is made and the heroin is purchased, the drug must be ingested as part of an almost ritualistic process. A safe place must be found where the addict, often in the company of other addicts, can inject the substance with a hypodermic syringe. The addict typically allows the solution to mix with blood by bringing blood back and forth into the syringe, or "booting." Some researchers see this as analogous to sexual intercourse, and many users describe it as more pleasurable and intense than sexual orgasm. In any event, as the short-term heightened feeling of euphoria that follows ingestion—the rush—subsides, the addict begins to experience the high, a feeling of general well-being that lasts about 4 hours. The cycle then needs to be repeated. "This is the 'addict's cycle'—an existence almost literally from fix to fix—with the necessary heroin-related activities in between" (M. Rosenbaum 1981: 15).

The heroin user recognizes the dangers of addiction, but "it is typical of the early experience of the addict-to-be that he knows or knows of people who use narcotics and who get away with it" (Duster 1970: 192). He sees himself as indestructible: "the tendency of the ego to treat the self as exempt from the experience of personal disaster."

Cocaine. Here are some typical steps involved in becoming a cocaine abuser (based on D. Smith 1986):

- *Experimental use.* The individual begins his or her initiation out of curiosity in a social situation in which some friends offer a "taste" of cocaine. Most of his or her friends are nonusers, and the subject uses cocaine only when it is offered to enhance feelings. Relationships remain normal, and no significant health or financial problems appear. There may even be an improvement in work performance and social functioning—gregariousness or extroversion.
- *Compulsive use.* The subject begins to buy cocaine and increases the number of friends who are users. Solitary use of cocaine follows, and use to enhance moods and performance and to ward off depression associated with the "crash" of coming down off cocaine continues to increase. Social disruptions appear, particularly mood swings, as well as health problems due to a lack of proper nutrition and sleep. Work performance begins to steadily deteriorate, and the abuser avoids nondrug-using

friends. He or she begins to encounter financial problems that result from supporting a growing cocaine habit.

■ *Dysfunctional use.* The abuser is preoccupied with drug use and associates only with cocaine-using friends. He or she may begin to deal in cocaine and/or to engage in other illegal or financially damaging activities to support the dependence on cocaine. Severe disruption of social life follows, including marital violence and divorce. Serious medical pathology appears, with a risk of seizure and toxic psychosis, paranoia, delusions, and hallucinations. The abuser has chronic sleep and nutritional problems as well. His or her physical appearance deteriorates; this is usually accompanied by a lack of concern with personal hygiene and dress. Compulsion, a loss of control, and an inability to stop despite adverse consequences lead the abuser to seek treatment, often because of pressure from family, friends, and/or employer and/or because of serious legal entanglements.

Early research (for example, Washton and Gold 1987) and journalistic sources reported that addiction to crack cocaine appeared to present a different progression because the speed with which this substance acts can lead to chronic habituation or addiction very quickly. In their research, however, Jeffrey Fagan and Ko-Lin Chin (1991) found no significant difference between the addictive qualities of crack and powdered cocaine. Crack users, however, more often reported an inability to stop using it. For reasons that have not yet been determined, crack has proven to be more popular than heroin among women, leading to a significant increase in child neglect and abuse as well as to increasing numbers of newborn children with cocaine in their urine and syphilis resulting from the sexual activity of their crack-abusing mothers. A seller describes a crack house as "full of young girls—fourteen, fifteen, sixteen years old. Some of these girls stayed for days at a time, getting high and having sex with these guys," any guy who offered drugs (T. Williams 1989: 108). Smoking crack reduces inhibitions while creating a desire for more drugs, leading female users to unprotected sexual behavior and the risk of sexually transmitted diseases, including AIDS. In their research Fagan and Chin found "no significant differences among those involved in crack, cocaine HCL [powdered cocaine], heroin or other drugs in the location, motivation or methods of introduction to their new drug" (1991: 327). Most (90 percent) were introduced to the new drug by family or friends, and they (71 percent) got it free. In their study Andrew Golub and Bruce Johnson (1994) found that older crack users were nearly all former heroin injecters or cocaine snorters, while crack tended to be the first hard drug for younger users.

Let us now examine some of the major sociological theories that help explain drug abuse.

Anomie

Derived from the Greek meaning "lack of law," **anomie** was used by sociologist Emile Durkheim (1858–1917) to describe an abnormal social condition wherein the cohesion of society is weakened by some crisis, such as an economic depression, that causes each

Substance Abuser Characteristics

"Regardless of social class differences, substance abusers share important similarities. All reveal some problems in socialization, cognitive/emotional skills, and overall psychological development, which is evident in their immaturity, poor self-esteem, conduct and character disorders, or antisocial characteristics. Typical features include low tolerance for all forms of discomfort and delay of gratification; inability to manage feelings (particularly hostility, guilt, and anxiety); poor impulse control (particularly sexual or aggressive); poor judgment and reality testing concerning consequences of actions; unrealistic self-appraisal in terms of a discrepancy between personal resources and aspirations; prominence of lying, manipulation, and deception as coping behaviors; and problems with authority and personal and social irresponsibility (i.e., inconsistency or failures in completing expected obligations and persistent difficulties in managing guilt)" (De Leon 1994: 19–20).

individual to pursue his or her own solitary interests without concern for the wider society. In 1938 Robert Merton "Americanized" the concept, arguing that no other society comes so close to viewing economic success as such an absolute value that the pressure to succeed tends to eliminate social constraint over the means employed to achieve success. In the United States, "good" (ambition) causes "evil" (deviance). According to Merton, anomie results when people, confronted by the contradiction between goals and means, "become estranged from a society that promises them in principle what they are denied in reality [economic opportunity]" (1964: 218). This sense of *strain* is particularly strong among the disadvantaged segments of our population whose use of drugs is endemic.

Response to Anomie

Strain leads to anomie, suffering to which people respond in one of four ways:

1. *Conformity.* Most scale down their aspirations and conform to conventional social norms.
2. *Rebellion.* Some rebel, rejecting the conventional social structure and seeking instead to establish a "new social order" through political action or alternative lifestyles.
3. *Innovation.* Some turn to innovation, which Merton defines as the use of illegitimate means to gain success, in particular professional and organized criminality, including drug trafficking.
4. *Retreatism.* The final response, retreatism, explains drug abuse: The individual abandons all attempts to reach conventional social goals in favor of a deviant adaptation.

The *retreat* into drug abuse allows the addict to expend time and energy to achieve an attainable goal—getting high. Dan Waldorf notes:

> The need for heroin requires an active life. The addict *may* be, as psychologists have claimed, depressed, he may be psychopathic, and he may use drugs to escape some reality in his life, but he is active in pursuit of a demanding life that requires considerable skill and ability to sustain. Addiction is *not* some aberrant, part-time leisure activity that one indulges in from time to time but that never engages one's life. On the contrary, addiction does engage the addict in an active life that has a precise purpose and satisfies a specific physical need. Whatever the individual's motives for using heroin or the ways in which a specific addict approaches his heroin use, he most certainly experiences an absorbing or engrossing drive, lives an active life, and is very much part of a social group. (1973: 10)

Edward Preble and John Casey argue that the behavior of the heroin addict is anything but an escape: "They are actively engaged in meaningful activities and relationships seven days a week. The brief moments of euphoria after each administration of a small amount of heroin constitute a small fraction of their daily lives. The rest of the time they are aggressively pursuing a career that is exacting, challenging, adventurous, and rewarding. They are always on the move and must be alert, flexible, and resourceful" (1995: 121).

Some heroin addicts view life as an adventure. As a San Francisco addict explained to John Irwin: "Cowboys and Indians at the Saturday matinee didn't have a life that was any more exciting than this. The cops are the bad guys, you are the glorious bandit. . . . The chase is on all day long. You awaken in the morning to shoot the dope you saved to be well enough to go out and get some more. First you have to get some money. To steal you have to outwit those you steal from, plus the police. It is very exciting" (1970: 19). The typical heroin addict, note Bertram Sackman and his colleagues, "exhibits as much pride in his heroin-getting skills as does the licit craftsman. He thinks about hustling and heroin, he talks about his exploits to other addicts, and his righteousness about heroin is rewarded by his women in the admiration and respect they accord him and his skills" (1978: 433). Being "in the life" is *reinforcing* (see Chapter 8).

According to Richard Cloward and Lloyd Ohlin (1960), however, the heroin addict is actually a *double failure*, unsuccessful at *both* legitimate and illegitimate enterprises—his or her crimes are typically high-risk, low-yield activities. In this case, the first response to anomie is *innovation;* when that fails to reduce the anomic condition, the addict moves to *retreatism.*

Problems with the Theory

Chein and his colleagues (1964) used a questionnaire to examine anomic attitudes. The questionnaires were administered to classes of eighth-grade male public school students in three neighborhoods with varying rates of delinquency—low, medium, and high (although even the "low" neighborhood had a relatively high rate of delinquency). Anomie was highly correlated with heroin use. But, as noted in Chapter 1, the drug-crime sequence is not at all certain. According to the Cloward and Ohlin thesis, delinquency/crime precedes drug dependence, but research has not clearly supported this contention. In any event, the successful and skilled (innovative) criminal is so rare that the double failure thesis must be questioned (Lindesmith and Gagnon 1964).

And, of course, anomie does not explain cocaine use by persons who are not retreatists and have achieved notable social and economic success in either criminal or noncriminal enterprises. Nor does it satisfactorily explain the relatively high rate of drug abuse among physicians, whose use of drugs is better explained by *access* than by anomie. Access, not anomie, is also put forth as an explanation for the high concentration of drug use in ghetto areas: Lack of viable economic opportunity induces more people to take the risks associated with drug trafficking, resulting in greater availability of illegal substances (Lindesmith and Gagnon 1964). Of course, greater access can be the result of anomie, drug trafficking being an innovative response to the anomic condition.

Working from a psychoanalytical model, Frederic Schiffer found that retreatism motivated cocaine abuse in the patients he treated, the drug taken because of a fear of failure: "Unconsciously, despair seemed familiar and inevitable, and success seemed foreign and unattainable" (1988: 134). In contrast to these views, Erich Goode declares that "anomie theory seems to explain no significant feature of drug use, abuse, or addiction" (1989: 64). For Elliott Currie, however, the breeding conditions for anomie are connected to drug abuse, and these conditions have grown more severe: "It is not just that material prospects have dimmed for the relatively young and poor, but that they have dimmed just when there has been an explosion of affluence and a growing celebration of material consumption at the other end" (1993: 145). This is exacerbated by the increasing gap between this country's wealthiest citizens and its poorest: Of the sixteen most industrialized nations, the United States has the widest gap between rich and poor, and its poor children are the worst off (Bradsher 1995a).

The Adaptive Model

Bruce Alexander sees drug dependence (compulsive as opposed to casual or recreational use) as functional. The addict's behavior is an attempt to deal with a failure to integrate; that is, "failure to achieve the kinds of social acceptance, competence, self-confidence, and personal autonomy that are the minimal expectation of individuals and society" (1990: 23). In the *adaptive model*, as in the retreatist perspective, the addict perceives the identity and life of an addict with its attendant misery, ill health, and social stigma to be less painful than the void of no identity at all. According to Alexander, persons who have not failed at integration and can form strong social bonds are not in danger of drug dependence. (This view is an important part of social control theory, discussed below.)

Drug dependence serves "as a strategy to remove the individual [a retreat] from competitive situations in which defeat is almost certain" (Alexander 1990: 25). This model contrasts with the *disease model* of drug dependence because it sees the addict as a healthy person who is a social, not biological or psychological, failure. The addict is not under the control of a drug, nor is his or her drug use "out of control"; the behavior is self-directed and purposeful, although not necessarily on a conscious level.

Differential Association

As proposed by Edwin Sutherland (1973), differential association explains how criminal behavior is transmitted. *Differential association* complements learning theory (discussed in Chapter 8): Criminal behavior is learned, and the principal learning occurs in intimate personal groups. The effectiveness of learning depends on the degree of intensity, frequency, and duration of the association. With respect to drug use, differential association can be conceived of as a scale in balance. On each side of the scale deviant and prosocial associations accumulate; at some theoretical point drug use will be initiated when there is an excess of deviant associations (drug abusers) over nondeviant or prosocial associations.

Robert Burgess and Ronald Akers (1969) reformulated Sutherland's central premise into a "differential association reinforcement theory": A person becomes delinquent if social norms or laws do not actually reinforce conforming legal behavior. Because behavior is shaped by positive reinforcement, if lawful behavior does not result in reinforcement, the strength of that lawful behavior is weakened, and a state of reinforcement deprivation results. This deprivation increases the probability that other—deviant—behaviors would be reinforced and strengthened. Members of the person's social group also make social reinforcement, such as social approval, esteem, and status, contingent upon the new deviant behavior.

In fact, initiation into drug use appears to be completely dependent on peer associations. "The first source of contact with the drug [heroin] was usually a friend," notes Troy Duster (1970: 180). The typical user receives his or her first "taste" free from new users who do not have expensive habits and will thus share their drugs. Most frequently he or she is introduced to heroin as a result of meeting a friend who was on his way to "cop" or was preparing a "fix": "he rarely sought out the drug the first time. Thus, initiation depended more on fortuitous circumstances than on a willful act by the new user" (P. Hughes 1977: 84).

In their study of heroin addicts in San Antonio, James Maddux and David Desmond (1981) found that only 4 percent obtained their first heroin directly from a dealer, and similar scenarios of heroin initiation are reported by Richard Rettig, Manual Torres, and Gerald Garrett (1977), and Chein and his colleagues (1964). Waldorf (1973: 31:) found a similar pattern and notes that heroin use is a social, not solitary, phenomenon: "Persons are initiated in a group situation among friends and acquaintances." The first experience with drugs, notes Duster (1970: 183), "is usually in a group situation." In England the situation is the same: Geoffrey Pearson (1987: 9) found that "the first time someone is offered heroin it will be by a friend. Or maybe by a brother or a sister. But always by someone well known, liked and even loved."

The relationship between initiation and friendship/kinship presents a problem for preventing "first use" of drugs: "In light of the decisive role of friendship networks in disseminating drugs, it is difficult to conceive of any effective form of conventionally conceived drug enforcement policy to control access at this level—quite simply, how might one be expected to police friendship?" (Advisory Council on Drug Misuse 1998: 30).

What of the relationship between parental use of psychoactive substances and the use of these substances by their children? (Peer relationships may simply serve as a mediating or intervening variable.) According to the theory of differential association, parental influence is responsible for generating the type of behavior that parents explicitly condemn in their children. However, in her research Denise Kandel found that "parental influence is relatively small, especially when compared with the influence of peers" (1974: 235). Peers provide social acceptance or reinforcement for the rules governing acceptance or conforming behavior valued by the peer group. To the adolescent, this reinforcement is typically more relevant than that provided by parents. Kandel concludes, however, that parents can enhance differential association: "When their friends use illegal drugs, children of nondrug-using parents are somewhat *less* likely to use illegal drugs, whereas children of drug-using parents are *more* likely to use drugs."

According to Coryl Jones and Robert Battjes, the use of certain drugs allows adolescents to emulate adults while rebelling against parental standards: "In emulation of their elders, adolescents use drugs to assuage immediate or anticipated discomfort, and, in rejection of their elders, they seize upon certain drugs of which their elders would disapprove. The use of illicit substances offers young adolescents the unique opportunity simultaneously to rebel against the rules their elders set down and to conform with the underlying attitudes which parental behavior manifests" (1987: 5).

However, an extensive study found that favorable parent-adolescent relations can offset personality risk factors for drug use and enhance personality protective factors against drug use. The study also found that peer drug use during adolescence was not a strong predictor of drug-use initiation during early adulthood (Morojele and Brook 2001).

Anomie and differential association help explain what Patrick Hughes (1977: 88) referred to as a heroin epidemic. In a Chicago-based study he posited a theory of heroin contagion in the form of micro- and macroepidemics: "The multiple drug using friendship group served as fertile soil for the growth of heroin addiction" into microepidemics, while "macroepidemics generally occurred in neighborhoods that had recently undergone rapid population change, leading to a breakdown in community stability and established mechanisms of social control [anomie]. In other words, not only had heroin addiction become rampant in these neighborhoods, but so had other forms of deviance as well." Hughes states that intensive treatment-outreach efforts can nip a new heroin-using network before it burgeons into an epidemic.

Identifying oneself as a "doper," "pothead," or "cokie" typically results from being enmeshed in a social network that includes others similarly situated. For some this becomes the primary reference group, and they may spend most of their time with other dopers, potheads, or cokies, withdrawing from nondrug-using social contacts. The substance becomes a symbol of group cohesion and unity, and provides a sense of belonging, thus offering strong support for continued use (Roffman and George 1988).

Social Control Theory

Social control theorists focus on why only a relatively few people engage in deviant behavior such as crime and drug abuse, and their answer is that the strength of an individual's bond to society is the determining factor. Youths who maintain strong attachments and commitment toward parents and school are less likely to engage in deviant behavior. According to control theorists, deviance "results when an individual's bond to society is weak or broken" (Hirschi 1969: 16). The strength of this social bond is determined by internal and external restraints. In other words, internal and external restraints determine whether we move in the direction of deviance or law-abiding behavior.

Internal restraints include what psychoanalytic theory (discussed in Chapter 8) refers to as the *superego*—they provide a sense of *guilt*. Dysfunction during early stages of childhood development, or parental influences that are not normative, can result in an adult who is devoid of prosocial internal constraints—sociopathology. (There is also evidence tying sociopathology to brain defects.) Criminal behavior, devoid of any genuine remorse, can be explained according to this theory. According to social control theory, deviants are poorly socialized, and the family is the basic unit for socialization. Thus, whether they are conceived of in terms of psychology or sociology, internal constraints are linked to the influence of the family (Hirschi 1969): Adolescent involvement with drugs and/or crime is therefore "highly correlated with family estrangement" (Brounstein et al. 1990: 10), an influence that can be supported or weakened by the presence or absence of significant external restraints.

External restraints include social disapproval linked to public shame and/or social ostracism and fear of punishment. In other words, people are typically deterred from criminal behavior by the possibility of being caught and the punishment that can result, ranging from public shame to imprisonment (and in extreme cases capital punishment). However, the strength of official deterrence—force of law—is measured according to two dimensions: risk versus reward. Risk involves the criminal justice system's ability to detect, apprehend, and convict the offender. The amount of risk is weighed against the potential rewards. Both risk and reward, however, are relative to one's socioeconomic situation. In other words, the less one has to lose, the greater the willingness to engage in risk. And the greater the reward, the greater the willingness to engage in risk. This theory explains why people in deprived economic circumstances would be more willing to engage in certain criminal behavior. However, the potential rewards and a perception of relatively low risk can also explain why individuals in more advantaged economic circumstances would engage in remunerative criminal behavior such as corporate crime.

Social control theory does not argue that only persons with weak societal ties will engage in drug use. Instead, it is the persistence of drug use that indicates a lack of societal bonds. Instead of conforming to conventional norms, through differential association some persons organize their behavior according to the norms of a delinquent or criminal group with which they identify or to which they belong. This is most likely to occur in environments characterized by relative social disorganization, where familial and communal controls are ineffective in exerting a conforming influence. "A similar process also helps explain why drugs are sometimes rampant in more affluent communities. Just as strong families and cultures can shield the materially deprived from drugs, so weakened families, the absence of available or concerned adults, and the pervasiveness of an insistent consumer culture can make the affluent more vulnerable" (Currie 1993: 103).

Another study revealed that family monitoring and rules, family conflict, and family bonding predict an adolescent's risk of illicit drug initiation. The researchers found that a warm and supportive family environment characterized by a strong bond to family members and a low level of family conflict predicted a lower risk for illicit drug initiation during adolescence. Thus, parental control and supervision characterized by close parental monitoring and clear family rules for children's behavior may significantly reduce the risk of illicit drug initiation throughout adolescence by affecting children's association with peers. These findings regarding family influences are consistent with findings from previous studies (Guo et al. 2002).

In a major study of the strength of family ties and risky behavior (cigarettes, marijuana, sex) by adolescents, researchers found that lower risk was closely related to a close-knit family. Family ties were found to be more important than peer relations (S. Gilbert 1997). In a longitudinal study designed to test social control theory, in particular that element relating poor interpersonal relations with deviance (in this case drug abuse), Denise Kandel and Mark Davies found no relationship between integration failure and drug abuse. In fact, they found illicit drug use to be "positively associated with intimacy among members of male friendship networks, whether intimacy refers to confiding or to interacting with friends. Further, the structure of the networks of illicit users is similar to that of nonusers. To the extent that some differences occurred, they tended to indicate closer friendships for drug users than nonusers" (1991: 459).

The researchers note that their findings tend to support *subcultural* (or cultural deviance) theory rather than control theory. George Vaillant (1983), a research psychiatrist, found that culture plays an important role in the genesis of alcoholism; that family practices—drinking habits into which a child is socialized—rather than a lack of social control (or even social distress), are a dominant factor. The idea that drug abuse, in particular alcoholism, is the result of a habit learned in accord with the same principles that govern other learning experiences is consistent with the behavior/learning theory of drug abuse (Bandura 1969; 1977).

Subcultures/Cultural Deviance Theory

Some sociologists explain deviant behavior as the result of persons conforming to subcultures to which they belong. "Subcultures are patterns of values, norms, and behavior which have become traditional among certain groups." They are "important frames of reference through which individuals and groups see the world and interpret it" (Short 1968: 11). A person without important bonds to conventional society but with strong ties to a drug-using subculture would be more likely to abuse drugs. Members of a drug subculture promote its values and norms to persons who are attracted to "the life"—socialization. The person who joins must reorder his or her life in conformity with the new subculture in order to remain a member in good standing, to be accepted by other members. The subculture provides rewards and punishments along the lines proposed by operant conditioning in order to retain the member's loyalty.

Albert Cohen (1965) argues that certain lower-class subcultures negate middle-class values, and this negation is a severe handicap because middle-class cultural characteristics are necessary to succeed in our society. These characteristics include:

- ambition
- a sense of individual responsibility
- skills for achievement
- ability to postpone gratification
- industry and thrift
- rational planning, such as budgeting time and money
- cultivation of manners/politeness
- control of physical aggression
- respect for property
- a sense of wholesome recreation

The norms of some lower-class subcultures, according to James Short (1968) and Walter Miller (1958), are simply not conducive to conventional types of achievement. The members of an adolescent street group adhere to the norms of a lower-class subculture, whose focal concerns are (Miller 1958):

- *Trouble.* Law-violating behavior
- *Toughness.* Physical prowess, daring
- *Smartness.* Ability to con others, shrewdness
- *Excitement.* Thrills, risk, danger
- *Fate.* Being lucky
- *Autonomy.* Independence of external restraint

Trouble often involves fighting or sexual adventures while drinking; troublesome behavior for women frequently means sexual involvement with disadvantageous consequences. Trouble-producing behavior is a source of status. Toughness evolves out of the significant proportion of lower-class males reared in female-dominated households and the resulting concern over homosexuality, which Miller contends runs through lower-class culture.

Gambling, also prevalent in lower-class culture, is rooted in the belief that life is subject to a set of forces over which there is little or no control—fate. Autonomy is often expressed in terms of "No one is going to push me around" and "I'm going to tell him to take this job and shove it." Such sentiments, however, often contrast with actual patterns of behavior; in other words, according to Miller, many lower-class individuals desire highly restrictive social environments such as the armed forces, prison, and drug treatment programs: "Being controlled is equated with being cared for" (1958: 13).

Chein and his colleagues note that "boys who become addicts are clearly related to the delinquent subculture. Even before they started using drugs regularly, most users have had friends who have been in jail, reformatory, or on probation" (1964: 13). Without exception, they found that addicts come from homes devoid of a father or strong father figure—female-dominated households. They are identified with what others have dubbed the *criminal underclass subculture* (B. Johnson et al. 1990), of which the drug subculture is an important component.

The concept of a drug subculture, notes John O'Donnell, implies that addicts are in contact with each other—differential association:

> In this contact, learning takes place. The learning can be of facts and techniques. For example, the neophyte can learn from more experienced addicts that his withdrawal symptoms are the result of not having his usual dose of narcotics, and will be relieved by a dose; that the intravenous route enhances the drug effect; how to obtain narcotics, or money for narcotics; new sources of narcotics; how to prepare narcotics for administration, and other knowledge of this kind. He will usually learn new attitudes too. He may learn to define himself as an addict, learn new justifications for his drug use, and new and negative attitudes toward the laws which try to prevent drug use. (1969: 84)

As the drug user comes to define himself or herself as an addict, the wider society perceives him or her as such in a process known as *labeling* (next section).

Drug cultures come in many different types. Some are linked to the use of particular substances, while others seem to be part of a larger subculture. Using participant observation, Patricia Adler provides an insider's look at a marijuana- and cocaine-smuggling subculture centered in the middle- and upper-class environs of the coastal communities of Southern California. She states: "This subculture provides guidelines for their dealing and smuggling, outlining members' rules, roles, and reputation. Their social life is deviant as well, as evidenced by their abundant drug consumption, extravagant spending, uninhibited sexual mores, and focus on immediate gratification" (1985: 1).

In general, cocaine abusers do not appear to present any clearly discernible subculture: Surveys of cocaine users have revealed that there is apparently no "typical" cocaine user (PCOC 1986). Heavy cocaine users fit no easy stereotype of drug abuse:

> A large proportion are successful, well-educated, upwardly mobile professionals in their early twenties and thirties. They are stockbrokers and lawyers and architects with sufficient disposable income to sink into a diversion that even at "social" use levels can cost $100 or more an evening. Many are, for the most part, otherwise law-abiding citizens who would cringe at being labeled criminals, even though they know what they are doing is illegal. A majority are men, but a growing number are women. And, as cocaine prices fall, more and more are teenagers and others for whom the

drug's exorbitant cost once kept it out of reach. (National Institute on Drug Abuse 1986: 1)

Cocaine in the form of crack, however, seems to have produced a drug subculture in poor neighborhoods of urban areas. "The subcultural patterns include an argot of terms that describes the activities having to do with crack, the various Crack combinations touted and paraphernalia needed for using, and the institution of base houses [where the substance is smoked] and crack houses [where the substance is purchased]" (Frank et al. 1987: 6). Blanche Frank and her colleagues point out that the development of this subculture helped to glamorize and thereby spread the use of crack.

Harold Finestone (1964) drew a portrait of the black heroin subculture in Chicago at the beginning of the 1950s. He found that the stereotypical addict eschewed violence, used a deliberately colorful vocabulary, and disdained work. (This contrasted with a small number of white addicts interviewed by Finestone, whose type of adjustment stressed violence.) These addicts, who Finestone (1964: 284) calls the "cats," had a lifestyle that centered on achieving "kicks." A kick is any act tabooed by conventional society "that heightens and intensifies the present moment of experience and differentiates it as much as possible from the humdrum routine of daily life." To the cat, heroin abuse provided the ultimate kick. A similar type of stereotypical heroin addict was found by Harvey Feldman (1977), who conducted his research in the late 1960s in a community pseudonymed "East Highland."

Symbolic Interactionism/Labeling

Symbolic interactionism is a sociological approach that appears in such perspectives as labeling or societal reaction theory. Its central premise is that people make their own reality:

> Symbolic interactionists suggest that categories which individuals use to render the world meaningful, and even the experience of self, are structured by socially acquired definitions. They argue that individuals, in reaction to group rewards and sanctions, gradually internalize group expectations. These internalized social definitions allow people to evaluate their own behavior from the standpoint of the group and in doing so provide a lens through which to view oneself as a social object. (Quadagno and Antonio 1975: 33)

Symbolic interactionism does not explain drug abuse because its focus is not on the behavior of the social actor but on how the behavior or person is viewed by others—by society. Thus, Kai Erikson states, "deviance is not a property *inherent* in any particular kind of behavior; it is a property *conferred* upon that behavior by people who come into direct or indirect contact with it" (1966: 6). In Chapter 1 we noted that certain harmful substances—alcohol and tobacco—can be lawfully manufactured, distributed, and possessed, while other chemicals are outlawed and the persons who choose to use them are labeled outlaws. In Chapter 2 we noted that at one time the users of certain substances—opiates and cocaine—were not seen as outcasts or criminals. After the Harrison Act, what had been lawful behavior became illegal, and a new class of criminals was created, as well as a lucrative new enterprise—drug trafficking. Using this perspective, Thomas Szasz argues that "before 1914 [and the Harrison Act] there was no 'drug problem' in the United States" (1974: 11). Thus, society is inclined to view those who abuse alcohol as suffering from a disease—alcoholism—while those who indulge in illegal chemicals are viewed—stigmatized—as deserving punishment. The societal interactionist view of drug use has important policy implications.

While those who abuse chemicals such as heroin and cocaine are labeled pejoratively, fired from employment, and subjected to law enforcement scrutiny, jail, and prison, the widespread acceptance of the traditional disease concept of alcoholism reduces the stigma associated with that problem. The disease model of alcoholism "provided a way for hundreds of thousands of alcoholics to make sense of their experience, to regain a measure of dignity and self-respect. And to begin to take control of and to rebuild their shattered lives" (Wallace 1993: 70).

Societal reaction has the effect of labeling—stigmatizing—certain actors, which causes a damaged self-image, deviant identity, and a host of negative social expectations. Furthermore, a damaged self-image can become a self-fulfilling prophecy. Edwin Schur notes that "once an individual has been branded as a wrong-doer, it becomes extremely difficult for him to shed that new identity" (1973: 124). During adolescence, "many youths engage in socially disruptive and health-endangering behavior," although "most adolescents who experiment with drugs or other health-compromising and illicit practices do not escalate their worrisome behavior" (Baumrind 1987: 14). This should caution us against unnecessarily labeling persons, particularly young persons. "Zero tolerance" may be *politically viable,* but it can significantly limit a young person's social and economic options in a way that does not encourage conforming behavior as an adult.

Labeling

"Young offenders in particular must be confronted with penalties that both deter them from future drug use and embarrass them among their peers. Today, many young offenders boast about their lenient treatment in the hands of the authorities and wear it as a badge of pride; corrections officials must make sure that when juveniles are caught using or selling drugs, their punishment becomes a source of shame. We need a mix of sanctions for juvenile drug use that includes school suspension, parental notification, and postponement of driver's license eligibility, and extends to weekends of 'community service' that involve arduous and unenviable public chores" (Office of National Drug Control Policy 1989: 25).

According to Edwin Lemert, the person labeled deviant reorganizes his or her behavior in accordance with the social reaction "and begins to employ his deviant behavior, or role based upon it, as a means of defense, attack, or adjustment to the overt and covert problems created by the subsequent societal reaction to him" (1951: 76). This *secondary deviance* is best exemplified by drug abusers who are forced to associate with other drug abusers and, furthermore, must often resort to crime (secondary deviance) in order to support their primary deviance—drug habits.

In the next chapter we will examine psychological theories that help explain drug use.

SUMMARY

Sociological studies and theories look at drug abuse in its social context, for instance, categorizing the stages of alcohol, heroin, and cocaine addiction and suggesting explanations for drug abuse. Anomie theory states that people denied opportunity that is due them in principle suffer from the strain of this dissonance and respond by conforming, rebelling, illegally innovating, or retreating. According to the theory, drug abusers choose the last, retreating from conventional social goals and competitive situations. The theory of differential association contends that drug behavior is learned behavior and the primary learning occurs in a small intimate group. The fact that initial drug use practically always occurs with adolescent friends is evidence for this theory. Social control theory states that the strength of the individual's social bonds predicts normative or deviant behavior, and internal and external restraints determine the strength of the bond. Subcultural theory explains drug use as the result of conforming to the norms of a deviant subculture. Symbolic interactionism contends that it is society's labeling of people and behaviors that determines society's response to those people and behaviors, rather than any attribute inherent to the person or behavior.

INTERNET CONNECTIONS

Canadian Centre on Substance Abuse: www.ccsa.ca
Crime theory: www.crimetheory.com
Drug Policy Research Center (part of RAND, major source of research and policy information): www.rand.org/multi/dprc

---

REVIEW QUESTIONS

1. According to the National Institute on Drug Abuse, what seven factors are associated with adolescent drug abuse?
2. What are the three stages to becoming an alcoholic?
3. What stages do heroin users and cocaine users go through on their way to addiction?
4. How does the theory of anomie explain drug abuse?
5. How does differential association explain the spread of drug abuse?
6. How does social control theory explain deviance, including drug abuse?
7. What is the connection between the delinquent subculture and drug abuse?
8. How does symbolic interactionism/labeling explain the "drug problem"?

CHAPTER 8

The Psychology of Drug Abuse

Being a drug abuser becomes a lifestyle. It cannot be treated as an isolated biological or pharmacological problem. —*Arnold M. Washton (PCOC 1984: 59)*

The addictive disorders are complex because they are influenced by genetic, familial, psychological, and sociocultural factors. —*American Psychiatric Association (1995: 5)*

The sociology of drug use, discussed in Chapter 7, notes that the phenomenon tends to be clustered in environments characterized by social conditions and relationships that cause despair, frustration, hopelessness, and general feelings of alienation. However, in these environments drug abusers represent only a small fraction of the populace. Why? Why do persons exposed to the same physical environment react differently to the use and abuse of drugs? Psychology, a discipline that focuses on the individual, provides some answers. In this chapter, for pedagogical purposes, psychological explanations are placed into two broad categories: clinical and behaviorist.

Psychology and Personality

Psychology examines individual human behavior, and clinicians attempt to treat abnormal or dysfunctional behavior. Some psychological theories of drug abuse are based on personality: "Drug addiction is primarily a personality disorder. It represents one type of abortive adjustment to life that individuals with certain personality predispositions may choose under appropriate conditions of availability and sociocultural attitudinal tolerance" (Ausubel 1978: 77). Robert Craig notes that the psychological literature supports such a conclusion: "[D]rug addicts have a paucity of major psychiatric syndromes and neuroses and a plethora of personality disorders and character disorders" (1987: 31). An extensive review of the literature on psychological testing of heroin addicts found them to be hostile, demanding, aggressive, rebellious, irresponsible, playful, and impulsive (Craig 1987). But many of these traits are also found in outstanding athletes. With respect to substance abusers in general, they "are characterized by disregard for established social customs, lack of control and foresight, inability to maintain lasting personal commitments, and the need for unusual and varied experiences" (Cox 1985: 233).

Part of the psychological explanation for drug abuse has been a presumed *addictive personality,* a psychological vulnerability resulting from problematic family relation-

Heroin users come in all types, including adolescents from upper-middle-class homes. Psychologists say that immature drug-dependent personalities ignore long-term negative consequences of behavior and opt for the short-term positive reinforcement that drugs provide.

© VCG/Getty Images

ships, inappropriate reinforcement, the lack of healthy role models, contradictory parental expectations, and/or an absence of love and respect. The psychologically immature drug-dependent personality seeks gratification on a primitive level or, according to the pleasure principle, finds drug use and its attendant behavior reinforcing. He or she ignores the long-term negative consequences of behavior and instead opts for the short-term positive reinforcement that drugs provide. Unfortunately, the search for the addictive personality—psychological variables that can predict future drug abuse—has not been fruitful (see Lang 1983). Peter Nathan (1988) points out that the search for predictors of drug dependence has discovered a variety of overt acts by prealcoholic and predrug abusers that reveal an unwillingness to accept societal rules. Beyond that, however, few consistent links have been found between other behaviors or personality factors and later abuse of alcohol and drugs. Furthermore, Nathan (1988) notes that large numbers of abusers have never demonstrated antisocial behavior in childhood and that a substantial number of antisocial or conduct-disordered children never develop alcohol or drug problems as adults.

Psychological theories can be broadly categorized into those following a Freudian or psychoanalytic strain and those following behaviorism or learning theory.

Psychoanalytic Theory and Drug Abuse

Psychoanalytic theory was fathered by Sigmund Freud (1856–1939). Although it has undergone change over the years, its basic proposition continues to be the influence of **unconscious** phenomena on human behavior. "Simply put, this concept says that people are not aware of the most important determinants of their behavior" (Cloninger, 1993: 25). According to Freud there are three types of mental phenomena:

- *Conscious.* What we are currently thinking about
- *Preconscious.* Thoughts and memories that can easily be called into consciousness
- *Unconscious.* Feelings and experiences that have been repressed and can be made conscious only with a great deal of difficulty and, nevertheless, exert a dominant influence over our behavior

Stages of Psychological Development

Freud posited that unconscious feelings and thoughts relate to stages of psychosexual development from infancy to adulthood. Psychoanalytic theory "conceives of the human being as a dynamic energy system consisting of basic drives and instincts which in interaction with the environment serve to organize and develop the personality through a series of developmental stages. Individuals from birth are pushed by these largely unconscious and irrational drives toward satisfaction of desires which are largely unconscious and irrational" (Compton and Galaway 1979: 90). Although we lack conscious memory of these stages, in later life they serve as a source of anxiety and guilt, psychoneurosis and psychosis. The stages overlap, and transition from one to the other is gradual. The time spans noted below are approximate and depend on individual and cultural differences. See Figure 8.1.

Oral Stage (Birth to 18 months).   During the oral stage the infant organizes his or her primitive impulses around the mouth, lips, and tongue, which are the predominant sexual organs during this stage. Desires and gratifications are mainly oral—sucking and

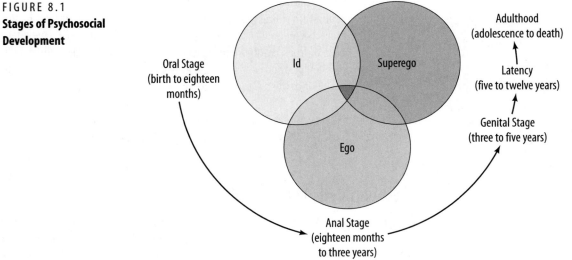

FIGURE 8.1
**Stages of Psychosocial
Development**

biting. The infant is unsocialized, devoid of all self-control, and narcissistic. In the normal infant, the source of pleasure becomes associated with the touch and warmth of the parent, who gratifies oral needs. When this is lacking, narcissism remains predominant, and in the narcissistically disturbed adult, drugs become a substitute for maternal warmth and self-esteem.

The infant's physiological balance is precarious, so that any environmental change may cause distress. The anxiety experienced in the helpless state of infancy is ameliorated by the discovery of a maternal object capable of providing nurture. The absence of warm mother-infant interaction and sensory deprivation during this stage causes the adult to use drugs as a means of reducing anxiety; drugs serve as a substitute for maternal attachment, and drug abuse is a regression back to an unfulfilled oral stage. Experiments conducted on animals reveal that the young of many species experience separation anxiety that can be ameliorated by opiates. "For human species, the experience of social attachments and comfort becomes inevitably bound up with the euphoria of human affection, intimacy, and love." Opiates apparently provide a substitute, albeit an inadequate one, for the absent maternal object (Levinthal 1988: 145).

During this stage the infant attempts to reach a state of homeostatic peacefulness, and this requires a responsive and supportive maternal object. Because of trauma or deficiencies experienced during this stage of development, "the infant may fail to achieve homeostatic balance, in the context of an attachment to a maternal object," and this can lead to drug abuse in the adult. The "substance, be it heroin or some other narcotic or stimulant, works at a physiologic and psychological representational level to facilitate the attainment of this basic homeostatic experience" (Greenspan 1978: 74).

Anal Stage (18 months to 3 years). As the infant moves into his or her second year, the "instinctual organization is beginning to organize around the mental representations concerned with anality" (Greenspan 1978: 76). The anus becomes the center of sexual desire and gratification during this stage, with pleasure closely associated with the retention and expulsion of feces. Physiologically the child is now able to control eliminatory processes. He or she typically experiences toilet training and becomes partially socialized, the beginning of a parental internalizing process that is completed during the genital stage that follows. During the anal stage children may act out destructive urges such as breaking toys or even injuring living organisms, insects, or small animals. A great deal of adult psychopathology, including violent behavior and sociopathic personality disorders, is traced back to this stage. Depressants such as heroin, alcohol, barbiturates, and tranquilizers can provide a way of managing sadistic and masochistic impulses—self-medication—that were not successfully dealt with during the anal stage. Such persons do not take depressants for pleasure but to control internal rage. (The policy implications of this theory mitigate against our current response to drug use.)

If development is thwarted during this stage, the infant does not succeed in achieving "an internal sense of mastery and delineation of self from the primary other"—the maternal figure. Drugs are used in an effort to obtain a state of mastery and clear demarcation from the maternal figure that is necessary to manage the transition to the genital stage. To gain greater independence, the infant must relinquish the dependent attachment to the maternal object, and if successful he or she can then move into the genital stage. In those who fail to accomplish this transition, substance abuse "is a defense against separation anxiety and its accompanying depression" (Greenspan 1978: 78).

Genital Stage (3 to 5 years). In this stage, which anticipates adulthood, the main sexual interest is assumed by the genitals and in normal persons is maintained by them thereafter. During this period boys experience strong attachments to their mothers (*Oedipus complex*) and girls to their fathers (*Electra complex*); both have incestuous fantasies, although they do not fully understand the mechanics of adult sexual relations. The child must begin to relinquish the dependent maternal/paternal attachment despite feelings of sadness in doing so. Drugs provide solace to the adult who was unable to deal with the ensuing depression of separation.

As noted in previous chapters, psychoactive drugs often affect sexual performance—by enhancing or depressing desire and/or performance. Drugs can provide a chemical means of dealing with disturbances experienced during the genital stage of development. Heroin, for example, may serve to suppress the sexual drive that is fixated in the genital stage; that is, the drug helps the person deal with unconscious (and guilt-provoking) incestuous wishes. Heroin causes a return to the oral stage, enabling the addict to avoid dealing with conflicts that were not adequately resolved.

Adolescence/Adulthood. The individual experiences a dramatic reawakening of genital interest and awareness. The incestuous wish, however, is repressed, and sexual interest is expressed in terms of mature (adult) sexuality. As noted above, drug use that substitutes for or enhances sexual activity allows the abuser to avoid or overcome the reawakening of incestuous sexual feelings that were never successfully reconciled during the genital stage. Furthermore, each stage is left behind but never completely abandoned. Some amount of psychic energy (*cathexis*) remains attached to earlier objects of psychosexual development. When the strength of the cathexis is particularly strong, it is expressed as a *fixation*. For example, instead of a boy transferring his affection to another woman in the adolescent-adult stage, he may remain fixated on his mother (or a girl on her father):

> At each stage, particular behaviors are important, but as we progress through the stages we use the behaviours associated with stages. So, in early stages, babies gain satisfaction from sucking (for example, at a mother's breast to satisfy the need for food). Later, sucking can also be satisfying—for example, in the use of cigarettes, sweets, or in sexual activities. However, adults have a wider range of satisfying activities to choose from. Some people become unconsciously attached to behaviour associated with particular stages (*fixation*). They are driven to seek that form of satisfaction to an unreasonable degree. Consequently they cannot use the full repertoire of behaviour available to them. (Payne, 1997: 73)

While the individual is experiencing each of these stages of development, corresponding psychic phenomena develop.

Divisions of the Psyche

Id. Each person is born with a mass of powerful drives, wishes, urges, and psychic tensions that are energized in the form of the *libido*. These seek immediate discharge or gratification. These **id** impulses are asocial, operating on the primitive level of pleasure and pain (that is, they are hedonistic), and from about birth to 7 months the id is the total psychic apparatus. Id drives are a central component of personality, impelling a person toward activity leading to cessation of the tension excitement it creates—satisfying the libido. For example, the hunger drive will result in activity that eventually satisfies (gratifies the id of) the person experiencing hunger. A craving for pleasure-producing chemicals will lead the id-driven person to seek drugs at considerable risk in order to satiate his or her desire, and the feelings of omnipotence that drugs can produce reinforce this drive.

Ego. Through the environment and training, infants learn to modify their expression of id drives and to delay immediate gratification. Ego development permits them to obtain maximum gratification with a minimum of difficulty—the **ego** tempers the id with reality and is the organism's contact with the real world. In normal development, the child learns to relinquish primitive id demands and to adapt behavior to social demands (Smart 1970). The stronger the ego, the stronger the individual's ability to tolerate frustration. Poor ego functioning, manifested by an inability to tolerate the psychological discomfort of frustration, can lead to the abuse of chemicals that lower the discomfort and provide immediate gratification. Furthermore, note Henry Krystal and Herbert Raskin, in the ego-deficient personality "drugs are used to avoid impending psychic trauma in circumstances which would not be potentially traumatic to other persons" (1970: 31); in other words, drug use reflects a dysfunction in reality testing. Through drug use, notes Sandor Rado (1981), reality is avoided, but only temporarily; when the chemical reaction subsides, reality returns with renewed vigor, and the subject again seeks relief through drugs. However, the psyche now finds that the same dosage brings diminished relief—tolerance has developed—leading to increasing dosages.

As a result of disturbances in psychosexual development, a person may remain at the ego level of development; in other words, "the child remains asocial or else behaves as if he had become social without having made actual adjustment to the demands of society. This means that he has not repudiated completely his instinctual wishes but has suppressed them so that they lurk in the background awaiting an opportunity to break through to satisfaction" (Aichhorn 1963: 4). Drug use, a reversion to gratifications associated with the oral stage, is a symptom of such a disturbance. Drug use is also associated with the ego's need to be in control of the source of pleasurable feelings—it is narcissistic (Rado 1981). Edward Khantzian (1980) states that heroin use is caused by the ego's need to control feelings of rage and aggression, emotions that relate to the anal stage of development.

The choice of drugs is either ego constricting or ego expanding. The weak ego structure of heroin users causes them to seek quiet and lonely lives—a tranquility through ego constriction that is aided by narcotics. Cocaine and amphetamine users, on the other hand, often come from households with warm mothers and fathers who are strong and encouraging. For them, stimulant use grows out of a self-directed and intensely competitive personality: "They take cocaine to expand their egos and their self-confidence" (Spotts and Shontz 1980: 65). The user of stimulants is suffering from anxiety brought on by a lack of stimulation: The ego is disturbed by the absence of stimuli, and intense stimulation is preferred by those using amphetamines and cocaine to ward off boredom and depression (Krystal and Raskin 1970).

In the course of normal development, over time the child integrates outer (social) discipline and imposes it upon him- or herself. The instinctual impulses are brought under his or her own control, and we get the beginning of a superego (Smart 1970).

Superego.   Oversimplified as the conscience, the **superego** is a counterforce to the id, exercising a critical influence, a sense of morality that controls behavior. Tied to overcoming the incestuous feelings of the genital stage, the superego serves as an internalized parent, meaning that behavior is no longer exclusively dependent on external forces (the ego level of control). Failures in superego development may leave a person without strong internal controls over id and ego impulses and can result in behavior that is harmful or destructive. The sociopath lacks sufficient superego strength, and the ego is insufficient to control powerful id impulses.

At the other extreme is an overactive superego that cannot make distinctions between *thinking* bad and *doing* bad. Unresolved conflicts of earlier development (for example, an Oedipus complex) and id impulses that are normally repressed or dealt with through other less destructive processes (such as reaction formation, discussed below) create a severe sense of guilt. This guilt is experienced (unconsciously) as a compulsive need to be punished, and to alleviate guilt the person commits acts for which punishment is virtually certain. August Aichhorn (1963) notes that such persons are victims of their own personalities. For them drugs accomplish a dual purpose: They reduce the anxiety caused by unresolved inner conflicts, while the deleterious aspects of drug abuse provide external punishment. According to Leon Wurmser (1978), society assists the drug abuser in this quest by imposing shame and punishment.

According to psychoanalytic theory, unconscious forces maintain a delicate balance as the person experiences life's various sociocultural and biological aspects. The balance is easily upset, crossing the very thin line between the normal and the neurotic, or between the neurotic and the psychotic. In fact, there is only a difference of degree between the *normal* and the *abnormal.* When repressed material begins to overwhelm the psyche and threatens to enter one's consciousness, external defense mechanisms come into play in the form of psychoneuroses and, in more serious cases, psychosis. These responses may take the form of phobias—to heights, insects, or closed spaces, for example. In the paranoid reaction, the person projects his or her thoughts onto imagined enemies; in the *reaction-formation,* the destructive urges of the anal stage can be channeled into prosocial activities—becoming a surgeon, a veterinarian, or a butcher, for example. The degree to which defense mechanisms cause the person to become dysfunctional provides an objective measurement of abnormality. The psychoneuroses, or the primitive defense mechanism that is drug abuse, allow psychic energy to be discharged without having to confront unconscious material (Wurmser 1978). In his cocaine-abusing patients, Frederic Schiffer (1988) found that drug usage was a self-medication aimed at alleviating the pain of early trauma. Cocaine abuse represented an unconscious, symbolic repetition of childhood trauma. Old psychological injuries were reinflicted by the drug, which also allowed the patient to unconsciously gain a (false) sense of control over these early difficulties, providing an opportunity to struggle against them again.

Drug Use and Adolescence

Psychoanalytic theory views drug abuse as a symptom of neuroses that manifest themselves during adolescence. We recognize that adolescents typically undergo periods of boredom, anxiety, anger, frustration, and even short-lived depression. A defining feature of adolescence "is the rapid and far-reaching changes occurring in virtually all aspects of life and the resultant high-level stress" (Newcomb and Bentler 1988: 11). Research has identified these factors as well as the peer group as being associated with drug abuse. The typical adolescent has not had sufficient experience in dealing with feelings of psychosocial stress in a mature—that is, adult—fashion. Psychoactive drugs can be seen as a form of self-medication in response to the stressful conditions of adolescence. These frequently include affective disorders: "Drugs of abuse and medications prescribed for affective disorders have common neurochemical effects that presumably treat the abnormality" (Bukstein, Brent, and Kaminer 1989: 1139).

It is normal for an adolescent to grapple with the problems of physiological and psychological development. The struggle for identity through a progressive process of relationships and experiences enables him or her to manage the complexities of adolescence. He or she becomes more competent and eventually moves into young adulthood. "Adolescence is a period of development involving transitions in the major physical, intellectual, psychosocial, and moral processes that make up a person. Transitional stages of development are by definition periods of disequilibration and disruption and, therefore, replete with opportunities for experiences that are both dangerous and growth-enhancing" (Baumrind 1987: 14).

"The adolescent addict, however, sidesteps such growth by at first simply avoiding the situations in which he can gradually acquire competence or by passively going along with the whims and decisions of others and eventually by substituting the anxiety-reducing 'normative' influence of the opiate drugs" (Chein et al. 1964: 202). As Otto Fenichel (1945) points out, euphoric substances protect against painful mental states. However, because of this, the adolescent's reality-testing (an ego function) ability remains primitive, and her or his ability to tolerate stress and frustration remains at an infantile (oral) level. Like the infant during the oral stage, the addict is motivated only by a need to immediately gratify his or her perceived needs. This type of behavior is governed only by the primitive id impulses—the pleasure principle—without any real concern for the results. As a result of their extensive longitudinal research, Michael

Newcomb and Peter Bentler conclude that adolescent drug use, "particularly of cannabis and hard drugs, has measurably negative effects on several critical areas of life functioning as a young adult" (1988: 240).

Heroin use typically begins during adolescence, with the drug serving as a means of avoiding psychologically demanding—but healthier—responses to developmental crisis, stress, deprivation, and other forms of emotional pain (Khantzian, Mack, and Schatzberg 1974). Sociopsychological growth and maturity require grappling with reality—as exercise aficionados will recognize: "No pain, no gain." Drug use reduces social competence and adaptive behaviors. The therapeutic community, a particular approach to treating drug abusers discussed in Chapter 9, responds to persons whose use of drugs is based on an inability to deal with the frustrations of reality.

Unresolved Parental Relationships. According to Freud, "from the time of puberty onward the human individual must devote himself to the great task of freeing himself from the parents; and only after this detachment is accomplished can he cease to be a child and so become a member of the social community" (1961: 345–46). Freud points out that in neurotics, such as addicts, this detachment is not accomplished because the neurotic has a distorted pathological relationship with his or her parents. This relationship is characterized by overdependence and fear of being rejected. While there is an identification with the father (or father figure), it is "at best laden with hostility" (Frazier 1962: 97). Isidor Chein and his colleagues (1964) found that addicts, as opposed to controls from the same environment, came from either single-parent households or from families where the father was usually distant, presented immoral models of behavior, was primarily concerned with day-to-day gratification of appetites, and impulsive. As would be expected, the fathers had unstable work histories, pessimistic and fatalistic attitudes toward the future, and low aspirations for their sons. The level of interaction between father and son was minimal. A 1999 study at Columbia University found that adolescents who do not get along well with their fathers are much more likely to use nicotine, alcohol, and illegal drugs than children from one-parent/mother-only households (Molotsky 1999).

The addict's relationship with his mother includes a long history of emotional deprivation:

> Frequently, a tense, dominant, autistic, unhappy mother forced the child into becoming an adjunct to herself rather than allowing him to develop as an independent person. The feeling of hostility toward the mother and the inability to form any close satisfactory relationships date back to these earliest years. The addict's conflicts reflect this oral deprivation in an infantile helplessness, and the drug helps him to regress to "happy" infancy that was never really happy. The effects of the drug handle his hostility and reduce tensions which are symptoms of these lifelong conflicts. The hostility toward the mother generally remains unconscious, but it is expressed through the drug which not only "destroys" the user but also symbolically destroys the mother whom he has incorporated through identification. (Frazier 1962: 98)

Ego Deficiencies. According to Robert Savitt, it is not euphoria that the addict seeks in narcotics but the satiated feeling reminiscent of infancy: "When an infant's basic needs for sustenance and love are fulfilled, he falls asleep" (1963: 45). Thus, the purported use of heroin for its euphoric properties is an exaggeration: "It would appear that the elation which the heroin addict experiences has been stressed out of proportion to the sleep or stupor which often soon follows. . . . Like the infant who alternates between hunger and sleep, the addict alternates between hunger for a drug and narcotic stupor" (1963: 44). The adolescent addict suffers from a narcissism (self-love), an infantile level of relating to others that retards the ability to form close, warm, emotional relationships. Other persons are simply instruments for his own purposes—even his own mother, whom he has not learned to differentiate as a portion of himself. Interpersonal relationships, even with parents, are shallow. Groups of "junkies" are tied together only by the one thing they share—drugs. It's an easy group, without demands, deliberate structure, or goals beyond those involving continued drug use. Stanley Greenspan states that "substance abuse could emanate from the lack of this basic ability of attaching to the human object" (1978: 74). A prominent feature of the family situation of the adolescent opiate addict "is the peculiarly close relationship between the addict and his mother. It is not a closeness of warmth or mutual regard so much as it is a clinging and feeling of being bound together" (Chein et al. 1964: 212).

Drug-dependent adolescents suffer from severe ego inadequacies. They have been found to be relatively unresponsive/indifferent to opportunities for education, work, or recreation; they have limited interests and curiosity. They appear to suffer from gross disturbances in early life, leading to a restricted pattern of responsiveness. They have poor reality testing and an inability to delay gratification or accept frustration; they react to criticism by withdrawal, giving up easily in school or employment situations; they are unable to form realistic goal orientations. While recognizing all of the dangers inherent in heroin use, addicts are unable to exercise restraint. They use heroin to deal with frustrations and pain; they are *retreatists* for whom heroin relieves anxiety, by changing feelings of tenseness and restlessness into feelings of comfort, relaxation, and peacefulness (Chein et al. 1964). Heroin helps overcome the usual tensions of adolescence. The heroin addict may also find heroin effective in thwarting feelings of intense destructiveness and sadism associated with a disturbance in the anal stage of development. The drug pacifies such drives, and the negative and punishing results of heroin addiction satisfy the super-ego's need to punish such feelings (Yorke 1970).

Regression to Infant Sexuality. There are significant sexual implications in drug use, particularly the intravenous use of heroin. "Addicts are persons who have a disposition to react to the effects of alcohol, morphine, or other drugs in such a way that they try to use these effects to satisfy the archaic oral longings which is sexual longing, a need for security, and a need for the maintenance of self-esteem simultaneously" (Fenichel 1945: 376). This pathology has its origins in infantile sexuality, both oral and genital. "The addict uses his addiction to express or act out repressed impulses and needs," and the discharge of psychic energy is pleasurable enough to replace other pleasurable activities, such as sex and eating (Chein et al. 1964: 235). The use of heroin is autoerotic, bypassing genital sex in favor of infantile or oral-stage eroticism (Yorke 1970).

Psychoanalytic theories of drug abuse have been criticized for their reliance on retrospective self-reports and individual case studies—limited methods lacking rigorous empirical grounding. This contrasts with the rigorous experimentation that underlies learning theory.

Behaviorism/Learning Theory

The second major school of psychological thought has its roots in the laboratory of experimental psychology with its dogs, pigeons, rats, monkeys, and mazes (see, for example, Rachlin 1991). Behaviorists typically reject psychoanalytic theory as unscientific, that is, lacking the rigorous testing to which learning theory has been subjected. Indeed, measurement of objective behavior is intrinsic to **learning theory,** which proceeds on the basis that all forms of behavior are conditioned: the result of learned responses to certain stimuli. Disturbed behavior such as drug abuse results from inappropriate conditioning (London 1964). To the behaviorist, a person is simply the sum product of his or her experience or learning, and learning is based on operant conditioning.

Operant Conditioning

The behaviorist stresses—and has been able to prove—that animal behavior can be modified through the proper application of operant conditioning: positive and negative **reinforcement.** Behavior is "*strengthened* by its consequences, and for that reason the consequences themselves are called 'reinforcers.' " (Skinner 1974: 40). When some aspect of (animal or human) behavior is followed by a certain type of consequence—a reward—it is more likely to be repeated. The reward is called **positive reinforcement.** If the probability of a behavior goes up after the *removal* of a stimulus, then **negative reinforcement** has occurred. "A negative reinforcer strengthens any behavior that reduces or terminates it" (Skinner 1974: 47). For example, the negative reinforcement that occurs when a heroin addict fails to ingest enough heroin—withdrawal symptoms—strengthens drug-seeking behavior. Both positive and negative reinforcers increase behavioral responses; they differ in their ordering relationship—positive reinforcers *follow* the behavior they reinforce, while negative reinforcers *precede* the behavior they reinforce. A person *works to receive* a positive reinforcer and *works to escape* a negative reinforcer. Punishment is the third general principle of operant conditioning. *Punishment* decreases the probability or frequency of a behavior (Bozarth 1994).

The noted behaviorist B. F. Skinner states that "punishment is easily confused with negative reinforcement, sometimes called 'aversive control.' The same stimuli are used,

Classical and Operant Conditioning

Behavioral psychology recognizes two basic types of processes associated with learning:

Classical conditioning involves the pairing of two stimuli, one of which elicits a reflex and one of which is neutral [food and the sounding of a bell, for example]. With repeated pairing of the two stimuli, the previously neutral stimulus [bell] becomes a conditioned stimulus and elicits the response [salivating, for example] in absence of the original eliciting stimulus [food].

Operant conditioning involves the repeated presentation or removal of a stimulus following a behavior to increase the probability of the behavior (i.e., reinforcement). A reinforcer is a stimulus that increases the probability of a behavior. If the probability of a behavior goes up following the presentation of some stimulus, then positive reinforcement has occurred. If the probability of a behavior goes up after the *removal* of a stimulus, then negative reinforcement has occurred. (Tilson 1993: 2)

and negative reinforcement might be defined as the punishment of not behaving, but punishment is designed to remove behavior from a repertoire, whereas negative reinforcement generates behavior" (1974: 63). As noted earlier, a particular psychoactive substance will be reinforcing to some persons or to most persons under certain conditions: for example, opiates when in pain. For most persons under ordinary circumstances, the same substance will not provide reinforcement—at least not reinforcement sufficiently positive to offset negative consequences—and they do not seek to repeat the behavior.

According to this view, drug use is merely the result of learning directly from others. Chein and his colleagues (1964) note that both processes involved with the use of heroin, excitement and the actions of the drug itself, become reinforcing, thus shaping—that is, molding—the behavior of the addict. Alfred Lindesmith (1968: 8) argues that a continuation of heroin use is based on negative reinforcement—"persons become addicts when they recognize or perceive the significance of withdrawal distress which they are experiencing" when they cease to use heroin. Lindesmith argues that substances such as cocaine and marijuana, on the other hand, are positive reinforcers because they are taken to enhance mood rather than to stave off withdrawal. From the discussion in Chapter 4, we know that Lindesmith's assertions are questionable: The physiological discomfort of heroin withdrawal is usually no greater than a bout with the flu; discontinuing the use of cocaine can produce depression; and sudden withdrawal from alcohol can be life threatening.

Behavior Modification

The abuse of stimulants and depressants can be explained by using learning theory. The use of cocaine, for example, can be quite rewarding: It elevates mood and provides a sense of well-being, strength, and energy, while discontinuing use provides negative reinforcement in the form of psychological depression or the "coke blues." Likewise, heroin use can be quite rewarding to the addict: It significantly reduces perceptions of physical and psychological pain, stress, and anxiety, and provides a sense of euphoria, while discontinuing use provides negative reinforcement in the form of uncomfortable physical and psychological withdrawal symptoms. Although initially chemicals such as cocaine or heroin may have been used for social reasons, these substances' ability to provide physiological and psychological rewards explains why addicts seek to continue use even in the face of considerable hardship—drugs overcome *competing reinforcers:* "The balancing of pleasurable or rewarding experiences and punishing or unpleasant experiences that occurs during the early weeks or months of drug involvement may be of critical importance. If the net impact of those experiences is highly positive, the effect or memory of that 'honeymoon' can remain remarkably strong over time, even as continuing reward diminishes and punishment increases, especially if alternative competitive behaviors are not exercised or reinforced as strongly" (Gerstein and Harwood 1990: 65).

Furthermore, while being known as a "junkie" or a "cokie" may have negative consequences in conventional society, it often provides positive reinforcement in that it allows entry and acceptance into a small clique that is the drug subculture: Daily activities can now be focused on a clearly identifiable goal—drugs. The sociological dimension of this concept appeared in Chapter 7 in the discussion of *anomie* and *retreatism.* Further, the illegal aspects of drug abuse provide a level of excitement that some persons may find rewarding. For drug users who must engage in criminality to support their habits, success in crime also provides an important source of reinforcement, particularly when they do not possess skills necessary to succeed in noncriminal endeavors that could offer a competing source of reinforcement.

Although a dose of intravenous methamphetamine would probably be physically pleasurable to anyone, Thomas Crowley (1981: 368) points out that not everyone who experiences the pleasure continues to use amphetamines. The person who continues use is more likely to be from an impoverished environment: "Users in impoverished environments, with few other reinforcers available, will probably seek drug reinforcement more actively. Similarly, long experience with disturbed, unloving parents seems to convince many young people that they can never achieve respect or love from others. These young people have not learned to expect reinforcement from their environment, and so they may more actively seek the predictable, regular reinforcement of drug abuse." Most persons who find the intake of certain substances rewarding do not become compulsive about continued use. Thus, while some persons become obese because of their eating habits, most people do not become compulsive overeaters. While certain foods are pleasing to most people—chocolate or ice cream, for example—relatively few respond by compulsive intake. While large numbers of Americans use alcoholic beverages, most avoid dependence.

Cognitive Learning Theory

Cognition refers to learning and memory, and cognitive processes cannot be observed the way outward behavior can. But many behaviorists believe that cognition plays a crucial role in learning theory in humans. "An important distinction in learning theory is between observable and unobservable behavior. Many behaviorists use 'behavior' only in reference to observable activity, but this is too restrictive. No matter what it is called, unobservable behavior, especially cognitive behavior, is important in people's lives. . . . A cognitive response is simply a thought or feeling, typically in reaction to some stimulus. But a thought or feeling may also serve as a stimulus for a subsequent response. So a cognitive event may act either as a stimulus or as a response, or as both, as these events often do" (Starkweather 1982: 37).

These behaviorists recognize that human behavior is more complex than that of other species—that, for example, human behavior is often mediated by beliefs and symbols. The readiness to fight or die for a cause—the cross, the star of David, the crescent, the red star—illustrates the abstract complexities of human behavior. This recognition has led to *cognitive learning theory,* the major tenets of which are that "human behavior is mediated by unobservables that intervene between a stimulus and a response to that stimulus. Beliefs, sets, strategies, attributions, and expectancies are examples of the types of mediating constructs currently considered crucial to an understanding of emotion and behavior" (S. Gold 1980: 8).

Furthermore, "the way an individual labels or evaluates a situation determines his or her emotional and behavioral responses to it." Thus, based on past learning, a twisted cross (swastika) may have a different meaning to a Jew than to a Navaho Indian (to whom it is a cosmic religious symbol). According to this approach, the drug abuser has difficulty in meeting societal demands or expectations, and this leads to anxiety. While anxiety is a universal experience, Steven Gold notes that drug abusers feel that "they cannot alter or control the situation; that they are powerless to affect their environment and decrease or eliminate the sources of stress" (1980: 9).

Persons facing persistent difficulties and anxieties in their lives and who are not prepared to cope with them may resort to analgesic drugs for comfort. "While enabling them to forget their problems and stress, the painkilling experience engendered by such drugs actually *decreases* the ability to cope. This is because such drugs depress the central nervous system and the individual's responsive capacity" (Peele 1980: 143). Heroin or alcohol provides relief from anxiety, and the user also attains temporary euphoria: "Under the influence of the drug the individual temporarily experiences an increased sense of power, control, and well-being." The drug acts as a powerful reinforcer—it can do for the abuser what he or she cannot do for him- or herself. However, these effects are short-lived, and after the drug wears off, the user finds that feelings of powerlessness return with a full fury, which leads to further use of the drug and a cycle of continuing drug abuse: "The reliance on drugs to cope with stress therefore creates a vicious cycle; the more drugs are used, the more the individual believes they are necessary. Each drug experience serves to confirm for users the belief that they are powerless to function on their own" (S. Gold 1980: 9). Behaviorists often refer to this state of thinking as "learned helplessness":

Through inappropriate reinforcement, the drug abuser *learns* that he or she can neither escape nor avoid the stimulus leading to drug use.

Stimulants such as amphetamine and cocaine provide not only primary reinforcement as a result of their impact on the central nervous system but also secondary reinforcement as the result of drug-induced behavioral change for those who wish to increase their assertiveness: Amphetamines, for example, can produce a sense of cleverness, clear thinking, energy, alertness, and loquaciousness (T. Crowley 1981).

Learning theory is difficult to apply in the treatment of drug abusers. As noted above, drugs are so reinforcing—providing immediate gratification for those who have *learned* to enjoy their use—that finding appropriate reinforcers that can successfully compete is quite difficult. Relapse after treatment can also be explained by learning theory, that is, the classical conditioned response: Certain cues associated with drug-taking behavior trigger a craving (Childress et al. 1993). These cues are discussed in Chapter 9. Agonists and antagonists, also discussed in Chapter 9, can be used to thwart the reinforcing quality of psychoactive substances. That chapter will also examine treatment programs that apply behavior theory.

A Psychosociological Dimension

Drug use has a sociopsychological dimension according to which the actor must *learn* that ingesting certain chemicals is desirable—intoxication, for example, is not inherently pleasurable. Expectations are based on learning and influence the direction of drug use. Thus, naive users, such as hospitalized patients given doses of morphine to relieve pain, do not experience euphoria and do not continue to seek out opiates when the pain

---

Psychoanalytic Learning Theory

Stanley Greenspan (1978:80) explains drug abuse by integrating behaviorism and psychoanalytic theory into a model that defines external experiences in terms of stimuli and reinforcers derived from psychosexual stages of development and the organization of id, ego, and superego. He states, for example, that "a substance abuser who achieves a basic and primitive homeostatic experience by using his addictive drug may be obtaining tremendous and potent reinforcement from the substance abuse. . . . Because of a lack of internalized control and the number of potent internal forces working from within, he tends to be vulnerable to environmental influences in rather dramatic ways and is sensitive to many potentially reinforcing events in his external environment [even though they may be destructive]."

subsides (Chein et al. 1964). Chein and his colleagues go so far as to state that opiates "are not inherently attractive, euphoric, or stimulant substances. The danger of addiction to opiates resides in the person, not in the drug" (1964: 348). Edward Brecher (1972: 13) notes that while there is "no doubt that the injection directly into a vein of a substantial dose of morphine or heroin produces a readily identifiable sensation," described by non-addicts as a sudden flush of warmth and by addicts as a rush, few nonaddicts perceive the rush as particularly pleasurable. R. M. Gilbert (1981: 386) states that just because "a substance *can* have a pharmacological effect, it does not automatically follow that use of the substance is caused by or maintained by that effect." (See also Becker 1966: "Becoming a Marijuana User.") A 16-year-old cigarette smoker reports: "The first time I tried it, last year, I was like, 'This is totally gross.' I was coughing, and I turned green, and I thought I was going to throw up. So I had to *learn* to like it" (Verhovek 1995: 1; emphasis added).

People who believe they are drinking alcohol when actually they have been given nonalcoholic substitutes get more relaxed and outgoing, and a party atmosphere develops (D. Wood 1991). Indeed, levels of sexual arousal increase when people given a placebo believe they have imbibed alcohol, although alcohol reduces sexual performance (Mendelson and Mello 1995).

With these explanations in mind, in the next chapter we will examine the variety of methods used to treat drug abusers and prevent drug abuse.

SUMMARY

Psychological theories of drug abuse center on the individual and fall into two general categories: psychoanalytic approaches and behaviorist approaches. Psychoanalytic theory's central propositions are that our unconscious exerts a dominant influence on our behavior, that the unconscious is related to stages in our psychosexual development, and that incomplete resolution of any of the stages finds expression in the entire range of adult behavior—from career choice to drug abuse. Developing during the psychological stages are the components of the human psyche: the id, primal drives and urges; the ego, reality check and social influence; and the super-ego, a sense of morality that controls behavior. Incomplete development of the ego or superego can also lead to drug abuse.

Behaviorism, or learning theory, states that all learning is based on operant conditioning—we become conditioned to respond to a stimulus in a certain way. That stimulus reinforces the behavior: It is called positive reinforcement if the probability of the behavior increases with the presentation of the stimulus, and it is called negative reinforcement if the probability of the behavior increases with the removal of the stimulus. A drug's impact on the CNS serves as positive reinforcement to continue drug use, and withdrawal symptoms serve as negative reinforcement to continue drug use.

INTERNET CONNECTIONS

American Academy of Addiction Psychiatry: www.aaap.org
American Psychological Association: www.apa.org

REVIEW QUESTIONS

1. What distinguishes psychological explanations of drug abuse from sociological explanations?
2. What is psychoanalytic theory's basic proposition?
3. How can problems experienced during the oral stage of development lead to drug abuse in the adult?
4. How can the use of depressants by an adult be connected to the anal stage of development?
5. What is the relationship between difficulty during the genital stage and drug abuse in adulthood?
6. How can drug abuse be explained by id drives?
7. How can drugs compensate for ego deficiencies?
8. How can a deficiency in superego development lead to drug abuse?
9. How can feelings of guilt generated by the superego lead to drug abuse?
10. How does psychoanalytic theory explain drug abuse during adolescence?
11. What basic belief underlies behaviorism/learning theory?
12. How does operant conditioning explain drug abuse?
13. How is psychoanalytic theory usually operationalized in the treatment of drug abusers?
14. How does behavior/learning theory explain drug abuse?
15. Why is it difficult to apply behavior theory in the treatment of drug abuse?
16. How do expectations based on learning influence individual drug use?

CHAPTER 9

Drug Abuse Treatment

Advances in science are rapidly dispelling both popular and clinical myths about drug abuse and addiction and what to do about them [although] scientific understanding has not yet totally displaced the moralizing that continues to shadow any discussion on this topic. —*Alan I. Leshner (1999a: 1)*

[T]reatment and prevention programs are frequently required to show that they are cost-effective, a standard never imposed on drug enforcement.
—*Robert MacCounand Peter Reuter (1997: 47)*

If treatment is conceived of as an ongoing process, rather than as a cure, a different, more optimistic notion of success emerges. —*Peggy Orenstein (2002: 74)*

There are probably as many approaches to treating and preventing drug abuse as there are theories explaining the phenomenon. Unfortunately, drug abuse is unlike diseases whose etiology and thus treatment and prevention appear to be clearly physiological. In fact, considering drug dependence as a "disease," in the narrow sense of that term, is controversial (see, for example, Wilbanks 1990; Maltzman 1994). As with other chronic illnesses, the National Institute on Drug Abuse (NIDA) recommends speaking in terms of remission and improvement, rather than cure, when discussing the treatment of substance abuse (*Drug Abuse* 1987) because the problem has proven to be quite intractable.

Adding to the problem's complexity are the incongruities discussed in Chapter 1: The moderate use of any variety of psychoactive substances—from nicotine to cocaine—may be the focus of a treatment response, not because of properties inherent in the chemicals themselves but because of the societal definition of *abuse*. Thus, in the United States the moderate use of alcohol, tobacco, or coffee is seen as clearly within the mainstream of acceptable behavior, while even the occasional use of heroin or cocaine is often seen as requiring treatment (if not imprisonment). The difficulty is apparent: Patients who do not feel ill, who do not want treatment, and are not dysfunctional are coerced into treatment by their families, their employers, or the criminal justice system. And, as Dean Gerstein and Henrick Harwood point out: "drug treatment is not designed for the low-intensity user who is readily able to control his or her level of consumption and for whom functional consequences have not yet accumulated" (1990: 69–70).

The Cure Industry

Like the quest for an explanation of drug abuse, the search for a cure, particularly a "magic bullet" in the form of a chemical cure, has a history that cautions us to be skeptical. Opiates were once presented as a cure for alcohol dependence; morphine was offered as a cure for opiate addiction; cocaine was offered as a cure for morphine addiction (though patients became dependent on cocaine while remaining addicted to morphine); heroin was proposed as a cure for morphine addiction; and methadone was presented as a cure for heroin addiction. In fact, the "cure industry" has a long and often less than honorable history.

The medical profession "often shared the distaste for drug users that permeated the society" (H. W. Morgan 1981: 65). Furthermore, the problem of addiction was only peripheral to the practice of most doctors, who typically sought to avoid association with the failure so common to treating drug dependence. This left a fertile field for the charlatan, and around the turn of the century the quest for a cure led to the development of an industry similar to that of patent medicines. Unregulated nostrums widely advertised as cures for drug dependence frequently contained alcohol, cocaine, and opiates. In 1906 these compounds came under regulation by the Pure Food and Drug Administration, which caused a significant decline in sales. In response, quacks began to portray themselves as outsiders feared by a medical establishment centered in the eastern United States. This approach had strong appeal, particularly in the South and Midwest, where anti-Eastern feelings ran deep.

Any number of (self-proclaimed) doctors operated clinics for the drug dependent and grew quite wealthy from their "cures." The most famous was Charles B. Towns, a Georgia farm boy, insurance salesman, and stockbroker. David Musto (1973) refers to Towns as the king of the cure proclaimers. Arriving in New York City in 1901, Towns spent several years as a partner in a stock brokerage firm that failed in 1904. Shortly afterward he began advertising a secret formula that would cure drug addiction. The medical profession was skeptical, but Towns and his cure were widely accepted and promoted even by federal agencies; a 1909 article in the *Journal of the American Medical Association* was also favorable. The Charles B. Towns Hospital proclaimed a cure rate of between 75 and 90 percent. Determining "success" was rather simple—if the patient never returned, he or she was "cured."[1] Eventually it was revealed that Towns' secret formula contained three ingredients: prickly ash bark, extract of hyoscyamus (henbane—a poisonous plant), and belladonna (deadly nightshade—a poisonous plant).

There were at the same time, however, sanatoriums whose approach to drug abuse was quite similar, if not identical, to that of many contemporary inpatient programs. The patient was withdrawn from drugs, sometimes with the aid of nonaddicting drugs. Before 1914 treating addiction was all the more difficult because morphine was usually available

---

[1]Bill Wilson, cofounder of Alcoholics Anonymous (AA), was a patient of the Towns Hospital, where according to AA publications he learned that alcoholism was a malady of mind, emotions, and body.

in a pure form that made withdrawal all the more difficult (H. W. Morgan 1981). The patient was given frequent baths, and as soon as he or she began to function more normally, a regimen of nourishing food and exercise was initiated. The patient, now withdrawn from drugs, engaged in such tasks as reading and gardening and was given a great deal of reassurance. The extent of the treatment often depended on a patient's ability to pay (H. W. Morgan 1981). More recently the profit that can accrue from treating certain types of substance abusers—such as those with appropriate health insurance—has led to the expansion of a private cure industry often based in health/hospital settings (Freudenheim 1987). These will be discussed later in the chapter.

For alcoholics, there were "inebriate homes" and asylums that operated on the fringes of religion, charity, and law enforcement. The different philosophies and treatment methods tended to merge over time: the medically oriented ones incorporating spiritual and religion-oriented remedies, and those operating on moral or religious principles integrating medical and psychological treatments. And as with the profit-making sector of drug addiction treatment, the alcohol cure industry became a business that promoted dubious notions hyped by unsupported claims. Indeed, many claimed success in treating both the drug- and alcohol-addicted (W. White 1998). Always pressed for sources of funding, these institutions were abandoned by the temperance movement and met their demise with the onset of Prohibition.

Chemical Treatments

A variety of treatment approaches use chemicals, often as a supplement to or in conjunction with some other form of treatment.

Opioid Antagonists

As part of the search for a magic bullet, scientists developed a number of heroin antagonists—substances that block or counteract the effects of opiates. These substances bind with opiate receptor sites, thereby preventing stimulation, or they displace an opiate already at the site. Some antagonists, such as cyclazocine and **naloxone,** have significant side effects. While cyclazocine taken orally effectively blocks the effects of heroin for 12 to 24 hours, it also produces nausea, sweating, a feeling of intoxication, anxiety, and hallucinations. Users suffer withdrawal symptoms when the substance is discontinued, although they do not develop a craving for it. A dose as small as .25 mg of naloxone will block the effects of heroin for 10 hours, but it is effective only when administered intravenously. Neither of these substances reduces the "drug hunger" of heroin addicts (DeLong 1972).

Naloxone is recommended for testing for opiate dependence (Narcon test) before admission to a methadone program (Judson and Goldstein 1986). It has no effect on the nondependent person, but causes immediate signs of heroin withdrawal in the opiate dependent. The substance is administered to persons seeking methadone because such

Thirteen Principles of Effective Drug Addiction Treatment

More than two decades of scientific research have yielded a set of fundamental principles that characterize effective drug abuse treatment. These thirteen principles are as follows:

1. *No single treatment is appropriate for all individuals.* Matching treatment settings, interventions, and services to each person's problems and needs is critical.

2. *Treatment needs to be readily available.* Treatment applicants can be lost if treatment is not immediately available or readily accessible.

3. *Effective treatment attends to multiple needs of the individual, not just his or her drug use.* Treatment must address the individual's drug use and associated medical, psychological, social, vocational, and legal problems.

4. *Treatment needs to be flexible* and to provide ongoing assessments of the person's needs, which may change during the course of treatment.

5. *Remaining in treatment for an adequate period of time is critical for treatment effectiveness.* The time depends on an individual's needs. For most, the threshold of significant improvement is reached at about three months in treatment. Additional treatment can produce further progress. Programs should include strategies to prevent leaving treatment prematurely.

6. *Individual and/or group counseling and other behavioral therapies are critical components of effective treatment for addiction.* In therapy, individuals address motivation, build skills to resist drug use, replace drug-using activities with constructive and rewarding nondrug-using activities, and improve problem-solving abilities. Behavioral therapy also facilitates interpersonal relationships.

7. *Medications are an important element of treatment for many patients,* especially when combined with counseling and other behavioral therapies. Methadone and levo-alpha-acetylmethadol (LAAM), disclosed later, help persons addicted to opiates stabilize their lives and reduce their drug use. Naltrexone (discussed later in the chapter) is effective for some opiate addicts and some patients with co-occurring alcohol dependence.

8. *Addicted or drug-abusing individuals with coexisting mental disorders should have both disorders treated in an integrated way.* Because these disorders often occur in the same individual, persons presenting for one condition should be assessed and treated for the other.

9. *Detoxification is only the first stage of addiction treatment* and by itself does little to change long-term drug use. Detoxification manages the acute physical symptoms of withdrawal. For some individuals it is a precursor to effective drug addiction treatment.

Continued

10. *Treatment does not need to be voluntary to be effective.* Sanctions or enticements in the family, employment setting, or criminal justice system can significantly increase treatment entry, retention, and success.

11. *Possible drug use during treatment must be monitored continuously.* Monitoring drug and alcohol use during treatment, through urinalysis, for example, can help the person withstand urges to use drugs. Such monitoring also can provide early evidence of drug use so that treatment can be adjusted.

12. *Treatment programs should provide assessment for HIV/AIDS, hepatitis B and C, tuberculosis, and other infectious diseases,* and counseling to help persons modify or change behaviors that place them or others at risk of infection. Counseling can help individuals avoid high-risk behavior and help people who are already infected manage their illness.

13. *Recovery from drug addiction can be a long-term process* and frequently requires multiple episodes of treatment. As with other chronic illnesses, relapses to drug use can occur during or after successful treatment episodes. Participation in self-help support programs during and following treatment often helps maintain abstinence.

Source: NIDA Notes (1999)

---

persons may not be opioid dependent or have only minimal dependence: "Treatment of these addicts with methadone raises important ethical and legal questions in view of the likelihood of producing physical dependence in previously nondependent persons" (Peachey and Lei 1988: 200). According to federal regulations, admission to methadone treatment is restricted to persons who have been addicted to heroin for at least 1 year. The antagonist nalorphine (Nalline) counters the depression of the central nervous system caused by opiates and is administered as an antidote for heroin overdose.

The National Institute on Drug Abuse was instrumental in developing **naltrexone** hydrochloride, a long-acting orally administered narcotic antagonist first synthesized in 1965 and marketed as Trexan by DuPont. This nonaddicting drug defeats the effects of opiates by occupying their receptor sites in the brain. It also displaces any agonists that are present, causing severe precipitated withdrawal in people who are opioid dependent. Naltrexone users often suffer from nausea and vomiting; less common side effects include headache, anxiety or depression, low energy, skin rashes, and decreased alertness. Discontinuing naltrexone will not cause withdrawal symptoms. Like any antagonist, naltrexone is effective only with patients motivated to give up the feeling of euphoria that opiates can provide. The manufacturer clearly states that it is recommended for use as an adjunct in the treatment of opioid abusers. "Treatment failure cannot be blamed on the failure of naltrexone to block opioids nor is treatment success likely to be the consequence of a use of naltrexone alone" (Ginzburg 1986: 5). There are about 2,000 persons being treated with naltrexone (Wren 1999d), and preliminary results are promising (Carroll et al. 2001).

Under the brand name Revia, naltrexone is being marketed for use in treating alcoholism (Leary 1995a). Alcohol causes the release of endorphins, believed to be a major factor in causing a person to continue drinking. Naltrexone blocks the endorphin-mediated rewarding effects of drinking alcohol.

Buprenorphine, which has a mixture of agonist and antagonist qualities, has been used experimentally to treat opiate dependence. It mimics the effects of opioids in some situations but blocks or reverses those effects in other situations by displacing opioids when they are present in excessive amounts. Pharmacologically it is related to morphine—it is a highly effective analgesic, 25 to 40 times more potent than morphine (Ling, Rawson, and Compton 1994). But buprenorphine is a partial agonist, which means it exhibits ceiling effects (increasing the dose only has effects to a certain level). Therefore, partial agonists usually have greater safety profiles than full agonists; they are less likely to cause respiratory depression, the major toxic effect of opiate drugs. Another benefit of buprenorphine is that the withdrawal syndrome is, at worst, mild to moderate and can often be managed without administration of narcotics (NIDA information).

In 2002, the Federal Drug Administration announced the approval of buprenorphine and buprenorphine-naloxone (partial opiate agonist with an opiate blocker). Taken orally, buprenorphine-naloxone does not produce euphoria and if injected, makes the user feel sick. It only needs to be taken every 1 to 3 days. As a result of the Drug Addiction Treatment Act of 2000, these drugs can be dispensed in a doctor's office instead of a clinic. The statute requires doctors to take an 8-hour course on the use of buprenorphine-naloxone, and each doctor or group practice is allowed to treat only thirty patients. In 2002, there were about 5,000 doctors qualified to offer the new drug, and there is no provision for Medicaid reimbursement (Markel 2002).

Chemicals for Detoxification

As in the past, contemporary treatment programs typically begin with detoxification—"a term left over from an obsolete theory that addicts suffer from an accumulation of toxins" (Dole 1980: 138)—with or without the assistance of drugs. Antagonists are sometimes used as an aid in heroin detoxification. Because of its potency, withdrawal from licit maintenance doses of methadone is generally accomplished by decreasing dosages. The antihypertension drug **clonidine** has been used to relieve many of the symptoms of opioid withdrawal, particularly those involving autonomic nervous system hyperactivity. The substance is nonaddicting (*Drug Abuse* 1987). Clonidine has been recommended by some physicians for the detoxification of methadone patients being maintained on relatively low dosages. Whereas methadone can be found in the patient's system more than a week after the last dose, clonidine has a shorter life. Thus, a clonidine patient can be placed on naltrexone immediately upon detoxification, whereas a methadone patient would experience unpleasant withdrawal symptoms under similar treatment (Ginzburg 1986).

In a controversial process referred to as "rapid detox," a heroin-addicted patient breathing through a respirator is strapped to a gurney and anesthetized. He or she then receives intravenous doses of the heroin antagonist naloxone. As naloxone pries off the opiate molecules from their receptor sites, the patient experiences "instant" withdrawal, which is complete in about four hours. Since the patient is unconscious, he or she avoids the usual discomfort that accompanies withdrawal, such as vomiting, shivering, and pain. After a night in intensive care, the patient can leave the hospital completely heroin free. Cost of the procedure can be as high as $8,500. Detoxification, of course, is simply a first step toward abstinence, and rapid detox is criticized for its expense while having no proven benefits of less costly approaches to withdrawal (Duenwald 2001). Indeed, making withdrawal relatively easy provides little incentive for remaining drug free.

Cocaine detoxification presents a serious problem because of the patient's craving for the drug. This may be associated with the depletion of dopamine, which, as noted in Chapter 5, is essential to maintain life. The extreme depression that occurs during the early days of abstinence, particularly with crack users, can lead to suicide. While withdrawal from opiates and cocaine can be accomplished without using other chemicals—although the patient may feel quite uncomfortable—detoxification from sedatives can lead to seizures and cardiac arrest and therefore must be accomplished by decreasing dosages.

The use of chemicals to facilitate drug withdrawal can serve to attract drug abusers into treatment and increases the probability that they will complete detoxification. However, at least with respect to heroin abusers, the use of chemicals has some troubling aspects: Addicts typically enter treatment when their habit is too expensive to support and they have to work quite hard simply to prevent the onset of withdrawal symptoms, while a high level of tolerance prevents achieving the high. Under such conditions addiction is no longer fun. "Then he enters a detoxification ward and is comfortably withdrawn from heroin. Detoxification is made so easy, compared to 'cold turkey,'[2] that addicts are not confronted with negatively reinforcing pharmacological and physiological aspects of addiction" (Bellis 1981: 139). Detoxification reduces the addict's tolerance so that the high can be enjoyed once again at an affordable price. Drug program staff "should not be surprised or miffed when addicts leave the detoxification ward and inject heroin within a few minutes or hours" (1981: 140).

Opioid Agonists

Certain synthetic substances have a chemical makeup similar to that of opioids. The most widely used agonist, **methadone,** a wholly synthetic narcotic, was developed in Germany (where it was named Dolophine in honor of Hitler) when access to morphine was

---

[2]A common symptom of withdrawal is piloerection—"goose flesh" (W. White 1998).

cut off during World War II. While it produces virtually the same analgesic and sedative effects as heroin and is no less addictive, orally administered methadone lasts longer. As opposed to the shorter-acting opiates such as heroin, the high it produces is less dramatic. While the effects of heroin wear off in 2 to 3 hours, the effects of oral methadone continue for 12 to 24 hours. Methadone can be prepared in a way that makes it difficult to inject, rendering it less likely to be diverted into the black market. After World War II, methadone was typically used in hospital settings to systematically detoxify persons addicted to opiates (Dole 1980; Gerstein and Harwood 1990).

The first clinical use of methadone to treat narcotic addiction occurred at the United States Public Health Hospital in Lexington, Kentucky, where it was substituted for morphine and heroin to help detoxify addicted patients. Withdrawal from heroin was made relatively painless by first administering doses equivalent to the patient's street use of heroin. The doses were then lowered until the patient was no longer addicted, a process that took 7 to 10 days (Blackmore 1979). During the early 1960s, when narcotic addiction once again emerged as a major national concern, Vincent Dole and Marie Nyswander of Rockefeller University reported on their successful use of methadone to treat heroin addicts in a dramatically new way—through maintenance.

Methadone—Magic Bullet? In 1964 Doctors Dole and Nyswander gave twenty-two hospitalized heroin addicts increasing doses of methadone until they reached a "stabilized state," meaning that they had neither withdrawal symptoms nor a craving for further increases in the dosage: "With repeated administration of a fixed dose, methadone loses its sedative and analgesic powers. The subject becomes tolerant" (Dole 1980: 146). The patients were then released, but they returned each day for an oral dose of methadone. The following year a research report by Dole and Nyswander (1965) revealed extraordinary results from this approach, which they ascribed to methadone's ability to provide a "pharmacological block" against heroin. Furthermore, it was theorized, heroin abuse in certain addicts results in a metabolic disorder that requires the continued ingestion of narcotics if the person is to remain homeostatic. With such disorders, methadone acts like any prescribed medicine, normalizing the patient's functioning.

Continuing research with additional patients provided further support for methadone maintenance—addict patients refrained from heroin use, secured employment, and avoided criminal activity. In 1966 Dole and Nyswander established a large outpatient methadone program at Beth Israel Hospital in New York City. Other programs followed. Dole and Nyswander (1966) intimated that they had discovered the magic bullet: methadone provides a *blockade* to the effects of heroin. (See Chambers and Brill, 1973, for a review of these early methadone experiments and treatment programs.)

The typical methadone program begins with a period of inpatient care during which low doses of methadone are substituted for heroin. (The patient is not informed of the dosage he or she receives.) The methadone is usually mixed with orange juice (which helps reduce its bitter taste) and consumed in front of a nurse. Slow increases in dosage reduce the high, which disappears once tolerance develops. Addicts subsequently report daily on an outpatient basis and are given take-home doses for weekends. As they progress, less than daily pickups are permitted. Patients usually provide a urine specimen before they are given methadone.

By the late 1960s a few thousand addicts were being maintained on methadone; by early 1973 there were approximately 73,000 (Danaceau 1974). This change was brought about by the Nixon administration, which was convinced that methadone could help reduce the crime rate—a cornerstone of the "law-and-order" presidency of Richard Nixon. Experts who knew better, argues Edward Jay Epstein, "chose not to deflate the unrealistic claim that methadone would substantially reduce crime" (1974: 22). They hoped that such programs would lure otherwise recalcitrant hard-core heroin addicts into treatment. Eventually, however, the "bad news" came out. Methadone was not the magic bullet. Indeed, there was no blockade but simply cross-tolerance—the patient maintained at significantly high doses of methadone would not experience the high from heroin. But methadone did not affect the euphoric rush. In fact, it was discovered that methadone patients, even those at high daily doses, were often abusing heroin as well as other drugs. Furthermore, while methadone maintenance was designed for heroin addicts, the problem was often one of polydrug use. In fact, cocaine is a major drug of abuse among methadone patients (C. O'Brien et al. 1990). Today there are about 180,000 methadone users nationally. (Eight states—Idaho, Mississippi, Montana, New Hampshire, North Dakota, South Dakota, Vermont, and West Virginia—prohibit methadone.)

It was further revealed that the figures given out by Dole and Nyswander were deceptive: The rate of "cure" attributed to methadone was better explained by the screening mechanisms used—older and more motivated addicts were preferred—and by the fact that unsuccessful cases were simply dropped from the program and the final tabulations. Methadone clinics came under severe attack by those associated with the drug-free therapeutic communities (discussed below), and by 1979 they were operating at about 90 percent of capacity (Blackmore 1979). Robert Newman states that "proponents of specific treatment approaches rarely missed an opportunity to make exaggerated claims for their own modality and to vilify publicly other therapeutic efforts" (1977: xx). Residents also strongly opposed the opening of methadone treatment centers in their communities— the NIMBY (not-in-my-backyard) syndrome.

No Magic Bullet, but Methadone Still Useful. This is not to say that methadone maintenance has no role in treating heroin addiction. Methadone maintenance appears to be quite beneficial to certain heroin abusers. It can act as a crutch for those motivated to give up heroin. The programs also attract addicts seeking a chemical cure, although the counseling and job assistance provided may be the real "cure." Even without such services, notes James DeLong (1972), methadone may have a placebo effect—the addict who believes that methadone is beneficial will find it so. To the extent that heroin addiction is explained by physiology, as discussed in Chapter 3—for example, that persons with abnormal endorphin levels compensate by ingesting heroin—methadone maintenance is the equivalent of providing insulin to diabetics.

If psychoanalytic theory is accurate, methadone may serve as an anti-aggression chemical for those heroin addicts whose drug use is based on a need to control the rage

Methadone and LAAM
Uses and Effects

Classification:	Narcotic
CSA Schedule:	Schedule I, II
Trade or Other Names:	Dolophine, Methadose, levo-alpha-acetylmethadol (LAAM), levomethadyl acetate
Medical Uses:	Analgesic, treatment of dependence
Physical Dependence:	High
Psychological Dependence:	High
Tolerance:	Yes
Duration (hours):	12–72
Usual Method:	Oral, injected
Possible Effects:	Euphoria, drowsiness, respiratory depression, constricted pupils, nausea
Effects of Overdose:	Slow and shallow breathing, clammy skin, convulsions, coma, possible death
Withdrawal Syndrome:	Watery eyes, runny nose, yawning, loss of appetite, irritability, tremors, panic, cramps, nausea, chills, and sweating

Source: Drug Enforcement Administration

and aggressive tendencies originating in a problematic anal stage of development (Khantzian 1980). In a review of evaluations of methadone maintenance programs, M. Douglas Anglin and William McGlothlin conclude that "methadone maintenance has been shown to effectively reduce drug use, dealing, and income-generating crime, and to a lesser extent to increase employment and family responsibility" (1985: 274). Furthermore, they note, methadone maintenance "appeals to a portion of the addict population that has not been amenable to other social intervention strategies." And methadone has proven effective in suppressing the administration of opiates in laboratory experiments with animals (Winger 1988).

There is some concern that older addicts who might have gone into remission without any intervention are nevertheless maintained on methadone—addicted. On the other hand, "patients who terminate before they have achieved stable social functioning are very unlikely to remain abstinent"; and "even patients who terminate under the best of

Methadone clinics across the country treat as many as 180,000 ex-heroin users every day. Methadone maintenance appears to be beneficial for certain addicts—it can act as a crutch for those motivated to give up heroin.

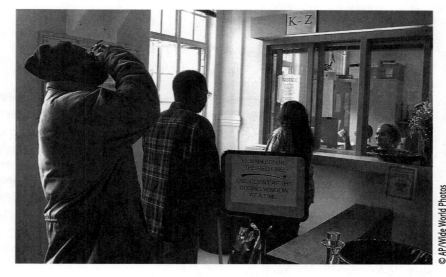

circumstances still may have less than a 50 percent chance of remaining abstinent as long as 3 years" (Hargreaves 1986: 70). Mary Kreek (1987) reports that only 20 to 30 percent of former "hard-core" heroin addicts remain heroin free for 3 years or more following discharge from a methadone maintenance program, which is about the same percentages generally reported for other treatment modalities, including residential drug-free or short-term methadone detoxification programs. Anglin and McGlothlin state that while methadone maintenance has not produced the wonderful results anticipated by early researchers, it makes a "real and beneficial contribution to reducing the social and individual costs associated with addiction" (1985: 274–75).

Critics of New York City's methadone programs argue that they discourage abstinence as an ultimate goal, thus prolonging dependency for those who might be able and willing to give up all drug use. They note that this dependency extends to employment: Fees from methadone patients on welfare is guaranteed, paid for by Medicaid, while those who are employed can usually only afford to pay a fraction of what Medicaid provides. Few programs offer vocational or job skills training (Massing 1999). Furthermore, methadone maintenance is predicated on the exclusiveness of heroin use, although heroin addicts are usually polydrug users who may continue use of illegal drugs even while being maintained on methadone (Inciardi, McBride, and Surratt 1998). When they enter treatment, methadone patients "frequently bring with them an inclination to experiment with a variety of other drugs and often view themselves as connoisseurs of drug-taking experiences. . . . Thus, continued use of other illicit drugs is frequently a problem in the treatment of a large percentage of methadone patients" (Platt et al. 1998).

The methadone maintenance program established at Beth Israel Medical Center in New York has continued to operate since its establishment by Dole and Nyswander. Beth Israel treats more than 8,000 patients, who make more than 1 million visits annually to the center's twenty-three outpatient clinics. Most patients have been in continuous treatment for more than 2 years; about one-half for more than 5 years. Treatment is voluntary—the program will not take coerced patients. Patients can remain on methadone for as long as they wish, or they can opt for detoxification. For the past decade the program has operated above capacity.

LAAM. Levo-alpha-acetylmethadol is used as a methadone substitute because it has the advantage of lasting up to 72 hours. LAAM also acts more slowly than methadone and does not produce a quick high (Schecter 1980; General Accounting Office 1990). This is both an advantage and a disadvantage. While LAAM's slow onset makes it an unlikely candidate for street diversion and use, addicts may be unwilling to stay with LAAM because of this quality (Ling, Rawson, and Compton 1994). LAAM was approved by the Food and Drug Administration as an opiate treatment medication in 1993. A 1997 study of heroin-dependent individuals treated with LAAM for 17 weeks revealed that they reduced their use of heroin by up to 90 percent (NIDA 1997).

Chemical Responses to Cocaine Abuse

In Chapter 5 you learned that the neurotransmitters dopamine and serotonin appear to play an important role in cocaine abuse. Cocaine agonists and antagonists—which typically impact on these neurotransmitters—have been tested as possible treatment agents, but no drug has emerged that effectively treats the cocaine-dependent patient (McCance 1997). Dopamine antagonists are available, but they "can produce serious and permanent motor disorders, unpleasant subjective effects, or increases rather than decreases in cocaine self-administration in experimental animals" (Winger 1988: 125). Medication may be used as an adjunct to treating cocaine abusers either to deal with the deleterious effects of cocaine use itself or to treat the underlying motivations for using cocaine. Medication may be needed by addicts who are suicide risks during the post-cocaine "crash" period characterized by a lack of energy and an inability to feel pleasure, or by those who exhibit transient psychotic states. Severe delusional states and paranoid reactions from excessive cocaine require medication.

As noted in Chapters 3 and 5, cocaine use may be a form of self-medication for those suffering from certain chemical deficiencies, particularly neurotransmitters that affect mood and activity levels. In fact, note Henry Spitz and Jeffrey Rosecan (1987), some cocaine abusers have been successfully treated with prescribed antidepressants, although crack addicts appear to be less amenable to such treatment (Kolata 1989a). Introduced in the 1950s, *tricyclic antidepressants* (TCAs) such as Tofranil (imipramine) treat depression by manipulating the level of several neurotransmitters.[3] They are used to treat cocaine depression, particularly in patients whose cocaine use appears to be a form of

---

[3]In many cases, TCAs have been replaced by Prozac (fluoxetine), which acts on a single neurotransmitter—serotonin. Fluoxetine has been used experimentally to treat cocaine abuse, but with minimal effect (Foltin and Fischman 1994).

self-medication to ward off depression: "[TCAs] appear to reverse some of the neurochemical effects of chronic cocaine administration" (Spitz and Rosecan 1987: 260). It is believed that TCAs may act as cocaine antagonists by displacing or blocking cocaine receptors in the CNS and may help to reduce the craving for cocaine.

In 1990 the National Institute of Mental Health won a patent for one TCA, *desipramine,* a cocaine substitute used to wean users off the drug. The substitute does not have any of the dangerous side effects of cocaine and is believed to reduce craving (Andrews 1990). It has since become the most widely studied medication for dealing with cocaine dependence. In limited clinical trials, desipramine has shown some ability to decrease the reinforcing effects of cocaine and to reduce the craving for it ("Drug Abuse" 1991; Kosten 1993). The substance is most effective with subjects who, in addition to cocaine dependence, suffer from depression (McCance 1997). *Lithium,* a standard drug for psychotic disorders, particularly depressive states, is used with patients whose cyclothymia (mild mood swings), manic depression, or bipolar disorder (extreme mood swings) preceded cocaine use.

Chronic cocaine use may deplete the neurotransmitter dopamine, causing a craving in dopamine receptors. *Bromocriptine,* a dopamine agonist used to treat Parkinson's disease, appears to bind to the dopamine receptors, thus reducing the craving for cocaine. It does, however, have serious side effects, including nausea, headaches, dizziness, abnormal involuntary movements, and psychosis. According to Rosecan and Nunes (1987), its use is justified only in treatment-resistant cases where recovery is hampered by severe craving. And while bromocriptine decreased cocaine use in laboratory monkeys, its chronic administration produced toxic effects including preconvulsive signs (Winger 1988). One study (Eiler, Schaefer, and Salstrom 1995) found little benefit in using bromocriptine to treat cocaine withdrawal, but Elinore McCance (1997) states that it still has potential as a possible treatment agent.

CRF Antagonists

As noted in Chapter 4, heroin addiction is believed related to the ability of the drug to reduce stress, thereby providing a basis for medicines that can serve the same purpose without the negative features of opiates. Several pharmaceutical companies are developing a class of medications, called *CRF antagonists,* that may help drug abuse patients avoid relapse by blocking the release of stress-causing hormones and neurotransmitters (Stocker 1999).

Psychological Treatments

Treatment based on psychological theories can be broadly divided into those that are psychoanalytically oriented—sometimes referred to as dynamic or clinical—and those that utilize some form of behaviorism. Some programs mix the two approaches.

A Psychoanalytic Approach

To the psychoanalyst,[4] symptoms of neurotic behavior such as drug abuse are tied to repressed material from early life—the developmental stages examined in Chapter 8. The symptoms will disappear when the repressed material is exposed under psychoanalytic treatment. Thus, the psychoanalyst seeks to make unconscious affect and memories available to the patient's consciousness (Holinger 1989). Psychoanalysis and the therapies based on it aim "at inducing the patient to give up the repressions belonging to his early life and to replace them by reactions of a sort that could correspond better to a psychically mature condition." To accomplish this a psychoanalyst uses *interpretation*—attempts to get the patient "to recollect certain experiences and emotions called up by them which he has at the moment forgotten or repressed" (Reiff 1963: 274). This is accomplished through *dream interpretation* and *free association*. While in a relaxed state, the patient is asked to say what comes to mind about any given element in a dream, or the therapist may ask the patient to let a proper name or even a number occur to him or her. The train of associations stirred up by the dream, the name, or the number becomes an entry point for the release of repressed material, which the analyst helps the patient interpret.

In order to re-create the emotional state originally attached to these associations, the therapist takes advantage of *transference,* the development of an emotional attitude, positive or negative, by the patient toward the therapist. Thus, the psychoanalyst may be emotionally (and unconsciously) perceived by the patient as a paternal or maternal figure in a re-creation of the emotions tied to very early psychic development.

In fact, psychoanalysis is rarely used to treat substance abusers, and there is a paucity of literature on treating substance abusers using this approach. This method requires highly skilled therapists, articulate patients—because psychoanalysis and the therapies based on it are "talking therapies"—and a long period of costly treatment: Psychoanalysis typically involves three to five 50-minute sessions a week for as long as 7 years, at $75 to $200 per session. There are few published reports of successful psychoanalytic treatment of drug-dependent persons, and those that exist deal almost exclusively with heroin addiction. As Clifford Yorke has pointed out with respect to heroin addicts, "the number of confirmed addicts seeking psychoanalytic treatment is almost certainly very small, the number of analysts prepared to accept them even smaller, and the number of addicts who pursue their treatment to conclusion smaller still" (1970: 156). In fact, Freud himself doubted the usefulness of psychoanalysis for treating drug addicts (Byck 1974).

Frederic Schiffer (1988) used short-term therapy based on a psychoanalytic model to treat cocaine addicts in a hospital and subsequently on an outpatient basis. He found their pathology to be based on psychologically abusive conditions covertly carried out by

---

[4]*Psychoanalyst* is not a restricted title like that enjoyed by psychiatrists, who must be physicians, or clinical psychologists, who must hold a doctorate in psychology. While there are certifying bodies for psychoanalysts, they do not enjoy a government-supported monopoly on the use of the title. There is a great deal of acrimony between psychologists and psychiatrists over who is qualified to practice psychoanalysis (Goleman 1988).

one or both parents during childhood. Patients were filled with a long-standing rage and pain that they could not understand. Therapy allowed the patient to understand and appreciate the cause of his (all patients were male) feelings. Finally, patients were helped to master their traumatic pasts by "reliving, in effect through the patient's memories and transference, the early trauma" (1988: 133). The goal of psychoanalytically oriented therapy is to foster insight and self-awareness, which helps the patient come to grips with his or her narcissistic disturbance that plays out as drug abuse (narcissistic tranquility). Substance abusers chemically extinguish unpleasant feelings and conflicts; self-awareness enables the patient to understand these emotions and thus learn to use nonchemical responses to them (Forrest 1985).

Psychology, notes James DeLong, has not found a consistent pathology among drug addicts: "No psychiatric diagnosis can be shown to apply to all heroin addicts or even to a majority of them" (1972: 224). George E. Woody and his colleagues argue, however, that "studies indicate that the types of psychiatric problems observed in addicts are similar to illnesses that are often treated with psychotherapy when they occur in nonaddicted populations" (1983: 639). In practice, therapists, while they may be steeped in psychoanalytic theory, generally avoid the psychoanalytical goal of effecting personality changes in drug abusers. Instead, they focus on improving the ego level of functioning by trying to help patients maintain constructive reality-based relationships, solve problems, and achieve adequate and satisfying social functioning within the existing personality structure. The focus of treatment is on the functions of the ego and its ability to adapt to stress and changes in the environment, *despite* inadequacies experienced during early stages of development. (For a comparison of the effectiveness of different forms of psychotherapy with opiate addicts, see Woody et al. 1983; for a discussion of the techniques of psychoanalytically based therapy with addicts, see Kaufman 1994). This is accomplished through encouragement and moral support, persuasion and suggestion, training and advice, reeducation and counseling—not psychoanalysis. The therapist maintains a substance-abuse orientation and typically focuses on identifying specific needs rather than intrapsychic processes. He or she will deal with impaired self-esteem and ability to form sound interpersonal relationships, characteristics that depend on healthy psychosocial development at early stages of life. While recognizing the unconscious etiology, the therapist focuses on the client's present and future reality. Abstinence, and not intrapsychic change, is the goal. For example, at City Roads, a short-term drug treatment program in London,

> the aims of counseling are to clarify *needs* and to build up the residents' motivation to do something about their needs. The first phase involves getting to know the resident, building up confidence and trust in City Roads. The very fact of sitting down and talking to a staff member who takes an interest in the resident is in itself fruitful. The resident starts to feel that someone cares. This was for them a very positive experience, which many drug abusers are not used to.
>
> The next step is "getting to the root of the problem," exploring the personal strengths and weaknesses and their origin, and the needs or problems under investigation are seen as psychological ones. People are seen as being unable to

Psychotherapeutic Success
A rigorous study that adhered to research protocols found that a combination of intensive individual and group counseling by credentialed psychotherapists for 9 months had a significant impact on drug-using behavior (Crits-Christoph et al. 1999).

take responsibility, unable to form relationships, depressed, bitter, angry, frustrated, and lacking in trust. The causes of these problems are thought to lie in past experiences, most commonly in an emotionally unstable childhood characterized by lack of parental care, alcoholism in the home, or an institutional upbringing, which are thought to lead to deprivation of warmth, care, and stability. (Jamieson, Glanz, and MacGregor 1984: 116–17; *edited*)

Behavior Modification

Behavior modification is a treatment approach based on learning theory. The strength of psychoactive substances as positive reinforcers and the negative reinforcement associated with abstinence provide conditioned responses that can explain the key difficulty in treating drug abusers: finding reinforcers that can successfully compete with these substances. Methadone's success in treating some heroin abusers can be explained in terms of behaviorism (Stitzer, Bigelow, and McCaul 1985). Furthermore, according to operant conditioning, for behavior modification to be effective, reinforcement, negative or positive, must follow immediately after the behavior is exhibited; this instant gratification is what makes drug use so reinforcing and why it is difficult to use behavior modification techniques with chronic drug users.

Aversion Treatment. Behavior modification can also attempt to shape behavior by applying punishment or aversive stimulation. Aversive control was depicted in Stanley Kubrick's motion picture *A Clockwork Orange*. In actual drug treatment, Anectine (succinylcholine), a muscle relaxant that causes brief paralysis but leaves the patient conscious, is injected into the subject immediately following the heroin cook-up ritual. The addict-patient remains conscious but is unable to move or breathe voluntarily, conditions that simulate the onset of death. The dangers of heroin use are recited while the patient remains paralyzed.

Drug antagonists can serve a similar function by rendering opiates or other substances either ineffective (lacking positive reinforcement) or extremely unpleasant (negative reinforcement or punishment). Disulfiram (Antabuse), metronidazole, or chlorpropamide can serve this purpose for alcohol abusers. **Antabuse,** the best known of these substances, disrupts the liver's metabolism, producing a severe reaction that includes stomach and head pain, extreme nausea, and vomiting. (Milder reactions can be triggered by any number of products that contain alcohol, such as cough medicine, mouthwash, or even skin creams.) In 1990 a patent was granted for a substance that has the appearance and smell of cocaine and even produces a numbing effect but is not psychoactive. The substance is used in conjunction with an aversive chemical (Andrews 1990). Other behavioral therapies use biofeedback and relaxation training, and sometimes assertiveness training, to prepare drug abusers to better cope with the stress and anxiety believed linked to drug use.

Research has discovered a connection between *cues* and drug use (see Chapter 3). The intensity of the drug euphoria burns emotional memories into brain circuits. These

Relapse

Three types of stimulus can trigger intense craving leading to renewed drug use (Hanson 2002b):

Priming. Just one exposure to a formerly abused substance can precipitate rapid resumption of abuse at previously established levels or greater.

Environmental cues. Exposure to people, places, or things associated with drug use can lead to resumption of abuse.

Stress. Acute and chronic stress can contribute to the establishment, maintenance, and resumption of drug abuse.

memories are encoded into a part of the brain—amygdala—that operates outside of conscious control to cause intense cravings for re-creating the euphoric experience. These are countered by desensitization treatment: "[P]atients are usually first relaxed, then given repeated exposure to a graded hierarchy of anxiety-producing stimuli (real or imaginal)" in order to provide a form of immunity (Childress, McLellan, and O'Brien 1985: 957). With voluntary patients, electric shocks may be self-administered whenever a craving for the chemical arises. Some researchers report that the use of chemical or electrical stimuli has not proven effective in producing a conditioned aversion in drug abusers, while success has been reported with verbal aversion techniques in which "a patient is asked to *imagine* strongly aversive stimuli (usually vomiting) in association with imaginal drug-related cues, scenes, and/or behavior" (Childress, McLellan, and O'Brien 1985: 951). Thus, *imagined* aversive stimuli may be superior to *real* aversive stimuli with the drug dependent (although this appears to run contrary to a great deal of research in operant conditioning). In any event, "aversive counterconditioning is not a substitute for support for life-enhancing behavior, rather it suppresses the undesirable behavior while other modalities support positive alternatives" (Frawley and Smith 1990: 21).

In an experiment using both chemical and verbal aversive techniques, cocaine abusers were provided with a nonpsychoactive substitute that smelled like cocaine and numbed the nose. The white substance was set out with a razor blade, straw, and mirrors for the preparation of "lines." The patient received an injection of nausea-producing drugs. Just before the onset of nausea, he or she snorted the lines of "coke." During the 3-hour recovery period, the patient was encouraged to dwell on the drug paraphernalia and pictures of cocaine and to pair the use of cocaine with negative consequences. After 6 months of in-hospital and outpatient booster treatments, the abstinence rate was 78 percent. Although a few patients had used cocaine again during the 6-month period, the relapses were quite brief (Frawley and Smith 1990).

Social Learning Theory Approach. *Social learning theory,* a variant of behaviorism, focuses on cognitive mediational processes. According to this view, people are active participants in their operant conditioning processes—they determine what is and what is not reinforcing. For example, as noted in Chapter 8, the actor must *learn* that ingesting certain chemicals is desirable. In other words, behavior is complex and reinforcement often abstract. Thus, notes Albert Bandura, "human beings can cognitively bridge delays between behavior and subsequent reinforcement without impairing the efficacy of incentive operations" (1974: 862). People have a unique capacity to use abstractions—symbols, such as the medals and trophies dear to any amateur athlete—as important reinforcers.

The drug abuser is seen as lacking the level of social competence necessary to cope adequately with a variety of situational demands. In using operant conditioning with drug abusers, the social learning theorist stresses patient analysis in order to discover the variables that are reinforcing. The therapist attempts to discover the situational demands and their related negative emotions that are related to the patient's drug use. The treatment begins with an assessment of the positive and negative aspects of drug use and a self-report on the type, amount, and frequency of drugs used. The assessment includes a focus on the social, physical, and emotional environments in which drug use occurs. After the assessment, the role of the therapist is to enable the patient to deal with triggering behavior so that it does not lead to drug use, with the patient's own report of the negative aspects of drug use serving as a motivator for adopting more positive coping strategies (Donovan 1988):

- Through a detailed examination of the antecedents and consequences of substance abuse, the therapist attempts to understand why patients may be more likely to use in a given situation and to understand the role that drugs play in their lives. This functional analysis is used to identify the high-risk situations in which they are likely to abuse drugs and, thus, to provide the basis for learning more effective coping behaviors in those situations.
- The therapist attempts to help patients develop meaningful alternative reinforcers to drug abuse, that is, other activities and involvements (relationships, work, hobbies) that serve as viable alternatives to cocaine abuse and help them remain abstinent.
- A detailed examination of the consequences, both long- and short-term, of cocaine and other substance abuse is employed as a strategy to build or reinforce the patient's resolve to reduce or cease substance abuse.

Cognitive Learning Theory Approach. Cognitive approaches in general tend to focus, not on the psychological causes of substance abuse, but rather on teaching abusers to understand their cravings and develop coping skills. This may include detailed planning on how to get from one day to the next without using drugs (Orenstein 2002).

In a cognitive approach developed by Ann Rose Childress (1993), the therapist first conducts a study to develop a set of cues that trigger drug cravings. Patients are then taught methods of combating the urges, including a planned delay before acting on a craving, having an alternative behavior planned for this delay period, and systematic relaxation to counter drug arousal. Other techniques include listening to a recording of positive/negative craving consequences, which instructs the addict to list the three most negative consequences of relapsing into drugs and the three most positive consequences of not acting on cravings. Negative imagery is used to encourage patients to remember their worst period of addiction—a type of scare tactic.

Fred Wright (1993) and his colleagues use the Socratic method—challenging questions and answers—to stimulate patients to examine and modify their drug-related beliefs. Patients are also taught to keep a log of their cravings; after each entry they write spontaneous negative thoughts.

Contingency Management and Contingency Contracting. Success in modifying behavior using learning theory has been experienced in the controlled setting of a total institution (Goffman 1961) such as a prison or hospital. In such environments important reinforcers can be manipulated by therapists, often in the form of contingency management and contingency contracting.

Sometimes referred to as the *token economy,* contingency management rewards residents for behavior classified as "therapeutic" by providing them with points or tokens that can be redeemed for items valued by the patient, such as snacks, television time, and weekend passes. Roy Pickens and Travis Thompson (1984) describe the program utilized in a drug treatment ward at the University of Minnesota Hospital where point transactions—added or subtracted—were recorded by staff members in a small booklet issued to each patient.

Points could be earned for engaging in personal-care activities such as cleaning the room or washing clothes, for doing chores such as preparing meals, for participating in ward activities, for attending classes aimed at helping residents think rationally about themselves, and for assertiveness and problem-solving that improved interpersonal skills. Extra points could be earned for good-quality participation; these were given to the resident at the end of each activity: "At this time a staff person marks the points earned in the patients' point booklets and briefly describes how the quality of their participation earned them extra points, or how they might improve their participation in the class to earn extra points" (1984: 55). Points earned were exchangeable for various goods or services, such as snacks, soft drinks, cigarettes, or personal care items. It is obvious that contingency management is not designed to directly impact on drug-using behavior but is a means of getting patients to participate in the therapeutic activities that have abstinence as a goal.

The University of Minnesota Hospital utilized contingency contracting in the form of "a formalized agreement between a staff person and the patient that specifies the manner in which learning principles are applied to the modification of the patient's behavior." The contingency contract was drafted and signed by the parties. The contract "details the specific behaviors to be changed, how such behaviors are to be monitored, and the contingencies [rewards or punishments] to be placed on the behaviors" (Pickens and Thompson 1984: 57). Contingency contracts were also used with patients during the first several weeks after discharge. The contracts were designed to allow for the implementation of behavioral contingencies in the patient's own home environment to reduce the likelihood of a return to drug use.

Stephen Higgens and Alan Budney (1993) describe a contingency management program for outpatient cocaine abusers that provides points for drug-free urine samples: The number of points multiplies when consecutive negative samples are submitted. The points can be exchanged for a variety of gift items. At the end of 3 months, patients are shifted from points/gifts to lottery tickets. Contingency management has been used by methadone clinics to treat patients who ingest opiates and other drugs while on methadone maintenance or methadone withdrawal programs. Rewards for a drug-free urine sample include a cash payment and methadone take-home privileges. Negative contingencies include the loss of cash payments or take-home privileges, daily urinalysis, and counseling (Stitzer et al. 1984; see also Magura et al. 1988; Kidorf and Stitzer 1996). Stephen Magura and his colleagues report that contingency management utilizing take-home privileges did not have a significant effect on most methadone patients whose poly-drug use included cocaine: Cocaine "seems especially attractive to patients and thus was resistant to behavioral modification" (1988: 117).

Contingency contracting with negative reinforcement has been used to ensure abstinence in cocaine treatment programs: "For example, a patient participating in such a contract will agree that, in the event of relapse, a previously drafted letter will be sent to his employer informing the latter of the patient's cocaine problem" (Kertzner 1987: 145). Robert Kertzner states that negative contingency contracting has been found to be very effective with patients who agreed to participate. However, one of the limitations of this strategy, he notes, is the large number of patients who decline to participate. "Others have modified this technique to include positive sanctions for continued abstinence, such as returning patients' money held in escrow" (1987: 146).

Group Treatment

Treatment using psychotherapeutic techniques or behavior modification may utilize casework—one-to-one counseling—or group approaches. According to Helen Northern: "one of the advantages of the uses of the group approach is that stimulation toward improvement arises from a network of interpersonal influences in which all members participate" (1969: 52). The basic theory underlying this approach is that peer interaction is more powerful than therapist-patient interactions within the one-to-one situation. In casework the relationship between therapist and patient may remain distant because the therapist typically lacks the all-important personal experience with drug abuse. In the group approach, the group, not the group leader-therapist, is the helping instrument, obviating the therapist's personal experience with drugs. Furthermore, many critical interpersonal behaviors that may not emerge in the casework approach, will emerge in a group (Flores 1988). "Group members are more likely to try new forms of behavior if these have been demonstrated effectively by others" (Kauffman, Dore, and Nelson-Zlupko 1995: 355).

Treatment groups are typically formed around one basic trait that all members share and from which the group derives its descriptive label. For example, they may be formed around cocaine abuse, with a subtrait being age or gender.[5] In general, notes Henry Spitz (1987), the more heterogeneous the group elements, the greater the intragroup tension that promotes interaction. The more homogeneous the group elements, the greater the basis for intermember trust and group cohesion. Groups may also be organized at different points in the treatment process, such as intake, detoxification, inpatient, and outpatient. There may also be groups for parents, siblings, and spouses. While group approaches have many advantages over casework, considerably fewer therapists are trained in the former than in the latter. Further, "patients whose motivation for change appears highly questionable should not be accepted into a group-oriented treatment program, because they usually have a negative, demoralizing impact on

---

[5]For a discussion in favor of women's therapy groups for drug addicts, see Kauffman, Dore, and Nelson-Zlupko 1995.

other patients who may be working hard to remain abstinent" (Washton, Stone, and Henrickson 1988: 380).

While group approaches may vary, "most professionals who work with alcoholics and addicts on a sustained basis agree that group therapy offers the chemically dependent individual unique opportunities to (1) share and to identify with others who are going through similar problems; (2) to understand their own attitudes about addiction and their defenses against giving up alcohol and drugs by confronting similar attitudes and defenses in others; and (3) to learn to communicate needs and feelings more directly" (Flores 1988: 7). Support provided by the group enables it to act as a catalyst for abstinence. (This has been the writer's experience working with groups of adolescent drug abusers.) Some researchers, however, advise caution: Group approaches "for youth with histories of antisocial behavior may be counterproductive; participants in a group may tend to validate and legitimize the antisocial behavior of the other group members" (Chavez and Sanchez-Way 1997: 17).

Drug Treatment Programs

The treatment of drug-dependent people presents an obvious problem: If we don't know the cause, how can we offer the "cure"? This problem is exacerbated by programs that fail to develop theory-centered treatment responses or to incorporate the results of research into their approach to clients. While matching patient needs with specific treatments is the norm in medicine, this approach may be missing even in drug programs housed in medical settings (Hester and Miller 1988). The admissions policies of some in-patient programs depend more on financial status than on matching patient needs and program resources. Often these are relatively new programs looking for middle- and upper-class patients, who are most likely to have third-party or insurance support. Assessment and intake are informal or based on available space. Mounting health-related costs have caused third-party payment organizations to "require treatment organizations to further document and better justify the need for treatment" (Winters and Henly 1988: 4). Indeed, the American Society of Addiction Medicine has established minimum criteria for inpatient drug and alcohol treatment for adults:

- severe but manageable withdrawal risk
- need for medical monitoring and a 24-hour structured setting
- high resistance despite negative consequences
- inability of outpatient treatment to curtail drug use
- home environment dangerous for recovery

Treatment can be accomplished in a variety of settings—voluntary, involuntary, inpatient, and outpatient. The cost of these programs varies according to whether they are inpatient or outpatient, the qualifications of their staff, and the length of treatment. A particularly vexing problem is community opposition to drug-treatment programs. Let us examine the settings and the treatments offered by some drug programs.

Summary of Psychological Treatment Approaches

Cognitive-Behavioral Therapy

Strategies based on the theory that learning processes play a critical role in the development of maladaptive behavioral patterns are referred to as cognitive-behavioral therapy. Individuals learn to identify and correct problematic behaviors. Specific techniques include exploring the positive and negative consequences of continued use, self-monitoring to recognize drug cravings early on and to identify high-risk situations for use, and developing strategies for coping with and avoiding high-risk situations and the desire to use. A central element of this treatment is anticipating the problems patients are likely to encounter and helping them develop effective coping strategies.

Supportive-Expressive Psychotherapy

This time limited therapy has two main components:

- *Supportive* techniques to help patients feel comfortable in discussing their personal experiences
- *Expressive* techniques to help patients identify and work through interpersonal relationship issues

Special attention is paid to the role of drugs in relation to problem feelings and behaviors, and how problems may be solved without recourse to drugs.

Individualized Drug Counseling

This treatment approach focuses directly on reducing or stopping the addict's illicit drug use. It addresses related areas of impaired functioning, such as employment status, illegal activity, and family/social relations, as well as the content and structure of the patient's recovery program. Through its emphasis on short-term behavioral goals, individualized drug counseling helps the patient develop coping strategies and tools for abstaining from drug use and then maintaining abstinence. The addiction counselor encourages 12-step participation (discussed later) and makes referrals for needed supplemental medical, psychiatric, employment, and other services. Individuals are encouraged to attend sessions one or two times per week.

Motivational Enhancement Therapy

This client-centered counseling approach for initiating behavior change helps clients to resolve ambivalence about engaging in treatment and stopping drug

Continued

use. This approach employs strategies to evoke rapid and internally motivated change in the client, rather than guiding the client stepwise through the recovery process. This therapy consists of an initial assessment battery session, followed by two to four individual treatment sessions with a therapist. The first treatment session focuses on providing feedback generated from the initial assessment battery to stimulate discussion regarding personal substance use and to elicit self-motivational statements. Motivational interviewing principles are used to strengthen motivation and build a plan for change. Coping strategies for high-risk situations are suggested and discussed with the client. In subsequent sessions, the therapist monitors change, reviews cessation strategies being used, and continues to encourage commitment to change or sustained abstinence. Clients are sometimes encouraged to bring a significant other to sessions. This approach has been used successfully with alcoholics and with marijuana-dependent individuals.

Behavioral Therapy for Adolescents

The principle that unwanted behavior can be changed by clear demonstration of the desired behavior and consistent reward of incremental steps toward achieving it is the basis for this approach. Therapeutic activities include fulfilling specific assignments, rehearsing desired behaviors, and recording and reviewing progress, with praise and privileges given for meeting assigned goals. Urine samples are collected regularly to monitor drug use. The therapy aims to equip the patient to gain three types of control:

> *Stimulus control* helps patients avoid situations associated with drug use and learn to spend more time in activities incompatible with drug use.
> *Urge control* helps patients recognize and change thoughts, feelings, and plans that lead to drug use.
> *Social control* involves family members and other people important in helping patients avoid drugs. A parent or significant other attends treatment sessions when possible and assists with therapy assignments and reinforcing desired behavior.

Multidimensional Family Therapy (MDFT) for Adolescents

An outpatient family-based drug abuse treatment for teenagers, MDFT views adolescent drug use in terms of a network of influences (that is, individual, family, peer, community) and suggests that reducing unwanted behavior and increasing desirable behavior occur in multiple ways in different settings. Treatment

Summary of Psychological Treatment Approaches, Continued

includes individual and family sessions held in the clinic, in the home, or with family members at the family court, school, or other community locations.

During individual sessions, the therapist and adolescent work on important developmental tasks, such as developing decision-making, negotiation, and problem-solving skills. Teenagers acquire skills in communicating their thoughts and feelings to deal better with life stressors and acquire vocational skills. Parallel sessions are held with family members. Parents examine their particular parenting style, learning to distinguish influence from control, and to have a positive and developmentally appropriate influence on their child.

Multisystemic Therapy

This approach addresses the factors associated with serious antisocial behavior in children and adolescents who abuse drugs. These factors include characteristics of the adolescent (for example, favorable attitudes toward drug use), the family (poor discipline, family conflict, parental drug abuse), peers (positive attitudes toward drug use), school (dropout, poor performance), and neighborhood (criminal subculture).

Source: NIDA information

Treatment Programs in the Criminal Justice System

About half the states have statutory provisions for the civil commitment of drug abusers (Leukefeld and Tims 1988), although few make any regular use of them. Civil commitment, or the nonpunitive incarceration of addicts for purposes of treatment, dates back to 1935, when a federal narcotic "farm" was opened in Lexington, Kentucky. A second was opened in 1938 in Fort Worth, Texas. Addict-patients who requested commitment and involuntary patients who had been prosecuted for criminal offenses spent 6 months at these facilities, which followed a standard course of withdrawal—physical restoration, psychological therapy in the form of individual and group counseling, and vocational counseling—after which patients returned to their communities. The physical structure of these facilities, however, resembled that of a modified prison, and security was strict (H. W. Morgan 1981). Reviews of the program were either mixed or inconclusive, and the federal government chose not to expand civil commitment. Despite this, in 1961, California enacted a program built on the Lexington model.

California Rehabilitation Center. In 1961 the California legislature established within the Department of Corrections the California Rehabilitation Center for the compulsory care of persons addicted to narcotics. In 1962 the U.S. Supreme Court ruled (in *Robinson v. California* 370 U.S. 660) that drug addiction was an illness, and therefore, a state could not make this status a crime. In that decision the Court also suggested that the Constitution would not be offended by involuntary civil commitment for the purpose of treating the illness of addiction. A later decision gave further support to the commitment-for-treatment approach, and in 1963 the legislature amended certain sections of the California Rehabilitation Act to emphasize treatment.

California statutes provide four methods of commitment (*All About the Civil Addict Program* 1994):

1. After a person has been convicted and sentenced to prison for a felony, the judge may suspend the sentence and order the district attorney to file for a narcotic petition. If the judge subsequently determines that the person is addicted or is in imminent danger of becoming addicted, execution of the sentence can be suspended and the offender placed in the California Rehabilitation Center (CRC) at Norco. Most residents at the CRC fall into this category.

2. After conviction for a misdemeanor and before or after sentencing, the judge can certify the case to superior court for a commitment petition. After an examination, the offender may be sent to the CRC.

3. Any interested party may report to the district attorney, under oath, his or her belief that another person is addicted to narcotics or is in imminent danger of becoming addicted. If sufficient evidence (probable cause) is present, the district attorney may petition the superior court for a period of commitment not to exceed 12 months.

4. Any person who believes that he or she is addicted or about to become addicted may report such belief to the district attorney, who can then petition the superior court for a period of commitment not to exceed 12 months.

The California Rehabilitation Center, which has the capacity for about 4,000 males and 800 females, is a medium security facility of the Department of Correction with open dormitories, double fences, and armed officers at the perimeter. It has remedial and high school educational facilities, as well as vocational training. Various self-help groups such as Alcoholics and Narcotics Anonymous may be joined voluntarily. Leisure activities include organized and individual athletics. Following institutional care, civil commitments are released to aftercare/parole supervision, which includes regular testing for drug use. Patients who fail to live up to the terms of release can be returned to the CRC. Release to aftercare and return to the CRC are decided by the Narcotic Addict Evaluation Authority. Felony commitments on aftercare who remain drug free for 12 or 16 months (depending on the length of the commitment) may receive early discharge. Research into the performance of released patients indicates that they did no better than addicts who received drug therapy in California prisons.

Federal Program. The federal government has a program similar to California's that provides for the commitment of drug users (the 1966 Narcotic Addict Rehabilitation Act—**NARA**). The act empowers a sentencing judge to commit drug-abusing defendants for a period of evaluation not to exceed 90 days. During that time the offender is evaluated by NARA staff from the Bureau of Prisons to ascertain his or her suitability for treatment. A report is then submitted to the judge, who can commit the defendant to the custody of the Surgeon General for treatment that may last up to 36 months; convicted offenders may be committed to the Bureau of Prisons for drug treatment for up to 10 years (but not to exceed the maximum sentence for their conviction), or placed on probation. Individuals who have not been charged with a federal crime can be committed by means of a petition submitted by the U.S. attorney on their behalf or on behalf of a relative. Involuntary patients have a right to a hearing with counsel to determine whether they are to be civilly committed. Treatment may last up to 42 months, although the institutional phase may last only 6 months (Kay 1973). Upon release from institutional treatment, patients can be required to participate in an aftercare program under the Probation Division of the U.S. Courts. A relapse can result in being reinstitutionalized.

Drug Courts

Established as a result of court and prison overcrowding, special drug courts have proven popular. In 1989 a special drug court was established by judicial order in Miami. This high-volume court expands on traditional drug-defendant diversion programs by offering a year or more of court-run treatment; defendants who complete this option have their criminal cases dismissed. Between 1991 and 1993 Miami influenced officials in more than twenty other jurisdictions to establish drug courts (*The Drug Court Movement* 1995).

Although they vary widely, common features of drug courts include a nonadversarial approach to integrating substance abuse treatment with criminal justice case processing. The focus is on early identification of eligible substance abusers and prompt placement in treatment, combined with frequent drug testing (Gebelein 2000).

The Madison County, Illinois, drug court was fueled by a 437 percent increase in drug arrests between 1988 and 1992. The program targets persons arrested on felony drug charges who are diagnosed with alcohol or drug dependence that could be treated on an outpatient basis. Those who successfully complete the program have their charges dismissed. The program provides job assistance, which includes vocational training and high school equivalency education. Initially, clients are scheduled for three to five intensive 3- to 4-hour counseling sessions per week. As they progress, the number and length of sessions is reduced. Depending on a client's progress, the program can be completed in about one year or less. Random drug tests are given, and failure to comply with program requirements results in prosecution for the original felony offense (Illinois Criminal Justice Authority 1999).

In Maricopa (Phoenix) County, Arizona, the goal of drug court is considerably different—to increase the number of drug cases entering the system. Using a catchy "do drugs, do time" slogan, law enforcement agencies targeted casual users to enforce a "zero tolerance" policy. Users are "held accountable" for their illegal drug use by a policy of arrest and threatened prosecution; those who accept the treatment option—which includes paying fees—avoid further court action (Hepburn, Johnston, and Rogers 1994).

A study of drug court participants in six U.S. cities found that judicial supervision coupled with treatment are powerful tools for responding to drug abusers, despite the fact that most participants enrolled to avoid incarceration and not for purposes of rehabilitation. Indeed, the study found that the threat of incarceration and frequent drug testing were essential to program success (National Institute of Justice 2002).

Treatment Alternative to Street Crime (TASC)

The federally funded **TASC** program initiated in 1972 to divert substance-abusing offenders from the court system and into community treatment stands somewhere between compulsory and voluntary treatment. Since its inception, it has been expanded to include persons on probation and parole. TASC identifies, assesses, and refers appropriate drug- and/or alcohol-dependent offenders accused or convicted of nonviolent crimes to community-based substance abuse treatment, as an alternative to or supplement to existing criminal justice sanctions and procedures (Cook and Weinman 1988). TASC monitors the client's progress in drug treatment and reports back to the criminal justice agency that made the referral. Those who fail to conform to program requirements face further criminal justice processing. Research into the effectiveness—reducing recidivism and drug use—of TASC, which operates in about thirty states, have generally been positive (Anglin, Longshore, and Turner 1999).

Coercive treatment, civil or criminal, appears to have a positive outcome (Anglin 1988; Anglin and Hser 1990a). Extensive research indicates that "coerced involvement in community-based programs and/or corrections-based treatment can have a substantial impact on the behavior of chronic drug-abusing offenders" (Anglin and Maughr 1992: 76). George Vaillant found that while the most effective motivation for abstinence is that narcotics are illegal, "the most potent treatment was compulsory supervision. Thus, if the addict is followed over time, external coercion of some kind appears a critical variable in facilitating abstinence" (1970: 494).

This was the author's experience when, as a parole officer he supervised heroin addicts in New York City (see Abadinsky 2003c). Close personal contact, unannounced home visits and searches, arm checks (for needle marks), and random urinalysis provided the ego and superego strengths for addicts to remain heroin free: "Besides offering addicts compulsory support and an 'external super-ego,' parole itself was probably a substitute for addiction in that it required ex-addicts to remain regularly employed" (Vaillant 1970: 495). The parole officer could redirect the considerable skills and energy required to be a successful heroin addict into seeking and maintaining legitimate employment (see also Eaglin 1986.) From the behaviorist view, the probation or parole officer provides the basis for operant conditioning—applying positive reinforcement for abstinence, and negative reinforcement for relapse.

In a study of compulsory treatment—residential treatment or imprisonment for felony offenders—Douglas Young (2002) found that mandatory treatment programs and progressively higher perceived legal pressure can increase treatment retention, and such retention is directly related to a positive treatment outcome for participants.

**The Therapeutic
Community in Sum**

"TCs are drug-free residential settings that use a hierarchical model
with treatment stages that reflect
increased levels of personal and
social responsibility. Peer influence, mediated through a variety
of group processes, is used to help
individuals learn and assimilate
social norms and develop more effective social skills. TCs differ from
other treatment approaches principally in their use of the community, comprising treatment staff
and those in recovery, as key
agents of change" (Therapeutic
Community" 2002: 1).

Therapeutic Community

Residential, self-help, drug-free treatment programs that have some common characteristics, including concepts adopted from Alcoholics Anonymous (AA), have come to be
known as **therapeutic communities** (TCs). "There is no such thing as an ex-addict,
only an addict who is not using at the moment; the emphasis on mutual support and aid;
the distrust of mental-health professionals; and the concept of continual confession and
catharsis. However, the TC has extended these notions to include the concept of a live-in
community with a rigid structure of day-to-day behavior and a complex system of punishment and rewards" (DeLong 1972: 190—91). George de Leon adds: "The primary
aims of the therapeutic community are a global change in lifestyle reflecting abstinence
from illicit substances, elimination of antisocial activity, increased employability, and
prosocial attitudes and values. A critical assumption in TCs is that stable recovery depends
upon a successful integration of these social and psychological goals. The rehabilitative
approach, therefore, requires multidimensional influences and training that, for most
clients, can only occur after an extended period of living in a 24-hour residential setting"
(1986b: 69).

The TC "views drug abuse as deviant behavior, reflecting impeded personality development and/or chronic deficits in social, educational and economic skills" (De Leon
1986a: 5; 2000). "A considerable number of [TC] clients never have acquired conventional lifestyles. Vocational and educational deficits are marked; mainstream values either are missing or unpursued. Most often, these clients emerge from a socially
disadvantaged sector where drug abuse is more a social response than a psychological
disturbance. Their TC experience can be termed *habilitation*—the development of a socially productive, conventional lifestyle for the first time in their lives" (De Leon 1994:
19). "According to the TC treatment perspective, drug abuse is a disorder of the whole person; the problem is the person, not the drug, and the *addiction* is only a *symptom* and
not the essence of the disorder" (Nielsen and Scarpitti 1997: 280).

TC Models. The therapeutic community becomes a surrogate family and a communal
support group for dealing with alienation and the drug abuse that derives from it. Its purpose, notes Mitchell Rosenthal (1973), is to strengthen ego functioning. Therapy, except for
the time spent asleep, is total. James DeLong (1972) notes that there is a quasi-evangelistic
quality to the "TC movement." The residences are often similar to the communes that
were popular during the late 1950s and 1960s counterculture movement, except they generally have a strict hierarchy and insist on rigid adherence to norms even more stringent
than those of the proverbial middle class. The model of all therapeutic communities, note
Jerome Platt and Christina Labate (1976), is Synanon, founded in 1958 by Charles E.
Dederich, a former alcoholic who was a participant in and advocate of the Alcoholics
Anonymous approach to substance abuse. (AA is discussed later in this chapter.) The
Synanon Foundation expanded rapidly into several states, with facilities run almost en-
tirely by ex-addicts.

Therapeutic communities such as Odyssey House, however, have been more receptive
to using professionals. The director of the New York–based Phoenix House, the largest

private, nonprofit drug treatment institution in the country, has long had a psychiatrist, Mitchell Rosenthal, as its executive director. David Bellis (1981: 155) is quite critical of therapeutic communities that resist professional involvement and instead use untrained staff and residents, "many hardly off heroin themselves," who, under no legal or professional oversight, unleash their own brand of "therapy" on addicts, many of whom are undergoing mandatory treatment because of a plea bargain, probation, or parole status. In his study of a failed therapeutic community, Robert Weppner (1983) points out that being a poorly educated ex-addict does not endow one with treatment skills.

While Synanon requires a lifetime commitment, most TCs have abandoned or modified this aspect of the Synanon model.[6] The TCs frequently offer vocational training and education to prepare residents to live in the community without continuous help from the TC. Indeed, George De Leon describes the TC as "community as method": *the purposive use of the peer community to facilitate social and psychological change in individuals*" (1995: 9; italics in original).

Life in the Therapeutic Community. A prominent feature of the TC has been the stiff entry requirement: a devastating initial interview that tests an applicant's motivation by focusing on his or her inadequacies and lack of success. Successful applicants must invest completely in the program, which encourages the resident to identify with the former addicts who run it and become resocialized into a drug-free existence. The new resident is isolated from all outside contacts, including family and friends. The withdrawal process is accomplished without drugs but with the support of other residents. Once withdrawal has been accomplished, a program of positive and negative reinforcement is implemented. The resident is assigned menial work projects, such as cleaning toilets, but given an opportunity to earn more prestigious assignments and greater freedom through conformity with the program. Transgressions are punished by public humiliation—reprimands, shaved heads, wearing a sign indicating the nature of the violation. Those who leave, relapse, and return are required to wear a sign announcing their situation. Shame and guilt are constantly exploited to force the addict to conform and to change his or her view of drugs (Platt and Labate 1976). There is little privacy. Drug use, physical violence, and sexual activity between residents are punished with expulsion.

Residents are kept busy in a highly structured environment that offers little time for idleness or boredom. They are expected to be active in all aspects of the TC program. Failing to do so becomes the subject of criticism at the encounter session, a central feature of the therapeutic process. The encounter is a relatively unstructured, leaderless group session in which members focus on a particular resident (who occupies the "hot seat") and bombard him or her with criticisms about attitude and behavior. The target is encouraged

---

[6]Dederich eventually transformed Synanon into a cultlike phenomenon. In 1980 he pled guilty to plotting to murder one of his Synanon critics, a lawyer representing former Synanon members who maintained they were held against their will. In poor health, Dederich received a sentence of 5 years' probation and was banned from participating in Synanon. In 1997, at age 83, Diderich died of a heart attack.

Phoenix House

At Phoenix House in the Bronx, every day begins the same. After a 30-minute breakfast at 7:00 A.M., there is an hour-long meeting that includes inspirational songs and skits written and performed by the residents. The rest of the day consists of seminars, classes to prepare for the general equivalency diploma, rap sessions, job assignments, and more meals and meetings. There is little free time until 9:00 P.M. Lights are out at 11:00 P.M. The 185-word Phoenix House philosophy is recited from memory at least twice a day. The weekend schedule is slightly more relaxed, with rented videos available and heavily supervised trips into New York. Most of the residents are between 20 and 40 years old and on welfare, which helps pay for their stay at the program. They typically have lengthy criminal records (Marriott 1989).

Odyssey House

Odyssey House operates a TC for pregnant women and those with young children. Housed on New York's Wards' Island, residents include about two dozen women and children. Some of the women are pregnant, and most have been abusing crack. The facility is underfunded and must depend on private donations to make up for inadequate government support. As a result, children's clothing and nursery toys are in short supply. The residents "participate in rigorous therapy, they are given parenting courses including such essentials as how to hold a baby and they must work at jobs. The overbearing and obnoxious scrape plates, while the shy and withdrawn are given pretty clothes and work as front-desk receptionists. But the most prized assignments are in the nursery. . . . Graduation requirements are stiff. Along with conquering addiction, women must complete the equivalent of high school, secure a driver's license and find a full-time job" (D. Martin 1990: 13).

to fight back—verbally—although the goal of such sessions is to destroy the rationalizations and defenses that help perpetuate irresponsible thought patterns and behavior— a resocialization process. "The style of the encounter, with its abrasive attacks and its permitted verbal violence . . . is designed to encourage the spewing out of pent-up hostility and anger, to force the patient to confront his maladaptive emotional response and behavior patterns" (Rosenthal 1973: 91). "TCs are successful because they provide the setting and the mechanisms for clients' learning new roles, attitudes, skills, and definitions of self. The most important mechanism for change is the community of peers who confront the client when old values or behaviors are displayed, who provide positive and negative reinforcements to elicit appropriate behavior, and who serve as role models for lifestyle changes" (Nielson and Scarpitti 1997: 281).

Dan Waldorf (1973) points out that the TC is an exciting, friendly, and highly moral—almost utopian—environment. But, notes Mitchell Rosenthal, it is not for all abusers: "Severe disturbances may be exacerbated by the TC regimen and may have an adverse effect not only on the disturbed client but also on the treatment environment and the progress of others in the treatment population. Also unsuitable for treatment are candidates whose drug involvement is of so limited a nature as to require a less rigorous intervention or who—despite the deleterious effects of drug abuse—are able to function with the help of a positive support network (e.g., family or significant others)" (1984: 55).

TCs in Prisons. TCs have been established in prisons in New York, California, and a number of other states (Pendergast et al. 2002). In these so-called "Stay 'N Out" therapeutic communities, inmates are recruited at state correctional facilities and housed in units segregated from the general population, although they eat and attend morning activities with other prisoners. The program, which lasts from 6 to 9 months, is staffed by graduates of community TCs and by ex-offenders with prison experience, who act as role models demonstrating successful rehabilitation.

> During the early phase of treatment, the major clinical thrust involves observation and assessment of client needs and problem areas. Orientation to the prison TC procedures occurs through individual counseling, encounter sessions, and seminars. Clients are given low-level jobs and granted little status. During the later phase of treatment, residents are provided opportunities to earn higher-level positions and increased status through sincere involvement in the program and hard work. Encounter groups and counseling sessions are more in-depth and focus on the areas of self-discipline, self-worth, self-awareness, respect for authority, and acceptance of guidance for problem areas. Seminars take on a more intellectual nature. Debate is encouraged to enhance self-expression and to increase self-confidence. (Wexler and Williams 1986: 224)

Upon release, prison TC graduates are encouraged to become part of the extensive community-based TC network. Research into the effect of the prison TC on parole success found that "Stay 'N Out" reduced recidivism (Wexler, Lipton, and Foster 1985; Wexler, Falkin, and Lipton 1990; Lipton 1995; Wexler et al. 1999).

Do TCs Work? There has been a great deal of controversy over the success rate of therapeutic communities, and most research has been inadequate or inconclusive. Many TCs release statistics that cannot withstand scrutiny by disinterested researchers. The arduous screening process keeps out many drug abusers who would probably fail the program, and an abuser's graduation from a TC does not necessarily mean that the program has succeeded. The TC insists on behavioral change that "is not away from antisocial behavior, that of the street addict, and toward the norms of the larger society, but toward norms accepted in the group alone" (Weppner 1983: xi). Those who need to manage in the community without the continuing support of the group are at risk, because they will return to the same environment that led to drug dependence in the first place, and they often bring with them all of the educational and vocational deficiencies they had upon entering. Those entering the TC with a greater degree of mental health, with limited or no attachment to a criminal subculture, and with employment skills are obviously better equipped to deal with post-TC existence.

Chemical Dependency (CD) Programs

As noted at the beginning of this chapter, during the past two decades the number of chemical dependency programs has increased. Some are profit making and others are nonprofit; many call themselves "therapeutic communities," although they differ dramatically from the TCs discussed above. These programs typically share a number of variables: They do a great deal of outreach—most employ a marketing person—and often advertise for clients likely to have health insurance, such as employed alcohol and cocaine abusers as opposed to heroin addicts, because the costs can run over $500 a day for inpatient care. Many CD programs are located in a health care facility, which typically increases the cost of treatment. Adding a chemical dependency program to a health care facility can help reduce the number of otherwise vacant beds that can be costly to any hospital. The treatment approach usually includes individual and group counseling, and the model tends to be eclectic rather than doctrinal.[7]

"Primarily they serve the more socially advantaged substance abusers whose fee for service is generally covered by insurance, in contrast to the major modalities whose costs are mostly tax subsidized. The treatment orientation of these programs is also varied, but mainly reflects a mix of traditional mental health and 12-Step perspectives [discussed below]. They offer a broad menu of services such as education, nutrition, relaxation training, recreation, counseling-psychotherapy, psychopharmacological adjuncts, and self-help groups" (De Leon 1995: 5). "CD programs do not require patients to perform housekeeping duties . . . [and they] are especially attractive to patients with greater initial functional and social resources who can afford the better facilities and amenities" (Gerstein 1994: 56).

The typical program is a 3- to 6-week intensive and highly structured inpatient regimen: "Clients begin with an in-depth psychiatric and psychosocial evaluation and then follow a general education-oriented program track of daily lectures plus two to three meetings per week in small task-oriented groups. Group education teaches clients about the disease concept of dependence, focusing on the harmful medical and psychosocial effects of illicit drugs and excessive alcohol consumption. There is also an individual prescriptive track for each client, meetings about once a week with a 'focal counselor,' and appointments with other professionals if medical, psychiatric, or family services are needed" (Gerstein and Harwood 1990: 171).

Harvey Siegel and his colleagues are critical: "Since it is the treatment professional who retains all responsibility for prescribing and implementing the necessary therapeutic activity, patients may have difficulty achieving ownership of their recovery program"

Private Hospital Drug Treatment

"Parents are often frightened by media hype or hospital treatment center advertisements that they have seen on television. Insurance coverage and the parents' willingness to have someone else deal with the 'abuse' are also factors. As a result, what may be experimental adolescent behavior becomes a reason to place an adolescent in an inpatient hospital treatment program. Such treatment programs are one of the few large-scale sources of profit for private hospitals. Managers of these programs have become desperate for adolescent admissions because of the vast overbuilding of these facilities that occurred during the 1980s" (G. Lawson 1992: 4).

---

[7]For a look at a theory-based approach to CD treatment, see Washton (1989).

(1995: 69). And **aftercare**—treatment and services following discharge—are typically meager. "Aftercare is considered quite important in CD [28-day] treatment, but relatively few program resources are devoted to it" (Gerstein 1994: 56). Patients are urged to participate in community 12-step groups. In fact, virtually all of the many programs that this author has examined throughout the country utilize an Alcoholics Anonymous or Narcotics Anonymous (NA) 12-step approach for both in- and outpatient treatment.

Alcoholics Anonymous

The Alcoholics Anonymous (AA) approach of using public confession and commitment and mutual aid concepts can be found in a number of nineteenth-century temperance organizations (White 1998). Alcoholics Anonymous was established during the 1930s by William ("Bill W.") Wilson (1895–1971), a financial investigator and alcoholic, and Robert ("Dr. Bob") Holbrook Smith (1879–1950), a physician and alcoholic. (Nan Robertson [1988b] presents a rather unflattering view of the two, particularly of Wilson, whom she refers to as a Wall Street hustler and compulsive womanizer.) Bill W. had joined the Oxford Group (renamed Moral Re-Armament in 1939), an international religious movement, as the result of the influence of another alcoholic whose religious experience appeared to act as a "cure." Bill W. was influenced by the work of William James (1842–1910), a psychologist and philosopher, particularly his *Varieties of Religious Experience* (1902).[8] As a member of the Oxford Group, Bill W. began dedicating his activities to curing alcoholics. His efforts were quite unsuccessful until he met Dr. Bob—also a member of the Oxford Group—in 1935 while on a business trip to Akron, Ohio. He helped Dr. Bob become abstinent, and the two recognized that success in helping alcoholics was not to be found in preaching abstinence, but rather in a fellowship where each alcoholic simply relates his or her story of drunkenness and conversion to a nonalcoholic lifestyle. The "listening" was as important as the "telling." "There could not have been just one founder of A.A.," notes Robertson, "because the essence of the process is one person telling his story to another as honestly as he knows how" (1988b: 34).

Early in 1939, Bill W. published *Alcoholics Anonymous*, which explained the philosophy and methods—the Twelve Steps of recovery—of his small association of alcoholics, and also contained case histories of some thirty recovered members. They became known as Alcoholics Anonymous after the title of Wilson's book, which AA members often refer to as "The Big Book" (it was quite bulky when originally published). Wilson, who died in 1971, was supported by the substantial royalties the book eventually generated. His wife, Lois Burnham, who died in 1988 at age 97, established Al-Anon for the family members of alcoholics. She was a nonalcoholic who patterned her organization on the AA model (Pace 1988). There are now similar groups for the family and friends of cocaine users—Co-Anon.

---

[8]It is ironic that William James typically found his religious and philosophical insights while intoxicated from nitrous oxide (Tymoczco 1996).

The AA Program

The AA program requires an act of surrender—an acknowledgment of being an alcoholic and of the destructiveness that results—a bearing of witness, and an acknowledgment of a higher power. While AA is nondenominational, there is a strong repent-of-your-sins revivalism—groups begin or end their meetings holding hands in a circle and reciting the Lord's Prayer or the Serenity Prayer: "God grant me the serenity to accept the things I cannot change; courage to change the things I can; and wisdom to know the difference" (DuPont and McGovern 1994: 27). As in Protestant revival meetings, the alcoholic/sinner seeks salvation through personal testimony, public contrition, and submission to a higher authority (Peele 1985; Delbanco and Delbanco 1995). Courts have ruled that Alcoholics Anonymous is a religion for purposes of state-church separation, thus rendering what transpires at AA meetings subject to the same protection as clergy-parishioner exchanges (Worth 2002). AA also provides "an important social network through which members learn appropriate behavior and coping skills in drinking situations and become involved in various (nondrinking) leisure activities with other recovering alcoholics" (McElrath 1995: 314).

According to their publications, AA recognizes the potency of shared honesty and mutual vulnerability openly acknowledged. The AA group supports each member in his or her effort to remain alcohol free. "Maintenance of sobriety depends on our sharing of our experiences, strength and hope with each other, thus helping to identify and understand the nature of our disease" (AA literature). AA offers a biological explanation for alcohol addiction, and the AA conceptual model is that alcoholism is a disease,[9] a controllable disability that cannot be cured—thus, there are no ex-alcoholics, merely recovering alcoholics. AA members are encouraged to accept the belief that they are powerless over alcohol, that they cannot control their intake, that total abstinence is required. New members are advised to obtain a sponsor who has remained abstinent and who will help the initiate work through the **twelve steps** that are the essence of the AA program. Those who are successful, "twelfth steppers," carry the AA message and program to other alcoholics—they become "missionaries" for AA.

AA, and groups based on the AA approach, "attempt to instill the substitution of more adaptive attitudes to replace habitual dysfunctional ones. The extreme use of denial and projection of responsibility for chemical dependency onto other people, circumstances, or conditions outside oneself is an example of a target behavior strongly challenged in the substance abuse self-help group. The familiar opening statement of 'I'm an alcoholic and/or drug addict' epitomizes the concrete representation that defense mechanisms of projection and denial run counter to the group culture and norms" (Spitz 1987: 160).

Because of their fear of losing employment, recovering alcoholics were often unwilling to admit their problem in front of others—hence strict anonymity became part of the AA approach. AA never uses surnames at meetings or in its publications. Accord-

---

[9]For a discussion of the model of alcoholism used in AA, see W. Miller and Kurtz (1994).

ing to an AA publication: "Individual anonymity is paramount. No AA member has the right to divulge the identity or membership of any other member. We must always maintain personal anonymity at the level of press, radio, TV and film" (hence the use of "Bill W." and "Dr. Bob"). However, "as a result of AA's popular success and the acceptance of the disease viewpoint," Stanton Peele notes that "prominent alcoholics today do not place the emphasis on anonymity that AA officially demands of its members: many public figures have described their alcoholism and their treatment before the camera" (1995: 46).

AA Organization

More than 50,000 AA groups are registered in the United States (Delbanco and Delbanco 1995). There is a minimum of formal organization, no power of punishment or exclusion in AA, and the only authority is shared experience. The basic AA unit is the local group, which is autonomous except in matters affecting other AA groups or the fellowship as a whole. "No group has powers over its members and instead of officers with authority, groups rotate leadership" (AA literature). A secretary chosen by the members plans the meetings and sets the agenda. In most local groups the position is rotated every 6 months. Delegates to the General Service Conference serve 2 years. There are twenty-one trustees, of whom seven are nonalcoholics who often work in the helping professions—social work or medicine—and who may serve for up to 9 years—alcoholic trustees may serve only 4 years.

There are no entry requirements or dues; "the hat is passed" at most meetings to defray costs. Some of this money goes to support a local service committee and the General Service Office in New York. AA does not engage in fund raising, and no one person is permitted to contribute more than $1,000. The sale of publications generates considerable income. The financial affairs of the General Service Office are handled by nonalcoholics: "The reason is that Bill Wilson and the early A.A.'s were afraid that if anybody running A.A. fell off the wagon, that would be bad enough, but if he were handling finances as well, the results could be disastrous" (Robertson 1988a: 57).

AA members typically attend four meetings a week for about 5 years, after which attendance is less frequent, or they may drop out completely when capable of functioning comfortably without alcohol. "The movement works in quiet and simple ways. Members usually give of themselves without reservation; exchange telephone numbers with newcomers; come to help at any hour when a fellow member is in crisis; are free with tips on how to avoid that first drink" (Robertson 1988a: 47).

The AA approach has been criticized because of its emphasis on total abstinence and its lack of research support: "The erstwhile abstainer who, for whatever reason, takes a drink may in effect be induced to go on a spree by the belief that this is inevitable. Spree drinking could also be induced by the fact that status in A.A. is correlated with length of sobriety. Years of sobriety with their attendant symbols and status can be obliterated by one slip, so the social cost of a single drink is as great as the cost of an all-out binge" (Ogborne and Glaser 1985: 176). Some 12-step groups "do not

Narcotics Anonymous

Nan Robertson (1988b) notes that some AA groups are less than accepting of persons addicted to substances other than alcohol—Bill Wilson was opposed to allowing heroin addicts to become part of AA. However, there are groups for drug abusers based on the 12-step approach, such as Narcotics Anonymous (NA) and Cocaine Anonymous (CA).

The Twelve Steps of Narcotics Anonymous

1. We admitted that we were powerless over our addiction, that our lives had become unmanageable.
2. We came to believe that a Power greater than ourselves could restore us to sanity.
3. We made a decision to turn our will and our lives over to the care of God as we understood Him.
4. We made a searching and fearless moral inventory of ourselves.
5. We admitted to God, to ourselves, and to another human being the exact nature of our wrongs.
6. We were entirely ready to have God remove all these defects of character.
7. We humbly asked Him to remove our shortcomings.
8. We made a list of all persons we had harmed, and became willing to make amends to them all.
9. We made direct amends to such people whenever possible, except when to do so would injure them or others.
10. We continued to take personal inventory and when we were wrong promptly admitted it.
11. We sought through prayer and meditation to improve our conscious contact with God as we understood Him, praying only for knowledge of His will for us and the power to carry that out.
12. Having had a spiritual awakening as a result of these steps, we tried to carry this message to addicts, and practice these principles in all our affairs.

NA publishes a monthly journal, *The NA Way*, which is filled with brief personal stories, news, and opinion. (Narcotics Anonymous World Service Office, PO Box 9999, Van Nuys, CA 91409; telephone 818-780-3951.) Local AA/NA chapters can be found in the telephone book.

consider members 'clean and sober' when they are using any psychoactive medication. Cases of adverse treatment consequences, even suicide, have resulted from well-meaning 12-step members dissuading individuals from taking prescribed medications" (DuPont and McGovern 1994: 56).

The Minnesota (12-Step) Model

One of the best examples of using the AA program in private inpatient chemical dependence treatment is the so-called *Minnesota model,* which integrates the twelve steps into the medical treatment of addiction (DuPont and McGovern 1994: xxii). The Hazelden Foundation in Center City, Minnesota, has inspired many similar programs in the United States and England, where substance abuse is seen as an incurable but controllable disease. Total abstinence and lifestyle improvement are the treatment goals. The 6- to 8-week program begins with an admissions assessment and detoxification that follows medical protocol. Individual counseling is provided by abusers "in recovery" and professional staff, including physicians, social workers, nurses, and clergy. Therapy groups take various forms, all of which are present and future oriented. They include problem solving, personal issues, decision making related to substance use, family sessions, and confrontations similar in process to those of the therapeutic community. Rounding out the program are lectures and videos on a variety of related topics, including AA/NA, the social and psychological aspects of substance abuse, and techniques for handling substance abuse problems, as well as reading and writing assignments. Aftercare usually involves attendance at AA or NA meetings (Cook 1988a). In a review of the Minnesota model research, Christopher Cook concludes: "Despite exaggerated claims of success, it appears to have a genuinely impressive 'track record' with as many as two-thirds of its patients achieving a 'good' outcome at 1 year after discharge" (Cook 1988b: 746). This treatment-rich private-sector approach to substance abuse is obviously quite expensive, and patients, who include such luminaries as Betty Ford and Elizabeth Taylor, therefore, are representative of the economically successful.

AA Alternatives

The spiritual dimension of AA and its insistence on a disease model of alcoholism—alcoholics cannot help themselves—have encountered opposition and led to the establishment of alternative groups, such as Rational Recovery (RR) and Secular Organization for Sobriety (SOS). Although it is a voluntary self-help group in the AA mode, RR rejects the 12-step approach as fostering dependency and instead argues that alcoholic participants are not powerless but fully capable of overcoming their addiction (Hall 1990). According to RR, alcoholism is not a disease but an individual shortcoming. Their approach emphasizes taking personal responsibility for behavior—there isn't any treatment for addiction other than voluntary abstinence.

RR uses "The Big Plan," a commitment never to drink again. It focuses on planning to prevent relapses and attempting to gain insight into how self-defeating beliefs encourage drinking behavior. Various strategies are discussed to deal with high-risk situations where temptations may run high (Galaif and Sussman 1995).

There are also groups that reject the total abstinence proviso of AA and, instead, emphasize sobriety—drinking in moderation—such as Moderation Management (MM). A national support organization, MM is designed for persons who want to limit, rather than eliminate, their drinking. While an estimated 30 percent of their members are on abstinence-based programs, most participants seek a way to control, but not eliminate, their use of alcohol. "An important Moderation Management recommendation is to go 30 days without alcohol" (Condor 2002a: Sec. 13: 1; 2002b). A similar program, Drink Wise, suggests 2 to 3 weeks without imbibing to reduce tolerance and gain control over the habit. Both programs call for keeping a "drink diary" to become more fully aware of alcohol-consumption patterns and temptations (Condor 2002b).

Moderation Management and Drink Wise promote tactics that lead to self-limits on alcohol consumption (Condor 2002a; 2002b). For example:

- Delay drinking by not having any alcohol until sitting down for dinner.
- Stay with beer or wine and avoid mixed drinks.
- Alternate between alcoholic drinks and other beverages, club soda with a splash of lemon or lime, for example.
- Never drink alcoholic beverages when you are thirsty.
- Develop a plan for drinking, such as one or two drinks and leaving after two hours at a party or bar.

Evaluating Treatment Effectiveness

How well do drug treatment programs perform? A straightforward answer to this question is not possible. A variety of programs—hospitals, public health agencies, independent organizations—offer treatment using an array of methodologies ranging from the twelve steps, to drug-free therapeutic communities, to methadone maintenance, while the intensity of services and staff qualifications vary significantly. And the client population is similarly complex: "They vary in age, social and economic background, number and types of drug abused, health status, and psychological well-being. Some have lengthy histories of addiction and treatment, while others are entering treatment for the first time in the early stages of dependence. Clients may be highly involved in criminal activity or may not have committed any crime other than drug possession" (Hubbard et al. 1989: 9). In general, "high-intensity" (long-term residential) treatment for high-severity users produces favorable outcomes for at least 5 years. For low-severity users, brief, low-intensity services have proven adequate and more cost effective (D. Simpson 2002).

There are additional problems with measuring the effectiveness of treatment for adolescents, as there are with providing them with appropriate programs. Adolescents go through distinctive developmental stages, and their substance abuse patterns differ from those of adults (Hser, Grella, et al. 2001).

Difficulties Measuring Effectiveness

Many programs purporting to treat specific types of substance abuse are not based on a scientific approach to such problems. They are not organized and structured according to controlled studies with random assignment, and they are often not eager for independent evaluation, which could affect their bottom line—finances. Evaluation requires a measurement of success, such as being drug free for a certain period of time. Tracking persons who complete treatment is often difficult if not impossible. Programs have different criteria for "completion." Some use length of time; others use number of visits or regularity of attendance. This makes it difficult to compare programs (E. Simpson 1989).

Evaluating drug treatment requires a comparison with a similar population that is not being treated or with other programs treating similar populations. In fact, any research efforts that do not include a control group are suspect, because in "the absence of a control group, it is difficult to determine whether unanticipated bias occurred in selecting the subjects for study, and whether the resulting experimental group is sufficiently representative for generalizations to be made about the outcome findings. Furthermore, without comparison groups, behavioral changes during and after treatment that result from the passage of time may wrongly be attributed to program activities" (Anglin and Hser 1990b: 408). However, withholding treatment from control groups has ethical, political, and legal dimensions (De Leon, Inciardi, and Martin 1995).

Some private treatment programs are quite selective. Their patients are required to have financial resources or employment that provides third-party coverage, which are social indicators of a better prognosis. Other programs accept persons with a host of social, psychological, and economic problems that are likely to impact upon prognosis. "In the real world of drug abuse treatment," note George De Leon, James Inciardi, and Steven Martin, "program staff choose the clients they feel are ready for treatment and are appropriate for a particular treatment modality" (1995: 88).

Patrick Biernacki (1986: 191) notes the serious problems in gauging the success of drug treatment programs. He asks, for example, what a 50 percent rate of success means: Would some, most, or all of the persons who were "successful" have abandoned drug addiction without treatment? In fact, he points out, drug treatment programs may be successful only with those persons who have resolved to stop using drugs: "Once addicts voluntarily have resolved to stop using drugs, treatment programs may then be able to help them realize their resolutions to change." (For a review of drug treatment outcome research and its methodological shortcomings, see Anglin and Hser 1990b; Moras 1993; De Leon, Inciardi, and Martin 1995.)

Researchers followed 581 male heroin addicts who had been admitted to the California Civil Addict Program (CAP) between 1962 and 1964. The average age of participants upon admission to CAP was 25. More than 60 percent had started using heroin before age 20. The men were, on average, 57 years old in 1996–97. Of the 242 subjects interviewed at that time, 21 percent tested positive for opiates. A total of 13.8 percent of the original 581 subjects had died by the time of the first interview; 27.7 percent had died by the time of the second interview; and 48.9 percent had died by the time of the latest interview. At the first interview, about 38 percent of the surviving sample had opiate-free urine tests; 41 percent were opiate free at the second interview; and 56 percent were opiate free at the last interview. Successful programming; aging out; or any combination of the two? ("33-Year Study Shows Severe Long-Term Effects of Heroin" 2001).

And how are we to interpret the effectiveness of adolescent programs, in which research found favorable reductions in drug use and criminal activity 1 year after treatment, but more than 25 percent still reported daily use of marijuana and heavy use of alcohol? How to interpret effectiveness of adolescent programs that result in a reduction in use, although a large proportion return to alcohol and drug use following treatment? (Hser, Grella et al. 2001).

Measuring AA/12-Step Effectiveness

Evaluations of AA encounter definitional problems from the start—programs and studies vary in their definitions and measurement of recovery, of success and failure, even of the term *alcoholism* itself (McElrath 1995). William R. Miller and Reid K. Hester, in a review of AA evaluation literature, state:

> Attempts to evaluate the effectiveness of A.A. have met with considerable, if not insurmountable, methodological problems, among them the very anonymity of members, which precludes systematic follow-up evaluation. Most studies have failed to include control groups (a near impossibility because of the availability of A.A. to all who are interested), have relied almost entirely upon self-report (often via mailed questionnaires) and upon abstinence as the sole criteria for success, have been plagued by sizable attrition rates and large selection confounds, and have failed to use single-blind designs, thus remaining open to criticisms of interviewer bias (particularly when the investigators have been "insiders"—members of A.A. themselves). (1980: 47)

While AA contends that upward of 75 percent of its members maintain abstinence, the evidence used to make this claim is typically testimonials of long-term, abstinent participants, which ignores dropouts, who may be more likely to continue or resume drug and alcohol use. Approximately 50 percent of AA participants will drop out within the first 3 months of attendance, and only about 13 percent of initial attendees will maintain a long-term relationship with AA (Fiorentine 1999*)*.

In his careful research, Geary Alford (1980) found that a residential treatment program for alcoholics that used the AA approach was highly effective: "Approximately 50% of the patients completing inpatient treatment were essentially abstinent, employed or productively functioning, *and* exhibited stable, adaptive social relationships at two years post-discharge. This figure increases to 56% if very light-moderate drinking is allowed." Alford and his colleagues report that an AA/NA model inpatient treatment program for adolescents, whose drug use was primarily alcohol or marijuana was successful: "Some 71% of male treatment completers and 79% of female treatment completers were found to be chemically abstinent or essentially abstinent at 6 months after discharge" (1991: 122). However, 2 years after treatment, the figure for men dropped to 40 percent, while 37 percent of those males who dropped out of the program were also found to be abstinent or essentially abstinent. Thirty percent of female noncompleters were abstinent or essentially abstinent after 2 years. As with the research reviewed by Miller and Hester (1980), Alford's (1980 and 1991) studies did not utilize a control group. In fact, AA successes appear to be concentrated among middle- and upper-class people with relatively stable lives before the onset of a drinking problem (Alexander 1990).

In an extensive research effort, Robert Fiorentine (1999) reports that any participation in 12-step programs is associated with lower levels of drug and alcohol use, and, not unimportantly, the magnitude of the association is about the same for both illicit drug and alcohol use. Less-than-weekly participants—who were more likely to be problematic drinkers—had levels of drug and alcohol use that were no different from nonparticipants. His findings suggest that weekly or more frequent 12-step participation is associated with drug and alcohol abstinence. However, *commitment* to attend a 12-step program may simply predict success; the program itself may actually do little or nothing to generate abstinence.

Despite the paucity of research on its effectiveness, the 12-step approach is very popular, some arguing that it has become a fad. The rise in the number of 12-step programs and members and the inclusion of 12-step philosophy in treatment programs are, of course, evidence only of its popularity, not of its effectiveness (Fiorentine 1999*)*. Groups such as Gamblers Anonymous, Overeaters Anonymous, Debtors Anonymous, and Sex Addicts Anonymous have been formed to address a host of social problems. While they claim inspiration from the AA 12-step approach, critics see them as groups for whiners who want an audience to dwell on their injured self (Delbanco and Delbanco 1995).

Measuring Other Chemical Dependency Programs

While treatment at most inpatient chemical dependency programs in the United States is based on a disease model built around an AA/12-step approach, there is an almost total lack of relevant research data on effectiveness (Gerstein and Harwood 1990; Galaif and Sussman 1995; Ogborne and Glaser 1985). Furthermore, most of these programs provide no aftercare but refer patients to AA, which deals with the problems of drinking but not with related or contributing problems such as unemployment and interpersonal skills or with drug use as a form of self-medication.

It is recognized that drug dependence is a career requiring treatment that is similarly oriented. "Many researchers, practitioners, and clinicians have assumed that treatment should occur once and should result in a cure if it is to be termed effective. Substance abuse does not appear to be the kind of problem that makes this orientation pragmatic. When the community in which people live is so strongly pro-intoxication, it is not surprising that treated persons are recruited back into the drug lifestyle." Therefore, "while treatment does not need to be applied forever, repeated episodes of treatment are probably necessary for most who develop serious problems with intoxicants" (Senay 1986: 143).

There is no clear research evidence on the effectiveness of short-term treatment, in- or outpatient treatment: "Given what is known about the importance of length of stay in treatment and the complexity of the recovery process in addiction, there is little likelihood that twenty-eight-day clinics or short-term modalities (one to six months) will yield positive outcomes" (De Leon 1990: 125). In fact, it may be the availability of legitimate economic opportunity rather than the mode of treatment that predicts post-treatment success. Without such opportunity, clients in disadvantaged groups will remain enmeshed in the drug-abuse subculture and continue to rely on income-generating crime (Anglin and Hser 1990b). In any event, after noting shortcomings in the research—they question the accuracy of self-reports by drug abusers—the General Accounting Office concludes (1998) that, while it may be overstated, drug abuse treatment is effective.

SUMMARY

Drug treatment in the early 1900s varied from chemical "cures," which were just as addictive as the drug the patient was being treated for, to sanatoriums where treatment was similar to many contemporary inpatient programs. Among the chemical treatments for drug abuse are the use of opioid antagonists to counteract the pleasurable effects of opiates, drugs such as clonidine to relieve withdrawal symptoms, and opioid agonists such as methadone that mimic the action of heroin but have less dramatic highs and last longer in the body. Methadone maintenance is a controversial treatment, whose advocates argue that it allows former heroin users to lead a "normal" life without having to undergo detoxification and without resorting to crime to support their drug habit. Critics argue that methadone maintenance perpetuates dependency and that polydrug users may continue to use other drugs during maintenance.

Psychological treatments include various forms of behavior modification, including aversion treatment and contingency management and contracting. Group treatment is predicated on the theory that peer interaction is more powerful than therapist-patient interactions because of the identification with others who have a similar problem.

Drug treatment programs include mandatory civil commitment, usually after a felony conviction; drug courts; and TASC programs. Therapeutic communities are residential self-help programs that offer a highly structured environment for withdrawal and ongoing behavior modification via positive and negative reinforcement to resocialize addicts into a drug-free life. Chemical dependency programs are inpatient, for-profit programs of 3 to 6 weeks that treat mostly drug abusers with health care insurance. Alcoholics Anonymous is a self-help program that consists of confession to addiction, sharing with other members, ongoing peer support, and working through the twelve steps of the program.

While drug treatment in general has been proven effective, the evaluation of specific programs is often difficult. In particular, chemical dependency programs and AA/12-step programs have been subjected to criticism for their lack of research support.

INTERNET CONNECTIONS

Alcoholics Anonymous: www.alcoholics-anonymous.org
Alcoholics Anonymous chapters: www.CyberSober.com
American Society of Addiction Medicine: www.asam.org
Betty Ford Center: www.bettyfordcenter.org
Caron Foundation: www.caron.org
Cocaine Anonymous: www.ca.org
Cognitive Behavioral Review: www.ccimrt.com
Drug Treatment Outcome Studies: www.datos.org
Father Martin's Ashley: www.fathermartinsashley.com

www.Moderation.org
Narcotics Anonymous: www.wsoinc.com
National Institute on Alcohol Abuse and Alcoholism: www.niaaa.nih.gov
New York State Office of Alcoholism and Substance Abuse Services: www.oasas.state.ny.us
Next Step Recovery Program: www.next-step-recovery.org
Prevention, Treatment and Recovery Programs: www.alchemyproject.net
Project Cork Office of Alcohol and Drug Programs: www.Dartmouth.edu/dms/cork
SMART Recovery: www.smartrecovery.org
Women for Sobriety: www.womenforsobriety.org
Wright State University Center for Interventions: www.med.wright.edu
Valley Hope: www.valleyhope.com

REVIEW QUESTIONS

1. Why has the medical profession historically avoided dealing with the problem of drug abuse?
2. What are the drawbacks of using heroin antagonists?
3. How have opioid agonists been used to deal with heroin addiction?
4. What are the advantages of using methadone maintenance rather than heroin maintenance?
5. What are the disadvantages of using methadone maintenance?
6. Why is it difficult, if not impossible, to use psychoanalysis to treat heroin addiction?
7. How is psychoanalytic theory usually operationalized in the treatment of drug abusers?
8. Why is it difficult to apply behavior theory in the treatment of drug abuse?
9. How is contingency management/contracting used in the treatment of drug abuse?
10. What is meant by the civil commitment of drug abusers?
11. What are drug courts?
12. What is the therapeutic community (TC) approach to drug abuse?
13. What are the criticisms of chemical dependency programs?
14. What is the Alcoholics Anonymous (AA)/12-step approach to dealing with substance abuse?
15. How do moderation management programs differ from Alcoholics Anonymous?
16. Why is it difficult to determine the effectiveness of the AA approach?
17. Why are health care facilities often eager to include a drug rehabilitation program as part of their services?
18. Why is it difficult to determine the success of any drug treatment programs?

CHAPTER 10

Drug Abuse Prevention

Many teachers, parents and politicians believe that drug education will deter young people from using drugs. However, evaluations of all kinds of drug education programmes in this country and all over the developed world show that drug education does not prevent young people using drugs. —*Julian Cohen (1996)*

In the early days of prevention education, young people were shown what drugs looked like, with warnings about what evil would befall them if these drugs were taken. In the 1980s, peers and adults were portrayed as vicious culprits exposing innocent children to drugs in the "just say no" campaigns. The more recent focus has been on concurrently teaching refusal skills and bolstering self-esteem with the belief that these will suffice to prevent experimentation with drugs. The problem with all of these prevention approaches is that there is no firm evidence that they work. —*J. Kelly Coker (2001: 71)*

Efforts at prevention attempt to reduce the supply or the demand for drugs of abuse. The former is the goal of drug-law enforcement (which will be examined in Chapter 12); the latter has been the goal of coercive legislation and education. "Considering the difficulty and cost of treating individuals with substance abuse problems, the prospect of developing effective substance abuse prevention programs has long held a great deal of appeal" (*Drug Abuse* 1987: 35). Unfortunately, effective prevention has proven to be as elusive as effective treatment (and effective law enforcement).

Models for Prevention

Based on extensive research, the National Institute on Drug Abuse recommends that prevention programs be designed to enhance "protective factors" and move toward reversing or reducing known "risk factors." Protective factors are those associated with reduced potential for drug use. Risk factors are those that make the potential for drug use more likely:

> *Protective factors* include strong and positive bonds within a prosocial family; parental monitoring; clear rules of conduct that are consistently enforced within the

family; involvement of parents in the lives of their children; success in school performance; strong bonds with other prosocial institutions, such as school and religious organizations; and adoption of conventional norms about drug use.

Risk factors include chaotic home environments, particularly in which parents abuse substances or suffer from mental illnesses; ineffective parenting, especially with children with difficult temperaments or conduct disorders; lack of mutual attachments and nurturing; inappropriately shy or aggressive behavior in the classroom; failure in school performance; poor social coping skills; affiliations with deviant peers or peers displaying deviant behaviors; and perceptions of approval of drug-using behaviors in family, work, school, peer, and community environments. (Lessons from Prevention Research 2001: 1)

Most efforts at prevention have focused on schools, and school-based antidrug programs are widespread. These programs have been dominated by three models (Ellickson 1995):

1. *Information model.* Assuming that children and adolescents will avoid drugs when they understand their potential hazards, this model seeks to impart information. Furthermore, the model assumes that students will develop negative attitudes that will deter them from using drugs. "In short, the information model posits a causal sequence leading from knowledge (about drugs) to attitude change (negative) to behavior change (nonuse)" (1995: 100). Sometimes the *shock* or *scare* is part of this approach, exemplified by "hard hitting" antidrug videos, talks by ex-junkies, or TV and billboard campaigns that focus on the horrors of drug use (J. Cohen 1996).

2. *Affective model.* Shifting the focus away from education, this model instead seeks to affect personality—the focus is on the individual rather than drugs per se, and it is assumed that young people of high self-esteem will not use drugs (J. Cohen 1996). "The model assumes that adolescents who turn to drugs do so because of problems within themselves—low self-esteem or inadequate personal skills in communication and decision making" (Ellickson 1995: 101). Affective model programs attempt to improve the affective skills (communication, decision making, self-assertion) believed related to drug use. In attempting to improve a student's self-image, the ability to interact within a group, and problem-solving ability, the model focuses on feelings, values, and self-awareness, and in some programs on personal values and choices.

3. *Social influence model.* Young people are seen as easy prey to peer pressure and in need of developing the skills to "say no to drugs." The approach assumes that young people lack the skills to make rational choices and that if they had these skills they would not use drugs (J. Cohen 1996). The social influence (SI) model is centered on external influences that push students toward drug use, especially peer pressure, as well as internal influences, such as the desire to be accepted by "the crowd." In order to deal with adolescent vulnerabilities, SI seeks to familiarize students with the pressures to use drugs, enabling them to develop resistance skills and techniques for saying no in those pressure situations.

Educating people, particularly elementary, high school, and college students (the primary population at risk), about the dangers of drug use would seem at first blush to be devoid of controversy and a sound response to the problem of drug abuse. After all, as Richard Brotman and Frederic Suffet (1975) point out, the thinking behind the idea appears to be quite rational: Provide valid information about the harmful consequences of drug abuse, and most persons will elect to avoid drugs. However, as Patricia Wald and Peter Hutt note, "There is substantial uncertainty and confusion in the area of drug education and prevention" because "there is no real evidence that such educational efforts are successful" (1972: 18). Indeed, as research by Isidor Chein and his colleagues (1964) revealed, youngsters with the greatest knowledge about drugs are the most susceptible to using drugs. And there is a substantial drug abuse problem among physicians, who presumably know a great deal about the dangers of drugs (Kennedy 1995).

Goodstadt points out that informational programs typically suffer from major weaknesses that may actually encourage drug use: "The unfortunate result is that young people may become more rather than less likely to experiment with drugs" (n.d.: 2). Dan Waldorf (1973) notes that in New York, heroin is seemingly everywhere in African American and Puerto Rican ghettos, where young people are exposed to it at an early age. They know about heroin and drug addicts through firsthand exposure; they witness the drugs being purchased and see addicts nodding on the streets and clustering in doorways, communal washrooms, and rooftops to "get off." They know addicts steal family belongings, which they sell for money to buy drugs. The real question, Waldorf states, is not why so many ghetto residents become drug abusers but why a majority avoid becoming addicted to a powerful substance that provides relief from an oppressive environment.

Information Model

The standard educational approach has been to present factual information concerning the dangers of substance abuse because it was assumed that increased knowledge would serve as an effective deterrent by enabling students to make rational decisions not to use drugs. Unfortunately this information has frequently been burdened with moral judgments about drug use (Zinberg 1984). The "scare" lecture of physical education teachers or nonschool personnel such as police officers has often been integral to this approach. While intended to frighten students away from dangerous substances, these lectures often contain so much misinformation or exaggeration that they raise students' skepticism and jeopardize all drug-education efforts. Young people have often found, through their own experiences of drug use and what friends tell them, that they have been lied to and thus mistrust adult sources of drug information (J. Cohen 1996; Brotman and Suffet 1975).

The American Social Health Association states that drug education "must avoid overconcentration on 'the drug problem.' Many youngsters, knowing more about drugs than their parents and teachers, will not accept moralization but will respect realistic, valid information derived from a credible source" (1972: 5). A different approach to educating youngsters about certain dangerous chemicals avoids exaggeration and scare tactics, relying instead on a factual presentation about dangerous substances and the body's reac-

Drug Education or Propaganda?

Drug education is often not based on the educational principles that underlie the teaching of other subjects, but instead tends to skew and censor information, to give a narrow view of drug use, and to tell young people what they should think and do. This is *propaganda,* not education. It often results in young people not being able to talk openly and honestly. Instead, they end up saying what they think their teachers or parents want to hear, not what they really believe. The gulf between adults and young people widens, open dialogue lessens, and young people with problems or concerns about drugs become less likely to approach adults for support (J. Cohen 1996).

Press release, Washington, D.C., January 23, 2003: The Office of National Drug Control Policy (ONDCP) today announced the launch of two new sets of advertisements, premiering during the Super Bowl and pregame show, designed to further educate Americans about the risks of drug use. Two of the ads aimed at teens are a response to research showing that American youth want to be provided with the facts about marijuana. A second pair of ads will follow up on the groundbreaking spots linking drugs, terror, and violence that were released during last year's Super Bowl. The ads are part of the ONDCP's National Youth Anti-Drug Media Campaign, which is designed to help America's youth reject illicit drugs.

In 2002, the administration of President George Bush initiated an antidrug campaign that featured an attempt to tie terrorism to the use of drugs. Ads on television and the print media depicted people saying: "I helped murder families in Colombia—it was just innocent fun." "I helped a bomber get a false passport—all the kids do it." "I helped blow up buildings—my life, my body." The commercial ends with a tag line: "Drug money supports terror. If you buy drugs, you might too" (A. Jones 2002).

tion to them, both the good and the bad. The goal is to provide information so that students can make informed decisions rather than to prevent drug use, which may be too much to expect from any educational program. There are some implementation problems with this approach:

- It may be opposed by public officials and/or parents who believe that schools should teach "proper" behavior, that is, *preach* on the evils of drug use.
- A great deal is not known about drugs of abuse.
- Depending on their ages, students may not be able to understand the information.

Providing greater knowledge about drugs may serve the unintended (or latent) function of piquing interest in and arousing curiosity about them and may possibly encourage

Scare Tactics

When it became obvious that scare tactics used by college antidrinking programs were not having their desired effect—indeed it was found that these tactics actually encouraged heavy drinking—emphasis shifted. Instead of posters showing students covered with vomit and cars wrecked by drunken drivers, the new campaign cites statistics that, in fact, reveal that most students drink in moderation. "Zero to three" read Frisbees handed out at one college, indicating the number of drinks most students have when they are at a party (Zernike 2000).

At the University of Arizona (UA), where it is known as the Social Norms Campaign, the focus is on educating students about accurate drinking norms on campus without the use of scare tactics or admonishments. "The social norms approach mandates that campaign messages consist of accurate majority (normative) statements that address campus drinking misconceptions." According to UA data, students overestimated the amount of alcohol their peers were consuming, and to correct this, ads were run in student publications, appropriate posters were mounted in residence halls, reinforced by bulletin board displays (Johannessen et al. 1999:5).

Peers, Volition, and Pleasure

"The emphasis on friendship as 'peer pressure' reflects a major difficulty in so much of the social discourse around drug-related issues—whether mass media, policy formulation, or academic debates—namely the absence of any notion of volition or desire. Health education discourses in particular have often been cleansed of any reference to the possibility that people might use drugs because they find them pleasurable" (Advisory Council on the Misuse of Drugs 1998: 36).

the more daring adolescents to seek out drugs (Wald and Abrams 1972: Goodstadt n.d.; Stuart 1974).

Some research indicates that drug addicts are quite familiar with the effects and dangers of the substances they abuse, but they either discount the risks or view them as minor and part of the "game" (see, for example, Hendler and Stephens 1977). Troy Duster reports that the *prospective* addict sees himself as an exception to the pattern of addiction he sees around him: "It is typical of the early experience of the addict-to-be that he knows of people who use narcotics and who get away with it . . . [in that] they are neither addicted nor are they known to the police. This double victory is witnessed by probably every individual who knowingly used heroin illegally for the first time" (1970: 192). However, while there is evidence that drug users know much more about drugs than do nonusers, "there is no evidence that increases in such knowledge stimulate use" (D. Hanson 1980: 273). "Simply providing the child with information about substance abuse would primarily alter the behavior of well-socialized children from cohesive families rather than those most at risk" (Dishion, Patterson, and Reid 1988: 90).

Goodstadt suggests acknowledging the positive reinforcements of drug use: "Drug use consequences are not all negative; if they were, nobody would continue to use drugs. Moderate use of some drugs offers physical, psychological, and social benefits for some people. Drug education programs that do not take into account this important aspect of the decision to start or continue using drugs diminish their credibility and effectiveness" (n.d.: 3). Julian Cohen (1996) concludes that the research evidence shows that appropriate drug education can increase drug knowledge, develop decision-making skills, and make young

Drug Education in High School

"Young people in this [high school] age group are more likely to be receiving conflicting messages about drugs. They will also be at different levels of knowledge and experience with drugs, even within the same class. Drug education may have lower priority in competition with other curriculum subjects and, whilst teachers also generally support the *principle* of drug education, some may feel that their own drug knowledge or understanding of cultural issues is deficient. All this at a time when teachers may in any case be losing ground to young people's friends and others in the credibility stakes" (*Drugs Prevention Initiative* 1999: 12).

...and College

Considering the high levels of drug use among college students, there is a need for universities to be targeted with drug information material. Research has revealed that it is frequency of drug use rather than the percentage of drug users per se that increases over time with this population, so emphasis should be on targeting drug information at those who are already drug users. Such information may encourage the formation of less positive attitudes, although there is a need for drug information to be balanced in order to appear credible (McMillan and Conner 2000).

people more discerning about what they actually do. This does not mean they will not use either legal or illegal drugs. In other words, drug education can play a role in reducing drug-related harm rather than preventing drug use.

And Goodstadt states: "Efforts to prevent drug abuse by reducing the most risky forms of drug use (for example, drinking and driving, cannabis use and gymnastics) need not condone illegal drug use" (n.d.: 3). Information programs should keep in mind that an 8-year study of adolescent drug use revealed that the vast majority of teenagers who occasionally use drugs suffer no long-lasting negative effects and cannot in later years be distinguished from those who abstained from drug use (Blakeslee 1988).

Affective Model

A broad approach to drug abuse prevention involves affective or humanistic education (although this term is likely to trigger negative responses in persons holding certain religious and social views). Public schools have turned away from the "scare 'em" approach in favor of one that emphasizes the judgment and social skills necessary to avoid substance abuse (Berger 1989). Some research indicates that this approach shows promise only with those youngsters who are not likely to become problem drug users in the first place. According to the U.S. Center for Substance Abuse Prevention, a "life skills" approach—problem-solving skills, decision-making skills, resistance skills against adverse peer influences, and social and communication skills—"is associated with short-term reductions in substance abuse among adolescents," and recommends that "life skills curricula should be recognized as an important component of effective substance abuse prevention programs for adolescents" (Chavez and Sanchez-Way 1997: 13, 14).

These affective efforts are designed to enhance self-esteem, to encourage responsible decision making, and to enrich students' personal and social development. The conceptual grounding for this approach was discussed in Chapter 8 as part of behaviorist/learning theory: prevention through the enhancement of social competence. This approach has research support (Pentz 1985).

The bases of this approach are assumptions that:

1. Substance abuse programs should aim at developing prevention-oriented decision making concerning the use of licit or illicit drugs.
2. Such decisions should result in fewer negative consequences for the individuals.
3. The most effective way of achieving these goals is by increasing self-esteem, interpersonal skills, and participation in alternatives to substance use. ("Drug Abuse" 1987: 35)

These assumptions are generally implemented through communication training, peer counseling, role playing, and assertiveness training. In the Los Angeles school system this approach has been implemented through Project D.A.R.E. and Reconnecting Youth discussed below.

Social Influence Model

The *social influence approach* attempts to "inoculate" students against using dangerous substances by making them aware of the social pressures they are likely to encounter and teaching skills that promote refusal.

The *social learning approach* views chemical abuse from the perspective of learning theory; that is, like other behavior, it is learned through modeling and reinforcement. Through instruction, demonstration, feedback, reinforcement, behavioral rehearsal (classroom practice), and extended practice through homework assignments, youngsters are taught life-coping skills that have a rather broad range of applications, including drug resistance. There is considerable variation in age groups and length of program. Some groups are led by adults, while others use peer leaders (see "Preparing for the Drug-Free Years" below).

Sample Programs

Project D.A.R.E

Drug Abuse Resistance Education, or **D.A.R.E.,** has proven popular with police departments throughout the United States. Any number of departments advertise the program on their police vehicles. The Los Angeles Police Department (LAPD) and the Los Angeles Unified School District jointly sponsor Project D.A.R.E., which is designed to equip fifth-, sixth-, and seventh-grade children with the skills and motivation they need to resist peer pressure to use drugs, alcohol, and tobacco. D.A.R.E.'s instructors are uniformed police officers on full-time duty with the project. All are veteran officers and volunteers carefully selected by D.A.R.E. supervisory staff and fully trained by officers and specialists from the school district.

> A D.A.R.E. police officer is assigned to teach in every elementary school under the LAPD's jurisdiction, offering the 17-session core curriculum to either fifth- or sixth-grade students. A junior-high program for seventh-graders, which includes early intervention with students deemed at risk, is also at full implementation in 58 junior high schools.

> In bringing the core curriculum to the elementary schools, D.A.R.E. officers are assigned to five schools per semester, and they visit each classroom once a week. Beyond this, the officers conduct one-day visits at other schools for an assembly program and follow-up visits in individual classrooms; hold formal training sessions on drug abuse for teachers; and conduct evening parent meetings. (DeJong 1987a: 4)

The use of uniformed police officers as instructors is seen as a key element in the program's success: "Police have knowledge of the drug scene and its impact on both individuals and society as a whole that regular classroom teachers cannot match. Indeed, many classroom teachers frankly admit their discomfiture in teaching lessons on drug abuse. For children this age, police hold a mystique. Kids respond to them" (DeJong 1987a: 7). And because the program "involves police officers in positive, nonpunitive roles, students are more likely to develop positive attitudes toward police officers and greater respect for the law" (1987a: 17). The D.A.R.E. curriculum ends with a schoolwide assembly that includes the reading of the winning "D.A.R.E. Pledges." Each student who completes the program receives a certificate of achievement signed by the chief of police and the superintendent of schools.

Reconnecting Youth

Reconnecting Youth is a peer group approach to building life skills for high school students who are at risk for dropping out. Designed to build resiliency, the program is presented in the form of a Personal Growth Class (PGC), typically delivered in daily 50- to 60-minute sessions during regular school hours by specifically trained school personnel (e.g., teachers, counselors, nurses) who work with students in a small-group format of 1:12 per class. An important component is the enhancement of learning skills: "One of the most important risk factors for substance abuse is academic failure" (*Drug Abuse Prevention for At-Risk Individuals* 1997: 17).

During the first 2 weeks, students are given an overview of the course as well as rules and expectations for working together as a group. Students learn about concepts such as inner strength, self-praise, and group praise, and they set goals for their participation in the class. This overview is followed by four life-skills training units:

1. *Self-esteem enhancement* provides the basis for training in the other units and includes visualization, relaxation techniques, self-praise, group praise, and liberal praise of others in the group. Students are encouraged to generate more and more positive self-portraits and, as these develop, to be able to make positive lifestyle changes.

2. *Decision making* is designed to help students enhance personal empowerment by learning to exercise greater freedom of choice and personal control over decisions. The benefits—increased self-esteem and improved mood—are emphasized. Participants examine how to make decisions in a group by reaching agreement and resolving conflicts: Stop an impulsive response; think of options; evaluate options in terms of whether each is helpful or hurtful; put into action the most helpful option; and self-praise for taking these steps.

3. *Personal control* over stress, depression, and anger. Students probe for what triggers feelings of depression and destructiveness, and they explore the effect of uncontrolled aggression on themselves and others. They practice strategies for dealing with stress, anger, and depression, with an emphasis on developing a repertoire of strategies that emphasize giving and receiving support from friends and others in their social network.

4. *Interpersonal communication* focuses on skills for communicating more effectively, and students practice ways of expressing concern for and developing healthy relationships with others at school.

As they develop, issues raised in the group become the basis for introducing and working on specific skills. At the beginning of a PGC class, for example, the group leader may start with a *check-in* to monitor all members of the group to assess how they are doing with respect to mood, school, and substance abuse control. The group works on setting the agenda for the day. The leader asks if anyone has individual issues for which they want group support and problem-solving time. Using group work and discussion skills, he or she is able to relate the students' issues to the planned skills training session and activities. "The challenge for the leader is to balance the students' daily needs with related skills building, skills application, and group problem solving applied to the students' current concerns and real-life issues" (*Drug Abuse Prevention for At-Risk Individuals* 1997: 61).

The program provides students with opportunities for prosocial recreation and school volunteer activities, designed to enhance self-esteem and school bonding. During the final 2 weeks of the class, students review what they have learned and celebrate their experiences.

Preparing for the Drug-Free Years (PDFY)

Established in 1987, **PDFY** empowers parents of children ages 8 to 14 to reduce risks that their children will abuse drugs and alcohol or develop other typical adolescent problems. PDFY is based on extensive research on factors that increase risk:

- Little parental supervision and monitoring

- Low degree of parent-child communication and interaction
- Poorly defined and communicated rules and expectations for children's behavior
- Inconsistent and excessively severe discipline
- Parental alcohol and drug use

Parents are recruited through public service announcements and advertisement, and since the program began, more than 120,000 families have been trained in five 2-hour or ten 1-hour sessions in more than thirty states and Canada. The focus is on strengthening family bonding (see "Social Control Theory" in Chapter 7), and children join their parents for a session that focuses on risk factors including friends who use drugs and how to resist peer pressure to use alcohol or other drugs. Sessions are typically conducted by two trained workshop leaders from the community aided by a curriculum kit that includes videos and family activity books.

Strengthening Families Program

This 7-week curriculum is designed for parents and youth aged 10–14. It aims at reducing substance abuse and other problem behavior during adolescence. "Intermediate objectives include improved parental nurturing and limit-setting skills, improved communication skills for both parents and youth, and youth prosocial skills development" (Molgaard, Spoth, and Redmond 2000: 2). Participants are recruited by a local family services agency that identifies a core group of parents and motivates them to recruit other families to the program. Recruitment material includes a motivational video and incentives such as $5 grocery certificates and fast-food coupons for youth.

There are separate skill-building sessions for parents and youth for the first hour followed by a second hour together in supervised family activities, during which facilitators offer assistance and model appropriate skills. The separate sessions contain parallel content; for example, while parents are learning how to use consequences when youth break rules, youth are learning about the importance of following rules. In small- and large-group discussions, the youth sessions "focus on strengthening goals for the future, dealing with stress and strong emotions, appreciating parents and other elders, increasing the desire to be responsible, and building skills to deal with peer pressure" (Molgaard, Spoth, and Redmond 2000: 2). Topics are presented in gamelike activities designed to keep participants engaged and sustain their interest while they are learning.

Parent sessions focus on understanding the developmental characteristics of young people, providing nurturing support, and dealing effectively with youth in everyday interactions. The need to set appropriate limits and to follow through with reasonable and respectful consequences is emphasized, as well as the sharing of beliefs and expectations regarding alcohol and drug use. The sessions include didactic presentations, role playing, group discussions, and the use of videotapes. "Two-thirds of each family session is spent within individual family units in which parents and youth participate in discussions on projects. The remaining time is spent in large-group skill building activities and games" (Molgaard, Spoth, and Redmond 2000: 2).

Effective Prevention Strategies

Prevention strategies targeting youth have evolved over the past 20 years as evaluation research reveals more about what works. Several strategies are used effectively, especially in combination:

- *Information dissemination.* This strategy provides awareness and knowledge of the nature and extent of alcohol, tobacco, and other drug use, abuse, and addiction and their effects on individuals, families, and communities, as well as information to increase perceptions of risk. It also provides knowledge and awareness of prevention policies, programs, and services. It helps set and reinforce norms (for example, underage drinking and drug dealers will not be tolerated in this neighborhood).
- *Prevention education.* This strategy aims to affect critical life and social skills, including decision making, refusal skills, critical analysis (for example, of media messages), and systematic and judgmental abilities.
- *Alternatives.* This strategy provides for the participation of targeted populations in activities that exclude alcohol, tobacco, and other drug use by youth. Constructive and healthy activities offset the attraction to, or otherwise meet the needs usually filled by, alcohol, tobacco, and other drug use.
- *Problem identification and referral.* This strategy calls for identification, education, and counseling for those youth who have indulged in age-inappropriate use of tobacco products or alcohol, or who have indulged in the first use of illicit drugs. Activities under this strategy would include screening for tendencies toward substance abuse and referral for preventive treatment for curbing such tendencies.
- *Community-based process.* This strategy aims to enhance the ability of the community to provide prevention and treatment services for alcohol, tobacco, and other drug use disorders more effectively. Activities include organizing, planning, enhancing efficiency and effectiveness of services implementation, interagency collaboration, coalition building, and networking. Building healthy communities encourages healthy lifestyle choices.
- *Environmental approach.* This strategy sets up or changes written and unwritten community standards, codes, and attitudes—influencing incidence and prevalence of alcohol, tobacco, and other drug use problems in the general population. Included are laws to restrict availability and access, price increases through "sin taxes," and community-wide actions.

Source: Indiana Prevention Resource Center at Indiana University

Prevention Research

A well-designed research effort found that a program based on a social influence model of prevention (Project ALERT) that seeks to motivate young people to resist drugs and helps them develop the skills to do so, can be effective in preventing or reducing adolescent use of cigarettes and marijuana. Students develop reasons for not using drugs and responses to internal and external pressures to use them. The 2-year research effort involved randomly selected seventh- and eighth-grade students across geographic, racial, and socioeconomic lines. ALERT had clearly positive results with respect to cigarette and marijuana use with both low- and high-risk students. The impact on alcohol consumption was negligible, and a "boomerang effect"—increased use of tobacco—was found for confirmed smokers (Ellickson and Bell 1990).

In Kansas City, Kansas, and Indianapolis, Indiana, beginning in the sixth and seventh grades, students were exposed to information about the dangers of drug use at school, at home, and in the community. Parents were trained to reinforce the antidrug message at home, and public service announcements were carried by news organizations throughout the community. Of the high school students who participated in the program, 1.6 percent said they had used cocaine in the last month, while 3.7 percent of the control group did. With respect to marijuana, the figures were 14.2 percent and 20.2 percent; alcohol, 36 percent and 50 percent; and cigarettes, 24 percent and 32 percent (Treaster 1990a; C. Johnson et al. 1990).

Research into eight programs using different prevention strategies found that each, in its own setting and in its own way, promoted supportive and caring relationships between youth and members of their families, their communities, and their peer groups. And each program implemented multifaceted interventions targeting the specific needs of its audiences. Each of the programs was successful either in increasing the latency of first alcohol, tobacco, and drug use, reducing the frequency of alcohol, tobacco, and drug use, or in effectively reducing risk factors and/or enhancing protective factors related to the development of substance use (*Guide to Science-Based Practices* 2001).

Two short-term reviews of Project D.A.R.E. (Nyre 1985; Aniskiewicz and Wysong 1990) have been positive: The program enhanced antidrug attitudes and knowledge while strengthening the social skills believed important in resisting drug use. A third evaluation (DeJong 1987b) contradicted these findings but, nevertheless, found that the D.A.R.E. students showed significantly less drug use. A subsequent analysis by Earl Wysong, Richard Aniskiewicz, and David Wright, which tracked a D.A.R.E. program for 5 years, found "no long-term effects for the program in preventing or reducing adolescent drug use" (1994: 467). In their review of eight D.A.R.E. studies, Susan Ennett and her colleagues (1994) did not find encouraging results. They also questioned the use of law enforcement personnel as teachers in the program, noting there are no studies on whether or not this is an effective use of police personnel. A controlled study of D.A.R.E. in Houston, Texas, found that drug, alcohol, and tobacco use increased among students exposed to the program (Gay 1999). Nevertheless, on July 8, 1999, White House Drug Czar Barry R. McCaffrey gave the keynote address at the 12th Annual National D.A.R.E. Officers Association

Training Conference. He praised D.A.R.E. both as a tool and as an important message to children about the positive role of police in the community.

Criticism of the program continued to grow. In an editorial, the conservative *Chicago Tribune* advised: "It's time to show D.A.R.E. the door. Year after year, about 80 percent of the elementary schools in the country allocate resources and classroom time for a curriculum that simply doesn't work, and few of them seem to care" (August 11, 1999: 18). In response to the increasing criticism, in 2001, the leaders of D.A.R.E. acknowledged its shortcomings and proposed changing the program accordingly. A new curriculum, focusing exclusively on middle and high schools was developed, and the role of police officers was significantly reduced (Zernike 2001). Nevertheless, research-based reports continued to criticize the program, and by 2003 state funding began to dry up, and more and more resource-starved police departments and school districts began dropping D.A.R.E. (Vogt 2003).

Harith Swadi and Harry Zeitlin state: "It must be our conclusion that the available methods of drug education that aim at preventing drug abuse are at least ineffective, if not counterproductive" (1987: 745). The National Institute on Drug Abuse notes that "Substance abuse prevention research remains in its infancy," that "we are still far from having a range of prevention strategies whose long-term efficacy is in little doubt" ("Drug Abuse" 1987: 50). The General Accounting Office (1987) reported to Congress that drug prevention efforts have been unevaluated or have shown little or no impact, and in 1990 William Bennett, the federal drug policy director at the time, stated before a congressional committee that drug education was not effective and that children were more likely to respond to law enforcement efforts and punishment (Berke 1990). Research has revealed that "simply giving information and training the child in self-control techniques would probably not be effective for the subset of children most at risk for later substance abuse. Even at age 10, this subset of most-at-risk children is already difficult to change, whether by family, teachers, or therapist" (Dishion, Patterson, and Reid 1988: 90).

Research has found that while it is relatively easy to increase knowledge and change attitudes, it is more difficult to bring about long-term sustained behavior change. "However, long-term changes can be achieved. The most persuasive support for this view comes from cigarette smoking. In 1972, about 46% of the British population smoked cigarettes and by 1992 this had been reduced to 30%. These gains were not won by one simple strategy nor by any interventions applied only in the short term. . . . Effecting health behaviour change through education is difficult but not impossible. It is likely to require perseverance, multiple approaches, and a long-term view" (Advisory Council on the Misuse of Drugs 1993: 16). Michael Goodstadt states that in the United States there is promising evidence regarding the impact of educational programs, based on smoking prevention studies "that offer approaches that can be applied to education about other drugs" (n.d.: 1–2). In fact, "Americans are smoking and drinking less . . . not because the Army imprisoned North Carolina tobacco farmers or bombed stills in Scotland, but because attitudes have been changing with the help of education and treatment programs" (May 1988: 12). And increased public awareness of the dangers of alcohol abuse, coupled with an emphasis on physical fitness and nutrition, has dramatically reduced alcohol consumption in the United States.

Prevention at the Community Level

The largest-ever study of community-based antidrug partnerships found that male residents served by Community Anti-Drug Partnerships funded by the Center for Substance Abuse Prevention had slightly lower rates—averaging about three percent—of alcohol and illicit drug use than their counterparts in nonpartnership communities. The study compared alcohol and other drug use in twenty-four communities that had antidrug partnership programs to twenty-four similar communities without such partnerships. Use rates were measured in 1994 and 1996 through a survey of 83,473 adults plus eighth- and tenth-grade students. Results for females were not nearly as encouraging: past-month and past-year alcohol and other drug-use rates were unchanged among women and girls between 1994 and 1996, and use of illicit drugs among eighth-grade girls in the partnership communities actually increased during that time period (Substance Abuse Resource Center 1999).

Technical Problems and Criticisms

The difficulty in producing and implementing effective drug abuse prevention programs may be related to some of the technical aspects of these programs. It may be—and there is evidence to support such a hypothesis—that instead of intervention models based on firm theoretical and empirical foundations, drug abuse prevention programs are too often "put together" and implemented by well-meaning but otherwise limited persons, which results in a naive or simplistic approach to a complex problem. For example, Patricia Bush and Ronald Iannotti (1987) note that programs designed to educate elementary school children about drug abuse often fail to consider cognitive development theory (originally developed by Jean Piaget). Thus they may be inappropriate for the children's developmental stage and a waste of resources. The U.S. Department of Education has attempted to deal with this problem by preparing a curriculum model that is grade-level specific: *Learning to Live Drug Free: A Curriculum Model for Prevention.*

School drug education staff are often more enthusiastic about their effectiveness than the empirical data would warrant. An evaluation of junior high school antidrug programs in the Kansas City, Missouri, area, for example, found that while school staff viewed the programs as beneficial and successful, outcome measurements did not support their optimism (Gilham, Lucas, and Siverwright 1997). In fact, support for drug prevention programs, note Aniskiewicz and Wysong (1990), may have more to do with politics than research. Such programs appear to rest less upon clear-cut evidence of effectiveness than upon their popularity as symbolic action against the "drug crisis." Being associated with such efforts can enhance the public standing of elected, police, and school officials.

Furthermore, "strategies which are adequate for preventing experimentation among those at low risk of engaging in serious antisocial behaviors may be wholly inadequate for

Another Prevention Problem

Research sponsored by the National Institute on Drug Abuse revealed that grouping high-risk youth in early adolescence for prevention program exposure may inadvertently reinforce problem behavior: They exhibited significantly worse behavior than those who received no intervention at all (Williams 2003).

preventing initiation and use by those who exhibit a 'deviance syndrome.' On the other hand, well-founded strategies for preventing drug abuse among those at highest risk for abuse may be inappropriate for those at risk of only becoming experimental users" (Hawkins, Lishner, and Catalano 1987: 78). Thus, a rational prevention program needs to establish and explicate its goals. "If the goal of prevention is to prevent serious maladaptive behavior associated with drug abuse in adolescence, then it may be desirable from an etiological perspective to focus prevention efforts on those youth who manifest behavior problems, including aggressive and other antisocial behaviors during the elementary grades. On the other hand, if the goal is to prevent experimentation with drugs, or to delay the age of experimentation in the general population, such highly focused efforts may by inappropriate" (Hawkins, Lishner, and Catalano 1987: 80).

Diana Baumrind cautions that "when socially deviant youths are required to participate in the school setting in peer-led denunciation of activities they value, they are more likely to become alienated than converted" (1987: 32). An 8-year study revealed that once an adolescent decides to use drugs in response to internal problems, peer-based prevention programs will not work (Blakeslee 1988). Michael Newcomb and Peter Bentler recommend that prevention and intervention "focus on the misuse, abuse, problem use, and heavy use of drugs to meet internal needs, cope with distress, and avoid responsibility and important life decisions and difficulties. The youngsters facing these tasks are in need of help, education, and intervention." They argue that it "is misleading to bask in the success of some peer programs that have reduced the number of youngsters who experiment with drugs (but would probably never have become regular users, let alone abusers) and ignore the tougher problems of those youngsters who are at high risk for drug abuse as well as other serious difficulties" (1989: 246).

An examination of the potential impact of a universal school-based prevention effort concludes that "it would not dramatically affect the course of drug use and the benefits would take years to accrue" (Caulkins et al. 1999: xxxi). However, "implementing model prevention programs seems to be justifiable in the sense that the benefits would likely outweigh the costs of the resources used" (1999: xxxii). Best estimates are that prevention reduces lifetime consumption of cigarettes by 2.1 percent, of alcohol by 2.2 percent, and of cocaine by 3.0 percent. While these numbers may seem relatively low, even small reductions in use can cause large decreases in social costs. With only 30 hours of programming, small reductions may be all that anyone should expect from prevention ("What Kind of Drug Use . . ." 2002).

SUMMARY

Three models for drug abuse prevention have been used in school-based programs. The information model presents factual information on drugs and the consequences of abuse on the assumption that knowledge will lead students to stay away from or stop using drugs. The affective model works to improve self-esteem and life skills to give students the tools to avoid drug use. The social influence model aims to give adolescents the information and skills to withstand peer pressure to use drugs. Drug abuse prevention programs include D.A.R.E. and Reconnecting Youth, two affective approaches that provide drug information and development of personal skills. PDFY and the Strengthening Families Program are social influence programs that focus on strengthening family bonds between parents and children. Research on prevention programs shows mixed results, but long-term behavior changes have occurred in alcohol and tobacco consumption.

INTERNET CONNECTIONS

American Council for Drug Education: www.acde.org

Center for Education and Drug Abuse Research (CEDAR): http://cedar.pharmacy.pitt.edu/main.html

Drugs Prevention Advisory Service (British government): www.homeoffice.gov.uk/dpas/links.htm

Indiana Prevention Resource Center: www.drugs.Indiana.edu

National Families in Action: www.emory.edu/NFIA

Partnership for a Drug-Free America: www.drugfreeamerica.org

Search Institute (youth abuse prevention): www.search-institute.org

Southwest Center for the Application of Prevention Technology: www.swcapt.org

Substance Abuse and Mental Health Services: www.samhsa.gov

Wisconsin Clearinghouse for Prevention Resources: www.uhs.wisc.edu/wch

---

REVIEW QUESTIONS

1. What drawbacks are inherent in educating youngsters about the dangers of drug abuse?
2. What is the affective, or humanistic, approach to drug education?
3. What is the social influence approach to drug abuse prevention?
4. What are the dangers of the "scare" approach to drug prevention?
5. What general conclusion have researchers reached about the usefulness of drug education programs?
6. Why is it crucial to aim a prevention program at a specific audience?
7. What are the technical problems encountered in implementing and evaluating drug prevention efforts?

CHAPTER 11

The Business of Drugs

Regardless of what we think we are trying to do, when we make it illegal to traffic in commodities for which there is an inelastic demand, the effect is to secure a kind of monopoly profit to the entrepreneur who is willing to break the law. In effect, we say to him: "We will set up a barrier to entry into this line of commerce by making it illegal and, therefore, risky; if you are willing to take the risk, you will be sheltered from the competition of those who are unwilling to do so. Of course, if we catch you, you may possibly (although not necessarily) be put out of business; but meanwhile you are free to gather the fruits that grow in the hothouse atmosphere we are providing for you. —*Herbert L. Packer (1968: 279)*

Changes as a Result of 9/11

"In the post 9/11 era of linking drugs with terror, of beefed-up border security and improved communication between international law-enforcement agencies in both intelligence-gathering and interdiction, the industry is likely to grow even more diffuse. Power will continue shifting from remote producers to highly specialized smuggling contractors, and outsourcing in general will become the crucial factor to survival and success" (Brzezinski 2002: 26).

This chapter examines the international and domestic traffic in illegal drugs, which by any estimate, is a multibillion-dollar-a-year industry with enormous profit to cost ratios. For example, heroin can be purchased in 700-gram units in Bangkok, Thailand, for between $7,500 and $9,500, and sold in the United States for $60–70,000. Because the product is illegal but nevertheless in great demand, drug trafficking is characterized by a level of free enterprise never envisioned by Adam Smith. It is a market totally devoid of legal constraints and one in which prices and profits are governed only by the law of supply and demand. Indeed, much like OPEC responds to the price of oil, "Colombian and Mexican drug importation organizations sometimes invoke artificial shortages, holding back stocks while building international inventories to induce drug famines and drive up the wholesale price" (Fuentes and Kelly 1999: 331).

The business of drugs shares common elements with the business of selling legal products: "It requires lots of working capital, steady supplies of raw materials, sophisticated manufacturing facilities, reliable shipping contractors and wholesale distributors, the all-important marketing arms and access to retail franchises for maximum market penetration" (Brzezinski 2002: 26).

As in any major industry, there are various functional levels: manufacturers, importers, wholesalers, distributors, retailers, and consumers. Workers in the drug business range from leaders of powerful international cartels to street dealers whose activities support a personal drug habit. At the manufacturing and importation levels, the drug business is usually concentrated among a relatively few persons who head major trafficking organizations; at the retail level it is filled with a large, fluctuating, and open-ended number of dealers and consumers. Because people at the highest levels of the drug trade are often connected by kinship and ethnicity, we will frequently refer to the ethnicity of criminal organizations in this chapter.

Young Mule

In 2002, a 12-year-old boy landed at Kennedy International Airport from Nigeria, but subsequently became ill on the cab ride to Brooklyn. After the cab driver took him to a hospital in Queens, the boy told officials that he had swallowed condoms filled with heroin, for which he was promised $1,900. The boy's father is in a federal prison in Virginia for drug offenses involving the use of students in their late teens and early 20s as drug couriers (Baker 2002).

Drugs are smuggled into the United States from both source and transshipment countries. Traffickers may use circuitous routes to avoid the suspicion normally generated by shipments from source countries. For example, cocaine may be shipped from Colombia to the African continent; from there it is moved to the United States as part of legitimate maritime cargo. Pleasure crafts and fishing vessels blend in with normal maritime traffic, and low-profile vessels fabricated of wood or fiberglass and measuring up to 40 feet in length are difficult to spot and do not readily appear on radar. Smugglers also use aircraft, landing on isolated runways and even highways or air-dropping their cargo. Motor vehicles using land routes across Canada and Mexico and "mules" carrying drugs that they have put in condoms round out the smuggling picture.

International Drug Trafficking[1]

For decades, the trafficking of heroin within the United States was principally controlled by traditional organized crime groups that lived and operated inside the country. In a drug trafficking network that became known as the French Connection, New York City–based crime families purchased heroin from Corsican sources, who worked with French sailors operating from Marseilles, to transship the drug directly to the United States. Ultimately, the heroin was distributed throughout the United States by domestic organized-crime families to street-level dealers working in low-income, minority communities. However, in 1972, the French Connection was effectively dismantled by French and U.S. drug agents, ending the domestic Mafia's monopoly on heroin distribution in the United States.

The demise of the French Connection, coupled with the subsequent emergence of criminal syndicates based in Colombia, marked a significant evolution in the international drug trade. These new traffickers introduced cocaine into the United States on a massive scale, launching unparalleled waves of drug crimes and violence. Throughout the 1980s and 1990s, the international crime syndicates continued to increase their wealth and dominance over the U.S. drug trade, overshadowing the domestic crime families.

Today, the traffic in illegal drugs, from manufacture to final street-level sale, is controlled by international organized-crime syndicates from Colombia, Mexico, and other countries. From their headquarters overseas, foreign drug lords produce and distribute unprecedented volumes of cocaine, methamphetamine, heroin, and marijuana throughout the United States. The international nature of the drug business is highlighted by Colombian authorities' seizure of tons of potassium permanganate, a chemical vital for producing cocaine, from the Republic of Korea being smuggled by Korean nationals.

These traffickers maintain tight control of their workers through highly compartmentalized cell structures that separate production, shipment, distribution, money laundering, communications, security, and recruitment. Traffickers have at their disposal the most technologically advanced airplanes, boats, vehicles, radar, communications equipment,

---

[1]Unless otherwise cited, information is from the Drug Enforcement Administration.

and weapons that money can buy. They have also established vast counterintelligence capabilities and transportation networks.

But, the international drug business has been forced to change operations in the wake of 9/11. Heightened border controls, for example, have made decentralization doubly important for Chinese, Colombian, or Nigerian trafficking organizations. Since the Colombian Cali and Medellín cartels were wiped out more than a decade ago, "virtually the entire narcotics trade has radically slimmed down. With the added pressure of 9/11 security measures, drug kingpins have adopted the mantra of their more enlightened corporate cousins, that size does not necessarily create efficiency and that to survive you have to stay nimble" (Brzezinski 2002: 26).

Colombia

Control of most of the world's cocaine industry remains in the hands of Colombian organizations. A nation of about 26 million, Colombia is the only South American country with both Pacific and Caribbean coastlines (see Figure 11.1). It is a nation that has been torn by political strife, with civil wars in 1902 and 1948. *La Violencia,* as the civil war of 1948 to 1958 is known, cost the lives of about 300,000 persons (Riding 1987). It ended when the Liberals and the Conservatives formed the National Front, but several Marxist insurgencies continued to threaten the stability of the central government. Not only was murder frequent but the methods used were often sadistic, such as the *corte de corbata*—the infamous "Colombian necktie"—in which the throat is cut longitudinally and the tongue pulled through to hang like a tie. Another practice, *no dejar la semilla* (don't leave the seed), includes the castration of male victims and the execution of women and children (Wolfgang and Ferracuti 1967).

La Violencia: The Violence Never Ended. In Colombia, drug traffickers exemplify a lack of belief in the legitimacy of the country's political and economic institutions. "Breaking the law—any law—is justified, and not just for the usual economic reasons that criminals favor. For traffickers, the law, law-enforcement officials, U.S. drug operatives, and drug-control organizations all represent the traditional elite, international imperialism, or other international competitive economic interests, none of which has any historical moral standing in their eyes. Therefore, moralistic arguments about restraining violent behavior do not capture these people's attention . . . [and] allows traffickers to garner enthusiastic support in some areas" (Tullis 1995: 66).

"At the root of Colombia's easy violence is an extraordinary indifference toward death" (Romoli 1941: 37). The homicide rate is ten times higher than that of the United States (Rohter 2000b). Murder is the leading cause of death for Colombian males aged 15 to 44 (Schemo 1997a). The country has the highest child murder rates in the world—street children kill each other, and hundreds are murdered by vigilante groups as part of their campaign of "social cleansing" (Luft 1995).

In this sociopolitical atmosphere, bandits have roamed freely, engaging in a combination of brigandage, terrorism, and revolution. In the northern cities of Barranquilla

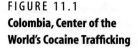

FIGURE 11.1
Colombia, Center of the World's Cocaine Trafficking

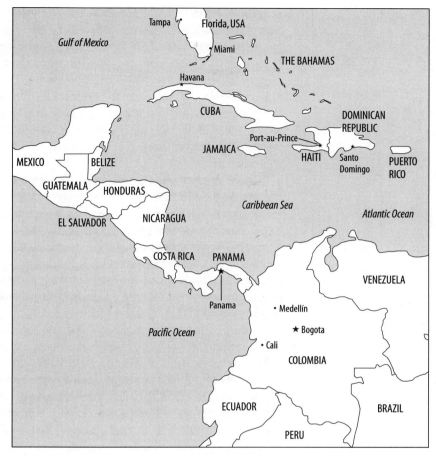

and Santa Marta and in La Guajira, smuggling (*contrabandista*) groups have operated for decades. Bandits, *contrabandistas,* and Guajiran Indians, often backed and financed by businessmen in Bogotá, have emerged as crime families, or the *narcomafia.* Members are often related by blood, marriage, or *compadrazgo* (fictional kinship). In a country where drug barons act as a state within a state, dozens of armed paramilitary groups "ply their murderous trade in the cities and countryside, sometimes selling themselves to the highest bidder as outmanned and intimidated judges and government officials feel helpless to stop them" (de Lama 1988: 5; Duzán 1994). These paramilitaries are sometimes allied with—sometimes fighting against—the drug traffickers, and they receive financial backing from wealthy landowners. In coca-growing regions, "guerilla and paramilitary groups substitute for the state in imposing a very authoritarian regime, defining and applying their own laws and regulations, and providing education, police, and civil justice to solve conflicts among the population. In exchange, these groups charge coca production and cocaine export taxes" (Thoumi 2002: 106).

For many decades, coca leaf was converted to cocaine base in Bolivia and Peru, and smuggled by small aircraft or boat into Colombia, where it was refined into cocaine in jungle laboratories. Laboratories have relocated to cities far from cultivation sites to be closer to sources of precursor chemicals and also because improved law enforcement methods facilitate the detection of jungle laboratories. Precursor chemicals are usually manufactured in the United States and Germany, and Panama and Mexico serve as major transit sources. Colombian cartels, using dummy companies and multiple suppliers, pay up to ten times the normal prices for these chemicals. Traffickers have also been stealing precursor shipments in transit from the point of entry into Colombia, en route to a legitimate end user.

Some Colombian traffickers set up laboratories in other Latin American countries and even the United States in response to increased law enforcement in Colombia and the increasing cost of ether, sulfuric acid, and acetone in Colombia. While sulfuric acid and acetone have wide industrial use in Colombia, ether does not, and each kilo of cocaine requires 17 liters of ether. The cost of these chemicals has increased as a result of controls imposed by the Colombian government on their importation and sale and of U.S. Drug Enforcement Administration efforts to disrupt the supply of chemicals essential in the cocaine refinement process. Acetone, sulfuric acid, and ether are widely available for commercial purposes in the United States.

In the past, because the quality of Colombian coca was significantly less than that grown in Peru and Bolivia, Colombia had not been a major coca producer. Success in eradicating coca in Bolivia and Peru[2] led to a major increase in Colombian coca cultivation, and in 1998, Colombia became the world's leading coca producer (Goering 1998; Krauss 2000). Colombian traffickers have achieved extraordinary levels of efficiency in extracting cocaine from their coca crops (Bureau for International Narcotics and Law Enforcement Affairs 2000). About three-quarters of the coca is grown in six rural provinces about the size of Kansas, southwest of Bogotá, with a population of about six million. The area is desperately poor and plagued by left- and right-wing paramilitary groups (Forero 2001a). Indeed, Colombia is the only country in Latin America still fighting a major guerrilla insurgency (Howe 2000).

The government has conceded to the main Marxist guerrilla group, the Revolutionary Armed Forces of Colombia (FARC), with about 18,000 fighters, an area in central Colombia about the size of Switzerland. FARC acts as a "labor organizer in the coca fields, keeping the price of a bushel up while taking a hefty percentage from the farmers" (Howe 2000: 38). In FARC-controlled areas, the economy is built on coca, and coca paste often serves as the local currency. Since paper currency is in short supply, "it is not unusual for people to be paid for their work in coca. They, in turn, pay for the necessities with the paste, which is soft and powdery like flour" (Forero 2001f: Sec. 4: 12). The traffickers buy the paste, process it into cocaine, and ship it by the ton to the United States, while FARC taxes the trade. "To prevent narcotraffickers from ripping off farmers, the rebels set a

Unique

Colombia is the only country in the world where the three main plant-based illegal drugs are produced in significant amounts: cocaine, heroin, and marijuana (Thoumi 2002).

---

[2]By 2002, coca was making a comeback in Peru, driven by a combination of poverty and soaring prices for coca (Forero 2002).

minimum price for a kilo of coca paste. They also tax the traffickers for protection of smuggling routes, the use of clandestine runways, the importation of cocaine-processing chemicals, and the export of every kilo of refined cocaine shipped from the region" (Semple 2000: 61; Guillermoprieto 2002).

Contesting the FARC and other leftist militias are right-wing paramilitaries that often receive assistance from wealthy landowners, ranchers, and the Colombian military (Forero 2001h). They are part of a loose-knit coalition, United Self-Defense Forces of Colombia (AUC)—about 11,000 strong and still growing—fighting Marxist guerrillas for control of poppy- and coca-producing regions. One group is headed by Carlos Castaño, in his mid-30s, whose 8,000 uniformed, well-trained, and well-armed men regularly do battle against leftist guerrillas. The group's methods are characterized by their nickname, "The Headcutters." Victims—anyone believed collaborating with leftists—are frequently kidnapped and usually found decapitated. Castaño finances his operation through drug trafficking and is believed to be an associate of the Montoya brothers, major cocaine traffickers in the Northern Valle de Cauca region. Ranchers who had been under siege from the guerrillas helped transform this small group of outlaws into a formidable army (Forero 2001h; Guillermoprieto 2002).

Operating out of the foothills of the Sierra Nevadas is another paramilitary headed by Hernán Giraldo, whose group, *Los Chamizos* (Charred Tree), numbers about 400. His men routinely kill suspected leftists, including university professors, student activists, and trade unionists. In 2000, at least 130 Colombian trade unionists were murdered (Forero 2001g). Giraldo is reputed to control a drug syndicate that exports more than $1 billion worth of cocaine to the United States and Europe, although he is not averse to other means of raising money. In 1995, his men kidnapped a wealthy local businessman and demanded a $1 million ransom. After the money was delivered, the victim was shot and his body carved up with chain saws. Three years later, Giraldo's men abducted the victim's widow and demanded a ransom of $5 million. After the money was delivered, she met the same fate as her husband.[3] Despite his notorious reputation, port authorities, police officials, and politicians are often eager to secure his largess, which has enabled him to elude capture (Schemo 1997b).

The militias have proven more effective against the guerrillas than government forces, and this has endeared them to elements of the population at risk. They have reinforced this support by building roads and schools in the areas from which they have driven the guerrillas (Forero 2001h; Guillermoprieto 2002).

In Medellín, both paramilitaries and drug traffickers make use of adolescent assassins formed into gangs under the control of young men whose services are for sale. These youngsters are protected from prosecution as adult murderers, although many die a violent death, by a law intended to foster rehabilitation (Griswold 2002).

---

[3]Kidnapping is a major source of funds for both right- and left-wing groups, as well as common criminals, in Colombia. In 2000, there were 3,076 reported, and many other kidnappings are hidden from authorities (Semple 2000).

The Cuban Role in Importing Cocaine. Until the early 1970s, the importation of cocaine into the United States was largely a Cuban operation, although the suppliers were Colombians. When Fidel Castro overthrew the corrupt dictatorial regime of Fulgencio Batista early in 1959, he expelled American gangsters who operated gambling casinos in Havana. Many of their Cuban associates fled to the United States, along with *narcotraficantes* who had distributed cocaine in Cuba. They settled primarily in the New York, New Jersey, and Miami areas and began to look for new sources of income. Many Cubans who fled with, or soon after, the Batista loyalists were organized and trained by the Central Intelligence Agency in an effort to dislodge Castro. After the Bay of Pigs debacle in 1961, members of the CIA-organized Cuban exile army were supposed to disband and go into lawful businesses. However, as Donald Goddard (1978: 44) points out, "They had no lawful business." Elements of these exile groups (they often overlapped) began to enter the cocaine business. At first they imported only enough cocaine to satisfy members of their own community, but by the mid-1960s the market had expanded way beyond the Cuban community, and so they began to import the substance in greater quantities.

During the latter half of the 1960s, Colombians began emigrating to the United States in numbers sufficient to establish communities in Miami, Chicago, Los Angeles, and New York. Many were illegal immigrants who entered the United States through the Bahamas carrying false documents such as phony Puerto Rican birth certificates and forged immigration papers of high quality. The Colombian traffickers became highly organized both in the United States and at home. By 1973 independent foreign nationals could no longer "deal drugs" in Colombia. In 1976 the Colombians became dissatisfied with their Cuban agents in the United States, who were reportedly making most of the profits and shortchanging the Colombians. Enforcers, often young men from Colombia's version of the "Wild West," the Guajira Peninsula, or from Barrio Antioquia, the slums of Medellín, were sent in and systematically executed Cubans in Miami and New York. By 1978 Cubans remaining in the cocaine business had become subordinate to the Colombians. Then the cocaine wars began between rival Colombian gangs, bringing terror to South Florida. Enforcers (*sicarios*) are well trained in their craft (Mowatt 1991) and are known to torture and mutilate their targets and members of their families—women and children and even pets are not spared.

Growing and Trafficking Cocaine in Colombia. The economic modernization of Colombia failed to bring about a corresponding respect for government. Delegitimization of government and *La Violencia* "left legacies which have worked to permit, if not encourage, the development of the cocaine industry" (Thoumi 1995: 84). Delegitimization spurred the development of smuggling, particularly export of products out of Colombia and into Venezuela and Ecuador—cattle, emeralds, coffee—providing experience in the contraband trade and money laundering. The propensity to use violence led to domination of potential Bolivian and Peruvian rivals in the cocaine business. "Aside from their disdain for Colombian institutions and their long criminal records, Colombian traffickers share other characteristics. They appear to be great believers in fate and providence and seem unmoved by normal considerations of personal danger. It is a perspective unaltered

The Cocaine Business: Good News, Bad News

The most striking change at the end of 1999 was the continuing, steady decline in the Andean coca crop. The most dramatic declines occurred in Peru and Bolivia, formerly the world's two principal coca producers. They now rank a distant second and third behind Colombia. The joint effort began in 1995 to sever the "air bridge" that carried Peruvian coca to Colombian refineries and then to eradicate coca crops. But Peru was not the only success story. During the same four-year period in Bolivia, Bolivian government eradication programs cut coca cultivation by more than half.

There was also some bad news. In 1999, coca cultivation in Colombia increased by 20%. The Colombian drug trade has been racing to make up for the shortfall in the other two Andean producers. Realizing that the only way to have a guaranteed source of coca was to plant it in lands under their immediate control, the Colombian syndicates have been steadily moving cultivation to the conflict-ridden south and southwest of the country. Since cocaine profits also in part fund Colombia's principal insurgency, the convergence of interests has led to expanded cultivation in guerrilla-dominated territory, where security conditions make it difficult for the central government to conduct eradication operations.

Another disturbing development is confirmation that the Colombian syndicates have achieved extraordinary levels of efficiency in extracting cocaine from their coca crops. Higher yielding varieties of coca are being grown in parts of Colombia. Colombian laboratory operators have also become more efficient in processing coca leaf into cocaine (Bureau for International Narcotics and Law Enforcement Affairs 2000).

by normal law-enforcement efforts and one that makes dealing with or trying to control them such a dangerous enterprise" (Tullis 1995: 67). Speculative capitalism, focus on very high short-term profits—a feature of Colombia's financial elite—provided the resources for development of a cocaine industry (Thoumi 1995).

Colombia is a relatively large country, and many regions have only a weak federal presence. "While Colombian authorities built suburbs and major highways between cities, they ignored vast sections of the country; much of rural Colombia is isolated by hilly, trackless terrain" (Duzán 1994: 63). Three steep Andean ranges run the length of Colombia, and impenetrable jungle covers the south: "The government didn't lose control of this half of Colombia; it never had it" (Robinson 1998a: 39). The vacuum left by the central government has proved ideal for coca cultivation and cocaine manufacture because it left areas where only local officials had to be bribed, a cheaper and less risky action (Thoumi 1995). In 1998, Colombia became the leading coca producer in the world—Peru had fallen to second place (Goering 1998). However, the quality of Colombian coca is significantly less than that grown in Peru and Bolivia. In response, traffickers have imported the type of coca native to Peru and, with the help of agronomists, have grafted it onto the weaker Colombian species to create a powerful hybrid (Rohter 1999a).

In the remote jungle areas where coca is cultivated, powerful Marxist guerrilla forces protect the crops and levy taxes on the drug business. They have been effective against Colombia's mostly poorly trained and motivated conscript military (Robinson 1998b; Rohter 1999b). And members of the Colombian military, often those trained by the United States, have been involved in widespread human rights abuses that generate support for the rebels and drug traffickers (Schemo and Golden 1998). Attempts to eradicate the crop have encountered stiff opposition from the subsistence farmers, for whom it is an economic lifeline ("Anti-Drug Efforts Encounter Resistance in Colombia" 1995).

The Revolutionary Armed Forces (FARC) has collected taxes from the traffickers and permitted them to operate in jungle areas controlled by FARC. Although it originated as a Marxist militia, in more recent years FARC has resembled organized banditry operating its own coca farms and laboratories in rural Colombia (Brooke 1995). In 1996, there were mass protests against the government's campaign to eradicate both coca and poppy crops in response to U.S. pressure. Colombia has been spraying herbicides from the air in several rural provinces. In support of these protests, FARC launched an attack on military and police installations, destroying two police stations and killing and abducting dozens of soldiers and police officers. At the end of 1998, in an effort to advance peace negotiations with FARC guerrillas, the Colombian government evacuated its security forces from a swath of Colombia as big as Switzerland (Schemo 1999).

Cells and Cartels. Colombia-based cocaine trafficking groups in the United States continue to be organized around *cells* that operate within a given geographic area. Since these cells are based on family relationships or close friendships, outsiders attempting to penetrate the cell run a high risk of arousing suspicion. Some cells specialize in a particular facet of the drug trade, such as cocaine transport, storage, wholesale distribution, or money laundering. Each cell, which may comprise ten or more employees, operates with little or no knowledge about the other cells. In this way, should one of the cells be compromised, the operations of the other cells would not be endangered.

A rigid top-down command and control structure is characteristic of these groups. The head of each cell reports to a regional director who is responsible for the overall management of several cells. The regional director, in turn, reports directly to one of the top drug lords, or his designate, based in Colombia. Trusted lieutenants of the organization in the United States have discretion in the day-to-day operations, but ultimate authority rests with the leadership in Colombia (Ledwith 2000).

Traffickers from Colombia are increasingly employing state-of-the-art encryption devices to translate their communications into indecipherable code. This evolving technology presents a significant impediment to law enforcement investigations of criminal activities. In the past, the necessity for frequent communication between drug lords in Colombia and their surrogates in the United States made the drug-trafficking organizations vulnerable to law enforcement wiretaps. Now, however, through the use of encryption technology, they can protect their electronic business communications from law enforcement interception and "hide" information that could be used to build criminal cases against them.

The most notorious drug cartels have been centered in Medellín and Cali. However, government efforts against the Medellín and Cali cartels have caused a balkanization of the cocaine trade in Colombia. A multiplicity of smaller organizations is filling the vacuum, and they maintain lower profiles in Colombia and the United States than their cartel predecessors. And while this fragmentation reduces efficiency, combating this multiplicity requires even more personnel and greater intelligence gathering efforts. Success against the major cartels has not affected the price of cocaine, which remains at about $12,000 to $18,000 a kilogram in Miami (Navarro 1998). Independent traffickers from Medellín and Cali who worked in the shadows of the major cartels have joined forces, and the cycle continues (NNICC 1998).

The DEA has identified major organizations based on the northern coast of Colombia that have deployed command and control cells in the Caribbean Basin to funnel tons of cocaine to the United States each year. Colombian managers dispatched to Puerto Rico[4] and the Dominican Republic operate these command and control centers and are responsible for overseeing drug trafficking in the region. These groups also direct networks of transporters that oversee the importation, storage, exportation, and wholesale distribution of cocaine destined for the continental United States. They have franchised to criminals from the Dominican Republic a portion of the mid-level wholesale cocaine and heroin trade on the U.S. East Coast. The Colombian groups remain, however, in control of the sources of supply. The Dominican trafficking groups, already firmly entrenched as low-level cocaine and heroin wholesalers in the larger northeastern cities, were uniquely placed to assume a far more significant role in this multibillion-dollar business.

The Dominican traffickers operating in the United States, and not the Colombians, are now the ones subject to arrest, while the top-level Colombians control the organization with sophisticated telecommunications. This change in operations reduces profits somewhat for the syndicate leaders. It succeeds, however, in reducing their exposure to U.S. law enforcement. When arrested, the Dominicans will have little damaging information that can be used against their Colombian masters. Reducing their exposure, together with sophisticated communications, puts the Colombian bosses closer to their goal of operating from a political, legal, and electronic sanctuary. Colombian drug traffickers' efforts to reduce their exposure are clearly linked to the 1997 change in Colombian constitutional law, which once again exposes the Colombians to extradition to the United States for drug crimes (Ledwith 2000).

Heroin Trafficking in Colombia. Since the 1980s Colombia has become a major poppy grower, and Colombians have become major heroin wholesalers. At the end of

---

[4]Puerto Rico, a 110-mile-long island with the third-busiest seaport in North America is ideal for smugglers, who have fewer problems getting cocaine to the United States because traffic from the island is not searched by customs agents.

1991, police raids in Colombia disclosed thousands of acres of poppy plants ("Colombian Heroin May Be Increasing" 1991). On the mountain slopes of Colombia's Andean rain forests, guerrillas and drug traffickers grow significant crops. On the hillsides of a reservation in the southern Colombian state of Cauca, 9,000 feet high, Guambiano Indians cultivate their most precious crop—gum from their poppies brings about $115 a pound and represents the difference between food and hunger. Nine other states are known to have poppy plantations (Tamayo 2001).

The purity level of Colombian heroin—it passes through fewer hands from "the farm to the arm" than the Asian variety—enables ingestion by sniffing and smoking, methods much safer than the injection, which is the only way to gain a potent high with weaker versions of the drug. By 1999, Colombia was believed to be the source of 70 percent of the heroin sold on the East Coast. In New York, Colombians caused a glut on the heroin market, with declining prices and street-sale purity as high as 90 percent. In the early (pre-Colombian) 1980s it was barely 5 percent (Wren 1999b).

While they may sell cocaine and heroin to wholesalers as part of a package deal (Navarro 1995), it appears that the major cocaine traffickers have not been involved in the heroin business, which is run by small independent organizations (Schemo 1997b). They typically use "swallowers" to get the drug into the United States: Poor Colombian women are recruited to swallow heroin packed into the cut-off fingers of surgical gloves. The $10,000 salary entails risks to life (the packets will disintegrate, causing a massive overdose if she does not arrive at her destination quickly enough) and liberty—being intercepted by customs officers using drug-sniffing dogs and body scanners (Wren 1999a).

The Mexican Route. During the 1980s, the Colombian drug lords relied heavily on organized groups from Mexico to transport cocaine into the United States after it was delivered to Mexico from Colombia. Currently, the greatest proportion of cocaine available in the United States is still entering through Mexico. Using their skills as seasoned drug traffickers with a long tradition of polydrug smuggling, crime lords from Mexico soon established cocaine trafficking routes and contacts. In the late 1980s, Colombia-based organizations, who had paid transporters from Mexico cash for their services, began to give them cocaine—in many cases up to half of the shipment—as payment for their services. As a result, the organizations from Mexico evolved from mere transporters of cocaine to major cocaine traffickers in their own right, and today pose a grave threat to the United States.[5] Mexican organized crime syndicates now control the wholesale distribution of cocaine in the western half and the Midwest of the United States (Ledwith 2000).

Mexico

Mexico is a nation of about 91 million persons, 75 percent of whom live in urban areas. Independence from Spanish rule in 1821 was followed by a series of revolutions, rigged

---

[5]For an examination of the trafficking organizations operating in one Mexican border city, see O'Day and Venecia (1999).

elections, and general turmoil. There was a war with the United States in 1848 and a French invasion and occupation from 1863 to 1867. In still another violent overthrow, Porfirio Diaz came to power in 1876 and ruled Mexico for 35 years. Out of the revolution that ousted Diaz emerged Mexico's dominant political party, known today as the PRI— *Partido Revolucionario Institucional.*

For decades after its founding, the PRI "was a tool of successive presidents using authoritarian methods to insure one-party rule" (Dillon 1999b: 1). The police forces—federal, state, and local—that evolved out of this atmosphere have been deployed not to protect but to control the population. Furthermore, police officers have been poorly paid, and it is understood that they can supplement their pittance with bribes as long as they remain loyal to the government (Dillon 1996). The PRI ruled Mexico for more than 70 years without any strong opposition, during which corruption became endemic.

From Heroin to Cocaine. The popular culture is infused with songs and ballads— *narco-corridos*—glamorizing drug trafficking. Major *narcotraficantes* are celebrated, along with their subculture of violence. Many songs contain references to an outlaw code of behavior, and music videos depict violence, including torture and the murder of police officers (Dillon 1999a). Mexico is the source of "brown" or "black tar" heroin, a less refined form of the substance that gained a foothold in the American drug market after the demise of the French Connection. While white heroin from the Golden Triangle and the Golden Crescent in Southwest Asia can approach 100 percent purity, Mexican brown generally ranges from 65 to 85 percent pure.

The poppy is not native to Mexico but was brought into the country at the turn of the century by Chinese laborers who were helping to build the railroad system. Chinese immigrants dominated heroin trafficking until anti-Chinese riots and property confiscations during the 1930s caused the trade to pass into Mexican hands (Lupsha 1991). Poppy fields are generally small and difficult to detect, although larger fields cultivated by more sophisticated growers have been discovered. The poppies are grown in remote areas of the Sierra Madre states of Durango, Sinaloa, and Chihuahua, as well as Sonora (the Mexican state just south of Arizona) (see Figure 11.2). Opium gum is then transported to nearby villages. *Acaparadores,* or gatherers, travel around the countryside buying large quantities of opium gum, which is flown to secret laboratories owned and operated by major heroin organizations. The conversion process takes about three days (although with special equipment and trained personnel it can be accomplished in one day). Once the chemists are finished, the heroin is moved to large population centers. From there, Mexican couriers transport the heroin to members of the trafficking organization in the United States.

In the early 1990s, the Mexicans struck a deal with the Colombians whose cocaine they were moving from Mexico into the United States on a contract basis: For every 2 kilograms of smuggled cocaine, the Mexicans keep 1 kilogram as payment in kind (O'Brien and Greenburg 1996; Wren 1996). Both sides benefited. The Colombians had an abundance of cocaine, and the Mexicans had a distribution network in the United States that they had previously used for heroin. This arrangement was aided by the North American Free Trade Act (NAFTA), which further opened the already porous borders with Mexico.

FIGURE 11.2   **Mexico and the States that Border It**

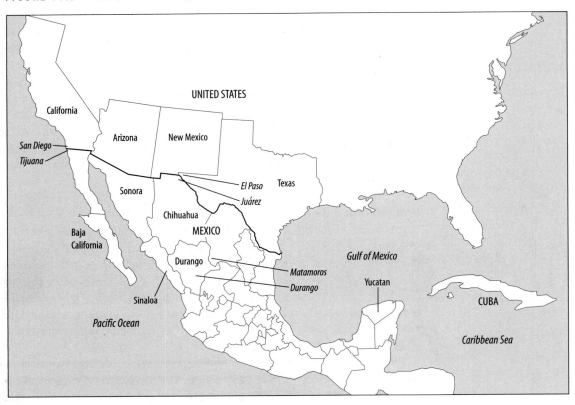

The relationship with the Colombians also led to structural changes, with some Mexican drug groups modeling their organizations along Colombian lines—compartmentalized units operating independently of each other but controlled hierarchically. They have also copied the Colombians in their attacks on journalists. The benefits to the Mexican traffickers were significant: Profits increased five to ten times. It also led to a dramatic increase in payments to public officials to protect their lucrative business (Golden 1997). This arrangement also had a certain logic for the Colombia-based traffickers who, in 1989, had been stunned by four costly cocaine seizures. Under the new payment plan, if a shipment was seized in a U.S. warehouse, the losses to the Colombia-based traffickers would be cut by half.

The markups for drug sales were so great that the new arrangement offered the traffickers from Mexico an opportunity to make far greater sums of money than they could have made being mere transporters for the traffickers from Colombia. More revenues meant more profits to invest in new distribution strategies. Eventually, the United States became divided into two marketing areas, the Mexico-based traffickers controlling the Midwest and West and the Colombia-based traffickers controlling the East. As a result, organized crime figures from Mexico began using their long-established contacts to emerge as major cocaine traffickers in their own right, especially after the arrest of the Cali cartel leaders in 1995. Currently, groups from Colombia and the Dominican Republic still control most of the cocaine trafficking along the East Coast, but in many areas, like New York State, they are being displaced by aggressive traffickers from Mexico. In 1998, there was a resurgence of heavy smuggling from the Bahamas and a corresponding drop-off on the southwest border, an indication that Colombians are concerned about the Mexicans becoming their competitors in the cocaine business.

In the 1980s, Mexican organizations had attempted to convert Peruvian coca paste into cocaine in Mexico-based laboratories. The end product, however, had the odor of kerosene, and the effort had to be abandoned in favor of buying the product from Colombians or acting as their shipping agents in return for half the load (McMahon 1995). It appears that the Mexicans have become more adept at this aspect of the cocaine business. In 1998, officials in Chicago seized 2,800 pounds of cocaine and $5 million at a West Side produce company being used to store drugs from Mexico (O'Connor 1998).

The drug trade is big business in poverty-wracked Mexico. Large traffickers have traditionally received protection from the highest levels of government and law enforcement. Indeed, some important traffickers have backgrounds in law enforcement. As Peter Lupsha notes, "For some of Mexico's top enforcement officials entrance into drug trafficking has simply been a lateral transfer" (1990: 12). This ugly facet of the drug trade was dramatically revealed when several Mexican law enforcement officers were implicated in the torture-murder of a U.S. drug agent. They were acting on orders from drug kingpin Rafael Caro Quintero. When Quintero and other members of his Guadalajara cartel were arrested, they were carrying credentials identifying them as agents of the Dirección Federal de Seguridad, the Mexican equivalent of the FBI. Sicilia Falcón, another leading Mexican trafficker, carried similar credentials (Lupsha 1991). In Rafael's hometown of Sinaloa, just south of Arizona, he and other members of the Caro Quintero clan are revered and are even the subjects of songs and legends (Bowden 1991).

The vast and remote 1,933-mile border between Mexico and the United States makes patrolling difficult and facilitates the transportation of drugs into Texas, California, Arizona, and New Mexico. Drugs are also secreted in a variety of motor vehicles and smuggled past official border entry points. Private aircraft make use of hundreds of small airstrips that dot the U.S.-Mexican border and dozens of larger airstrips on the Yucatán Peninsula to move heroin north.

Mexican Methamphetamine Labs. While they are latecomers to the trade, Mexican drug organizations have become dominant in the manufacture and distribution of methamphetamine. They import precursor chemicals from Asia and Europe and convert them into "speed" in Mexican-based laboratories. The drugs are then smuggled into the United States (Dillon 1995). Methamphetamine provides Mexican organizations an opportunity for profit that does not have to be shared with others, as does cocaine with Colombians, for example. And the profits are substantial, usually a tenfold return on an investment (Arax and Gorman 1995).

Better organization and an extensive drug portfolio has enabled Mexican organizations to diversify by dividing operations into heroin, cocaine, marijuana, and now methamphetamine units. Mexican involvement with the substance apparently began when the Hells Angels motorcycle club turned to them in order to avoid the hazards posed by methamphetamine manufacture: It is explosive, the chemicals are caustic, inhalation can be fatal, and the strong odor can alert law enforcement. Eventually, the Mexicans improved on the methods learned from the bikers, and now it is the bikers who typically buy for distribution from the Mexicans (Arax and Gorman 1995).

By 1995 it became apparent that Mexican drug trafficking was dominated by about a half dozen *padrones* (bosses), leaders of several cartels, who were sometimes allied, sometimes in competition, and sometimes in violent conflict, although gun battles have been infrequent. They are often referred to by their geographic location, such as the "Gulf cartel." While they operate out of discrete sites in Mexico, their stature "comes not from controlling territory so much as from the international scope of their contacts and their ability to operate across Mexico with Government protection" (Golden 1995: 8). Thus, the leader of the infamous Juárez cartel in the state of Chihuahua, Amado Carrillo-Fuentes, resided in Culiacan, in the neighboring state of Sinaloa, which is actually the home of another cartel by that name.

While major international trafficking organizations have traditionally specialized in one substance—heroin or cocaine—in several cases commodity lines have become blurred: Colombians, historically cocaine traffickers, have become involved in the heroin business, while Mexicans, traditionally heroin traffickers, have become major cocaine dealers.

The Golden Triangle

The Golden Triangle of Southeast Asia encompasses approximately 150,000 square miles of forested highlands, including the western fringe of Laos, the four northern provinces of Thailand, and the northeastern parts of Myanmar (formerly Burma). Myanmar accounts for about 90 percent of the total heroin production of the Golden Triangle[6] and is the world's second largest source of heroin and opium. The country is also a major producer of methamphetamine (Mydans 2003). These countries emerged from colonial rule with relatively weak central governments. Their rural areas were inhabited by bandits and paramilitary organizations such as the Shan United Army. Colonial officials, particularly the French, used these organizations and indigenous tribes against various insurgent groups, particularly those following a Marxist ideology. As support for overseas colonies dwindled at home, French officials in Southeast Asia utilized the drug trade to finance their efforts. Golden Triangle opium was shipped to Marseilles, where the Corsican underworld processed it into heroin for distribution in the United States.

---

[6]Drug traffickers in Myanmar have diversified into methamphetamine, which is being smuggled into other Asian countries.

FIGURE 11.3   **Major Asian Opium Regions**

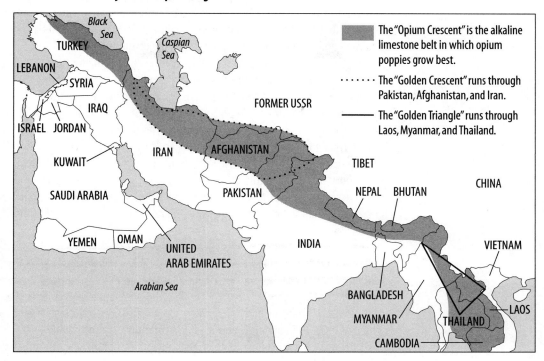

The French withdrew from Southeast Asia in 1955, and several years later the United States took up the struggle against Marxist groups—the Vietnam War is part of this legacy. The CIA waged its own clandestine war. Again, heroin played a role, for many of the indigenous tribal groups organized by the CIA cultivated opium. In Laos and South Vietnam, corrupt governments were heavily involved in heroin trafficking, making the substance easily available to American GIs (A. McCoy 1972; 1991). This long-standing tradition of using drugs to help finance military efforts continues in this part of the world (see Figure 11.3).

Shan United Army/Mong Tai Army. The Shan States, an area somewhat larger than England, lie on a rugged, hilly plateau in the eastern part of central Myanmar, flanking the western border of China's Yunnan Province. The Shan States contain an array of tribal and linguistic groupings. The largest group is the Shans, who speak Thai and thus have more in common with their neighbors in Thailand than with Myanmar. The Shans are lowland rice cultivators, but hill tribes on the mountain ridges around them cultivate opium. During British colonial rule (1886–1948), the Shan States were administered independently from what was then Burma, and the Shan princes enjoyed a great deal of autonomy. Burma won independence in 1948: The Shans, with great misgivings, agreed to join the Union of Burma in return for statehood and guarantees of a number of ministry posts. As a final incentive, the Shans were given the right to secede after 1957. Since a coup in 1962, Burma has been dominated by a repressive military dictatorship. In 1989 the country changed its name to Myanmar. Brutality against ethnic minorities and collaboration with drug trafficking continues.

The Burmese government's heavy-handed approach to the Shan States set the stage for revolution. Official Burmese financial policies were devastating to many hill farmers, who turned more and more to poppy cultivation as a cash crop outside of central government control (Delaney 1977). Shan princes (known as *sawbwas*) "had been encouraged to introduce the opium poppy to their fiefdoms by the British as far back as 1866 and opium shops had been opened throughout Burma to retail the narcotics to licensed addicts" (Bresler 1980: 67). In later years, the British made a number of efforts to abolish opium cultivation in the Shan States, although they were never completely successful (A. McCoy 1972). In any event, many Shans blamed their princes for accommodating the central government, and traditional systems of authority deteriorated.

Originally known as the Shan United Army (SUA), the Mong Tai Army (MTA), under the leadership of Chang Chifu, who is half-Chinese, half-Shan and better known as *Khun Sa,* resorted to opium trafficking in order to purchase arms and support its independence movement (Delaney 1977). The SUA/MTA came to dominate the opium trade along the Thai-Burma border, where about 400,000 hill tribesmen had no source of income other than heroin (Permanent Subcommittee on Investigations 1981a). The SUA/MTA was able to control both the shipments of opium and the production of heroin in its laboratories.

In the 1980s the Thai government succeeded in driving the MTA out of Thailand and back into Burma, but the group continued to dominate opium traffic, taxing drug caravans crossing their territory. In 1990 the Shans suffered significant setbacks: Khun Sa was indicted for drug trafficking by a federal grand jury, and the United States offered a $3 million reward for his capture and conviction in an American court. And his Mong Tai Army suffered defeats by the primitive but ferocious Wa tribesmen (Schmetzer 1990).

In 1994, a joint U.S./Thai operation ("Tiger Trap") closed the Thai/Myanmar border in areas where the MTA operates. This cut off Khun Sa's ability to move heroin into Thailand and curtailed purchase of supplies for his forces. Later that year, Thai police arrested thirteen major MTA brokers who had been indicted by a federal grand jury in New York. The squeeze was complete in 1995 when the Myanmar army moved against Khun Sa, whose forces were low on food, ammunition, and medical treatment for their wounded. Shortly afterward, ethnic strife broke out: The rank-and-file ethnic Shans mutinied against the MTA, whose top officers are ethnic Chinese (Shenon 1996). Khun Sa began secret negotiations with Myanmar, and in 1996 a deal was made. In front of reporters from Thailand, the 61-year-old Khun Sa submitted his resignation—he was retiring to raise chickens, he told them—and disbanded the MTA. The Myanmar government refuses to extradite him, and until his health deteriorated, Khun Sa regularly golfed with the generals against whom he fought a protracted guerrilla war (Wren 1998a). As a result, the amount of Southeast Asian heroin entering the United States dropped dramatically (replaced by heroin from Colombia).

United Wa State Army. Until 1989 another formidable private army in the Golden Triangle served the Burmese Communist Party (BCP). The BCP force had in the past received support from the People's Republic of China. After Beijing cut off this aid in order to improve relations with Burma, the BCP, following a long-established precedent in the region, went into the opium business. The BCP controlled much of the poppy-producing area and received opium as a form of tax and tribute from local farmers, which it then refined into heroin in its own laboratories.

In 1989 its ethnic rank-and-file Wa tribesmen—fierce warriors whose ancestors were headhunters—rebelled, and the BCP folded as an armed force (Haley 1990). Most Wa political groups reached an accommodation with the Myanmar ruling junta, while one faction of the Wa organized as the United Wa State Army (UWSA). Headquartered on the border of China's Yunnan Province, the UWSA uses heroin—and more recently methamphetamine—trafficking as a means of funding efforts against Burmese control (Witkin and Griffin 1994). There are nearly one million Wa who straddle the border between Myanmar and China, and the UWSA has an estimated strength of 15,000 to 20,000 men, well armed with ground-to-air missiles and modern communications equipment. In 1997, a Myanmar military patrol of thirty men stumbled onto a Wa drug caravan smuggling methamphetamine into Thailand and was wiped out. For the Wa, profits from methamphetamine production and smuggling have surpassed heroin. Ironically, the Wa routinely execute anyone caught dealing heroin for local use (Wren 1998b). "Since the surrender of the SUA/MTA, the UWSA has reigned supreme in narcotics production in Burma," the world's largest producer of heroin (NNICC 1998: 50).

Thailand. Whatever its source, Southeast Asian opium in the form of morphine base or of almost pure heroin is usually brokered in Thailand, which has modern communications and transportation systems. A nation of 50 million people, Thailand is almost as large as France. A staunch anticommunist ally of the United States, Thailand sent troops to fight alongside American soldiers in Korea and Vietnam. In addition to its role in drug trafficking, Thailand, with an estimated 50,000 active brothels, has a reputation of being the "world's biggest whorehouse" (Schmetzer 1991c). Thailand is also a major consumer of methamphetamine smuggled in from Myanmar (Mydans 2003). In 1991 a military coup—one of seventeen since 1932—overthrew the democratically elected Thai government.

"In Southeast Asia, not only did the British and French opium monopolies create massive addict populations, but they also inadvertently formed a smuggling network that was crucial to the post-World War II heroin epidemic. Although the colonial administrations reaped huge profits, they never became involved in the drug's distribution and sale. That work was left to each colony's licensed opium merchant. Invariably they were Chinese" (Posner 1988: 66).

Bangkok has a large population of Thai-born Chinese, called *Haw,* who are known by Thai names but maintain close ties with compatriots in Hong Kong, Yunnan

Province,[7] Amsterdam, and British Columbia. From Bangkok, Chinese criminal organizations have flooded their China white into major cities of Europe, Canada, and the United States. At the center of much of this drug trafficking are the *triads*.

Triads.   Secret societies have a long history in China, some dating back to the beginning of the common era (Fong 1981; Chin 1990). An important part of these societies are the triads and their American offshoots—tongs and Chinatown gangs. They draw their strength from the unique cultural dynamics of Chinese society in which loyalty to family and friends is a moral imperative (J. Liu et al. 1998). "Chinese are born into a hierarchically organized society, *guanxi,* in which they never see themselves or others as free individuals, but as bound to others in an ever expanding web of social relations having mutual obligate bonds of varying strength" (W. Myers 1995: 3).

In this cultural setting, notes Willard Myers (1995), law is marginalized, relegated to a position well below mediative mechanisms within a particularistic social order of human relationships. These cultural manifestations, while not ipso facto criminal, facilitate criminal organization. Of particular interest are persons of Cantonese and Fukienese heritage,[8] who as immigrants throughout the world were subjected to pernicious discrimination to which they responded by relying on cultural attributes that provided great advantages in business, both legal and illegal. And *guanxi* is global, providing a dynamic for international business, both legal and illegal. The triad phenomenon is a natural extension of these cultural attributes.

The term *triad* refers to the Chinese societies' common symbol: an equilateral triangle representing the three basic Chinese concepts of heaven, earth, and man. These groups, based in Hong Kong and Taiwan, engage in highly ritualized dress and behavior—secret hand signs, passwords, and blood oaths are used in elaborate initiation ceremonies (Carter 1991b).

The triad phenomenon is believed to have originated in opposition to the Ch'ing dynasty established by the conquering Manchus in 1644 (Fong 1981). The Ch'ing dynasty ended in 1911 with the success of Dr. Sun Yat-sen (1866–1925), who had been a triad member. Many triad members turned to criminal activities: gambling, loan-sharking, extortion, and trafficking in opium from the Golden Triangle of Southeast Asia. This trade was strengthened considerably by the activities of Chinese Nationalist forces in the Golden Triangle. Chiang Kai-shek, himself a triad member, is reputed to have used triads in his war against the Communists and labor unions. Triads were suppressed with a great deal

---

[7]Because it is located next to the Golden Triangle, China's Yunnan ("south of the clouds") province, with a population that includes twenty of the country's minority groups, has been a center for drug trafficking. High-quality heroin passes easily over borders that were opened for trade more than a decade ago, supported by rampant corruption among the police and other officials. The traffickers are well armed and gunfights are frequent, and the army has been used extensively to combat the drug gangs (Tyler 1995a).

[8]Competition between members of these two groups, in both licit and illicit spheres, has led to violence in a number of American cities (W. Myers 1995).

of violence on the mainland by Mao Tse-Tung when his Communist forces defeated Chiang's Nationalist Army in 1947. Triad members who fled to Taiwan with Chiang Kai-shek were tightly controlled by the Kuomintang, the Nationalist Party, and were unable to expand their criminal operations on the island (Chin 1990).

Thousands of other triad members fled into the British colony of Hong Kong, which already had locally organized triads that dated back to the early twentieth century. The indigenous Hong Kong triads began as guilds and benevolent societies. They extended into criminal activities and actively collaborated with the Japanese during Japan's World War II occupation of the colony. In the postwar era, they emerged as powerful criminal societies (Chin 1995).

The drug-trafficking triads expanded their operations during the Vietnam War, when thousands of GIs were attracted to the potent heroin of Southeast Asia. When the Americans withdrew from Vietnam, the triads followed the market and internationalized their drug operations. Since many soldiers were stationed in Europe, a major triad marketplace developed there, with operations headquartered in Amsterdam.

Heroin manufactured in the Golden Triangle is smuggled into China's Yunnan Province and transported eastward to the coast and beyond. It is also smuggled through the Laos People's Democratic Republic and Vietnam into the Guanxi Autonomous Region and Guangdong Province of China. Other important transit routes bring heroin from the Golden Triangle to major cities on the southeast Asian peninsula, where it is to be sold on the illicit markets there or transported to other parts of the world.

The Golden Crescent

The Golden Crescent of Southwest Asia includes parts of Iran, Afghanistan, and Pakistan (see Figure 11.3). The region has limestone-rich soil, a climate and altitude ideal for poppy cultivation, and, like the Golden Triangle, a ready abundance of cheap labor for the labor-intensive production of opium. In Pakistan the typical poppy farmer lives in semiautonomous northern tribal areas outside the direct control of the central government in Islamabad. The Pakistani authorities have little control in these areas and must appeal to tribal leaders to move against the region's dozens of illegal processing laboratories. In northwest Pakistan's Karakoram Mountains, 1 acre of poppies yields about a dozen kilos of opium gum; 10 kilos of opium gum can be converted into 1 kilo of base morphine. The wholesaling is accomplished in lawless border towns such as Landi Kotal, which is about three miles from the Afghan border.

Afghan opium is processed into heroin in local laboratories or shipped—generally aboard donkeys, but sometimes aboard jeeps bought with U.S. funds—to processing plants in Pakistan (Burns 1990; NNICC 1998). Much of the heroin trade in and from Pakistan is controlled by a consortium of three Quetta-based families, referred to as the Quetta Alliance. Quetta, a border city of more than 1 million persons, is filled with Afghan refugees, poverty, and drug addicts.

Although these groups appear to be independent, they cooperate with each other when such cooperation is to their mutual benefit. Extensive corruption efforts shield them

Though Pakistani officials have little control in the prevention of drug exportation, they do manage to seize some heroin destined for the United States. Most heroin trade in Pakistan is controlled by the Quetta Alliance.

© Francoise de Mulder/CORBIS

from law enforcement, and many family members hold provincial-level political offices (NNICC 1998).

Unlike Southeast Asia, Afghanistan's rugged terrain and the martial tradition of its tribes kept it free of colonialism. Western interest in this nation of about 27 million was limited until the Soviet invasion. The Pashtuns, a tribal group that populates Pakistan's Northwest Frontier Province, make up about 40 percent of the inhabitants of Afghanistan. The border dividing Pashtuns in Pakistan from their tribal brethren in Afghanistan was drawn by the British more than a century ago, and is generally ignored—there are few border patrols in the region (Ahmed-Ullah 2001). Known as exceptional warriors, the Pashtuns are also the major drug traffickers in the region. Along with other Islamic groups, many Pashtuns fought a guerrilla war against the Soviet-backed regime in Kabul. In late 1979, the Soviets rolled their tanks into the opium provinces of Afghanistan. "Suddenly, the tribes which had spent the last decade maneuvering their heavily armed drug caravans past the increasingly troublesome patrols of the U.S. Drug Enforcement Administration's agents found themselves flung into the limelight as the new anti-communist 'crusaders.' " (Levins 1980: 201).

U.S. anti-Soviet efforts in Afghanistan were orchestrated by the CIA, which adopted a benign attitude toward drug trafficking. As the conflict wound down, the United States became increasingly concerned with rebel drug activity. Opium is the cash crop that has traditionally enabled feuding tribes in Afghanistan and in Pakistan's Northwest Frontier Province to purchase weapons and ammunition. In 1991, U.S. officials announced that they would no longer provide military assistance to Afghan rebels. Prior to its disintegration, the Soviet Union also agreed to stop aiding the Afghan government. The following year, *mujahedin* forces entered Kabul without encountering any resistance, and the war officially ended, but warfare between rebel groups continued, supported by heroin. By

1998, the Islamic fundamentalist Taliban movement, made up primarily of Pashtuns, controlled most of the country, and Afghanistan became one of the world's largest producers of heroin (Wren 1998c; U.S. Department of State 1998). Until 2001, the country was the world's second largest grower of the opium poppy, producing about one-third of the heroin entering the United States, and about 80 percent of the heroin consumed in Europe. Despite the severe economic ramifications, in 2001, the Taliban leadership banned the growing of poppies as a sin against the teachings of Islam. Compliance was immediate and thorough (Bearak 2000). However, a United Nations report offered a cynical explanation for the new policy: The Taliban were stockpiling opium and heroin, suggesting that production was halted to keep heroin prices from plummeting (Lederer 2001a).

In any event, in the wake of the September 11, 2001, terrorist attacks and U.S. military action, the Taliban government told farmers they were once again free to grow the opium poppy. With the collapse of the Taliban, the poppy once again became an indispensable crop in parts of Afghanistan: "There is no other way to survive," notes one farmer. A pound of raw opium can be sold for $100 or more, more than one hundred times what fruits and vegetables will bring. By the end of 2002, Afghanistan was again the world's leader in opium production (Torriero 2002; Waldman 2002; Rohde 2002).

The United States has pressured Pakistan to move against poppy cultivation, but the infusion of hundreds of thousands of Afghan tribesmen into Pakistan has made this difficult, if not impossible. Tribesmen in Pakistan are now armed with rocket-propelled grenade launchers and automatic weapons to protect miles of poppy plants, pledging to die fighting rather than give up their best cash crop. Furthermore, there is a growing domestic market for heroin in Pakistan: While most poppies now grow on the Afghan side of the border and are shipped to Europe and America in the form of powdered heroin, Pakistan's heroin-smoking population has grown, with estimates as high as 1 million users.

Iran has been fighting a deadly battle against heavily armed Afghan traffickers and has lost several thousand men in the effort. The traffickers, equipped with anti-aircraft missiles, night-vision goggles, and satellite telephones, are better armed than their opponents in Iranian law enforcement (Moore 2001). And the entry of so much heroin into the country has caused a serious domestic drug abuse problem in Iran (Barraclough 1999). Turkey, which serves as a land bridge to markets in the West for heroin from the Golden Crescent, is fighting a similar battle. Kurdish separatists and Turkish criminal groups (*babas*) have important connections in the Western drug market. They move heroin across the highways of Turkey and into Europe where other criminal organizations, in particular Mafia and Camorra groups, distribute the drug throughout the European market. Morphine base is frequently transported by ship through the Suez Canal into Turkey.

The nations of Central Asia that surround Afghanistan, such as Tajikistan, have a predominantly young, rapidly growing and poverty-stricken population. Add heroin to this mix, and you get an expanding addict population and drug organizations taking advantage of porous borders and easily bribed officials. "The drug business sustains up to 50 percent of the Tajik economy and props up its currency, if only because of the great number of people it employs" (Orth 2002: 168). For many of the warlords who are part of the post-Taliban Afghan government, heroin was the way they supported their armed followers. Islamic terrorist groups also operate in this region, and heroin provides them with an invaluable source of funds. And the corruption-drug connection reaches into the highest ranks of the Russian military (Orth 2002).

For a while, the Soviet invasion disrupted normal drug-trade routes into Iran and Turkey. As a result, morphine base was moved out of Afghanistan into Pakistan through the Khyber Pass and into the port city of Karachi or on to Delhi or Bombay. India, with borders on both the Golden Triangle and the Golden Crescent, has become a major transshipment center for heroin entering Europe and the United States. In addition to receiving heroin, Indian criminal groups ship the precursor chemical acetic anhydride to drug cartels in Afghanistan, Pakistan, and Burma/Myanmar (Hazarika 1993).

Balkan overland routes, disrupted by war in the former Yugoslavia, have now shifted to Bulgaria, Romania, and Czechoslovakia. Countries of Eastern Europe, Poland in particular, whose police forces are underfunded, have become important drug transshipment points (Bonner 1995).

Nigeria

Nigerian involvement in international drug trafficking is remarkable—the country produces no precursor chemicals or drugs, and it is not contiguous to major drug producer or consumer states (P. Williams 1995). But Nigeria is a major trafficking hub and the base for criminal organizations responsible for a significant amount of heroin used in the United States. In addition to drugs, these organizations are involved in collateral activities such as money laundering, document, immigration, and financial fraud (U.S. Department of State 1999). Nigeria has become a major transshipment center for Golden Crescent heroin and cocaine, primarily from Brazil. Organized along familial and tribal lines, high-level traffickers seldom deal with outsiders (NNICC 1998). Nigerian couriers based in Lagos travel to Pakistan to obtain heroin or to Brazil to obtain cocaine, then continue on commercial flights to their final destinations; or they return to Nigeria to repackage the drugs into smaller amounts for smuggling throughout the world. Nigerian students or poor residents of Lagos are used as mules. They receive a few thousand dollars a trip for bringing in 100 grams, usually by swallowing drug-filled condoms.

At home, most Nigerians earn about $300 a year, and the country is infamous for its high level of official corruption—false birth certificates and passports are easy to obtain (M. Jones 1993). In the capital of Lagos, multimillionaire drug barons rule vast organizations, at the bottom of which are the drug couriers, who take most of the actual risks (Treaster 1992). In 1991 a Nigerian-Chicago connection was uncovered that used the Philippines as a transshipment point. Asian women transported heroin from Bangkok to Manila, where Caucasian-American women received the drugs for transportation to the United States. This elaborate setup was designed to reduce the suspicion that would accompany Asian women flying from Thailand to the United States. Couriers carried between 4.5 and 6.5 pounds of heroin and were paid $20,000 plus expenses (Schmetzer 1991a).

In 1996, thirty-four persons in three countries were arrested for being part of a Nigerian drug ring that had been in business for 15 years. The group's leader, known as "the Policeman" for his ability to impose discipline, was living in Bangkok. While members operated out of London, Amsterdam, Pakistan, New York, and Detroit, most of those arrested were in Chicago where the group was headquartered at an African women's boutique in the Edgewater neighborhood on the city's North Side. Heroin phone orders were delivered to Chicago by female couriers who usually traveled with children from Bangkok, taking circuitous routes through Europe, Guatemala, and finally Mexico, before reaching the United States (J. O'Brien 1996; A. Martin and O'Brien 1996).

In 1997, Nigerian organizations began using express mail services with shipments routed through European countries. Drugs can be mailed anonymously to fictitious persons or mail drops, which decreases the risk and cost associated with couriers. According to the Drug Enforcement Administration, Nigerians dominate the shipment of Southeast Asian heroin into the United States and Latin American cocaine into Europe (Dellios 1998). Nigerian wholesalers have developed close ties to street gangs in a number of urban areas, especially those with established Nigerian communities, particularly Chicago, where they have ties to the notorious Gangster Disciples (discussed below) (NNICC 1998).

Domestic Drug Trafficking

The enormous profits that accrue in the drug business are part of a criminal underworld where violence is always an attendant reality. Drug transactions must be accomplished without recourse to the formal mechanisms of dispute resolution that are usually available in the world of legitimate business. This reality leads to the creation of private mechanisms of enforcement. The drug world is filled with heavily armed and dangerous persons in the employ of the larger cartels, although even street-level operatives are often armed. These private resources for violence serve to limit market entry, to ward off competitors and predatory criminals, and to maintain internal discipline and security within an organization.

In several areas of the country, particularly in New York City and Los Angeles, the relatively stable neighborhood criminal organizations that dominated the heroin and cocaine trade found new competitors: youthful crack dealers. Entry into the crack trade requires only a small investment: An ounce of cocaine converts to 2,500 milligrams of crack. Street gangs or groups of friends and relatives have entered the market, often resulting in competition that touches off explosive violence involving the use of high-powered handguns and automatic weapons.

Jeffrey Fagan and Ko-Lin Chin state that this violence was to be expected for two reasons:

> First, crack selling was concentrated in neighborhoods where social controls had been weakened by intensified social and economic dislocations in the decade preceding the emergence of crack. Second, the rapid development of new drug-selling

---

Barbaric Violence, Rational Violence

"Regular displays of violence are essential for preventing rip-offs by colleagues, customers, and professional holdup artists. Indeed, upward mobility in the underground economy of the street-dealing world requires a systematic and effective use of violence against one's colleagues, one's neighbors, and, to a certain extent, against oneself. Behavior that appears irrationally violent, 'barbaric,' and ultimately self-destructive to the outsider, can be reinterpreted according to the logic of the underground economy as judicious public relations and long-term investment in one's 'human capital development' " (Bourgois 1995: 24).

---

groups following the introduction of crack brought with it competition. Accordingly, violence within new selling groups *internally* to maintain control and violence *externally* to maintain selling territory (product quality) was more likely to characterize the unstable crack markets than the more established drug markets and distribution systems. (1991: 325)

The dramatic drop in homicides during the 1990s has been linked to the decline of crack (Butterfield 1997). In New York City, "in communities that used to have more open-air crack markets than grocery stores, where children grew up dodging crack vials and gunfire, the change from a decade ago is startling. On the surface, crack has disappeared from much of New York, taking with it the ragged and violent vignettes that were a routine part of street life" (Egan 1999c: 1). And the New York experience has been experienced by other major cities that were plagued by the crack epidemic. There was a dramatic change in attitude toward crack, and "crackheads" became community pariahs. The remaining crack market has moved indoors, or dealers use cell phones to arrange sales, typically to users who are considerably older than the adolescents who once made up the core of the crack scene.

Dominicans

The Dominican Republic, with a population of 8 million, occupies about two-thirds of the Caribbean island of Hispaniola, which it shares with Haiti. While the Dominican Republic is not as depressed as Haiti, in the mid-1960s political unrest and economic upheavals caused many residents to seek their fortunes by going north. In New York City, Dominicans who have legally entered the United States number about 350,000; thousands more are illegal aliens. Some of these immigrants, legal and illegal, have entered the drug trade. Known as Dominican-Yorks, the traffickers keep a low profile in the United States, returning their profits to cities in the Dominican Republic such as San Francisco de Macoris, a city conspicuous for its wealth in a country where the per capita income is less than $900 a year (French 1991).

The center of the Dominican wholesale trade in crack is the uptown Manhattan neighborhood of Washington Heights. In recent years, some of the leaders have slipped out of New York and are running operations from their homeland, where corruption is endemic among airport officials and law enforcement. Until 1998, the Dominican Republic refused to extradite its citizens for crimes committed in the United States. In that year, two notorious traffickers were sent to New York, where they were wanted for drug trafficking and murder.

Dominicans have demonstrated the necessary talent for moving large amounts of heroin, crack cocaine, and, more recently, ecstasy at the street level. They purchase heroin and cocaine directly from Asian and Colombian importers, sharing a common language and entrepreneurial values with the latter. Ecstasy is purchased in the Netherlands. Dominicans have apparently applied their well-known skills as tradesmen and merchants to become New York City's top traffickers and have captured markets in Pennsylvania. They also control a significant portion of the cocaine trafficking in New England. Dominicans generally provide top-quality uncut drugs at competitive prices, avoiding the common practice of diluting the product as it passes through the distribution chain. Often operating out of grocery stores, bars, and restaurants in Latino neighborhoods, they employ a variety of marketing gimmicks to move their product. In Philadelphia they sold heroin packets with lottery tickets attached that a winner could use to claim an additional twelve packets. The structure of Dominican drug-trafficking organizations is based on familial or regional loyalties.

Dominicans developed a reputation as reliable dealers who promptly pay their suppliers and avoid violence to muscle in on others or maintain exclusive control of a particular market. Instead, they compete on the basis of efficiency and pricing, allowing them to avoid high-profile violence (Pennsylvania Crime Commission 1990). However, while "early Dominican gangs were known for keen marketing techniques . . . their successors in the 1990s mark out their territories" and use violence to maintain hegemony (Kleinknecht 1996: 260–61). Several Dominican groups have become noted for their excessive violence, both to maintain discipline and to deal with competitors. In one instance, "The Company," a Brooklyn-based gang, even lured a police officer to his death (Wren 1998c).

Dominicans have come to dominate the middle echelon between the Colombians and the street dealers of cocaine and heroin in the New York City area and into New England (Wren 1998a; Rohter and Krauss 1998b). In part, this is a result of Colombian dissatisfaction with their Mexican counterparts (discussed earlier). By 1995, major Colombian organizations had established themselves in the Dominican Republic to coordinate activities with their Dominican partners. "While the bulk of Colombian cocaine and heroin continues to move through Mexico, the Colombian traffickers have in the last few years come full circle, returning to the Caribbean as a base of operations." And the influence of drug money on the island has been pervasive: "Office buildings, hotels and shopping centers are springing up in Santo Domingo, Santiago, and San Francisco de Macoris—often in the gaudy style that some describe as narcodeco" (Rohter and Krauss 1998a: 6). Police corruption is widespread and often coordinated with law enforcement counterparts in Colombia.

**Colombian Cocaine
via Haiti**

In a two-week period, authorities investigating Haitian drug trafficking have seized nearly 3,000 pounds of cocaine and four ships docked along the Miami River. The seizures resulted from a long-term investigation of trafficking through Haiti, a transshipment point of drugs grown in Colombia and destined for the United States (La Corte 2000).

Drug traffickers take advantage of the fact that the region of Central America and the Caribbean is located between major drug-producing areas and significant illicit drug markets, that there are hundreds of relatively small islands with myriad cays in the Caribbean, and the socioeconomic situation in most of the countries in the region is difficult. The relatively weak institutional and political situation in some of the countries and the large number of political entities in the Caribbean pose challenges to efforts to ensure strategic coordination in the fight against illicit drug trafficking and abuse.

In the Caribbean, a common practice is to air-drop illicit drug consignments into coastal waters and then have them picked up by speedboat. Private vessels, fishing boats, cruisers, and pleasure ships are also increasingly being used in maritime drug trafficking. Because of the increased efforts by the authorities of some countries to combat drug-related crime, drug traffickers have turned to quickly moving their operations to weaker jurisdictions. In addition, illicit drug stockpiling in isolated locations has become a more common practice.

The Dominicans and their Colombian partners have made Haiti, which (along with the Dominican Republic) lies roughly between Colombia and Florida, the fastest growing transit point for cocaine being shipped to the United States. Haiti has proven attractive to the traffickers because it is the poorest country in the hemisphere, making it relatively cheap to find criminal labor and bribe officials. The police had to be created from scratch after the old force was abolished in the wake of the American troop landing in 1994; they have limited training and resources. The Haitian Coast Guard consists of ten boats, only half of which are operating at any given time (Rohter and Krauss 1998a).

Black Drug Organizations

A variety of black criminal groups exist throughout the United States. Some are home grown, such as the Gangster Disciples; others, such as Jamaican posses, are imported. There are important black criminal organizations in the heroin business, particularly in New York, Detroit, Chicago, Philadelphia, and Washington, D.C. While blacks have traditionally been locked out of many activities associated with organized crime (labor racketeering and loan-sharking, for example) because of prejudice, *dope is an equal opportunity employer.* African American criminal groups made important strides in the heroin business when the Vietnam War exposed many black soldiers to the heroin markets of the Golden Triangle—previously, black groups were dependent on organized crime families for their heroin. As a result of their overseas experience, black organizations were able to bypass traditional organized crime and buy directly from suppliers in Thailand. Let us look at one of the more important of these organizations.

Gangster Disciples. The Gangster Disciples (GD) was formed as the result of the 1969 merger of two South Side gangs. In 1974, leadership was assumed by Larry Hoover, born in Jackson, Mississippi, in 1951. This, despite a 1973 conviction for planning and ordering the murder of a man who had held up a GD drug house. Hoover has been incarcerated ever since, serving a 150-year sentence. Nevertheless, GDs are active in selling cocaine and heroin throughout Chicago, a number of suburban areas, and in several states, including Wisconsin, Indiana, Missouri, Oklahoma, and Georgia. They also extort money from other drug dealers for the right to sell in areas in which the GDs assert control. Independent dealers who have achieved a level of success are typically approached by GD representatives and told to choose from three alternatives: (1) join the Gangster Disciples; (2) stop selling drugs; or (3) die.

Lower-ranking members who actually sell the drugs at the retail level get to enjoy most of the profit they make; they do not necessarily share it with higher-ranking members or the organization as a whole. Instead, the hierarchy makes considerable income from wholesaling drugs to these members. As noted several times earlier, a criminal organization can exhibit a formal structure, while its economic activities may actually involve small firms or partnerships among members and include nonmember associates—the formal structure is not necessarily the same as the economic structure. However, the Gangster Disciples' size—about 6,000 members—requires a more corporate-like structure. Business activities—primarily drug trafficking—are closely related to their structure. Thus, the GDs have been able to pool drug profits, street taxes, and membership dues to establish and operate legitimate businesses, including apartment buildings, sometimes for the purpose of money laundering and to serve as centers for illegal operations.

Political involvement by the Gangster Disciples has been extensive, at least in part to aid in the parole release efforts of their imprisoned leader. Under the name of "21st Century VOTE," they engaged in voter registration drives and have supported unsuccessful candidates for the city council. Nevertheless, in 1995, Hoover and thirty-eight GDs were named in an indictment charging 149 counts of criminal conduct involving their drug-trafficking operations. Authorities devised a prison visitor's pass with a hidden transmitter, and Hoover was recorded passing orders to lieutenants who visited him at the Vienna Correctional Center. One of those convicted was a Chicago police officer who had been assigned to the Gang Crimes Unit. During the GD trials it was revealed that the offices of 21st Century VOTE served as a drop-off site for street taxes collected by gang members. In 1997, Hoover was convicted of forty counts of drug trafficking and given six additional life sentences (O'Connor 1997). In 1999, three GD officers who had vied for gang leadership were sentenced to life imprisonment for supervising a multimillion-dollar cocaine operation (O'Connor 1999).

As a result of the imprisonment or indictment of virtually its entire hierarchy, the gang is having difficulties maintaining discipline and thwarting encroachments by rival groups. Street taxes often go unpaid/uncollected, and since the 1995 indictments, several members have been killed by other GD members or rival gangs selling drugs where the GDs claim hegemony.

Street-Level Drug Business

Below the wholesale level, cocaine or heroin is an easy-entry business, requiring only a source and funds. Any variety of groups can come together to deal heroin, such as street gangs in many urban areas. Jerome Skolnick and his colleagues (1990) distinguish be-

Dr. Dealer

The 48-year-old physician set up a pain management practice in Portsmith, Ohio. At about the same time, police noticed a startling rise in drug-related crime. Undercover agents were dispatched to the pain clinic. With little or no physical examination, each paid $200 and was given a prescription for OxyContin, the powerful synthetic opiate. In a subsequent raid, agents found almost $500,000 in cash and passbooks for offshore accounts ("The 'Poor Man's Heroin'" 2001).

tween two types of street gangs. *Cultural gangs* are strongly grounded in a neighborhood identity; members may be involved in crime, including drug trafficking. *Entrepreneurial gangs* are organized for the express purpose of distributing drugs. The first type is maintained by loyalty to the gang and the neighborhood; the second is based on continuing economic opportunity. In the cultural gang, involvement in drug use and dealing can serve as membership requirements; stature in the group may be linked to success in the drug trade. Unlike the entrepreneurial gangs, these groups define themselves in terms of brotherhood, are highly protective of their turf, and engage in nonutilitarian violence with other gangs. While the cultural gang is not organized expressly to sell drugs, "the gang organization facilitates that activity" (1990: 7). However, the low level of cohesiveness, loose organization, high member turnover, and unstable leadership typical of most street gangs mitigate against their being effective drug entrepreneurs (Klein, Maxson, and Cunningham 1991). "Because youth [*cultural*] gangs generally are involved only in street-level drug distribution, the proceeds of which typically are used for personal consumption, providing legitimate ways of earning money may be an effective intervention strategy. Suppression approaches (formal and informal social control procedures) may be more effective with drug [*entrepreneurial*] gangs" (Howell and Gleason 1999: 9).

Some street gangs have also been expanding their organizations and drug markets to other states. Los Angeles gangs, in particular the Crips, have moved into Seattle, Denver, Minneapolis, Oklahoma City, St. Louis, and Kansas City as well as smaller cities throughout California. Along with their smaller rivals, the Bloods, they moved east with startling speed: "Neither gang is rigidly hierarchical. Both are broken up into loosely affiliated neighborhood groups called 'sets,' each with 30 to 100 members. Many gang members initially left Southern California to evade police. Others simply expanded the reach of crack by setting up branch operations in places where they visited friends or family members and discovered that the market was ripe" (Witkin 1991: 51). In 1992, its was reported that the Crips, or perhaps older former members of the gang, had developed direct ties with the Medellín cartel ("FBI Says Los Angeles Gang Has Drug Cartel Ties" 1992).

Thomas Mieczkowski (1986) studied the activities of a loosely organized retail heroin group in Detroit—The Young Boys, Inc. At the center of their activities is a crew boss, who receives his supply of heroin from a drug-syndicate lieutenant. The *crew boss* gives a consignment of heroin to each of his seven to twenty *runners,* young (16 to 23 years old) African American males whom he recruits. Afterward, each runner takes his station on a street adjacent to a public roadway to facilitate purchases from vehicles. To avoid rip-offs and robberies, each crew is guarded by armed men, including the crew boss himself. Runners reported earning about $160 for a 10 1/2 hour workday.

Participants in these drug networks tend to be the most serious drug delinquents, who are frequently hired by adult or older adolescent street drug sellers as runners. Loosely organized into crews of three to twelve, each boy generally handles small quantities of drugs—for example, two or three packets or bags of heroin. They receive these units "on credit," "up front," or "on loan" from a supplier and are expected to return about 50 to 70 percent of the drug's street value.

In addition to distributing drugs, these youngsters may act as lookouts, recruit customers, and guard street sellers from customer-robbers. They typically are users of marijuana and cocaine, but not heroin. Moreover, in some cities, dealers and suppliers prefer to hire distributors who do not "get high" during an operation. But their employment as runners is not generally steady; it is interspersed with other crimes including robbery, burglary, and theft.

A relatively small number of youngsters who sell drugs develop excellent entrepreneurial skills. Their older contacts come to trust them, and they parlay this trust to advance in the drug business. By the time they are 18 or 19 they can have several years of experience in drug sales, be bosses of their own crews, and handle more than $500,000 a year. (Chaiken and Johnson 1988: 12)

The net profits in heroin for most participants at the street level, however, are rather modest. While dealers typically work long hours and subject themselves to substantial risk of violence and incarceration, their incomes generally range from $1,000 to $2,000 a month. Less successful participants eke out a living that rivals minimum wage. Many are involved to support their own drug habits, to supplement earnings from legitimate employment, or both.

The sale of cocaine and crack is carried out by thousands of small-time operators who may dominate particular local markets—a public housing complex, city blocks, or simply street corners. Control is exercised through violence. Income is modest considering the dangers of death or imprisonment, and the sellers often work for less than minimum wage—for example, $30 a day for acting as a lookout, or 50 cents for each vial of crack sold. They might earn $100 to $200 per week for long hours under unpleasant conditions without unemployment compensation, medical insurance, or any of the usual benefits of legitimate employment. A study in Washington, D.C., found that a majority of drug sellers in the sample did not sell drugs on a daily basis. Their median annual income was about $10,000; those who sold daily earned about $3,600 monthly (Reuter, MacCoun, and Murphy 1990).

The domestic business of cocaine requires only a connection to a Colombian source and sufficient financing to initiate the first buy. Any variety of persons several steps removed from the Colombian source are involved in the domestic cocaine business. Because the cocaine clientele is traditionally at least middle income, distributors likewise tend to come from the (otherwise) respectable middle class. The popularity of crack, however, dramatically altered the drug market at the consumer level, in particular the age of many retailers. James Inciardi and Anne Pottieger, experienced drug researchers, were shocked by the youthfulness of crack dealers compared with those involved in the heroin business: "While both patterns ensnare youth in their formative years, crack dealers are astonishingly more involved in a drug-crime lifestyle at an alarmingly younger age" (1991: 269).

At the retail level, sellers frequently deal several different drugs. Heroin dealers added cocaine to their portfolio when that substance started becoming popular at the end of the 1970s, and more recently crack dealers have reflected a shift in the market by also selling heroin (Chitwood, Comerford, and Weatherby 1998). It is common for long-term users of cocaine to use a depressant to "mellow out." Alcohol is frequently used for this purpose, but cocaine users with access to it prefer heroin.

Marcia Chaiken and Bruce Johnson state that small drug sales are common among adult users and that some adolescents distribute drugs without being involved in more serious criminal activity. They sell drugs to adolescent friends and relatives less than once a month to support their own drug use, and "most of these adolescents do not consider these activities 'serious' crimes" (1988: 10). They rarely have contact with criminal justice agencies: "Since these youths conceal their illicit behavior from most adults, and are likely to participate in many conventional activities with children their age, criminal justice practitioners can take little direct action to prevent occasional adolescent sellers from distributing drugs and recruiting new users" (1988: 11).

The Street-Level Drug Market. Like more conventional consumer items, drugs sold at the street level often carry a name and/or logo to promote "brand name" loyalty. "Among the more important marketing techniques are attractive packaging (stamps), name recognition (brand names), and consumer involvement and camaraderie around drug-consuming activities (product name contests). Moreover, product names . . . reflect strong, positive attributes and notions of success, strength, power, excitement, and wealth, encourage consumers to make symbolic connections with these products" (Waterston 1993: 117).

As in other stages of the drug trade, the street-level business is filled with violence. Paul Goldstein reports that violence in the drug trade is sometimes the result of brand deception:

> Dealers mark an inferior quality heroin with a currently popular brand name. Users purchase the good heroin, use it, then repackage the bag with milk sugar for resale. The popular brand is purchased, the bag is "tapped," and further diluted for resale.
>
> These practices get the real dealers of the popular brand very upset. Their heroin starts to get a bad reputation on the streets and they lose sales. Purchasers of the phony bags may accost the real dealers, complaining about the poor quality and demanding their money back. The real dealers then seek out the purveyors of the phony bags. Threats, assaults, and/or homicides may ensue. (1985: 497)

In the drug business, Goldstein (1985) notes, norm violations—for example, a street-level dealer failing to return sufficient money to his superior in a drug network—often result in violence. Violence almost invariably results from the robbery of a drug dealer. No dealer who wishes to remain in the business can allow himself to be robbed without exacting vengeance. Death is also the punishment for a norm violation that, although serious, is nevertheless widespread in the drug business: informing. Informing may be the means of eliminating competition or exacting vengeance for the sale of poor-quality dope, but more often, informing results from an attempt to gain leniency from the criminal justice system.

Occasionally, distinct patterns of injury can be recognized. For example, drug runners—teenagers who carry drugs and money between sellers and buyers—are seen in emergency rooms with gunshot wounds to the legs and knees. A more vicious drug-related injury emerged in the western part of the United States. In this injury, known as "pithing," the victim's spinal cord is cut, and he or she is left alive but paraplegic (De La Rosa, Lambert, and Gropper 1990).

Domestic Production of Marijuana, Methamphetamine, and Other Drugs

The business of drugs involves substances other than cocaine and heroin. Most of these substances, such as PCP, LSD, methamphetamine, and barbiturates, are produced in domestic laboratories; marijuana is also grown in the United States. The persons and groups that manufacture and traffic in these substances are quite varied. They fit into no particular ethnic pattern—white, rural, working- and middle-class persons are as likely to be involved as any identifiable racial or ethnic group. For example, there is little or no pattern to marijuana trafficking in the United States. It is an easy-entry business, and a number of relatives, friendship groups, and former military veterans have come together to "do marijuana."

In rugged rural western North Carolina, for example, the same county that historically produced moonshine whiskey now has extensive marijuana cultivation. Patches of marijuana can be grown undetected in remote areas, where it blends with crops or vegetation. For the farmer of this illicit crop, a single plant will bring hundreds if not thousands of dollars on the street. During the July 2002 harvesting season, law enforcement officers seized more than 2,000 plants with an estimated street value of $4 million (Cantrell 2002).

Less than a dozen chemists are believed to be manufacturing nearly all of the LSD available in the United States. Some have probably been operating since the 1960s. LSD manufacturers and traffickers can be separated into two groups. The first, located in Northern California, is composed of chemists (commonly referred to as "cooks") and traffickers who work together in close association; typically, they are major producers capable of distributing LSD nationwide. The second group is made up of independent producers who, operating on a comparatively limited scale, can be found throughout the country; their production is intended for local consumption (Drug Enforcement Administration n.d.a).

LSD chemists and top-echelon traffickers form an insiders' fraternity of sorts. They have remained at large because there are so few of them. Their exclusivity is not surprising given that LSD synthesis is a difficult process to master. Although cooks need not be formally trained chemists, they must adhere to precise and complex production procedures. In instances where the cook is not a chemist, the production recipe most likely was passed on by personal instruction from a formally trained chemist. At the highest levels of the traffic, where LSD crystal is purchased in gram or multigram quantities from wholesale sources of supply, it rarely is diluted with adulterants, a common practice with cocaine, heroin, and other illicit drugs. However, to prepare the crystal for production in retail dosage units, it must be diluted with binding agents or dissolved and diluted in liquids. The dilution of LSD crystal typically follows a standard, predetermined recipe to ensure uniformity of the final product. Excessive dilution yields less potent dosage units that soon become unmarketable (Drug Enforcement Administration n.d.a).

Production of methamphetamine has blossomed in parts of rural America. "In Texas, most of the labs are located in rural areas and are reportedly set up and run by local residents. The predominant pattern for methamphetamine lab operations in the plains of West Texas and in heavily wooded East Texas is similar to the operation of small scale production and distribution of moonshine whiskey during the prohibition era: individually owned and operated, with networks of local users, but also with connections for export to urban population centers" (Spence 1989: 6). In Arkansas, outlaw chemists have been stealing ammonia used for fertilizer for conversion to methamphetamine using the "Nazi method," so called because German troops used anhydrous ammonia in World War II (Parker 1999). In 2002, in the state of Washington's rural Snohomish County, there were more methamphetamine lab seizures than in New York, Pennsylvania, and New England combined (Egan 2002).

The number of meth labs seized in North Carolina has increased dramatically, from 18 in 2000, to 34 in 2001, and 48 in the first six months of 2002. About half of these seizures have been in the rural mountain area in the western part of the state. Similar activity has been reported in rural communities in Tennessee and Georgia. While inexpensive for dealers to set up, the cost to the taxpayers for cleanup ranges from $2,000 to $20,000 per lab and is accomplished by crews wearing hazardous material suits for protection from fumes and deadly liquids. The suits, which range in cost from $700 to $2,000, frequently need to be disposed of after one use (Brevorka 2002).

As noted earlier, in recent years there has been an increase in the involvement of Mexican gangs operating in Southern California, where they produce methamphetamine in unpopulated desert areas. "Once the domain of outlaw biker gangs, the nation's meth trade has been taken over by Mexican drug families in the rural belt from San Diego County to Redding. Operating from Sinaloa and other states deep inside Mexico, these families oversee teams of cookers dispatched to orchards, cotton fields, chicken ranches, and abandoned dairies north of the border" (Arax and Gorman 1995: 1).

Although the vast majority of MDMA/ecstasy consumed domestically is produced in Europe—primarily the Netherlands and Belgium—a limited number of MDMA labs operate in the United States. In recent years, Israeli crime syndicates, some composed of Russian émigrés associated with Russian organized crime syndicates, have forged relationships with Western European traffickers and gained control over a significant share of the European market. The Israeli syndicates are currently the primary source for U.S. distribution groups.

Overseas ecstasy trafficking organizations smuggle the drug in shipments of 10,000 or more tablets via express mail services, couriers aboard commercial airline flights, or through air freight shipments from several major European cities to cities in the United States. The drug is sold in bulk quantity at the mid-wholesale level in the United States for approximately eight dollars per dosage unit. The retail price of MDMA sold in clubs in the United States is $20 to $30 per dosage unit. Ecstasy traffickers use brand names and logos as marketing tools and to distinguish their product from that of competitors. The logos are produced to coincide with holidays or special events. Among the more popular logos are butterflies, lightning bolts, and four-leaf clovers.

Money Laundering

Drug traffickers operating at the upper levels of the business have a serious problem: what to do with the large amounts of cash the business is continually generating? Ever since Al Capone was imprisoned for income-tax evasion, successful criminals have sought to launder their illegally secured money. Further complicating the problem is that this cash is frequently in small denominations. In some cases "laundering" may simply be an effort to convert the cash into one or more cashier's checks or secure $100 bills so that the sums of money are more easily handled—500 bills weigh about one pound; $1 million in twenties weighs about 100 pounds.

To avoid IRS reporting requirements under the Bank Secrecy Act, transfers of cash to cashier's checks or $100 bills must take place in amounts under $10,000—or through banking officials who for a fee (generally 5 percent) agree not to fill out a Currency Transaction Report (**CTR**). A CTR is required for each deposit, withdrawal, or exchange of currency or monetary instruments in excess of $10,000. It must be submitted to the IRS within 15 days of the transaction. In 1984, tax amendments extended the reporting requirements to anyone who receives more than $10,000 in cash in the course of a trade or business. A **CMIR** (Currency and Monetary Instrument Report) must be filed for cash or certain monetary instruments exceeding $10,000 in value that enter or leave the United States. Federal Reserve regulations require banks to file suspicious-activity reports when they suspect possible criminal wrongdoing in transactions. Attempts to strengthen these regulations have met vigorous opposition from the banking industry (Wahl 1999).

Modern Money Laundering

"Modern financial systems permit criminals to transfer instantly millions of dollars through personal computers and satellite dishes. Money is laundered through currency exchange houses, stock brokerage houses, gold dealers, casinos, automobile dealerships, insurance companies, and trading companies. The use of private banking facilities, offshore banking, free trade zones, wire systems, shell corporations, and trade financing all have the ability to mask illegal activities. The criminal's choice of money laundering vehicles is limited only by his or her creativity" (U.S. Department of State 1999: 3). The international trade in gold has proven to be an excellent vehicle for concealing the source of funds. Drug profits are used to buy gold, which is then legally exported for the jewelry trade and sold, the money returning to the original sources—"laundered" (D. Kaplan 1999).

Currency Exchanges and Smurfs

Currency exchanges (*casas de cambio*) have sprouted up along the Texas-Mexico border. These poorly regulated enterprises accept (illegally) large amounts of cash. They pool many customers' funds into one account and deposit the money in a domestic or foreign bank, keeping records on what is owed to each customer. When a foreign drug trafficker wants to send money to his own country, the *casa* operator wires the funds from the bank to the trafficker's foreign account(s). Even when a U.S. bank completes a CTR, it names the *casa* as the owner of the funds, not the actual owner. In the Houston area, in addition to *casas,* there are *giro* (wire) houses. In general, the *giros* move drug money to Colombia, while the *casas* move Mexican drug money (Webster and McCampbell 1992).

In some schemes money launderers use dozens of persons (called "smurfs") to convert cash into money orders and cashier's checks that do not specify payees or that are made out to fictitious persons. Each transaction is held to less than $10,000 to avoid the need for a CTR. One ring operating out of Forest Hills, New York, employed dozens of persons who used about thirty banks in New York and New Jersey to launder about $100 million a year for the Cali cartel. The checks were pasted between the pages of magazines and shipped to Cali; from there the money was transferred to banks in Panama. In 1989, sixteen persons were indicted when one of the banks became suspicious of the unusual amount of cash transactions and reported them to federal authorities (T. Morgan 1989). "Smurfing" has now been made a federal crime, and increased bank scrutiny has made tellers suspicious of cash transactions just under $10,000. In response, smurfs have reduced transactions to as low as $5,000 and often make dozens of transactions in a day, typically in banks that do not usually have long lines (Walter 1990).

Money laundering has been greatly facilitated by advances in banking technology. It has become increasingly difficult for the government to effectively monitor banking transactions. "An alternative to physically removing money from the country is to deposit the cash, then transfer the funds electronically to other domestic and foreign banks, financial institutions, or securities accounts. Swiss law enforcement officials report that when money is transferred by wire to Switzerland, it seldom comes directly from the country of origin, rather it is 'prewashed' in a third country such as Panama, the Bahamas, the Cayman Islands, or Luxembourg" (Webster and McCampbell 1992: 4). The sheer volume of wire transfers makes accounting difficult—one major bank in New York handles about 40,000 wires each business day.

A customer can instruct his or her personal computer to direct a bank's computer to transfer money from a U.S. account to one in a foreign bank. The bank's computer then tells a banking clearinghouse that assists in the transfer—no person talks to another. While depositing more than $10,000 in cash into an account requires the filing of a CTR, the government receives more than 7 million such reports annually and is hopelessly behind in reviewing them. The daily average volume of American transactions is about $7 billion. On one day it actually amounted to $1.25 trillion (Labaton 1989).

A typical overseas laundering scheme might work like this: A lawyer acting on behalf of a client creates a "paper" (or "boilerplate") company in any one of a number of countries that have strict privacy statutes, for example, Panama, which has over 200,000 companies registered. The funds to be laundered are transferred physically or wired to the company's account in a local bank. The company then transfers the money to the local branch of a large international bank. The paper company is then able to borrow money from the United States (or any other) branch of this bank, using the overseas deposit as security (Walter 1990). Or an employment contract is set up between the launderer and his or her "paper" company for an imaginary service for which payments are made to the launderer. In some cases, the lawyer may also establish a "boilerplate bank"—like the company, this is a shell. Not only does the criminal get his money laundered, but he also earns a tax write-off for the interest on the loan. Under the Bank Secrecy Act, however, wiring or physically transporting cash or other financial instruments out of the country in excess of $10,000 must be reported to the Customs Service. Once the money is out of the United States, however, it may be impossible for the IRS to trace it. Liechtenstein, population 32,000, has 80,000 trust companies and associated banks whose transactions are protected by bank secrecy laws; the tiny principality has been a favorite for money laundering by the Sicilian Mafia, Colombian drug cartels, and Russian organized crime (Tagliabue 2000).

Another method of laundering funds without actually moving cash out of the country involves otherwise legitimate companies that import goods from the United States. Representatives of the Cali cartel in the United States paid for imported goods with dollars that went to the exporters. In return, the participating companies paid the cartel in Colombia at slightly less than the true exchange rate (Krauss and Frantz 1995). Or, instead of shipping currency, drug proceeds are used to purchase easily sold goods such as expensive liquor or electronic products. These are shipped to Colombia and sold at a 20 to 30 percent discount (Sanger 1995).

Our examination of the business of illegal drugs provides a framework for understanding the problems that confront law enforcement officials trying to constrain trafficking in dangerous drugs, the topic of the next chapter.

SUMMARY

Political instability, lack of respect for the rule of law, low standards of living, and good growing conditions for opium poppies or coca have contributed to the rise of international drug trafficking areas. Violence is endemic in the trafficking business, both international and domestic. Colombia is the center of the world's cocaine industry; Colombians used to ship through the Caribbean but now move the drug through Mexico, where payment is one-half the shipment. Mexican traffickers convert home-grown opium to heroin, smuggle Colombian cocaine into the United States, and manufacture and distribute methamphetamine. The Golden Triangle of Southeast Asia is a major opium-producing region, where the sale of drugs has long funded guerrilla warfare in Myanmar; the heroin produced is usually brokered in Thailand. The Golden Crescent of Southwest Asia also has an ideal climate for producing opium, which has provided money for weapons for feuding groups in Afghanistan and Pakistan's Northwest Frontier Province. Nigeria is a major transshipment center for heroin from the Golden Crescent and Brazilian cocaine.

Dominicans dominate the mid-level cocaine business in New York City and New England. Black criminal organizations operate the heroin business in several big cities: New York, Detroit, Chicago, Philadelphia, and Washington, D.C. Street-level drug business is operated mainly by gangs—cultural gangs or entrepreneurial gangs. Surprisingly, profits at the street level are mostly modest; some sellers risk their lives for minimum wage or less. Small, varied groups produce the marijuana, LSD, and methamphetamines in the United States. Rural America is becoming known for drug production, similar to the production of moonshine in Prohibition days.

Drug traffickers use many methods for laundering the large amounts of cash they receive: currency exchanges, smurfs, electronic transfer, and paper companies. The advent of electronic banking is adding to difficulties of tracking illegal profits.

INTERNET CONNECTIONS

Bureau for International Narcotics and Law Enforcement Affairs: www.state.gov/www/global/narcotics_law/sites
International Narcotics Control Board: www.incb.org
Office of National Drug Control Policy: www.whitehousedrugpolicy.gov
United Nations Office for Drug Control and Crime Prevention: www.undcp.org

REVIEW QUESTIONS

1. How did the demise of the French Connection change the drug business?
2. Why has it been so difficult for the Colombian government to wipe out the growing of coca?
3. How are Colombian cartels organized?
4. What is the relationship between Colombian and Mexican drug organizations?
5. How has the popularity of crack cocaine affected the business of drugs?
6. What are the major heroin-producing areas of the world?
7. What is the link between politics and the production of heroin in the Golden Triangle?
8. What has been the traditional role of Chinese organizations in drug trafficking?
9. Why is it impossible to control the production of opium in the Golden Crescent?
10. Why is the drug business typically violent?
11. Why is the street-level drug business an easy-entry enterprise?
12. What is the purpose of money laundering?
13. What are the various ways money laundering can be accomplished?

CHAPTER 12

Drug Laws and Law Enforcement

Drug laws reflect the decision of some persons that other persons who wish to consume certain substances should not be permitted to act on their preferences. Nor should anyone be permitted to satisfy the desires of drug consumers by making and selling the prohibited drug.... [The] most important characteristic of the legal approach to drug use is that these consumptive and commercial activities are being regulated by force.

—*Randy Barnett (1987: 73)*

"The most important precipitating factor in narcotic addiction is degree of access to narcotic drugs" (Ausubel 1980: 4), an assertion supported by research into heroin consumption (Anglin 1988). This is why narcotic usage is higher in the inner city than in the suburbs and why the incidence of narcotic addiction in the United States approached the zero level during World War II. "Thus, no matter how great the cultural attitudinal tolerance for addictive practices is, or how strong individual personality predispositions are, nobody can become addicted to narcotic drugs without access to them. Hence the logic of a law enforcement component in prevention" (Ausubel 1980: 4).

If drug abuse is seen as based on some combination of susceptibility and availability—"that drug abuse occurs when a prone individual is exposed to a high level of availability" (R. Smart 1980: 46)—it follows that a considerable reduction in availability can reduce drug abuse.[1] Availability also involves questions of cost—at some point the cost of purchasing a drug can reduce to near zero its availability to potential abusers, and law enforcement efforts can affect the cost of illegal drugs.

Before we can examine the strategies and techniques used by law enforcement agencies to deal with drug trafficking and to reduce the availability of drugs of abuse, we need to consider three issues that severely constrain law enforcement in general and drug-law enforcement in particular: constitutional limitations, jurisdictional limitations, and corruption.

Constitutional Constraints

Law enforcement in the United States operates under significant constitutional constraints, generally referred to as *due process*—literally meaning the *process that is due* a person before something disadvantageous can be done to him or her. Due process re-

---

[1]That is, of course, if we discount the abuse of alcohol and the possibility/probability that persons unable to secure their preferred drug will switch to alcohol.

strains government from arbitrarily depriving a person of life, liberty, or property. There is an inherent tension between society's desire for security and safety and the value we place on liberty. Herbert Packer (1968) refers to this as a conflict between two conceptual models of criminal justice—crime control and due process. (A *conceptual model* is a way of representing an idea that facilitates discussion and understanding of the reality represented by the model.)

Conceptual Models of Criminal Justice

The **crime control model** "is based on the proposition that the repression of criminal conduct is by far the most important function to be performed by the criminal justice process" (Packer 1968: 158). The stress is on achieving the greatest amount of societal security and safety. Effective crime control requires a high level of efficiency: The system must be able to investigate, apprehend, prosecute, and convict a large proportion of criminal offenders. However, the system must respond to these cases with only limited resources. Consequently, efficiency demands that cases be handled speedily, with a minimum of formality and without time-consuming challenges. This efficiency can be accomplished only by a presumption of guilt: "The supposition is that the screening processes operated by the police and prosecutors are reliable indicators of probable guilt" (1968: 160). To maximize crime control after this screening, the system must move expeditiously to conviction and sentencing. The crime control model is characterized by a high level of confidence in the ability of police and prosecutors to separate the guilty from the innocent. It conflicts with the due process model.

The **due process model** stresses the need for protecting individual freedoms. It assumes that the criminal justice system is deficient and stresses the possibility of error: "People are notoriously poor observers of disturbing events—the more emotion-arousing the context, the greater the possibility that recollection will be incorrect; confessions and admissions by persons in police custody may be induced by physical or psychological coercion so that the police end up hearing what the suspect thinks they want to hear rather than the truth; witnesses may be animated by a bias or interest that no one would trouble to discover except one specially charged with protecting the interests of the accused (as the police are not)" (Packer 1968: 163).

Due process confronts crime control and its need for efficiency and speed with an obstacle course of formalities, technicalities, and civil rights: "Power is always subject to abuse—sometimes subtle, other times, as in the criminal justice process, open and ugly. Precisely because of its potency in subjecting the individual to the coercive power of the state, the criminal justice process must . . . be subjected to controls that prevent it from operating with maximal efficiency" (1968: 166). The due process model requires the system to slow down until it "resembles a factory that has to devote a substantial part of its input to quality control" (p. 165)—these are the equivalent of due process guarantees.

Due process, while it protects individual liberty, also benefits the criminal population by guaranteeing the right to remain silent (Fifth Amendment), the right to counsel (Sixth Amendment), the right to be tried speedily by an impartial jury (Sixth Amendment), and the right to confront witnesses (Sixth Amendment). The Fourth Amendment and the *exclusionary rule* are particularly important for drug-law enforcement.

The Fourth Amendment and the Exclusionary Rule

The Fourth Amendment guarantees that "the right of the people to be secure in their persons, houses, papers and effects, against unreasonable searches and seizures shall not be violated, and no Warrants shall issue, but upon probable cause, supported by Oath or affirmation, and particularly describing the place to be searched, and the persons or things to be seized." In practice, information sufficient to justify a search warrant in drug cases is difficult to obtain; unlike such conventional crimes as robbery and burglary, there is an absence of innocent victims who will report the crime. The exclusionary rule is the court's way of enforcing the Fourth Amendment; it provides that evidence obtained in violation of the Fourth Amendment cannot be entered as evidence in a criminal trial (*Weeks v. United States,* 232 U.S. 383, 1914; *Mapp v. Ohio,* 357 U.S. 643, 1961). Note that there are a number of exceptions that are beyond the scope of this book. The purpose of the exclusionary rule is to control the behavior of law enforcement agents; for example, making drug enforcement efforts that violate the Constitution not worth the effort.

To respond effectively to drug trafficking, law enforcement officials require information about the activities of suspected traffickers. The Fourth Amendment and Title III of the Omnibus Crime Control and Safe Streets Act of 1968 (18 U.S.C. Section 2510–520) place restraints on how the government can secure this information. Thus, in order to surreptitiously intercept conversations by wiretapping telephones or using electronic devices ("bugging"), officials must secure a court order that, like a search warrant, must be

---

Crime Control v. Due Process

The conflict between the crime control and due process models of criminal justice can be conceived of as a zero-sum continuum: Court decisions or legislation that move criminal justice toward one model do so at the expense of the other. Exceptions to the exclusionary rule, for example, while they may increase the efficiency of law enforcement efforts against drug trafficking, also reduce the courts' ability to control police misconduct.

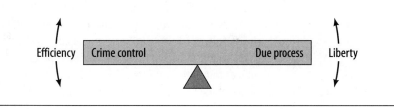

based upon information sufficient to meet the legal standard of probable cause. When an order to intercept electronic communications is secured (generally referred to as a "Title III"), it is quite limited, requires extensive documentation, and demands that the persons intercepted be notified after the order expires. These requirements make electronic surveillance expensive, in terms of personnel hours expended, and difficult to accomplish properly.

The supervision of drug-law enforcement agents is also difficult, because they typically operate covertly or undercover. This means that "legal control over agents is problematic, and the circumstances of arrest are often such that there is a great temptation to perjury, violation of the exclusionary rule, misuse of informants, discretionary dropping, overlooking and altering charges, and other violations of procedural and/or legal rules" (J. Williams, Redlinger, and Manning 1979: 6). The greater the pressure on law enforcement officers "to do something about drugs," the greater the temptation to avoid the significant constraints of due process and take unlawful (though often effective) shortcuts.

Jurisdictional Limitations

Domestic Branches and Levels

The Constitution provides for a form of government in which powers are diffused horizontally and vertically. This is accomplished by three branches—legislative, judicial, and executive—and four levels of government within each branch—federal, state, county, and municipal (Figure 12.1). Although each level of government has responsibilities for responding to drug abuse and drug trafficking, there is little or no coordination among them. Each level responds to the problem of drugs independently of the others. Federalism was part of a deliberate design to help protect us against tyranny; unfortunately, it also provides us with a level of inefficiency that significantly handicaps efforts to curtail drug trafficking.

On the federal level, a host of executive branch agencies (to be examined later), ranging from the military to the Federal Bureau of Investigation, are responsible for combating drug trafficking. A separate federal judicial system is responsible for trying drug cases, and a legislative branch is responsible for enacting drug legislation and allocating funds for federal drug-law enforcement efforts. At the local level are about 20,000 police agencies. Each state has state-level drug-law enforcement agents, a state police or similar agency, and agencies that manage prisons and the parole system (if one exists). County government is usually responsible for prosecuting defendants, and a county-level agency, usually the sheriff, is responsible for operating jails. The county may also have a police department with drug-law enforcement responsibilities under, or independent of, the sheriff's office, and almost every municipality has a police department whose officers enforce drug laws. Each of these levels of government has taxing authority and allocates resources with little or no consultation with other levels of government. The sum total is a degree of inefficiency surpassing that of most democratic nations.

FIGURE 12.1   **Governmental Complexity**

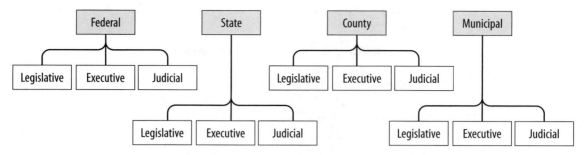

U.S. efforts against drug abuse are also limited by national boundaries: Cocaine and heroin originate where U.S. law enforcement has no jurisdiction. The Bureau of International Narcotics Matters within the Department of State has primary responsibility for coordinating international programs and gaining the cooperation of foreign governments in antidrug efforts. But the bureau has no authority to force governments to act in a manner beneficial to U.S. efforts in dealing with cocaine or heroin. Elaine Sciolino (1988: E3) reports that it "has little influence even within the department [of State]. Foreign Service officers," she states, "readily admit that they try to avoid drug-enforcement assignments because they generally do not result in promotions." The State Department also collects intelligence on policy-level international narcotics developments, while the Central Intelligence Agency collects strategic narcotics intelligence and is responsible for coordinating foreign intelligence on narcotics. The CIA, however, has often protected drug traffickers who have provided useful foreign intelligence. U.S. efforts against drug trafficking are often sacrificed to foreign policy (Sciolino and Engelberg 1988).

International Efforts

In 1988 the International Convention Against Illicit Traffic in Narcotic Drugs and Psychotropic Substances was adopted in Vienna, with two main purposes:

> First, to establish an internationally recognized set of offenses relating to drug trafficking that are to be criminalized under the domestic law of the parties to the convention; and second, to create a framework for international cooperation to enhance the prospect that traffickers and others who profit from trafficking will be brought to justice. . . .
>
> The Convention focuses on the eradication of drugs and drug-producing laboratories; the international transportation of precursor chemicals used to produce illegal drugs; the tracing of laundered drug trade profits back to the drug cartels; and the worldwide extradition of drug criminals so that they can have no safe havens. Significantly, the Convention obligates parties to make money laundering an extraditable offense, to afford the widest measure of international mutual legal assistance in

judicial proceedings, and to cooperate closely to enhance the effectiveness of law enforcement actions to suppress narcotics trafficking and related offenses. (Thornburgh 1989: 59)

In 1994 Bill Clinton signed legislation authorizing the president to provide assistance for the prevention and suppression of international drug trafficking and money laundering. While international law (multinational treaties) provides the basis for eradicating illicit poppy and coca cultivation, adherence to treaties depends on a level of cooperation often sacrificed on the altar of domestic economic and political realities (discussed in Chapter 13). Under treaties, coca- and poppy-producing countries are to limit their cultivation acreage to a level in line with *legitimate* world needs. Strict controls over growers require them to deliver their crops to a government monopoly to prevent diversion to the black market. Crops growing wild are to be destroyed. The price paid by the government, however, is not competitive with that offered by traffickers, and the illegal diversion of coca or opium is the only significant source of cash for many peasant growers, whose standard of living is already marginal. Attempts to substitute other cash crops have met with only limited success, because such programs cannot challenge the reality of the marketplace. As noted in Chapter 11, coca and poppy are grown in regions where governments often have only nominal control.

Jurisdictional limitations, however, can sometimes overcome constitutional restrictions. For example, because the Bill of Rights applies only to actions of the U.S. government, the Fourth Amendment and exclusionary rule do not govern seizures in foreign countries by those nations' police. This holds even when the evidence seized is from U.S. citizens; thus it would be admissible in an American court (Anderson 1992). Furthermore, the Supreme Court has held that constitutional protections do not obtain in U.S. government actions against foreign nationals on foreign soil. In *United States v. Verdugo-Urquidez* (110 S.Ct. 1056 1990), a Mexican national suspected in the 1985 torture-murder of a Drug Enforcement Administration (DEA) agent, was apprehended by Mexican police on a U.S. warrant and turned over to U.S. marshals at the California border. At the request of the DEA, Mexican police, without a warrant, searched the fugitive's two residences and seized incriminating documents, which were turned over to the DEA. The evidence was ruled admissible.

In a 1992 ruling on another case involving the DEA agent's murder, the Supreme Court ruled that kidnapping a suspect on foreign soil does not prevent the suspect from being tried in the United States. In this case (*United States v. Alvarez Machain,* 504 U.S.), Mexican bounty hunters kidnapped a medical doctor and took him to El Paso; they were paid $20,000 and given the right to settle with their families in the United States. The Mexican government reacted with outrage to the decision.

Corruption

In the previous chapter we examined the complex world of drug trafficking and the enormous profits that accrue to many of those involved. The easy availability of large sums of money and the clandestine nature of the business make drug-law enforcement vulnerable to corruption. There are two basic strategies available to law enforcement agencies—reactive and proactive—and many use a combination of both.

Reactive law enforcement has its parallel in fire fighting: Firefighters remain in their fire stations, equipment at the ready, until they get a call for service. Reactive law enforcement encourages citizens to report crimes; the agency will then respond to the reports. This type of law enforcement is used for dealing with such conventional criminal behavior as murder, rape, assault, robbery, burglary, and theft—all likely to be reported to the police. (It should be noted, however, that with the exception of murder and auto theft, studies indicate that most of these crimes are *not* reported to the police.)

Proactive law enforcement requires officers/agents to seek out indications of criminal behavior, always a necessity when the criminal violation includes victim participation (e.g., gambling, prostitution, and drugs). These crimes are often described as consensual or "victimless," although they clearly have victims who are unlikely to report the crime to the police. The problem of corruption is in part tied to the proactive strategy.

Exposure to Temptation

In order to seek out criminal activity in the most efficient manner possible, proactive law enforcement officers must conceal their identities and otherwise deceive the criminals they are stalking. As James Wilson (1978: 59) points out, both reactive and proactive law

On Being Shocked

We should be shocked not that there are police officers on the take but that there are police officers not on the take. In 2003, making $50,000 a year, they arrest people who are driving cars worth several times that (Boaz 1990). The French Connection heroin case, the subject of a best-selling book and an Academy Award–winning movie (Best Picture and Best Actor of 1971), is an example.

In 1962 Detectives Eddie "Popeye" Egan (played in the movie by Gene Hackman) and his partner Sonny Grosso (played by Roy Scheider) smashed an international drug ring that was smuggling Turkish heroin into New York from Marseilles. That same year, the drugs seized in connection with the case—57 pounds of almost pure heroin—were vouchered with the police property clerk by Detectives Egan and Grosso. In 1972 the Police Commissioner of the city of New York held a news conference: The French Connection heroin, he announced, had been stolen and replaced with white flour. Several days later, an inventory of the property clerk's office revealed that additional heroin was missing: A total of nearly 400 pounds had been stolen—*by police officers* (Wallance 1981). In 1989 a DEA supervisory agent who had worked on the French Connection case was indicted for transporting more than 62 pounds of cocaine from Miami to Boston (Berke 1989).

**Mexican Drug Czar
Sentenced**

A Mexican court sentenced army general and national antidrug chief Gutierrez Rebollo to 32 years and 40 years for taking bribes from the Juarez cartel to ease its operations while cracking down on those of its rivals. A codefendant, the state police chief in the western state of Jalisco, was sentenced to 21 years (Associated Press 2000a).

enforcement officers are exposed to opportunities for graft, but the latter are more severely tested: The reactive officer, "were he to accept money or favors to act other than as his duty required, would have to conceal or alter information about a crime already known to his organization." The proactive agent, however, "can easily agree to overlook offenses known to him but to no one else or to participate in illegal transactions (buying or selling drugs) for his own rather than for the organization's advantage." Undercover officers pretending to be criminals are difficult to supervise; the agency they work for often knows only what the agents tell it.

There is also corruption in foreign countries that grow, process, or serve as transshipment stations for illegal substances.[2] In fact, the corrupt official is an essential ingredient in the drug business, according to the President's Commission on Organized Crime. The commission concluded that: "Corruption linked to drug trafficking is a widespread phenomenon among political and military leaders, police and other authorities in virtually every country touched by the drug trade. The easily available and enormous amounts of money generated through drug transactions present a temptation too great for many in positions of authority to resist" (PCOC 1968: 178). And in addition to corruption, there is the problem of brutality. The military in many drug source and transshipment countries have earned widespread condemnation for violating basic human rights.

Informants

Corruption is often intertwined with the problem of informants. Informants come in two basic categories—the "good citizen" and the "criminal." The former is such a rarity, particularly in drug-law enforcement, that we will deal only with the criminal informant, the individual who helps law enforcement in order to further his or her own personal ends. These ends include vengeance, efforts to drive competition out of business, and/or financial rewards, but most frequently the information is given to "work off a beef"—secure leniency for criminal activities that have become known to the authorities. Jerald Cloyd (1982: 188n) found that one federal district had a specified menu for every "beef": For each arrest resulting from informant assistance and yielding approximately the same amount of drugs that the defendant is being charged with, there is "a reduction of charges by one count. Being charged with two counts (one count of possession, one of possession with intent to sell), one arrest would get her a reduction of one count (felony possession) in exchange for an expedient plea of guilty. One good arrest and a guilty plea would reduce the charge to misdemeanor possession. Two good arrests would get her case dismissed.

Despite law enforcement agency regulations, often "while serving as informers, suspects are allowed to engage in illegal activity" notes Joseph Goldstein (1982: 37). "Continued use of narcotics is condoned; the narcotics detective generally is not concerned

---

[2]For an examination of corruption in Mexico, see Gomez-Cespedes (1999) and O'Day and Venecia (1999).

Corruption: A Sampler "Ripped from the Headlines"

"12 Capital Officers Face Drug Charges." *New York Times* (December 16, 1993: 12)

"9 New Orleans Police Officers Are Indicted in U.S. Drug Case." *New York Times* (December 8, 1994: 8)

"Charges Filed Against Five Men in [Philadelphia] Drug Squad." *New York Times* (March 2, 1995: 10)

"Officer Admits That He Sold Cocaine Taken from Dealers." *New York Times* (December 7, 1995: 20)

"Ex-Officer Sentenced in a [St. Louis] Drug-Ring Case." *New York Times* (March 27, 1996: 11)

"Franklin Park [Illinois] Cop Pleads Guilty to Drug Deal." *Chicago Tribune* (March 29, 1997: 5)

"Gresham District [Chicago] Cops Are Guilty in Drug Sting." *Chicago Tribune* (December 23, 1997: 1)

"FBI Operation Nets 44 Officers [in Ohio] Charged in Cocaine Trafficking." *Chicago Tribune* (January 22, 1998: 14)

"[Chicago] Officer Confessed to Drug Runs, Agent Says." *Chicago Tribune* (May 8, 1998: Sec. 2: 6)

"U.S. Indicts [Chicago] Cop as Drug Kingpin." *Chicago Tribune* (April 9, 1999: 1)

"Police Drug Scandal Touches Sheriff's Department." *Chicago Tribune* (March 16, 2000: Sec. 2: 1)

"Chicago Cop Ferried $12 Million in Coke, Prosecutors Allege." *Chicago Tribune* (September 20: Sec. 2)

"[NYPD] Detectives Called Drug Couriers." *New York Times* (October 26, 2000: C20)

"10 Cops Arrested on Federal Charges of Aiding Traffickers." *Chicago Tribune* (March 23, 2001: 8)

"Ex-Cops Sentenced in Huge Drug Sting." *Chicago Tribune* (August 10, 2002: 12)

"Sting Snags Cop in Drug Cash Theft." *Chicago Tribune* (September 7, 2002: 15)

"Indicted Police Officer Tests Positive for Cocaine." *Chicago Tribune* (January 30, 2003): Sec. 2: 3.

"Ex-Cop Held in Drug Theft, Sale: Cocaine Evidence Fueled a Lavish Lifestyle." *Chicago Tribune* (February 7, 2003): Sec. 2: 1, 7.

Informing for Profit

While the behavior of criminal informants is usually motivated by a desire to avoid or ameliorate imprisonment, informing can also be quite profitable, as the case of Philip Han reveals. Between 1987 and 1990, the stylishly dressed 35-year-old member of the Ghost Shadows gang in New York's Chinatown received more than $400,000 for aiding the DEA. Before that, Han served a 4-year term for murder conspiracy.

"DEA informants, working on commission, were kept so busy [during the 1980s] that at times the 300 registered informers outearned investigators, annually pulling down $50,000 to $75,000 in their constant quest to bring us information" (Stutman and Esposito 1992: 42).

…and for Freedom

In an effort to convict Manuel Noriega, federal prosecutors dropped three life terms and reduced the sentences of four convicted high-level drug traffickers by 546 years. The men testified against the former Panamanian strongman, and two were freed in 1991. Each had been given a new identity and government financial support worth hundreds of thousands of dollars. Some of the informants don't need government largesse; they have been permitted to keep the profits of their drug dealings—millions of dollars—in return for testifying against Noriega (Lubasch 1990; Richey 1991).

---

with the problem of informants who make buys and use some of the evidence themselves." Goldstein points out that although "informers are usually warned that their status does not give them a 'license to peddle,' possession of a substantial amount of narcotics may be excused" (1982: 37).

Obviously, the more involved in criminal activity the informer—"snitch" or CI (confidential informant)—is, the more useful is his or her assistance. This raises serious ethical and policy questions. Should the informant be given immunity from lawful punishment in exchange for cooperation? If so, who is to make that determination? The agent who becomes aware of the informant's activities? His or her supervisor? The prosecutor who is informed of the situation? A trial judge? Should a murderer be permitted to remain free because he or she is valuable to law enforcement efforts in drug trafficking? Should a drug addict-informant be allowed to continue his or her abuse in order to keep in touch with traffickers? If so, doesn't this contradict the goal of drug statutes, which is to curtail drug abuse? Should the government encourage informants even if they face serious physical danger, and they usually do? Most drug agents would argue, however, that without informants there can be no effective drug-law enforcement. The issues are complex, and without definitive answers.

Other Dangers

Special agents from the U.S. Customs Service and Drug Enforcement Agency used a battering ram to enter the posh California residence, and they responded with automatic weapons when fired upon by the occupant. The agents thought they were raiding the headquarters of a heavily armed drug gang who protected the house with vicious rottweilers; the badly wounded computer executive thought he was defending his house against home invaders. No drugs, dogs, or weapons were found. Information leading to the raid was provided by a confidential informant who was subsequently convicted of perjury (Katel 1995).

Based on information supplied by a confidential informant, New York City police officers broke down the door of a Brooklyn apartment and tossed a stun grenade. The residents, including an 18-year-old retarded girl who was being bathed, were handcuffed. No guns; no drugs—but a multimillion-dollar lawsuit (M. Cooper 1998).

In 1998, in Houston, Texas, six police officers, acting on an informant's tip, burst into the apartment of a Mexican immigrant and shot him twelve times. No drugs or evidence of illegal activity was found (Lyman 1998).

There are other dangers with informants. In South Florida, for example, given the number of law enforcement agencies and "given their heavy dependence on intelligence, it is inevitable that there are informants who inform on other informants, who are probably informing on them. A consequence of that is selective prosecution: arbitrary decisions made by police officers and agents as to who will go to jail and who will be allowed to remain on the street. Given the vast amounts of money at stake in the drug business, selective prosecution raises the specter of corruption" (Eddy, Sabogal, and Walden 1988: 85).

Working closely with informants is potentially corrupting. The informant helps the agent enter an underworld filled with danger—as well as great financial rewards. There is always concern that the law enforcement agent may become something else to the informer—a friend, an employee, an employer, a partner. The rewards can be considerable: Agents can confiscate money and drugs from other traffickers or receive payment for not arresting traffickers; at the same time they can improve their work record by arresting competing dealers. It is often only a small step from using drug traffickers as informants to going into business with them.

Statutes and Legal Requirements

The legal foundation for federal drug-law violations is Title II of the Comprehensive Drug Abuse Prevention and Control Act of 1970, as amended (usually referred to as the Controlled Substances Act [**CSA**]). Among the provisions of the CSA is a set of criteria for placing a substance in one of five schedules (see Table 12.1). Following the federal model, most states have established the five-schedule system, but many "have chosen to reclassify particular substances within those five schedules. Variation also exists in the number of schedules employed by the states [North Carolina, for example, uses six] and in the purpose of these schedules" (*Illicit Drug Policies* 2002: 8). Massachusetts categorizes drugs based on the penalty rather than the federal scheme of potential for abuse and medical use. Like federal law, state statutes refer to the drug involved (e.g., cocaine or heroin), the action involved (simple possession, possession with the intent to sell, sale, distribution, or trafficking), and the number of prior offenses. And across states there is significant variation in the penalties for cocaine, marijuana, methamphetamine, and ecstasy-related offenses (*Illicit Drug Policies* 2002).

Persons involved in the illegal drug business can be arrested and prosecuted for a number of different offenses: manufacture, importation, distribution, possession, sale; or conspiracy to manufacture, import, distribute, possess, or sell; or failure to pay the required income taxes on illegal income. Possession of drugs may be *actual*—for example, actually on the person, in pockets or in a package that he or she is holding; or *constructive*—not actually *on* the person, but under his or control, directly or through other persons. Possession must be proven by a legal search, which usually requires a search warrant as per the Fourth Amendment (an important exception is at ports of entry). A search warrant requires the establishment of probable cause—providing a judge with sufficient evidence of a crime to justify a warrant. Drugs can easily be secreted in any variety of places, including inside the human body. Federal trafficking penalties are shown in Table 12.2.

Based on the Ecstasy Anti-Proliferation Act of 2000, the U.S. Sentencing Commission raised (for judges) the guideline sentences for trafficking MDMA: for 800 pills—about 200 grams—the sentence increased from 15 months to 5 years. For 8,000 pills, from 41 months to 10 years.

Conspiracy

Conspiracy is an agreement between two or more persons to commit a criminal act; the agreement becomes the *corpus* (body) of the crime. Conspiracy requires proof (beyond a reasonable doubt) that two or more persons planned to violate drug laws and that at least one overt act in furtherance of the conspiracy was made by a conspirator (for example, the purchase of materials to aid in the transportation or dilution of illicit drugs). Conspiracy statutes are valuable tools for prosecuting drug offenders because:

- Intervention can occur before the commission of a substantive offense.
- A conspirator cannot shield himself or herself from prosecution because of a lack of knowledge of the details of the conspiracy or the identity of co-conspirators and their contributions.
- An act or declaration by one conspirator committed in furtherance of the conspiracy is admissible against each co-conspirator (an exception to the hearsay rule).

TABLE 12.1   **Schedule of Controlled Substances**

Schedule I

A. The drug or other substance has a high potential for abuse.

B. The drug or other substance has no currently accepted medical use in treatment in the United States.

C. There is a lack of accepted safety for use of the drug or other substance under medical supervision.

Schedule II

A. The drug or other substance has a high potential for abuse.

B. The drug or other substance has a currently accepted medical use in treatment in the United States or a currently accepted medical use with severe restrictions.

C. Abuse of the drug or other substances may lead to severe psychological or physical dependence.

Schedule III

A. The drug or other substance has a potential for abuse less than the drugs or other substances in Schedules I and II.

B. The drug or other substance has a currently accepted medical use in treatment in the United States.

C. Abuse of the drug or other substance may lead to moderate or low physical dependence or high psychological dependence.

Schedule IV

A. The drug or other substance has a low potential for abuse relative to the drugs or other substances in Schedule III.

B. The drug or other substance has a currently accepted medical use in treatment in the United States.

C. Abuse of the drug or other substance may lead to limited physical dependence or psychological dependence relative to the drugs or other substances in Schedule III.

Schedule V

A. The drug or other substance has a low potential for abuse relative to the drugs or other substances in Schedule IV.

B. The drug or other substance has a currently accepted medical use in treatment in the United States.

C. Abuse of the drug or other substance may lead to limited physical dependence or psychological dependence relative to the drugs or other substances in Schedule IV.

Source: Drug Enforcement Administration.

TABLE 12.2 **Federal Trafficking Penalties: Narcotic Penalties and Enforcement Act of 1986**

CSA Schedule	Drug/Quantity	Penalty
I and II	Heroin, 1 kg mixture Cocaine, 5 kg mixture Cocaine Base, 50 gram mixture PCP, 100 gram or 1 kg mixture LSD, 10 gram mixture Fentanyl, 400 gram mixture Fentanyl Analog, 100 gram mixture	**First Offense:** Not less than 10 years. Not more than life. If death or serious injury, not less than 20 years, not more than life. Fine of not more than $4 million individual, $10 million other than individual. **Second Offense:** Not less than 20 years. Not more than life. If death or serious injury, not less than life. Fine of not more than $8 million individual, $20 million other than individual.
	Heroin, 100 gram mixture Cocaine, 500 gram mixture Cocaine Base, 5 gram mixture PCP, 10 gram or 100 gram mixture LSD, 1 gram mixture Fentanyl, 40 gram mixture Fentanyl Analog, 10 gram mixture	**First Offense:** Not less than 5 years. Not more than 40 years. If death or serious injury, not less than 20 years, not more than life. Fine of not more than $2 million individual, $5 million other than individual. **Second Offense:** Not less than 10 years. Not more than life. If death or serious injury, not less than life. Fine of not more than $4 million individual, $10 million other than individual.
	Others*/Any Amount	**First Offense:** Not more than 20 years. If death or serious injury, not less than 20 years, not more than life. Fine $1 million individual, $5 million not individual. **Second Offense:** Not more than 30 years. If death or serious injury, life. Fine $2 million individual, $10 million not individual.
III	All/Any Amount	**First Offense:** Not more than 5 years, fine not more than $250,000 individual, $1 million not individual. **Second Offense:** Not more than 10 years, fine $500,000 individual, $2 million not individual.
IV	All/Any Amount	**First Offense:** Not more than 3 years, fine not more than $250,000 individual, $1 million not individual. **Second Offense:** Not more than 6 years, fine not more than $500,000 individual, $2 million not individual.
V	All/Any Amount	**First Offense:** Not more than 1 year, fine not more than $100,000 individual, $250,000 not individual. **Second Offense:** Not more than 2 years, fine not more than $200,000 individual, $500,000 not individual.

*Does not include marijuana, hashish, or hash oil.

Source: Drug Enforcement Administration.

■ Each conspirator is responsible for the substantive crimes of co-conspirators; even late joiners can be held liable for prior acts of co-conspirators if the latecomer's agreement is given with full knowledge of the conspiracy's objective.

There are three basic types of conspiracy:

1. *Wheel conspiracies.* One person at the "hub" conspires individually with two or more persons, who make up the "spokes" of the wheel. For the conspiracy to be (legally) complete, the wheel needs a "rim": Each spoke must be aware of and agree with the others in pursuit of one objective.

2. *Chain conspiracies.* Like the lights on a Christmas tree, each conspirator depends on the successful participation of every other member. Each member is a "link," who in order to complete the conspiracy, must understand that the success of the scheme depends upon everyone in the chain.

3. *Enterprise conspiracies.* Part of the **RICO** (Racketeer Influenced and Corrupt Organizations) statute of the Organized Crime Control Act of 1970, the enterprise conspiracy avoids the practical limitations inherent in proving wheel and chain conspiracies. The statute makes it a separate crime to conspire to violate drug laws as part of an agreement to participate in an enterprise by engaging in a pattern of racketeering activity. Members of the conspiracy need not know each other or even be aware of each other's criminal activities. All that needs to be shown is each member's agreement to participate in the organization—the "enterprise"—by committing two or more acts of racketeering, such as gambling or drug violations, within a 10-year period. The enterprise conspiracy facilitates mass trials, with each member of the enterprise subject to the significant penalties—20 years imprisonment on each count—that can result from a conviction.

The Continuing Criminal Enterprise (**CCE**) statute is similar in purpose to RICO, but targets only illegal drug activity. The statute makes it a crime to commit or conspire to commit a continuing series of felony violations of the 1970 Drug Abuse Prevention and Control Act when the violations are undertaken in concert with five or more persons. The courts have ruled that "series" requires three or more violations. "For conviction under this statute, the offender must have been an organizer, manager, or supervisor of the continuing operation and have obtained substantial income or resources from the drug violations" (Carlson and Finn 1993: 2). In 1999, the Supreme Court ruled (*Richardson v. United States* No. 97-8629) that juries must agree on which specific illegal acts were committed by a defendant, rather than simply finding that he or she committed a series of drug violations without specifying which ones. The 6–3 decision will make it harder to convict persons for violating the CCE.

Tax Violations

In 1927 the Supreme Court decided the case of *United States v. Sullivan* (274 U.S. 259), which denied the claim of self-incrimination as an excuse for failure to file income tax on illegally gained earnings. This decision enabled the federal government to successfully prosecute Al Capone and members of his organization. Drug entrepreneurs have devised ways to successfully evade taxes by, for example, dealing in cash, keeping minimal records, and setting up fronts. This is countered by the indirect method known as the *net worth theory*: "The government establishes a taxpayer's net worth at the commencement of the taxing period [which requires substantial accuracy], deducts that from his or her net worth at the end of the period, and proves that the net gain in net worth exceeds the income reported by the taxpayer" (E. Johnson 1963: 17–18). In effect, the Internal Revenue Service reconstructs the total expenditures of the taxpayer by examining his or her standard of living and comparing it with reported income. The government can then maintain that the taxpayer did not report his or her entire income; the government does not have to show a probable source of the excess unreported gain in net worth.

Money Laundering Control Act

The attorney general of the United States has pointed out that so much cash is involved in large, illicit drug-trafficking operations that tracking the money from these drug activities is often a more fruitful investigative endeavor than tracking the underlying criminal activities (Thornburgh 1989). Before the passage of the Money Laundering Control Act of 1986 (Title 18 U.S.C. sections 1956 and 1957), money laundering was not a federal crime, although the Department of Justice had used a variety of federal statutes to successfully prosecute money-laundering cases. The act consolidated these statutes with the goal of increasing prosecutions for this offense. Money laundering was made a separate federal offense punishable by a fine of $500,000 or twice the value of the property involved, whichever is greater, and 20 years imprisonment. Title 18 U.S.C. Section 981 provides for the civil confiscation of any property related to a money-laundering scheme. Legislation enacted in 1988 allows the government to file a suit claiming ownership of all cash funneled through operations intended to disguise their illegal source. The courts can issue an order freezing all contested funds until the case is adjudicated (Weinstein 1988).

A person is guilty of money laundering if he or she, knowing that the property involved represents the proceeds of an illegal activity, attempts to conceal or disguise the nature, location, source, ownership, or control of the proceeds or attempts to avoid a transaction-reporting requirement. Furthermore, whoever transports or attempts to transport a monetary instrument or funds out of the United States in an attempt to conceal or disguise the nature, location, source, ownership, or control of the proceeds to avoid a transaction-reporting requirement, with the intent to promote an unlawful activity or with the knowledge that the monetary instrument or funds represent the proceeds of an unlawful activity, shall be guilty of money laundering. For a conviction under section 1957 the prosecutor must prove:

1. that the defendant engaged in a monetary transaction in excess of $10,000;
2. that the defendant knew the money to be the fruit of criminal activity; and
3. that the money was in fact the fruit of a specified unlawful activity (Weinstein 1988).

Until 1988 the act permitted the Department of Justice to prosecute attorneys and seize fees obtained from tainted sources. Defense attorneys argued that this created a situation "in which a defendant cannot retain an attorney because of the government's threat of criminal and civil sanctions against any attorney who takes the case" (Weinstein 1988: 381). The defendant is left without a free choice of attorneys and thus, must depend upon a public defender who may not be familiar with the complexities of RICO prosecutions. Supporters of this legislation argue that criminals who have grown wealthy from crime are not entitled to any greater consideration with respect to legal representation than their less successful criminal colleagues, who are often represented by public defenders. On November 18, 1988, President Ronald Reagan signed the antidrug abuse bill, which contains an amendment to 18 U.S.C. Section 1957, effectively excepting defense attorneys' fees from the criminal money-laundering provisions. Thus, while criminal-defense fees could still be subject to forfeiture, the attorney who accepts tainted fees is exempt from criminal prosecution. In 1989 the Supreme Court, in a 5–4 decision, ruled that the government, under the Comprehensive Forfeiture Act, can freeze the assets of criminal defendants before trial (*Caplin and Drysdale v. United States,* 491 U.S. 616; *United States v. Monsanto,* 491 U.S. 600).

Seizure and Forfeiture of Assets

Federal and state statutes provide for the forfeiture of property used in criminal activity or secured with the fruits of criminal activity. Forfeiture has proved particularly useful in dealing with drug traffickers. There are four types of forfeitable items:

1. *Contraband,* such as controlled substances, are illegal to possess and may be seized and destroyed without a court order.
2. *Derivative contraband* includes conveyances used to transport contraband, such as aircraft, vessels, and motor vehicles. While not illegal in themselves, they are classified as contraband when used in furtherance of a criminal act.
3. *Direct proceeds* are usually cash.
4. *Derivative proceeds* include real estate and stock.

In practice, vehicles and cash are the most frequently seized assets, because the pursuit of real property requires extensive financial investigation. "The investigative expense may be cost effective," however, if "the property is valuable and the potential for disrupting the criminal organization is high" (Stellwagen 1985: 5).

There are two types of forfeiture proceedings: criminal and civil. *Criminal forfeiture* is applicable only as part of a successful criminal prosecution. "The defendant in the criminal case must be convicted of the crime involving the property, or the property cannot be subject to forfeiture" (Poethig 1988: 11). Thus, the government can use criminal forfeiture to seize the home of a *convicted* drug dealer who used it to store drugs. *Civil forfeiture,* on the other hand, does not require criminal charges; civil forfeiture can proceed even in the absence of a criminal prosecution and has certain advantages over criminal forfeiture: The level of evidence required is considerably less than that in a criminal action, and the considerable due process guarantees accruing to a criminal defendant are not applicable in a civil action. Interestingly, civil forfeiture proceedings are brought against property involved in a criminal offense, not against a person. "Possession of the property in and of itself may not be illegal, but the property may be subject to seizure and forfeiture because of the way it was used. No criminal charge or conviction need exist against the owner of the property for the civil case to occur" (Poethig 1988: 11). Thus, the government can use civil forfeiture to seize an automobile used to transport drugs, even if no conviction resulted from this activity.

RICO and the 1984 Comprehensive Forfeiture Act (CFA) provide for the seizure of assets under certain conditions. The CFA "creates a rebuttable presumption that any property of a person convicted of a drug felony is subject to forfeiture if the government establishes by a preponderance of evidence that the defendant acquired the property during the period of violation or within a reasonably short period thereafter, *and* there was no likely source for the property other than the violation" (PCOC 1986: 274). Much of the money taken in forfeitures goes into state and local law enforcement efforts. To stop commuter customers from driving into New York City to purchase drugs, law enforcement officials have been seizing the cars of those making drug purchases. Some vehicles have been returned to their owners when the owners were not the ones arrested; hundreds of others have been auctioned off.

In any number of jurisdictions, disputes have arisen over how to allocate the fruits of seized assets. Because these funds do not incur a political cost—not being linked to taxes—they are highly valued. However, "once the money reaches the local police, it often can become a political football with law enforcement and politicians squabbling over how to spend it" (Soble 1991: 23). In several California communities, for example, police officials wanted to put the money into drug-law enforcement, but elected officials insisted instead on increasing the uniformed police force. There is also concern that pressure to produce revenue will encourage legally questionable activity and even alter the basic goal of drug-law enforcement.

Intertwined with this concern is one expressed over the seizure of property owned by innocent third parties. Three fraternity houses seized at the University of Virginia in 1991, for example, were owned by alumni, not the current occupants, some of whom were arrested for drug violations. (Two houses were returned before the 1991 school year began.) Innocent parties can be deprived of a residence, vehicle, business, or cash until they are able to prove they were not involved in law-violating activity—a reversal of the normal presumption of innocence. To get back seized property, the owner needs an attorney, and litigation can take several months without any guarantee of success. For persons who make the "mistake" of traveling with large amounts of cash—particularly if they are black, Hispanic, or Asian—the results can be more than an inconvenience. A study by the *Pittsburgh Press* revealed several cases in which the cash of innocent persons was seized at airports and kept for years without any criminal charges being filed (Schneider and Flaherty 1991). "Overcoming the burden of proof can be hard even for the most upright citizens. How does a mother prove she didn't know her son was using the family car to transport drugs? How does a landlord prove he didn't know a tenant was a drug dealer?

. . . The effort is also expensive, and even if you win, you're still out the money to pay your lawyer, which can be more than the value of the property you've recovered" (Chapman 1992: 23). In 1996, the Supreme Court determined that property can be seized even when the owner was innocent of any wrongdoing. In this case, *Bennis v. Michigan* (517 U.S. 1163), a jointly owned car was impounded after the husband used it to solicit a prostitute. In response to these criticisms, in 2000, the 1984 statute was revised to require the government to prove confiscated property either had been used for illegal activity or was purchased with the proceeds of criminal activity.

Forfeiture has also been criticized as a plea bargaining device for drug kingpins. They negotiate lighter sentences by promising to reveal hidden assets and not put up court challenges to their seizure. Law enforcement agencies, eager for additional funds, promote leniency for those at the top of the drug trafficking ladder, while those down below, without substantial hidden assets, face significant penalties (Navarro 1996).

Grand Jury

A grand jury is made up of fifteen to twenty-three citizens selected to hear evidence against accused persons and to determine whether sufficient evidence exists to bring these persons to trial—to *indict* them. While not all states use grand juries to indict defendants, all states and the federal government empower the grand jury to conduct investigations of criminal activity, usually pertaining to official corruption. The Organized Crime Control Act of 1970 requires that a *special grand jury* be convened at least every 18 months in federal districts of more than 1 million people; it may also be convened at the request of a federal prosecutor, and its life may be extended to 36 months. The special grand jury is often used to investigate drug-law violations.

The broad investigative powers of the grand jury permit jurors to consider tips and rumors as well as more substantial evidence offered by the prosecutor. Even illegally secured evidence may be used as a basis for questioning witnesses. A grand jury can issue subpoenas for documents and persons. Federal (and most state) grand juries do not permit witnesses to be accompanied by counsel (although defendants are free to leave the grand jury room to consult with their attorneys). Testimony before a grand jury is given under oath and recorded, although the proceedings are secret until released by the court. Witnesses who invoke their constitutional right to remain silent can be granted immunity, which requires that they testify or suffer summary incarceration for the remainder of the life of the grand jury.

Law Enforcement Agencies

As noted earlier, local efforts against drug trafficking are usually directed at mid-level dealers, although most frequently it is the low-level street dealer who is arrested and prosecuted at the local level. Federal drug-law enforcement seeks to disrupt illicit trafficking organizations and to reduce the availability of drugs for illicit use. This is accomplished in three ways (Comptroller General 1983: 3):

- Arrest, prosecution, and incarceration of traffickers and the immobilization of trafficking organizations eliminate some capacities for supplying illicit drugs.
- Removal of drugs from the distribution networks directly reduces supply.
- Seizure of equipment and operating resources leaves the drug networks at least inconvenienced, at best crippled.

On the federal level, because the United States, unlike most other democratic nations, does not have a national police force, the job of carrying out these objectives falls on a confusing number of agencies in several departments—Transportation, Justice, Treasury, Defense—whose responsibilities for enforcing drug laws often overlap. This fragmentation is the result of the ad hoc creation of law enforcement agencies at the national level—each time a particular problem arose, an agency was established without significant attention to the problem of coordination. We will discuss the agencies in the order listed in Table 12.3.

Drug Enforcement Administration (DEA)

The DEA evolved out of several predecessor agencies, particularly the Federal Bureau of Narcotics (see Chapter 2). It is a single-mission agency responsible for enforcing federal statutes dealing with controlled substances by investigating alleged or suspected major

---

Levels of Drug-Law Enforcement

There are five levels of drug-law enforcement (Kleiman 1985):

1. *Source control.* This comprises actions aimed at limiting cultivation and production of poppies and opium, coca and cocaine, and marijuana. Both the State Department and the Drug Enforcement Administration have agents assigned to foreign countries.
2. *Interdiction.* The interception of drugs being smuggled into the United States is primarily the role of the Coast Guard and Customs Service.
3. *Domestic distribution.* The disruption of high-level trafficking is usually the responsibility of the Drug Enforcement Administration and the Federal Bureau of Investigation.
4. *Wholesaling.* The focus on mid-level dealing is usually the role of state and local law enforcement.
5. *Street sales.* Low-level dealing, often by addicts supporting their own drug habits, is usually left to local law enforcement.

TABLE 12.3
Federal Drug-Law Enforcement Agencies

Department of Justice

Drug Enforcement Administration

Federal Bureau of Investigation

Immigration and Naturalization Service

Marshals Service

Department of the Treasury

Bureau of Alcohol, Tobacco, and Firearms

Customs Service

Internal Revenue Service

Department of Transportation

Coast Guard

Department of Defense

Air Force

Army

Navy

Postal Service

Postal Inspection Service

DEA Antecedent Agencies

1973–present: Drug Enforcement Administration

1968–1973: Bureau of Narcotics and Dangerous Drugs

1930–1968: Federal Bureau of Narcotics

1927–1930: Bureau of Prohibition

1915–1927: Bureau of Internal Revenue

drug traffickers. The DEA is also responsible for regulating the legal trade in such controlled substances as morphine, methadone, and barbiturates. Diversion agents conduct accountability investigations of drug wholesalers, suppliers, and manufacturers. They inspect the records and facilities of major drug manufacturers and distributors, and special agents investigate instances in which drugs have been illegally diverted from legitimate sources. DEA special agents are also stationed in sixty-five countries (Thornburgh 1989), where their mission is to gain cooperation in international efforts against drug trafficking and to help train foreign enforcement officials.

The basic approach to DEA drug-law enforcement is the *buy and bust* or the *controlled buy*. Typically, a drug agent is introduced to a seller by an informant. The agent arranges to buy a relatively small amount of drugs and then attempts to move farther up the organizational ladder by increasing the amount purchased. When arrests are made, DEA agents attempt to "flip" the suspect—convince him or her to become an informant—particularly if the person has knowledge of the entire operation, so that a conspiracy case can be effected. As discussed earlier in the chapter, the use of informants is problematic.

"Mule Skinning"

DEA special agents, working with state and local police agencies, monitor airports at key junctions for drugs entering the United States. In addition to such primary ports of entry as South Florida, Los Angeles, and New York City, they also cover such secondary locations as Atlanta and Chicago, where travelers frequently change planes. Using a *drug courier profile* developed over the past 15 years, the agents look for specific clues—primary and secondary characteristics—that have been proven to characterize persons ("mules") most likely to be carrying wholesale quantities of illegal substances.

Seven primary characteristics:

1. Arrival from or departure to an identified foreign source country (such as Colombia) or domestic source city (such as Miami)
2. Carrying little or no luggage or empty suitcases
3. Unusual travel patterns—for example, short turnaround times for lengthy airplane trips
4. Use of an alias
5. Possession of large amounts of currency
6. Purchasing airline tickets using small bills
7. Unusually nervous

Four secondary characteristics:

1. Exclusive use of public transportation, particularly cabs, to and from the airport
2. Making phone calls immediately after deplaning
3. Providing a phony telephone number when purchasing airline tickets
4. Excessive travel to a source country or distribution city or cities

While these primary and secondary characteristics may be consistent with lawful behavior, they also indicate a person who should be questioned. Passengers meeting enough profile characteristics may be approached and questioned—asked for identification and travel documentation. Agents are particularly interested in signs of excessive nervousness. If such signs are observed, agents will ask the passenger to consent to a drug search, which can include a cavity search. The rare refusal may result in detention and the securing of a drug-sniffing dog and/or a search warrant. At times, agents discover large amounts of cash that cannot be accounted for. This is seized until its "lawful" owner appears to claim it, a highly unlikely event. If a courier is arrested, efforts are made to "flip" the mule in order to implicate the person picking up the drugs.

Continued

Although its use is controversial, the profile permits drug agents to act in the absence of specific information (the sort usually provided by criminal informants). The use of the profile and the seizure of any evidence discovered have been upheld by the courts as legitimate law enforcement tools, the Fourth Amendment notwithstanding. In 1989 the Supreme Court, in a 7–2 decision, ruled that the profile provides a "reasonable basis" to suspect that a person is transporting drugs. The case involved Andrew Sokolow, who in July 1984 flew from Honolulu to Miami and returned to Hawaii 48 hours later. Sokolow, dressed in a black jumpsuit and gold jewelry, purchased two airline tickets in Miami for $2,100 in cash taken from a roll of $20 bills containing about twice that amount. He was traveling under a name that did not match his telephone listing. Sokolow did not check any luggage and appeared to be very nervous. After stopping him in Honolulu, drug agents used a drug-sniffing dog, which led them to 1,063 grams of cocaine in Sokolow's carry-on luggage. Writing for the Court, Chief Justice William H. Rehnquist stated that, "while a trip from Honolulu to Miami, standing alone, is not a cause for any sort of suspicion, here there was more: surely few residents of Honolulu travel from that city for 20 hours to spend 48 hours in Miami during the month of July." The Court, however, did not base its decision on the existence or use of the DEA drug profile; according to the decision, agents must justify their decision to stop a suspect on the basis of their own observations and experience.

While the profile has proven useful in interdiction efforts, it is not without controversy because its use appears to relate to ethnicity and race; the darker a person's skin, the more likely it is that he or she will be targeted. A stop can involve several hours of detention and accompanying humiliation. Nevertheless, the practice has been extended to highways, where vehicles and their occupants, if they fit certain profiles, are subjected to a stop and interrogation.

Sources: Crank and Rehm (1992); Hedgepath (1989); Elsasser (1989); Greenhouse (1989); Belkin (1990)

Federal Bureau of Investigation (FBI)

The FBI is as close to a federal police force as exists in the United States. Its broad investigative mandate was expanded in 1982, when the FBI was given concurrent jurisdiction with the DEA for drug-law enforcement and investigation. In addition, the administrator of the DEA is now required to report to the director of the FBI, who has overall responsibility for supervising drug-law enforcement efforts and policies. Despite its increased mandate, the primary role of the FBI is to deal with espionage—it is the only law enforcement agency having jurisdiction over this activity. The dramatic changes in what was known as the Eastern (Communist) bloc have led to the reassignment of hundreds of FBI agents from counterespionage to more conventional criminal activity, such as drug trafficking.

Immigration and Naturalization Service (INS)

The primary role of the INS is to prevent illegal entry into the United States and to apprehend those who have entered illegally. Border Patrol officers check suspicious persons within 100 miles of border areas likely to be used as illegal crossing points, and they often arrest persons transporting drugs.

Internal Revenue Service (IRS)

The mission of the IRS is to encourage and achieve the highest possible degree of voluntary compliance with tax laws and regulations. When such compliance is not forthcoming or not feasible, as in the case of drug traffickers, the Criminal Investigation Division receives the case. Agents examine bank records, canceled checks, brokerage accounts, property transactions, and purchases, compiling a financial biography of the subject's lifestyle in order to prove that proper taxes have not been paid. As a result of the excesses revealed in the wake of the Watergate scandal, Congress enacted the Tax Reform Act of 1976, which reduced the law enforcement role of the IRS and made it difficult for law enforcement agencies (other than the IRS) to gain access to income tax returns. Amendments in 1982 reduced the requirements and permitted the IRS to better cooperate with the efforts of other federal law enforcement agencies investigating drug traffickers.

Marshals Service

The Marshals Service is the oldest federal law enforcement agency, dating back to 1789. During the period of westward expansion, the U.S. marshal played a significant role in the "Wild West." Today, marshals provide security for federal court facilities, transport federal prisoners, serve civil writs issued by federal courts, and investigate and apprehend certain federal fugitives. Marshals are responsible for seizing, managing, and disposing of forfeited properties and assets from major drug cases. The Marshals Service's most important task relative to drug trafficking is its responsibility for administering the Witness Protection Program.

Witness Protection Program. Because of the potentially undesirable consequences for a witness who testifies in a drug trafficking case, efforts have been made to protect such witnesses from retribution. The Witness Protection Program was authorized by the Organized Crime Control Act of 1970:

> The Attorney General of the United States is authorized to rent, purchase, modify, or remodel protected housing facilities and to otherwise offer to provide for the health,

safety, and welfare of witnesses and persons intended to be called as Government witnesses, and the families of witnesses and persons intended to be called as Government witnesses in legal proceedings instituted against any person alleged to have participated in an organized criminal activity whenever in his judgment testimony from, or a willingness to testify by, such a witness would place his life or person, or the life or person of a member of his family or household, in jeopardy. Any person availing himself of such an offer by the Attorney General to use such facilities may continue to use such facilities for as long as the Attorney General determines the jeopardy to his life or person continues.

The program was given over to the Marshals Service to administer. There was logic behind this arrangement (Permanent Subcommittee on Investigations 1981b: 54): "Law enforcement officers wanted the protecting and relocating agency to be in the criminal justice system but to be as far removed as possible from both investigating agents and prosecution. That way the Government could more readily counter the charge that cooperating witnesses were being paid or otherwise unjustifiably compensated in return for their testimony."

Bureau of Alcohol, Tobacco, and Firearms (ATF)

ATF dates back to 1791, when a tax was placed on alcoholic spirits. It eventually evolved into the Prohibition Bureau, which with the repeal of Prohibition became known as the Alcohol Tax Unit. In 1942 the bureau was given jurisdiction over federal firearms statutes and in 1970 over arson and explosives. ATF agents often encounter drug traffickers during their investigation of firearms and explosives violations. They have been particularly active in efforts against outlaw motorcycle clubs, who typically traffic in firearms and drugs.

Coast Guard

The Coast Guard, part of the Department of Transportation, is responsible for drug interdiction at sea. Coast Guard personnel do not have to establish probable cause before boarding a vessel at sea. "Responsible in large part for U.S. drug interdiction efforts, the Coast Guard's strategy has been mainly directed toward intercepting mother ships as they transit the major passes of the Caribbean. To effect this "choke point" strategy, the Coast Guard conducts both continuous surface patrols and frequent surveillance flights over waters of interest, and boards and inspects vessels at sea" (PCOC 1986: 313).

Smugglers bringing drugs from Colombia across the Caribbean to the Florida coast carry extra fuel for the 700-mile round-trip in boats that are 30 to 45 feet long, capable of carrying 3,000 pounds of cocaine, and travel at nearly 70 miles per hour. In response, in 1999, the Coast Guard reinstituted a tactic last employed during Prohibition: Helicopter-borne sharpshooters disable the engines of speedboats refusing to follow the orders of Coast Guard vessels (Stout 1999).

Customs Service

The Customs Service was established in 1789 to collect duties on various imports. Customs inspectors examine cargoes and baggage, articles worn or carried by individuals, and vessels, vehicles, and aircraft entering or leaving the United States. The frontiers of the United States, to the north and the south, "are the longest undisputed, undefended borders on earth" (Weiner 2002: 14). The more than 20,000 agents are deployed at airports, ports of entry, and northern and southern borders.

Special teams of inspectors and canine enforcement officers concentrate on cargo and conveyances considered high risk. In 1981 the Customs Service established the Office of Intelligence to better manage information and target suspects; it participates in several multiagency programs designed to combat organized criminal activities in drug trafficking. The service works with commercial carriers, often signing cooperative agreements, to enhance the carriers' ability to prevent their equipment from being used to smuggle drugs. Special agents of the Customs Service are responsible for carrying out investigations into drug smuggling and currency violations as part of money-laundering schemes.

The Customs Service is not hampered by Fourth Amendment protections that typically restrain domestic law enforcement. Customs agents do not need probable cause or warrants to engage in search and seizure at ports of entry; certain degrees of suspicion will suffice. The typical customs case is a "cold border bust," the result of an entry checkpoint search. Because it is impractical if not impossible to thoroughly search most vehicles and persons entering the United States, customs agents have developed certain techniques for minimizing inconvenience to legitimate travelers and shippers while better targeting those most likely to be involved in smuggling activity. Besides being alert to various cues that act as tip-offs, the officials at border-crossing points have computers containing information such as license plate numbers and names of known or suspected smugglers.

Special teams of U.S. Customs inspectors and canine enforcement officers examine cargo imported into the United States. Agents don't need probable cause or warrants to search for drugs at ports of entry.

© Amy C. Etra/PhotoEdit

Drug Smuggling Interceptions

A light gray spray-painted bust of Jesus composed of molded cocaine

5 pounds of cocaine packed in condoms surgically implanted in a sheepdog

37 pounds of cocaine packed in condoms and inserted in the rectums of live boa constrictors

1,000 pounds of cocaine packed in hollow plaster shells shaped and painted to resemble yams

6,000 pounds of cocaine packed in kilo bricks inside ice-packed cases of broccoli

2,000 pounds of cocaine in the soles of a shipment of sneakers

16 tons of cocaine inside concrete fence posts

3,000 pounds of cocaine hidden beneath a shipment of iced fish fillets

Two rust-colored beds with Colombian heroin molded into ornate scrollwork on the headboards and footboards.

Sources: Speart (1995); Associated Press (1999c)

Persons arrested by the Customs Service become targets for offers of plea bargaining in efforts to gain their cooperation in follow-up enforcement efforts by the DEA; they are pressured to become informants in return for some form of leniency.

As the result of the September 11, 2001, attacks, Customs Service priorities have shifted to intercepting potential terrorists seeking to enter the United States. Along with the INS, customs agents have become the front line in protecting the U.S. from terrorist enemies.

The Coast Guard and Customs Service are hampered by the need to patrol more than 12,000 miles of international boundary, crossed by more than 420 billion tons of goods and 270 million persons each year. About half the drugs entering the United States come through commercial ports, where they are secreted in tightly sealed steel containers, 20 or 40 feet long, 12 feet high, and 8 feet wide, millions of which enter the country every year. Customs officials can inspect only a small number (about 10 percent) of these containers, and without advance information, the drugs typically pass right through the ports. Drugs that are intercepted are easily replaced (Treaster 1990b).

The Military

The most controversial federal agency involved in drug-law enforcement is the Department of Defense (DoD). In 1878, congressional Democrats enacted the *Posse Comitatus* (literally, "force of the county") Act to stop Republican presidents from using the army to

Changing Customs

In general, Customs can detain passengers for any period of time without judicial approval. Dogged by investigations and lawsuits alleging abusive searches, the Customs Service said that it will obtain the approval of a federal magistrate when it wants to hold a passenger suspected of smuggling drugs for more than 4 hours. Under the policy change, after a person has been held for 4 hours, customs agents must present a case to a federal magistrate showing that it has "reasonable suspicion" to keep the passenger in custody.

If the magistrate deems that there isn't reasonable suspicion to hold the passenger, he or she is released. If the magistrate determines there is reasonable suspicion, then Customs can continue to hold a passenger and, following appropriate procedures, can subject the passenger to more advanced body searches, such as a medically supervised X ray at a hospital, or a monitored bowel movement.

The agency is facing numerous lawsuits alleging that people were singled out for body searches because of their race and gender. Customs, which has taken a number of steps to respond to criticism over its body search procedures, will help passengers who have been detained but weren't found to have smuggled drugs if their travel plans are disrupted. They will help such people arrange for airline, hotel, or transportation and pick up the tab (Aversa 1999).

U.S. Customs workers in Miami use a torch to open a secret compartment containing cocaine on a seized cargo ship. Smugglers had stashed more than 2,000 pounds of cocaine on the ship's keel.

© Reuters Newmedia Inc./CORBIS

(Almost) Undetectable Cocaine

In 1991, federal agents raided several houses in south Florida where they discovered a rather unique method of disguising cocaine for smuggling purposes. Agents found hundreds of pounds of harmless-looking black plastic molds into which cocaine had been blended, making detection using routine methods impossible. In fact, only the discovery of chemicals used in cocaine processing alerted agents to the blend. The drug is extracted from the plastic in much the same way that it is removed from the coca plant. The plastic is about one-quarter cocaine and can be made into any shape, allowing cocaine to be smuggled in the form of toys, glasses, camera lenses, or any plastic product (Rhor 1991).

further Reconstruction in the states of the erstwhile Confederacy. The act (as amended) makes it a crime to use the military as a domestic police force: "Whoever, except in cases and under circumstances expressly authorized by the Constitution or Act of Congress willfully uses any part of the Army or Air Force as a posse comitatus or otherwise to execute the laws shall be fined not more than $10,000 or imprisoned not more than two years or both" (18 USCA sec. 1385 (1984). In 1956, Congress added the Air Force to the Posse Comitatus Act, while the Navy and Marines promulgated administrative restrictions.

Until 1981 DoD limited its involvement to lending equipment and training civilian enforcement personnel in the use of military equipment. In that year, as part of a new "War on Drugs," Congress amended the Posse Comitatus Act, authorizing a greater level of military involvement in civilian drug enforcement, particularly the tracking of suspect ships and planes and the use of military pilots and naval ships to transport civilian enforcement personnel. As a result of this legislation, DoD provided surveillance and support services, using aircraft to search for smugglers and navy ships to tow or escort vessels seized by the Coast Guard to the nearest U.S. port. The legislation authorized the military services to share information collected during routine military operations with law enforcement officials and to make facilities and equipment available to law enforcement officials.

Further amendments to the 1981 legislation led to the use of military equipment and personnel in efforts against cocaine traffickers in Bolivia, Colombia, and Peru. These amendments permit the use of such personnel and equipment if the Secretary of State or the Secretary of Defense and the Attorney General jointly determine that an emergency exists, in that the scope of specific criminal activity poses a serious threat to the interests of the United States. Combined operations involving U.S. Army Special Forces, DEA agents, U.S. Border Patrol officers, and Bolivian police and military officers have been successful in destroying hundreds of coca-paste laboratories in the coca-growing Champare region. In 1999, a U.S. spy plan crashed in an isolated region of Colombia, killing five U.S. soldiers and revealing their controversial role in antidrug efforts. As FARC guerrillas

Department of Defense

DoD has extraordinary technical capabilities developed from its long experience in monitoring the skies and the waters for incoming Soviet or other hostile military aircraft, warships, and missiles. DoD adds the ability to alert law enforcement agencies to the presence of suspected drug smugglers by means of an existing detection system along the southern U.S. border and in the Caribbean Basin (Mabry 1995).

Corrupting the Navy

In 1996, twenty-one American sailors were arrested in Italy by the Naval Criminal Investigative Service whose agents were able to infiltrate a Nigerian drug ring that paid the defendants to carry bags of cocaine and heroin across European borders. A lieutenant commander was the highest ranking member of the group ("Navy Holds 21 Sailors . . ." 1996).

. . . and the Marines

In 2002, at the Camp Lejune Marine base in North Carolina, the Naval Criminal Investigation Service arrested eighty-four marines and sailors (and ninety-nine civilians) and seized $1.4 million in drugs. The suspects were accused of trafficking in ecstasy, cocaine, LSD, and methamphetamine (Kilian and Mendell 2002). Shortly afterward, the eighty-four military personnel were convicted and sentenced to prison terms ranging from 3 to 19 years ("84 Military Personnel Convicted. . . ." 2002).

---

continue to finance their revolution through trafficking in cocaine and heroin, the U.S. struggle against drug trafficking and the fight against Marxist insurgencies have become blurred.

The 1981 statute and subsequent amendments maintain the prohibition against the involvement of U.S. military personnel in arrest and seizure activities. This prohibition was based on the fear that further DoD involvement in drug-law enforcement could:

- compromise U.S. security by exposing military personnel to the potentially corrupting environment of drug trafficking (Sciolino and Engelberg 1988);
- impair the strategic role of the military; and
- present a threat to civil liberties.

Despite this fear, in 1988 legislation was overwhelmingly approved to dramatically expand the role of the military and allow the arrest of civilians under certain circumstances.

The U.S. Department of State uses *former* military pilots to fly helicopter gunships, transport planes, and crop dusters used by U.S. and foreign drug agents in countries where U.S. military operations are barred. Early in 1990, hundreds of National Guardsmen who as a *state* militia are not governed by the Posse Comitatus Act, were deployed to search for drugs along the border with Mexico and at ports of entry. Guardsmen routinely aid in California antidrug efforts. U.S. military officials have traditionally opposed the involvement of the armed forces in law enforcement. In 1989 and early 1990 their position was tempered by the reality of military budget cutbacks. The use of the military in the war on drugs

DoD and Dope

U.S. Army Colonel James Hiett has been in command of 200 American military personnel waging a campaign against drug trafficking in Colombia. In 1999, a criminal complaint filed in Brooklyn federal court accused his wife of using the special mail service at the American embassy in Bogotá to smuggle drugs into the United States (Watson 1999). Mrs. Hiett pled guilty, and in 2000 the colonel was implicated in the case; he also pled guilty (Feuer 2000; Hays 2001).

justifies a level of funding that might otherwise be difficult to defend before Congress and the public. Nevertheless, the Pentagon continues to resist further military involvement in domestic law enforcement ("Military Doesn't Seek Big Role in Drug War . . ." 1995).

Postal Inspection Service

The Postal Inspection Service, among its several responsibilities, investigates the use of the mails to transport drugs.

Strike/Task Forces

To overcome the inefficient competitive efforts and "turf-protecting" proclivities of enforcement agencies, since 1966 the federal government has utilized task forces in response to organized crime. That year, the Department of Justice established the "Buffalo Project" in upstate New York, bringing together personnel from a number of federal enforcement agencies. The success of the project led to the establishment of a strike force in every city known to have organized crime (Mafia) groups. In his 1982 "War on Drugs" speech, President Ronald Reagan announced the creation of regional Organized Crime Drug Enforcement Task Forces (OCDETF), and by the end of 1983, twelve were located in such core cities as New York, Los Angeles, and Detroit. In 1984, a thirteenth, the Florida/Caribbean, was added.

"The Task Force Program relies largely on the Continuing Criminal Enterprise statutory provision and the Racketeer Influenced and Corrupt Organizations (RICO) statutes. The conviction rate in cases reaching disposition is approximately 95 percent. State and local officers participate in nearly one-half of the Task Force investigations" (PCOC 1985: 319). Local enforcement officers may be sworn in as special U.S. marshals, which allows them to enforce federal statutes and to cross jurisdictional boundaries that typically inhibit local enforcement agencies. Guidelines for the Organized Crime Drug Enforcement Task Force specify that a case is appropriate for Task Force adoption if it:

- appears to involve major drug-trafficking figures;
- requires the resources and expertise of another agency because of possible violations other than those involving narcotics;
- has serious investigative ramifications extending to other geographical jurisdictions; and/or
- requires the assistance of an Assistant U.S. Attorney during the early stages of an investigation.

INTERPOL

The International Police Organization, known by its radio designation INTERPOL, assists law enforcement agencies with investigative activities that transcend international boundaries. INTERPOL meant very little to the United States law enforcement community until 1968 when Iran announced that it was going to end its ban on opium production. At the same time, there appeared to be an epidemic of drug use in the United States. A U.S. (INTERPOL) National Central Bureau (NCB) was quickly activated in Washington.

There are about 150 INTERPOL members; a country becomes a member merely by announcing its intention to join. In each member country there is an NCB that acts as a point of contact and coordination with the General Secretariat in Lyons, France. INTERPOL has a headquarters staff of around 250, about 60 of whom are law enforcement officers from about forty different countries. A large communications facility links 72 member countries into a radio network; other nations use Telex or cable facilities. INTERPOL is under the day-to-day direction of a secretary general; it is a coordinating body and has no investigators or law enforcement agents of its own.

The U.S. NCB receives about twelve thousand requests for assistance from federal, state, and local law enforcement agencies each year. These are checked and coded by technical staff and entered into the INTERPOL Case Tracking System (ICTS), a computer-controlled index of persons, organizations, and other crime information items. The ICTS conducts automatic searches of new entries, retrieving those that correlate with international crime. The requests are forwarded to senior staff members who serve as INTERPOL case investigators. These are usually veteran agents from a federal agency whose experience includes work with foreign police forces. Each investigator is on loan from his or her principal agency.

Requests for investigative assistance include a whole range of criminal activity—murder, drug violations, illicit firearms traffic—and often involve locating fugitives for arrest and extradition. The bureau also receives investigative requests for criminal histories, license checks, and other ID verifications (Fooner 1985). The Financial and Economic Crime Unit at INTERPOL headquarters facilitates the exchange of information about offshore banking and money-laundering schemes. Monitoring this type of activity can sometimes lead to identifying suspects involved in drug trafficking who had previously escaped detection.

Street-Level Law Enforcement

Efficient street-level enforcement, argues Mark Moore (1977), is a strategy worth pursuing, even if there is *displacement*—sellers moving to new locations and becoming more cautious. Jonathan Caulkins (1992) agrees that even when there is complete displacement, benefits to society accrue. Because street-level enforcement makes sellers more cautious and thus more difficult to find, the buyer is forced to spend more time searching for a connection and less time searching for money (criminal opportunity) or actually using drugs. Under such conditions, many may be motivated to seek treatment, although there is often a shortage of available treatment programs. New users in particular will have difficulty "scoring." If this situation becomes widespread, profits from drug wholesaling will drop as if there were a drop in consumer demand.

Drug Checkpoints

In 2000, the Supreme Court ruled (*Indianapolis, et al. v. Edmond, et al.,* No. 99-1030) that absent any suspicion, police checkpoints that briefly detain drivers and use drug-sniffing dogs are a violation of the Fourth Amendment. Checkpoints are permitted, however, for discovering and taking intoxicated drivers off the road because that protects public safety.

In Lynn, Massachusetts, a drug task force made up of six state police officers and a city detective was deployed to decrease the flagrant selling of heroin in the city's High Rock area. Open drug dealing poses special threats. "Some neighborhood residents, particularly children, may become users; and . . . the behavior of buyers and sellers will be disruptive or worse. In poor neighborhoods, the opportunity for quick money offered by the illicit market may compete with entry-level licit jobs and divert labor-market entrants from legitimate careers. When the drug sold is heroin, residents are likely to be bothered by users 'nodding' in doorways and heroin-using prostitutes soliciting" (Kleiman 1988: 10). The goal was achieved, and drugs were harder to purchase in the area. This led to an increase in the number of persons seeking treatment for drug abuse. A significant reduction in street crime was also reported for the area (Kleiman 1988). The drying up of immediate sources of heroin can potentially reduce experimentation, although long-term users ("junkies") will merely be inconvenienced. The time and energy required to establish new sources, however, might otherwise be spent on drug use and criminality. If treatment is available, the crackdown may serve as an incentive for entering a treatment program.

In New York City, a 1984 street-level enforcement effort known as Operation Pressure Point (OPP) was designed to improve the quality of life and reduce drug-related crime in an area of the city's Lower East Side. Drug trafficking in the area had become so blatant that residents and their political representatives demanded police action. OPP instituted aggressive patrolling by uniformed officers, cleared abandoned buildings and parks of drug users, and sent out detectives to make "buy-and-bust" arrests. The risk of arrest increased dramatically for both buyers and sellers, with the result that most abandoned the area and others resorted to low-profile trafficking. OPP followed up these activities with programs designed to strengthen the community and increase cooperation with and support for the police. The program achieved its goals, and neighborhood residents reported being very satisfied. Similar operations in other parts of New York City, however, have not been as successful (Zimmer 1990).

Street-level enforcement is expensive and, if it is to be more than briefly effective, must be combined with sufficient prison space to accommodate the increase in population. In an attempt to stem the 1985 crack epidemic in New York City, police initiated a street-level crackdown with impressive results: Crack arrests and jailings reached record levels; felony drug arrests went up 21 percent the first year and 70 percent the next. Total jail sentences for drug felonies increased by 60 percent in 1987. Nevertheless, the street price of crack steadily dropped. And in response to the stepped-up police activity, crack dealers began recruiting thousands of young addicts to make street sales, overwhelming a number of city neighborhoods as well as the city's overextended police force. Placing unusually large resources in one area also raises the possibility that the problem will be displaced into areas where law enforcement efforts are less concentrated. Furthermore, the reduction of crime in Lynn, Massachusetts, discussed earlier, was short-lived, and a similar crackdown in Lawrence, Massachusetts, actually resulted in an increase in crime, particularly burglary and robbery (A. Barnett 1988; Bouza 1990: 47).

In New York, in response to intensive police efforts against street dealing, sellers moved away from high-profile and vulnerable street sales, to mobile delivery services using pagers and/or cellular telephones. As a result of the extra costs associated with this type of drug trafficking, both in terms of the equipment and time spent making deliveries, sellers began dealing only with those who could purchase large amounts at once with the attendant risk of increased consumption. These buyers may become dealers to their friends. This strategy can also move drug selling from urban areas into the suburbs, making drugs more accessible to those who were reluctant to purchase in neighborhoods with which they are not familiar.

Street-level enforcement efforts bring with them the specter of corruption and related abuses: "Bribery, perjured testimony, faked evidence and abused rights in the past have accompanied street-level narcotics enforcement. Indeed, it was partly to avoid such abuses that many police departments began concentrating on higher-level traffickers and restricted drug efforts to special units" (Moore and Kleiman 1989: 8). These special units have brought problems of their own; New York provides an example. In 1971, in order to centralize drugs, vice, and organized-crime enforcement and to prevent corruption through stricter supervision, the city established the Organized Crime Bureau. Early in 1992, the police department's chief of inspectional services submitted a confidential report citing recent cases in which the bureau's narcotic officers were accused of lying to strengthen cases and to obtain search warrants—there were no accusations of corruption. The report noted: "Of all units in the department, the greatest integrity hazards and vulnerability exist in narcotics" (Raab 1992).

Issues in Drug-Law Enforcement

Besides those discussed at the beginning of this chapter, several perplexing issues complicate drug-law enforcement. The first involves measuring success: How can we determine whether drug law enforcement in general, or specific activities in particular, are success-

The 100 to 1 Ratio: Crack Penalties and Race

Cocaine in the form of crack is most likely to be used and sold by African Americans, while powdered cocaine is often used and sold by whites. Under federal statutes, "It takes one hundred times the amount of powder cocaine to equal the same sentence as crack cocaine" (*Illicit Drug Policies,* 2002: 134). A cocaine dealer would have to sell $75,000 worth of the drug in powdered form to get the same mandatory 5-year federal sentence that a crack dealer would receive for selling $750 worth. And "crack is the only drug that carries a mandatory prison term for possession, whether or not the intent is to distribute" (C. Jones 1995: 9).

ful? What criteria can provide a standard for measuring success? The number of persons arrested, convicted, imprisoned? The amount of drugs seized? The level of purity or price of the product sold on the streets? The number of persons admitted to hospital emergency rooms for drug overdoses? The number of persons seeking admission to drug treatment programs? In practice, we use all of these, with often confusing results. For example, *increased* arrests and drug seizures have often been accompanied by *declining* prices and greater levels of purity. A 1983 report by the Comptroller General points out that while enhanced federal resources increased the amount of illegal drugs seized, purity at the retail level increased while prices fell. The Comptroller General also revealed that some drug seizures are counted several times by different agencies eager to claim credit and increase their "stats." Sometimes there is triple counting: The Coast Guard typically turns its interdicted drugs over to Customs, while the seizure may be the result of intelligence information developed by DEA, with all three agencies including the amount in their totals.

Successful law enforcement efforts, at least in theory, should reduce the available supply of drugs while driving up the price and reducing purity. When the level of purity dips below some hypothetical level but the price remains high, the abuser will no longer find it worth his or her while to make a purchase. Either the abuser will switch to a more readily available chemical—perhaps alcohol—or abandon drug use completely. In fact, successful law enforcement efforts may cause a switch from a less dangerous substance—for example, marijuana—to a more dangerous substance, such as heroin. This situation apparently occurred when, in 1969, Operation Intercept at the Mexican border effectively choked off supplies of marijuana. "There was an upsurge in heroin use among urban, white, middle-class high school students shortly after Operation Intercept" (Zinberg and Robertson 1972: 210). More recent successful campaigns against marijuana may be causing an increase in the use of alcohol, particularly among adolescents. Increases in law enforcement do not necessarily translate into reductions in supply: A widely heralded (by politicians) 1986 $1.7 billion federal antidrug law resulted in an increase in drug seizures and arrests with no discernible impact on supply (J. Johnson 1987).

The structure of the drug market, as noted in Chapter 11, makes it the last refuge of laissez-faire capitalism: How does law enforcement affect the price of illegal drugs? Mark Kleiman (1985: 69) states that the key to analyzing this question "is the response of drug purchasers to increasing drug prices." If there is a reduction in supply and a corresponding increase in price, will the amount of drug consumption remain unchanged? Is demand relatively inelastic to price? If demand is relatively elastic, consumption will decrease as price goes up. This will cause a decrease in the profits of drug traffickers. If, however, demand is inelastic, drug-law enforcement may actually increase the profits of traffickers—those who elude arrest and prosecution will reap higher prices. With respect to heroin, Kleiman notes, consumption is likely to decrease in the long run as addicts, unable to keep up with the increase in price, enter drug treatment or find alternative drugs. The issue with respect to cocaine is more difficult. Cocaine has typically been relatively expensive, although the introduction of crack has altered the market. Nevertheless, Kleiman argues, an increase in price as a result of law enforcement efforts is likely to increase the profits of cocaine traffickers—it is a market relatively impervious to price.

At the domestic distribution level, successful law enforcement efforts whittle down the number of persons involved in drug trafficking. This may leave a void at certain levels of distribution that, in a seller's market, will simply attract new entrepreneurs. Furthermore, the better-organized groups resist and survive law enforcement efforts. Thus, the level of law enforcement vigor and ability determines whether certain groups will come to dominate the drug trade and bring a concomitant increase in profits by virtue of oligopolistic (scarcity of sellers) market circumstances. On the other hand, reduced law enforcement allows more groups to remain in business, with a corresponding reduction in profits resulting from a more competitive market. Under such conditions, organizations equipped with resources for violence may be tempted to use force to reduce competition.

Steven Wisotsky (1987) argues that, at least in theory, combating cocaine abuse should be significantly easier than battling heroin abuse. The major traffickers operate out of Colombia with major supply lines more restrictive than those for heroin (which comes from several continents). However, there are analogs for many popular drugs of abuse. Successful interdiction may reduce the amount of heroin and cocaine entering the United States, but if demand remains unchanged, underground chemists will be inspired to greater creativity. Indeed, experienced cocaine users cannot tell the difference between cocaine and synthetic substances that mimic cocaine; heroin addicts often prefer the synthetic opiate fentanyl to the diluted heroin typically available on the streets.

Another issue is the argument that the substantial investment in drug-law enforcement increases criminality—drug abusers committing crimes to support habits—and also diverts resources that could be better utilized to deal with more serious criminality. Police, prosecutors, and judges are occupied with drug-law enforcement, and our jails, prisons, and probation and parole systems are overcrowded. Our drug enforcement agents are exposed to great danger, both from a most violent class of criminals and from being around the drugs themselves.

Our "war" on drugs is really a fight against socioeconomic dynamics reputed to be unconquerable: the profit motive and the law of supply and demand. In the next chapter, we will examine U.S. policy for responding to drug abuse.

SUMMARY

U.S. law enforcement efforts against drug trafficking must work within the constraints of the Constitution and the various jurisdictions involved. The criminal justice system must balance crime control to protect the security and safety of society and due process to protect the rights of each individual. The Fourth Amendment, which protects people from unreasonable search and seizure, and the exclusionary rule, which states that evidence obtained illegally is not admissible, are particular legal constraints on drug-law enforcement. Access to large amounts of drugs and the profits they generate are potentially corrupting influences on drug-law enforcement.

Drug traffickers are usually prosecuted using the conspiracy laws, especially RICO; tax evasion laws; and money-laundering statutes. Federal drug-law enforcement agencies span several departments: Justice, Treasury, Transportation, and Defense; their functions include (1) arrest, prosecution, and imprisonment of drug traffickers; (2) removing drugs from the trafficking networks; and (3) seizing equipment and resources of the drug networks. Street-level drug-law enforcement can improve the quality of residential life but may displace drug dealing and drug-related crime into other areas.

INTERNET CONNECTIONS

Drug Enforcement Administration: usdoj.gov/dea
International Narcotics Control Board: incb.org
Bureau for International Narcotics and Law Enforcement Affairs: state.gov/www/global/narcotics_law/sites

---

REVIEW QUESTIONS

1. In terms of reducing drug use, how do cost and availability explain the purpose of drug-law enforcement?
2. What is the relationship between drug-law enforcement and the two models of criminal justice—crime control and due process?
3. How do constitutional and jurisdictional limitations constrain drug-law enforcement?
4. How does the *exclusionary rule* restrain drug-law enforcement agents?
5. Why is the supervision of law enforcement agents particularly difficult in drug-law enforcement?
6. What are the two main purposes of the 1988 International Convention Against Illicit Traffic in Narcotic Drugs and Psychotropic Substances?
7. Why is corruption a bigger problem in drug-law enforcement than in other areas of law enforcement?
8. What problems arise in using criminal informants in drug-law enforcement?
9. What are the offenses for which persons involved in drug trafficking may be prosecuted?
10. What is the difference between *actual* and *constructive* possession of dangerous drugs?
11. What two legal elements are necessary to support a charge of conspiracy?
12. What is the advantage of using conspiracy statutes when dealing with drug-trafficking organizations?
13. What is the difference between criminal and civil forfeiture?
14. Why is civil forfeiture controversial?
15. What powers of a grand jury make it a useful tool in drug investigations?
16. Why is federal drug-law enforcement so fragmented in the United States?
17. Why is the use of the U.S. military in drug-law enforcement so controversial?
18. What are some of the latent, unintended negative consequences of successful drug-law enforcement?
19. What are the responsibilities of each of these federal agencies with respect to drug-law enforcement?
    a. Coast Guard
    b. Customs Service
    c. Drug Enforcement Administration
    d. Federal Bureau of Investigation

e. Immigration and Naturalization Service
f. Internal Revenue Service
g. Military
h. Marshals Service

20. What is a controlled buy?
21. What is the strike/task force concept, and what is its purpose?
22. Why is it difficult to measure success in drug-law enforcement?
23. How can drug-law enforcement actually increase the profits of some traffickers?
24. What are the advantages and disadvantages of concentrating drug-law enforcement efforts at the street level?

CHAPTER 13

Drug Abuse Policy

American drug policy has been frozen in place since crack cocaine hit the cities in the mid-1980s. These policies are punitive (in both rhetoric and reality), divisive (certainly by race, probably by age and perhaps by class), intrusive (in small ways for many and in large ways for some) and expensive ($30 billion to $35 billion annually). Yet the nation has a drug problem more severe than that of any other rich Western society, whether measured in terms of the extent of drug use, drug-related AIDS cases, or the level of violence and corruption associated with these drugs. —*Peter Reuter (2001: 15)*

Out of the history we explored in Chapter 2, there developed two basic models for responding to the use of dangerous substances. The first is a *disease model:* The abuser is "helpless" and "blameless," analogous to the cancer or coronary patient. The model defines substance abuse as a disease to be prevented or treated, just like any other public health problem. The second is a *moral-legal model* that defines alcohol and other psychoactive drugs as either legal or illegal and attempts to control availability through penalties. The moral-legal model utilizes three methods to control potentially dangerous drugs in the United States:

1. *Regulation.* Certain substances that may be harmful to their consumers can be sold with only a minimum of restrictions. These substances are heavily taxed, providing government with an important source of revenue. Alcoholic beverages and tobacco products are subjected to disproportionate taxation, and their sale is restricted to those above a certain age. Special licenses are usually required for the manufacture, distribution, and sale of regulated substances.

2. *Medical auspices.* The use of certain potentially harmful substances is permitted under medical supervision. Under this model the medical profession is given control over legal access to specific substances having medical uses because taken under the direction of a physician, their value outweighs their danger (J. Kaplan 1983a). In this category would be barbiturates, amphetamines, certain opiates (morphine and codeine), and heroin substitutes such as methadone.

3. *Law enforcement.* Statutory limitations make the manufacture or possession of certain dangerous substances a crime and empower specific public officials to enforce these statutes. Certain other substances are permitted under medical auspices, but punishment is specified for persons possessing these substances outside of accepted medical practice. Thus, heroin has no permissible use in the United States—an absolute prohibition—while other psychoactive substances, such as

morphine and Seconal (secobarbital sodium), are permissible for medical use but illegal under any other circumstances.

The official response to a particular substance—regulation as opposed to law enforcement—determines the manner in which the user will be treated. Thus, the alcoholic is typically viewed according to the disease model, while the user of illegal drugs has the criminal label attached. From the Civil War until the 1920s the U.S. response to dangerous drugs moved from permissiveness to one of rigid law enforcement—from the public health model to the moral-legal model. The practical effect of this change was "to define the addict as a criminal offender" (Schur 1965: 130), leading to the creation of a vast black market in which drug entrepreneurs quickly filled the void left by the withdrawal of lawful sources: "In the 1920s this country had a large number of addicts, but they were not regarded as criminals by the law; in general, they did not commit crimes and conducted their lives much the same way as the nonaddict population did. Clinics and private physicians were free to prescribe maintenance doses. It was the outlawing of the addictive drug that gave rise to an illegal market controlled by organized crime; and it is the exorbitant cost of the outlawed drug that has driven addicts into criminal activity to support their habit" (National Council on Crime and Delinquency 1974: 4).

Drug policy in the United States has been guided by "commonly shared simplifications"—in particular, the belief that "drug problems are largely attributable to morally compromised or pathological individuals who were not properly inculcated in childhood with normal American values such as self-control and respect for the law. These individuals must be disciplined and punished by authorities to deter them from involvement (for pleasure or profit) with inherently dangerous, addicting drugs" (Gerstein and Harwood 1990: 41).

Drug use, notes Gresham Sykes, "became defined as a fundamental affront, part of a larger pattern challenging society with an alternative view of a meaningful life." The wrongdoing of the drug user was "moved into the category of the most serious offense—treason—where the individual forsakes his society for an enemy allegiance" (1967: 77). A "clearer case of misapplication of the criminal sanction," writes Herbert Packer (1968: 333), "would be difficult to imagine." Post-Harrison Act efforts against certain psychoactive chemicals were based on their potential to harm users. Policy has now come full circle and the user is the target of vigorous enforcement efforts: "We must focus responsibility and sanctions on illegal drug users" (White House Conference for a Drug Free America 1988: 9).

Incongruities Between Facts and Policies

Before examining current policy in the United States, we need to return to the first chapter and recall some of the incongruities. Of the most widely used psychoactive drugs, heroin and cocaine (except for limited topical use) are banned; barbiturates, tranquilizers, and amphetamines are restricted; while alcohol, caffeine, and nicotine products are freely available. These inconsistencies make any response to the problem of substance abuse difficult. How do you tell the progeny of cigarette-smoking, coffee- and alcohol-drinking, sedative-using parents that drugs should not be used for recreational purposes? Therefore, "a major step toward developing sounder policy with respect to drugs would be to use that label for alcohol and nicotine (as the scientific literature already does), and to make an augmented Office of Drug Control Policy responsible for coordinating federal policy toward alcohol and nicotine as part of the overall national drug control strategy" (Reuter and Caulkins 1995: 1061).

To what extent does knowledge actually affect drug policy? While nicotine and alcohol are clearly dangerous psychoactive chemicals—*drugs*—semantic fiction portrays them otherwise: Statutory vocabulary and social folklore have established the fiction that alcohol and nicotine are not really drugs at all (National Commission on Marijuana and Drug Abuse 1973). Furthermore (the commission points out), to do otherwise would be inconsistent with our stated policy goal of eliminating drug abuse—an admission that we can never eliminate the drug use problem. Joseph Gusfield (1975) suggests that we distinguish between *scientific* knowledge—the body of facts and theories related to drug use—and *political* knowledge, which concerns public attitudes toward drug use, including scientific knowledge. Norman Zinberg (1984: 200) states that in the field of drug use, the truth will not necessarily set one free. The scientific truth, he notes, is that not all psychoactive drug use is misuse; but because this contravenes formal social policy, those who present this message run the risk that "their work will be interpreted as condoning use."

Our response to easily abused substances is not based on the degree of danger inherent in their use. Indeed, measured on any dimension, alcohol is a more serious drug of abuse than marijuana, though this is not reflected in our legal system. Furthermore, many dangerous substances—amphetamines, barbiturates, and a variety of sedatives—were actively promoted for use in dealing with anxiety, stress, obesity, or insomnia. Famous abusers of these substances, such as Marilyn Monroe and Elvis Presley—commemorated on our postage stamps—are representative of a large abusing population not subjected to arrest and imprisonment. The pushers of these substances—the drug companies and their willing partners in the medical profession—are not arrested or prosecuted.

That some drugs are outlawed while others are legally and widely available is better understood in terms other than those of science or medicine—in terms of the tobacco industry, the alcoholic-beverage industry, the drug-manufacturing industry, and the media. In addition to political contributions, the purveyors of legal psychoactive substances are able to protect their interests through advertising and by employing media specialists. In fact, the public's knowledge of and response to the "drug problem" is mediated through newspapers and television. Frightening news stories create pressure for more vigorous drug enforcement, which increases drug-fighting budgets, which yield more arrests (L. Hunt 1977). The resulting statistics are then viewed as proof of a growing drug problem.

> ### Accomplices to Terror
>
> In the wake of the September 11 terrorist attacks, the administration of President George W. Bush initiated a television campaign linking drugs to terrorism. Buying drugs, the splashy commercials announced, meant handing money to the September 11 terrorists and their ilk. As part of this multimillion-dollar campaign, supporting ads were run in more than 200 newspapers. Problems with this approach are obvious. The most widely used illegal drug in the United States is marijuana, a domestic product. And, of course, U.S. allies, such as Afghanistan's Northern Alliance, have a long history of drug trafficking (Bendavid 2002).

Hunt concludes that public fear not only may be exaggerated but also may feed upon itself through media sensationalism.

The "volume of attention generated when the national press converges on a story, like drugs, virtually demands a political response. In their haste, these [politicians'] reactions may not always be carefully considered" (Merriam 1989: 21). "Convergence" occurs when media sources discover an issue and respond to each other "in a cycle of peaking coverage, before largely dismissing the issues" (Reese and Danielian 1989: 30). In 1989, for example, President George Bush (Sr.) made a major television address during which he "declared war" on drugs. For the next week, network news averaged four stories each evening on drugs, and an opinion poll indicated that 64 percent of the public viewed drugs as America's most important problem. A year later, that figure had fallen to 10 percent as new problems received presidential attention (Oreskes 1990).

With these incongruities serving as a backdrop, let us critically examine U.S. drug policy on reducing the supply of drugs and reducing demand for them.

One DEA Agent's Lament

"It is both sobering and painful to realize, after twenty-five years of undercover work, having personally accounted for at least three thousand criminals serving fifteen thousand years in jail, and having seized several tons of illegal substances, that my career was meaningless and had absolutely no effect whatsoever in the so-called war on drugs" (Levine 1990: 11).

Supply Reduction Through Criminal Sanction

In a free market economy, in theory, reducing the supply of a product will drive up the price and thus reduce demand and consumption. But in the drug economy, an increase in price may just raise the revenue for traffickers because there is no significant decrease in consumption. The evidence is that there is not a single documented instance in which one or a succession of high-level drug cases coincided with a substantial reduction in consumption in a city (Kleiman 1989). John DiNardo (1993: 63) failed to find "any significant effects of law enforcement on the price of cocaine faced by users." (See also Caulkins, Crawford, and Reuter 1993.) Thus, enforcement to reduce the supply of drugs may eliminate the less-organized criminal distributors, resulting in an increase in the profits of criminal organizations strong enough and ruthless enough to survive (Kleiman 1989).

Overflowing Prisons

An alternative strategy, focusing on lower-level dealers, presents two additional problems. First, there is a political problem in going after small wrongdoers while largely ignoring the big ones (Kleiman 1985). And second, there is a practical concern: the cost of arresting, prosecuting, and imprisoning large numbers of people. However, this approach was the mainstay of the so-called (Governor) "Rockefeller Laws" in New York during the 1970s. As a result, the time needed to dispose of drug cases nearly doubled between 1973 and 1976, and by mid-1976, the system was approaching collapse. Research indicates that the use of drugs increased during this time, as did drug-related crimes such as burglary, robbery, and theft (Joint Committee on New York Drug Law Evaluation 1977).

In 1987 the strategy recommended by Kleiman caused New York City to establish special courts to rapidly dispose of felony drug cases through plea bargaining because the regular criminal courts were being flooded with arrests of street-level drug dealers. Because of the volume, it was taking 6 to 12 months to dispose of a case, which created a chaotically overcrowded situation on Riker's Island, the city jail for persons awaiting trial (Raab 1987). In the decade from 1981 to 1991, the average daily jail population in New York City increased 170 percent. The *New York Times* concluded that "New York City's war on drugs has resulted in so many arrests that there are simply not enough prosecutors, judges, Legal Aid lawyers or probation officers to give adequate attention to each of the thousands of cases, let alone courtrooms to try the suspects in or jail cells to hold the convicts" ("Drug Arrests and the Courts' Pleas for Help" 1989: E6).

Other states followed New York's lead, with similar results. The number of people convicted of drug felonies in state courts increased almost 70 percent from 1988 to 1990. In Cook County (Chicago), Illinois, the chief criminal court judge stated that drug cases were overwhelming the county's court system (O'Connor 1990). In the federal courts,

---

A Racist Drug War?

A study conducted by *USA Today* revealed that African Americans are four times as likely as whites to be arrested on drug charges, even though both groups use drugs at about the same rate; and blacks are more likely to be imprisoned for drug charges than non-Hispanic whites (Meddis 1993).

The war on drugs also exacerbates racial disparities related to health and well-being in minority communities: (1) Federal law prohibits ex-prison inmates from receiving any federal benefits for five years if the conviction was for drug trafficking; (2) they are also barred from Temporary Assistance to Needy Families and food stamps; (3) they become ineligible for federal education assistance for one year after conviction, two years after a second conviction, and indefinitely after a third ("How the War on Drugs Influences . . ." 2001).

Increased drug arrests have overtaxed the legal system and the capacity of prisons and jails. During the 1990s, more and more drug offenders were released early under the supervision of parole officers. Here, a parolee submits to a drug patch test.

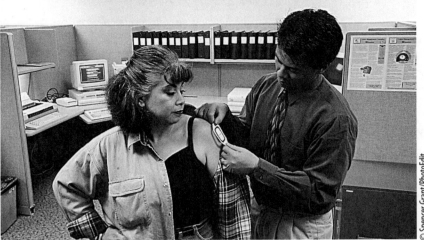

© Spencer Grant/PhotoEdit

the number of drug arrests has so backed up the system that judges are unable to attend to civil cases, resulting in increasing delays despite a drop in the number of civil filings in the past few years. The federal prison system is operating at more than 119 percent of capacity.

In New York, from 1976 to 1991, the prison population tripled to about 60,000 inmates, and by 1998 the number had reached more than 70,000—138 percent of capacity. In California the prison population rose from 22,000 in 1982 to 102,000 in 1991; by 1998 the figure was more than 147,000 and now exceeds 160,000. Between 1980 and 1986, New Jersey's prison population increased by 136 percent, and Virginia's by 111 percent. In Illinois in 1999, more than 41,000 inmates inhabited state correctional facilities designed for 16,492—almost 150 percent of capacity.

In 1993, a federal court judge returned control of Tennessee's prison system to the state—Tennessee prisons had been under federal supervision since 1981 because of overcrowding. In 1985, the state of Texas signed an agreement to end overcrowding in its prison system; Texas had been under federal supervision since a judge ruled that conditions in its prisons violated constitutional guarantees against cruel and unusual punishment. To meet constitutional standards, Texas has been granting time off for good behavior at the rate of up to 90 days for every 30 days served. Nevertheless, by 1998, Texas had more than 140,000 inmates and ranks number one in rates of incarceration (U.S. Department of Justice statistics). Jails throughout the United States are already being operated severely over capacity, and any strategy causing a significant increase in the inmate population could be disastrous.

The General Accounting Office (1991) found that overcrowded jails and prisons, the result of increased drug arrests and prosecutions, resulted in more offenders being placed in probation and parole systems, which, in turn, has generally decreased the level of supervision of probationers and parolees. It has also led to emergency prison release

Do as I Order, Not as I Do?

In 1997, Texas governor George W. Bush signed a bill authorizing judges to imprison persons convicted of possessing 1/28 of an ounce of cocaine. In 1999, as a Republican presidential candidate, Governor Bush was asked by reporters if he had ever used cocaine. He refused to answer the question.

programs and an increase in plea bargaining—a system that is spinning its wheels. Jails and prisons are scarce resources because of their exorbitant cost: The annual per inmate cost of imprisonment ranges as high as $30,000 and the cost of building a prison is as high as $100,000 per cell. Are scarce tax dollars being spent wisely in the "war" on drugs? A report by the RAND Drug Policy Research Center concluded that mandatory minimum prison sentences for low-level drug violators are "not justifiable on the basis of cost-effectiveness at reducing cocaine consumption, cocaine expenditures, or drug-related crime" (Caulkins et al. 1997: xvi). And a study of similar convicted drug offenders found that those "placed on probation [have] substantially lower recidivism rates than those who were sentenced to prison" (Spohn and Holleran 2002: 351).

Manhattan district attorney Robert M. Morgenthau (1988: 27) has noted that "we are putting more drug dealers in jail for longer terms than ever before." But "not only have we not 'conquered drugs,' but drugs are more available on the streets of our cities than ever before." "Long sentences for serious crimes have intuitive appeal. They respond to deeply held beliefs about punishment for evil actions, and in many cases ensure that, by removing a criminal from the streets, further crimes that would have been committed will not be. But in the case of black-market crimes like drug dealing, a jailed supplier is often replaced by another supplier if demand remains" (Caulkins et al. 1997: xxv). In 1996, and again in 1998, Arizona voters took matters into their own hands and enacted propositions

Marijuana Policy

The cannabis policy debate in the United States and many other Western countries has often been represented as a forced choice between two positions: "doves" who argue that cannabis use is harmless, and hence it should be legalized; and "hawks" who argue that cannabis use is harmful to health, and hence should continue to be prohibited. This false antithesis has prevented a realistic appraisal of the adverse health effects of cannabis. It has meant that the public have been exposed to two polarized views of the adverse health effects of cannabis dictated by their proponents' views on the legal status of cannabis. The doves focus on the modest health risks of intermittent cannabis use; the hawks emphasize the worst-case interpretation of the evidence on the risks of chronic cannabis use. There seems to be an implicit agreement between doves and hawks that the acute health effects of intermittent cannabis use provide at best a weak justification for prohibition. The doves stress that there is no risk of overdose from cannabis. The hawks respond by pointing to the possibility of death or serious injury in a motor vehicle accident if cannabis users drive, and to the social consequences of engaging in risky sexual and other behavior while intoxicated by cannabis (W. Hall 1999: 1).

Winning the War by Getting Tough

- The 32-year-old real estate attorney and Harvard Law School graduate was sentenced to 15 years in prison for possession of cocaine. The police discovered 36 grams (28.35 grams equals 1 ounce) of diluted cocaine in a raid on the attorney's home in Hoffman Estates, Illinois. Authorities had been tipped off by a boarder seeking leniency for a drug conviction of his own.
- A 49-year-old dockworker was flagged down by an acquaintance and for $5 agreed to drive him to a hamburger stand. Once there, the friend was arrested by federal agents for dealing drugs. The dockworker, who had no criminal record, was convicted of conspiracy and received a 10-year sentence as mandated by the 1986 Anti-Drug Abuse Act. He will be eligible for release after serving 8.5 years.
- In St. Louis, a 24-year-old mother of three young children received a mandatory 11.5-year federal prison sentence without possibility of parole for her minor role in a cocaine deal. It was her first offense, and evidence indicates that her involvement was the result of a combination of fear and ignorance.
- In California, a 36-year-old Mexican American field worker, the mother of five daughters who does not speak English, was found guilty of transporting several hundred pounds of cocaine and heroin into the United States. Susana claimed that she did not know that the van, which was not hers, contained drugs; at trial it was not proven that she did know. Her 10-year sentence does not permit parole but does allow about 16 months off for good behavior.

Sources: "New Drug Law Leaves No Room for Mercy" (1989); Tackett (1990); Chapman (1991b).

---

that mandate treatment instead of imprisonment for drug offenders (Egan 1999b). Nevertheless, in 2000, 743,000 persons were incarcerated for marijuana possession, the highest number ever (Haynes 2002).

Would Changing the Penalties Help?

What about a policy of incarceration for only the most serious criminal offenders, such as robbers, among the drug-abusing population? Unfortunately, this is not feasible: "Existing criminal justice practices would fail to detect most persons who actually are robber-dealers" (B. Johnson, Lipton, and Wish 1986: 187). In their study, Bruce Johnson and his colleagues found that none of the high-rate addict-robbers were ever arrested for robbery. In fact, "less than 1 percent of self-reported crimes by cocaine-heroin abusers result in an arrest; the higher the crime rate, the lower the possibility of arrest per thousand crimes" (1986: 4).

Drug Availability

"As far as drug availability is concerned, the drug war has been a total failure. Drugs are as widely available now as they ever have been" (Gazzaniga 1995: 50).

In a report to the Ford Foundation, Patricia Wald and Peter Hutt (1972: 37) recommended reducing penalties to a fine or abolishing penalties completely for those possessing drugs for personal use: "If this were done, drug users—but not drug traffickers—could then be handled on a public health and social-welfare basis. . . . Law-enforcement efforts would, and in our opinion should, continue, but they would be directed at illegal distribution. And illegal drugs would remain subject to confiscation wherever found." In Switzerland and the Netherlands (discussed in Chapter 14), there has been an unofficial policy of tolerating small-time drug sellers and their customers, as long as they do not become public nuisances. At best, law enforcement efforts, states Kleiman, can prevent the "effective decriminalization" of drugs, the point at which trafficking "is so open and flagrant that demand increases because the apparent social disapproval is reduced" (1989: xviii).

Increasing penalties for drug trafficking seems an unrealistic strategy because sentences for trafficking are already high—40 years for a second offense—and because capital punishment (for drug-transaction-related murders) has now become part of the federal effort against drugs. (Severe penalties encourage in traffickers the mind-set that they have little or nothing to lose by using violence in their attempts to avoid arrest and prosecution.)

Penalties in Other Nations. Some third-world countries execute drug dealers, but the impact of this policy is questionable. For example, while Malaysia imposes the death penalty for anyone found trafficking in heroin or marijuana, the substances are readily available even to foreigners traveling through that country. The Drug Enforcement Administration points out that "despite severe penalties, no significant diminution of trafficking or production occurred" (1991: 9). Draconian attempts to deal with opium and heroin abuse in Iran have proven unsuccessful. Smugglers and traffickers have been hung at a rate of about six hundred a year since 1988 (Ghazi 1991). (The U.S. State Department has accused Iran of executing political prisoners under the guise of drug trafficking cases [Tyler 1991].)

The People's Republic of China routinely executes drug traffickers found in possession of a pound or more of heroin; in 1994 more than 466 were killed in Yunnan Province alone (Tyler 1995a). On one day in 1999, China executed at least 71 people as part of its antidrug campaign (Associated Press 1999b). Despite the executions, drug trafficking continues to thrive, particularly in Yunnan and Guangdong provinces in southern China, and the country has become a transshipment point for Golden Triangle and Golden Crescent heroin.

Centralize Federal Drug-Law Enforcement?

Increasing the government's drug-law enforcement ability—for example, by improving enforcement resources and centralizing the operational command structure of the executive branch—can bring its own dangers. These are stressed by Edward Jay Epstein (1977: 8), who argues that President Richard Nixon used "the war on heroin" to "set up a series of special units which, it was hoped, would conduct clandestine surveillance of

Drug Justice

Under a Michigan "get tough on drugs" law, the mandatory term for possession of more than 650 grams (about 23 ounces) of an illegal drug exceeds that for either rape or second-degree murder. By 1992 more than 160 persons were serving life sentences without parole for drug offenses. One was Gary Fannon. Fannon had just completed high school and was planning a career as an auto mechanic when he was approached by an undercover Michigan police officer. The officer, who was later fired for drug use, paid Fannon to purchase drugs for him, the amounts getting larger and larger until he bought 2.2 pounds for $32,000. Although he had no prior criminal record, Fannon was sentenced to life without parole. While the Michigan law was upheld by the U.S. Supreme Court (*Harmelin v. Michigan,* 111 S.Ct. 2680, 1991), in 1992 the state supreme court ruled it unconstitutional: The justices found the denial of parole to be unconstitutionally harsh—it is the penalty for first-degree murder—and ordered those sentenced under the law to be considered for parole after 10 years.

In 1991, the Minnesota Supreme Court found unconstitutional and discriminatory against African Americans a state law providing 20 years in prison for crack possession but only 5 years for possession of powdered cocaine. In 1988, of the persons charged with crack possession in Minnesota, 96.6 percent were black, while those charged with possessing cocaine hydrochloride were 79.6 percent white.

Sources: Cauchon (1992); Associated Press (June 15, 1992); Associated Press (December 13, 1991).

both government officials and newsmen during his first administration." On the basis of an executive order, the Office of Drug Abuse Law Enforcement (ODALE) was established with agents requisitioned from the Bureau of Narcotics and Dangerous Drugs, Customs, IRS, and the Bureau of Alcohol, Tobacco and Firearms. This strike force was funded by the executive branch (Law Enforcement Assistance Administration), thus bypassing the need for congressional approval. A special-action office was set up in the White House to work with ODALE; it included Watergate participants Egil Krogh, G. Gordon Liddy, and E. Howard Hunt (McWilliams 1992). Had the Watergate scandal not intervened, Epstein (1977: 252) argues, the drug superagency proposed by the administration "might have served as the strong investigative arm for domestic surveillance that President Nixon had long quested after." As noted in the previous chapter, inefficient law enforcement is the price we pay for our constitutional form of government.

In theory, if at some point the price rises significantly and/or the amount available for consumption falls off considerably, abusers will seek treatment or give up their drug-

A Sting Hurts

U.S. Drug Enforcement (DEA) agents hid 100 pounds of cocaine on a Belize Air International Flight going from Miami to Honduras. Hoping to track and capture drug smugglers, the DEA did not inform the three crew members, the three passengers, or Honduran officials. In Honduras, the cocaine was discovered and the passengers and crew detained and subjected (they allege in a lawsuit) to 12 days of electric shock and rubber hose beatings. The six were released when U.S. officials acknowledged the sting ("Victims of Botched U.S. Drug Sting Sue" 1995).

using habits. Indeed, research has found that the amount of heroin use is related to price (Bach and Lantos 1999). But experience reveals that when drug abusers are unable to secure their preferred substance, they frequently switch to other substances that may be even more harmful. We have already seen that heroin and cocaine have analogs produced in the United States. As long as demand remains strong, we can anticipate that successful interdiction will encourage the production of domestic inorganic (agonists) depressants and stimulants. However, with respect to heroin, increases in cost lead to more addicts seeking methadone treatment (Bach and Lantos 1999).

Enforcement Results

Richard Cowan (1986: 27) argues that federal efforts against cocaine led to the development of crack: *"The iron law of drug prohibition is that the more intense the law enforcement, the more potent the drug will become.* The latest stage of this cycle has brought us the crack epidemic." Free market conditions provide an incentive for traffickers to improve the attractiveness of their product. Jeffrey Fagan and Ko-Lin Chin (1991)

Winning Battles, Losing Wars

Reducing the market for illegal drugs can have unpleasant outcomes because "competition will increase among dealers, perhaps violently. In addition, because selling cocaine has been the primary source of earnings for poor adult males dependent on cocaine, these individuals may turn to other forms of crime to finance their continued consumption, relying more on muggings, burglary, and shoplifting for income, just as heroin users/dealers have done for many years" (Drug Policy Research Center 1992).

point out that crack was the subject of an ingenious production and marketing strategy (see also Witkin 1991). A glut of cocaine forced prices down in 1983, but even lower prices did not keep up with production: "At this point, a new product was introduced which offered the chance to expand the market in ways never before possible: crack, packaged in small quantities and selling for $5 and sometimes even less—a fraction of the usual minimum for powder—allowed dealers to attract an entirely new class of consumers. Once it took hold this change was very swift and very sweeping" (T. Williams 1989: 7).

Crack never became a mainstream drug, and by 1990 the epidemic had peaked, but heroin use increased. Because heroin had lost its dominant market position to cocaine, purity levels increased substantially, drawing in new users who snorted or smoked the substance instead of injecting it intravenously in the more traditional manner. But the "crack scare" of the 1980s left in its wake new laws and greater use of imprisonment, adding significantly to an already overcrowded prison system (Egan 1999a). As David Musto notes: "History shows that excessive use of a drug at one time does not mean that such a high rate will continue indefinitely; the drug may fade in esteem and usage, even to the vanishing point. Reasonable drug policies must take into account the long-term perspective. We should avoid hastily surrendering to defeat at a time of extensive use nor declare victory after a long and deep decline in drug use" (1998: 58).

Insofar as drug abuse is caused by societal deficiencies in education, housing, and other quality-of-life variables, the more we expend on law enforcement, the less we have available to deal with these social ills, which continue to foster greater drug abuse. Not only are we spinning our wheels in the mud, but the faster we go, the deeper the hole becomes. Furthermore, "when criminals are the most successful people in a community, the effect on that community's natural order is devastating. The authority of parents, schools, religious leaders, and (legal) businesspeople is undermined, and violent criminals become role models" (Boaz 1990: 3).

Conclusion

Wisotsky (1987) argues that our law enforcement efforts have failed and will continue to do so. He certainly has the lessons of history and classical economics on his side. "Stop talking about winning drug wars," states Trebach (1987: 383). "In the broadest sense, there is no way to win because we cannot make the drugs or their abusers go away. They will always be with us. We have never run a successful drug war and never will." Nevertheless, more extreme measures are being considered such as shooting down aircraft suspected of transporting drugs. Legislation to accomplish this was introduced into the Senate in 1989 but ran into a storm of opposition from pilots fearful of possible mistakes. The Mexican government reports, however, that they have shot down aircraft suspected of carrying drugs when the planes refuse to respond to warnings. Peru has done the same, and this has cost the lives of innocent travelers on commercial airliners.

We must recognize a troubling aspect of drug trafficking: It operates according to the powerful forces of free market capitalism. It is paradoxical that politicians who argue that capitalism defeated communism in Eastern Europe also talk of defeating the business of drugs. They fail to recognize that these same forces are operating in the drug trade—and that government cannot compete effectively with the free market.

Supply Reduction by Controlling Drugs at Their Source

The current U.S. policy of attempting to control drugs at their source has had unintended consequences: displacement of production and human rights violations.

The "Balloon Effect" and Human Rights Violations

The successful effort to force Turkey to curtail its production of opium in the 1970s resulted in a concomitant rise in production in Mexico and Southeast Asia. Mexican antidrug efforts have led to a rise in poppy production in neighboring Guatemala, whose government is ill equipped to respond to the problem (Sheppard 1990). Crackdowns in Colombia succeeded in displacing the problem into other countries: Ecuador and Brazil now have cocaine-processing laboratories; Argentina, Uruguay, and Chile have emerged as major money-laundering centers; drug-related corruption scandals have hit Argentina and Venezuela, which, along with Chile, serve as major cocaine transshipment centers (Nash 1992).

Bolivia reduced coca cultivation by more than half, but at a price: According to the Human Rights Watch-Americas, pressure on the government of Bolivia to deal with coca cultivation has led to widespread trampling of civil rights and physical abuse of citizenry (Vivanco 1995). Using similar methods, Peru has also cut coca cultivation by more than half. "Peru leads the world in documented cases of disappearances of people taken prisoner by security forces" (Brooke 1991b: 6). In response to declines in these source countries, the Colombian wholesalers who bought Bolivian and Peruvian coca reacted by increasing domestic production. (C. Krauss 1999a).

Coca production in Colombia has more than doubled from 1995 to 2000—the country is now the source of more than 500 tons of cocaine a year, 90 percent of the world's supply. The breakup of the powerful Medellín and Cali drug cartels spurred coca cultivation in more remote regions of the country and resulted in alliances between new drug gangs and leftist guerrillas. Added to this volatile mix are right-wing paramilitary forces who, like their left-wing enemies, are supported by the drug trade. "Feeling relatively safe on their native soil, native coca-growing syndicates have invested heavily in developing more potent strains, some of which can be harvested in as little as 60 days" (Rohter 2000b). Colombian syndicates have achieved extraordinary levels of efficiency in extracting cocaine from their coca crops. Higher-yielding varieties of coca are being grown in parts of Colombia. Likewise, Colombian laboratory operators are more efficient in processing coca leaf into cocaine base than they had been previously (U.S. Department of State 2000).

After Congress approved a Clinton administration allocation of $1.6 billion to help the Colombian government fight drug traffickers, an editorial in the *Chicago Tribune* (March 12, 2000: 18) argued: "This policy threatens to entangle the U.S. in a decade-old foreign guerilla war while doing nothing to dampen the engine that ultimately drives narcotrafficking: America's roughly $50 billion a year appetite for illicit drugs." The editorial, after noting the Colombian army's and its right-wing paramilitary allies' involvement in massive human rights violations, stated: "It would be repugnant to funnel American aid to a foreign army with such bloody credentials."

Economic Importance of the Coca Crop in Peru and Bolivia

In Peru and Bolivia inhabitants of coca-growing areas are strongly opposed to U.S.-inspired efforts to eradicate their most important cash crop, and both countries face Marxist insurgencies that are particularly strong in these remote regions. Unfortunately, in addition to providing a livelihood for impoverished Bolivian farmers, cocaine brings into Bolivia more money than all legal exports combined.

In Peru's Upper Huallaga Valley, which extends for 200 miles along the Huallaga River, an estimated 60,000 families depend on coca as a cash crop for their survival. Large-scale eradication, notes Alan Riding (1988: 6), could "provoke a social convulsion, forcing thousands of families to leave the area" and creating deep resentment that Marxist guerrillas exploit. And "coca is Peru's largest export, earning more than one billion dollars a year. As many as one million of the country's twenty-one million citizens are involved in the trade" (Massing 1990: 26). Under President Alberto K. Fujimori, Peruvian armed forces have been shooting down planes suspected of transporting drugs—about twenty-five aircraft met this fate. This strategy succeeded in breaking the "air bridge," and when the price of coca leaf dropped more than 60 percent in 1995, farmers began abandoning the crop. With U.S. help, Peruvian officials began teaching farmers to raise coffee instead of coca. By 1999, however, traffickers had reopened some air routes and replaced others with river, road, and sea channels, once again making coca profitable, and the crop rebounded (C. Krauss 1999b). Government anti-coca efforts in Bolivia left thousands of Indian farmers without a source of income and helped generate violent protests that left several soldiers, police officers, and farmers dead (Associated Press 2000b).

Wisotsky (1987: 57) states that "in both Peru and Bolivia, the failure of coca control is not a temporary aberration but a function of culture, tradition, and the weakness and poverty of underdevelopment. These basic social conditions render effective enforcement against coca impossible. Widespread corruption in the enforcement agencies, the judiciary, and elsewhere in government is endemic. Indeed, the central governments do not necessarily control major portions of the coca-growing countryside, where the traffickers rule like feudal lords." Participation in the illicit cocaine economy, writes Edmundo Morales (1986: 157), "is inevitable. Not only is the natives' traditional way of life intertwined with coca, but their best cash crop is the underground economy for which no substitute has yet been provided."

Crop Eradication or Substitution

Crop-substitution programs have been part of the U.S. effort to control drugs at their source, but have met with only limited success. As long as demand remains high, the price offered for poppy or coca will be many times that received for conventional crops.

Coca

"Not only is coca fully integrated into Andean society but it is also an integral part of the region's ecosystem—a stubborn and dismaying biological fact impeding those who would like to make it disappear. As a cultivated plant, coca is nearly ideal. It has few predators and pests. . . . The plant will grow in soils too poor and on slopes too steep to support other crops, will live for forty years or more, and will tolerate many harvests a year" (Weil 1995: 72).

A View from Latin America

Thirteen persons, including jurists, doctors, artists, religious leaders, and three former Latin presidents—Belisario Betancur of Colombia, Violeta Chamorro of Nicaragua, and Nobel Peace Prize Laureate Oscar Arias of Costa Rica—signed a letter stating that the U.S.-led military-style war on drugs is a failure and should be changed to focus more on ending the demand for drugs and drug money. "The escalation of a militarized drug war in Colombia and elsewhere in the Americas threatens regional stability, undermines efforts towards demilitarization and democracy and has put U.S. arms and money into the hands of corrupt officials and military . . . units involved in human rights abuses." It is time to admit, the letter continued "that after two decades, the U.S. war on drugs—both in Latin American and in the United States—is a failure." Despite spending tens of billions of dollars for raids on drug labs, crop eradication and arrests and imprisonment at home, "today in the U.S., illicit drugs are cheaper, more potent and more easily available than two decades ago" (Jelnik 1999).

There are other problems: In 1991 the leader of a Peruvian coca-growers association who had agreed to a crop-substitution program was murdered, reputedly by corrupt government officials earning money from the cocaine business (Strong 1992).

Attempts to eradicate the crop by cutting or burning result in healthier and more bountiful growth, while uprooting coca plants causes the soil to become unproductive for as long as 8 to 10 years (Morales 1989). An eradication program in the Upper Huallaga Valley was established with U.S. funding in 1982, but since that time about forty of its workers have been murdered. The United States subsequently suspended the program (Massing 1990).

An alternative is the use of aerial herbicides that are either sprayed or dropped as pellets and that melt into the soil when it rains. The United States has been conducting research on a variety of environmentally safe herbicides. The most successful herbicides, however, kill many species of plants, including crop plants, and they remain in the soil, affecting future plantings. Environmentalists have raised objections to the use of herbicides, and the companies that produce them are concerned about potential liability and fear that their employees in South America may become targets of retribution by trafficking organizations (Riding 1988). Furthermore, Lee McIntosh (1988: 26) has found that a "single genetic mutation can give rise to complete resistance in a similar herbicide. This implies it may be necessary continually to spray different classes of herbicides in the future." The human and political dangers inherent in this approach to drug control should serve as a restraining influence.

Successful eradication and interdiction efforts can affect both availability and price. However, because of the pattern of price markups in the cocaine business, efforts to eradicate

Cost at the Source

"It costs cocaine refiners only 30 cents to purchase the coca leaf needed to produce a gram of cocaine, which sells for about $150 in the United States. Even if the price of the leaves needed for that gram of the finished product doubled, it would be negligible. And if retail prices don't rise, then consumption in the United States will not decline" (Reuter 2000: 29).

crops or supply routes that increase the cost of the coca leaf tenfold add only 5 percent to the retail consumer price, while doubling seizures from importers increases consumer cost by only 10 percent (Passell 1990).

If all of the coca that the producing countries of Latin America have publicly committed themselves to eradicate were actually eradicated, the effect in the United States would be minimal. It is likely that African, Middle Eastern, and Southeast Asian areas would be able to cultivate enough to meet consumer demand in coca indefinitely (as they have done with opium). It should be noted that coca leaf has been grown commercially in Indonesia, Malaysia, Nigeria, Sri Lanka, and Taiwan. Indeed, the crop grown in Java and Taiwan contained more than twice the cocaine than the varieties grown in Latin America (Karch 1998). Edward Epstein (1988: 25) points out that "the entire cocaine market in the United States can be supplied for a year by a single cargo plane." Furthermore, as noted in previous chapters, curtailing importation without affecting demand provides an incentive for greater domestic efforts: the production of synthetic analogs for cocaine and heroin and stronger strains of marijuana.

The inventive marijuana horticulturists of California are using a new, faster-growing, highly potent strain that matures in 3 months (older strains require 4 months). The cultivation of this new strain has been discovered in the national forests of Northern California. (Growing marijuana on federal lands was made a felony in 1987, punishable by a prison term of up to 10 years.)

In response to law enforcement efforts against imported marijuana, some innovative growers have established elaborate underground farms equipped with diesel-powered lights and ventilation systems. Their use of hydroponic technology—growing plants in water to which nutrients have been added—has helped make marijuana the number one cash crop

Aerial marijuana searches continue to locate illegal farms, but as this photo shows, clever cultivators have gone underground. Innovations can include diesel-powered lights, ventilation systems, and hydroponic technology.

© Owen Franken/Getty Images

in the United States. In response, the DEA has been subpoenaing the records of businesses selling hydroponic equipment in order to discover indoor marijuana growers. These records contain the names of mostly legitimate growers paying by check or credit card—marijuana traffickers usually pay cash—who may be subjected to DEA inquiries (Bishop 1991).

Drug Enforcement and Foreign Policy

There is evidence that U.S. efforts against drug trafficking are often secondary to foreign policy considerations. The Anti-Drug Abuse Act of 1986, for example, requires the president to "certify" to Congress that producer and transshipment nations have made adequate progress in attacking drug production and trafficking. Without certification, a country can lose aid, loans, and trade preferences. Elaine Sciolino (1988) reports that the law has numerous loopholes allowing several nations to be certified despite their failure to cooperate in the war against drugs. In 1990, of the twenty-four major drug-producing and drug-transiting countries, only four—Afghanistan, Myanmar, Iran, and Syria— were denied certification.

At the other extreme, the United States has turned to the military in Guatemala, a major producer of opium and a leading transshipment point for Colombian cocaine, to take the lead in efforts against trafficking. The Guatemalan military, however, has been responsible for human rights abuses that have plagued the country (Gruson 1990).

For many years we tolerated the drug-trafficking activities of our Central American ally, General Manuel Noriega. When his politics took on a decidedly anti-U.S. tone, in 1988 the general was indicted and apprehended, following the "Operation Just Cause" invasion of Panama. (For a discussion of Noriega, his relationship with the United States, and drug dealing, see Dinges 1990; Kempe 1990.) According to Thomas A. Constantine, retired director of the Drug Enforcement Administration, the administration of Bill Clinton was more concerned about trade and other economic issues in their relationship with Mexico than with corruption and drug trafficking (Golden 1999).

Peter Andreas and his colleagues note that "after more than a decade of U.S. efforts to reduce the cocaine supply, more cocaine is produced in more places than ever before. Curiously, the U.S. response to failure has been to escalate rather than reevaluate." And they state: "The logic of escalation in the drug war is in fact strikingly similar to the arguments advanced when U.S. counterinsurgency strategies, undercut by ineffective and uncommitted governments and security forces, were failing in Vietnam: 'We've just begun to fight.' 'We're turning the corner.' " Andreas and his colleagues argue that "since failure can so easily be used to justify further escalation, how do we know whether we are really turning the corner or simply running around in a vicious circle?" (1991–92: 107).

Demand Reduction by Drug Testing

The President's Commission on Organized Crime (1986), in what has become its most controversial recommendation, suggested extensive drug testing as a device for reducing consumer demand. Public and private employers began testing new and ongoing employees, generating criticism and lawsuits. Drug testing of prospective employees has become almost routine at many major corporations. About 61 percent of major U.S. companies administer pre-employment drug tests, and more than 500 school districts have screening programs (D. Hawkins 2002).[1] The military has extended its program of drug testing, and various levels of government have initiated the testing of employees in critical areas involving public safety, particularly law enforcement and transportation. Some states have reacted to increasing protests about the practice by enacting legislation barring random testing of employees, and in a number of states the practice is thwarted by constitutional provisions guaranteeing individuals the right to privacy.

Case Law Results

In states with privacy provisions, for an intrusive act such as mandatory drug testing to be constitutional, there must be a "compelling interest." In a 1987 case, a computer programmer dismissed from her job for refusing to take a drug test on the grounds of personal privacy was awarded $485,000—a San Francisco jury failed to find "compelling interest." That city has subsequently enacted an ordinance prohibiting mandatory testing except when an employer has reason to believe—"reasonable suspicion"—that an employee is impaired because of drug use (Bishop 1987).

In 1989, the Supreme Court upheld the testing of railroad employees for drugs after an accident and ruled that personnel of the U.S. Customs Service in sensitive positions must submit to drug testing, even in the absence of "individualized suspicion" (*Skinner v. Railway Labor Executives' Association,* 109 S.Ct. 1402; *National Treasury Employees Union v. von Raab,* 109 S.Ct. 1384). In a 6-month study completed in 1990, slightly more than 3 percent of 65,000 U.S. transportation workers tested positive for drugs—mostly marijuana and cocaine—as did 4.2 percent of applicants for such positions (Cawley 1990). Lower federal courts have rejected the testing of *public* employees suspected of using drugs in a manner that does not affect job performance; the U.S. Constitution does not similarly protect *private* employees. In an Oregon case, the U.S. Supreme Court (6–3) approved of the random urinalysis of public school athletes as a condition of their continued participation (*Vernonia School District v. Acton,* 515 U.S. 646 [1995]).

In 2002, the Court, in a 5–4 decision (*Board of Education v. Earls,* No. 01-332), extended *Vernonia* by upholding an Oklahoma school district's policy of requiring students engaged in virtually all extracurricular school activities to submit to random drug testing. The majority opinion written by Justice Clarence Thomas stated that given the epidemic of drug use by youngsters and the schools' "custodial responsibilities," drug testing was entirely reasonable. That led hundreds of school boards across the country, mostly in smaller districts, to consider proposals for testing students (Lewin 2002).

---

[1]In Alabama, where the legal age for smoking tobacco products is 19, about a dozen school districts test for nicotine in addition to alcohol and illegal drugs (Giuffrida 2002).

Drug Testing Process

Drug testing has spawned a growth industry. The National Institute on Drug Abuse (NIDA) certifies drug testing firms, a necessity for securing federal contracts. NIDA has certified about fifty labs, which must maintain stringent standards in areas such as sample collection, storage, personnel, laboratory controls, and testing procedures and accuracy. Table 13.1 summarizes the pros and cons of the various testing methods; the most common is urinalysis.

Urinalysis. Primarily because of its low cost—about five dollars a test—the enzyme-multiplied immune test is the most frequently used urinalysis (Wish n.d.). "These tests depend on a chemical reaction between the specimen and an antibody designed to react to a specific drug. The chemical reaction causes a change in the specimen's transmission of light, which is measured by a machine. If the reading is higher than a given standard, the specimen is positive for the drug" (n.d.: 2). Eric Wish notes that there have been complaints of relatively high rates of false positives using this test, sometimes as a result of commonly used licit drugs cross-reacting with the test's antibody. "Sloppy recording procedures by laboratory staff and failure to maintain careful controls over the chain of custody of the specimen can also produce serious test errors" (n.d.: 2).

The most accurate test, gas chromatography/mass spectroscopy, notes Wish (n.d.), is relatively expensive—about $100 per specimen for screening and confirmation—but so is the cost of firing or not hiring someone because of a false positive. Drug testing programs often use the enzyme-multiplied immune test for an initial screening and then submit all positives for gas chromatography/mass spectroscopy (GC-MS). But GC-MS is not perfect. "The test works by extracting and heating molecules from a sample and using an electric field to separate and identify them." At best, however, this is 95 to 99 percent accurate. And some labs, as a cost-saving device, "look for only a few fragments of the drug molecules which raises the risk of mistaking legitimate medicines, herbs, and foods like poppy seeds for illegal drugs" (D. Hawkins 2002: 47).

Hair Analysis. Collecting hair samples is easy and is not subject to evasive actions designed to produce false negatives—shampooing, for example, has no effect. Hair analysis has been used for some time to detect exposure to such toxic metals as mercury and lead. In a process similar to urinalysis, dissolved hair shafts reveal whether drugs are in the blood. Because of the unique qualities of hair growth—about one-half inch a month—it may be possible to determine the amount of drug use over a period of several months and whether it is increasing or decreasing. There are complications, however: The test can also be positive for those who come into contact with drugs via touching the skin or sweat of a user or through exposure to air where the substance has been smoked (Baumgartner, Hill, and Blahd 1989). And contaminants can be discriminatory in their impact: "Drug molecules, whether ingested or picked up from the environment, have an affinity for the pigment melanin and bind more strongly to dark hair than light" (D. Hawkins 2002: 48). Hair analysis has been suggested as an initial screening method for drug use, positives to be corroborated by urinalysis/GC-MS (Magura, Kang, and Shapiro 1995; Mieczkowski 1995; D. Hawkins 2002).

TABLE 13.1   **Pros and Cons of Various Drug Testing Methods**

Type of Test	Pros	Cons	Window of Detection
Urine	■ Highest assurance of reliable results. ■ Least expensive. ■ Most flexibility in testing different drugs, including alcohol and nicotine. ■ Most likely of all drug-testing methods to withstand legal challenge.	■ Specimen can be adulterated, substituted, or diluted. ■ Limited window of detection. ■ Test sometimes viewed as invasive or embarrassing. ■ Biological hazard for specimen handling and shipping to lab.	■ Typically 1 to 5 days.
Hair	■ Longer window of detection. ■ Greater stability (does not deteriorate). ■ Can measure chronic drug use. ■ Convenient shipping and storage (no need to refrigerate). ■ Collection procedure not considered invasive or embarrassing. ■ More difficult to adulterate than urine. ■ Detects alcohol/cocaine combination use.	■ More expensive. ■ Test usually limited to basic 5-drug panel. ■ Cannot detect alcohol use. ■ Will not detect very recent drug use (1 to 7 days prior to test).	■ Depends on the length of hair in the sample. Hair grows about a half-inch per month, so a 1 1/2-inch specimen would show a 3-month history.
Oral Fluids	■ Sample obtained under direct observation. ■ Minimal risk of tampering. ■ Noninvasive. ■ Samples can be collected easily in virtually any environment. ■ Can detect alcohol use. ■ Reflects recent drug use.	■ Drugs and drug metabolites do not remain in oral fluids as long as they do in urine. ■ Less efficient than other testing methods in detecting marijuana use.	■ Approximately 10 to 24 hours.
Sweat Patch	■ Noninvasive. ■ Variable removal date (generally 1 to 7 days). ■ Quick application and removal. ■ Longer window of detection than urine. ■ No sample substitution possible.	■ Limited number of labs able to process results. ■ People with skin eruptions, excessive hair, or cuts and abrasions cannot wear the patch. ■ Passive exposure to drugs may contaminate patch and affect results.	■ Patch retains evidence of drug use for at least 7 days, and can detect even low levels of drugs 2 to 5 hours after last use.

Source: Office of National Drug Control Policy (2002a).

Security companies investigate drug residues in the workplace by using portable machines that can identify vapors from minuscule particles of heroin, cocaine, and methamphetamines. Samples are gathered at such critical areas as doorknobs or desktops by cloth or vacuum cleaners and analyzed through gas chromatography, a process that separates out compounds according to their boiling points. A readout indicates the type of substance detected ("Sniffing for Drugs by Testing Vapors" 1991).

Sweat Patch.   For this type of test, a Band-Aid-like patch is attached to the skin to collect sweat for up to 7 days and subsequently lab tested for drug residue. If the patch is removed, it cannot be reattached. This test is often used by probation and parole agencies. However, drug molecules from clothes or other people can penetrate the patch and trigger a false positive (D. Hawkins 2002).

Testing Problems

At best, drug testing can only determine that the subject has used a drug recently; it cannot determine when or how much. Tests cannot discern the casual user from a chronic one. There is concern over the inadequacy of testing—false positives that could destroy the careers of innocent employees. In 2000, the U.S. Department of Health and Human Services revealed that the shortcomings of drug testing laboratories were jeopardizing the jobs of innocent employees (Zuckerman 2000).

The rationale behind drug testing is confused and ironic: Employers are interested in having a drug-free workplace because controlled substances are presumed to be detrimental to job performance. If this is so, then monitoring job performance—a rather routine managerial task—makes more sense than drug testing, since some people will perform quite well even though their urine reveals drugs. Persons who lawfully come into contact with cocaine, such as plastic surgeons and drug-law enforcement officers, will test positive for the substance, as will anyone exposed to crack-cocaine fumes, even though the dose is far too low to produce symptoms (Karch 1996).

Another standard explanation is that impaired workers represent a workplace hazard. This may indeed be true, but drug testing does not reveal impairment, and impaired workers are most likely to be alcohol abusers. There is a lack of documentation proving that workers testing positive for illegal drugs have a higher rate of accidents (Noble 1992). Sound public relations may better explain workplace drug testing than sound public policy.

The criminal justice system uses drug testing in making bail or pretrial release decisions, and in probation and parole supervision.

Drug Testing as Failed Policy

A federally financed study of 76,000 students found that drug testing had no effect on drug use—does not change "hearts and minds" (Winter 2003).

Demand Reduction by Criminal Prosecution for Fetal Liability

The prosecution of drug-using pregnant women for fetal endangerment, delivering drugs to a minor, or child abuse dates back to the end of the 1980s, when drug abuse was high in the political consciousness of elected officials, and an increasing number of "drug babies" were being reported. It is estimated that about 350,000 infants annually are exposed prenatally to some form of illegal drug (Nolan 1990). Prosecution is sometimes used to coerce women into drug treatment, although drug treatment programs may not be readily available, and those that are may be unwilling or unable to provide for pregnant clients.

The first woman convicted for delivering a controlled substance to her fetus, in Florida in 1990, was sentenced to a year in a drug treatment program and 14 years probation; her conviction was upheld by a state appeals court the following year but was later voided by the Florida Supreme Court (Lewin 1991; 1992). In 1991 the Michigan Court of Appeals ruled that a woman who took crack hours before giving birth could not be charged with delivering cocaine to her son through the umbilical cord. In response to the decision, the Muskegon County prosecutor defended his decision to charge the woman: "This is a major health care crisis and we must use whatever means we can to reach a solution" (Wilkerson 1991: 13). Health care officials who supported the woman expressed fear that prosecuting drug-using pregnant women will drive them away from prenatal care. Courts have dismissed similar cases in North Carolina, Ohio, and Florida (Lewin 1991).

Despite considerable concern about the high rate of cocaine use among pregnant women, studies have failed to find a homogeneous pattern of fetal effects, and there is little consensus on the adverse effects of the drug (Finnegan et al. 1994). In a study of birth outcomes and developmental growth of children exposed to drugs in utero, infants varied in their birth outcomes, with a majority evidencing no significant problems (Cosden, Peerson, and Elliott 1997). An overwhelming majority of women using cocaine also ingest other drugs, including nicotine, alcohol, marijuana, and opiates. And many suffer from sexual and physical abuse (Finnegan 1993). It is difficult to separate the effects of cocaine from other potential hazards to the fetus: "Women who use cocaine during pregnancy also engage in other behaviors, such as alcohol and tobacco use, that are risk factors for poor pregnancy outcome. In addition, they often live in circumstances that, in themselves, create an environment that fosters poor developmental outcome. To understand the unique or independent effects of cocaine exposure during pregnancy, it is critical to separate factors that correlate with prenatal cocaine use and with the outcome, both at birth and during the postpartum period" (Richardson and Day 1999: 234).

While we know that women who abuse heroin during pregnancy frequently give birth to infants suffering from Neonatal Abstinence Syndrome—the newborn suffers withdrawal symptoms—we do not know if there are long-range effects directly attributable to the use of drugs. As with cocaine, it is difficult, if not impossible, to separate the effects of drugs from the effects of poverty and poor prenatal care. Furthermore, the fetus can be endangered by any number of maternal behaviors not related to *illegal* drug use, for example, "too much or too little exercise, an inadequate or harmful diet, or use of cigarettes, alcohol [6,000 to 8,000 born annually with fetal alcohol syndrome], and other [lawful] drugs" (Nolan 1990: 13–14). Other risks include the general environment and specific workplace exposures.

Research has revealed that infants (about 750,000 per year) exposed to a high level of cigarette smoke (one pack or more per day) suffer from decreased birth weight, head circumference, and body length; there are also increased rates of spontaneous abortions and bleeding during pregnancy. An estimated 5,600 infants die each year as a result of smoking by their pregnant mothers. A study in 1994 revealed that mothers who smoke as few as 10 cigarettes a day cause their children under 5 years old to test positive for cancer-causing compounds (Hilts 1994).

And what of the liability of the father who is using illegal drugs or alcohol or tobacco? Recent research suggests that psychoactive substances are hazardous to spermatozoa

(Finnegan 1993). Furthermore, what of the societal responsibility to provide adequate prenatal care for all pregnant women? The nonmedical use of controlled substances is only one facet of a significantly greater social problem that will not be resolved by a simplistic recourse to criminal law.

An equally pressing problem is the cost of providing for infants of drug-abusing mothers: Foster care for one child ranges from $15,000 to $20,000 a year. New York City has responded to this problem by permitting drug-abusing mothers to keep their children at home under the intensive supervision of a social worker (Treaster 1991). A study in Illinois found that while white and African American women show similar rates of illegal drug use during pregnancy, "the black women are more likely to be reported to authorities" (Olen 1991: Sec. 3: 14). Illinois is one of a number of states where medical personnel are required to report suspected prenatal drug use to authorities. But there are few places in the state to care for babies born with drugs in their bloodstream, so they are usually sent home with their mother with some type of outpatient help and monitoring (Poe and Searcey 1996).

Demand Reduction by Expanding Treatment

Justifying Treatment

"Treatment and prevention programs are frequently required to show that they are cost-effective, a standard never imposed on drug enforcement" (MacCoun and Reuter 1997: 47).

While the core of the U.S. response to drug use has centered on enforcement, expanding the availability of treatment may be more productive for reducing demand. There is almost universal agreement that without reduced demand, our efforts will remain ineffective.

The cost effectiveness of *treatment versus law enforcement* is emphasized by Peter Rydell and Susan Everingham. They argue that $246 million would have to be spent on domestic law enforcement to achieve the same reduction in drug use that could be achieved by spending $34 million on treatment. And no assumption is made about the long-range effect of treatment—abstinence—on the individual abuser: "The cost advantage is so large that even if the after-treatment effect is ignored, treatment is still more cost-effective than law enforcement" (1994: xv).

Mandatory Treatment

It is the possession of controlled substances that constitutes a crime—an addict is not a criminal by virtue of his or her addiction. In *Robinson v. California* 370 U.S. 660 (1962), the Supreme Court ruled that persons cannot be prosecuted for "being under the influence" or for "internal possession" of illegal drugs. The Court, in that same decision, upheld the civil commitment of drug addicts for purposes of *treatment* (similar to commitment of the mentally ill): "A state might determine that the general health and welfare require that the victims of these and other human afflictions might be dealt with by compulsory treatment, involving quarantine, confinement, or sequestration." Some twenty-seven states have made such a determination and enacted legislation that permits the civil commitment of drug addicts (J. Kaplan 1983b). Only California and New York, however, have made extensive use of such statutes.

As noted in Chapter 9, in 1961 the California legislature passed comprehensive legislation raising the penalties for drug violations and providing for the compulsory civil commitment of narcotic addicts. In its first 12 years, the California Civic Addict Program admitted more than 18,000 addicts for treatment. Most of those committed to the program, however, were persons who had been convicted of felony crimes, with a much smaller number convicted of misdemeanors, and an even smaller amount committed without any criminal charges at all (R. Wood 1973). While the California program continues to operate, the New York program was discontinued in 1974 after an enormous expenditure of tax dollars with, at best, questionable results.

Bruce Johnson and his colleagues (1986) argue in favor of mandatory treatment, because almost all objective evidence suggests that drug treatment has an important impact on heroin-cocaine abuser criminality. The cost of such a policy, they note, would be prohibitive unless treatment was on an outpatient basis, a method they support. Because most heroin and cocaine abusers have come into contact with the criminal justice system, all criminal defendants should be subjected to drug tests, which, if positive, should require mandatory treatment. Johnson and his colleagues argue that drug treatment should be part of any sentence for convicted drug abusers and that postrelease treatment should be a condition of probation/parole supervision, with a careful monitoring of urine for at least 1 year (see, for example, Benedict, Huff-Corzine, and Corzine 1998). This writer has supervised heroin addicts on parole in New York, and their careful monitoring by a parole officer does ensure a high rate of abstinence, at least during the period of supervision. But in any number of jurisdictions, supervision in the community is superficial, with caseloads so large that they cannot be adequately monitored. Offenders who violate the conditions of supervision by using drugs often go unnoticed or unpunished, remaining at liberty until they are arrested again for another drug offense (Abadinsky 2003a).

Measuring the Result of Policy Changes

A major problem with instituting any changes in policy is measurement of results. Increases or decreases in the number of persons using illegal substances cannot be measured with any accuracy, and the statistics that are often presented as "data" are usually meaningless. There are no direct measures of the incidence of drug use in the general population; all estimates are derivative, such incidence or prevalence being inferred from various data gathered by law enforcement or medical sources.

Patrick Biernacki (1986: 189) points out that "it cannot be determined with any degree of certainty what effect U.S. drug policy has had on the addict population. What we do know is that the indicators used to estimate the size of the addict population at any one time are unreliable. For example, if the number of hospital emergency room admissions for heroin overdoses drops, does this indicate the effectiveness of police control methods, or the successful treatment of addicts? Or can the drop in admissions be attributed to a change in drug preference? Or to an increase in the number of natural recoveries?"

Natural recovery, or the abandoning of heroin use, was discovered among returning Vietnam veterans on a relatively large scale (Robins 1973, 1974; Robins et al. 1980).[2] To the extent that we have been able to measure the effect of our drug policy, the results, but not necessarily the claims, have not been clear.

Now that we have examined drug policy in the United States, in the next chapter we will consider more radical changes, some of which are being or have been adopted by European countries.

SUMMARY

U.S. drug abuse policy is filled with incongruities and inconsistencies, starting with which drugs are legal and which are not. Scientific knowledge about drug effects is not the determining factor; rather political knowledge is. Attempting to reduce the supply of illegal drugs has led to overflowing prisons and the availability of more potent drugs, without any measurable drop in consumption. Attempting to reduce supply by eradicating drugs at their source has led to displacement of production to other countries and massive human rights violations. On the demand side, drug testing is an unproven tool of fear; prosecution for fetal liability has not been used often and leaves many questions unanswered. Expanding treatment and mandatory treatment for convicted drug felons offer the best hope for curtailing the demand for drugs. Unfortunately, measuring results of policy changes is nearly impossible.

INTERNET CONNECTIONS

Community Anti-Drug Coalitions: www.cadca.org

Drug Policy Alliance (liberal drug policy group): www.dpf.org

Drug Strategies (mainstream group promotes more effective drug policy): www.drugstrategies.org

DrugSense (drug policy reform group): www.drugsense.org

FAS Drug Policy Project (American Federation of Scientists opposing current drug policy): www.fas.org/drugs

Institute for a Drug-Free Workplace (corporate financed policy group): www.drugfreeworkplace.org

Mothers Against Drunk Driving: www.madd.org

REVIEW QUESTIONS

1. What are the differences between *scientific* and *political* knowledge?
2. Why have some psychoactive drugs been outlawed while others are legally and widely available?
3. What are the disadvantages of focusing law enforcement on low-level dealers?
4. What are some of the unanticipated results of drug-law enforcement?
5. How does the "natural law" of capitalism mitigate against effective drug-law enforcement?
6. Why is criminal prosecution for fetal liability a questionable policy?

---

[2]On natural recovery among middle-class addicts, see Granfield and Cloud (1996).

7. What are the drawbacks in controlling such drugs as cocaine and heroin at their source countries?
8. Why is drug treatment more cost effective than drug-law enforcement?
9. Why is it difficult, if not impossible, to measure the success of any change in drug policy?

CHAPTER 14

Drug Maintenance, Decriminalization, and Harm Reduction

The easy cynicism that has grown up around the drug issue is no accident. Sowing it has been the deliberate aim of a decades-long campaign by proponents of legalization, critics whose mantra is "nothing works," and whose central insight appears to be that they can avoid having to propose the unmentionable—a world where drugs are ubiquitous—if they can hide behind the bland management critique that drug control efforts are "unworkable." —National Drug Control Strategy (2002: 3)

There is little question that if the production, sale, and possession of alcohol and tobacco were criminalized, the health costs associated with their use and abuse could be reduced. But most Americans do not believe that criminalizing the alcohol and tobacco markets would be a good idea. Their opposition stems largely from two beliefs: that adult Americans have the right to choose what substances they will consume and what risks they will take, and that the economic costs of trying to coerce so many Americans into abstaining from those substances would be enormous and the social costs disastrous.

—Ethan Nadelmann (1988: 97)

What should we as a nation do about drug use? What are our options beyond enforcement? In this chapter we look at some other possibilities.

Decriminalization of Drugs of Abuse

John Kaplan poses the following policy question: "Could we not lower the total social costs of heroin use and the government response to it by allowing the drug to be freely and cheaply available in liquor stores, or as an over-the-counter drug?" (1983b: 101). Such policy would be consistent with the U.S. approach to other unhealthy habits such as cigarette smoking, drinking alcohol, and overeating, or to sports such as mountain climbing, skydiving, automobile and motorcycle racing, football, and boxing—an acknowledgment of an individual's freedom to enjoy him- or herself or to earn money, even through activities that may be injurious to that person's health. In fact, deliberately engaging in dangerous pursuits can be explained by these activities causing release of potentially reinforcing neurotransmitters such as dopamine or endorphin.

Edward Brecher notes that most of the harmful aspects of heroin use are the result of its being illegal: "Many American morphine and heroin addicts before 1914 led long, healthy, respectable, productive lives despite addiction—and so do a few addicts today. The sorry plight of most heroin addicts in the United States results primarily from the high price of heroin, the contamination and adulteration of the heroin available on the black market, the mainlining of the drug instead of safer modes of use, the laws against heroin and the ways in which they are enforced, the imprisonment of addicts, society's attitudes toward addicts, and other nonpharmacological factors" (1972: 528). Drug czar Barry McCaffrey argues that "addictive drugs were criminalized because they are harmful; they are not harmful because they were criminalized"—but he avoids any reference to nicotine and alcohol (press release June 15, 1999). James Ostrowski notes, "Our attempt to protect drug users from themselves has backfired, as it did during the prohibition of alcohol. We have only succeeded in making drug use much more dangerous and driving it underground, out of the reach of moderating social influences" (Committee on Law Reform 1987: 6). Furthermore, imprisonment serves as a form of networking and recruitment for drug dealers and their clients (Currie 1993).

The Pros

The practical advantages of a drug maintenance/decriminalization policy are impressive:

1. There would be a reduction in the resources necessary for drug-law enforcement. Federal, state, and local governments spend billions of tax dollars annually for drug-law enforcement; additional billions are spent on imprisonment and probation and parole supervision of drug users. These resources could be shifted to other areas of crime control and to drug treatment and prevention. Jonathan Caulkins and his colleagues caution that if the money saved from not having to enforce drug prohibition were used to fund drug prevention, "even by our most optimistic estimates of prevention's effectiveness" it would not offset any increase in use resulting from relaxation of controls (1999: xxx).

2. The low cost of psychoactive substances would curtail secondary criminality needed to support an expensive drug habit. It would obviate the need to trade sex for drugs, a practice that has helped to spread AIDS.

3. Criminal organizations supported by drug trafficking would no longer remain viable, unless, of course, they moved into other criminal activities.

4. The aggressive marketing by traffickers aimed at expanding customer bases would no longer be operative; this marketing resulted in the widespread use of crack cocaine.

5. Those dependent on heroin, cocaine, or other currently illegal psychoactive substances could lead more normal lives, the time and energy needed to maintain the habit could be channeled into more constructive pursuits, and abusers would have an opportunity to become contributing members of society. For example, it is not the drug but the law that makes heroin hazardous to the addict. Opiates, like widely

prescribed sedatives, provide relief from anxiety, distress, and insomnia to persons who would have difficulty functioning normally in the absence of such substances. Similar arguments can be made for cocaine and other substances. For those who accept the disease theory of addiction—that some persons take heroin or cocaine to compensate for a physiological deficiency—decriminalization is a reasonable suggestion. Allowing these people access to drugs is analogous to the diabetic's need for insulin. Some researchers have found a strong correlation between poor mental health and drug abuse: Drugs are frequently self-prescribed by persons to deal with their mental problems, and psychoactive drugs do alleviate, at least temporarily, psychological discomfort, enabling the person to relax and/or function more effectively.

6.   The intravenous use of heroin would not necessarily involve the danger of hepatitis or AIDS because each user would have his or her own hypodermic kit. In the United States, while the incidence of AIDS among the homosexual population has stabilized, the disease is spreading quickly among drug addicts. Decriminalization would also make many drugs available in liquid form for oral ingestion. Under government oversight, drugs would be distributed in precisely measured doses, free of any dangerous contaminants. The chance of a drug overdose would thus be reduced.

7.   Decriminalization would enable the use of social controls that inhibit antisocial, albeit lawful, behavior. Because drugs are illegal, users avoid detection and are shielded from social pressure. "Therefore, illicit drug users generally escape the potent forms of social control that are applied to smokers and drunk drivers" (Alexander 1990: 8).

The Cons

There are, of course, important disadvantages:

1.   Cocaine, amphetamines, and heroin freely available to adults could be abused by youngsters as easily as cigarettes and alcohol are. Restrictions on these items have not proven effective in keeping the substances away from young people (see, for example, Feder 1996a). Those adolescents motivated toward drug use are unlikely to be thwarted by legislative acts and law enforcement efforts. Zimring and Hawkins point out, however: "To the extent that prohibition policies make drugs more difficult or more expensive for adults to acquire, the same policies will mean that young persons will encounter a prohibited drug less often and will often be unable to afford the purchase even when a source is located" (1992: 121)

2.   More people would be tempted to try legalized controlled substances, and abuse-related problems might increase accordingly. As noted earlier, because of easier access, medical practitioners have a higher rate of drug use than the general population. The Presidents Commission on Organized Crime stated that "legalization would almost certainly increase demand, and therefore spread this destruction" (1986: 331). The American Academy of Psychiatrists in Alcoholism and Addictions (AAPAA) argues against legalization of drugs because "increased availability will lead to increased use,

abuse and addiction to illegal substances, and . . . there is no rational plan for distribution of these drugs that would not be hazardous and full of ethical problems" (AAPAA Board of Directors, September, 1990). Robert Peterson (1991) argues that drug prohibition, as contrasted with the devastation caused by a lack of similar controls over alcohol, saves billions of dollars and thousands of lives each year. Chanoch Jacobsen and Robert Hanneman (1992) state that the illegitimacy of drug abuse allows for the activation of informal social controls through families, peers, and community that restrain drug abuse.

However, opiates are not seductive substances that "hook" the unsuspecting and the innocent. A study of 11,882 hospital patients treated with pain-killing drugs revealed that only 4 became addicted. A study of more than 10,000 burn victims who received injections of narcotics for weeks or months found not a single case of addiction attributed to this treatment (Melzack 1990). Russell Portnoy, M.D., director of analgesic studies in the Pain Service at Sloan-Kettering Memorial Hospital, points out, "Just as the vast majority of people who drink do not become alcoholics, those who are treated with opioid for pain do not become addicts" (Goleman 1987: 10; Brownlee and Schrof 1997). While two out of every three Americans consume alcohol, 10 percent of the drinkers account for half of all the alcohol consumed in the United States.

3. Legalizing all psychoactive substances would signal an acceptance of their use similar to the acceptance of alcohol and tobacco. Most users of alcohol do not become addicted, but Kaplan (1983b) argues that we do not know whether this would hold true for such drugs as heroin. Studies indicate that rats and monkeys perform considerable amounts of work to earn injections of heroin or cocaine but do not respond so eagerly to alcohol. However, as noted previously, many persons have used opiates without becoming addicted: hospital patients experiencing pain, "chippers" and "weekenders" who use heroin much as a social drinker uses alcohol, and soldiers returning to the United States who used high-quality heroin while in Vietnam. Soldiers discontinued use when they were no longer confronted by the anxiety and depression of the Vietnam experience and when the cheap, high-quality heroin to which they had grown accustomed was no longer available (Robins 1973, 1974; Robins et al. 1980). The availability of cheap heroin in the United States, argues Wilson (1990), might have kept these veterans addicted. And the availability of cheap drugs may lead to greater use by pregnant women.

4. The easy availability of legal heroin, cocaine, and other currently illegal psychoactive substances would reduce the incentive for those already addicted or habituated to enter drug treatment or otherwise to seek a drug-free existence. Of course, there is no reason to believe that a drug-free existence will facilitate a constructive, crime-free lifestyle in most persons currently using psychoactive substances. Most heroin addicts, for example, go right on using heroin despite the threat or actuality of imprisonment, and often despite efforts to cure the affliction.

The legal availability of heroin, however, could prolong heroin addiction beyond the age (35 to 40) at which spontaneous remission typically occurs. Recall that availability of cheap high-grade heroin in Vietnam helps explain its widespread use by U.S. servicemen (Zinberg 1984). Indeed, by 1999, it was apparent that the increasing use of heroin in the United States was the result of the drug being purer, cheaper, and readily available for intravenous use, or sniffing and smoking. New users are often white and from more affluent backgrounds than typical heroin addicts in the past (Wren 1999b).

Policy Issues

Focus on Causes

In order to develop a policy that answers these serious concerns, we need to understand the cause(s) of drug use. Are some persons more vulnerable than others? As earlier chapters have shown, we do not know why some persons use/abuse drugs while others with similar access do not. We do not know why some persons who experiment with certain drugs become dependent while others do not. Any discussion of drug policy is conditioned on views of drug abuse and on the particular theory that one adopts:

- Drug abuse is a disease with a physiological basis.
- Drug abuse is a psychological condition or personality disorder.
- Drug abuse is a response to oppressive social conditions.
- Drug abuse is simply the pleasure-seeking activity of hedonistic persons.

We know that there is a very high correlation between urban poverty and heroin and cocaine use. A great deal of drug use, it seems, feeds upon human misery. "Britain first came to experience widespread and serious problems of drug misuse amidst the economic downturn of the early 1980s which devastated the local economies of many local industrial working class communities. Subsequently, chronic drug-related problems have become established as a common feature of the social landscape in many neighborhoods in this condition. Under such circumstances, local efforts to curb drug misuse are likely to be severely handicapped unless supported by wider schemes of urban regeneration, access to jobs and training, and other initiatives to combat social exclusion" (Advisory Council on the Misuse of Drugs 1998: 40). Similarly, a serious effort to deal logically with drugs in the United States would require greater efforts to reduce the ills of urban America. The policy of drug warriors seldom reflects on social conditions as a source of drug misuse.

Chein and his colleagues extend this argument further: "Is a society which cannot or will not do anything to alleviate the miseries which are, at least subjectively, alleviated by drugs better off if it simply prevents the victims of these miseries from finding any relief?" (1964: 381). Furthermore, remember that much of the damage inflicted by drugs is the result of their illicit status and not from their pharmacology.

Among those strongly opposed to drug decriminalization, however, are many leaders of the African American community. They have expressed the view that such programs are merely schemes designed to tranquilize members of the minority community who would be attracted by the availability of cheap drugs to alleviate their social and psychological frustrations. Some would abandon protest and political activity for the "easy fix," and such programs would saddle the minority community with lifelong abusers robbed of the incentive to give up drugs.

Congressman Charles B. Rangel of Harlem, while chairman of the House Select Committee on Narcotics Abuse and Control, vigorously opposed any type of drug maintenance program or decriminalization. He states that while "illegal drug-trafficking violence would end under decriminalization, a new crime source would be created by the influx of new addicts" and "hyperactive reactions to such drugs as cocaine will spur criminal behavior" (1990: 14).

Emergence of Decriminalization as a Policy Issue

Until 1988, the debate over drug decriminalization remained basically academic—that is, discussed seriously only by a few university educators and liberal or libertarian political ideologues. In that year, drugs became a—possibly *the*—*major* political issue of the presidential campaign. In response to the obvious—that antidrug efforts have not had any significant effect—*Time* magazine (30 May 1988) presented a cover article on the issue: "Should Drugs Be Made Legal?" In a balanced presentation, *Time* outlined the benefits and disadvantages of such a proposal and concluded that "even though corner drug shops are not going to pop up anytime soon, nor should they, the hot new debate over legalization is a significant one. It reflects the widespread and understandable dismay over antidrug efforts that have gone to such discomforting lengths as to call in the military without noticeably making a dent in the crime and abuse problem."

No Loans for Student Drug Offenders

U.S. Department of Education regulations, based on a law enacted in 1998, bar students convicted of drug offenses from receiving federal college tuition aid: A first possession conviction bars aid for a year, while a sales conviction will bar aid for 2 years. Students convicted of possessing drugs for a second time will lose aid for 2 years; a third time, permanently. A student convicted twice of selling drugs will lose aid permanently. Some students can retain eligibility by completing a drug rehabilitation program. Students must report any drug convictions on federal financial aid forms, including Pell grants and student loans. Students who lie will have to return any aid received and may be prosecuted (McQueen 1999).

Two Models of Drug Maintenance/Decriminalization

1. Dangerous drugs can be dispensed only through government-controlled clinics or specially licensed medical personnel and only for short-term treatment purposes; unauthorized sale or possession entails criminal penalties. Long-term maintenance is limited to the use of methadone. This is basically the approach currently used in England.
2. Dangerous drugs can be prescribed by an authorized medical practitioner for treatment or maintenance; criminal penalties are imposed for sale or possession outside medical auspices. This is the old British system.
3. Dangerous drugs can be sold and used as tobacco and alcohol products are; that is, nonprescription use by adults is permitted. This was the case in the United States before the Harrison Act.

Pat O'Malley and Stephen Mugford (1991) argue for a more limited version:

1. Providing safer options, for example, by making coca tea readily available, but significantly limiting cocaine and severely restricting crack, which, along with morphine and heroin, would be available only through prescription or licensing arrangements. There would be no incentives to attract new users.
2. Offering and encouraging safer ingestion. For example, smoking opium would be readily available but intravenous drug use severely restricted.
3. Permitting cultivation and possession of small amounts of marijuana and criminalizing large-scale operations.
4. Banning prodrug advertising—including for tobacco and alcohol products—while encouraging education and antidrug advertising, which would be financed through drug-related tax revenues.

The following year, the *New York Times* reported that while popular opinion still opposed decriminalization, debate over the issue had intensified: "It has become a staple of editorial pages, letters to the editor, talk shows on television and radio and public lectures. And many who do not go as far as advocating legalization show a new interest in the subject" (Corcoran 1989: 9). The discussion of decriminalization brought a hostile response from William Bennett, then the "drug czar" (actually, federal director of drug policy). He argued that any public discussion of the issue only worsens the problem and undermines efforts to combat drug abuse (Sly 1989).

Medical Maintenance as a Policy for Heroin?

Kaplan (1983b) argues that the inability to predict the consequences of making heroin freely available mitigates against a policy of drug legalization. Nadelmann responds that "the case for legalization [of heroin, cocaine, and marijuana] is particularly convincing when the risks inherent in alcohol and tobacco use are compared with those associated with illicit drug use" (1988: 91). Chein (et al. 1964) and Trebach (1982) recommend a more modest policy: placing greater trust in the medical profession and allowing physicians to treat addicts with a variety of drugs, including heroin. They recommend that clinics be established to implement this policy. (Such clinics have never been popular with community residents, and it would be difficult to open them in most neighborhoods.)

Any person shown to be addicted to heroin could receive prescriptions for this drug. Determining whether a person is addicted and how much heroin he or she should be given would be left to the medical profession. Trebach notes that some drugs would be diverted into the black market, but the market in illegal heroin is already considerable.

Legalization would, of course, reduce the price of heroin, thereby reducing the incentive for dealing in the substance. This policy, Trebach argues, would attract heroin addicts in large numbers and cause significant decreases in crime. Such clinics would also offer a wide variety of social services, including help in becoming drug free (which would be encouraged—but not imposed—by clinic staff).

What About Cocaine?

Although cocaine abuse is a major problem, fewer researchers are calling for its decriminalization (Wisotsky 1987; O'Malley and Mugford 1991). Kaplan (1983b) notes that monkeys who become addicted to heroin will increase their dosage to a relatively high level and then stabilize the amount and work to earn food or other rewards; laboratory animals given unlimited access to cocaine, however, will continue to increase self-injected doses of the substance until the supply is cut off or they die from debilitation (see Dworkin et al. 1987). Of course, monkeys do many things that humans do not, and this may be one of them. However, while satiety for heroin can be satisfied by substituting methadone, cocaine may induce greater craving. Thus providing clinic doses of cocaine may stimulate rather than reduce the demand for street cocaine (*Problems of Drug Dependence* 1997). Interestingly, Brecher (1972)—writing on behalf of Consumers Union—advocates legalizing heroin for addicts but takes no similar position with respect to cocaine (or amphetamines).

Comparison to Legal Substances

Wisotsky (1987) argues that we have continuously focused on the negatives of substances whose nonmedical use is subjected to criminal sanctions. Yet these substances provide not only relief from anxiety, but also euphoria, a sense of enhanced well-being, and experiences that the user obviously finds pleasing. While these substances carry some dangers, so do a host of other substances such as tobacco, alcohol, and even certain foods whose abuse can lead to obesity and high blood pressure, not to mention firearms, skydiving, mountain climbing, motorcycle and automobile racing, and any number of dangerous pastimes that people find pleasurable—that produce a "high." Why pick on chemicals, or rather on the specific chemicals we have chosen to control with criminal sanctions? To the person whose appetite appears insatiable, certain food—sometimes referred to as junk food—is addicting, yet we do not restrict the intake of potentially harmful foods that have little, if any, nutritional value.

The noted economist Ludwig von Mises, a favorite of many political conservatives, argues:

> Opium and morphine are certainly dangerous, habit-forming drugs. But once the principle is admitted that it is the duty of government to protect the individual against his own foolishness, no serious objections can be advanced against further encroachments. A good case could be made out in favor of the prohibition of alcohol and nicotine. And why limit the government's benevolent providence to the protection of the individual's body only? Is not the harm a man can inflict on his mind and soul even more disastrous than any bodily evils? Why not prevent him from reading bad books and seeing bad plays? The mischief done by bad ideologies surely, is much more pernicious, both for the individual and for the whole society, than that done by narcotic drugs. (1949: 728–29)

Nadelmann adds: "There is little question that if the production, sale, and possession of alcohol and tobacco were criminalized, the health costs associated with their use and abuse could be reduced. But most Americans do not believe that criminalizing the alcohol and tobacco markets would be a good idea. Their opposition stems largely from two beliefs: that adult Americans have the right to choose what substances they will consume and what risks they will take, and that the economic costs of trying to coerce so many Americans into abstaining from those substances would be enormous and the social costs disastrous" (1988: 97).

Canadian Cannabis

"Studies on cannabis use in Canada have demonstrated that 25 years of criminalization have had no significant deterrent effect, while the costs of criminalizing cannabis continue to rise" (Law Commission of Canada 2003: 11).

"Most people," states Wisotsky, "will not *permit* themselves to become addicted, just as most people will not consistently overeat to the point of obesity." With respect to heroin and cocaine, the "dominant pattern consists of controlled recreational use or social use, not chronic, compulsive, or obsessive use" (1987: 207). Zinberg (1984) points out that U.S. policies have failed to distinguish between the controlled user of psychoactive substances and the one for whom drug use has become dysfunctional. The use of drugs in the United States is widespread, and most of those ingesting psychoactive chemicals, from alcohol and marijuana to heroin and cocaine, do not become dysfunctional. However, the President's Commission on Organized Crime recommended that: "No Federal, State, or local government funds should go directly or indirectly to programs that counsel 'responsible' drug use or condone illicit drug use in any way" (1986: 483).

It appears irrational to give the dysfunctional alcoholic a "legal pass" while subjecting the controlled user of marijuana, heroin, or cocaine to criminal sanctions—sanctions that can result in labeling that, in itself, may be socially, psychologically, and economically debilitating. In fact, much of what society decries about drug abuse is the result of our policy of criminal sanctions. With a redefinition of the problem, Wisotsky (1987: 214) asserts, "drug abuse would become like any other health problem, managed

Dangers of Drug Law Enforcement

In response to New York City's intensified war against drug sellers, dealers have adopted more perilous tactics:"Five or six times each month, undercover investigators are now forced to use cocaine or heroin at gunpoint, to prove to dealers that they can be trusted. At least twice a month, an officer is shot or otherwise wounded during a staged purchase" (Kocieniewski 1998: 18).

by research, prevention, education and treatment," an approach that could be funded by the considerable amount of money now expended on drug-law enforcement. This approach would help destroy heroin and cocaine cartels that threaten the integrity and stability of a number of nations faced with Marxist insurgencies while reducing the everyday dangers to which we expose the public and drug-law enforcement agents.

Efforts to Decriminalize Marijuana

There has been some movement toward decriminalization with respect to marijuana: Possession for personal use has been decriminalized in some states, and some authorities have proposed legalization and taxation. Although the state supreme court in Alaska decriminalized the possession of small amounts of marijuana in 1975, 15 years later voters passed a ballot initiative making it illegal once again. (Marijuana was also recriminalized in Oregon.) There is no evidence to indicate that legal changes have resulted in a marijuana-abuse problem in these states. European countries such as the Netherlands and Spain have similarly decriminalized the possession of marijuana for personal use. In the Netherlands, thousands of "coffee shops" sell marijuana and hashish under government regulation (discussed later).

In 2002, England established a policy of not arresting persons for possessing small amounts of marijuana for personal use. This was apparently based on a 6-month experiment in South London's Braxton, where people caught smoking marijuana were given warnings rather than being arrested. The policy is not without its critics, as residents complained of the openness of marijuana smoking and the fact that sellers often peddle an array of illegal substances, not just marijuana. In response, Parliament increased penalties for drug selling, particularly of heroin and cocaine (Lyall 2002).

In the United States, the decriminalization of marijuana appears to have considerable opposition. Polls show that most Americans oppose decriminalization and that the adverse effects of alcohol and tobacco do not justify decriminalization of marijuana (PCOC 1986: 483). The PCOC suggests that laws in certain states that decriminalized the possession of marijuana are equivalent to condoning the use of drugs and should be reconsidered.

In 1992 the U.S. Public Health Service rescinded approval of marijuana for a handful of carefully screened patients suffering from AIDS, cancer, or glaucoma. In an editorial, the *Chicago Tribune* argued that "apparently the federal government just wants to have nothing more to do with marijuana, no matter who might benefit." The reason: "It doesn't want to be embarrassed politically by having to admit that marijuana might not be all bad, that it may have some benign uses after all" (March 16, 1992: 20). In 1999, residents of Washington, D.C. voted overwhelmingly to permit the medical use of marijuana, but the referendum was effectively nullified by Congress. About a dozen states have decriminalized marijuana possession, and eight states have laws allowing patients to use marijuana with a doctor's recommendation, but federal law prohibits the practice (Haynes 2002; Adams 2002). The vehemence of government opposition is characterized by a statement issued by the U.S. Office of Narcotics and Drug Control policy with respect to the cultivation of hemp for its fiber, particularly in the American apparel and paper in-dustries: "Legalizing hemp production would send a confusing message to our youth concerning marijuana. Also, it may lead to the *de facto* legalization of marijuana culti-vation" (July 29, 1997).

Containment in Zurich

A somewhat ambiguous middle position was adopted in Zurich—a policy of contain-ment. Vigorous police action drove hard-core users into a park near the heart of the city where open drug sale and use were tolerated. "Needle Park" accommodated about 400 hard-core users of heroin and cocaine and about 3,000 others who passed through daily. An AIDS prevention program was established in the park, and free needles were distributed as part of the effort. Social workers attempted to guide users into treatment programs, and volunteers provided free lunches. Because of the number of drug overdoses—an average of twelve daily—five doctors had to be stationed in the park. Urination killed off all the trees and flowers.

Drug users were drawn to the park from throughout Europe, an important factor leading to the park's demise: In 1992 the park was shut; remains sealed behind a 10-foot iron fence (Treaster 1990c; R. Cohen 1992). The drug market in Zurich did not end with the closing of the park; it moved a half mile away to a little-used railway station. There, a policy of tolerance again ensued until increasing violence, including the murder of four dealers, led to a 1995 government crackdown, and the area was closed off with razor wire and steel fencing (Cowell 1995).

In 1997, the Swiss public voted to continue a program that permits hard-core heroin addicts to receive their drugs from the government. Three times a day, enrolled addicts visit authorized centers where they pay a modest fee and receive heroin that they inject at antiseptic clinic tables. As part of the program, participants are enrolled in health, social, and psychological services, and abstinence programming is available (Olson 1997; Asso-ciated Press 1997b). Switzerland, with a population of about seven million has about 30,000 drug addicts.

Needle-Exchange Programs

In the United States, only six states allow the purchase of syringes without a prescription and do not have laws prohibiting their possession (G. Judson 1995), although addicts may be unwilling to absorb the cost of purchasing them.[1] In an effort to reduce the spread of AIDS among intravenous (IV) drug users, and to reduce AIDS among infants of addict mothers, a number of needle-exchange programs have been initiated. It was discovered that intravenous-drug abusers who are also diabetic do not get AIDS. At first this appeared

[1]In 1992 Connecticut changed its law to permit the purchase and possession of hypodermic nee-dles without a prescription. As a result, the number of AIDS cases fell by 40 percent (G. Judson 1995).

connected to their diabetes, but it was subsequently explained by their legal access to hypodermic needles (Chapman 1991a). A study by researchers from Yale University found that a needle-exchange program in New Haven, Connecticut, reduced new infections among intravenous drug users by more than 30 percent (Navarro 1991).

In 1988 a service agency in Portland, Oregon, became the first to distribute free needles as part of a pilot project involving 125 addicts. Oregon has no law restricting the distribution of hypodermic needles, but addicts frequently do not have the necessary funds to purchase them. Officials in a number of foreign cities have been distributing needles, but "proposals to hand out clean needles have touched off intense debate in cities from San Francisco to Boston. Opponents among law-enforcement, political, religious and drug treatment officials contend that free needles would promote drug use" (Lambert 1988: 7).

Nevertheless, by 1992, eight U.S. cities had needle-exchange programs. Half of them are in the state of Washington (Navarro 1992). Switzerland and the Netherlands distribute hypodermic needles to reduce the spread of AIDS (Bollag 1989), as does almost every country in Western Europe. Australia has a needle- and syringe-exchange program, which has been operating in the state of New South Wales since 1986. While Australia has a relatively high number of AIDS cases and IV drug users, there are very few intravenous drug users with AIDS (Wodak 1990; Wodak and Lurie 1997).

In 1995 a report by the National Academy of Sciences commissioned by Congress found that programs that encourage drug abusers to exchange used needles for new ones greatly reduce the spread of AIDS (Leary 1995b). In 1997, the American Medical Association endorsed the concept of using needle-exchange programs to combat AIDS. Nevertheless, in 1998, President Clinton, fearing criticism from congressional Republicans, refused to lift a 1989 federal ban on financing for programs that distribute clean needles to drug addicts, even though government scientists reported that such programs do not encourage drug use and could save lives by reducing the spread of AIDS (Stolberg 1998).

Harm Reduction

Like Switzerland, a number of European countries have been exploring a third model of response to drug abuse—harm reduction.[2] **Harm reduction** is offered as an alternative to the *supply reduction* strategy—aggressive law enforcement and pressure on producer nations—and the *demand reduction* strategy—treatment and prevention. This alternative recognizes that while abstinence is desirable, it is not a realistic goal. Instead, this approach examines harm from two points of view: harm to the community and harm to the drug user. The focus, then, is on lowering the amount of harm to each. "Each policy or programmatic decision is assessed for its expected impact on society. If a policy or program is expected to reduce aggregate harm, it should be accepted; if it is expected to increase aggregate harm, it should be rejected. The prevalence of drug use should play no special and separate role"

---

[2]For a general discussion of the role of law enforcement in harm reduction, see Caulkins and Heinz (2002).

(Reuter and Caulkins 1995: 1060). As Jonathan Caulkins notes, however, "attempting to translate the concept of harm reduction into formal terms brings out key philosophical questions that must be addressed. How does one measure harm? How does one aggregate and compare different types of harm? Which (whose) harms count?" (1996: 232).

Principles of Harm Reduction

At present there is no agreement in the addiction literature or among practitioners as to the definition of harm reduction, but in harm reduction approaches, the use of drugs is accepted as a fact and focus is placed on reducing harm while use continues. The main characteristics or principles of harm reduction are as follows (Conley et al. n.d.):

- *Pragmatism.* Harm reduction accepts that some use of mind-altering substances is a common feature of human experience. It acknowledges that, while carrying risks, drug use also provides the user with benefits that must be taken into account if drug-using behavior is to be understood. From a community perspective, containment and amelioration of drug-related harms may be a more pragmatic or feasible option than efforts to eliminate drug use entirely.
- *Humanistic values.* The drug user's decision to use drugs is accepted as fact. This doesn't mean approval. No moralistic judgment is made either to condemn or to support use of drugs, regardless of the level of use or mode of intake. The dignity and rights of the drug user are respected.
- *Focus on harms.* The fact or extent of a person's drug use per se is of secondary importance to the risk of harms consequent to use. Harms addressed are related to health, social, economic, and other factors affecting the individual, the community, and society as a whole. Therefore, the first priority is to decrease the negative consequences of drug use to the user and to others, as opposed to focusing on decreasing the drug use itself. Harm reduction neither excludes nor presumes the long-term treatment goal of abstinence. In some cases, reduction of level of use may be one of the most effective forms of harm reduction. In others, alteration to the mode of use may be more effective.
- *Balancing costs and benefits.* A pragmatic process of identifying, measuring, and assessing the relative importance of drug-related problems, their associated harms, and costs/benefits of intervention is carried out in order to focus resources on priority issues. The analysis extends beyond the immediate interests of users to include broader community and societal interests. Because of this rational approach, harm reduction approaches theoretically lend themselves to evaluation of impacts in comparison to some other, or no, intervention. In practice, however, such evaluations are complicated because of the number of variables to be examined in both the short and long term.
- *Priority of immediate goals.* Most harm-reduction programs have a hierarchy of goals, with the immediate focus on proactively engaging individuals, target groups, and communities to address their most pressing needs. Achieving the most immediate and realistic goals is usually viewed as first steps toward risk-free use, or, if appropriate, abstinence.

As a harm reduction measure, needle exchange programs are considered a small but important step in curbing HIV, which can spread through shared and dirty needles.

© A. Ramey/PhotoEdit

Reducing the Risky Consequences of Drug Use

In the view of Alan Marlatt, Julian Somers, and Susan Tapert (1993), harm reduction seeks to avoid marginalizing drug users because more can be done to control the often destructive behavior of drug abusers when they are "normalized." While abstinence is an ultimate objective, in the continuum shown in Figure 14.1, the authors posit *any* steps that decrease risk are worthwhile goals.

The focus is on reducing the risky consequences of drug use rather than on reducing drug use per se. In contrast to the "war" analogy and "total victory" rhetoric, this view

---

Example: Harm Reduction Information, Methamphetamine

Speed has the ability to make you feel good. You can have intense feelings of pleasure and well-being and be able to function at top speed, getting lots of work or studying done or dancing all night. Of course, with the up, comes the down. There are not-so-pleasurable effects of using speed also. Like other drugs, the more you use speed, the more your body needs. This is called tolerance. Tolerance occurs more rapidly when speed is injected or smoked. Speed tells your body that you don't need food or sleep, so you are extremely tired and depleted when you take a break. Depression, nightmares, and insomnia are also side effects of using speed. Then there's the crash. To avoid crashing, people often take more speed, which intensifies the negative effects of the crash when it does come, and the crash always comes (Harm Reduction Coalition 1998).

FIGURE 14.1
Risk Continuum

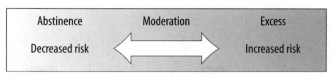

supports small steps that reduce harm. For example, intravenous use would be made safer with needle-exchange programs. The next step would be to encourage safer methods of ingestion. Risk would be further reduced by substituting methadone for heroin or other legal substances for cocaine and then by moderating the use of drugs—including nicotine and alcohol—en route to abstinence when this is possible. Related risk-taking behavior would also be targeted in an effort to deal with AIDS and other sexually transmitted diseases; in this case the focus of harm reduction would be on reducing the frequency of high-risk sexual activity by promoting less risky sexual practices, monogamous sex, and the use of birth control.

Harm Reduction in the United Kingdom

The harm reduction approach is more easily achieved in England, where controlled substances can be prescribed for those dependent upon them. In the province of Merseyside, a severely disadvantaged region whose largest city is Liverpool, vestiges of the "old British system" remain, with addicts taking home injectable opiates. But Merseyside has also introduced a comprehensive harm reduction policy. "By no means soft on drugs, the Drug Squad of the Merseyside police force arrest and charge a greater number of people for drug offenses than all other provincial forces" (O'Hare 1992: xiv). Nevertheless, their focus on harm reduction means that first offenders found in possession of any drug are cautioned—harm reduction aims at "avoiding the amplification of a drug-using career that may stem from a first conviction" (1992: xiv).

As part of a harm reduction approach to battle an alarming number of AIDS cases, physicians in Edinburgh are permitted to prescribe oral doses of nearly any drug craved by abusers. And there is indeed harm reduction: Great Britain has the lowest rate of AIDS in Europe (Schmidt 1993). In Britain, harm reduction principles are not seen as incompatible with vigorous street policing—"indeed in many circumstances they actually require it" (Advisory Council on the Abuse of Drugs 1994: 2). While American "drug warriors" have frequently denounced the harm reduction approach as capitulation (or worse), the British Advisory Council on the Abuse of Drugs, whose membership includes police executives, recommends "the wider adoption of harm reduction principles in developing law enforcement strategies" (1994: 83).

The harm reduction approach is popular throughout Europe, where officials generally avoid the "drug warrior" approach typical of the United States. Since 1990, the International Harm Reduction Association has been holding an annual conference in various cities—not in the United States—throughout the world. The U.S.-based Harm Reduction Coalition has been holding annual conferences since 1996. The country most identified with a national policy of harm reduction is the Netherlands.

The British Response: "Old" and "New" Systems

The first British drug control laws (passed in 1916) dealt with cocaine, a substance being used by soldiers on leave from World War I. The government had difficulty translating the statute, and in response the Ministry of Health formed a committee of physicians that moved the problem of drug abuse toward a medical response (Stimson and Oppenheimer 1982). The committee noted that some medical experts favored a program of providing diminishing doses until the patient became drug free. Other physicians argued that some addicts will never be able to live drug free, and for them, after all other treatment had proven unsuccessful, heroin maintenance was suggested—*if not cure, then care.* Most important, the committee report stated that drug abuse is a *disease,* not an indulgence (Trebach 1982). The *British system* that resulted from the committee's report gave the medical profession almost unhindered freedom to treat drug addicts by means of providing drugs.

Problems developed in the 1950s when a substantial market in heroin tablets grew in London. Most of the new addicts were young recreational users whose lifestyles were more deviant than those of the older class of addicts. A 1966 report concluded that the problem was caused by a handful of doctors who were over-prescribing heroin, which was being diverted into a black market. As a result, the use of opiates and cocaine to treat addiction was restricted to specially licensed physicians and drug treatment clinics. Between the late 1970s and the early 1980s, there was a large growth in the volume of smokable and injectable heroin in all parts of the United Kingdom. This problem continued throughout the 1980s during which there was a growth in the acid house music culture with major media coverage of MDMA (ecstasy) and other hallucinogenic drugs. In 1999, cocaine was determined to be overtaking heroin in popularity (Murray and Tendler 1999). Today, specially licensed doctors can provide heroin or cocaine for drug treatment, but this has become rare. Instead of heroin, most licensed physicians and clinics prescribe methadone for oral ingestion, although any medical doctor can provide the drug as an analgesic for physical pain.

The modern British system involves two barely compatible policies operating at the same time: a political policy and a services policy. The political policy focuses on supply reduction and penal policies in a belief that elimination of drug use is possible. The services policy focuses on local prevention campaigns and providing a variety of local services, including needle-exchange schemes, advice and counseling services, and a variety of prescribing options from short-term outpatient detoxification to long-term prescribing and rehabilitation. "At the heart of this approach is the view that drug use cannot be eliminated, but its most harmful consequences for the individual, society, and public health can be moderated." (Turner 1991: 184–85).

The Merseyside Model

At present, the only truly comprehensive harm reduction program is in Merseyside, England: needle exchange, counseling, prescription of drugs including heroin, and employment and housing services. Many levels of service and a wide variety of agencies are involved, and services are integrated to provide drug users with help when they need it. Pharmacists play a vital role in the workings of the Merseyside system. Some fill prescriptions for smokable drugs in the form of "reefers," which provide an alternative to injection and produce the "buzz" that some intravenous users crave. To prepare reefers, drugs such as heroin and methadone are injected into either herbal or regular cigarettes. Clients who have received injectable prescriptions for more than 10 years are now voluntarily switching to reefers in an attempt to stop injecting. In addition to reefers, pharmacists dispense drugs in the form of ampules, liquid, and aerosols.

The Merseyside police have become national leaders in developing a cooperative harm reduction strategy with the regional health authority. The police sit on health authority drug-advisory committees and employ health authority officers in police training courses involving the drugs/HIV issue. They have also agreed not to conduct surveillance on treatment centers, to refer arrested drug offenders to services, not to bring charges for possession of syringes to be exchanged, and to publicly support syringe exchange.

A key feature of the Merseyside police strategy has been to use resources to deal with drug traffickers while operating a cautioning policy toward drug users. Cautioning involves confiscating the drug, taking an offender to a police station, recording the incident, and formally warning the offender that any further unlawful possession of drugs will result in prosecution. The offender must also meet certain conditions, such as not having a previous drug conviction and not having an extensive criminal record. He or she is given information about treatment services in the area, including syringe exchanges. On the second and third occasions they are sent to court and fined for possession of small quantities or sentenced for possession of large amounts. If an addict becomes registered by getting in touch with service agencies, he or she is legally entitled to carry drugs for personal use. The overall effect of this policy is to steer users away from crime and possible imprisonment (Riley, n.d.).

Dutch Drug Policy

The Netherlands is one of the most densely populated countries in the world, with about sixteen million people in an area about the size of South Carolina. The Dutch believe strongly in individual freedom, and government is expected to avoid becoming involved in matters of morality and religion. At the same time, there is a strong sense of responsibility

Jars of marijuana line a coffee shop counter in the Netherlands. Some coffee shops not only offer choices of java, they offer different kinds of cannabis, which is legal. The Dutch consider marijuana a "soft" drug.

© Owen Franken/CORBIS

for the well-being of the community. The Netherlands has an extensive system of social security, while health care and education are accessible to everyone (Bullington 1999; Barnard 1998). Accordingly, drug treatment programs are readily available (deKort and Cramer 1999).

Dutch policy is based on the idea that drug use is a fact of life and needs to be discouraged in as practical a manner as possible (Barnard 1998). In place of prohibitionism's "war on drugs" and "user accountability," the Dutch have implemented a pragmatic and nonmoralistic approach whose main objective is to minimize the risks associated with drug use, both for users themselves and for those around them. The Dutch distinguish between "soft" drugs such as marijuana and "hard" drugs such as heroin, cocaine, and ecstasy. The idea is to separate the market so users of soft drugs are less likely to come into contact with hard drugs and will not suffer the negative consequences of labeling (discussed in Chapter 7): If young people become stigmatized they are more likely to start using more dangerous drugs (deKort and Cramer 1999).

During the 1970s possession or sale of small amounts of marijuana (30 grams, reduced to 5 grams in 1995) was virtually decriminalized, and the substance remains widely available in so-called coffee shops (MacCoun and Reuter 1997); trafficking in hard drugs can bring a 12-year sentence. While drug users are rarely arrested, those involved in secondary criminality are prosecuted, and drugs are not a mitigating circumstance (Silvas 1994). "Criminalization of the consumer is considered a harmful way of discouraging drug use" (Wever 1994: 64).

Dutch Policy Change to Harm Reduction

Extensive social services in the Netherlands provide aid to drug abusers that is not available in many other countries, including the United States. Nevertheless, in the early 1980s downtown areas of larger Dutch cities became increasingly dominated by a highly visible population of untreated drug users. This fostered a change in approach, which had focused almost exclusively on promoting abstinence. Treatment was expanded to deal with the host of social and physical problems experienced by abusers. Harm reduction became the focus: If abstinence is not possible, then safer use of drugs and safer sex practices should be the near-term goals. Drug abusers are now provided with health-related education, and a wide variety of treatment programs is readily available, including methadone maintenance (Wever 1994).

Drug abuse prevention efforts in the Netherlands treat alcohol and tobacco, as well as heroin and cocaine, as *dangerous* drugs—legal versus illegal is not considered a sound basis for differentiation. This avoids the double standard that provokes cynicism in young people. The focus is on *risky behavior,* which also includes eating disorders. The policy seeks to deglamorize drugs and stresses individual responsibility for the consequences of substance abuse. Persons are cautioned against using dangerous substances while being provided with information on how to reduce the risks for those who insist on experimenting with drugs (Marshall and Marshall 1994). As noted earlier, there are extensive treatment programs for those who become drug dependent.

Ineke Marshall and Chris Marshall note the differences between the Dutch and the American approach to drugs: "The American mass media, public, politicians, and educators appear to devote considerably more resources and energy to issues related to drug prevention than is the case in Holland. Differences in intensity of prevention efforts reflect fundamental differences in the definition of drugs as a social problem in the U.S. and Netherlands: In the U.S., drugs are viewed as a terrible evil to be fought with heavy arms (both in terms of prevention and repression); in the Netherlands, from a policymaker's viewpoint, drugs are viewed as a 'normal' social and health risk controlled by minimal measures or even ignored (e.g., cannabis, XTC)" (1994: 226). They conclude that the "Dutch pragmatic approach has prevented the use of radical measures such as forced treatment, drug testing at the workplace, and fear-inducing information campaigns— 'solutions' which may give the appearance of a tough approach, but which frequently cause more problems than they solve."

Problems Encountered by the Dutch

The Dutch approach has had problems. From 1979 to 1983 Amsterdam permitted drug-use rooms where drugs could be consumed. It eventually became obvious that drug dealers were in charge, and the group norm within these centers was aimed at maintaining high levels of drug use and criminality. In 1983, the centers were closed and more emphasis was given to police interventions and public order problems. By the early nineties, the "coffee houses" were becoming increasingly commercial and rapidly multiplying. Since they operated on the margins of society, there was the very real prospect of becoming centers of criminal activity—receiving stolen goods, for example—and they were attracting increasing numbers of foreigners. In response, new restrictions were announced: no more than 5 grams per transaction and, due to an increase in marijuana use among schoolchildren, a ban on those under 18 years old. Local authorities were given the power to ban or close coffee shops, and their numbers began to fall. Their regulation is now largely a local affair (deKort and Cramer 1999).

Dutch drug policy led to an influx of heroin users from other countries. In part, this appears to be the unanticipated result of success in lowering the use of heroin—methadone maintenance is readily available—which caused a decrease in price and attracted users from elsewhere (Korf, Riper, and Bullington 1999). In defending the Dutch approach, Herbert Barnard (1998), counselor for health and welfare at the Netherlands Embassy in Washington, D.C., states that their policy has kept the number of heroin addicts relatively low compared with that in many countries, and that population is rather stable and rapidly aging. Furthermore, the number of addicts infected with HIV is exceptionally low. He argues that despite the fact that marijuana is readily available, the rate of cannabis use in the Netherlands is lower than in the United States. "A situation often encountered in other nations, where the user—in most cases a minor—runs the risk of getting into trouble with the police, is seen as highly undesirable in the Netherlands."

Larry Collins (1999) disputes this view. He states that marijuana use is a serious problem in the Netherlands. However, based on the figures he presents, marijuana use is actually greater in the United States. Collins argues that because of the Netherlands' liberal attitude, that country has become a mecca for drug traffickers and drug trafficking. Holland has the world's biggest seaport (Rotterdam) and has been attractive to shippers of lawful—and unlawful—goods.

Collins notes that much of the ecstasy entering other European countries originates in the Netherlands. The Dutch have recognized this problem by setting up a special national unit to combat synthetic drugs. But MDA-type synthetic drugs such as MDMA remain a problem to which the Dutch have responded with a public campaign on their dangers and, in line with the harm reduction approach, by providing first-aid resources where the substance is most likely to be used. Indeed, because certain chemical configurations of MDA are more dangerous than others, Dutch policy provides pill testing for potential consumers. Crack cocaine has also been a problem in Holland, although its use is primarily among a stable subset of polydrug users who also abuse heroin and methadone (deKort and Cramer 1999).

Canada Changes Direction

Despite opposition from the United States, Canada is slowly moving in the Western European direction of harm reduction. Part of a larger concern with the issue of what behavior constitutes a crime, the Law Commission of Canada (2003) is examining the effects of criminalizing drug use. Meanwhile, Canada, which has already decriminalized marijuana use for medical purposes, is considering permitting possession of small amounts of marijuana for personal use. Following the lead of Switzerland, a project is under way in Toronto, Vancouver, and Montreal to see if crime and health problems can be reduced by giving hard-core heroin addicts prescriptions (Krauss 2003).

Vancouver, a port city that serves as an entry point for Asian drugs, has an active and open drug subculture. In a drug-infested neighborhood, a window sign in a long-abandoned storefront announces "Safer Injection Site"—a place where twenty-five heroin and cocaine addicts arrive every night to inject their drugs. A registered nurse dispenses fresh needles, sterile water, and advice on how to maintain veins. While technically illegal, the operation is condoned by the new mayor who was elected by a landslide on a platform of more treatment for addicts and regulated injection sites (Krauss 2003).

Conclusion

Suggesting a comprehensive policy acceptable to mainstream America does not take a great deal of imagination—but it would take a great deal of money. The level of funding required to institute most of these recommendations makes them unrealistic in the present United States—we already spend about $4 billion a year on controlling illegal drugs, with more than half going for drug-law enforcement.

Reducing the consumption of drugs by increasing law enforcement and large-scale treatment programs does not solve such significant sociological problems as lack of educational and employment opportunity and residential instability. We know that drug abuse is not randomly dispersed over the population but is concentrated in areas of poverty. Insofar as drug abuse is the result of despair, frustration, hopelessness, and alienation, programs directed only at the symptom—drug abuse—cannot succeed. Elliott Currie (1993) points out that drug abuse is not an isolated problem within stricken inner-city communities but part of a syndrome that includes family disintegration, child abuse/neglect, delinquency, and alcohol abuse. Successful treatment of individual drug abusers would not stem the tide of new entries generated by unchanged social conditions that serve as a fertile breeding ground. "Even the best, most comprehensive programs to help addicts transform their lives will inevitably be compromised if we do not simultaneously address the powerful social forces that are destroying the communities to which they must return" (1993: 279).

No author enjoys ending a book on a note of pessimism. Defeatism is anathema to the American culture—Yankee ingenuity can overcome any problem, just as we have overcome the Nazis, the Communists, the Iraqis, and a host of diseases. But reality indicates that some problems, particularly social ones—crime and poverty, for example—can be intractable. The United States has the widest gap between rich and poor in the industrialized world, and that gap is growing (Bradsher, 1995b, 1995c). David Bellis states that "resolving issues like poverty, crime and addiction, especially in isolation from one another, and unmediated by economic, social and political factors may be impossible" (1981: xiv).

That our current strategies in response to drug abuse have failed is obvious. Despite the dramatic pronouncements of several administrations and continued posturing of elected officials, we have been unable to stem the flow of heroin and cocaine into the United States and are unlikely to do so in the future. Our success against foreign marijuana has led to

A Comprehensive Program for Responding to Drug Abuse

1. Institute educational programs at the elementary, high school, and college levels that fully present all aspects of the use of psychoactive chemicals, including moderation and controlled use. Unfortunately, to date there has been little evidence to indicate that educational efforts actually reduce the use of drugs, although they may encourage a more rational or controlled use.

2. Decriminalize marijuana for personal use to conserve valuable resources and to avoid stigmatizing persons unnecessarily. Breaking the connection between marijuana and hard drugs may also help keep young people away from hard drugs. Furthermore, notes Richard Cowan (1986), effective law enforcement against marijuana drives up the price and may move users toward more readily available crack cocaine.

3. Reduce the supply of drugs by enhancing domestic law enforcement; that is, significantly increase personnel and equipment for the Coast Guard, Customs, and DEA. (The FBI should not have drug-law enforcement responsibilities, because this merely increases interagency conflict and detracts from the major law enforcement role of that agency, which includes combating espionage and terrorism.)

4. Reduce the supply of drugs at source countries; that is, provide more technical support and equipment and greater financing for crop-substitution and eradication programs.

5. Reduce the consumer market by expanding local law enforcement efforts, and place all convicted drug abusers on intensive probation supervision or

improvements in domestic cultivation, so that the home-grown crop is now preferred by pot connoisseurs. There is every reason to believe that if efforts to eradicate coca and poppy cultivation in source countries and/or to improve antismuggling techniques ever succeeded, it would simply spur the domestic production of cocaine and heroin substitutes. Furthermore, as indicated in Chapters 9 and 10, there is no evidence that widespread educational efforts have, or ever will, significantly reduce the number of persons using drugs or that treatment programs will be any more successful. And there remains the problem of widespread deprivation: "We are far from suggesting that all types and levels of drug use are at all times and in all circumstances deprivation-related. What we do, however, feel confident in asserting is that deprivation relates statistically to types and intensities of drug use which are problematic" (Advisory Council on Drug Misuse 1998: 111).

Our current policy of "shared simplifications" (Gerstein and Harwood 1990) appears to reflect the popular will: allowing the majority of society to be against drug abuse, while remaining free to abuse alcohol and tobacco. In other words, laws and law enforcement efforts against substances desired by a substantial minority of our citizenry provide sym-

---

A Comprehensive Program for Responding to Drug Abuse, Continued

incarceration followed by intensive parole supervision. This would require a significant increase in local law enforcement personnel assigned to drug-law enforcement, an expansion of correctional facilities (which are already overtaxed), and a significant increase in probation and parole personnel.

6. Drastically expand the availability of treatment programs, enabling every substance abuser—including those addicted to nicotine and alcohol—to have access to treatment. Continue research efforts into the causes of substance abuse and the effectiveness of various approaches to treatment.

7. Provide educational and vocational programs for drug abusers who have enrolled in treatment programs. In addition to the problem of financing such efforts, there is the problem of equity: Should only drug abusers be entitled to receive educational and vocational services, or should these be made available to all disadvantaged persons?

8. Enact and enforce legislation prohibiting employment discrimination against former substance abusers.

This comprehensive program would require a significant expenditure of tax dollars. A *Newsweek* poll revealed that while Americans were in favor of increasing penalties and additional funding for treatment and law enforcement, 63 percent opposed an increase in personal income taxes to support these goals (September 18, 1989).

---

bolic opposition for the majority without actually impairing their own freedom to enjoy dangerous substances and activities—a policy most Americans would be pleased to "drink to."

SUMMARY

Besides enforcement and treatment, the United States has other drug-use options, and one is decriminalization. Arguments in favor of decriminalization include reduction in money spent on drug-law enforcement, reduction in crime and in sexually transmitted diseases by drug users supporting expensive habits, reduction in extent of criminal organizations, decline in marketing of drugs by distributors, normalization of drug users' lives, decline in diseases spread through unclean hypodermics, and the rise of social controls to inhibit antisocial drug behavior. The arguments against decriminalization include expanded potential for use by minors, possible increase of abuse because of availability, appearance of social acceptance of drug use, and reduced incentive for treatment or abstinence. Policy issues that need to be addressed include determination of the causes of drug abuse, medical maintenance, the double standard with regard to lawful drugs, the possible decriminalization of marijuana, and the helpfulness of needle-exchange programs.

Another alternative approach is that of harm reduction, which generally refers to strategies that place first priority on reducing the negative consequences of drug use for the individual and for the community. Harm reduction is a many-pronged approach that includes such efforts as needle-exchange programs, methadone maintenance, and encouragement of less risky sexual practices. The harm reduction approach has been used in Great Britain, where success is shown in the lowest AIDS rate in Europe, and in the Netherlands, where a clear distinction is made between hard drugs and soft drugs.

A comprehensive policy in the United States would take a great amount of money but would include educational programs, decriminalization of marijuana for personal use, enhancement of domestic law enforcement, reducing supply at source countries, expansion of local law enforcement with intensive probation and parole supervision, and expansion of treatment programs.

INTERNET CONNECTIONS

DrugText (international harm reduction policy group): www.drugtext.org
Drug Watch International (Anti-legalization policy group): www.drugwatch.org
Harm Reduction Coalition: www.harmreduction.org

REVIEW QUESTIONS

1. What are the arguments for legalizing/decriminalizing drugs in the United States?
2. What are the possible drawbacks of legalizing/decriminalizing drugs in the United States?
3. If drug use is related to a physiological condition—an endorphin deficiency, for example—what policy implications are suggested?
4. What is the harm reduction approach to drug abuse?
5. Why is it easier to institute a harm reduction approach in England than in the United States?
6. What is the Merseyside model?
7. What are the characteristics of the approach to drug use in the Netherlands?
8. What are the advantages of a needle-exchange program?

Glossary

acetaldehyde By-product of the metabolism of alcohol

ADAM Arrestee Drug Abuse Monitoring

addiction A preoccupation with the use of psychoactive substances, characterized by neurochemical and molecular changes in the brain

adrenaline Epinephrine; hormone secreted by the adrenal gland that arouses the sympathetic nervous system

aftercare Treatment that follows discharge from a residential treatment program

agonist Drug that has an effect similar to another drug; cocaine and amphetamine are norepinephrine agonists.

Amanita muscaria Hallucinogenic mushroom; fly agaric

amphetamine Artificially produced central nervous system stimulant

amygdala Part of forebrain that plays a role in emotional learning

analog A chemical compound similar to another drug in its effects but slightly different in its chemical structure

angel dust Street name for phencyclidine (PCP)

anhedonia Inability to feel pleasure

anomie A condition characterized by estrangement from society as a result of being unable to achieve financial success through legitimate avenues

Antabuse Drug that produces unpleasant reactions when used with alcohol

antagonist Drug that counters or blocks the effects of another drug

ATF Bureau of Alcohol, Tobacco, and Firearms

autonomic nervous system Part of the peripheral nervous system responsible for regulating the activity of involuntary bodily functions such as that of the heart and lungs. It includes the sympathetic and parasympathetic nervous systems.

axon The fiberlike extension of a neuron by which the cell sends information to target cells

barbiturates CNS depressants

behavior modification Treatment approach based on learning theory

benzodiazepines Drugs that relieve anxiety or are prescribed as sedatives; among the most widely prescribed medications, including Valium and Librium

blood alcohol level (BAL) Amount of alcohol in the blood: the legal standard is .08 or .10 as measured by a breathalyzer test

blood-brain barrier System that filters blood for toxins before it can enter the brain

BNDD Bureau of Narcotics and Dangerous Drugs

buprenorphine Drug that blocks the action of opiates by occupying their receptor sites

Cannabis sativa L. The hemp plant from which marijuana and hashish are derived

catecholamines The neurotransmitters dopamine, epinephrine, and norepinephrine active in the brain and sympathetic nervous system

CCE Continuing Criminal Enterprise (conspiracy statute similar to RICO)

cell body That part of a neuron to which the dendrites and axons are attached

central nervous system (CNS) Brain and the spinal vertebrae that carry information to the brain

China white Southeast Asian heroin of high purity

chipper Occasional user of heroin

cirrhosis Scarring of the liver as a result of alcohol abuse

classical conditioning Learning in which a primary stimulus that naturally produces a specific response is repeatedly paired with a neutral stimulus. With repeated pairing, the neutral stimulus becomes a conditioned stimulus that can evoke a response similar to that of the primary stimulus.

clonidine Antihypertension drug used to relieve many symptoms of opioid withdrawal, particularly those involving autonomic nervous system hyperactivity

club drugs General term for a number of illicit drugs, primarily synthetic, that are most commonly encountered at nightclubs and raves. The drugs include MDMA, ketamine, Rohypnol, GHB, and GBL.

CMIR Currency and Monetary Instrument Report

CNS Central nervous system

crack Smokable form of cocaine

crank Street name for methamphetamine

crime control model A conceptual model of criminal justice that emphasizes repression of criminal conduct to protect society

cross-tolerance Tolerance to one substance that carries over to another

CSA Controlled Substances Act (Title II of the Comprehensive Drug Abuse Prevention and Control Act of 1970, as amended)

D.A.R.E. Drug Abuse Resistance Education

DAWN Drug Abuse Warning Network

DEA Drug Enforcement Administration

delirium tremens (DTs) A severe symptom of alcohol withdrawal

dendrite A treelike extension of the neuron cell body. Along with the cell body, it receives information from other neurons.

designer drugs Analogs of restricted drugs that have psychoactive properties

disease model Explanation for drug use based on deficiencies or abnormalities in a person's physical or psychological makeup

distillation Process used to produce ethanol

dopamine (DA) A stimulating (catecholamine) neurotransmitter present in regions of the brain that regulate movement, emotion, motivation, and feelings of pleasure; its absence results in Parkinson's disease.

drug A substance having mood-altering, psychoactive effects

drug abuse Excessive use of psychoactive substances

due process model A conceptual model of criminal justice that emphasizes the need to protect individual freedoms

ecstasy Common name for 3, 4-methylenedioxymethamphetamine (MDMA); designer drug having hallucinogenic and amphetamine-like characteristics

ego The psyche's contact with reality that maximizes gratification with a minimum of difficulties

endorphins Neurotransmitters produced in the brain that generate cellular and behavioral effects similar to morphine

epinephrine A hormone, released by the adrenal medulla and the brain, that acts with norepinephrine to activate the sympathetic division of the autonomic nervous system; sometimes called adrenaline

FBN Federal Bureau of Narcotics (1930–1968)

fentanyl Potent opiate agonist

fermentation process by which yeast interacts with plant sugars to produce alcohol

fetal alcohol syndrome Affliction that results from drinking during pregnancy

formication Sensations of insects crawling under the skin, caused by cocaine and amphetamine

freebase Separating the crystalline base of cocaine hydrochloride to enable smoking

GABA Gamma-aminobutyric acid; a receptor that restrains neuron activity

gateway drug Substances that presage use of other psychoactive drugs; for example, nicotine leading to marijuana leading to heroin

GBL Gamma-butyrolactone; a GHB precursor that is colorless, odorless, virtually tasteless, and in very low doses a CNS depressant. In higher doses it can produce unconsciousness and respiratory failure.

GHB Gamma-hydroxybutyrate; similar to Rohypnol, it is colorless, odorless, virtually tasteless, and in very low doses a CNS depressant. In higher doses it can produce unconsciousness and respiratory failure.

half-life The time it takes for one-half of a drug to be eliminated from the body

hallucinogen Natural or artificial chemicals that can produce distortions of reality

harm reduction An alternative model of response to drug abuse that focuses on reducing the amount of harm to the community and to the individual drug user while acknowledging that drug use cannot be prevented

hashish More potent form of marijuana

heroin an opiate produced from and more powerful than morphine

HEW Department of Health, Education, and Welfare (now Health and Human Services)

high Euphoria or feeling of well-being enjoyed by a substance user

homeostasis A state of equilibrium or balance achieved through the self-adjusting characteristics of the body

hypothalamus Brain structure that integrates information from a variety of sources and is the control center of the central nervous system

id The part of the human psyche composed of powerful basic urges, for example, hunger

inhalant Volatile solvent (glue, paint thinner), aerosol (spray paint), anesthetic (laughing gas), or volatile nitrate whose vapors cause intoxication

IRB International Reform Bureau

ketamine Surgical anesthetic related to phencyclidine (PCP)

kindling Drug reaction that reoccurs without continued ingestion

Korsakoff syndrome A disease associated with chronic alcoholism characterized by memory loss and psychotic behavior

LAAM *See* Levo-alpha-acetylmethadol

learning theory Concept that all behavior is shaped by its consequences

levo-alpha-acetylmethadol (LAAM) Opiate agonist similar to methadone used to treat heroin addiction

LSD (lysergic acid diethylamide) Hallucinogen that can be produced artificially or from ergot

MAO inhibitors Drugs used to treat depression by controlling the reuptake of serotonin

marijuana A leaf similar to tobacco that when smoked can produce stimulant and hallucinogenic reactions

Marinol Trade name for delta-9 tetrahydrocannabinol (THC), the active ingredient in marijuana that is used in medicine

MDMA *See* ecstasy

medial forebrain bundle Brain pathway that produces pleasure when stimulated

mescaline Hallucinogen found in the peyote cactus

methadone Opiate agonist used to treat heroin addiction

methamphetamine Powerful CNS stimulant

monoamine oxidase (MAO) Chemicals in the presynaptic terminals that control the level of neurotransmitters

morphine opiate derivative used to relieve pain

naloxone Opiate antagonist

naltrexone Opiate agonist that is longer lasting than naloxone

NARA Narcotic Addict Rehabilitation Act

narcotic CNS depressant

nativism An ideology favoring established residents over, and prejudice against, newer immigrants

negative reinforcement Removal of a stimulus that increases the likelihood of a behavior

neuron Nerve cell for the transmission of information, characterized by long fibrous projections called axons and shorter, branchlike projections called dendrites

neurotransmitter A chemical released by neurons at a synapse for the purpose of relaying information via receptors

NHSDA National Household Survey on Drug Abuse

NIDA National Institute on Drug Abuse

NMDA A receptor that promotes communication necessary to encode memories, generate thoughts, and make decisions

NNICC National Narcotics Intelligence Consumers Committee

norepinephrine A neurotransmitter produced in the brain and in the peripheral nervous system that governs arousal and elevates mood

ONDCP Office of National Drug Control Policy

operant conditioning Repeated presentation or removal of a stimulus (reinforcer) following a behavior to increase the probability of the behavior. If the probability of a behavior increases after removal, negative reinforcement has occurred.

opioid A substance derived from opium

opium Psychoactive sap of the poppy plant

oxycodone Synthetic version of morphine

parasympathetic nervous system A branch of the autonomic nervous system concerned with the conservation of the body's energy and resources during relaxed states

Parkinson's disease Neurological disorder caused by a dopamine deficiency and characterized by muscular rigidity and difficulty starting movements, tremors, and loss of balance

PCOC President's Commission on Organized Crime

PCP Phencyclidine

PDFY Preparing for the Drug-Free Years

peripheral nervous system A division of the nervous system consisting of all nerves that are not part of the brain or spinal cord

peyote cactus plant whose "buttons" have hallucinogenic properties

polydrug use Use of more than one psychoactive drug

positive reinforcement A stimulus that increases the likelihood that a behavior will be repeated

Prohibition Period of 1930–1933 when alcohol as a beverage was outlawed in the United States

psilocybin Hallucinogen found in certain mushrooms

psychedelic Another term for hallucinogen

psychoactive referring to a substance that affects the central nervous system

psychoanalytic theory Belief that unconscious material controls conscious behavior

receptor sites Sites consisting of molecules on the surface or inside cells where neurotransmitters attach and exert their effects

reinforcement Consequence of a behavior that increases the likelihood that it will reoccur

reuptake A process by which released neurotransmitters are absorbed for subsequent reuse

reverse tolerance Increase in the reaction to a drug that develops after chronic use; sensitization

RICO Racketeer Influenced and Corrupt Organizations

Rohypnol A benzodiazepine (sedative) widely prescribed in Europe but not approved for use in the United States. Known as "roofies" or "rope," it is often ingested with alcohol or marijuana

sedative CNS depressant that can produce calm and induce sleep

selective tolerance Tolerance that develops to one or more, but not all, aspects of a drug's effects

self-medicating Nonmedical use of psychoactive substances in response to physiological and/or psychological difficulties

serotonin (SE) A neurotransmitter that elevates mood; antidepressant drugs often stimulate the release of serotonin.

substance abuse Harmful use of a psychoactive substance(s)

superego Conscience-like mechanism that exerts a sense of morality

sympathetic nervous system A branch of the autonomic nervous system responsible for mobilizing the body's energy and resources during times of stress and arousal

synapse A gap between two neurons that functions as the site of information transfer from one neuron to another

TASC Treatment Alternative to Street Crime

theory Building block for scientific knowledge that organizes events, explains past events, and predicts future ones

therapeutic community Residential drug treatment program based on Alcoholics Anonymous, emphasizing addicts helping one another to become socially conforming persons

tolerance Progressive ability of the body to adapt to the effects of a drug used at regular and frequent intervals, making the drug less effective; higher doses of a drug are required to produce the same effect.

toluene Ingredient in inhalants that causes intoxication

transporter Protein on the surface of a sending neuron that carries a neurotransmitter back inside the neuron

twelve steps Principles upon which Alcoholics Anonymous and similar programs are based

unconscious According to psychoanalytic theory, repressed feelings and experiences that exert an influence over conscious behavior

Volstead Act Federal statute for enforcing the Eighteenth (Prohibition) Amendment

withdrawal Unpleasant symptoms that result when an addicted person fails to ingest a sufficient amount of addictive substance

References

Abadinsky, Howard
2003a   *Organized Crime,* 7th ed. Belmont, CA: Wadsworth.
2003b   *Law and Justice: An Introduction to the American
         Legal System,* 5th ed. Upper Saddle River, NJ: Prentice-
         Hall.
2003c   *Probation and Parole: Theory and Practice,* 8th ed.
         Upper Saddle River, NJ: Prentice-Hall.
Abel, Ernest L., ed.
1978   *The Scientific Study of Marijuana.* Chicago: Nelson-Hall.
Abrahart, David
1998   "Concerning Lysergic Acid Diethylamide (LSD) and
         Mental Health." Master of Arts thesis, Department of
         Mental Health Studies, University of Portsmouth,
         England.
Adams, Jane Meredith
2002   "Medical Marijuana Users Sue U.S. Officials." *Chicago
         Tribune* (October 10): 12.
Addiction Research Unit/SUNY at Buffalo
1998   *Dopamine.* Internet.
Adler, Patricia A.
1985   *Wheeling and Dealing: An Ethnography of an Upper-
         Level Drug-Dealing and Smuggling Community.*
         New York: Columbia University Press.
Adrade, Xavier, Stephen J. Sifaneck, and Alan Neaigus
1999   "Dope Sniffers in New York City: An Ethnography of
         Heroin Markets and Patterns of Use." *Journal of Drug
         Issues* 22 (2): 271–98.
Advisory Council on the Misuse of Drugs
1998   *Drug Misuse and the Environment.* London: Home
         Office.
1994   *Police, Drug Misusers and the Community.* London:
         Home Office.
1993   *Drug Education in Schools: The Need for New
         Impetus.* London: Home Office.
Agar, Michael
1973   *Ripping and Running: A Formal Ethnography of
         Urban Heroin Addicts.* New York: Seminar Press.
Ahmed-Ullah, Noreen S.
2001   "Pashtun Identity Defies Colonial Line." *Chicago
         Tribune* (November 6): 15.
Aichhorn, August
1963   *Wayward Youth.* New York: Viking.
Alexander, Bruce K.

1990   "Alternatives to the War on Drugs." *Journal of Drug
         Issues* 20 (1): 1–27.
Alford, Geary S.
1980   "Alcoholics Anonymous: An Empirical Outcome Study."
         Addictive Behaviors 5: 359–70.
Alford, Geary S., Roger A. Koehler, and James Leonard
1991   "Alcoholics Anonymous-Narcotics Anonymous Model
         Inpatient Treatment of Chemically Dependent
         Adolescents: A 2-Year Outcome Study." *Journal of
         Studies on Alcohol* 52 (March): 118–26.
All About the Civil Addict Program
1994   Norco, CA: California Narcotic Addict Evaluation
         Authority.
Allen, Frederick
1998   "American Spirit." *American Heritage* (May/June):
         82–92.
Alvarez, A.
2001   "Drugs and Inspiration." *Social Research* 68 (Fall):
         779–95.
American Heart Association
1999   "More Bad News for Cocaine Users: Drug Can Triple
         Risk of Aneurysm" (November 9): Internet.
American Heritage Dictionary
2000   Boston: Houghton-Mifflin.
American Psychiatric Association (APA)
1995   *Psychiatric Services for Addicted Patients.*
         Washington, DC: APA.
1994   *Diagnostic and Statistical Manual of Mental
         Disorders,* 4th ed. Washington, DC: APA.
American Social Health Association
1972   *Guidelines: A Comprehensive Community Program
         to Reduce Drug Abuse.* Overview I. NY: American
         Social Health Association.
Anderson, Austin A.
1992   "Transnational Crimes: A Global Approach." *FBI Law
         Enforcement Bulletin* (March): 26–32.
Andreas, Peter R., Eva C. Bertram, Morris J. Blackman, and
Kenneth E. Sharpe
1991–92 "Dead End Drug Wars." *Foreign Policy* (Winter):
         106–28.
Andrews, Edmund L.
1990   "2 Treatments for Cocaine Addiction." *New York Times*
         (July 21): 18.

Angier, Natalie
1995   "Variant Gene Tied to a Love of New Thrills." *New York Times* (January 2): 1, B9.
1991   "Moderate Drinking Cuts Risk of Heart Disease, Study Says." *New York Times* (August 24): 10.

Anglin, M. Douglas
1988   "The Efficacy of Civil Commitment in Treating Narcotic Addiction." Pages 8–34 in *Compulsory Treatment of Drug Abuse: Research and Clinical Practice.* Rockville, MD: National Institute on Drug Abuse.

Anglin, M. Douglas and Yih-lng Hser
1990a   "Legal Coercion and Drug Abuse Treatment: Research Findings and Social Policy Implications." Pages 151–76 in *Handbook of Drug Control in the United States,* edited by James A. Inciardi. Westport, CT: Greenwood.
1990b   "Treatment of Drug Abuse?" Pages 393–460 in *Drugs and Crime,* edited by Michael Tonry and James Q. Wilson, Chicago: University of Chicago Press.

Anglin, M. Douglas, Douglas Longshore, and Susan Turner
1999   "Treatment Alternative to Street Crime: An Evaluation of Five Programs." *Criminal Justice and Behavior* 26 (June): 168–95.

Anglin, M. Douglas and Thomas H. Maughr II
1992   "Ensuring Success in Interventions with Drug-Using Offenders." *Annals* 521 (May): 66–90.

Anglin, M. Douglas and William McGlothlin
1985   "Methadone Maintenance in California: A Decade's Experience." Pages 219–80 in *The Year Book of Substance Use and Abuse,* edited by Leon Brill and Charles Winick. New York: Human Services Press.
1990   "Treatment of Drug Abuse." Pages 393–460 in *Drugs and Crime,* edited by Michael Tonry and James Q. Wilson. Chicago: University of Chicago Press.

Anglin, M. Douglas and George Speckart
1988   "Narcotics Use and Crime: A Multisample, Multimethod Analysis." *Criminology* 26 (May): 197–233.

Aniskiewicz, Rick and Earl Wysong
1990   "Evaluating DARE Drug Education and the Multiple Meanings of Success." *Policy Studies Review* 9 (Summer): 727–47.

Anslinger, Harry J. and William F. Tompkins
1953   *The Traffic in Narcotics.* New York: Funk and Wagnalls.

Anthony, James C. with Valerie Forman
2000   "At the Intersection of Public Health and Criminal Justice Research on Drugs and Crime." Draft of a paper for the Drugs and Crime Research Forum.

"Anti-Drug Efforts Encounter Resistance in Colombia"
1995   *New York Times* (December 12): 4.

Arax, Mark and Tom Gorman
1995   "The State's Illicit Farm Belt Export." *Los Angeles Times* (March 13): 1, 16, 17.

Asbury, Herbert
1950   *The Great Illusion: An Informal History of Prohibition.* Garden City, NY: Knopf.

Ashley, Richard
1975   *Cocaine: Its History, Use and Effects.* New York: St. Martin's Press.

Associated Press
2002   "Doctor Sentenced for OxyContin Deaths." *New York Times* (March 23): 11.
2000a   "Ex-Mexico Drug Czar Gets More Jail" (February 22): Internet.
2000b   "Economic Protests Disrupt Bolivia." *Chicago Tribune* (April 10): 11.
1999a   "Alcohol-Linked Road Death at Low." Internet.
1999b   "China Executes at Least 71 in a Day." Internet.
1999c   "Cocaine Seized in Fish Shipment." Internet.
1999d   "Study Links Cigars to High Risk of Cancer." *New York Times* (June 10): 24.
1998   "Alcohol, Violence Link Still Strong, U.S. Says." *Chicago Tribune* (April 6): 5.
1997a   "High Nicotine Levels Found in Smoking Moms' Babies." *Chicago Tribune* (March 20): 13.
1997b   "Swiss Back Heroin Project." *New York Times* (September 29): 1.
1995   "5,600 Infant Deaths Tied to Mothers' Smoking." *New York Times* (April 13): 11.

Ausubel, David P.
1980   "An Interactional Approach to Narcotic Addiction." Pages 4–7 in *Theories on Drug Abuse: Selected Contemporary Perspectives,* edited by Dan J. Lettieri, Mollie Sayers, and Helen Wallenstein Pearson. Rockville, MD: NIDA.
1978   *What Every Well-Informed Person Should Know About Drug Addiction.* Chicago: Nelson-Hall.

Avants, S. Kelly, Arthur Margolin, Thomas R. Kosten, and Ned L. Cooney
1995   "Differences Between Responders and Nonresponders to Cocaine Cues in the Laboratory." *Addictive Behaviors* 20 (March/April): 214–24.

Aversa, Jeannine
1999   "Customs Changing Search Policy." Associated Press (August 11).

Bach, Peter B. and John Lantos
1999   "Methadone Dosing, Heroin Affordability, and the Severity of Addiction." *American Journal of Public Health* 5 (May): 662–65.

Baer, John S.
2002   "Student Factors: Understanding Individual Variation in College Drinking." *Journal of Studies on Alcohol* 14 (March): 40–53.

Bailey, Pearce
1974   "The Heroin Habit," pages 171–76 in *Yesterday's Addicts; American Society and Drug Abuse, 1865–1920,* edited by Howard Wayne Morgan. Norman, OK: University of Oklahoma Press.

Baker, Al
2002   "Boy, 12, Flies into U.S. After Swallowing Heroin in Condoms." *New York Times* (April 12): 24.

Ball, John C., Lawrence Rosen, Ellen G. Friedman, and David N. Nurco
1979   "The Impact of Heroin Addiction upon Criminality." Pages 163–69 in *Problems of Drug Dependence 1979,* edited by Louis S. Harris. Rockville, MD: NIDA.

Balster, Robert L.
1988   "Pharmacological Effects of Cocaine Relevant to Its Abuse." Pages 1–13 in *Mechanisms of Cocaine Abuse and Toxicity,* edited by Doris Clouet, Khursheed Asghar, and Roger Brown. Rockville, MD: NIDA.

Balter, Mitchell B.
1974   "Drug Abuse: A Conceptual Analysis and Overview of the Current Situation." Pages 3–21 in *Drug Use: Epidemiological and Sociological Approaches,* edited by Eric Josephson and Eleanor E. Carroll. New York: Wiley.

Bandura, Albert
1974   "Behavior Theory and the Models of Man." *American Psychologist* 29 (December): 860–66.
1969   *Principles of Behavior Modification.* New York: Holt, Rinehart and Winston.

Barnard, Herbert P.
1998   "The Netherlands' Drug Policy: 20 Years of Experience." Royal Netherlands Embassy, Washington, DC: Internet.

Barnett, Arnold
1988   "Drug Crackdowns and Crime Rates: A Comment on the Kleiman Paper." Pages 35–42 in *Street-Level Drug Enforcement: Examining the Issues,* edited by Marcia R. Chaiken. Washington, DC: U.S. Government Printing Office.

Barnett, Randy E.
1987   "Curing the Drug-Law Addiction: The Harmful Side Effects of Legal Prohibition." Pages 73–102 in *Dealing with Drugs: Consequences of Government Control,* edited by Ronald Hamowy. Lexington, MA: D.C. Heath.

Barraclough, Colin
1999   "Iran Confronts a Long Hidden Problem: Drugs." *New York Times* (August 29): 10.

Baumgartner, Werner A., Virginia Hill, and William H. Blahd
1989   "Hair Analysis for Drugs of Abuse." *Journal of Forensic Sciences* 34 (November): 1433–53.

Baumrind, Diana
1987   "Familial Antecedents of Adolescent Drug Use: A Developmental Perspective." Pages 13–44 in *Etiology of Drug Abuse: Implications for Prevention,* edited by Coryl LaRue Jones and Robert J. Battjes. Rockville, MD: NIDA.

Bearak, Barry
2001   "At Heroin's Source, Taliban Do What 'Just Say No' Could Not." *New York Times* (May 24): 1, 12.
2000   "Distress in the Opium Bazaar: 'Can't Make a Profit.'" *New York Times* (March 3): 4.

Beck, Jerome and Marsha Rosenbaum
1994   *Pursuit of Ecstasy: The MDMA Experience.* Albany, NY: SUNY Press.

Becker, Howard S.
1977   "Knowledge, Power, and Drug Effects." Pages 167–90 in *Drugs and Politics,* edited by Paul E. Rock. New Brunswick, NJ: Transaction Books.
1967   "History, Culture, and Subjective Experience: An Exploration of the Social Bases of Drug-Induced Experiences." *Journal of Health and Social Behavior* 8: 163–76.

Beeching, Jack
1975   *The Chinese Opium Wars.* New York: Harcourt Brace Jovanovich.

Begley, Sharon
1999   "Hope for Snow Babies." *Pressweek* (September 29): 62–63.

Behind Bars: Substance Abuse and America's Prison Population
1998   New York: National Center on Addiction and Substance Abuse at Columbia University.

Belenko, Steven
1993   *Crack and the Evolution of Anti-Drug Policy.* Westport, CT: Greenwood.

Belenko, Steven and Ko-Lin Chin
1989   "Typologies of Criminal Careers Among Crack Arrestees." Paper presented at the annual meeting of the American Society of Criminology, Reno, November.

Belkin, Lisa
1990   "Airport Anti-Drug Nets Snare Many People Fitting 'Profiles.'" *New York Times* (March 20): 1, 11.

Bellis, David J.
1981   *Heroin and Politicians: The Failure of Public Policy to Control Addiction in America.* Westport, CT: Greenwood.

Belluck, Pam
2003   "Methadone, Once the Way Out, Suddenly Grows as a Killer Drug." *New York Times* (February 9): 1, 20.

Bendavid, Naftali
2002   "Critics Decry Ads Linking Drugs, Terror." *Chicago Tribune* (March 24): 1, 17.

Benedict, William Reed, Lin Huff-Corzine, and Jay Corzine
1998   "'Clean Up and Go Straight': Effects of Drug Treatment on Recidivism Among Felony Probationers." *American Journal of Criminal Justice* 22 (2): 169–87.

Bennett, David H.
1988   *The Party of Fear: From Nativist Movements to the New Right in American History.* Chapel Hill, NC: University of North Carolina Press.

Bennett, William Ira
1988   "Patterns of Addiction." *New York Times Magazine* (April 10): 60–61.

Berger, Joseph
1989   "Judgment Replaces Fear in Drug Lessons." *New York Times* (October 30): 1, 8.

Berke, Richard L.
1990   "Bennett Doubts Value of Drug Education." *New York Times* (February 3): 1, 9.

1989   "Corruption in Drug Agency Called a Crippler of Inquiries and Morale." *New York Times* (December 17): 1, 22.

Berkow, Robert, ed.
1982   *The Merck Manual of Diagnosis and Therapy.* Rahway, NJ: Merck Sharp and Dohme.

Biernacki, Patrick
1986   *Pathways from Heroin Addiction: Recovery Without Treatment.* Philadelphia: Temple University Press.

Binder, Arnold and Gilbert Geis
1983   *Methods of Research in Criminology and Criminal Justice.* New York: McGraw-Hill.

Bishop, Katherine
1991   "Business Data Is Sought in Marijuana Crackdown." *New York Times* (May 24): B9.
1987   "Ex-Employee Wins Drug Testing Case." *New York Times* (October 31): 18.

Blackmore, John
1979   "Diagnosis: Heroin Addiction. Prescription: Methadone." *Corrections Magazine* 5 (December): 24–31.

Blakeslee, Sandra
1998   "Two Studies Shed New Light on Cocaine's Effect on Brain." *New York Times* (May 14): 18.
1997   "Studies of Brain Find Marijuana Can Have the Same Effect as Other Drugs." *New York Times* (June 27): 13.
1996   "Complex and Hidden Brain in the Gut Makes Cramps, Butterflies, and Valium." *New York Times* (January 23): B5.
1995   "Popular Drug May Damage Brain." *New York Times* (August 15): B10.
1994   "Yes, People Are Right. Caffeine Is Addictive." *New York Times* (October 5): B9.
1991   "Finding the Secrets of Caffeine, the Drug." *New York Times* (August 7): B6.
1989   "Crack's Toll Among Babies: A Joyless View of Even Toys." *New York Times* (September 18): 1, 12.
1988   "8-Year Study Finds 2 Sides to Teen-Age Drug Use." *New York Times* (July 21): 1, 13.

Bloom, Floyd E.
1993   "Brain Research for Today and Tomorrow: Recent Advances and Research Frontiers." Pages 9–26 in *International Research Conference on Biomedical Approaches to Illicit Drug Demand Reduction,* edited by Christine R. Hartel. Washington, DC: U.S. Government Printing Office.

Bluhm, Judy
1987   *When You Face the Chemically Dependent Patient: A Practical Guide for Nurses.* St. Louis, MO: Ishiyaku EuroAmerica.

Blum, Kenneth, Ernest Noble, Peter Sheridan, Anne Montgomery, Terry Ritchie, Puduer Jagadeeswaran, Harou Nogami, Arthur Briggs, and Jay Cohn
1990   "Allec Association of Human Dopamine D2 Receptor Gene in Alcoholism." *Journal of the American Medical Association* 263 (April, 18): 2055–60.

Blum, Richard H. and Associates
1969   *Society and Drugs.* San Francisco: Jossey-Bass.

Boaz, David, ed.
1990   *The Crisis in Drug Prohibition.* Washington, DC: Cato Institute.

Bolla, Karen I., Jean-Lud Cadet, and Edythe D. London
1998   "The Neuropsychiatry of Chronic Cocaine Abuse." *Journal of Neuropsychiatry* 1 (Summer): 280–89.

Bollag, Burton
1989   "Swiss-Dutch Drug Stance: Tolerance." *New York Times* (December 1): 4.

Bonner, Raymond
1995   "Drug Smuggling Growing in Ex-Communist Lands." *New York Times* (June 5): 2.

Bonnie, Richard J. and Charles H. Whitebread II
1970   "The Forbidden Fruit and the Tree of Knowledge: An Inquiry into the Legal History of American Marijuana Prohibition." *Virginia Law Review* 56 (October): 971–1203.

Bonson, Katherine R., Steven Grant, Carlo Contoreggi, Jonathan Links, Janet Metcalfe, Lloyd Weyl, Varughese Kurian, Monique Ernst, and Edythe London
2002   "Neural Systems and Cue-Induced Cocaine Craving." *Neuropsychopharmacology* 26 (3): 376–86.

Bourgois, Philippe
1995   *In Search of Respect: Selling Crack in El Barrio.* Cambridge, England: Cambridge University Press.

Bourne, Peter
1990   "Our Dubious Crusade in Colombia." *Chicago Tribune* (July 2): 11.

Bouza, Anthony
1990   *The Police Mystique: An Insider's Look at Cops, Crime, and the Criminal Justice System.* New York: Plenum.

Bowden, Charles
1991   "La Virgen and the Drug Lord." *Phoenix* (March): 96–103.

Bozarth, Michael A.
1994   "Pleasure Systems in the Brain." Pages 5–16 in *Pleasure: The Politics and the Reality,* edited by D. M. Warburton. New York: John Wiley & Sons.

Bradsher, Keith
1995a   "Low Ranking for Poor American Children." *New York Times* (August 14): 7.
1995b   "Gap in Wealth in U.S. Called Widest in West." *New York Times* (April 17): 1, C4.
1995c   "Widest Gap in Incomes? Research Points to U.S." *New York Times* (October 27): C2.

Bray, Robert M. and Mary Ellen Mardsden, eds.
1999   *Drug Use in Metropolitan America.* Thousand Oaks, CA: Sage.

Brecher, Edward M. and the Editors of Consumer Reports
1972   *Licit and Illicit Drugs.* Boston: Little, Brown.

Bresler, Fenton
1980   *The Chinese Mafia.* New York: Stein and Day.

Brevorka, Jennifer
2002   "Meth Lab Seizures on Rise in North Carolina."
        Asheville Citizen-Times (July 22): 1, 5.
Brewington, Vincent, Michael Smith, and Douglas Lipton
1994   "Acupuncture as a Detoxification Treatment: An
        Analysis of Controlled Research." *Journal of Substance
        Abuse Treatment* 11 (No. 4): 289–307.
Brody, Jane E.
2001   "An Old Enemy, Smoking, Hangs Tough." *New York
        Times* (December 11): D7.
1997   "Many Smokers Who Can't Quit Are Mentally Ill, a
        Study Shows." *New York Times* (August 27): B10.
1995   "Tourette Syndrome Can't Be Cured, but Knowledge
        Often Reduces Suffering." *New York Times* (March 1):
        B8.
1988   "Personal Health." *New York Times* (April 21): 24.
1987   "Role of Heredity in Alcoholism." *New York Times*
        (August 14): 14.
Brooke, James
1995   "Colombia's Rebels Grow Rich from Banditry." *New
        York Times* (July 2): 1, 4.
1991a   "In Brazil, A Plague Hits Port." *New York Times* (July
        22): 6.
1991b   "Marxist Revolt Grows Strong in the Shantytowns of
        Peru." *New York Times* (November 11): 1, 6.
Brotman, Richard and Frederic Suffet
1975   "The Concept of Prevention and Its Limitations."
        Annals 417 (January): 53–65.
Brounstein, Paul J., Harry P. Hatry, David M. Altschuler, and
Louis H. Blair
1990   *Substance Use and Delinquency Among Inner-City
        Adolescent Males.* Washington, DC: Urban Institute.
Brown, Ethan
1999   "Clear and Present Danger." *New York* (November 22):
        43–45.
Browne, Malcolm W.
1989   "Problems Loom in Effort to Control Use of Chemicals
        for Illicit Drugs." *New York Times* (October 24):
        17, 21.
Brownlee, Shanon
1999   "Inside the Teen Brain." *U.S. News & World Report*
        (August 9): 44–53.
Brownlee, Shanon and Joannie M. Schrof
1997   "The Quality of Mercy." *U.S. News & World Report*
        (March 17): 54–62, 65–67.
Brust, John C. M.
1999   "Substance Abuse, Neurobiology, and Ideology."
        Neurology and Public Health 56 (December):
        Internet.
Brzezinski, Matthew
2002   "Re-Engineering the Drug Business." *New York Times
        Magazine* (June 23): 24–29, 46, 54, 56.
Buchanan, David R.
1992   "Social History of American Drug Use." *Journal of
        Drug Issues* 22 (Winter): 31–52.

Bukstein, Oscar, David A. Brent, and Yifrah Kaminer
1989   "Comorbidity of Substance Abuse and Other Psychiatric
        Disorders in Adolescents." *American Journal of
        Psychiatry* 146 (September): 1131–41.
Bullington, Bruce
1999   "Editor's Introduction: The 'Golden Age' of Dutch Drug
        Policy?" *Journal of Drug Issues* 29 (3): 443–50.
Bureau for International Narcotics and Law Enforcement Affairs
2000   *International Narcotics Control Strategy Report.*
        Washington, DC: U.S. Department of State.
Burgess, Robert L. and Ronald L. Akers
1969   "Differential Association-Reinforcement Theory of
        Criminal Behavior." Pages 291–320 in *Behavioral
        Sociology,* edited by Robert L. Burgess and Don Bushell,
        Jr. New York: Columbia University Press.
Burns, John F.
2002   "Afghan Warlords Squeeze Profits from the War on
        Drugs, Critics Say." *New York Times* (May 5): 14.
1990   "Afghans: Now They Blame America." *New York Times
        Magazine* (February 4): 23–29, 37.
Burns, R. Stanley and Alan Done
1980   "Special Management Procedures for Emergency
        Medical Staff." Pages 95–120 in *Phencyclidine
        Abuse Manual,* edited by Mary Tuma McAdams,
        Ronald L. Linder, Steven E. Lerner, and Richard
        Stanley Burns. Los Angeles: University of California
        Extension.
Burros, Marian
1996   "In an About-Face, U.S. Says Alcohol Has Health
        Benefits." *New York Times* (January 3): 1, B6.
Burros, Marian and Sarah Jay
1996   "Concern Is Growing over an Herb That Promises a
        Legal High." *New York Times* (April 10): B1, 8.
Bush, Patricia J. and Ronald Iannotti
1987   "The Development of Children's Health Orientations
        and Behaviors: Lessons for Substance Abuse
        Prevention." Pages 45–74 in *Etiology of Drug Abuse:
        Implications for Prevention,* edited by Coryl LaRue
        Jones. Rockville, MD: NIDA.
Byck, Robert, ed.
1974   *Cocaine Papers: Sigmund Freud.* New York:
        Stonehill.
"Canadian Study Quantifies Link Between Substance Abuse and
Crime: Alcohol Abuse Associated with Violent Offenses"
2002   *Alcoholism and Drug Abuse Weekly* 14 (May 13):
        2–5
Cantrell, Geoffrey
2002   "Valuable Marijuana Crop Found in Madison."
        Asheville Citizen-Times (July 24): B1.
Carlson, Kenneth and Peter Finn
1993   *Prosecuting Criminal Enterprises.* Washington, DC:
        Bureau of Justice Statistics.
Carpenter, Cheryl, Barry Glassner, Bruce D. Johnson, and
Julia Loughlin
1988   *Kids, Drugs, and Crime.* Lexington, MA: D.C. Heath.

Carroll, Kathleen, Samuel Ball, Charla Nich, Patrick O'Connor, Dorothy Eagan, Tami Frankforter, Elisa Triffleman, Julia Shi, and Bruce Rounsaville
2001   "Targetting Behavioral Therapies to Enhance Naltrexone Treatment of Opioid Dependence." *Archives of General Psychiatry* 58 (August): 755–83.

Carroll, Linda
2002   "Marijuana's Effects: More Than Munchies." *New York Times* (January 29): D6.
2000   "Genetic Studies Promise a Path to Better Treatment of Addictions." *New York Times* (November 14): D6.

Carter, Hodding IV
1991a   "King of the Jungle." *M Inc.* (March): 84–91.
1991b   "Day of the Triads." *M Inc.* (June): 68–73.

Cashman, Sean D.
1981   *Prohibition.* New York: Free Press.

Catanzarite, Anne M.
1992   *Managing the Chemically Dependent Nurse.* Chicago: American Hospital Publishing.

Cauchon, Dennis
1992   "Michigan Drug Law: No Exceptions, No Mercy." *USA Today* (April 7): 3.

Caulkins, Jonathan P.
1997   "Is Crack Cheaper Than (Powder) Cocaine?" *Addiction* 92: 1437–43.
1996   "What Does Mathematical Modeling Tell Us About Harm Reduction?" *Drug and Alcohol Review* 15: 231–35.
1994   "What Is the Average Price of an Illicit Drug?" *Addiction* 89 (July): 815–19.
1992   "Thinking About Displacement in Drug Markets: Why Observing Change of Venue Isn't Enough." *Journal of Drug Issues 22* (Winter): 17–30.

Caulkins, Jonathan P., Gordon Crawford, and Peter Reuter
1993   "Simulation of Adaptive Response: A Model of Drug Interdiction." *Mathematical and Computer Modelling* 17 (No. 2): 37–52.

Caulkins, Jonathan P., Patricia A. Ebener, and Daniel F. McCaffrey
1995   "Describing DAWN's Dominion." *Contemporary Drug Problems* 22 (Fall): 547–67.

Caulkins, Jonathan P. and H. John Heinz III
2002   "Law Enforcement's Role in a Harm Reduction Regime." *Contemporary Issues in Crime and Justice* 64 (January): 1–12.

Caulkins, Jonathan P., C. Peter Rydell, Susan Everingham, James Chiesa, and Shawn Bushway
1999   *An Ounce of Prevention, a Pound of Uncertainty: The Cost-Effectiveness of School-Based Drug Prevention Programs.* Santa Monica: RAND.

Caulkins, Jonathan P., C. Peter Rydell, William L. Schwabe, and James S. Chiesa
1997   *Mandatory Minimum Drug Sentences: Throwing Away the Key or the Taxpayer's Money?* Santa Monica: RAND.

Cawley, Janet
1990   "3% Fail Drug Tests in Transit Industries." *Chicago Tribune* (July 11): 9.

Center on Addiction and Substance Abuse
1994   "Relationship Between Cigarette Smoking and Heroin, Cocaine and Crack." Press release, March 10.

Center for Disease Control
1999   *CDC, Morbidity and Mortality Weekly Report* 48 (36) (September 17): 796.

Chaiken, Jan M. and Marcia R. Chaiken
1990   "Drugs and Predatory Crime." Pages 203–39 in *Drugs and Crime,* edited by Michael Tonry and James Q. Wilson. Chicago: University of Chicago Press.

Chaiken, Marcia R. and Bruce D. Johnson
1988   *Characteristics of Different Types of Drug-Involved Offenders.* Washington, DC: National Institute of Justice.

Chambers, Carl D. and Leon Brill
1973   *Methadone: Experiences and Issues.* New York: Behavioral Publications.

Chambliss, William
1973   *Functional and Conflict Theories of Crime.* New York: MSS Modular Publications.

Chapman, Stephen
1992   "The Awful Price of Fighting the War on Drugs." *Chicago Tribune* (May 21): 23.
1991a   "Do We Want to Save Addicts or Kill Them?" *Chicago Tribune* (February 21): 23.
1991b   "In the Drug War, Bigger Sentences for Smaller Crimes." *Chicago Tribune* (June 9): Sec. 4: 3.

Chavez, Nelba and Ruth Sanchez-Way
1997   *Selected Findings in Prevention.* Washington, DC: U.S. Substance Abuse and Mental Health Services Administration.

Chavkin, Wendy
2001   "Cocaine and Pregnancy—Time to Look at the Evidence. (Commentary)." *Journal of the American Medical Association* 285 (March 28): Internet.

Chein, Isidor, Donald L. Gerard, Robert S. Lee, and Eva Rosenfeld
1964   *The Road to H: Narcotics, Delinquency, and Social Policy.* New York: Basic Books.

Chermack, Stephen T. and Stuart P. Taylor
1995   "Alcohol and Human Physical Aggression: Pharmacological Versus Expectancy Effects." *Journal of Studies on Alcohol* 56 (July): 449–56.

Cheung, Yuet W., Patricia G. Erickson, and Tammy C. Landau
1991   "Experience of Crack Use: Findings from a Community-Based Sample in Toronto." *Journal of Drug Issues* 21 (Winter): 121–40.

Childress, Ann Rose
1993   "Medications in Drug Abuse Treatment." Summary in *NIDA Second National Conference on Drug Abuse Research and Practice: An Alliance for the 21st Century,* pp. 73–75. Rockville, MD: NIDA.

Childress, Ann Rose, Anita Hole, Ronald Ehrman, Steven Robbins, A. Thomas McLellan, and Charles O'Brien
1993   "Cue Reactivity and Cue Reactivity Interventions in Drug Dependence." Pages 73–95 in *Behavioral Treatments for Drug Abuse and Dependence,* edited

by Lisa Simon Onken, John D. Blaine, and John J. Boren. Rockville, MD: NIDA.

Childress, Ann Rose, A. Thomas McLellan, and Charles P. O'Brien
1985   "Behavioral Therapies for Substance Abuse." *International Journal of the Addictions* 20: 947–69.

Childress, Ann Rose, P. David Mozley, William McElgin, Josh Fitzgerald, Martin Reivich, and Charles O'Brien
1999   "Limbic Activation During Cue-Induced Cocaine Craving." *American Journal of Psychiatry* 156 (January): 11–18.

Chin, Ko-Lin
1995   "Triad Societies in Hong Kong." *Transnational Organized Crime* 1 (Spring): 47–64.
1990   *Chinese Subculture and Criminality: Non-traditional Crime Groups in America.* Westport, CT: Greenwood.

Chin, Ko-Lin and Jeffrey Fagan
1990   "The Impact of Crack on Drug and Crime Involvement." Paper presented at the annual meeting of the American Society of Criminology, Baltimore, November.

Chitwood, Dale D., Mary Comerford, and Norman L. Weatherby
1998   "The Initiation of the Use of Heroin in the Age of Crack." Pages 51–76 in *Heroin in the Age of Crack-Cocaine,* edited by James A. Inciardi and Laura D. Harrison. Thousand Oaks, CA: Sage.

Chitwood, Dale D., James E. Rivera, and James A. Inciardi
1996   *The American Pipe Dream: Crack Cocaine and the Inner City.* Ft. Worth: Harcourt Brace.

Christian, Sue Ellen
2000   "Teen's Death Sheds Light on a Volatile Party Drug." *Chicago Tribune* (February 7): 1, 34.

Cintron, Myrna
1986   "Coca: Its History and Contemporary Parallels." Pages 25–51 in *Drugs in Latin America,* edited by Edmundo Morales. Williamsburg, VA: College of William and Mary.

Clines, Francis X. and Barry Meier
2001   "Cancer Painkillers Pose New Abuse Threat." *New York Times* (February 9): 1, 18.

Cloninger, Susan C.
1993   *Theories of Personality: Understanding Persons.* Upper Saddle River, NJ: Prentice-Hall.

Cloward, Richard A. and Lloyd E. Ohlin
1960   *Delinquency and Opportunity.* New York: Free Press.

Cloyd, Jerald W.
1982   *Drugs and Information Control: The Role of Men and Manipulation in the Control of Drug Trafficking.* Westport, CT: Greenwood.

Clymer, Adam
1994   "Senate Told That Cigarettes Are Entry into Hard Drugs." *New York Times* (March 11): 12.

Coffey, Thomas A.
1975   *The Long Thirst: Prohibition in America, 1920–1933.* New York: Norton.

Cohen, Albert K.
1965   *Delinquent Boys.* New York: Free Press.

Cohen, Julian
1996   "Drug Education: Politics, Propaganda and Censorship." *The International Journal of Drug Policy* 7 (No 3): Internet.

Cohen, Roger
1992   "Amid Growing Crime, Zurich Closes a Park It Reserved for Drug Addicts." *New York Times* (February 11): 11.

Coker, J. Kelly
2001   "Four-Fold Prevention: Strategies to Prevent Substance Abuse Among Elementary School-Aged Children." *Professional School Counseling* 5 (October): 70–75.

Collins, James J., Robert L. Hubbard, and J. Valley Rachel
1985   "Expensive Drug Use and Illegal Income: A Test of Explanatory Hypotheses." *Criminology* 23 (November): 743–64.

Collins, Larry
1999   "Holland's Half-Baked Drug Experiment." *Foreign Affairs* 78 (May/June): 82–98.

"Colombian City Basks in Terror's End"
1991   *New York Times* (December 12): 9.

"Colombian Growth Hurt By Cocaine"
1991   *New York Times* (February 19): C1.

"Colombian Heroin May Be Increasing"
1991   *New York Times* (October 27): 10.

Colorado Alcohol and Drug Abuse Division
1987   *Drug Use Trends in Colorado.* Denver.

"Coming to Grips with Alcoholism"
1987   *U.S. News & World Report* (November 30): 56–63.

Comings, David E.
1996   "Genetic Factors in Drug Abuse and Dependence." Pages 16–38 in *Individual Differences in the Biobehavioral Etiology of Drug Abuse,* edited by Harold W. Gordon and Meyer D. Glantz. Rockville, MD: NIDA.

Committee on Law Reform of the New York County Lawyers Association
1987   *Advisory Reports. Part I: Why Cocaine and Heroin Should Be Decriminalized. Part II: Why Cocaine and Heroin Should Not Be Decriminalized.* New York: Photocopied.

Compton, Beaulah and Burt Galaway
1979   *Social Work Processes,* 2nd ed. Homewood, IL: Dorsey Press.

Comptroller General
1988a   *Controlling Drug Abuse: A Status Report.* Washington, DC: General Accounting Office.
1988b   *Drug Control: U.S.-Mexico Opium Poppy and Marijuana Aerial Eradication Program.* Washington, DC: General Accounting Office.
1983   *Federal Drug Interdiction Efforts Need a Strong Central Oversight.* Washington, DC: General Accounting Office.

Condor, Bob
2002a   "Getting a Grip." *Chicago Tribune* (June 30): Section 13: 1, 4–5.
2002b   "Learning to Sip: A New Progam Helps Problem Drinkers Cut Back on Alcohol" *New York Daily News* (August 12): 42–44.

Conley, Peter, David Hewitt, Wayne Mitic, Christiane Poulin, Diane Riley, Robin Room, Ed Sawka, Eric Single and John Topp
n.d.   "Harm Reduction: Concepts and Practice: A Policy Discussion Paper." Ottawa: Canadian Centre on Substance Abuse (CCSA) National Working Group on Policy: Internet.

Cook, Christopher C. H.

1988a   "The Minnesota Model in the Management of Drug and Alcohol Dependency: Miracle, Method or Myth? Part I. The Philosophy and the Programme." *British Journal of Addiction* 83: 625–34.

1988b   "The Minnesota Model in the Management of Drug and Alcohol Dependency: Miracle, Method or Myth? Part II. Evidence and Conclusions." *British Journal of Addiction* 83: 735–48.

Cook, L. Foster and Beth A. Weinman

1988   "Treatment Alternatives to Street Crime." Pages 99–105 in *Compulsory Treatment of Drug Abuse: Research and Clinical Practice,* edited by Carl G. Leukefeld and Frank M. Tims. Rockville, MD: NIDA.

Coomber, Ross

1999   "The Cutting of Heroin in the United States in the 1990s." *Journal of Drug Issues* 29: 17–36.

Cooper, James

1998   "Statement Presented at the Joint New York Assembly Committee on Alcoholism and Drug Abuse and Committee on Health Hearings, New York City, December 11."

Cooper, Michael

1998   "Police Raid Wrong Apartment in Brooklyn." *New York Times* (May 8): 17.

Corcoran, David

1989   "Legalizing Drugs: Failures Spur Debate." *New York Times* (November 27): 9.

Cosden, Merith, Stacey Peerson, and Katherine Elliott

1997   "Effects of Prenatal Drug Exposure on Birth Outcomes and Early Child Development." *Journal of Drug Issues* 27: 525–39.

Courtwright, David T.

1982   *Dark Paradise: Opiate Addiction in America Before 1940.* Cambridge, MA: Harvard University Press.

Cowan, Richard C.

1986   "A War Against Ourselves: How the Narcs Created Crack." *National Review* (December 5): 26–31.

Cowell, Alan

1995   "Zurich's Open Drug Policy Goes into Withdrawal." *New York Times* (March 12): 3.

Cox, W. Miles

1985   "Personality Correlates of Substance Abuse." Pages 209–46 in *Determinants of Substance Abuse: Biological, Psychological, and Environmental Factors,* edited by Mark Galizio and Stephen A. Maisto. New York: Plenum.

Crack and Cocaine

2001   Washington, DC: NIDA.

Craig, Robert J.

1987   "The Personality Structure of Heroin Addicts." Pages 25–36 in *Neurobiology of Behavioral Control in Drug Abuse,* edited by Stephen I. Szara. Rockville, MD: NIDA.

Crank, John P. and Lee R. Rehm

1992   "From Drug Courier Profiles to Officer Awareness: A Study of a State Drug Interdiction Program." Paper presented at the Annual Meeting of the Academy of Criminal Justice Sciences, Pittsburg, March.

Crits-Christoph, Paul, Lynne Siqueland, Jack Blaine, Arlene Frank, Lester Luborsky, Lisa Onken, Larry Muenz, Michael Thase, Roger Weiss, David Gastfriend, George Woody, Jacques Barber, Stephen Butler, Dennis Daley, Ihsan Salloum, Sarah Bishop, Lisa Najavits, Judy Lis, Delinda Mercer, Margaret Griffin, Karla Moras, and Aaron Beck

1999   "Psychosocial Treatments for Cocaine Dependence." *Archives of General Psychiatry* 56 (June): 493–502.

Crowley, Geoffrey

1996   "Herbal Warning." *Pressweek* (May 6): 60–67.

Crowley, Thomas J.

1981   "The Reinforcers for Drug Abuse: Why People Take Drugs." Pages 367–81 in *Classic Contributions in the Addictions,* edited by Howard Shaffer and Milton Earl Burglass. New York: Brunner/Mazel.

Currie, Elliott

1993   *Reckoning: Drugs, the Cities, and the American Future.* New York: Hill and Wang.

Cushman, Paul, Jr.

1974   "Relationship Between Narcotic Addiction and Crime." *Federal Probation* 38 (September): 38–43.

Danaceau, Paul

1974   *Methadone Maintenance Programs: The Experience of Four Programs.* Washington, DC: Drug Abuse Council, Inc.

Davenport-Hines, Richard

2002   *The Pursuit of Oblivion: A Global History of Narcotics.* New York: Norton.

Davis, Joel

1984   *Endorphins: New Waves in Brain Chemistry.* Garden City, NY: Doubleday.

DeJong, William

1987a   *Arresting the Demand for Drugs: Police and School Partnership to Prevent Drug Abuse.* Washington, DC: National Institute of Justice.

1987b   "A Short Term Evaluation of Project DARE: Preliminary Indications of Effectiveness." *Journal of Drug Education* 17: 279–94.

de Kort, Marcel and Ton Cramer

1999   "Pragmatism Versus Ideology: Dutch Drug Policy Continued." *Journal of Drug Issues* 29 (3) 473–92.

De Lama, George

1988   "Besieged Colombia Becoming the Lebanon of Latin America." *Chicago Tribune* (November 20): 5.

Delaney, William P.

1977   "On Capturing an Opium King: The Politics of Law Sik Han's Arrest." Pages 67–88 in *Drugs and Politics,* edited by Paul E. Rock. New Brunswick, NJ: Transaction Books.

De La Rosa, Mario, Elizabeth Y. Lambert, and Bernard Gropper, eds.

1990   *Drugs and Violence: Causes, Correlates, and Consequences.* Rockville, MD: NIDA.

Delbanco, Andrew and Thomas Delbanco
1995   "AA at the Crossroads." *New Yorker* (March 20): 50–63.
De Leon, George
2000   *The Therapeutic Community: Theory, Model, and Method.* New York: Springer.
1995   "Residential Therapeutic Communities in the Mainstream: Diversity and Issues." *Journal of Psychoactive Drugs* 27 (No. 1): 3–15.
1994   "The Therapeutic Community: Toward a General Theory and Model." Pages 16–53 in *Therapeutic Community: Advances in Research and Application,* edited by Frank M. Tims, George De Leon, and Nancy Jainchill. Rockville, MD: NIDA.
1990   "Treatment Strategies." Pages 115–38 in *Handbook of Drug Control in the United States,* edited by James A. Inciardi. Westport, CT: Greenwood.
1986a   "The Therapeutic Community for Substance Abuse: Perspective and Approach." Pages 5–18 in *Therapeutic Communities for Addictions,"* edited by George De Leon and James T. Ziegenfuss, Jr. Springfield, IL: Charles C. Thomas.
1986b   "Program-Based Evaluation Research in Therapeutic Communities." Pages 69–87 in *Drug Abuse Treatment Evaluation: Strategies, Progress, and Prospects,* edited by Frank M. Tims and Jacqueline P. Ludford. Rockville, MD: NIDA.
De Leon, George, James A. Inciardi, and Steven S. Martin
1995   "Residential Drug Abuse Treatment Research: Are Conventional Control Designs Appropriate for Assessing Treatment Effectiveness?" *Journal of Psychoactive Drugs* 27 (No. 1): 85–91.
Dellios, Hugh
1998   "Once Just a Supplier, Nigeria Develops Heroin Woes." *Chicago Tribune* (July 29): 4.
DeLong, James V.
1972   "Treatment and Rehabilitation." Pages 173–254 in *Dealing with Drug Abuse: A Report to the Ford Foundation.* New York: Praeger.
Dembo, Richard, Linda Williams, Alan Getreu, Lisa Genung, James Schmeidler, Estrellita Berry, Eric Wish, and Lawrence Voie
1991   "A Longitudinal Study of the Relationship Among Marijuana/Hashish Use, Cocaine Use, and Delinquency in a Cohort of High Risk Youths." *Journal of Drug Issues* 21: 271–312.
De Quincey, Thomas
1952   *The Confessions of an English Opium-Eater.* London: J. M. Dent. First published in 1821.
Dettling, Michael, Andreas Heinz, Peter Dufeu, Hans Rommelspacher, Klaus-Jürgen Gräf, and Lutz Schmid
1995   "Dopaminergic Responsivity in Alcoholism: Trait, State, or Residual Marker?" *American Journal of Psychiatry* 152 (9): 1317–21.
Dickson, Donald T.
1977   "Bureaucracy and Morality: An Organizational Perspective on a Moral Crusade." Pages 31–52 in *Drugs and Politics,* edited by Paul E. Rock. New Brunswick, NJ: Transaction Books.
Dillon, Sam
1999a   "Mexico's Troubadors Turn from Amor to Drugs." *New York Times* (February 19): 4.
1999b   "Ruling Party, at 70, Tries Hard to Cling to Power in Mexico." *New York Times* (March 4): 1, 12.
1996   "Mexicans Tire of Police Graft as Drug Lords Raise Stakes." *New York Times* (March 21): 3.
1995   "Speed Carries Mexican Drug Dealer to the Top." *New York Times* (December 27): 6.
DiNardo, John
1993   "Law Enforcement, the Price of Cocaine and Cocaine Use." *Mathematical and Computer Modelling* 17 (No. 2): 53–64.
Dinges, John
1990   *Our Man in Panama: How General Noriega Used the United States—and Made Millions in Drugs and Arms.* New York: Random House.
Dishion, Thomas J., Gerald R. Patterson, and John R. Reid
1988   "Parent and Peer Factors Associated with Drug Sampling in Early Adolescence: Implications for Treatment." Pages 69–93 in *Adolescent Drug Abuse: Analyses of Treatment Research,* edited by Elizabeth R. Rahdert and John Grabowski. Rockville, MD: NIDA.
Dole, Vincent P.
1980   "Addictive Behavior." *Scientific American* 243: 138–54.
Dole, Vincent P. and Marie F. Nyswander
1966   "Rehabilitation of Heroin Addicts After Blockade with Methadone." *New York State Journal of Medicine* 66 (April): 2011–17.
1965   "A Medical Treatment for Diaectylmorphine (Heroin) Addiction." *Journal of the American Medical Association* 193 (August): 146–50.
Donovan, Dennis M.
1988   Assessment of Addictive Behaviors: Implications of an Emerging Biopsychosocial Model." Pages 3–48 in *Assessment of Addictive Behaviors,* edited by Dennis M. Donovan and G. Alan Marlatt. New York: Guilford.
Dotson, James W., Deborah L. Ackerman, and Louis Jolyon West
1995   "Ketamine Abuse." *Journal of Drug Issues* 25 (Fall): 751–57.
Doyle, A. Conan
1899   *Memoirs of Sherlock Holmes.* New York: Harper and Brothers.
Drug Abuse
1991   *See Drug Abuse and Drug Abuse Research*
1987   *See Drug Abuse and Drug Abuse Research*
Drug Abuse and Drug Abuse Research
1991   Rockville, MD: NIDA.
1987   Rockville, MD: NIDA.
Drug Abuse Prevention for At-Risk Individuals
1997   Rockville, MD: NIDA.

"Drug Arrests and the Courts' Pleas for Help"
1989   *New York Times* (April 9): E6.
The Drug Court Movement
1995   Washington, DC: National Institute of Justice.
Drug Enforcement Administration
n.d.a   *LSD Manufacture.* Internet.
n.d.b   *LSD Use and Effects.* Internet.
1995   *LSD in the United States.* Washington, DC.
1994   *Crack Cocaine.* Washington, DC.
1991   *Worldwide Heroin Situation.* Washington, DC.
Drug Policy Research Center
1992   "Cocaine: The First Decade." Issue Paper 1, April.
Drug Use Summary
2003   Office of National Drug Control Policy (ONDCP). Washington, DC.
Drugs of Abuse
1989   Washington, DC: Drug Enforcement Administration.
Drugs Prevention Initiative
1999   London: Home Office.
Duenwald, Mary
2001   "Fresh Look at a Fast Way to Kick a Heroin Habit." *New York Times* (December 4) 0: D6, 8.
Dunwiddie, Thomas V.
1988   "Mechanisms of Cocaine Abuse and Toxicity: An Overview." Pages 337–53 in *Mechanisms of Cocaine Abuse and Toxicity,* edited by Doris Clouet, Khursheed Asghar, and Roger Brown. Rockville, MD: NIDA.
DuPont, Robert L. and John P. McGovern
1994   *A Bridge to Recovery: An Introduction to 12-Step Programs.* Washington DC: American Psychiatric Press.
Duster, Troy
1970   *The Legislation of Morality: Law, Drugs, and Moral Judgment.* New York: Free Press.
Duzán, Maria
1994   *Death Beat.* New York: HarperCollins.
Dworkin, Steven I., Nick E. Goeders, John Grabowski, and James E. Smit
1987   "The Effects of 12-Hour Limited Access to Cocaine: Reduction in Drug Intake and Mortality." Pages 221–25 in *Problems of Drug Dependence, 1986,* edited by Louis S. Harris. Rockville, MD: NIDA.
Dworkin, Steven I. and Raymond C. Pitts
1994   "Use of Roden Self-Administration Models to Develop Pharmaco-Therapies for Cocaine Abuse." Pages 88–112 in *Neurobiological Models for Evaluating Mechanisms Underlying Cocaine Addiction,"* edited by Lynda Erinoff and Roger M. Brown. Rockville, MD: NIDA.
Eaglin, James B.
1986   *The Impact of the Federal Drug Aftercare Program.* Washington, DC: Federal Judicial Center.
Eddy, Paul, with Hugo Sabogal and Sara Walden
1988   *The Cocaine Wars.* New York: Norton.
Egan, Timothy
2002   "Meth Building Its Hell's Kitchen in Rural America." *New York Times* (February 6): 14.

1999a   "The War on Crack Retreats, Still Taking Prisoners." *New York Times* (February 28): 1, 20–21.
1999b   "In States' Anti-Drug Fight, a Renewal for Treatment." *New York Times* (June 10): 1, 22.
1999c   "A Drug Ran Its Course, Then Hid with Its Users." *New York Times* (September 19): 1, 27.
"84 Military Personnel Convicted in Drug Case at Camp Lejune"
2002   *New York Times* (July 4): 8.
Eiler, Kathryn, Melodie R. Schaefer, and Daniel Salstrom
1995   "Double-Blind Comparison of Bromocriptine and Placebo in Cocaine Withdrawal." *American Journal of Drug and Alcohol Abuse* 21 (No. 1): 65–79.
Elifson, Claire Sterk, and Kirk W. Elifson
1993   "The Social Organization of Crack Cocaine Use: The Cycle in One Type of Base House." *Journal of Drug Issues* 23 (Summer): 439–41.
Ellickson, Phyllis L.
1995   "Schools." Pages 93–120 in *Handbook on Drug Prevention,* edited by Robert H. Coombs and Douglas Ziedonis. Boston: Allyn and Bacon.
Ellickson, Phyllis L. and Robert M. Bell
1990   "Drug Prevention in Junior High: A Multi-Site Longitudinal Test." *Science* 247 (March 16): 1299–1305.
Ellis, Lee
1990   "Universal Behavioral and Demographic Correlates of Criminal Behavior: Toward Common Ground in the Assessment of Criminological Theories." Pages 36–49 in *Crime in Biological, Social, and Moral Contexts,* edited by Lee Ellis and Harry Hoffman. Westport, CT: Praeger.
Elsasser, Glen
1989   "Suspicion Is Ruled Ample Basis for Drug Search." *Chicago Tribune* (April 4): 3.
Engel, Madeline H.
1974   *The Drug Scene.* Rochelle Park, NJ: Hayden Book Co.
Ennett, Susan T., Nancy S. Tobler, Christopher L. Ringwalt, and Robert L. Flewelling
1994   "How Effective Is Drug Abuse Resistance Education? A Meta-Analysis of Project DARE Outcome Evaluations." *American Journal of Public Health* 84 (No. 9): 1394–1401.
Epstein, Edward Jay
1988   "The Dope Business." *Manhattan, inc.* (July): 25–27.
1977   *Agency of Fear: Opiates and Political Power in America.* New York: G.P. Putnam's Sons.
1974   "Methadone: The Forlorn Hope." *The Public Interest* 36 (Summer): 3–24.
Epstein, Joan F. and Joseph C. Gfroerer
1997   *Heroin Abuse in the United States.* Substance Abuse and Mental Health Services Administration. Internet.
Erikson, Kai T.
1966   *Wayward Puritans.* New York: Wiley.
Fact Sheet: Drug Related Crime 1994
1995   Washington, DC: National Institute of Justice.

Fagan, Jeffrey and Ko-Lin Chin
1991   "Social Processes of Initiation into Crack." *Journal of Drug Issues* 21: 313–43.

"Far East Sopranos"
2003   *U.S. News & World Report* (January 27): 34.

Farabee, David, Vandana Joshi, and M. Douglas Anglin
2001   "Addiction Careers and Criminal Specialization." *Crime and Delinquency* 47 (April): 196–220.

Faupel, Charles E. and Carl B. Klockars
1987   "Drugs-Crime Connections: Elaborations from the Life Histories of Hard-Core Heroin Addicts. *Social Problems* 34 (February): 316–33.

Fay, Peter Ward
1975   *The Opium War: 1840-1842.* Chapel Hill, NC: University of North Carolina Press.

"FBI Says Los Angeles Gang Has Drug Cartel Ties"
1992   *New York Times* (January 10): 8.

"FDA: Date-Rape Drug Has Medical Use"
2002   *Chicago Tribune* (July 18): 16.

Feder, Barnaby J.
1996a   "A Study Finds That Teen-Agers Are Buying Cigarettes with Ease." *New York Times* (February 16): 10.
1996b   "Increase in Teen-Age Smoking Sharpest Among Black Males." *New York Times* (May 24): 9.

Feldman, Harvey
1977   "Street Status and Drug Use." Pages 207–22 in *Drugs and Politics,* edited by Paul E. Rock. New Brunswick, NJ: Transaction Books.

Fenichel, Otto
1945   *The Psychoanalytic Theory of Neuroses.* New York: Norton.

Feuer, Alan
2000   "U.S. Colonel Is Implicated in Drug Case." *New York Times* (April 4): 20.

Fields, Richard
2001   *Drugs in Perspective,* 4th ed. New York: McGraw-Hill.

Finestone, Harold
1964   "Cats, Kicks, and Color." Pages 281–97 in *The Other Side,* edited by Howard S. Becker. New York: Free Press.

Finnegan, Loretta
1993   "Discussant and Discussion." Pages 189–207 in *International Research Conference on Biomedical Approaches to Illicit Drug Demand Reduction,* edited by Christine R. Hartel. Washington, DC: U.S. Government Printing Office.

Finnegan, L. P., A. P. Streissguth, G. Koren, D. Neuspiel, and K. Kaltenbach
1994   "The Teratogenicity of the Drugs of Abuse: A Symposium." Pages 51–54 in *Problems of Drug Dependence, 1993. Vol. I.,* edited by Louis S. Harris. Rockville, MD: NIDA.

Fiorentine, Robert
1999   "After Drug Treatment: Are 12-Step Programs Effective in Maintaining Abstinence?" *American Journal of Drug and Alcohol Abuse* 25 Feb: Internet.

Fishbein, Diana H., David Lozovsky, and Jerome H. Jaffe
1989   "Impulsivity, Aggression, and Neuroendocrine Responses to Serotonergic Stimulation in Substance Abusers." *Biological Psychiatry* 25: 1049–66.

Fishbein, Diana H. and Susan E. Pease
1990   "Neurological Links Between Substance Abuse and Crime." Pages 218–43 in *Crime in Biological, Social, and Moral Contexts,* edited by Lee Ellis and Harry Hoffman.Westport, CT: Praeger.

Flores, Philip J.
1988   *Group Psychotherapy with Addicted Populations.* New York: Haworth.

Foderaro, Lisa W.
1995   "Can Problem Drinkers Really Just Cut Back?" *New York Times* (May 28): 15.

Foltin, Richard W. and Marian W. Fischman
1994   "Cocaine: Self-Administration Research: Treatment Implications." Pages 139–62 in *Neurobiological Models for Evaluating Mechanisms Underlying Cocaine Addiction,* edited by Lynda Erinoff and Roger M. Brown. Rockville, MD: NIDA.

Fong, Mak Lau
1981   *The Sociology of Secret Societies: A Study of Chinese Secret Societies in Singapore and Peninsular Malaysia.* Oxford: Oxford University Press.

Fooner, Michael
1985   *A Guide to Interpol.* Washington, DC: U.S. Government Printing Office.

Forero, Juan
2002   "Farmers in Peru Are Turning Again to Coca Crop." *New York Times* (February 14): 3.
2001a   "New Challenge to the Bogota Leadership." *New York Times* (May 6): 8.
2001b   "No Crops Spared in Colombia's Coca War." *New York Times* (January 31): 1, 8.
2001c   "In the War on Coca, Colombian Growers Simply Move Along." *New York Times* (March 17): 1, 5.
2001d   "Europe Expands as Market for Colombian Cocaine." *New York Times* (May 29): 1, 9.
2001e   "Rightist Chief in Colombia Shifts Focus to Politics." *New York Times* (June 7): Internet.
2001f   "Where a Little Coca Is as Good as Gold." *New York Times* (July 8): Sec. 4: 12.
2001g   "Union Says Coca-Cola in Colombia Uses Thugs." *New York Times* (July 26): 6.
2001h   "Ranchers in Colombia Bankroll Their Own Militia." *New York Times* (August 8): 1, 6.

Forrest, Gary G.
1985   "Psychodynamically Oriented Treatment of Alcoholism and Substance Abuse." Pages 307–36 in *Alcoholism and Substance Abuse: Strategies for Clinical Intervention,* edited by Thomas E. Bratter and Gary G. Forrest. New York: Free Press.

Frank, Blanche, Gregory Rainone, Michael Maranda, William Hopkins, Edmundo Morales, and Alan Kott
1987   "A Psycho-Social View of 'Crack' in New York City." Paper presented at the American Psychological Association Convention, New York City, August 28.

Franklin, Stephen
1987   "Detroit Wages All-Out War Against Crack." *Chicago Tribune* (December 13): 29.

Frawley, P. Joseph and James W. Smith
1990   "Chemical Aversion Therapy in the Treatment of Cocaine Dependence as Part of a Multimodal Treatment Program: Treatment Outcome." *Journal of Substance Abuse Treatment* 7: 21–29.

Frazier, Thomas L.
1962   "Treating Young Drug Abusers: A Casework Approach." *Social Work* 7 (July): 94–101.

Fredlund, Eric V., Richard T. Spence, Jane C. Maxwell, and Jennifer A. Kavinsky
1990   *Substance Abuse Among Youth Entering Texas Youth Commission Facilities, 1989: Final Report.* Austin: Texas Commission on Alcohol and Drug Abuse.

French, Edward D., Stefanie Levenson, and Angelo Ceci
1990   "Characterization of the Actions of Phencyclidine Midbrain Dopamine Neurons." Pages 255–63 in *Problems of Drug Dependence 1989,* edited by Louis S. Harris. Rockville, MD: NIDA.

French, Howard W.
1991   "Filthy Rich with a Drug Connection." *New York Times* (August 6): 6.

Freud, Sigmund
1961   *A General Introduction to Psychoanalysis.* New York: Washington Square Press. Originally published in 1924.

Freudenheim, Milt
1987   "Specialty Health Care Booms." *New York Times* (November 24): 25, 26.

Friedman, David P.
1993   "Introduction to the Brain: A Primer on Structure and Function of the Brain's Reward Circuitry." Pages 53–62 in *International Research Conference on Biomedical Approaches to Illicit Drug Demand Reduction,* edited by Christine R. Hartel. Washington, DC: U.S. Government Printing Office.

Fuentes, Joseph R. and Robert J. Kelly
1999   "Drug Supply and Demand: The Dynamics of the American Drug Market and Some Aspects of Colombian and Mexican Drug Trafficking." *Journal of Contemporary Criminal Justice* 15 (November): 328–51.

Galaif, Elisha and Steve Sussman
1995   "For Whom Does Alcoholics Anonymous Work?" *International Journal of the Addictions* 30 (No. 2): 161–84.

Gandossy, Robert P., Jay R. Williams, Jo Cohen, and H. J. Harwood
1980   *Drugs and Crime: A Survey and Analysis of the Literature.* Washington, DC: U.S. Government Printing Office.

Gawin, Frank H., M. Elena Khalsa, and Everett Elinwod., Jr.
1994   "Stimulants." Pages 111–39 in *The American Psychiatric Press Textbook of Substance Abuse Treatment,* edited by Marc Galanter and Herbert D. Kleber. Washington, DC: American Psychiatric Press.

Gay, Bruce
1999   "Drug Education Programs Fail in Houston." *Society* 36 (Jan-Feb): Internet.

Gazzaniga, Michael S.
1995   "Legalizing Drugs: Just Say Yes." *National Review* (July): 44–51.

Geary, Nori
1987   "Cocaine: Animal Research Studies." Pages 19–47 in *Cocaine Abuse: New Directions in Treatment and Research,* edited by Henry I. Spitz and Jeffrey S. Rosecan. New York: Brunner/Mazel.

Gebelein, Richard S.
2000   "The Rebirth of Rehabilitation: Promise and Perils of Drug Courts." *Sentencing and Corrections* 6 (May): 1–7.

Gelernter, Joel, David Goldman, and Neil Risch
1993   "The A1 Allele at the D2 Dopamine Receptor Gene and Alcoholism." *Journal of the American Medical Association* 269 (April 7): 1673–77.

General Accounting Office
1998   *Drug Abuse Treatment Data Limitations Affect the Accuracy of National and State Estimates of Need.* Washington, DC.
1993   *Drug Use Measurement: Strengths, Limitations, and Recommendations for Improvement.* Washington, DC.
1991   *The War on Drugs: Arrests Burdening Local Criminal Justice Systems.* Washington, DC.
1990   *Methadone Maintenance: Some Treatment Programs Are Not Effective; Greater Federal Oversight Needed.* Washington, DC.
1987   *Drug Abuse Prevention: Further Efforts Needed to Identify Programs that Work.* Washington, DC.

George, William H. and Jeanette Norris
n.d.   "Alcohol, Disinhibition, Sexual Arousal, and Deviant Sexual Behavior." *Health and Research World* posted by the Indiana Prevention Resource Center: Internet.

Gerstein, Dean R.
1994   "Outcome Research: Drug Abuse." Pages 45–64 in *The American Psychiatric Press Textbook of Substance Abuse Treatment,* edited by Marc Galanter and Herbert D. Kleber. Washington, DC: American Psychiatric Press.

Gerstein, Dean R. and Henrick J. Harwood, eds.
1990   *Treating Drug Problems, Vol. I: A Study of the Evolution, Effectiveness, and Financing of Public and Private Drug Treatment Systems.* Washington, DC: National Academy Press.

Ghazi, Katayon
1991   "Drug Trafficking Is Thriving in Iran." *New York Times* (December 4): 7.

Gilbert, R. M.
1981   "Drug Abuse as Excessive Behavior." Pages 382–95 in *Classic Contributions in the Addictions,* edited by Howard Shaffer and Milton Earl Burglass. New York: Brunner/Mazel.

Gilbert, Susan
1997   "Youth Study Elevates Family's Role." *New York Times* (September 10): B10.
1996   "Doctors Found to Fail in Diagnosing Addictions." *New York Times* (February 14): B4.

Gilham, Steven A., Wayne L. Lucas, and David Siverwright
1997   "The Impact of Drug Education and Prevention
        Programs: Disparity Between Impressionistic and
        Empirical Assessments." *Evaluation Review* 21
        (October): 589–613.
Ginzburg, Harold M.
1986   *Naltrexone: Its Clinical Utility.* Rockville, MD: NIDA.
Giuffrida, Greg
2002   "Schools Use Testing to Smoke Out Tobacco Use."
        Chicago Tribune (October 8): 8.
Glassman, Alexander H. and George F. Koob
1996   "Psychoactive Smoke." *Nature* 379 (February 22):
        677–78.
Glassner, Barry and Julia Loughlin
1989   *Drugs in Adolescent Worlds: Burnouts to Straights.*
        Houndmills, England: Macmillan.
Goddard, Donald
1978   *Easy Money.* New York: Farrar, Straus and Giroux.
Goering, Laurie
1998   "In Peru, Battle Against Flow of Drugs Moves to
        Amazon River Maze." *Chicago Tribune* (June 30): 6.
Goffman, Erving
1961   *Asylums: Essays on the Social Situation of Mental
        Patients and Other Inmates.* Garden City, NY:
        Doubleday.
Gold, Mark S.
1994   "Neurobiology of Addiction and Recovery: The Brain,
        the Drive for the Drug, and the 12-Step Fellowship."
        Journal of Substance Abuse Treatment 11 (No. 2):
        99–97.
1984   *800-Cocaine.* New York: Bantam.
Gold, Mark S., Charles A. Dackis, A. L. C. Pottash, Irl Extein, and
Arnold Washton
1986   "Cocaine Update: From Bench to Bedside." *Advances
        in Alcohol and Substance Abuse* 5 (Fall/Winter):
        35–60.
Gold, Steven
1980   "The CAP Control Theory of Drug Abuse." Pages 8–11
        in *Theories on Drug Abuse: Selected Contemporary
        Perspectives,* edited by Dan J. Lettieri, Mollie Sayers, and
        Helen Wallenstein Pearson. Rockville, MD: NIDA.
Goldberg, Carey
1999   "Study Details Smoking Fad Among Youth." *New York
        Times* (September 17): 12.
Goldberg, Jeff
1988   *Anatomy of a Scientific Discovery.* New York: Bantam.
Golden, Tim
1999   "U.S. Brushed Aside Mexican Role, Former Drug Chief
        Says." *New York Times* (November 26): 12.
1997   "Mexico and Drugs: Was the U.S. Napping?" *New York
        Times* (July 11): 1, 10.
1995   "Mexican Connection Grows as Cocaine Supplier to
        U.S." *New York Times* (July 30): 1, 8.
1991   "Mexican Panel Faults Army in Death of Drug Agents."
        New York Times (December 7): 3.
Goldsmith, Neal M. and Rick Doblin
1995   "'Ecstasy' Drug Tests Employed High Doses." Letter to
        the *New York Times* (August 24): 14.

Goldstein, Avram
2001   *Addiction: From Biology to Drug Policy,* 2nd ed.
        New York: Oxford University Press.
Goldstein, Joseph
1982   "Police Discretion Not to Invoke the Criminal
        Process." Pages 33–42 in *The Invisible Justice System:
        Discretion and the Law,* 2nd edition, edited by
        Burton Atkins and Mark Pogrebin. Cincinnati:
        Anderson.
Goldstein, Paul J.
1985   "The Drugs/Violence Nexus: A Tripartite Conceptual
        Framework." *Journal of Drug Issues* 15 (Fall):
        493–506.
Goldstein, Paul J., Patricia Bellucci, Barry J. Spunt, and
Thomas Miller
1991   "Volume of Cocaine Use and Violence: A Comparison
        Between Men and Women." *Journal of Drug Issues* 21:
        345–67.
Goleman, Daniel
1990   "Scientists Pinpoint Brain Irregularities in Drug
        Addicts." *New York Times* (June 26): B5.
1989   "Lasting Costs for Child Are Found from a Few Early
        Drinks." *New York Times* (February 16): 20.
1988   "Psychologists and Psychiatrists Clash over Hospital and
        Training Barriers." *New York Times* (May 17): 21.
1987   "Physicians Said to Persist in Undertreating Pain and
        Ignoring the Evidence." *New York Times* (December
        31): 10.
Golub, Andrew and Bruce D. Johnson
1994   "Cohort Differences in Drug-Use Pathways to Crack
        Among Current Crack Abusers in New York City."
        Criminal Justice and Behavior 21 (December):
        403–22.
Gomez-Cespedes, Alejandro
1999   "The Federal Law Enforcement Agencies: An Obstacle in
        the Fight Against Organized Crime in Mexico." *Journal
        of Contemporary Criminal Justice* 15 (November):
        352–69.
Gomez, Linda
1984   "America's 100 Years of Euphoria and Despair." *Life*
        (May): 57–68.
Goode, Erica
1998   "Nerve Damage to Brain Linked to Heavy Use of Ecstasy
        Drug." *New York Times* (October 30): 22.
Goode, Erich
1989   *Drugs in American Society,* 3rd ed. New York: Knopf.
1972   *Drugs in American Society.* New York: Knopf.
Goodstadt, Michael S.
n.d.   *Drug Education.* Rockville, MD: NIDA.
Grady, Denise
1998   "Hardest Habit to Break: Memories of the High." *New
        York Times* (October 27): D1, 9.
1996   "Engineered Mice Mimic Drug Use and Mental Illness."
        New York Times (February 20): B5, B8.
Granfield, Robert and William Cloud
1996   "The Elephant That No One Sees: Natural Recovery
        Among Middle-Class Addicts." *Journal of Drug Issues*
        26 (Winter): 45–61.

Greenberg, Brigitte
1999   "Study: Alcohol Cuts Stroke Risk." Associated Press
         (November 17) Internet.
Greenfeld, Lawrence A.
1998   *Alcohol and Crime.* Washington, DC: Bureau of Justice
         Statistics.
Greenhouse, Linda
1990   "Use of Illegal Drugs as Part of Religion Can Be
         Prosecuted, High Court Says." *New York Times* (April
         18): 10.
1989   "High Court Backs Airport Detention Based on Profile."
         New York Times (April 4): 1, 10.
Greenspan, Stanley I.
1978   "Substance Abuse: An Understanding from
         Psychoanalytic Developmental and Learning Theory
         Perspectives." Pages 73–87 in *Psychodynamics of
         Drug Dependence,* edited by Jack D. Blaine and
         Demetrious A. Julius. Rockville, MD: NIDA.
Griffiths, Roland R.
1990   "Caffeine Abstinence Effects in Humans." Pages
         129–30 in *Problems of Drug Dependence
         1990,* edited by Louis S. Harris. Rockville, MD:
         NIDA.
Griffiths, Roland R., Suzette Evans, Stephen Heisman, Kenzie
Preston, Christine Sannerud, Barbara Wolf, and Phillip Woodson
1990   "Low-Dose Caffeine Physical Dependence in Humans."
         *Journal of Pharmacology and Experimental
         Therapeutics* 255 (No. 3): 1123–32.
Grinspoon, Lester
1987   "Cancer Patients Should Get Marijuana." *New York
         Times* (July 28): 23.
1979   *Psychedelic Drugs Reconsidered.* New York: Basic
         Books.
Grinspoon, Lester and James B. Bakalar
1985   *Cocaine: A Drug and Its Social Evolution: Revised
         Edition.* New York: Basic Books.
1976   *Cocaine: A Drug and Its Social Evolution.* New York:
         Basic Books.
Grinspoon, Lester and Peter Hedblom
1975   *The Speed Culture: Amphetamine Use and Abuse in
         America.* Cambridge, MA: Harvard University Press.
Griswold, Eliza
2002   "The 14-Year Old Hit Man." *New York Times
         Magazine* (April 28): 62–65.
Grob, Charles S., Russell E. Poland, Linda Chang, Thomas Ernst
1996   "Psychobiologic Effects of 3,4-methylenedioxy-
         methamphetamine in Humans: Methodological
         Considerations and Preliminary Observations."
         Behavioural Brain Research 73: 103–7.
Groopman, Jerome
2001   "Eyes Wide Open." *New Yorker* (Decmber 3): 52–57.
Grosswirth, Marvin
1982   "Medical Menace: Doctors Hooked on Drugs." *Ladies
         Home Journal* (February): 94, 141–44.
Gruson, Lindsey
1990   "U.S. Pinning Hopes on Guatemalan Army for Stability
         and War Against Drugs." *New York Times* (July 5): 4.

Guardia, José, Ana Catafau, Fanny Batlle, Juan Carlos Martin,
Lidia Segura, Begona Gonzalvo, Gemma Prat, Ignasi Carrió, and
Miguel Casas
2000   "Striatal Dopaminergic D_2 Receptor Density Measured
         by [^{123}] Iodobenzamide SPECT in the Prediction of
         Treatment Outcome of Alcohol-Dependent Patients."
         American Journal of Psychiatry 157 (1): 127–29.
Guide to Science-Based Practices
2001   Washington, DC: Substance Abuse and Mental Health
         Services Administration.
Guillermoprieto, Alma
2002   "Waiting for War." *New Yorker* (May): 48–55.
Gulley, Joshua M., Cecelia McNamara, Thomas Barbera, Mary Ritz,
and Frank George
1995   "Selective Serotonin Reuptake Inhibitors on Ethanol-
         Reinforced Behavior in Mice." *Alcohol* 12 (May/June):
         177–81.
Guo, Jie, Karl G. Hill, J. David Hawkins, Richard F. Catalano, and
Robert D. Abbott
2002   "A Developmental Analysis of Sociodemographic,
         Family, and Peer Effects on Adolescent Illicit Drug
         Initiation." *Journal of the American Academy of
         Child and Adolescent Psychiatry* 41 (July): 838–46.
Gusfield, Joseph R.
1975   "The (F)Utility of Knowledge? The Relation of Social
         Science to Public Policy Toward Drugs." *Annals* 417
         (January): 1–15.
1963   *Symbolic Crusade: Status Politics and the American
         Temperance Movement.* Urbana, IL: University of
         Illinois Press.
Haley, Bruce
1990   "Burma's Hidden Wars." *U.S. News & World Report*
         (December 10): 44–47.
Hall, Trish
1990   "New Way to Treat Alcoholism Discards Spiritualism of
         A.A." *New York Times* (December 24): 1, 10.
Hall, Wayne
1999   "Appraisals of the Adverse Health Effects of Cannabis
         Use: Ideology and Evidence." *Drug Policy Analysis
         Bulletin.* Internet.
"Hallucinogens and Dissociative Drugs"
2000   *NIDA Research Report.* Rockland, MD: NIDA.
Hanbauer, Ingeborg
1988   "Modulation of Cocaine Receptors." Pages 44–54 in
         Mechanisms of Cocaine Abuse and Toxicity, edited by
         Doris Clouet, Khursheed Asghar, and Roger Brown.
         Rockville, MD: NIDA.
Hanson, David J.
1980   "Drug Education: Does It Work?" Pages 251–82 in
         Drugs and the Youth Culture, edited by Frank S.
         Scarpitti and Susan K. Datesman. Beverley Hills: Sage.
Hanson, Glen R.
2002a   "Drug Abuse, Gender Matters." *NIDA Notes* 17 (2): 3, 4.
2002b   "New Insights into Relapse." *NIDA Notes* 17 (3): 3–4.
2001   "Looking the Other Way: Rave Promoters and Club
         Drugs." Hearing before the Senate Caucus on
         International Narcotics Control (December 4).

Hargreaves, William A.
1986 "Methadone Dosage and Duration for Maintenance Treatment." Pages 19–79 in *Research on the Treatment of Narcotic Addiction: State of the Art,* edited by James R. Cooper, Fred Altman, Barry Brown, and Dorynne Czechowicz. Rockville, MD: NIDA.

Harm Reduction Coalition
1998 "Effects, Tolerance & Addiction." Internet.

Harris, Louis S., ed.
1999 *Problems of Drug Abuse, 1998.* Rockville, MD: NIDA.

Harris, Louis S.
1993 "Opiates: A History of Opiates and Their Use in Treatment." Pages 85–90 in *International Research Conference on Biomedical Approaches to Illicit Drug Demand Reduction,* edited by Christine R. Hartel. Washington, DC: U.S. Government Printing Office.

Hartel, Christine R., ed.
1993 *International Research Conference on Biomedical Approaches to Illicit Drug Demand Reduction.* Washington, DC: U.S. Government Printing Office.

Hawkins, Dana
2002 "Tests on Trial: Jobs and Reputations Ride on Unproven Drug Screens." *U.S. News & World Report* (August 12): 46–48.

Hawkins, J. David, Denise M. Lishner, and Richard F. Catalano
1987 "Childhood Predictors and the Prevention of Adolescent Substance Abuse." Pages 75–126 in *Etiology of Drug Abuse,* edited by Coryl LaRue Jones and Robert Battjes. Rockville, MD: NIDA.

Hawley, Thersa Lawton, Tamara G. Halle, Ruth E. Drasin, and Nancy G. Thomas
1995 "Children of Addicted Mothers: Effects of the 'Crack Epidemic' on the Caregiving Environment and the Development of Preschoolers." *American Journal of Orthopsychiatry* 65 (July): 364–79.

Haynes, V. Dion
2002 "Nevada Blazes Trail for Legal Marijuana." *Chicago Tribune* (August 9): 1, 14.

Hays, Tom
2001 "Army Colonel to Plead Guilty." Associated Press (April 4): Internet.

Hazarika, Sanjoy
1993 "Indian Heroin Smugglers Turn to New Cargo." *New York Times* (February 21): 8.

Hedgepath, William
1989 "'Mule Skinner.'" *Atlanta* (March): 61–62, 93–101.

Helmer, John
1975 *Drugs and Minority Oppression.* New York: Seabury Press.

Henderson, Leigh A.
1994a "About LSD." Pages 37–53 in *LSD: Still with Us After All These Years,* edited by Leigh A. Henderson and William Glass. New York: Lexington Books.
1994b "Adverse Reactions to LSD." Pages 55–75 in *LSD: Still with Us After All These Years,* edited by Leigh A. Henderson and William Glass. New York: Lexington Books.

Hendler, Harold I. and Richard C. Stephens
1977 "The Addict Odyssey: From Experimentation to Addiction." *International Journal of the Addictions* 12: 25–42.

Hepburn, John R., C. Wayne Johnston, and Scott Rogers
1994 *Do Drugs. Do Time: An Evaluation of the Maricopa County Demand Reduction Program.* Washington, DC: National Institute of Justice.

Hester, Reid K. and William R. Miller
1988 "Empirical Guidelines for Optimal Client-Treatment Matching." Pages 27–38 in *Adolescent Drug Abuse: Analyses of Treatment Research,* edited by Elizabeth R. Rahdert and John Grabowski. Rockville, MD: NIDA.

Higgens, Stephen T. and Alan Budney
1993 "Treatment of Cocaine Dependence Through the Principles of Behavior Analysis and Behavioral Psychology." Pages 97–121 in *Behavioral Treatments for Drug Abuse and Dependence,* edited by Lisa Simon Onken, John Blaine, and John Boren. Rockville, MD: NIDA.

Hilts, Philip J.
1995 "Survey Finds Surge in Smoking by Young." *New York Times* (July 20): C19.
1994 "Children of Smoking Mothers Show Carcinogens in Blood." *New York Times* (September 21): 16.
1990 "How the Brain Is Stimulated by Marijuana Is Discovered." *New York Times* (July 21): 1, 5.

Himmelstein, Jerome L.
1983 *The Strange Career of Marijuana: Politics and Ideology of Drug Control in America.* Westport, CT: Greenwood.

Hirschi, Travis
1969 *Causes of Delinquency.* Berkeley: University of California Press.

Ho, David
1999 "Survey Finds Teen Drug Use Stable." Associated Press (December 17): Internet.

Hobson, Katherine
2002 "Danger at the Gym." *U.S. News & World Report* (January 21): 59.

Hoffmann, Norman G., Patricia A. Harrison, and Susan G. Streed
1991 "Outcome Evaluation." Pages 137–54 in *Substance Abuse Services: A Guide to Planning and Management,* edited by Joseph Westermeyer and Ronald Krug. Chicago: American Hospital Association.

Holinger, Paul C.
1989 "A Developmental Perspective on Psychotherapy and Psychoanalysis." *American Journal of Psychiatry* 146 (November): 1404–12.

Hollon, Tom
2002 "Phenotype Offers New Perception on Cocaine: Researchers Say Glutamate Is More Essential to Addiction than Dopamine." *The Scientist* 16 (January 21): 16–17.

Holloway, Marguerite
1991 "Rx for Addiction." *Scientific American* (March): 94–103.

Hormes, Joseph T., Christopher M. Filley, and Neil L. Rosenberg
1986   "Neurologic Sequelae of Chronic Solvent Vapor Abuse." *Neurology* 36 (May): 698–702.

Horowitz, Craig
1996   "The No-Win War." *New York* (February 5): 23–33.
"How the War on Drugs Influences the Health and Well-Being of Minority Communities"
DPRC (Drug Police Research Center) *Newsletter* (June): 1–3.

Howe, Benjamin Ryder
2000   "Out of the Jungle." *nn* (May): 32–38.

Howell, James C. and Debra Gleason
1999   *Youth Gang Drug Trafficking* Washington, DC: Office of Juvenile Justice and Delinquency Prevention.

Hser, Yih-Ing, Christine Grella, Robert Hubbard, Shih-Chao Hsieh, Bennett Fletcher, Barry Brown, and M. Douglas Anglin
2001   "An Evaluation of Drug Treatments for Adolescents in 4 U.S. Cities." *Archives of General Psychiatry* 58 (July): 689–95.

Hubbard, Robert L., Mary Ellen Marsden, J. Valley, Rachel Henrick, J. Harwood, Elizabeth Cavanaugh, and Harold Ginsberg
1989   *Drug Abuse Treatment: A National Study of Effectiveness.* Chapel Hill, NC: University of North Carolina Press.

Hughes, John R.
1990   "Nicotine Abstinence Effects." Page 123 in *Problems of Drug Dependence 1989,* edited by Louis S. Harris. Rockville, MD: NIDA.

Hughes, Patrick H.
1977   *Behind the Wall of Respect.* Chicago: University of Chicago Press.

Huizinga, David H., Scott Menard, and Delbert S. Elliott
1989   "Delinquency and Drug Use: Temporal and Developmental Patterns." *Justice Quarterly* 6 (September): 419–55.

Humphries, Drew and David F. Greenberg
1981   "The Dialectics of Crime Control." Pages 209–54 in *Crime and Capitalism,* edited by David F. Greenberg. Palo Alto, CA: Mayfield.

Hunt, Leon Gibson
1977   *Assessment of Local Drug Abuse.* Lexington, MA: D.C. Heath.

Hunt, Walter A.
1983   "Ethanol and the Central Nervous System." Pages 133–63 in *Medical and Social Aspects of Alcohol Abuse,* edited by Boris Tabakoff, Patricia Sutker, and Carrie Randall. New York: Plenum.

Hyman, Steven E. and Eric J. Nestler
1996   "Initiation and Adaptation: Paradigm for Understanding Psychotropic Drug Action." *American Journal of Psychiatry* 153 (February): 151–62.

Ihde, Aaron J.
1982   "Food Controls under the 1906 Act." Pages 40–50 in *The Early Years of Federal Food and Drug Control,* edited by James Harvey Young. Madison, WI: American Institute of the History of Pharmacy.

Ikonomidou, Chrysanthy, Petra Bittigau, Masahiko Ishimaru, David Wozniak, Christan Koch, Kerstin Genz, Madelon Price, Vanya Stefovska, Friederlke Hörster, Tanya Tenkova, Krikor Dikranian, and John Olney
2000   "Ethanol-Induced Apoptotic Neurodegeneration and Fetal Alcohol Syndrome." *Science* 287 (February 11): 1056–60.

Illicit Drug Policies: Selected Laws from the 50 States
2002   Chicago: Robert Wood Johnson Foundation.

Illinois Criminal Justice Authority
1999   "Drug Court Provides Treatment Alternative to Incarceration." *On Good Authority* 2 (April): 1–4.

Inciardi, James A.
1986   *The War on Drugs: Heroin, Cocaine, Crime, and Public Policy.* Palo Alto, CA: Mayfield.
1981   "Heroin Addiction and Street Crime." Pages 53–60 in *International Narcotics Trafficking,* hearings before the Permanent Subcommittee on Investigations, November 10–13, 17, 18. Washington, DC: U.S. Government Printing Office.

Inciardi, James A., Duane McBride, and Hilary L. Surratt
1998   "The Heroin Street Addict: Profiling a National Population." Pages 31–50 in *Heroin in the Age of Crack-Cocaine,* edited by James A. Inciardi and Laura D. Harrison. Thousand Oaks, CA: Sage.

Inciardi, James A. and Anne E. Pottieger
1991   "Kids, Crack, and Crime." *Journal of Drug Issues* 21: 257–70.

Inhalants
2003   NIDA. Internet.

Institute for Study of Drug Dependence, ISDD
1987   *Drug Abuse Briefing.* London: ISDD.

Inverarity, James M., Pat Lauderdale, and Barry Field
1983   *Law and Society: Sociological Perspectives on Criminal Law.* Boston: Little, Brown.

Irwin, John
1970   *The Felon.* Englewood Cliffs, NJ: Prentice-Hall.

Izenwasser, Sari and Ellen M. Unterwald
1994   "Sensitization and Tolerance to Cocaine." Pages 71–73 in *Problems of Drug Dependence, 1993,* edited by Louis S. Harris. Rockville, MD: NIDA.

Jacob, Peyton III and Alexander Shulgin
1994   "Structure-Activity Relationships of the Classic Hallucinogens and Their Analogs." Pages 74–91 in *Hallucinogens: An Update,* edited by Geraline C. Lin and Richard A. Glennon. Rockville, MD: NIDA.

Jacobsen, Chanoch and Robert A. Hanneman
1992   "Illegal Drugs: Past, Present and Possible Futures." *Journal of Drug Issues* 22 (Winter): 105–20.

Jamieson, Anne, Alan Glanz, and Susanne MacGregor
1984   *Dealing with Drug Misuse: Crisis Intervention in the City.* London: Tavistock.

Jelnik, Pauline
1999   "Latin Leaders: U.S. Drug War Failed." Associated Press (November 3).

Johannessen, Koreen, Carolyn Collins, Beverly Mills-Novoa, and Peggy Glider
1999   *A Practical Guide to Alcohol Abuse Prevention: A Campus Case Study in Implementing Social Norms and Environmental Management Approaches.* Tucson: University of Arizona.

Johnson, Bruce D., Kevin Anderson, and Eric C. Wish
1989   "A Day in the Life of 105 Drug Addicts and Abusers: Crimes Committed and How the Money Was Spent." *Sociology and Social Research* 72: 185–91.

Johnson, Bruce D., Paul Goldstein, Edward Preble, James Schmeidler, Douglas Lipton, Barry Spunt, and Thomas Miller
1985   *Taking Care of Business: The Economics of Crime by Heroin Abusers.* Lexington, MA: D.C. Heath.

Johnson, Bruce D., Andrew Golub, and Jeffrey Fagan
1995   "Careers in Crack, Drug Use, Drug Distribution, and Nondrug Criminality." *Crime and Delinquency* 41 (July): 275–95.

Johnson, Bruce D., Douglas S. Lipton, and Eric D. Wish
1986   *Facts About the Criminality of Heroin and Cocaine Abusers and Some New Alternatives to Incarceration (Research Summary).* New York: Narcotic and Drug Research, Inc.

Johnson, Bruce D., Terry Williams, Koja A. Dei, and Harry Sanabria
1990   "Drug Abuse in the Inner City: Impact on Hard-Drug Users and the Community." Pages 9–67 in *Drugs and Crime,* edited by Michael Tonry and James Q. Wilson. Chicago: University of Chicago of Press.

Johnson, Bruce D., Eric C. Wish, James Schmeidler, and David Huizinga
1991   "Concentration of Delinquent Offending: Serious Drug Involvement and High Delinquency Rates." *Journal of Drug Issues* 21: 205–29.

Johnson, C. Anderson, Mary Ann Pentz, Mark Weber, James Dwyer, Neal Baer, David MacKinnon, William Hansen, and Brian Flay
1990   "Relative Effectiveness of Comprehensive Community Programming for Drug Abuse Prevention with High-Risk and Low-Risk Adolescents." *Journal of Consulting and Clinical Psychology* 58 (August): 447–56.

Johnson, Earl, Jr.
1963   "Organized Crime: Challenge to the American Legal System." *Criminal Law, Criminology, and Police Science* 54 (March): 1–29.

Johnson, Julie
1987   "Two Reagan Officials Report Limited Success in Drug War." *New York Times* (December 9): 53.

Johnson, Patrick B., Sharon M. Boles, and Herbert D. Kleber
2000   "The Relationship Between Adolescent Smoking and Drinking and Likelihood Estimates of Illicit Drug Use." *Journal of Addictive Diseases* 19 (2): 75–81.

Joint Committee on New York Drug Law Evaluation
1977   *The Nation's Toughest Drug Law: Evaluation of the New York Experience.* New York: Association of the Bar of the City of New York.

Jones, Allison North
2002   "Strong Views, Pro and Con, on Ads Linking Drug Use to Terrorism." *New York Times* (April 2): C7.

Jones, Charisse
1995   "Crack and Punishment: Is Race the Issue?" *New York Times* (October 16): 1, 9.

Jones, Coryl LaRue and Robert J. Battjes
1987   "The Context and Caveats of Prevention Research on Drug Abuse." Pages 1–12 in *Etiology of Drug Abuse: Implications for Prevention,* edited by Coryl LaRue Jones and Robert J. Battjes. Rockville, MD: NIDA.

Jones, Kenneth L., Louis W. Shainberg, and Curtis O. Byer
1979   *Drugs and Alcohol,* 3rd ed. New York: Harper and Row.

Jones, Mark
1993   "Nigerian Crime Networks in the United States." *International Journal of Offender Therapy and Comparative Criminology* 37 (1): 59–73.

Jourbert, Lucien
1987   "The Oral Dose Is Safer," Letter to the *New York Times* (August 15): 14.

Judson, Barbara A. and Avram Goldstein
1986   "Uses of Naloxone in the Diagnosis and Treatment of Heroin Addiction." Pages 1–18 in *Research on the Treatment of Narcotic Addiction: State of the Art,* edited by James R. Cooper, Fred Altman, Barry S. Brown, and Dorynne Czechowicz. Rockville, MD: NIDA.

Judson, George
1995   "Study Finds AIDS Risk to Addicts Drops if Sale of Syringes Is Legal." *New York Times* (August 30): 1, 12.

Kajdasz, D. K., J. W. Moore, H. Donepudi, C. E. Cochrane, and R. J. Malcolm
1999   "Cardiac and Mood-Related Changes During Short-Term Abstinence from Crack Cocaine: The Identification of Possible Withdrawal Phenomena." *American Journal of Drug and Alcohol Abuse* 25(4): 629–37.

Kandel, Denise K.
1974   "Interpersonal Influences on Adolescent Illegal Drug Use." Pages 207–40 in *Drug Use: Epidemiological and Sociological Approaches,* edited by Eric Josephson and Eleanor E. Carroll. New York: Wiley.

Kandel, Denise K. and Mark Davies
1991   "Friendship Networks, Intimacy, and Illicit Drug Use in Young Adulthood: A Comparison of Two Competing Theories." *Criminology* 29 (August): 441–67.

Kaplan, David
1999   "The Golden Age of Crime." *U.S. News & World Report* (November 29): 42–44.

Kaplan, John
1983a   "Drugs and Crime: Legal Aspects." Pages 643–52 in the *Encyclopedia of Crime and Justice,* edited by Sanford H. Kadish. New York: Free Press.

1983b   *The Hardest Drug: Heroin and Public Policy.* Chicago: University of Chicago Press.

Karch, Steven B.
1998   *A Brief History of Cocaine.* Boca Raton: CRC Press.

1996   *The Pathology of Drug Abuse: Second Edition.* Boca Raton: CRC Press.

Katcher, Leo
1959   *The Big Bankroll: The Life and Times of Arnold Rothstein*. New York: Harper & Brothers.

Katel, Peter
1995   "Justice: The Trouble with Informants." *Pressweek* (January 30): 48.

Kauffman, Eda, Martha Morrison Dore, and Lani Nelson-Zlupko
1995   "The Role of Women's Therapy Groups in the Treatment of Chemical Dependence." *American Journal of Orthopsychiatry* 65 (July): 355–63.

Kaufman, Edward
1994   *Psychotherapy of Addicted Persons*. New York: Guilford Press.

Kay, David C.
1973   "Federal Civil Commitment in the Federal Medical Program for Opiate Addicts." Pages 17–35 in *Yearbook of Drug Abuse*, edited by Leon Brill and Earnest Harms. New York: Behavioral Publications.

Kempe, Frederick
1990   *Divorcing the Dictator: America's Bungled Affair with Noriega*. New York: Putnam's.

Kennedy, Randy
1995   "Death Highlights Drug's Lethal Allure to Doctors." *New York Times* (November 11): 1, 10.

Kerr, Peter
1988   "Crime Study Finds High Drug Use at Time of Arrest." *New York Times* (January 22): 1, 9.

Kertzner, Robert M.
1987   "Individual Psychotherapy of Cocaine Abuse." Pages 138–55 in *Cocaine Abuse: New Directions in Treatment and Research*, edited by Henry I. Spitz and Jeffrey S. Rosecan. New York: Brunner/Mazel.

Khantzian, Edward J.
1985   "The Self-Medication Hypothesis of Addictive Disorders: Focus on Heroin and Cocaine Dependence." *American Journal of Psychiatry* 142: 1259–64.

1980   "An Ego/Self Theory of Substance Dependence: A Contemporary Psychoanalytic Perspective," Pages 29–33 in *Theories on Drug Abuse: Selected Contemporary Perspectives*, edited by Dan J. Lettieri, Mollie Sayers, and Helen Wallenstein Pearson. Rockville, MD: NIDA.

Khantzian, Edward J., John E. Mack, and Alan F. Schatzberg
1974   "Heroin Use as an Attempt to Cope: Clinical Observations." *American Journal of Psychiatry* 131 (February): 160–64.

Kidorf, Michael and Maxine L. Stitzer
1996   "Contingent Use of Take-Home and Split Dosing to Reduce Illicit Drug Use of Methadone Patients." *Behavior Therapy* 27 (Winter): 41–51.

Kilian, Michael and David Mendell
2002   "$1 Million in Drugs Seized in Base Sting." *Chicago Tribune* (July 3): 10.

King, Rufus
1969   *Gambling and Organized Crime*. Washington, DC: Public Affairs Press.

Kinlock, Timothy W., Thomas E. Hanlon, and David N. Nurco
1998   "Heroin Use in the United States: History and Present Developments." Pages 1–30 in *Heroin in the Age of Crack-Cocaine*, edited by James A. Inciardi and Laura D. Harrison. Thousand Oaks, CA: Sage.

Kirsebbaum, Susan
2002   "Darling, Pass the Xanax: Trading Prescription Painkillers and Sedatives Is the Latest Trend at Parties." *Harper's Bazaar* (May): 108–10.

Klam, Matthew
2001   "Experiencing Ecstasy." *New York Times Magazine* (January 21): 38–43, 64, 68, 78–79.

Kleiman, Mark A. R.
1992   *Against Excess: Drug Policy for Results*. New York: Basic Books.

1989   *Marijuana: Costs of Abuse, Costs of Control*. New York: Greenwood.

1988   "Crackdowns: The Effects on Intensive Enforcement on Retail Heroin Dealing." Pages 3–18 in *Street-Level Drug Enforcement: Examining the Issues*, edited by Marcia R. Chaiken. Washington, DC: U.S. Government Printing Office.

1985   "Drug Enforcement and Organized Crime." Pages 67–87 in *The Politics and Economics of Organized Crime*. Lexington, MA: D.C. Heath.

Klein, Malcolm, Cheryl L. Maxson, and Lea C. Cunningham
1991   "'Crack,' Street Gangs, and Violence." *Criminology* 29 (November): 623–50.

Kleinknecht, William
1996   *The New Ethnic Mobs: The Changing Face of Organized Crime in America*. New York: Free Press.

Kocieniewski, David
1998   "In Drug War, Risky Tactic Yields a Fatality." *New York Times* (January 21): 18.

Kolata, Gina
1997   "Hard-Core Smokers, Last Ditch Remedies." *New York Times* (July 29): B9.

1996   "The Unwholesome Tale of the Herb Market." *New York Times* (April 21): 6E.

1989a   "Medications May Ease Craving for Cocaine." *New York Times* (March 7): 21, 23.

1989b   "In Cities, Poor Families Are Dying of Crack." *New York Times* (August 11): 1, 10.

1989c   "Experts Finding New Hope on Treating Crack Addicts." *New York Times* (August 24): 1, 9.

1988   "Drug Researchers Try to Treat a Nearly Unbreakable Habit." *New York Times* (June 25): 1, 9.

Koerber, Brendan I.
1997   "Extreme." *U.S. News & World Report* (July 30): 50–60.

Koob, George F., Barak Caine, Athina Markou, Luigi Pulvirenti, and Freidbert Weiss
1994   "Role for the Mesocortical Dopamine System in the Motivating Effects of Cocaine." Pages 1–16 in *Neurobiological Models for Evaluating Mechanisms Underlying Cocaine Addiction*,"

edited by Lynda Erinoff and Roger M. Brown. Rockville, MD: NIDA.

Korf, Dirk J., Heleen Riper, and Bruce Bullington
1999   "Windmills in Their Minds? Drug Policy and Drug Research in the Netherlands." *Journal of Drug Issues* 29 (3): 451–72.

Kosten, Thomas R.
1993   "Clinical and Research Perspectives on Cocaine Abuse: The Pharmacology of Cocaine Abuse." Pages 48–56 in *Cocaine Treatment: Research and Clinical Perspectives,* edited by Frank M. Tims and Carl G. Leukefeld. Rockville, MD: NIDA.

Kotulak, Ronald
2002a "Experts Say Love of Nicotine Is All in the Mind." *Chicago Tribune* (March 14): 1, 18.
2002b "Traffic Signal: Red Light, Green Light and Booze." *Chicago Tribune* (September 29): Sec 2: 1, 7.
1997   "Unlocking Secrets of Alcohol's Grip." *Chicago Tribune* (August 24): 1, 16.

Krauss, Clifford
2003   "Canada Parts with the U.S. on Drugs." *New York Times* (May 19): 9.
2000   "Bolivia Wiping Out Coca, at a Price." *New York Times* (October 23): 10.
1999a "Bolivia, at Some Risk, Is Making Big Gains in Eradicating Coca." *New York Times* (May 9): 6.
1999b "Peru's Drug Successes Erode as Traffickers Adapt." *New York Times* (August 19): 3.
1991   "U.S. Military Team to Advise Peru in War Against Drugs and Rebels." *New York Times* (August 7): 1, 6.

Krauss, Clifford and Douglas Frantz
1995   "Cali Drug Cartel Using U.S. Business to Launder Cash." *New York Times* (October 30): 1, 13.

Krauss, Melvyn B. and Edward P. Lazear, eds.
1991   *Searching for Alternatives: Drug Control Policy in the United States.* Stanford, CA: Hoover Institution.

Kreek, Mary Jeanne
1997   "Goals and Rationale for Pharmacotherapeutic Approach in Treating Cocaine Dependence: Insights from Basic and Clinical Research." Pages 5–35 in *Medication Development for the Treatment of Cocaine Dependence: Issues in Clinical Efficacy Trials* edited by Betty Tai, Nora Chiang, and Peter Bridge. Rockville, MD: NIDA.
1987   "Tolerance and Dependence: Implications for the Pharmacological Treatment of Addiction." Pages 53–62 in *Problems of Drug Dependence, 1986,* edited by Louis S. Harris. Rockville, MD: NIDA.

Kristoff, Nicholas D.
1999   "1492: The Prequel." *New York Times Magazine* (June 6): 80–86.

Krystal, Henry and Herbert A. Raskin
1970   *Drug Dependence: Aspects of Ego Function.* Detroit: Wayne State University Press.

Kummer, Corby
1999   "Smoky Scotch." *Atlantic Monthly* (December): 115–19.

Labaton, Stephen
1989   "New Tactics in the War on Drugs Tilt Scales of Justice Off Balance." *New York Times* (December 29): 1, 14.

La Corte, Rachel
2000   "Haitian Cocaine Seized in Florida." Associated Press (February 8): Internet.

Lambert, Bruce
1996   "Fears Prompting Crackdown on Legal Herbal Stimulant." *New York Times* (April 23): 12.
1988   "Drug Addicts in Portland, Ore., to Get Free Hypodermic Needles." *New York Times* (June 10): 7.

Lamour, Catherine and Michael R. Lamberti
1974   *The Second Opium War.* London: Allen Lane.

Lane, Charles, Douglas Waller, Brook Larmer, and Peter Katel
1992   "The Newest War." *Pressweek* (January 6): 18–23.

Lang, Alan R.
1983   "Addicting Personality: A Viable Construct?" Pages 157–235 in *Commonalities in Substance Abuse and Habitual Behavior,* edited by Peter K. Levison, Dean R. Gerstein, and Deborah R. Maloff. Lexington, MA: D.C. Heath.

Latimer, Dean and Jeff Goldberg
1981   *Flowers in the Blood: The Story of Opium.* New York: Franklin Watts.

LaVelle, Marianne
2000   "Teen Tobacco Wars." *U.S. News & World Report* (February 7): 14–16.

Law Commission of Canada (LCC)
2003   *What Is a Crime? Challenges and Alternatives, Discussion Paper.* Ottawa: LCC.

Lawson, Gary W.
1992   "A Biopsychological Model of Adolescent Substance Abuse." Pages 3–10 in *Adolescent Substance Abuse,* edited by Gary W. Lawson and Ann W. Lawson. Gaithersburg, MD: Aspen Publications.

Leary, Warren E.
1997   "Researchers Investigate (Horrors!) Nicotine's Potential Benefit." *New York Times* (January 14): B11.
1995a "Drug for Heroin Addiction Is Being Marketed for Treatment of Alcoholism." *New York Times* (January 18): 12.
1995b "Report Endorses Needle Exchanges as AIDS Strategy." *New York Times* (September 20): 1, 14.

Lederer, Edith M.
2001a "Taliban a Heroin Trader, UN Panel Says." *Chicago Tribune* (May 27): 6.
2001b "With Taliban Gone, Opium Farmers Return to Their Only Cash Crop." *New York Times* (November 26): B1, 4.

Ledwith, William E. (Chief of International Operations, DEA)
2000   "Statement Before the House Government Reform Committee, Subcommittee on Criminal Justice, Drug Policy, and Human Resources." February 15.

Lee, Rensselaer, III
1995   "Drugs in Communist and Former Communist Countries." *Transnational Organized Crime* 1 (Summer): 193–205.

Lemert, Edwin M.
1951   *Social Pathology.* New York: McGraw-Hill.
Lerner, Steven E.
1980   "Phencyclidine Abuse in Perspective." Pages 13–23 in
         Phencyclidine Abuse Manual, edited by Mary Tuma
         McAdams, Ronald L. Linder, Steven E. Lerner, and
         Richard Stanley Burns. Los Angeles: University of
         California Extension.
Leshner, Alan I.
1999a   "Editorial: Science Is Revolutionizing Our View of
         Addiction—and What to Do About It." *American
         Journal of Psychiatry* 156 (January): 1–3.
1999b   "Research Shows Effects of Prenatal Cocaine Are Subtle
         but Significant." *NIDA Notes* 14 (3): 3–4.
Lessons from Prevention Research
2001   Washington, DC: NIDA.
Levine, Michael
1990   *Deep Cover.* New York: Delacorte.
Levins, Hoag
1980   "The Kabul Connection." *Philadelphia* (August):
         114–20; 192–203.
Levinthal, Charles F.
1988   *Messengers of Paradise: Opiates and the Brain.*
         Garden City, NY: Doubleday.
Lewin, Tamar
2002   "With Court Nod, Parents Debate School Drug Tests."
         New York Times (September 29): 1, 27.
1992   "Drug Verdict over Infants Is Voided." *New York Times*
         (July 24): B6.
1991   "Guilt Upheld for Drug Delivery by Umbilical Cord."
         New York Times (April 20): 1, 6.
Li, Guohua, Gordon S. Smith, and Susan P. Baker
1994   "Drinking Behavior in Relation to Cause of Death
         Among U.S. Adults."*American Journal of Public
         Health* 84 (No. 9): 1402–06.
Lidz, Charles W. and Andrew L. Walker
1980   *Heroin, Deviance and Morality.* Beverley Hills: Sage.
Lin, Geraline and Richard A. Glennon, eds.
1994   *Hallucinogens: An Update.* Rockville, MD: NIDA.
Linder, Ronald L., with Steven E. Lerner and R. Stanley Burns
1981   *PCP: The Devil's Dust.* Belmont, CA: Wadsworth.
Lindesmith, Alfred C.
1968   *Addiction and Opiates.* Chicago: Aldine.
Lindesmith, Alfred C. and John H. Gagnon
1964   "Anomie and Drug Addiction." Pages 158–88 in
         Anomie and Deviant Behavior, edited by Marshall B.
         Clinard. New York: Free Press.
Ling, Walter, Richard A. Rawson, and Margaret A. Compton
1994   "Substitution Pharmacotherapies for Opioid
         Addiction: From Methadone to LAAM and
         Buprenorphine." *Journal of Psychoactive Drugs* 26
         (No. 2): 119–28.
Lipton, Douglas S.
1995   *The Effectiveness of Treatment for Drug Abusers
         Under Criminal Justice Supervision.* Washington, DC:
         National Institute of Justice.

Liu, Jainhong, Dengke Zhou, Allen Liska, Steven Messner,
Marvin Krohn, Lening Zhang, and Zhou Lu
1998   "Status, Power, and Sentencing in China." *Justice
         Quarterly* 15 (June): 289–300.
Liu, Liang Y.
1994   *Substance Use Among Youths at High Risk of
         Dropping Out: Grades 7-12 in Texas, 1992.* Austin:
         Texas Commission on Alcohol and Drug Abuse.
London, Perry
1964   *The Modes and Morals of Psychotherapy.* New York:
         Holt Rinehart and Winston.
Lubasch, Arnold H.
1990   "Trial Shows the Rich Rewards of a Federal Drug
         Informant." *New York Times* (November 4): 23.
Luft, Kerry
1995   "For Busted Drug Lord, Terror Too Crass." *Chicago
         Tribune* (June 15): 3.
Lukas, Scott E.
1996   *Proceedings of the National Consensus Meeting on
         the Use, Abuse and Sequelae of Abuse of
         Methamphetamine with Implications for Prevention,
         Treatment and Research.* Rockville, MD: U.S.
         Department of Health and Human Services Substance
         Abuse and Mental Health Services.
Lupsha, Peter A.
1995   "Transnational Narco-Corruption and Narco
         Investment: A Focus on Mexico." *Transnational
         Organized Crime* 1 (Spring): 84–101.
1991   "Drug Lords and Narco-Corruption: The Players
         Change but the Game Continues." *Crime, Law and
         Social Change* 16: 41–58.
1990   "The Geopolitics of Organized Crime: Some Comparative
         Models from Latin American Drug Trafficking
         Organizations." Paper presented at the annual meeting of
         the American Society of Criminology, Baltimore, November.
Lyall, Sarah
2002   "Easing of Marijuana Laws Angers Many Britons." *New
         York Times* (August 12): 3.
Lyman, Rick
1998   "Rights Query on Killing of Immigrant." *New York
         Times* (October 21): 18.
Mabry, Donald J.
1995   "The U.S. Military and the War on Drugs." Pages 43–60
         in *Drug Trafficking in the Americas,* edited by Bruce
         M. Bagley and William O. Walker III. New Brunswick,
         NJ: Transaction Publishers.
MacCoun, Robert, Beau Kilmer, and Peter Reuter
2002   "Research on Drug-Crime Linkages: The Next
         Generation." Drugs and Crime Research Forum draft.
MacCoun, Robert and Peter Reuter
1997   "Interpreting Dutch Cannabis Policy: Reasoning by
         Analogy in the Legalization Debate. *Science* 278
         (October): 47–52.
MacDonald, James and Michael Agar
1994   "What Is a Trip—and Why Take One?" Pages 9–36 in
         LSD: Still with Us After All These Years, edited by Leigh

A. Henderson and William J. Glass. New York: Lexington Books.

Maddux, James F. and David P. Desmond
1981   *Careers of Opioid Users.* New York: Praeger.

Magura, Stephen, Cathy Casriel, Douglas Goldsmith, David Strug, and Douglas Lipton
1988   "Contingency Contracting with Polydrug-Abusing Methadone Patients." *Addictive Behaviors* 13: 113–18.

Magura, Stephen, Sung-Yeon Kang, and Janet L. Shapiro
1995   "Measuring Cocaine Use by Hair Analysis Among Criminally-Involved Youth." *Journal of Drug Issues* 25 (Fall): 683–701.

Maltzman, Irving
1994   "Why Alcoholism Is a Disease." *Journal of Psychoactive Drugs* 26 (January/March): 13–31.

Manderson, Desmond
1999   "Symbolism and Racism in Drug History." *Drug and Alcohol Review* 18 (2): 179–86.

Mansnerus, Laura
1996   "Timothy Leary, Pied Piper of Psychodelic 60's, Dies at 75." *New York Times* (June 1): 1, 11.

Margolick, David
1991   "Ex-Kent Smoker Blames Filter of Past for Illness." *New York Times* (August 30): B6.

Markel, Howard
2002   "For Addicts, Relief May Be an Office Visit Away." *New York Times* (October 27): WK 14.
2000   "For Some, Marijuana Grows Mean." *New York Times* April 30: D5.

Marlatt, G. Alan, Julian M. Somers, and Susan F. Tapert
1993   "Harm Reduction: Application to Alcohol Abuse Problems." Pages 147–66 in *Behavioral Treatments for Drug Abuse and Dependence,* edited by Lisa Simon Onken, John D. Blaine, and John J. Boren. Rockville, MD: NIDA.

Marlowe, Ann
1999   *How to Stop Time: Heroin from A to Z.* New York: Basic Books.

Marriott, Michael
1995   "Half Steps vs. 12 Steps." *Pressweek* (March 27): 62.
1989   "Struggle and Hope from the Ashes of Drugs." *New York Times* (October 22): 1, 22.

Marshall, Ineke Haen and Chris E. Marshall
1994   Drug Prevention in the Netherlands: A Low Key Approach." Pages 205–31 in *Between Prohibition and Legalization: The Dutch Experiment in Drug Policy,* edited by Ed. Leuw and I. Haen Marshall. Amsterdam: Kugler Publications.

Martin, Andrew and John O'Brien
1996   "Alleged Drug Hub Didn't Fit the Area." *Chicago Tribune* (October 13): 1, 21.

Martin, B. R., S. Childers, A. Howlett, R. Mechoulam, and R. Pertwee
1994   "Cannabinoid Receptors: Pharmacology, Second Messenger Systems and Endogenous Ligands." Pages 55–60 in *Problems of Drug Dependence, 1993. Vol. I,* edited by Louis S. Harris. Rockville, MD: NIDA.

Martin, Douglas
1990   "A Big Bribe Helps Mothers Flee the Seduction of Crack." *New York Times* (March 7): 13.

Massing, Michael
1999   "The Real Methadone Problem." *New York* (January 11): 40–43, 102.
1990   "In the Cocaine War, the Jungle Is Winning." *New York Times Magazine* (March 4): 26, 88, 90, 92.

Mathias, Robert
2002   "Chronic Solvent Abusers Have More Brain Abnormalities and Cognitive Impairments Than Cocaine Abusers." *NIDA Notes* 17 (4): 5–6, 12.
2000a   "Pathological Obesity and Drug Addiction Share Common Brain Characteristics" *NIDA Notes* 16 (4): 11, 13.
2000b   "Methamphetamine Brain Damage in Mice More Extensive Than Previously Thought." *NIDA Notes* 15 (4): 1, 10.
1999   "Study Shows How Genes Can Help Protect from Addiction." *NIDA Notes* 14 (March): 5, 9.

Mathias, Robert and Patrick Zickler
2001   "NIDA Conference Highlights Scientific Findings on MDMA/Ecstasy." *NIDA Notes* 16 (5): 1, 5–8, 12.

Mattison, J. B.
1883   "Opium Addiction Among Medical Men." *Medical Record* 23 (June 9): 621–23. Reproduced in Morgan, 1974, pages 62–66.

May, Clifford D.
1988a   "Drug Enforcement: Once-Lonely Voice Finds an Audience." *New York Times* (June 6): 12.
1988b   "Coca-Cola Discloses an Old Secret." *New York Times* (July 1): 25, 29.

Mayes, Linda G.
1992   "Prenatal Cocaine Exposure and Young Children's Development." *Annals* 521 (May): 11–27.

McBride, Duane C. and Clyde B. McCoy
1981   "Crime and Drug-Abusing Behavior." *Criminology* 19 (August): 281–302.

McCance, Elinore F.
1997   "Overview of Potential Treatment Medications for Cocaine Dependence." Pages 36–72 in *Medication Development for the Treatment of Cocaine Dependence: Issues in Clinical Efficacy Trials,* edited by Betty Tai, Nora Chiang, and Peter Bridge. Rockville, MD: NIDA.

McConnaughey, Janet
2000   "Study: Smoking's Dangers Immediate." Associated Press (March 9): Internet.

McCoy, Alfred W.
1991   *The Politics of Heroin: CIA Complicity in the Global Heroin Trade.* Brooklyn: Lawrence Hill Books.
1972   *The Politics of Heroin in Southeast Asia.* New York: Harper and Row.

McCoy, H. Virginia, Christine Miles, and James A. Inciardi
1995   "Survival Sex: Inner-City Women and Crack-Cocaine." Pages 172–77 in *The American Drug Scene: An Anthology,* edited by James A. Inciardi and Karen McElrath. Los Angeles: Roxbury.

McDonald, Scott B.
1988   *Dancing on a Volcano: The Latin-American Drug Trade.* New York: Praeger.

McElrath, Karen
1995   "Alcoholics Anonymous." Pages 314–17 in *The American Drug Scene: An Anthology,* edited by James A. Inciardi and Karen McElrath. Los Angeles: Roxbury.

McFarland, George C.
1989   *Drug Abuse Indicators Trend Report, District of Columbia.* Washington, DC: Alcohol and Drug Abuse Services Administration.

McGehee, Daniel S., Mark Heath, Shari Gelber, Piroska Devay, and Lorna Role
1995   "Nicotine Enhancement of Fast Excitatory Synaptic Transmission in CNS by Presynaptic Receptors." *Science* 269 (September 22): 1692–96.

McIntosh, Lee
1988   "Letter to the Editor." *New York Times* (June 29): 26.

McKim, William A.
1991   *Drugs and Behavior: An Introduction to Behavioral Pharmacology,* 2nd ed. Englewood Cliffs, NJ: Prentice-Hall.

McMahon, Colin
1995   "Mexicans Make Their Mark in Drug Game as Middlemen." *Chicago Tribune* (September 18): 1, 14.

McMillan, Brian and Mark Conner
2000   "Drug Use and Cognitions About Drug Use Amongst Students: Changes over the University Career." *Journal of Youth and Adolescence* 31 (June): 221–30.

McNeil, Donald G., Jr.
2002   "Study in Primates Shows Brain Damage from Doses of Ecstasy." *New York Times* (September 27): 26.

McQueen, Anjetta
1999   "No Loans for Student Drug Offenders." Associated Press (October 26).

McWilliams, John C.
1992   "Through the Past Darkly: The Politics and Policies of America's Drug War." Pages 5–41 in *Drug Control Policy: Essays in Historical and Comparative Perspective,* edited by William O. Walker III. University Park, PA: Pennsylvania State University.

MDMA (Ecstasy)
2002   Washington, DC: Office of National Drug Control Policy.

Meddis, Sam
1993   "Is the Drug War Racist?" *USA Today* (July 23): 1, 2.

Meier, Barry
2001   "At Painkiller Trouble Spot, Signs Seen as Alarming Didn't Alarm Drug's Maker." *New York Times* (December 10): 16.

Meier, Barry and Melody Peterson
2001   "Sales of Painkiller Grew Rapidly, but Success Brought a High Cost." *New York Times* (March 5): 1, 15.

Meltzer, Herbert L.
1979   *The Chemistry of Human Behavior.* Chicago: Nelson-Hall.

Melzack, Ronald
1990   "The Tragedy of Needless Pain." *Scientific American* 262 (February): 27–33.

Mendelson, Bruce D. and Linda Harrison
1989   *Drug Use in Denver and Colorado.* Denver: Colorado Alcohol and Drug Use Division.

Mendelson, Jack H. and Nancy K. Mello
1995   "Alcohol, Sex, and Aggression." Pages 50–56 in *The American Drug Scene: An Anthology,* edited by James A. Inciardi and Karen McElrath. Los Angeles: Roxbury.

Merlin, Mark David
1984   *On the Trail of the Ancient Opium Poppy.* Rutherford, NJ: Fairleigh Dickinson University Press.

Merriam, John E.
1989   "National Media Coverage of Drug Issues, 1983-1987." Pages 21–28 in *Communication Campaigns About Drugs: Government, Media, and the Public,* edited by Pamela J. Shoemaker. Hillside, NJ: Lawrence Erlbaum.

Merton, Robert
1964   "Anomie, Anomia, and Social Interaction." Pages 213–42 in *Anomie and Deviant Behavior,* edited by Marshall B. Clinard. New York: Free Press.
1938   "Social Structure and Anomie." *American Sociological Review* 3: 672–82.

"Methamphetamine: Abuse and Addiction"
2002   NIDA: Internet.

Methamphetamine Abuse and Addiction
1999   Washington, DC: NIDA.

Mieczkowski, Thomas
1995   *Hair Analysis as a Drug Detector.* Washington, DC: National Institute of Justice.
1986   "Geeking Up and Throwing Down: Heroin Street Life in Detroit." *Criminology* 24 (November): 645–66.

"Military Doesn't Seek Big Role in Drug War, Pentagon Says"
1995   *New York Times* (September 10): 13.

Miller, Norman S.
1995   *Addiction Psychiatry: Current Diagnosis and Treatment.* New York: Wiley.

Miller, Norman S. and Mark S. Gold
1990   "Benzodiazepines: Reconsidered." *Advances in Alcohol and Substance Abuse* 8 (3/4): 67–81.

Miller, Walter B.
1958   "Lower Class Culture as a Generating Milieu of Gang Delinquency." *Journal of Social Issues* 14: 5–19.

Miller, William R. and Reid K. Hester
1980   "Treating the Problem Drinker: Modern Approaches." Pages 11–141 in *The Addictive Behaviors,* edited by William R. Miller. New York: Pergamon.

Miller, William R. and Ernest Kurtz
1994   "Models of Alcoholism Used in Treatment: Contrasting AA and Other Perspectives with Which It Is Often Confused." *Journal of Studies on Alcohol* 55 (March): 159–66.

Milloy, Ross E.
2002   "A Forbidding Landscape That's Eden for Peyote." *New York Times* (May 7): 14.

Minnesota Department of Human Services
1987   *Chemical Dependency Program Division Biennial Report.* St. Paul.

Mintz, John
1997   "Getting a Financial High from Rope." *Washington Post National Weekly Edition* (January 13): 18–19.

Miotto, Karen and Brett Roth
2001   *GHB Withdrawal Syndrome.* Austin: Texas
        Commission on Alcohol and Drug Abuse.
Mises, Ludwig Von
1949   *Human Action: A Treatise on Economics.* New Haven,
        CT: Yale University Press.
Misner, Dinah L. and James M. Sullivan
1999   "Mechanism of Cannabinoid Effects on Long-Term
        Potentiation and Depression in Hippocampal CA1 Neurons."
        Journal of Neuroscience 19 (August): 6795–6805.
Molgaard, Virigina K., Richard L. Spoth, and Cleve Redmond
2000   *Competency Training.* Washington, DC: Office of
        Juvenile Justice and Delinquency Prevention.
Molotsky, Irvin
1999   "Study Links Teen-Age Substance Abuse and Parental
        Ties." *New York Times* (August 31): 14.
Moody, John
1991   "A Day with the Chess Player." *Time* (July 1): 34–36.
Moore, Mark H.
1977   *Buy and Bust: The Effective Regulation of
        an Illicit Market in Heroin.* Lexington, MA: D.C.
        Heath.
Moore, Mark H. and Mark A. R. Kleiman
1989   *The Police and Drugs.* Washington, DC: U.S.
        Government Printing Office.
Moore, Molly
2001   "Iranians Wage War on Afghan Drugs." *Chicago
        Tribune* (July 19): 10.
Morales, Edmundo
1989   *Cocaine: White Gold Rush in Peru.* Tucson: University
        of Arizona Press.
1986   "Coca and Cocaine Economy and Social Change in the
        Andes of Peru." *Economic Development and Social
        Change* 35: 144–61.
Moras, Karla
1993   "Substance Abuse Research: Outcome Measurement
        Conundrums." Pages 217–48 in *Behavioral
        Treatments for Drug Abuse and Dependence,* edited
        by Lisa Simon Onken, John D. Blaine, and John J.
        Boren. Rockville, MD: NIDA.
Morgan, Howard Wayne
1981   *Drugs in America: A Social History, 1800-1980.*
        Syracuse, NY: Syracuse University Press.
Morgan, Howard Wayne, ed.
1974   *Yesterday's Addicts: American Society and Drug
        Abuse, 1865-1920.* Norman, OK: University of
        Oklahoma Press.
Morgan, Thomas
1989   "16 Charged in Scheme to Launder Millions." *New
        York Times* (May 14): 24.
Morgenthau, Robert M.
1988   "We Are Losing the War on Drugs." *New York Times*
        (February 16): 27.
Morojele, Neo K. and Judith S. Brook
2001   "Adolescent Precursors of Intensity of Marijuana
        and Other Illicit Drug Use Among Adult Initiators."
        Journal of Genetic Psychology 162 (December):
        430–51.

Moss, Andrew
1977   "Methadone's Rise and Fall." Pages 135–53 in *Drugs
        and Politics,* edited by Paul E. Rock. New Brunswick,
        NJ: Transaction Books.
Mowatt, Twig
1991   "For Killers Who Seek a New Job." *New York Times*
        (August 14): 4.
Murphy, Dean E.
2003   "Jurors Who Convicted Marijuana Grower Seek New
        Trial." *New York Times* (February 5): 13.
Murray, Ian and Stewart Tendler
1999   "Cocaine Deaths on the Increase." *London Times*
        (August 9): 6.
Musto, David
1998   "The American Experience with Stimulants and
        Opiates." Pages 51–78 in *Perspectives on Crime and
        Justice: 1997-1998 Lecture Series.* Washington, DC:
        National Institute of Justice.
1987a   "The History of Legislative Control over Opium,
        Cocaine, and Their Derivatives." Pages 37–71 in
        *Dealing with Drugs: Consequences of Government
        Control,* edited by Ronald Hamowy. Lexington, MA:
        D.C. Heath.
1987b   *The American Disease: Origins of Narcotic Control,
        Expanded Edition.* New York: Oxford.
1973   *The American Disease: Origins of Narcotic Control.*
        New Haven, CT: Yale University Press.
Mydans, Seth
2003   "Thailand Police Crack Down in Deadly Fight Against
        Drugs." *New York Times* (February 17): 6.
1989   "Vast Drug Cache and $10 Million Discovered in Raid
        in Los Angeles." *New York Times* (September 30): 1, 9.
Myers, Linnet
1995   "Europe Finds U.S. Drug War Lacking in Results."
        Chicago Tribune (November 2): 1, 24, 25.
Myers, Willard H., III
1995   "Orb Weavers—The Global Webs: The Structure and
        Activities of Transnational Ethnic Chinese Groups."
        Transnational Organized Crime 1 (Winter):
        1–36.
Nadelmann, Ethan A.
1993   *Cops Across Borders: The Internationalization of U.S.
        Criminal Law Enforcement.* University Park, PA:
        Pennsylvania State University Press.
1988   "U.S. Drug Policy: A Bad Export." *Foreign Policy* 70
        (Spring): 83–108.
Nahas, Gabriel and Nicholas A. Pace
1993   "Marijuana as Chemotherapy Aid Poses Hazards."
        Letter to the *New York Times* (December 4): 14.
Nash, Nathaniel C.
1992   "Cocaine Invades Chile, Scorning the Land Mines."
        New York Times (January 23): 6.
1991   "10 Die a Day, or Disappear, and Peru Goes Numb."
        New York Times (July 14): 2E.
Nathan Peter E.
1988   "The Addictive Personality Is the Behavior of the
        Addict." *Journal of Consulting and Clinical
        Psychology* 56 (April): 183–88.

National Commission on Marijuana and Drug Abuse
1973   *Drug Abuse in America: Problem in Perspective.*
        Washington, DC: U.S. Government Printing Office.
National Council on Crime and Delinquency
1974   "Drug Addiction: A Medical, Not a Law Enforcement
        Problem." *Crime and Delinquency 20* (January):
        4–9.
National Drug Control Strategy
2002   Washington, DC: U.S. Government Printing Office.
National Institute of Justice
2002   *An Honest Chance: Perspectives on Drug Courts:
        Executive Summary.* Internet.
National Institute on Alcohol Abuse and Alcoholism (NIAAA)
1997   *Ninth Special Report to the U.S. Congress on Alcohol
        and Health.* Rockville, MD: NIAAA.
1992   "NIAA's Genetic Research." *Alcohol Alert Supplement*
        (No. 18): 1–2.
National Institute on Drug Abuse (NIDA)
1999a   Press release, April 20.
1999b   Press release, June 14.
1999c   Press release, June 22.
1999d   Press release, September 1.
1999e   Press release, August 1.
1998a   *Nicotine Addiction.*
1998b   Press release, May 6.
1998c   Press release, May 13.
1998d   Press release, February 3.
1997   Press release, June 24.
1991   *Drug Abuse and Drug Abuse Research.*
1987   *Drug Abuse and Drug Abuse Research.*
1986   "Cocaine Use in America." *Prevention Networks*
        (April): 1–10.
Navarro, Mireya
1998   "Upgraded Drug Traffic Flourishes on Old Route."
        New York Times (May 31): 14.
1996   "When Drug Kingpins Fall, Illicit Assets Buy a
        Cushion." *New York Times* (March 19): 1, C19.
1995   "Drug Sold Abroad by Prescription Becomes
        Widely Abused in U.S." *New York Times*
        (December 12): 1, 9.
1992   "New York City Resurrects Plan on Needle Swap." *New
        York Times* (May 14): 1, B8.
1991   "Yale Study Reports Clean Needle Project Reduces AIDS
        Cases." *New York Times* (August 1): 1, 12.
"Navy Holds 21 Sailors in Italy in Smuggling"
1996   *New York Times* (May 29): 13.
Nelson, Jack E., Helen W. Pearson, Mollie Sayers, and
 Thomas J. Glynn
1982   *Guide to Drug Abuse Research Terminology.*
        Washington, DC: Government Printing Office.
"New Drug Law Leaves No Room for Mercy"
1989   *Chicago Tribune* (October 5): 28.
"New Hazard of Drinking in Pregnancy Is Found"
1996   *New York Times* (January 3): 9.
New York State Division of Substance Abuse Services
1986   *Annual Report.* Albany.

Newcomb, Michael D.
1995   "Identifying High-Risk Youth: Prevalence and Patterns
        of Adolescent Drug Use." Pages 7–35 in *Adolescent
        Drug Abuse: Clinical Assessment and Therapeutic
        Interventions,* edited by Elizabeth Rahdert and
        Dorynne Czechowicz. Rockville, MD: NIDA.
Newcomb, Michael D. and Peter M. Bentler
1989   "Substance Use and Abuse Among Children and
        Teenagers." *American Psychologist 44* (February):
        242–48.
1988   *Consequences of Adolescent Drug Use.* Newbury Park,
        CA: Sage.
1986   "Cocaine Use Among Adolescents: Longitudinal
        Associations with Social Context, Psychopathology, and
        Use of Other Substances." *Addictive Behavior* 11: 263–73.
Newman, Robert G.
1977   *Methadone Management, Findings, and Prospects
        for the Future.* New York: Academic Press.
NIAAA. *See* National Institute on Alcohol Abuse and Alcoholism.
Nichols, David E. and Robert Oberlender
1989   "Structure-Activity Relationships of MDMA-like
        Substances." Pages 1–28 in *Pharmacology and
        Toxicology of Amphetamine and Related Designer
        Drugs,* edited by Khursheed Asghar and Errol De Souza.
        Rockville, MD: NIDA.
"Nicotine Addiction"
2001   *NIDA Resaearch Report.* Rockville, MD: NIDA.
NIDA. *See* National Institute on Drug Abuse.
NIDA Notes
1999   "Thirteen Principles of Effective Drug Addiction
        Treatment." National Clearinghouse for Alcohol and
        Drug Information 14 (5) (December). www.nida.nih.gov.
Nielson, Amie L. and Frank R. Scarpitti
1997   "Changing the Behavior of Substance Abusers: Factors
        Influencing the Effectiveness of Therapeutic Communities."
        Journal of Drug Issues 27 (Spring): 279–98.
Nieves, Evelyn
1991   "Tainted Drug's Death Toll Rises to 10, Officials Say."
        New York Times (February 4): C11.
NNICC
1998   *The Supply of Illicit Drugs to the United States.*
        Washington, DC: National Narcotics Intelligence
        Consumers Committee.
Noble, Barbara Presley
1992   "Testing Employees for Drugs." *New York Times* (April
        12): F27.
Nolan, Kathleen
1990   "Protecting Fetuses from Prenatal Hazards: Whose
        Crimes? What Punishment?" *Criminal Justice Ethics* 9
        (Winter/Spring): 13–23.
Northern, Helen
1969   *Social Work with Groups.* New York: Columbia
        University Press.
Nunes, Edward V. and Jeffrey S. Rosecan
1987   "Human Neurobiology of Cocaine." Pages 48–94 in
        Cocaine Abuse: New Directions in Treatment and

Research, edited by Henry I. Spitz and Jeffrey S. Rosecan. New York: Brunner/Mazel.

Nurco, David N., John C. Ball, John W. Shaffer, and Thomas Hanlon
1985   "The Criminality of Narcotic Addicts." *Journal of Nervous and Mental Disorders* 173: 94–102.

Nyre, George F.
1985   *Final Evaluation Report, 1984-1985: Project DARE.* Los Angeles: Evaluation and Training Institute.

O'Brien, Charles P., Arthur Alterman, Dan Walter, Anna Rose Childress, and A. T. McLellan
1990   "Evaluation of Treatment for Cocaine Dependence." Pages 78–83 in *Problems of Drug Dependence 1989,* edited by Louis S. Harris. Rockville, MD: NIDA.

O'Brien, John
1996   "Chicago at Heart of Heroin Case." *Chicago Tribune* (October 12): 1, 9.

O'Brien, John and Jan Crawford Greenburg
1996   "Raids Reveal How Little Guys Climb the Drug Ladder." *Chicago Tribune* (May 3): 1, 21.

O'Brien, Robert and Sidney Cohen
1984   *Encyclopedia of Drug Abuse.* New York: Facts on File.

O'Connor, Matt
1999   "3 Who Succeeded Hoover Get Life Terms." *Chicago Tribune* (January 9): 5.
1998   "Raiders Net Millions, Ton of Cocaine." *Chicago Tribune* (May 28): Sec. 2: 7.
1997   "Hoover, 6 Others Convicted; Seen as Blow to Gang." *Chicago Tribune* (May 10): 1, 12.
1990   "Drug Court a Success, but It's Not Enough." *Chicago Tribune* (February 22): 1, 2.

O'Day, Patrick and Rex Venecia
1999   "Cazuelas: An Ethnographic Study of Drug Trafficking in a Small Mexican Border Town." *Journal of Contemporary Criminal Justice* 15 (November): 421–43.

O'Donnell, John A.
1969   *Narcotic Addicts in Kentucky.* Washington, DC: U.S. Government Printing Office.

Oetting, E. R. and Fred Beauvais
1990   "Adolescent Drug Use: Findings of National and Local Surveys." *Journal of Consulting and Clinical Psychology* 58 (August) 385–94.

Office of National Drug Control Policy (ONDCP)
2002a   *Robypnol.* Washington, DC: ONDCP.
2002b   *What You Need to Know About Drug Testing in Schools.* Washington, DC: U.S. Government Printing Office.
2001   *National Drug Control Strategy: 2001 Report.* Washington, DC: U.S. Government Printing Office.
2000   *National Drug Control Strategy: 2000 Report.* Washington, DC: U.S. Government Printing Office.
1998   *Robypnol.* Washington, DC: ONDCP.
1995a   *National Drug Control Strategy.* Washington, DC: U.S. Government Printing Office.

1995b   *Pulse Check: National Trends in Drug Abuse.* Washington, DC: U.S. Government Printing Office.
1989   *National Drug Strategy.* Washington, DC: U.S. Government Printing Office.

Ogborne, Alan C. and Frederick B. Glaser
1985   "Evaluating Alcoholics Anonymous. Pages 176–92 in *Alcoholism and Substance Abuse,* edited by Thomas E. Bratter and Gary G. Forrest. New York: Free Press.

O'Hare, P. A.
1992   "Preface: A Note on the Concept of Harm Reducation." Pages xiii–xvii in *The Reduction of Drug Related Harm,* edited by P. A. O'Hare, R. Newcome, A. Matthews, E. C. Buning, and E. Drucker. London: Routledge.

Olen, Helaine
1991   "Racial Tinge to Drug Testing of New Moms." *Chicago Tribune* (December 19): 14.

Olson, Elizabeth
1997   "Swiss to Weigh Fate of Clinics Offering Legal Heroin." *New York Times* (September 28): 3.

O'Malley, Pat O. and Stephen Mugford
1991   "The Demand for Intoxicating Commodities: Implications for the 'War on Drugs.'" *Social Justice* 18 (Winter): 49–75.

ONDCP. *See* Office of National Drug Control Policy.

Orenstein, Peggy
2002   "Staying Clean." *New York Times Magazine* (February 10): 34–39, 50–51, 74–75.

Oreskes, Michael
1990   "Drug War Underlines Fickleness of Public." *New York Times* (September 6): 12.

Orth, Maureen
2002   "Afghanistan's Deadly Habit." *Vanity Fair* (March): 150–52, 165–77.

Pace, Eric
1988   "Lois Burnham Wilson, a Founder of Al-Anon Groups, Is Dead at 97." *New York Times* (October 4): 15.

Packer, Herbert L.
1968   *The Limits of the Criminal Sanction.* Stanford, CA: Stanford University Press.

Palfai, Tibor and Henry Jankiewicz
1991   *Drugs and Human Behavior.* Dubuque, IA: Wm. C. Brown.

Parker, Suzi
1999   "Ammonia's New Cachet." *U.S. News & World Report* (September 27): 37.

Parrott, Andy C.
1999   "Does Cigarette-Smoking Cause Stress?" *American Psychologist* 54 (October): 817–20.

Parsons, Loren H., Friedbert Weiss, and George F. Koob
1998   "Serotonin1B Receptor Stimulation Enhances Cocaine Reinforcement." *Journal of Neuroscience* 18 (December):10078–89.

Passell, Peter
1990   "Cocaine Policy: Gauging Success." *New York Times* (June 6): C2.

Payne, Malcolm
1997   *Modern Social Work Theory,* 2nd ed. Chicago: Lyceum.
PCOC. *See* President's Commission on Organized Crime.
Peachey, J. E. and H. Lei
1988   "Assessment of Opioid Dependence with Naloxone."
         British Journal of Addiction 83: 193–201.
Pear, Robert with Denise Grady
2003   "Government Moves to Curtail the Use of Diet
         Supplement." *New York Times* (March 1): 1, 13.
Pearson, Geoffrey
1987   *The New Heroin Users.* Oxford: Basil Blackwell.
Peele, Stanton
1995   *Diseasing of America.* San Francisco: Jossey-Bass.
1985   *The Meaning of Addiction: Compulsive Experience
         and Its Interpretation.* Lexington, MA: D.C. Heath.
1980   "Addiction to an Experience: A Social-Psychological
         Theory of Addiction." Pages 142–44 in *Theories of
         Drug Abuse: Selected Contemporary Perspectives,*
         edited by Dan J. Lettieri, Mollie Sayers, and Helen
         Wallenstein Pearson. Rockville, MD: NIDA.
Pendergast, Michael, David Farabee, Jerome Cartier, and
Susan Henkin
2002   "Involuntary Treatment Within a Prison Setting:
         Impact on Psychosocial Change During Treatment."
         Criminal Justice and Behavior 29 (February): 5–26.
Pennsylvania Crime Commission (PCC)
1990   *Organized Crime in Pennsylvania: A Decade of
         Change, 1990 Report.* Conshohocken, PA: PCC.
Pentz, Mary Ann
1985   "Social Competence and Self-Efficacy as Determinants
         of Substance Abuse in Adolescence." Pages 117–42 in
         Coping and Substance Abuse, edited by Saul Shiffman
         and Thomas Ashby Wills. Orlando: Academic Press.
Permanent Subcommittee on Investigation, U.S. Senate
1981a   *International Narcotics Trafficking.* Washington, DC:
         U.S. Government Printing Office.
1981b   *Witness Security Program.* Washington, DC: U.S.
         Government Printing Office.
"Peruvian Plane Is Shot Down in Error; 17 Die"
1991   *Chicago Tribune* (July 11): 11.
Peterson, Robert C., ed.
1980   *Marijuana Research Findings: 1980.* Rockville, MD:
         NIDA.
Peterson, Robert E.
1991   "Legalization: The Myth Exposed." Pages 324–55 in
         *Searching for Alternatives: Drug Control Policy in the
         United States,* edited by Melvyn B. Krauss, and Edward
         P. Lazear. Stanford, CA: Hoover Institution.
Physicians' Desk Reference, 57th Edition
2003   Montvale, NJ: Thomson PDR.
Pickens, Roy W. and Travis Thompson
1984   "Behavioral Treatment of Drug Dependence." Pages
         53–67 in *Behavioral Intervention Techniques in
         Drug Dependence Treatment,* edited by John
         Grabowski, Maxine L. Stitzer, and Jack E. Henningfield.
         Rockville, MD: NIDA.

Platt, Jerome J. and Christina Labate
1976   *Heroin Addiction: Theory, Research, and Treatment.*
         New York: John Wiley.
Platt, Jerome J., Mindy Widman, Victor Lidz, and Douglas Marlowe
1998   "Methadone Maintenance Treatment: Its Development
         and Effectiveness After 30 Years." Pages 160–87 in *Heroin
         in the Age of Crack-Cocaine,* edited by James A. Inciardi
         and Laura D. Harrison. Thousand Oaks, CA: Sage.
Poe, Janita and Dionne Searcey
1996   "Few Options Are Open for Drug Babies." *Chicago
         Tribune* (January 31): Sec. 2: 1, 4.
Poethig, Margaret
1988   "Q & A: Seizing the Assets of Drug Traffickers." *The
         Compiler* 8 (Winter): 11–12.
Pollan, Michael
1995   "How Pot Has Grown." *New York Times Magazine*
         (February 19): 31–35, 44, 50, 56–57.
"The 'Poor Man's Heroin'"
2001   *U.S. News & World Report* (February 12): 27.
Posner, Gerald L.
1988   *Warlords of Crime: Chinese Secret Societies—The New
         Mafia.* New York: McGraw-Hill.
Post, Robert M. and Susan R. B. Weiss
1988   "Psychomotor Stimulant vs. Local Anesthetic Effects
         of Cocaine: Role of Behavioral Sensitization and
         Kindling." Pages 217–38 in *Mechanisms of
         Cocaine Abuse and Toxicity,* edited by Doris Clouet,
         Khursheed Asghar, and Roger Brown. Rockville, MD:
         NIDA.
Preble, Edward and John J. Casey
1995   "Taking Care of Business—The Heroin Addict's Life on
         the Street." Pages 121–32 in *The American Drug
         Scene: An Anthology,* edited by James A. Inciardi and
         Karen McElrath. Los Angeles: Roxbury.
Prescott, Carol A. and Kenneth S. Kendler
1999   "Genetic and Environmental Contributions to Alcohol
         Abuse and Dependence in a Population-Based Sample
         of Male Twins." *American Journal of Psychiatry* 156
         (January): 34–40.
President's Commission on Organized Crime (PCOC)
1986   *America's Habit: Drug Abuse, Drug Trafficking, and
         Organized Crime.* Washington, DC: U.S. Government
         Printing Office.
1985   *Organized Crime and Heroin Trafficking.*
         Washington, DC: U.S. Government Printing Office.
1984   *Organized Crime and Cocaine Trafficking.*
         Washington, DC: U.S. Government Printing Office.
"Principles of Nerve Cell Communication"
1997   *Alcohol Health and Research World* 21 (2): 107–8.
Problems of Drug Dependence 1997
1997   Rockville, MD: NIDA.
Quadagno, Jill S. and Robert J. Antonio
1975   "Labeling Theory as an Oversocialized Conception of
         Man: The Case of Mental Illness." *Sociology and Social
         Research* 60 (October): 30–41.
"Quitting Caffeine Can Bring on the Blahs"

1991 *Chicago Tribune* (August 18): 24.

Raab, Selwyn
1992 "Chief Seeks Action on Narcotics Unit." *New York Times* (January 9): B8.
1987 "New York Establishes Special Courts to Hasten Disposal of Drug Cases," *New York Times* (June 7): 17.

Rachlin, Howard
1991 *Introduction to Modern Behaviorism.* New York: W.H. Freeman.

Rado, Sandor
1981 "The Psychoanalysis of Pharmacothymia (Drug Addiction)." Pages 77–94 in *Classic Contributions in the Addictions,* edited by Howard Shaffer and Milton Earl Burglass. New York: Brunner/Mazel.

Rangel, Charles B.
1990 "Letter to the Editor: 'What's Wrong with Legalizing Drugs?'" *New York Times* (Jul 24): 14.

Ray, Oakley
1978 *Drugs, Society, and Human Behavior.* St. Louis: C.V. Mosby.

Reese, Joel
2000 "Problem Drug." *Chicago* (April): 51–60.

Reese, Stephen D. and Lucig H. Danielian
1989 "Intermedia Influence and the Drug Issue: Converging on Cocaine." Pages 29–45 in *Communication Campaigns About Drugs: Government, Media, and the Public,* edited by Pamela J. Shoemaker. Hillsdale, NJ: Lawrence Erlbaum.

Reiff, Phillip
1963 *Freud, Therapy and Techniques.* New York: Crowell-Collier.

Rettig, Richard P., Manuel J. Torres, and Gerald R. Garrett
1977 *Manny: A Criminal Addict's Story.* New York: Houghton-Mifflin.

Reuter, Peter
2001 "Supply-Side Drug Control." *Milken Institute Review* (First Quarter): 14–23.
2000 "One Tough Plant." *New York Times* (March 31): 29.
1999 "Drug Use Measures: What Are They Really Telling Us?" *National Institute of Justice Journal* (April): 12–19.

Reuter, Peter and Jonathan P. Caulkins
1995 "Redefining the Goals of National Drug Policy: Recommendations from a Working Group." *American Journal of Public Health* 85 (August): 1059–63.

Reuter, Peter, Robert MacCoun, and Patrick Murphy
1990 *Money from Crime: A Study of the Economics of Drug Dealing in Washington, D.C.* Santa Monica: RAND.

Rhodes, Jean E. and Leonard Jason
1990 "A Social Stress Model of Substance Abuse." *Journal of Consulting and Clinical Psychology* 58 (August): 395–401.

Rhor, Monica
1991 "Nearly Undetectable Cocaine Found." *Chicago Tribune* (June 27): 31.

Richardson, Gale A. and Nancy L. Day
1999 "Studies of Prenatal Cocaine Exposure: Assessing the Influence of Extraneous Variables." *Journal of Drug Issues* 29 (2): 225–36.

Richey, Warren
1991 "Prosecutors' Deal with Criminals: Testify Against Noriega and Go Free." *Chicago Tribune* (November 27): 4.

Riding, Alan
1988 "Dispute Impeding U.S. War on Coca." *New York Times* (June 28): 1, 6.
1987 "Colombia's Drugs and Violent Politics Make Murder a Way of Life." *New York Times* (August 23): E3.

Riley, Diane
n.d. "The Harm Reduction Model: Pragmatic Approaches to Drug Use from the Area Between Intolerance and Neglect." Canadian Centre on Substance Abuse: Internet.

"Ritalin"
2001 NIDA Infofax. Internet.

Robertson, Nan
1988a "The Changing World of Alcoholics Anonymous." *New York Times Magazine* (February 21): 40–44, 47, 57, 92.
1988b *Getting Better: Inside Alcoholics Anonymous.* New York: William Morrow.

Robins, Lee N.
1974 *The Vietnam Drug User Returns.* Washington, DC: U.S. Government Printing Office.
1973 *A Followup of Vietnam Drug Users.* Washington, DC: U.S. Government Printing Office.

Robins, Lee N., John E. Helzer, Michi Hesselbrock, and Eric Wish
1980 "Vietnam Veterans Three Years After Vietnam: How Our Study Changed Our View of Heroin." Pages 213–30 in *The Yearbook of Substance Use and Abuse, Volume II,* edited by Leon Brill and Charles Winick. New York: Human Services Press.

Robinson, Linda
1998a "Is Colombia Lost to Rebels?" *U.S. News & World Report* (May 11): 38–42.
1998b "Land for Peace in Colombia." *U.S. News & World Report* (November 23): 37.

Rocha, Beatriz, Kimberly Scearce-Levie, José Lucas, Noboru Hiroi, Nathalie Castanon, John Crabbe, Eric Nestler, and René Hen
1998 "Increased Vulnerability to Cocaine in Mice Lacking the Serotonin-1B Receptor." *Nature* 393 (May 14): 175–78.

Roffman, Roger A. and William H. George
1988 "Cannabis Abuse." Pages 325–63 in *Assessment of Addictive Behaviors,* edited by Dennis M. Donovan and G. Alan Marlatt. New York: Guilford.

Rohde, David
2002 "Afghans Lead World Again in Poppy Crop." *New York Times* (October 28): 8.

Rohter, Larry
2000a "Driven by Fear, Colombians Leave in Droves." *New York Times* (March 5): 8.
2000b "Weave of Drugs and Strife in Colombia." *New York Times* (April 21): 1, 10, 11.

1999a "Colombia Tries, Yet Cocaine Thrives." *New York Times* (November 20): 6.

1999b "Colombian Army Hopes to Get Fighting Fit, No Easy Task." *New York Times* (December 5): 17.

1991 "From Brazil to Peru to Jamaica, Gun Smugglers Flock to Florida." *New York Times* (August 11): 1, 13.

1988a "U.S. Accusations on Drugs Outrage Mexicans." *New York Times* (April 29): 5.

1988b "Who Is the Enemy in Mexico Drug War?" *New York Times* (July 24): 7.

Rohter, Larry and Clifford Krauss

1998a "Dominicans Allow Drugs Easy Sailing." *New York Times* (May 10): 1, 6.

1998b "Dominican Drug Traffickers Tighten Grip on the Northeast." *New York Times* (May 11): 12, 17.

Romach, Myroslava K., Paul Glue, Kyle Kampman, Howard Kaplan, Gail Somer, Sabrina Poole, Laura Clarke, Vicki Coffin, James Cornish, Charles O'Brien, and Edward Sellers

1999 "Attenuation of the Euphoric Effects of Cocaine by the Dopamine D1/D5 Antagonist Ecopipam." *Archives of General Psychiatry* 56 (December): 1101–6.

Romoli, Kathleen

1941 *Colombia.* Garden City, NY: Doubleday, Doran.

Rosecan, Jeffrey S. and Edward V. Nunes

1987 "Pharmacological Management of Cocaine Abuse." Pages 255–70 in *Cocaine Abuse: New Directions in Treatment and Research,* edited by Henry I. Spitz and Jeffrey S. Rosecan. New York: Brunner/Mazel.

Rosecan, Jeffrey S., Henry I. Spitz, and Barbara Gross

1987 "Contemporary Issues in the Treatment of Cocaine Abuse." Pages 299–323 in *Cocaine Abuse: New Directions in Treatment and Research,* edited by Henry I. Spitz and Jeffrey S. Rosecan. New York: Brunner/Mazel.

Rosenbaum, Marsha

1981 *Women on Heroin.* New Brunswick, NJ: Rutgers University Press.

Rosenbaum, Ron

1988 "High Life: The Social Rise of Timothy Leary." *Vanity Fair* (April): 132–44; 154.

Rosenfeld, Richard and Scott H. Decker

1999 "Are Arrest Statistics a Valid Measure of Illicit Drug Use? The Relationship Between Criminal Justice and Public Health Indicators of Cocaine, Heroin, and Marijuana Use." *Justice Quarterly* 16 (September): 685–99.

Rosenkranz, Keith

2003 "High Fliers." *New York Times* (January 23): 27.

Rosenthal, Elisabeth

1993 "Patients in Pain Find Relief, Not Addiction, in Narcotics." *New York Times* (March 28): 1, 11.

Rosenthal, Mitchell S.

1984 "Therapeutic Communities: A Treatment Alternative for Many but Not All." *Journal of Substance Abuse Treatment* 1: 55–58.

1973 "New York City Phoenix House: A Therapeutic Community for the Treatment of Drug Abusers and Drug Addicts." Pages 83–102 in *Yearbook of Drug Abuse,* edited by Leon Brill and Earnest Harms. New York: Behavioral Publications.

Rothman, Richard B.

1994 "A Review of the Effects of Dopaminergic Agents in Humans: Implications for Medication Development." Pages 67–87 in *Neurobiological Models for Evaluating Mechanisms Underlying Cocaine Addiction,* edited by Lynda Erinoff and Roger M. Brown. Rockville, MD: NIDA.

Rowell, Earle Albert and Robert Rowell

1939 *On the Trail of Marijuana: The Weed of Madness.* Mountain View, CA: Pacific Press.

Royal College of Psychiatrists

1987 *Drug Scenes: A Report on Drug Dependence.* London: Gaskell.

Russell, Francis

1975 *A City in Terror—1919—The Boston Police Strike.* New York: Viking.

Rydell, C. Peter and Susan S. Everingham

1994 *Controlling Cocaine: Supply Versus Demand Programs.* Santa Monica: RAND.

Sackman, Bertram S., M. Maxine Sackman, and G. G. DeAngelis

1978 "Heroin Addiction as an Occupation: Traditional Addicts and Heroin-Addicted Polydrug Users." *International Journal of the Addictions* 13: 427–41.

Sanger, David E.

1995 "Money Laundering, New and Improved." *New York Times* (December 24): E4.

Santana, Rosa Maria

1996 "Drinking Blamed for Death of Teenager." *Chicago Tribune* (January 3): Sec. 2: 6.

Savitt, Robert A.

1963 "Psychoanalytic Studies on Addiction: Ego Structure in Narcotic Addiction." *Psychoanalytic Quarterly* 32: 43–57.

Sawyers, June

1988 "When Opium Was Really the Opiate of the Masses." *Chicago Tribune Magazine* (January 3): 5.

Schecter, Arnold

1980 "Long-Acting Methadone (Levo-Alpha-Acetylmethadol) in the Treatment of Opiate Dependence." Pages 99–112 in *The Yearbook of Substance Use and Abuse: Volume II,* edited by Leon Brill and Charles Winick. New York: Human Sciences Press.

Schemo, Diana Jean

1999 "Bogotá Sees Drug War as Path to Peace." *New York Times* (January 6): 11.

1997a "Players Are Main Danger in Noisy Colombian Game." *New York Times* (December 26): 10.

1997b "Heroin Is Providing a Growth Industry for Colombia." *New York Times* (March 30): 3.

Schemo, Diana Jean and Tim Golden

1998 "Bogotá Aid: To Fight Drugs or Rebels?" *New York Times* (June 2): 1, 12.

Schiffer, Frederic

1988 "Psychotherapy of Nine Successfully Treated Cocaine Abusers: Techniques and Dynamics." *Journal of Substance Abuse Treatment* 5: 131–37.

Schmetzer, Uli
1991a   "Burmese Heroin Plagues China, U.S." *Chicago Tribune* (May 2): 1, 14.
1991b   "China Declares a 'Peoples War' on Drugs." *Chicago Tribune* (July 3): 2.
1991c   "Slave Trade Survives, Prospers Across Asia." *Chicago Tribune* (November 15): 1, 18.
1990   " 'Prince of Death' Is a Wanted Man." *Chicago Tribune* (March 21): 21.

Schmidt, William E.
1993   "To Battle AIDS, Scots Offer Drugs to Addicts." *New York Times* (February 8): 3.

Schneider, Andrew and Mary Pat Flaherty
1991   "Drug Law Leaves Trail of Innocents." *Chicago Tribune* (August 11): 1, 13.

Schnoll, Sidney H.
1979   "Pharmacological Aspects of Youth Drug Abuse." Pages 255–75 in *Youth Drug Abuse,* edited by George M. Beschner and Alfred S. Friedman. Lexington, MA: D.C. Heath.

Schuckit, Marc A.
1985   "Genetics and the Risk for Alcoholism." *Journal of the American Medical Association* 254: 2614–17.

Schur, Edwin H.
1973   *Radical Non-Intervention: Rethinking the Delinquency Problem.* Englewood Cliffs, NJ: Prentice-Hall.
1965   *Crimes Without Victims: Deviant Behavior and Public Policy. Abortion, Homosexuality, Drug Addiction.* Englewood Cliffs, NJ: Prentice-Hall.

Schuster, Charles R.
1993   "A Natural History of Drug Abuse." Pages 37–51 in *International Reseach Conference on Biomedical Approaches to Illicit Drug Demand Reduction,* edited by Christine R. Hartel. Washington, DC: U.S. Government Printing Office.

Sciolino, Elaine
1988   "Diplomats Do Not Hurry to Enlist in the War on Drugs." *New York Times* (February 21): E3.

Sciolino, Elaine and Stephen Engelberg
1988   "Narcotics Effort Foiled by U.S. Security Goals." *New York Times* (April 10): 1, 10.

Scott, Michael S.
2002   *Rave Parties.* Washington, DC: U.S. Department of Justice.

Seligmann, Jean and Patricia King
1996   " 'Roofies': The Date-Rape Drug." *Pressweek* (February 26): 54.

Semple, Kirk
2001   "Colombia's Cocaine Frontier." *Mother Jones* (November/December): 58–63.

Senay, Edward C.
1986   "Clinical Implications of Drug Abuse Treatment Outcome." Pages 139–50 in *Drug Abuse Treatment Evaluation: Strategies, Progress, and Prospects,* edited by Frank M. Tims and Jacqueline P. Ludford. Rockville, MD: NIDA.

"Sexual Dysfunction and Addiction Treatment"
2000   *Addiction Treatment Forum* 9 (Spring): 1, 6–8

Shenk, Joshua Wolf
1999   "America's Altered States." *Harper's Magazine* (May): 38–52.

Shenon, Philip
1996   "Opium Baron's Rule May End with Surrender in Myanmar." *New York Times* (January 6): 4.
1990   "Peru Drug Fund Used in War, Aide Says." *New York Times* (June 21): 3.

Sheppard, Nathaniel, Jr.
1990   "Guatemalan Climate: Good for Poppy Fields, Drug Traffickers." *Chicago Tribune* (September 23): 12.

Sher, Kenneth J.
1991   *Children of Alcholics: A Critical Appraisal of Theory and Research.* Chicago: University of Chicago Press.

Shiffman, Saul and Mark Balabanis
1995   "Associations Between Alcohol and Tobacco." Pages 17–36 in *Alcohol and Tobacco: From Basic Science to Clinical Practice.* Bethesda, MD: National Institute on Alcohol Abuse and Alcoholism.

Short, James F., Jr.
1968   *Gang Delinquency and Delinquent Subculture.* New York: Harper and Row.

Siegal, Harvey A., Richard Rapp, Casey Kelliher, James Fisher, Joseph Wagner, and Phyllis Cole
1995   "The Strengths Perspective of Case Management: A Promising Inpatient Substance Abuse Treatment Enhancement." *Journal of Psychoactive Drugs* 27 (No. 1): 67–72.

Siegel, Ronald K.
1989   *Intoxication: Life in Pursuit of Artificial Paradise.* New York: E.F. Dutton.

Siegel, Shepard
1988   "Drug Anticipation and the Treatment of Dependence." Pages 1–24 in *Learning Factors in Substance Abuse,* edited by Barbara A. Ray. Rockville, MD: NIDA.

Silvas, Jos
1994   "Enforcing Drug Laws in the Netherlands." Pages 41–58 in *Between Prohibition and Legalization: The Dutch Experiment in Drug Policy,* edited by Ed. Leuw and I. Haen Marshall. Amsterdam: Kugler Publications.

Simpson, Dwyne
2002   "We Know It Works; Now Let's Make It Better." *Drugs and Alcohol Findings* 7: 7.

Simpson, Edith E.
1989   "Adherence to Cigarette, Marijuana, and Cocaine Treatment Programs: A Survival Analysis." Paper presented at the annual meeting of the American Society of Criminology, Reno, November.

Sinclair, Andrew
1962   *The Era of Excess: A Social History of the Prohibition Movement.* Boston: Little, Brown.

Sinclair, Upton
1981   *The Jungle.* New York: Bantam. Originally published in 1906.

Skinner, B. F.
1974   *About Behaviorism.* New York: Knopf.

Skolnick, Jerome H., Theodore Correl, Elizabeth Navarro, and Roger Rabb
1990 "The Social Structure of Street Drug Dealing." *American Journal of Police* 9: 1–41.

Sly, Liz
1989 "Bennett Attacks Drug Legalization." *Chicago Tribune* (December 14): 24.

Smart, Frances
1970 *Neurosis and Crime.* New York: Barnes and Noble.

Smart, Reginald G.
1980 "An Availability-Proneness Theory of Illicit Drug Abuse." Pages 46–49 in *Theories on Drug Abuse: Selected Contemporary Perspectives,* edited by Dan J. Lettieri, Mollie Sayers, and Helen Wallenstein Pearson. Rockville, MD: NIDA.

Smith, David E.
1986 "Cocaine-Alcohol Abuse: Epidemiolgical, Diagnostic and Treatment Considerations." *Journal of Psychoactive Drugs* 18 (April-June): 117–29.

Smith, David E., ed.
1979 *Amphetamine Use, Misuse, and Abuse.* Boston: G.K. Hall and Co.

Smith, David E. and Donald R. Wesson
1994 "Benzodiazepines and Other Sedative-Hypnotics." Pages 179–90 in *The American Psychiatric Press Textbook of Substance Abuse Treatment,* edited by Marc Galanter and Herbert D. Kleber. Washington, DC: American Psychiatric Press.

"Sniffing for Drugs by Testing Vapors"
1991 *New York Times* (October 9): C7.

Snyder, Solomon H.
1989 *Brainstorming: The Science of Politics and Opiate Research.* Cambridge, MA: Harvard University Press.
1986 *Drugs and the Brain.* New York: *Scientific American.*
1977 "Opiate Receptors and Internal Opiates." *Scientific American* (March): 44–56.

Soble, Ronald L.
1991 "Seized Assets Underwrite the War on Drugs." *Los Angeles Times* (April 16): 3, 23.

Society for Neuroscience (SNS)
2002 *Brain Facts: A Primer on the Brain and Nervous System.* Washington, DC: SNS.

Speart, Jessica
1995 "The New Drug Mules." *New York Times Magazine* (June 11): 44-45.

Speckart, George and M. Douglas Anglin
1987 "Narcotics Use and Crime: An Overview of Recent Research Advances." *Contemporary Drug Problems* 16 (Winter): 741–69.
1985 "Narcotics and Crime: An Analysis of Existing Evidence for a Causal Relationship." *Behavioral Sciences and the Law* 3: 259–82.

Spence, Richard T.
1989 *Current Substance Abuse Trends in Texas.* Austin: Texas Commission on Alcohol and Drug Abuse.

Spillane, Joseph F.
2000 *Cocaine: From Medical Marvel to Modern Menace in the United States, 1884-1920.* Baltimore: Johns Hopkins University Press.

Spitz, Henry I.
1987 "Cocaine Abuse: Therapeutic Group Approaches." Pages 156–201 in *Cocaine Abuse: New Directions in Treatment and Research,* edited by Henry I. Spitz and Jeffrey S. Rosecan. New York: Brunner/Mazel.

Spitz, Henry I. and Jeffrey S. Rosecan
1987 "Overview of Cocaine Abuse Treatment." Pages 97–118 in *Cocaine Abuse: New Directions in Treatment and Research,* edited by Henry I. Spitz and Jeffrey S. Rosecan. New York: Brunner/Mazel.

Spohn, Cassia and David Holleran
2002 "The Effect of Imprisonment on Recidivism Rates of Felony Offenders: A Focus on Drug Offenders." *Criminology* 40 (May): 329–57.

Spotts, James V. and Franklin C. Shontz
1980 "A Life-Theme Theory of Chronic Drug Abuse." Pages 59–70 in *Theories on Drug Abuse: Selected Contemporary Perspectives,* edited by Dan J. Lettieri, Mollie Sayers, and Helen Wallenstein Pearson. Rockville, MD: NIDA.

Starkweather, C. Woodruff
1982 "Techniques of Therapy Based on Cognitive Learning Theory." Pages 37–47 in *Communication Disorders: General Principles of Therapy,* edited by William H. Perkins. New York: Thieme-Stratton.

Stearns, Peter N.
1998 "Dope Fiends and Degenerates: The Gendering of Addiction in the Early Twentieth Century." *Journal of Social History* 31 (Summer): 809–14.

Stellwagen, Lindsey D.
1985 *Use of Forfeiture Sanctions in Drug Cases.* Washington, DC: National Institute of Justice.

Sterling, Claire
1990 *Octopus: The Long Reach of the Sicilian Mafia.* New York: Simon and Schuster.

Stevens, Jay
1987 *Storming Heaven: LSD and the American Dream.* New York: Atlantic Monthly Press.

Stimson, Gerry V. and Edna Oppenheimer
1982 *Heroin Addiction: Treatment and Control in Britain.* London: Tavistock.

Stitzer, Maxine L., George E. Bigelow, Ira A. Liebson, and Mary E. McCaul
1984 "Contingency Management of Supplemental Drug Use During Methadone Maintenance Treatment." Pages 84–103 in *Behavioral Intervention Techniques in Drug Abuse Treatment,* edited by John Grabowski, Maxine L. Stitzer, and Jack E. Henningfield. Rockville, MD: NIDA.

Stitzer, Maxine L., George E. Bigelow, and Mary McCaul
1985 "Behavior Therapy in Drug Abuse Treatment: Review and Evaluation." Pages 31–50 in *Progress in the*

Development of Cost-Effective Treatment for Drug Abusers, edited by Rebecca S. Ashery. Rockville, MD: NIDA.

Stocker, Steven
1999 "Studies Link Stress and Drug Addiction." *NIDA Notes* 14 (April): 12–15.

Stolberg, Sheryl Gay
1999a "Government Study of Marijuana Sees Medical Benefits." *New York Times* (March 18): 1, 20.
1999b "Restrictions Eased for Studies on Marijuana as Medicine." *New York Times* (May 22): 11.
1998 "President Decides Against Financing Needle Programs." *New York Times* (April 21): 1, 18.

Stout, David
1999 "Coast Guard Using Sharpshooters to Stop Boats." *New York Times* (September 14): 16.

Strong, Simon
1992 "Peru Is Losing More Than the Drug War." *New York Times* (February 17): 11.

Stryker, Jeff
2001 "For Partygoers Who Can't Say No, Experts Try to Reduce the Risks." *New York Times* (September 25): D5.

Stuart, Richard B.
1974 "Teaching Facts About Drugs: Pushing or Preventing?" *Journal of Educational Psychology* 66 (April): 189–201.

Stutman, Robert M. and Richard Esposito
1992 *Dead on Delivery: Inside the Drug Wars, Straight from the Street.* New York: Warner.

Substance Abuse and Mental Health Services Administration
1999 "Press Release" (June 23): Internet.

Substance Abuse Resource Center
1999 "Study Says Community Partnerships Can Reduce Drug Use" (December 23): Internet.

Sugarman, Barry
1974 *Daytop Village: A Therapeutic Community.* New York: Holt, Rinehart and Winston.

Sunderwirth, Stanley G.
1985 "Biological Mechanisms: Neurotransmission and Addiction." Pages 11–19 in *The Addictions: Multidisciplinary Perspectives and Treatments,* edited by Harvey B. Milkman and Howard J. Shaffer. Lexington, MA: D.C. Heath.

Suro, Roberto
1992 "In Bad Lands of Texas, Drug Traffickers Reopen Old Routes." *New York Times* (February 7): 9.

Sutherland, Edwin
1973 *On Analyzing Crime.* Edited by Karl Schuessler. Chicago: University of Chicago Press.

Swadi, Harith and Harry Zeitlin
1987 "Drug Education for School Children: Does It Really Work?" *British Journal of Addiction* 82: 741–46.

Swan, Neil
n.d. "Researchers Probe Which Comes First: Drug Abuse or Antisocial Behavior." *Drug Abuse Prevention Research and the Community.* Washington, DC: NIDA.

Sykes, Gresham M.
1967 *Crime and Society,* 2nd ed. New York: Random House.

Szasz, Thomas
1974 *Ceremonial Justice: The Ritual Persecution of Drugs, Addicts, and Pushers.* Garden City, NY: Doubleday.

Tackett, Michael
1990 "Minor Drug Players Are Paying Big Prices." *Chicago Tribune* (October 15): 1, 9.

Tagliabue, John
2000 "The Prince and His Black Sheep: This Is No Liechtenstein Fairy Tale." *New York Times* (April 8): 4.

Tamayo, Juan O.
2001 "Colombia's Heroin Trade Is Flourishing." *Chicago Tribune* (August 24): 6.

Tancer, Manuel and Charles R. Schuster
1997 "Serotonin and Dopamine System Interactions in the Reinforcing Properties of Psychostimulants: A Research Strategy." *Pressletter of the Multidisciplinary Association for Psychedelic Studies* 7 (Summer): Internet.

Tarter, Ralph E.
1988 "Are There Inherited Behavioral Traits That Predispose to Substance Abuse?" *Journal of Consulting and Clinical Psychology* 56 (April): 189–96.

Tarter, Ralph E., Arthur I. Alterman, and Kathleen L. Edwards
1985 "Vulnerability to Alcoholism in Men: A Behavior-Genetic Perspective." *Journal of Studies on Alcohol* 46 (July): 329–56.

"Teenage Drug Use Drops to an 8-year Low"
2002 *New York Times* (July 18): 17.

Terry, Charles E. and Mildred Pellens
1928 *The Opium Problem.* New York: The Committee on Drug Addictions in Collaboration with the Bureau of Social Hygiene, Inc.

"Therapeutic Community"
2002 National Institute on Drug Abuse Research Report, Washington, DC: U.S. Department of Human Services.

"33-Year Study Shows Severe Long-Term Effects of Heroin"
2001 *Brown University Digest of Addiction Theory and Application* 20 (June): 16–20.

Thomas, Josephine
2001 "Maternal Smoking During Pregnancy Associated with Negative Toddler Behavior and Early Smoking Experimentation." *NIDA Notes* 16 (1): 1, 4–5.

Thornburgh, Dick
1989 *Drug Trafficking: A Report to the President.* Washington, DC: U.S. Government Printing Office.

Thoumi, Francisco E.
2002 "Illegal Drugs in Colombia: From Illegal Economic Boom to Social Crisis." *Annals* 582 (July): 102–16.
1995 "The Size of the Illegal Drug Industry." Pages 77–96 in *Drug Trafficking in the Americas,* edited by Bruce M. Bagley and William O. Walker III, New Brunswick, NJ: Transaction Publishers.

Tilson, Hugh A.
1993 "Neurobehavioral Methods Used in Neurotoxicology." Pages 1–33 in *Assessing Neurotoxicity in Drugs of Abuse,* edited by Lynda Erinoff. Rockville, MD: NIDA.

Tindall, George B.
1988   *America: A Narrative History. Vol. 2*. New York: Norton.

Torriero, E. A.
2002   "Afghan Officials Struggle to Stop Opium Bonanza."
        Chicago Tribune (March 3): 6.

Tortora, Gerard J.
1983   *Principles of Human Anatomy,* 3rd ed. New York:
        Harper and Row.

Treaster, Joseph B.
1992   "Nigerian Connection a New Threat in Heroin War."
        New York Times (February 15): 1, 10.

1991   "Plan Lets Addicted Mothers Take Their Newborns
        Home." *New York Times* (September 19): 1, 16.

1990a   "Programs Find Adolescents' Use of Cocaine Can Be
        Curtailed." *New York Times* (June 2): 10.

1990b   "Bypassing Borders, More Drugs Flood Ports." *New
        York Times* (April 29): 1, 18.

1990c   "At City's Heart, Carnival for Haunted." *New York
        Times* (September 27): 4.

Trebach, Arnold S.
1987   *The Great Drug War: A Radical Proposal That
        Could Make America Safe Again.* New York:
        Macmillan.

1982   *The Heroin Solution.* New Haven, CT: Yale University Press.

Trends in Heroin
1994   Washington DC: DEA.

Tullis, LaMond
1995   *Unintended Consequences: Illegal Drugs and Drug
        Policies in Nine Countries.* Boulder: Lynne Reinner.

Turner, David
1991   "Pragmatic Incoherence: The Changing Face of
        British Drug Policy." Pages 175–90 in *Searching
        for Alternatives: Drug Control Policy in the
        United States,* edited by Melvyn B.Krauss and
        Edward P. Lazear. Stanford, CA: Hoover
        Institution.

Tyler, Patrick E.
1995a   "China Battles a Spreading Scourge of Illicit Drugs."
        New York Times (November 15): 1, 7.

1995b   "Heroin Influx Ignites a Growing AIDS Epidemic in
        China." *New York Times* (November 28): 3.

1991   "Teheran Convicts Nine in Opposition." *New York
        Times* (September 22): 9.

Tymoczco, Dmitri
1996   "The Nitrous Oxide Philosopher." *Atlantic Monthly*
        (May): 93–101.

Uelmen, Gerald F. and Victor G. Haddox, eds.
1983   *Drug Abuse and the Law.* New York: Clark Boardman.

"Update on Nicotine Addiction and Tobacco Research"
2000   *NIDA Notes* 15 (5): 15.

U.S. Department of State
2000   Policy and Program Overview for 1999. Washington,
        DC: Bureau for International Narcotics and Law
        Enforcement Affairs.

1999   *Money Laundering and Financial Crimes.*
        Washington, DC: Bureau for International Narcotics
        and Law Enforcement Affairs.

1998   *International Narcotics Control Strategy Report.*
        Washington, DC: U.S. Department of State.

"U.S. Resists Easing Curb on Marijuana"
1989   *New York Times* (December 31): 14.

Vaillant, George E.
1983   *The Natural History of Alcoholism.* Cambridge, MA:
        Harvard University Press.

1970   "The Natural History of Narcotic Drug Addiction."
        Seminars in Psychiatry 2 (November): 486–98.

Valenzuela, C. Fernando
1997   "Alcohol and Neurotransmitter Interactions." *Alcohol
        Health and Research World* 21 (2): 144–48.

Van Dyke, Craig and Robert Byck
1982   "Cocaine." *Scientific American* 246 (March):128–41.

Varisco, Raymond
2000   "Drug Abuse and Conduct Disorder Linked to Maternal
        Smoking During Pregnancy." *NIDA Notes* 15 (5): 5.

Verhovek, Sam Howe
1995   "Young, Carefree and in Love with Cigarettes."
        New York Times (July 30): 1, 10.

Vest, Jason
1997   "DEA to Florists: The Poppies Are Unlovely." *U.S. News
        & World Report* (March 17): 49.

"Victims of Botched U.S. Drug Sting Sue"
1995   *Chicago Tribune* (January 24): 7.

Visher, Christy A.
1990   "Linking Criminal Sanctions, Drug Testing, and Drug
        Abuse Treatment: A Crime Control Strategy for the
        1990s." *Criminal Justice Policy Review* 3: 329–43.

Vivanco, José Miguel
1995   "Letter to the New York Times: 'U.S. Aids Bolivia in
        Trampling Rights.'" *New York Times* (July 18): 14.

Vogt, Amanda
2003   "Now Many 'Just Say No' to DARE." *Chicago Tribune*
        (January 26): 1, 14.

Volkow, Nora D., Gene-Jack Wang, Joanna Fowler, Jean Logan,
Samuel Gatley, Andrew Gifford, Robert Hitzemann, YuShin Ding,
and Naomi Pappas
1999a   "Prediction of Reinforcing Responses to Psychostimulants
        in Humans by Brain Dopamine$_2$ Receptor Levels."
        American Journal of Psychiatry 156 (September):
        1440–43.

Volkow, Nora D., Gene-Jack Wang, Joanna Fowler, Jean Logan,
S. John Gatley, Christopher Wong, Robert Hitzemann, and
Naomi Pappas
1999b   "Reinforcing Effects of Psychostimulants in Humans
        Are Associated with Increases in Brain Dopamine and
        Occupancy of D$_2$ Receptors." *Journal of
        Pharmacology and Experimental Therapeutics* 291
        (October): 409–15.

2001   "Association of Dopamine Transporter Reduction with
        Psychomotor Impairment in Methamphetamine
        Abusers." *American Journal of Psychiatry* 3 (March):
        377–382.

Vorenberg, James and Irving F. Lukoff
1973   "Addiction, Crime, and the Criminal Justice System."
        Federal Probation 37 (December): 3–7.

Wahl, Melissa
1999   "Hitting a Wall of Opposition." *Chicago Tribune*
        (February 4): Sec. 3: 1, 4.
Wald, Matthew
2002   "Hidden Plague of Alcohol Abuse by the Elderly." *New
        York Times* (April 2): D7.
Wald, Patricia M. and Annette Abrams
1972   "Drug Education." Pages 123–72 in *Dealing with
        Drug Abuse: A Report to the Ford Foundation.* New
        York: Praeger.
Wald, Patricia M. and Peter Barton Hutt
1972   "The Drug Abuse Survey Project: Summary of Findings,
        Conclusions, and Recommendations." Pages 3–61 in
        *Dealing with Drug Abuse: A Report to the Ford
        Foundation.* New York: Praeger.
Waldman, Amy
2002   "A Village at Source of Heroin Trade Fears the
        Eradication of Its Poppies." *New York Times* (March
        12): 12.
Waldorf, Dan
1973   *Careers in Dope.* Englewood Cliffs, NJ: Prentice-Hall.
Walker, William O., III, ed.
1992   *Drug Control Policy: Essays in Historical and
        Comparative Perspective.* University Park, PA:
        Pennsylvania State University.
Wallace, John
1993   "Modern Disease Models of Alcoholism and
        Other Chemical Dependencies: The New
        Biopsychosocial Models." *Drugs and Society* 8 (1):
        69–87.
Wallance, Gregory
1981   *Papa's Game.* New York: Ballantine.
Walter, Ingo
1990   *Secret Money: The World of International Financial
        Secrecy.* New York: Harper Business.
"War on Drugs Is Lost"
1996   *National Review* (February 12): 34–48.
Washton, Arnold M.
1989   *Cocaine Addiction: Treatment, Recovery, and
        Relapse Prevention.* New York: Norton.
Washton, Arnold M. and Mark S. Gold
1987   "Recent Trends in Cocaine Abuse as Seen from the
        '800-Cocaine Hotline.'" Pages 10–22 in *Cocaine: A
        Clinicians Handbook,* edited by Arnold M. Washton
        and Mark S. Gold. New York: Guilford.
Washton, Arnold M., Nannette S. Stone, and Edward C. Henrickson
1988   "Cocaine Abuse." Pages 364–89 in *Assessment of
        Addictive Behaviors,* edited by Dennis M. Donovan and
        G. Alan Marlatt. New York: Guilford.
Washton, Arnold M. and Nanette Stone-Washton
1993   "Outpatient Treatment of Cocaine and Crack Addiction: A
        Clinical Perspective." Pages 15–30 in *Cocaine Treatment:
        Research and Clinical Perspectives,* edited by Frank M.
        Tims and Carl G. Leukefeld. Rockville, MD: NIDA.
Waterston, Alisse
1993   *Addicts in the Political Economy.* Philadelphia:
        Temple University Press.

Watlington, Dennis
1987   "Between the Cracks." *Vanity Fair* (December):
        146–51, 184.
Watson, Russell
1999   "Coke and Mrs. Colonel." *Pressweek* (August 16): 37.
Webster, Barbara and Michael S. McCampbell
1992   *International Money Laundering: Research and
        Investigation Join Forces.* Washington, DC: National
        Institute of Justice.
Weil, Andrew
1995   "The New Politics of Coca." *New Yorker* (May 15):
        70–80.
Weiner, Eric
1989   "Mexico Shooting Down Drug Planes, Officials Say."
        New York Times (December 8): 11.
Weiner, Tim
2002   "Border Customs Agents Are Pushed to the Limit." *New
        York Times* (July 25): 14.
Weingarten, Paul
1989   "Profits, Perils Higher for Today's Bootleggers." *Chicago
        Tribune* (September 14): 1, 22.
Weinstein, Adam K.
1988   "Prosecuting Attorneys for Money Laundering: A New
        and Questionable Weapon in the War on Crime." *Law
        and Contemporary Problems* 51 (Winter): 369–86.
Weisheit, Ralph A.
1990   "Cash Crop: A Study of Illicit Marijuana Growers."
        Working draft for the National Institute of Justice.
1989   "Domestic Marijuana Growers: Mainstreaming
        Deviance." Paper presented at the annual meeting
        of the American Society of Criminology, Reno,
        November.
Weiss, Roger D. and Steven M. Mirin
1987   *Cocaine.* Washington, DC: American Psychiatric Press.
Weppner, Robert S.
1983   *The Untherapeutic Community: Organizational
        Behavior in a Failed Addiction Treatment Program.*
        Lincoln, NE: University of Nebraska.
Wesson, Donald R. and David E. Smith
1985   "Cocaine: Treatment Perspectives." Pages 193–203 in
        *Cocaine Use in America: Epidemiologic and Clinical
        Perspectives,* edited by Nicholas J. Kozel and Edgar H.
        Adams. Rockville, MD: NIDA.
1977   *Barbiturates: Their Use, Misuse, and Abuse.* New
        York: Human Sciences Press.
Westermeyer, Joseph and Ronald S. Krug, eds.
1991   *Substance Abuse Services: A Guide to Planning and
        Management.* Chicago: American Hospital Association.
Wever, Leon
1994   "Drugs as a Public Health Problem." Pages 59–74 in
        *Between Prohibition and Legalization: The Dutch
        Experiment in Drug Policy,* edited by Ed. Leuw and I.
        Haen Marshall. Amsterdam: Kugler Publications.
Wexler, David B.
1996   "Editorial." *American Journal of Psychiatry* 153: 4–5.
Wexler, Harry K., George DeLeon, George Thomas, David Kressel,
and Jean Peters

1999 "The Amity Prison TC Evaluation: Reincarceration Outcomes." *Criminal Justice and Behavior* 26 (June): 147–67.

Wexler, Harry K., Gregory P. Falkin, and Douglas S. Lipton
1990 "Outcome Evaluation of a Prison Therapeutic Community for Substance Abuse Treatment." *Criminal Justice and Behavior* 15: 71–92.

Wexler, Harry K., Douglas S. Lipton, and Kenneth Foster
1985 "Outcome Evaluation of a Prison Therapeutic Community for Substance Abuse Treatment: Preliminary Results." Paper presented at the American Society of Criminology, San Diego, November.

Wexler, Harry K. and Ronald Williams
1986 "The Stay 'N Out Therapeutic Community: Prison Treatment for Substance Abusers." *Journal of Psychoactive Drugs* 18 (July-September): 221–30.

"What Kind of Drug Use Does School-Based Prevention Prevent?"
2002 *Drug Policy Research Center Newsletter* (June): Internet.

Wheat, Sue and Philip Withers Green
1999 "Leaf in the Lurch." *Geographical* (September): 42–48.

White, Peter
1989 "Coca—An Ancient Herb Turns Deadly." *National Geographic* (January): 3–47.

White, William L.
1998 *Slaying the Dragon: The History of Addiction Treatment and Recovery in America.* Bloomington, IN: Chestnut Health Systems.

White House Conference for a Drug Free America
1988 *Final Report.* Washington, DC: U.S. Government Printing Office.

Whiteacre, Kevin W. and Hal Pepinsky
2002 "Controlling Drug Use." *Criminal Justice Policy Review* 13 (March): 21–31.

Whitlock, Rod Van, Howard Collings, and Cathleen Burnett
1990 "Relationship Between Cocaine Use and Severity of Crime." Paper presented at the annual meeting of the American Society of Criminology, Baltimore, November.

Wicker, Tom
1987 "Drugs and Alcohol." *New York Times* (May 13): 27.

Wiebe, Robert H.
1967 *The Search for Order: 1877-1920.* New York: Hill and Wang.

Wilbanks, William
1990 "The Danger in Viewing Addicts as Victims: A Critique of the Disease Model of Addiction." *Criminal Justice Policy Review* 3: 407–22.

Wilkerson, Isabel
1991 "Court Backs Woman in Pregnancy Drug Case." *New York Times* (April 3): 13.

Williams, Jay R., Lawrence J. Redlinger, and Peter K. Manning
1979 *Police Narcotics Control: Patterns and Strategies.* Washington, DC: U.S. Government Printing Office.

Williams, Jill Schlabig
2003 "Grouping High-Risk Youths for Prevention May Harm More Than Help." *NIDA Notes* 17 (No. 5): 1, 6.

Williams, Phil
1995 "The New Threat: Transnational Criminal Organizations and International Security." *Criminal Organizations* 9 (3 and 4): 3–19.

Williams, Terry
1989 *The Cocaine Kids: The Inside Story of a Teenage Drug Ring.* Reading, MA: Addison-Wesley.

Willoughby, Alan
1988 *The Alcohol Troubled Person: Known and Unknown.* Chicago: Nelson-Hall.

Wilson, James Q.
1990 "Against the Legalization of Drugs." *Commentary* 89 (February): 21–28.
1978 *The Investigators: Managing FBI and Narcotics Agents.* New York: Basic Books.
1975 *Thinking About Crime.* New York: Basic Books.

Winerip, Michael
1998 "Binge Nights: The Emergency on Campus." *New York Times Education Life* (January 4): 28–31, 42.

Winger, Gail
1988 "Pharmacological Modifications of Cocaine and Opioid Self-Administration." Pages 125–36 in *Mechanisms of Cocaine Abuse and Toxicity,* edited by Doris Clouet, Khursheed Asghar, and Roger Brown. Rockville, MD: NIDA.

Winter, Greg
2003 "Study Finds No Sign That Testing Deters Students' Drug Use." *New York Times* (May 17): 1, 14.

Winter, Jerrold C.
1994 "The Stimulus Effects of Serotonergic Hallucinogens in Animals." Pages 157–82 in *Hallucinogens: An Update,* edited by Geraline C. Lin and Richard A. Glennon. Rockville, MD: NIDA.

Winters, Ken C. and George Henly
1988 "Assessing Adolescents Who Abuse Chemicals: The Chemical Dependency Adolescent Assessment Project." Pages 4–18 in *Adolescent Drug Abuse: Analyses of Treatment Research,* edited by Elizabeth R. Rahdert and John Grabowski. Rockville, MD: NIDA.

Wise, Roy A.
1994 "Cocaine Reward and Cocaine Craving: The Role of Dopamine in Perspective." Pages 191–206 in *Neurobiological Models for Evaluating Mechanisms Underlying Cocaine Addiction,* edited by Lynda Erinoff and Roger M. Brown. Rockville, MD: NIDA.

Wish, Eric
n.d. *Drug Testing.* Rockville, MD: National Institute of Justice.

Wish, Eric D. and Bruce Johnson
1986 "The Impact of Substance Abuse on Criminal Careers." Pages 52–88 in *Criminal Careers and Career Criminals,* edited by Alfred Blumstein, Jacqueline Cohen, Jeffrey A. Roth, and Christy A. Visher. Washington, DC: National Academy Press.

Wishart, David
1974   "The Opium Poppy: The Forbidden Crop." *Journal of Geography* 73 (January): 14–25.

Wisotsky, Steven
1987   *Breaking the Impasse in the War on Drugs.* Westport, CT: Greenwood.

Witkin, Gordon
1991   "The Men Who Created Crack." *U.S. News & World Report* (August 19): 44–53.

Witkin, Gordon and Jennifer Griffin
1994   "The New Opium Wars." *U.S. News & World Report* (October 10): 39–44.

Wodak, Alex
1990   "Needle Exchange Succeeding in Australia." Letter to the *New York Times* (March 26): 14.

Wodak, Alex and Peter Lurie
1997   "A Tale of Two Countries: Attempts to Control HIV Among Injecting Drug Users in Australia and the United States." *Journal of Drug Issues* 27: 117–34.

Wolfe, Tom
1968   *The Electric Kool-Aid Acid Test.* New York: Farrar, Straus and Giroux.

Wolfgang, Marvin E. and Franco Ferracuti
1967   *The Subculture of Violence: Toward an Integrated Theory in Criminology.* London: Tavistock.

Wood, Daniel
1991   "Bar Lab Challenges the Alcohol Mystique." *Chicago Tribune* (February 24): Sec. 5: 6.

Wood, Roland W.
1973   "18,000 Addicts Later: A Look at California's Civil Addict Program." *Federal Probation* 38 (March): 26–31.

Woodiwiss, Michael
1988   *Crime, Crusades and Corruption: Prohibition in the United States, 1900–1987.* Totawa, NJ: Barnes and Noble.

Woods, James R., Jr.
1993   "Effects of Drugs of Abuse on Mother and Fetus." Pages 179–87 in *International Research Conference on Biomedical Approaches to Illicit Drug Demand Reduction,* edited by Christine R. Hartel. Washington, DC: U.S. Government Printing Office.

Woody, George E., Lester Lubrosky, A. Thomas McLellan, Charles O'Brien, Aren Beck, Jack Blaine, Ira Herman, and Anita Hole
1983   "Psychotherapy for Opiate Addicts: Does It Help?" *Archives of General Psychiatry* 40 (June): 639–45.

Worth, Robert F.
2002   "Judge's Ruling on Statements to A.A. Is Overturned." *New York Times* (July 18): 19.

Wren, Christopher S.
1999a   "Pipeline of Poor Smuggles Heroin." *New York Times* (February 21): 28.
1999b   "A Purer Form of Heroin Lures New Users to a Long, Hard Fall." *New York Times* (May 9): 27.

1999c   "Bid for Alcohol in Antidrug Ads Hits Resistance." *New York Times* (May 31): 1, 8.
1999d   "In Battle Against Heroin, Scientists Enlist Heroin." *New York Times* (June 8): D1, 6.
1999e   "The Opposing Camps Square Off at a Congressional Hearing About Drug Legalization." *New York Times* (June 20): 20.
1999f   "Bird Food Is a Casualty of the War on Drugs." *New York Times* (October 3): 14.
1998a   "Road to Riches Starts in the Golden Triangle." *New York Times* (May 11): 8.
1998b   "Afghanistan's Opium Output Drops Sharply, U.N. Survey Shows." *New York Times* (September 27): 11.
1998c   "Drug Officials Sense a Shift in Dominicans." *New York Times* (August 14): 16.
1996   "Mexican Role in Cocaine Is Exposed in U.S. Seizure." *New York Times* (May 3): C19.

Wright, Fred D., Aaron T. Beck, Cory F. Newman, and Bruce S. Liese
1993   "Cogntive Therapy of Substance Abuse: Theoretical Rationale." Pages 123–46 in *Behavioral Treatments for Drug Abuse and Dependence,* edited by Lisa Simon Onken, John D. Blaine, and John J. Boren. Rockville, MD: NIDA.

Wurmser, Leon
1978   "Mr. Pecksniff's Horse? (Psychodynamics in Compulsive Drug Use)." Pages 36–72 in *Psychodynamics of Drug Dependence,* edited by Jack D. Blaine and Demetrios A. Julius. Rockville, MD: NIDA.

Wysong, Earl, Richard Aniskiewicz, and David Wright
1994   "Truth and DARE: Drug Education to Graduation and as Symbolic Politics." *Social Problems* 41 (August): 448–72.

Ynclan, Nery
2002   "Web Site Gives Addicts Support on the Road." *Chicago Tribune* (October 13): Sec. C10.

Yorke, Clifford
1970   "A Critical Review of Some Psychoanalytic Literature on Drug Addiction." *British Journal of Medical Psychology* 43: 141–59.

Young, Douglas
2002   "Impact of Perceived Legal Pressure on Retention in Drug Treatment." *Criminal Justice and Behavior* 29 (February): 27–55.

Young, James Harvey
1961   *The Toadstool Millionaires: A Social History of Patent Medicines in America Before Federal Regulation.* Princeton: Princeton University Press.

Zahniser, Nancy R., Joanna Peris, Linda Dwoskin, Pamela Curella, Robert Yasuda, Laurie O'Keefe, and Sally Boyson
1988   "Sensitization to Cocaine in the Nigrostriatal Dopamine System." Pages 55–77 in *Mechanisms of Cocaine Abuse and Toxicity,* edited by Doris Clouet, Khursheed Asghar, and Roger Brown. Rockville, MD: NIDA.

Zernike, Kate
2001   "Antidrug Program Says It Will Adopt a New Strategy." *New York Times* (February 15): 1, 23.

2000   "New Tactic on College Drinking: Play It Down." *New York Times* (October 3): 1, 21.

Zickler, Patrick

2002   "Study Demonstrates That Marijuana Smokers Experience Significant Withdrawal." *NIDA Notes* 17 (3): 7, 10.

2001a   "Genetic Variation in Serotonin System May Play a Role in Smoking Initiation." *NIDA Notes* 17 (2): 7, 14.

2001b   "Cues for Cocaine and Normal Pleasures Activate Common Brain Sites." *NIDA Notes* 16 (2): 1, 5, 7.

2000   "Brain Imaging Studies Show Long-term Damage from Methamphetamine Abuse." *NIDA Notes* 15 (3): 11, 13.

1999   "Twin Studies Help Define the Role of Genes in Vulnerability to Drug Abuse." *NIDA Notes* 14 (4): 1, 5, 8.

Zielbauer, Paul

2000   "New Campus High: Illicit Prescription Drugs." *New York Times* (March 24): 1, 19.

Zimmer, Lynn

1990   "Proactive Policing Against Street-Level Drug Trafficking." *American Journal of Police* 9: 43–74.

Zimring, Franklin E. and Gordon Hawkins

1992   *The Search for Rational Drug Control.* New York: Cambridge University Press.

Zinberg, Norman E.

1984   *Drug, Set, and Setting: The Basis for Controlled Intoxicant Use.* New Haven, CT: Yale University Press.

Zinberg, Norman E., Wayne M. Harding, Shirley M. Stelmack, and Robert A. Marblestone

1978   "Patterns of Heroin Abuse." Pages 10–24 in *Recent Developments in Chemotherapy of Narcotic Addiction,* edited by Benjamin Kissin, Joyce H. Lowinson, and Robert B. Millman. New York: New York Academy of Sciences.

Zinberg, Norman E. and John A. Robertson

1972   *Drugs and the Public.* New York: Simon and Schuster.

Zuckerman, Laurence

2000   "Workers Get Greater Drug Test Protection." *New York Times* (December 15): 20.

Author Index

Subject Index

Photo Credits

Chapter 1
Page 2 © Richard Hutchings/PhotoEdit

Chapter 4
Page 83 © Ric Ergenbright/CORBIS
Page 87 © Grant LeDuc/Stock, Boston

Chapter 5
Page 117 © J. Pickerell/The Image Works
Page 120 © Schwartz/Black Starr

Chapter 6
Page 153 © Scott Houston/Corbis Sygma
Page 161 © Dennie Cody/Getty Images

Chapter 7
Page 168 © Michael Jang/Getty Images

Chapter 8
Page 187 © VCG/Getty Images

Chapter 9
Page 213 AP/Wide World Photos

Chapter 11
Page 282 © Francoise de Mulder/CORBIS

Chapter 12
Page 224 © Amy C. Etra/PhotoEdit
Page 226 © Reuters Newmedia Inc./CORBIS

Chapter 13
Page 342 © Owen Franken/Getty Images

Chapter 14
Page 376 © A. Ramey/PhotoEdit
Page 380 © Owen Franken/CORBIS

Timeline
Front endsheet 1: © Hulton Getty
Front endsheet 2: © Roger Ressmeyer/CORBIS